AQA A-level

Law

For Year 2

2

Jacqueline Martin

Nicholas Price

Richard Wortley

Approval message from AQA

This textbook has been approved by AQA for use with our qualification. This means that we have checked that it broadly covers the specification and we are satisfied with the overall quality. Full details of our approval process can be found on our website.

We approve textbooks because we know how important it is for teachers and students to have the right resources to support their teaching and learning. However, the publisher is ultimately responsible for the editorial control and quality of this book.

Please note that when teaching the *AQA A-level Law* course, you must refer to AQA's specification as your definitive source of information. While this book has been written to match the specification, it cannot provide complete coverage of every aspect of the course.

A wide range of other useful resources can be found on the relevant subject pages of our website: www.aqa.org.uk.

HODDER EDUCATION
AN HACHETTE UK COMPANY

Please note that AQA does not review or approve any of the weblinks mentioned in the book.

The Publishers would like to thank the following for permission to reproduce copyright material.

Photo credits

p.3 © Steven Purcell/Alamy Stock Photo; **p.2** © Michael Stephens/PA Archive/ PA Images; **p.28** © Science & Society Picture Library/Getty Images; **p.61** © REX/ Shutterstock; **p.95** © Trinity Mirror/Mirrorpix/Alamy Stock Photo; **p.157** © Allstar Picture Library/Alamy Stock Photo; **p.159** © Trinity Mirror/Mirrorpix/Alamy Stock Photo; **p.165** © Sailesh Patel/Shutterstock; **p.168** © Photosorensen/Shutterstock; **p.174** © blue light images/Alamy Stock Photo; **p.178** © WavebreakMediaMicro/stock. adobe.com; **p.187** © Homer Sykes/Alamy Stock Photo; **p.199** © Eric James/Alamy Stock Photo; **p.203** © Lordprice Collection/Alamy Stock Photo; **p.205** © Victor/stock. adobe.com; **p.238** © Stephen Barnes/Alamy Stock Photo; **p.266** © Robert Przybysz/ Shutterstock; **p.272** © ZUMA Press, Inc./Alamy Stock Photo; **p.291** © Gary Lucken/ Alamy Stock Photo; **p.298** © Everett Collection Historical/Alamy Stock Photo; **p.307** © The Travel Library/REX/Shutterstock; **p.314** © Prometheus72/Shutterstock; **p.331** © Janine Wiedel Photolibrary/Alamy Stock Photo; **p.339** © Huntstock, Inc/Alamy Stock Photo; **p.346** © Crown copyright; **p.358** © David Ball/Alamy Stock Photo; **p.361** © TopFoto.co.uk; **p.375** © Lee Martin/Alamy Stock Photo; **p.389** © Hadrian/Shutterstock.

Acknowledgements

p.9 Reprinted with permission of *Independent*; **p.10** Reprinted with permission of TRINITY MIRROR PUBLISHING LIMITED; **pp.19–20** Reprinted with permission of *Darlington and Stockton Times*; **p.24** Reprinted with permission of *The Times*/News Licensing; **pp.33–4** © Guardian News and Media; **pp.60–1** Reprinted with permission of *Metro*; **p.67** Reprinted with permission of Press Association; **p.184** © Guardian News and Media; **pp.254–5** Reprinted with permission of *Daily Mail*; **p.312** © Guardian News and Media; **pp.325–6** Reprinted with permission of Health Service Journal; **p.381** Reprinted with permission of Adam Ramsay; **p.383** data obtained from National Strategy for Police Information Systems.

Every effort has been made to trace all copyright holders, but if any have been inadvertently overlooked, the Publishers will be pleased to make the necessary arrangements at the first opportunity.

Although every effort has been made to ensure that website addresses are correct at time of going to press, Hodder Education cannot be held responsible for the content of any website mentioned in this book. It is sometimes possible to find a relocated web page by typing in the address of the home page for a website in the URL window of your browser.

Hachette UK's policy is to use papers that are natural, renewable and recyclable products and made from wood grown in well-managed forests and other controlled sources. The logging and manufacturing processes are expected to conform to the environmental regulations of the country of origin.

Orders: please contact Hachette UK Distribution, Hely Hutchinson Centre, Milton Road, Didcot, Oxfordshire, OX11 7HH. Telephone: +44 (0)1235 827827. Email education@hachette. co.uk Lines are open from 9 a.m. to 5 p.m., Monday to Friday. You can also order through our website: www.hoddereducation.co.uk

ISBN: 978 1 5104 0174 7

© Jacqueline Martin, Nicholas Price, Richard Wortley 2018

First published in 2018 by

Hodder Education,
An Hachette UK Company
Carmelite House
50 Victoria Embankment
London EC4Y 0DZ

www.hoddereducation.co.uk

Impression number   10 9 8 7 6

Year   2022

Cover photo © fStop Images GmbH /Alamy Stock Photo

Illustrations by Aptara Inc., Peter Lubach and Ian Foulis

Typeset in Caecilia LT Std/45 Light, 9.5/13.5 pts. by Aptara Inc.

Printed in India

A catalogue record for this title is available from the British Library.

Contents

Tort law

Human rights

Preface

This book and Book 1 *AQA A-level Law for Year 1 and AS* are written for the AQA specification for A-level Law. The order of topics covered follows that of the AQA specification. There is also a chart setting out the coverage of the specification and where to find the related material in this book.

As well as factual material on the topics, evaluation is included for all areas where it is required by AQA's specification.

The content is broken up into manageable 'bites', and throughout we have used features which have proved popular in previous texts for A-and AS-level

Law. These include key facts charts, case charts, highlighting cases and diagrams.

Activities for students are also included. These are based on a variety of sources, such as newspaper and internet articles, research material and decided cases. There are also application tasks so that students can practise applying the law to given scenarios.

The law is as we believe it to be on 1 March 2018.

Jacqueline Martin

Nick Price

Richard Wortley

Tables of legislation

Acts

Secondary legislation

International conventions and other provisions

Table of cases

Introduction

This book has been written and designed for the new AQA A-level Law specification, introduced for first teaching in September 2017. It supplements *AQA A-level Law for Year 1 and AS*, and together the books cover the content required for AQA A-level Law for first examination in 2019.

Book 1 covers the content that is typically taught in the first year of the course, including an introduction to the nature and rule of law, the civil and criminal court systems and any alternatives available, the personnel involved in the legal system and how civil and criminal cases are funded. It also deals with how laws are made and how they are used in court. The book also contains some specific areas of criminal and civil law.

In the criminal law section, the general rules and content of criminal offences are covered, with particular emphasis on non-fatal offences against the person. In the civil law section, the emphasis is on the law of tort, particularly the rules of negligence and of occupiers' liability and the remedies that can be claimed.

In this book, the topics of Book 1 are developed further, and it is likely that teachers will cover its content in the second year of the course. Criminal law is explored in greater depth, as the book considers fatal offences and some property offences, together with the rules of some part and full defences. Knowledge and understanding of tort law are extended by considering some further actions relating to land and vicarious liability. Optional topics of contract law and human rights are encompassed. Some theoretical issues are also covered, including issues of law and morality, law and justice, and law and society.

Books 1 and 2 together cover the content required for the AQA A-level Law specification. To view the full specification, and examples of assessment material, visit **www.aqa.org.uk**.

How to use this book

Each chapter has a range of features that have been designed to present the course content in a clear and accessible way, to give you confidence and to support you.

Learning objectives

Each chapter starts with a list of what is to be studied and how this relates to the specification.

Key terms

Key terms, highlighted in bold in the text, are defined.

Key fact tables

These provide a summary of key facts.

Tables of key cases

These include descriptions of cases and comments on the points of law they illustrate.

Tips

These are suggestions to help further your learning.

Case studies

These provide examples of cases to illustrate points of law.

Extension activities

These include challenging questions and activities to help advance your understanding.

Look online

These weblinks will help you with further research and reading on the internet.

In the news

Real events relating to specific areas of law are covered.

Summary

These boxes contain summaries of what you have learned in each section.

Activities

These appear throughout the book and have been designed to help you apply your knowledge and develop your understanding of various topics.

Practice questions

These help you test your knowledge.

Book coverage of specification content

A-level content	Covered in
3.1 THE NATURE OF LAW AND THE ENGLISH LEGAL SYSTEM	
Nature of law	Book 1 Chapters 1.1, 1.2, 1.3 and 1.4
Nature of law: law and society	
The role law plays in society	Book 2 Chapter 1.1
The effect of law on enforceable rights and the balance required between competing interests (e.g. public and private)	Book 2 Chapter 1.2
The meaning and importance of fault in civil and/or criminal law	Book 2 Chapter 1.3
Nature of law: law and morality	Book 2 Chapter 2
The distinction between law and morality and the diversity of moral views in a pluralist society	Book 2 Chapters 2.1 and 2.2
The relationship between law and morality and its importance	Book 2 Chapter 2.3
The legal enforcement of moral values	Book 2 Chapter 2.4
Nature of law: law and justice	Book 2 Chapter 3
The meaning of justice and theories of justice	Book 2 Chapter 3.1
The extent to which the law (civil and/or criminal) achieves justice	Book 2 Chapter 3.2
The rule of law	Book 1 Chapter 2
Law making: parliamentary law making	Book 1 Chapter 3
Law making: delegated legislation	Book 1 Chapter 4
Law making: statutory interpretation	Book 1 Chapter 5
Law making: judicial precedent	Book 1 Chapter 6
Law making: law reform	Book 1 Chapter 7
Law making: the European Union	Book 1 Chapter 8
The legal system: the civil courts and other forms of dispute resolution	Book 1 Chapters 9 and 10
The legal system: the criminal courts and lay people	Book 1 Chapters 11, 12, 13, and 14
The legal system: legal personnel and the judiciary	Book 1 Chapters 15 and 16
The legal system: access to justice and funding	Book 1 Chapter 17
3.2 CRIMINAL LAW	
The rules of criminal law	Book 1 Chapter 18
Theory in criminal law	Book 2 Chapter 4
Harm as the basis for criminalising conduct	Book 2 Chapter 4.3

A-level content	Covered in
Autonomy, fault and individual responsibility	Book 2 Chapter 4.4
Principles in formulating rules of criminal law: ■ fair labelling ■ correspondence ■ maximum certainty ■ no retrospective liability	Book 2 Chapter 4.7
General elements of liability	Book 1 Chapters 19, 20 and 21
Fatal offences against the person	
Common law offence of murder Voluntary manslaughter: ■ loss of control ■ diminished responsibility	Book 2 Chapters 5 and 6.2 Book 2 Chapter 6.3
Common law offence of involuntary manslaughter: ■ unlawful act manslaughter ■ gross negligence manslaughter	Book 2 Chapter 7.2 Book 2 Chapter 7.3
Non-fatal offences against the person	Book 1 Chapter 22
Property offences	
Theft (s 1 Theft Act 1968)	Book 2 Chapter 8
Robbery (s 8 Theft Act 1968)	Book 2 Chapter 9
Preliminary offence	
Attempt (s 1 Criminal Attempts Act 1981)	Book 2 Chapter 10
Defences: capacity defences	
Insanity	Book 2 Chapter 11.1
Automatism	Book 2 Chapter 11.2
Intoxication	Book 2 Chapter 11.3
Defences: necessity defences	
Self-defence/prevention of crime	Book 2 Chapter 12.1
Duress	Book 2 Chapter 12.2
Duress of circumstances	Book 2 Chapter 12.3
3.3 TORT	
The rules of tort law	Book 1 Chapter 23
	Book 2 Chapter 13.1
Theory of tort law	
Basic understanding of the public policy factors governing the imposition of a duty of care (the *Caparo* three-part test) in a claim for physical injury to people and damage to property	Book 1, Chapter 24.1
Basic understanding of the policy factors governing imposition of liability for pure economic loss and psychiatric injury	Book 2 Chapters 13.2, 14.1 and 14.2

A-level content	Covered in
Basic understanding of the factors governing the objective standard of care in an action for negligence	Book 1 Chapter 24.2
Basic understanding of the factors governing the grant of an injunction as a remedy, and the way in which conflicting interests are balanced	Book 1 Chapter 26.4
Basic understanding of the nature and purpose of vicarious liability	Book 2 Chapter 16
Liability in negligence for physical injury to people and damage to property	Book 1 Chapter 24
Liability in negligence for economic loss and psychiatric injury	
Liability for pure economic loss caused by negligent acts and negligent misstatements	Book 2 Chapter 14.1
Liability for psychiatric injury sustained by primary and secondary victims	Book 2 Chapter 14.2
Occupiers' liability	Book 1 Chapter 25
Nuisance and the escape of dangerous things	
Private nuisance	Book 2 Chapter 15.1
The rule in *Rylands v Fletcher*	Book 2 Chapter 15.2
Vicarious liability	
Nature and purpose of vicarious liability	Book 2 Chapter 16.1
Testing of employment status	Book 2 Chapter 16.2
Other areas of vicarious liability	Book 2 Chapter 16.4
Defences	
Contributory negligence	Book 1 Chapter 24.5.1
Consent (*volenti non fit injuria*)	Book 1 Chapter 24.5.2
Defences specific to private nuisance and the rule in *Rylands v Fletcher*	Book 2 Chapter 15
Remedies	Book 1 Chapter 26
3.4 LAW OF CONTRACT	
The rules of contract law	
Rules and principles of contract law concerning formation, terms, vitiating factors, discharge of a contract and associated remedies	Book 2 Chapter 17.1
Theory of contract law	
Analysis and evaluation of the voluntary nature of a contract and of principles governing contract law, with particular reference to the issues specified below: ■ outline of the theory of freedom of contract and the competing need to protect the consumer ■ outline of the distinction between offers, offers in unilateral contracts and invitation to treat; outline of acceptances, including the rationale for the postal rule and its relationship to electronic communications ■ outline of the rationale for consideration, and of the relationships between consideration and privity, and between consideration and economic duress ■ outline of the nature and effectiveness of exemption clauses ■ outline of the nature and effectiveness of remedies, including specifically consumer remedies	Book 2 Chapter 17.2

A-level content	Covered in
Essential requirements of contract	
Offer and acceptance	Book 2 Chapter 18
Consideration and privity, intention to create legal relations	Book 2 Chapter 19
Contract terms: general	
Express and implied terms	Book 2 Chapter 20.1
Conditions, warranties and innominate terms	Book 2 Chapter 20.2
Contract terms: specific terms implied by statute law in relation to consumer contracts	

Consumer Rights Act 2015:
■ terms implied into a contract to supply goods:
  ■ section 9 (satisfactory quality)
  ■ section 10 (fitness for particular purpose)
  ■ section 11 (description)
■ Remedies for the breach of a term implied into a contract to supply goods:
  ■ section 20 (short term right to reject)
  ■ section 23 (right to repair or a replacement)
  ■ section 24 (right to a price reduction or a final right to reject)
■ Terms implied into a contract to supply services:
  ■ section 49 (reasonable care and skill)
  ■ section 52 (performance within a reasonable time)
■ Remedies for the breach of a term implied into a contract to supply services:
  ■ section 55 (right to repeat performance)
  ■ section 56 (right to a price reduction)
	Book 2 Chapter 20.5

Contract terms: exclusion clauses	
Basic understanding of the nature of exclusion and limitation clauses	Book 2 Chapter 21.1
Common law control of exclusion clauses: rules relating to incorporation; brief understanding of the rules relating to construction	Book 2 Chapter 21.1
Statutory control of exclusion clauses: Unfair Contract Terms Act 1977 (s 2 and s 3); Consumer Rights Act 2015 (s 31, s 57 and s 65)	Book 2 Chapter 21.2
Vitiating factors	
Misrepresentation (nature, types and remedies)	Book 2 Chapters 22.2, 22.3 and 22.4
Economic duress (definition and remedies)	Book 2 Chapters 22.5 and 22.6
Discharge of a contract	
Performance	Book 2 Chapter 23.2
Breach (actual and anticipatory breach)	Book 2 Chapter 23.3
Frustration	Book 2 Chapter 23.4
Remedies	
Compensatory damages (including categories of recoverable loss, causation, remoteness and mitigation)	Book 2 Chapter 24.2
Equitable remedies of specific performance and rescission	Book 2 Chapter 24.3
Termination of contract for breach	Book 2 Chapter 24.4

A-level content	Covered in
3.5 HUMAN RIGHTS	
Rules in human rights law	
Rules and principles of law relating to the rights to life, to liberty and security of person, to privacy, to freedom of expression, and to freedom of assembly and association, as recognised by the European Convention on Human Rights and in the United Kingdom	Book 2 Chapter 25.1
Theory in human rights	
Theories of rights	Book 2 Chapter 25.2
Rights contrasted with liberties	Book 2 Chapter 25.3
The scope of 'fundamental' human rights	Book 2 Chapter 25.4
Human rights in international law	
The Second World War and its aftermath	Book 2 Chapter 26
The United Nations and the Universal Declaration of Human Rights 1948	
The Council of Europe and the European Convention on Human Rights 1953	
Human rights in the United Kingdom prior to the Human Rights Act 1998	
The status of the European Convention on Human Rights in the United Kingdom, and the impact of decisions of the European Court of Human Rights	Book 2 Chapters 27.1 and 27.2
Human Rights in the United Kingdom after the enactment of the Human Rights Act 1998	
Extent and method of incorporation and interpretation of the provisions of the European Convention on Human Rights	Book 2 Chapter 27.3
Impact on constitutional arrangements and on law in the United Kingdom, including entrenched nature of the Human Rights Act 1998 in the devolutionary settlement of Scotland and Northern Ireland	Book 2 Chapter 27.4
Criticisms of human rights	Book 2 Chapter 27.5
Article 2 of the European Convention on Human Rights 1953	
Article 2.1: right to life	Book 2 Chapter 28.1
Article 2.2: justified exceptions	Book 2 Chapter 28.2
Article 5 of the European Convention on Human Rights 1953	
Article 5.1: right to liberty and security of person	Book 2 Chapter 29.1
Article 5.1a–5.1c: justified deprivation of liberty – lawful arrest or detention	Book 2 Chapter 29.2
Article 5.2–5.5: additional requirements to justify deprivation of liberty in cases of lawful arrest or detention	Book 2 Chapter 29.2
Article 8 of the European Convention on Human Rights 1953	
Article 8.1: right to respect for private and family life, home and correspondence	Book 2 Chapter 30.1
Article 10 of the European Convention on Human Rights 1953	
Article 10.1: right to freedom of expression: ■ receive information and ideas ■ communicate information and ideas	Book 2 Chapter 31

A-level content	Covered in
Article 11 of the European Convention on Human Rights 1953	
Article 11.1: right to freedom of peaceful assembly and to freedom of association with others	Book 2 Chapter 32.1
Restrictions	
Restrictions on the rights under Article 8.1–8.2	Book 2 Chapter 30.2
Restrictions on the rights under Article 10.1–10.2	Book 2 Chapter 31.2
Restrictions on the rights under Article 11.1–11.2: general requirements relating to restrictions	Book 2 Chapter 32.2
Enforcement	
Claims before the European Court of Human Rights; the role of domestic courts; the effect of decisions on states and claimants	Book 2 Chapters 33.1 and 33.2
The process of judicial review	Book 2 Chapter 33.4
Human rights and English law	
The right to life: an outline of criminal and civil law provisions and investigatory procedures ■ Homicide and associated offences (including the defence of self-defence/prevention of crime) ■ Obligations on police and others in planning dangerous operations ■ Protective policing ■ Civil law negligence ■ Independent investigation of deaths in custody or attributable to agents of the State	Book 2 Chapter 28.2 Book 2 Chapter 29.2
Deprivation of liberty	Book 2 Chapter 30.5
Privacy and communication: criminal and civil law provisions which protect or restrict the rights	Book 2 Chapter 31.3
Expression, assembly and association: in addition to relevant provisions identified above which impact on the balance between privacy and the right to freedom of expression, assembly and association	Book 2 Chapter 32.3
Reform	
Reform of the protection of human rights in the UK	Book 2 Chapter 27.5

Nature of law

1 Law and society

After reading this chapter, you should be able to:
- Understand the role law plays in society
- Understand the effect of law on enforceable rights and the balance required between competing interests (for example public and private)
- Understand the meaning and importance of fault in civil and/or criminal law

1.1 The role law plays in society

1.1.1 What is society?

According to sociologists, a society is a group of people with common territory, interaction and culture. There are many individuals in society who share aspects of their culture, such as language, beliefs, values, behaviour and material objects that make up their way of life. Members of a society will not necessarily have every aspect of culture in common. This may appear to give separate societies within a geographical country, such as where there is apartheid or large groups of people with the same ethnicity living close to each other.

Society today is very complex and every state has different groups within society. Pluralism is a term used when smaller groups within a larger society maintain their unique cultural identities, and their values and practices are accepted by the wider culture provided they are consistent with the laws and values of the wider society.

1.1.2 Pluralism

In the context of this chapter, **pluralism** may be defined as a form of society in which the members of minority groups maintain their independent cultural traditions while being a part of society as a whole. A pluralist believes that the existence of different types of people, beliefs and opinions within a society is a good thing. This requires tolerance from everyone concerned.

Pluralism is not the same as multiculturalism. Multiculturalism lacks a dominant culture. If the dominant culture is weakened, societies can easily pass from cultural pluralism into multiculturalism, without any intentional steps being taken by that

society. If communities function separately from each other, or compete with one another, they are not considered culturally pluralistic.

Key term

Pluralism – a form of society in which the members of minority groups maintain their independent cultural traditions.

The United Kingdom is a society composed of many groups of people, some of whom originally belonged to other societies. There is a long history of invasion, such as the Romans, the Vikings and the Norman Conquest. Since the Norman Conquest there have been many examples of relatively large immigrations to the United Kingdom, such as the Huguenots who, in the seventeenth and eighteenth centuries, left their homes in France to escape persecution. The influence of the British Empire and Commonwealth enabled immigration from many parts of the world. Successive governments have either encouraged or discouraged immigration from different countries and of different groups.

Members of a particular culture, religion or immigrant society tend to congregate together for comfort and also to preserve the cultural identity of their society. Some practices that are common in other societies will inevitably offend or contradict the values and beliefs of society as a whole. Groups seeking to become part of a pluralistic society often have to give up many of their original traditions in order to fit in. This is known as assimilation, and can be seen in the gradual loss of immigrant's language as they assimilate society's use of English as the language of society in the UK.

However, in pluralistic societies, groups do not have to give up all of their former beliefs and practices. Many groups within a pluralistic society retain their traditions, such as Chinese communities celebrating the Lunar New Year.

UK society has people from different societies who blend together into a single mass. In a pluralistic society, no single group is officially considered more influential than another. However, powerful informal mechanisms, such as prejudice and discrimination, work to keep many groups out of the political process or out of certain neighbourhoods, or to prevent free expression of their values and beliefs. The role of law includes the regulation and control of society.

Chinese New Year parade in Manchester

1.1.3 Law in society

The rule of law cannot exist without a transparent legal system. Law attempts to control society through regulation. This requires a clear set of laws that are freely and easily accessible to all, strong enforcement structures, and an independent judiciary to protect citizens against the arbitrary use of power by the state, individuals or any other organisation. Lord Bingham, at the end of the twentieth century, held office successively as Master of the Rolls, Lord Chief Justice of England and Wales and Senior Law Lord of the United Kingdom, the only person ever to hold all three offices. In 2010 he published *The Rule of Law,* in which he identified the core principle of the rule of law as being:

> **...that all persons and authorities within the state, whether public or private, should be bound by and entitled to the benefit of laws publicly and prospectively promulgated and publicly administered in the courts.**

He set out the rule of law through eight principles which society, the state and the judiciary must embrace. His principles are these:

1 The state must abide by both domestic and international law. This means no government has the ability to act at whim.

2 People should only be punished for crimes set out by law.

3 Questions on the infringement of rights should be subject to the application of law, not discretion.

4 The law should be accessible, clear, precise and open to public scrutiny.

5 All people should be treated equally.

6 There must be respect for human rights.

7 Courts must be accessible, affordable and cases should be heard without excessive delay.

8 The means must be provided for resolving, without prohibitive cost or inordinate delay, *bona fide* disputes which the parties themselves are unable to resolve.

Lord Bingham

These principles result in certain roles for law in society:

1   To protect people from harm – typically by the mechanisms of the criminal law with respect to harm by other people or by dangerous things such as unsafe machinery or pollution.
2   To ensure a common good – by providing facilities for all such as education and health care.
3   To settle arguments and disputes – this is the idea of a civil justice system.

These roles result in regulating and controlling society and make a balance between competing interests within society. These principles and roles highlight the importance of fault as a basis for law in society.

Tip

When considering law and society, consider the balance of interests between the state, the majority of society and minorities within society. Does the state protect minorities or does it persecute them?

1.1.4 Social control

Much of the balance between different sectors of society is aimed to achieve **social control**, which may be either informal or formal. Informal social control occurs through the family, the peer group, the local community and societal group. Formal social control occurs through specific social agencies which have the role of maintaining order in society. This is the criminal justice system, including the police force, the judiciary, the probation and prison services as well as law makers – Parliament through Acts of Parliament and through delegating its powers to local law makers such as local councils and the judiciary in its interpretation and application of the law. The civil justice system also does this so that disputes can be settled through formal mechanisms trusted by society.

Social control is important because without it there would be the likelihood of anarchy. Social control should protect those less able to protect themselves, such as children, disabled people or those who are ill.

Key term

Social control – the ways in which our behaviour, thoughts and appearance are regulated by the norms, rules, laws and social structures of society.

Rosco Pound's book, *Social Control Through Law*, was published in 1942. He suggested that the subject matter of law involves examining manifestations of human nature which require social control to assert or realise individual expectations. Pound formulated a list of social-ethical principles, with a three-fold purpose:

1   They identify and explain human claims, demands, or interests of a given social order.
2   They express what the majority of individuals in a given society want the law to do.
3   They guide the courts in applying the law.

He states that individual interests, public interests and social interests overlap and that claims, demands and desires can be placed in all three categories. Rights, unlike interests, have many different meanings.

The increasing rate of litigation in society can be seen as a result of the decline of the family's and religious institutions' control over an individual's behaviour. The result is that the law exerts greater control over the public and private lives of most members of society. Law is now the paramount agency of social control.

Social control entails rules of behaviour that should be followed by the members of a society. Some of the rules of conduct fall into the realm of good manners as the culture defines them. As such they describe behaviour that is socially desirable but not necessarily compulsory. Other rules of conduct are not optional and are enforced by laws.

Some areas of law are confusing because they are inconsistent or open to interpretation in different situations. Killing another individual is considered to be a serious crime except when it is done in battle during a war. There is a distinction between murder, manslaughter and other crimes where a death has occurred such as causing death by dangerous driving. The offence of murder has a mandatory life sentence. Other offences involving death do not. There is a wide disparity in sentencing for the same offence.

Look online

Read this article online and discuss whether the sentence was appropriate for this crime: www.thestar.co.uk/whats-on/out-and-about/death-crash-driver-freed-1-316624.

Suicide is not a crime. The law on assisted suicide indicates the confusion there is in the law. Assisting a suicide is a crime. Those convicted could face up to 14 years in prison. Whether there is a prosecution is a matter of prosecution policy. The policy should be to balance the interests of the individual against society's view of what is right.

The policy includes a list of public interest factors that will influence whether or not someone is prosecuted for assisting suicide. In cases of encouraging or assisting suicide, prosecutors must apply the public interest factors in making their decision. A prosecution will usually take place unless the prosecutor is sure that there are sufficient public interest factors against it. This is balancing interests in practice.

A prosecution is less likely if:

- the person made a voluntary, informed decision to end his or her life
- the assister was wholly motivated by compassion
- the assister tried to discourage the person, and
- the assister's actions could be seen as reluctant encouragement or assistance.

The policy says that police and prosecutors should take a common sense approach to financial gain. If compassion was clearly the only reason behind the assister's actions, the fact that he or she may have gained some benefit will not usually be a factor in favour of prosecution. This is hardly clear for a situation like that of Debbie Purdy who had multiple sclerosis (MS). Shortly after her diagnosis in 1995, she began to think about how to have choice and control over her death. She argued that it was against her human rights not to know if her husband would be prosecuted if he went abroad with her so that she could die in a country where assisted suicide is legal. In 2009, she won her case in the House of Lords. The judges said that the law was not clear enough about when people would be prosecuted for encouraging or assisting suicide and guidelines have been drawn up.

Criminal and civil disputes are rarely simple matters in any society. Laws may be open to interpretation, and there is often a difference of opinion about the evidence. In criminal law, when guilt is established, there can be a difference of opinion about the appropriate punishment. In civil law, there may be disagreement about the quantum of damages or the wording of an injunction. Because these issues are open to differing conclusions, most societies settle legal cases in a manner agreed by the entire community, or at least a representative sample of it.

The jury system is based on this idea, but jurors do not choose the sentence, only whether or not the defendant is guilty. The assumption is made that jurors will come to an understanding that would be acceptable to a 'reasonable man'. In most societies in the past, the reasonable man was thought to be male and judges were also almost exclusively male. Women and children were not thought to be reasonable, nor were uneducated poor men. Subsequently, they were excluded from being jurors and judges. Society today has changed and the law recognises this. However, although the law recognises equality, it does not always enforce it.

1.2 The effect of law on enforceable rights and the balance required between competing interests (such as public and private)

Through regulation by the law, control of society is expected to be effected. The notion of fault in this context will be explored later in this chapter in the context of criminal law and the law of tort. These two areas of law also balance conflicting interests in society. Examples can be seen in the conflict between every individual and the criminal law, for example where defences such as insanity and loss of control are in issue. In the law of tort, there is a balance to be made between the victim and the tortfeasor;

this balance may well be viewed through damages, even though money cannot fully balance a loss of life or the loss of expectation of a long life. The way in which the law attempts to balance conflicting interests will now be discussed in the context of contract law and human rights law.

When considering the balance of interests, there are three questions to consider:

1 What interests can be identified?
2 What is the conflict between these interests?
3 What is the legal mechanism by which the conflict is mediated?

1.2.1 The balance of competing interests in contract law

In contract law, the courts are often confronted with the interests of two innocent parties, both of whom believe they have a plausible legal argument.

What interests can be identified?

In any contract there are two obvious interests – the two parties to the contract. Each party to the contract wants to get the best deal possible. However, the two parties rarely are acting as equals in the negotiations. The law recognises this by categorising parties to a contract as consumers or traders, to use the nomenclature of the Consumer Rights Act 2015. The state also wants to ensure that the different interests are served by the law and that regulations ensure protection and encourage a thriving economy, whether the contract is between two individuals who may each be considered a consumer, or two businesses who can be seen as traders.

Similarly, the parties can be seen as buyer and seller of goods or buyer of services and provider of services (or a mixture of both), with parties being consumers or traders (businesses).

Third parties also have potential interest in a contract where the subject matter of the contract may benefit them. Examples of this include where someone is given a present and the present then proves to not work correctly, or where one person books a holiday for a group of friends.

What is the conflict between these interests?

The conflict arises from the desire of a stronger party to dictate the terms of a contract. This can be seen in a number of areas. Most obviously, this comes with respect to written terms in a contract. If there is complete freedom of contract, the only option for a weaker party is to decline to accept an offer that has terms that seem unacceptable and so decline to make a contract.

The conflict also arises from the principle that only a party to a contract can take legal action upon it. This means that those who are not a party to the contract cannot enforce any rights they might have had if they had made the contract directly.

What is the legal mechanism by which the conflict is mediated?

The law addresses these conflicts in a number of ways including:

- by implying terms in contracts between traders and consumers through the Consumer Rights Act 2015
- by regulating the legal effectiveness of exclusion clauses in contracts not covered by the Consumer Rights Act 2015
- through the Contracts (Rights of Third Parties) Act 1999
- through judicial creativity with respect to remedies.

Implied terms in contracts between traders and consumers through the Consumer Rights Act 2015
Law controls the way in which sectors of society can impose their will and profit from others through legislation such as the Consumer Rights Act 2015. This Act is sometimes criticised for protecting consumers in society at the expense of business. The Consumer Rights Act 2015 brings together rights and remedies available to consumers when making a contract with a business. The law is supposed to be straightforward so that consumers can buy and businesses can sell to them knowing what must be done. When problems arise, disputes should be sorted out more quickly and cheaply. The difficulty with this is that many consumers do not know their rights and some businesses try to avoid their duties. The lack of access to the law for many on the basis of ignorance and cost still means that many people in society do not attempt to enforce their rights and business still holds sway, particularly businesses with a poor record of ethical dealings.

For details of the rights of consumers, see Chapter 20, section 20.5.

By regulating the legal effectiveness of exclusion clauses in contracts not covered by the Consumer Rights Act 2015

This applies to non-consumer contracts – not just contracts between businesses, but also those where someone who would normally be considered a consumer is involved, but the subject matter does not fall within the scope of the Consumer Rights Act 2015. An example of this latter category would be a rental agreement on a flat or house. Here there is often an imbalance between the parties and successive legislation has failed to prevent illegal actions and unfair contracts imposed by so called 'rogue landlords'. The article below shows that local authorities are having to take steps to redress this imbalance between many members of society and an unscrupulous few.

In the news

Council crackdown on rogue landlords to improve housing standards

North Lincolnshire Council is looking to launch a new licence for private landlords, aimed at protecting their most vulnerable residents and raising housing standards in the private rented sector for the benefit of tenants.

Many landlords in areas of Scunthorpe act responsibly but unfortunately this is not the case across the board. As a result, in some properties residents live in inadequate conditions that the property owners are doing little about.

The new scheme would require all private landlords within the designated area to apply for a licence for each property they let out. The licence would then last for five years.

To become licence-holders, landlords would have to meet certain standards before they could legally rent out a property. A set of conditions would also be attached to the licence regarding the standard and management of the property itself. The licence would ensure that all the houses in this area are fit for tenants to live in and they have the full range of facilities they need.

Cllr Richard Hannigan, Deputy Leader of North Lincolnshire Council, said:

> This scheme is not meant to stop people renting privately in Scunthorpe town centre, nor is it to deter landlords from renting out their properties. This new licence will root out and tackle rogue landlords who are taking advantage of their tenants by allowing them to live in unacceptable conditions.
>
> We recognise and thank many of the landlords in this area who are good landlords; they should have no problems achieving a licence for their properties. However, this new licence will ensure all landlords in the area take responsibility for the homes they let and their tenants.
>
> Bringing in a set of standards for landlords and their properties will have a knock-on effect on the neighbourhood, helping to keep it cleaner, reducing anti-social behaviour, and making it altogether a nicer place to live.

Before bringing into effect the new licensing scheme, the council will be consulting with residents, landlords and other affected parties to gather information and opinions on how the licence will help.

Source: Adapted from an article on the North Lincolnshire Council website, 22 September 2017

While few landlords will deliberately include the right to use violence to evict a tenant, many will use exclusion clauses and related notices to try to evade their legal responsibilities. Even where the law on exclusion clauses makes the term unenforceable, the mere existence of the term will put many off complaining or trying to enforce their rights. Exclusion clauses are terms in a contract that exclude or limit liability for a breach of the contract. They may also attempt to exclude liability in other areas of law, for example under the tort of negligence. Exclusion clauses also include terms in a contract that limit liability for a breach of contract or other loss.

The judiciary has moved from the idea of freedom of contract seen in *L'Estrange v Graucob* (1934) to find ways of reducing or extinguishing the effect of some exclusion clauses, particularly those contained in notices with decisions such as *Olley v Marlborough Court Hotel* (1949), but the effect of the decisions left an inconsistency in approach to the protection of those in a weaker bargaining position affected by the existence of the exclusion clause, as can be seen in the cases of *Spurling v Bradshaw* (1956) and *Hollier v Rambler Motors* (1972). Parliamentary efforts such as the Unfair Contract Terms Act 1977 can be criticised for using expressions such as 'so far as is fair and reasonable', which could be seen as a license to litigate – litigation that is not supported by legal funding and which is discouraged by the effort involved and lack of confidence in the legal system to provide a remedy without undue risk to the claimant and which, if successful, might be enforced successfully against the defendant.

It should also be noted that many businesses with a large customer base in the UK make it a term of the contract that the law is a foreign law; for example, Amazon refers to the law of Luxembourg in some terms and conditions and Spotify to the law of Sweden. While these legal systems may be perfectly satisfactory in balancing the interests, for example of the business and its consumer customers, it remains another daunting hurdle for any who might have a legitimate claim to make.

The Contracts (Rights of Third Parties) Act 1999

We have seen a shift in the law as stated by judges with respect to third party rights in contract over the years from the approach in *Tweddle v Atkinson* (1861), where the claim failed as the claimant was not a party to the contract and so had no legal interest in the case. This strict rule has been modified by the 1999 Act, but this Act has had little practical effect as many contracts exclude its effect and there has not been any test of the reasonableness of such an exclusion clause to date.

An example from a barrister's chambers is:

> ❝ This Agreement governs the rights and obligations of the Barrister and the Authorised Person towards each other and confers no benefit upon any third party (including the Lay Client). The ability of third parties to enforce any rights under the Contracts (Rights of Third Parties) Act 1999 is hereby excluded. ❞

Source: http://onepumpcourt.co.uk/standard-contractual-terms/

Judicial creativity with respect to remedies

The law states that only a party to a contract may sue on it and gain a remedy. However, in *Jackson v Horizon Holidays* (1975) the House of Lords awarded the claimant damages on his own behalf and on behalf of his family for their disappointment over a package holiday that failed to match the advertised description. This award was made even though Mr Jackson was the only member of his family who was a party to the contract for the holiday.

There are of course many reasons to applaud this decision, but it might well be argued that this just decision is actually no more than an implied application of the law of agency. Despite this, many still have difficulty successfully claiming from travel companies and airlines.

1.2.2 The balance of competing interests in human rights law

Human rights law balances the individual and his or her freedoms under the European Convention on Human Rights (ECHR) with the law of the state. The balance is between the human rights of the individual and the state and its organs. This may be reflected in civil law or criminal law, or both together. It does this in three ways:

1 All UK law must be interpreted, so far as it is possible to do so, in a way that is compatible with rights under the Convention.

2 If an Act of Parliament breaches these rights, the legislation is incompatible with Convention rights. The law remains valid. However, it remains up to Parliament to decide whether or not to amend the law.

3 It is unlawful for any public authority to act incompatibly with human rights, unless required by a statutory duty to do so. Where an individual's rights have been violated, he or she can bring court proceedings against the public authority.

If a declaration of incompatibility is made, the Government has the choice of:

- doing nothing
- changing the offending law or the practice
- making a remedial order; this can include amending an Act or a piece of secondary legislation, and under s 10 of the Human Rights Act (HRA) 1998 a piece of legislation can be repealed by ministerial order (a 'Henry VIII clause').

Such a declaration should only be made as a last resort, and s 3 requires the courts to do all they can to achieve compatibility. They should not rewrite legislation or do anything that undermines the relationship between the legislature and the courts.

> See Chapter 29 for details of the case of *R (on the application of T, JB and AW) v Chief Constable of Greater Manchester, Secretary of State for the Home Department and Secretary of State for Justice* (2013).

Related changes continue to be proposed to refine the law on human rights in the UK.

In the news

Rules on childhood criminal records should be relaxed, MPs say

Rules governing the disclosure of childhood criminal records should be relaxed, a new Commons report says, claiming Britain's current system could be falling short of its international obligations.

According to the report from Westminster's Justice Select Committee, violent offences committed under the age of 18 should not always be automatically flagged up in checks as it prevents children from moving on from their past and 'creates barriers to rehabilitation'.

Calling for a major overhaul of the scheme, the MPs warn the current system undermines the principles of youth justice, adding that rules could mean the Government is falling short of the UK's obligations under the UN Convention on the Rights of the Child.

The committee said the problems caused by the disclosure regime could affect significant numbers of people. In 2014/15, 26 per cent of standard Disclosure and Barring Service (DBS) checks and 23 per cent of enhanced checks related to subjects who were under 18 at the time of a conviction.

Most sex offences cannot be filtered and the report raises concerns over the implications for children penalised for 'sexting'. It says: 'We do not think that the difficult problem of sexual offending by children is assisted by giving them a record of a non-filterable sexual offence.'

The assessment suggests a number of features that could be included in a new filtering scheme for offences committed in childhood.

'The Government confirmed to us that its primary objective in youth justice is to stop people being drawn into crime, with consequent blighting of the life chances, as well as harm being caused to victims and communities,' said Bob Neill, the chair of the Justice Select Committee.

'But these laudable aims are systematically undermined by the current disclosure regime; mistakes made as a teenager can follow someone around for decades and create a barrier to rehabilitation, as well as profound problems with access to employment and education.'

Witnesses who gave evidence to the MPs also highlighted the adverse effect of childhood criminal records on individuals' access to employment, education, housing, insurance and visas for travel. They added that it also had a 'discriminatory impact' on particular groups, including those within the care system and Black, Asian and Minority Ethnic (BAME) groups.

'Overall, the inquiry evidence strongly supported the case for changing the criminal records disclosure system,' the report added. 'For young adults, the majority of those who expressed a view thought that reform was also needed.'

Under the Rehabilitation of Offenders Act 1974, individuals are not required to divulge past convictions and cautions once they have become 'spent' – meaning a certain period of time has passed.

But there are some circumstances when disclosure can be requested, and employers are required to carry out checks when hiring people for certain roles, such as work with children or vulnerable adults.

MPs called for the filtering process – the framework that regulates when someone has to disclose convictions and cautions even though they are spent – to be 'radically revised'.

The scheme was introduced so that someone who would otherwise be required to disclose all of his or her criminal history would not be required to do so if the convictions or cautions were for old and minor offences.

Source: Adapted from an article by Ashley Cowburn in the Independent online, 26 October 2017

1.3 The meaning and importance of fault in civil and/or criminal law

Fault, in a legal sense, is some form of wrongdoing. This might be an offence in criminal law or being negligent in the civil law of tort. Fault is the term used to describe the idea of blameworthiness. It then usually ensures that the person at fault has legal responsibility. Sometimes a person can be at fault even if the offence or action carried out is termed 'no fault'.

1.3.1 Examples of liability depending upon fault

There are many examples of liability depending on fault in both civil and criminal law that are studied in this specification. Some examples are set out below, but you can use any others you choose.

Criminal law examples

In criminal law, there is a general presumption that liability is based upon fault. A person should not be held liable for a criminal offence unless he or she is to some extent blameworthy, or at fault. This underpins the concept of *mens rea* in a criminal offence, as it is what is in a person's mind that distinguishes between an accident and a criminal offence. For example, kicking someone rather than the ball in a game of football will not normally be considered criminal. It is part and parcel of the game, and only becomes criminal when the kick is deliberately intended to cause an injury so that the necessary element of *mens rea* can be established. Usually such incidents are dealt with under the laws of football or, on occasions, in civil law.

The general rule is that the *actus reus* must be voluntary, which has been examined in the case of *Hill v Baxter* (1958). However, fault can occur where the defendant omits, or fails, to do something when a duty has been imposed. This has been seen in the cases such as *R v Dytham* (1979), *R v Stone and Dobinson* (1977), *R v Pittwood* (1902) and *R v Miller* (1983).

> See AQA *A-level Law for Year 1 and AS*, Chapter 19 for details of these cases.

Causation in both criminal and civil law also illustrates the way in which fault is seen as a basic constituent of the law. The criminal law case of *White* (1910) shows that the law treats the concept of fault

in a manner that might not necessarily appeal to all members of society; the fact that White was not guilty of killing his mother as she died from natural causes rather than the poison he had administered to her would make many in society believe he should be found guilty of something. This is rectified by the possibility of guilt of other offences such as attempted murder or administering a noxious thing under s 23 of the Offences Against the Person Act 1861. The choice of offence means that the law can ensure the best chance of conviction where a person is considered to be at fault criminally – see, for example, the choice of offence in the article reproduced here.

In the news

Young woman appears in court accused of forcing a man to smoke cannabis at knife-point

A young woman was charged at Teesside Magistrates' Court with two counts of affray and one count of administering a 'poison or noxious thing'. It is alleged that the defendant held a knife to the victim and forced him to smoke cannabis. Because of the seriousness of the charges, the case was referred to the Crown Court.

Source: Adapted from an article by James Cain in Gazette Live online, 17 April 2017

In civil law, this is mirrored in the principle of factual causation, although it may be there is no other avenue for redress available as in *Barnett v Kensington and Chelsea Hospital* (1969).

The availability of a defence recognises that the defendant may have committed the *actus reus* of an offence, with the appropriate *mens rea*, but still not be at fault, for example in the defences of self-defence or insanity.

> See Chapter 12, section 12.1 for information on the defence of self-defence and Chapter 11, section 11.1 for information on the defence of insanity.

Similarly, the partial defences to a charge of murder show that the law recognises that not all killings are equally blameworthy and the level of fault perceived may result in conviction for a lesser, but nonetheless serious offence. Society accepts this and also puts pressure on the law to reflect concerns on the way in which the law operates. This can be seen in the strength of feeling that there is with respect to violence against women, particularly in a domestic context. The difficulty is that the law lags in this area, if only in its enforcement. This has been the case for many years, as in famous cases such as that of *R v Ahluwalia* (1992).

Look online

Look up this case online and consider the sentencing: www.independent.co.uk/news/uk/brutalised-wife-appeals-against-murder-verdict-kiranjit-ahluwalia-given-a-life-sentence-for-killing-1534433.html.

Extension activity

Research what happened as a result of pressure brought about in the *Ahluwalia* case (and similar cases). What can you find in the press about domestic violence and society's failings today? List the cases and make notes to develop an argument that the law is not reflecting the needs of society in the areas of domestic violence and also of stalking.

With offences of strict liability, while it can be argued that they are not truly criminal, the *actus reus* still has an element of fault – at least in the sense that someone has responsibility for the event that has occurred, whether it is exceeding the speed limit or a question of health and safety. Society views this as important for the safety and security of all members of society including the person responsible, and again demonstrates that fault is an essential part of the criminal law.

Whatever the offence in criminal law, conviction results in a sentence being imposed. Section 143(1) of the Criminal Justice Act 2003 provides:

> " In considering the seriousness of any offence, the court must consider the offender's culpability in committing the offence and any harm which the offence caused, was intended to cause or might foreseeably have caused. "

Culpability can be equated to fault or blameworthiness and so reflects the essential nature of fault in criminal law. A note to paragraph 1.7 of the Sentencing Council's Guidelines states:

> " Note: There are offences where liability is strict and no culpability need be proved for the purposes of obtaining a conviction, but the degree of culpability is still important when deciding sentence. The extent to which recklessness, knowledge or negligence are involved in a particular offence will vary. "

Extension activity

Read the Sentencing Council's Guidelines and write down how these can be viewed as informing law and society, law and justice in particular. You can find them online at: www.sentencingcouncil.org.uk/wp-content/uploads/web_seriousness_guideline.pdf.

One example of the importance of fault and the use of sentencing can be seen in the case of *R v Clarke* (2017).

R v Clarke (2017)

Clarke and another appellant, Cooper, aged 101 and 96 respectively, were sentenced to imprisonment for historic sex offences. In terms of sentencing, there is 'a limited degree of mercy' to be shown on account of the defendant's age and likelihood of reoffending. However, culpability must be taken into account.

The court stated:

> " Whilst we consider that an offender's diminished life expectancy, his age, health and the prospect of dying in prison are factors legitimately to be taken into account in passing sentence, they have to be balanced against the gravity of the offending, (including the harm done to victims), and the public interest in setting appropriate punishment for very serious crimes. Whilst courts should make allowance for the factors of extreme old age, we consider that the approach of taking them into account in a limited way is the correct one. "

1.3.2 Fault in civil and criminal law

We have seen that causation is relevant in both civil and criminal law. Negligence, however, is an area of civil law that is used in the offence of gross negligence manslaughter, as seen in the case of *Adomako* (1995).

> For case details of *R v Adomako* (1995), see Chapter 7, section 7.3.

The law provides for a criminal conviction where the defendant had no *mens rea* based on intent or recklessness but the jury considers the negligence to be so bad as to be criminal.

Civil law

While civil law is concerned with weighing the interests of the two parties to an action and providing the most suitable remedy where appropriate, one part, the law of tort, is concerned with civil wrongs. In most areas of tort, liability will only be imposed where a party is at fault.

The award of damages in negligence is compensatory and is intended to restore the claimant to his or her pre-accident position, so far as money can do this. The defendant's fault is linked to the extent of harm that has been caused. However, where the defendant contributes to his or her own harm or injury, the rules of contributory negligence will apply, as this splits fault between the two parties.

> For more information about damages in negligence, see *AQA A-level Law for Year 1 and AS*, Chapter 24.

Occasionally exemplary damages may be awarded. Here, the fault is considered so extreme as to go beyond what would normally be awarded, thus showing the importance of fault. In *Treadaway v Chief Constable of West Midlands* (1994), the claimant had been tortured by the police into making a confession to a crime, and subsequently sentenced to 15 years' imprisonment. Exemplary damages of £50 000 were awarded against the police, as they had shown total disregard for the law. Interestingly, the decision not to prosecute the police for any offence of assault against Treadaway was reviewed, but the police remained protected and there is no proper reflection of the fault of the parties.

Vicarious liability can occur without any fault. In the criminal case of *Harrow LBC v Shah* (1999), it can be argued that the guilty shop owner had no fault, merely responsibility. In civil law, the principle of vicarious liability has a potentially similar effect.

> See *AQA A-level Law for Year 1 and AS*, Chapter 21, section 21.3.2 for discussion of *Harrow LBC v Shah and Shah* (1999). For more information on vicarious liability, see Chapter 16 of this book.

The Consumer Rights Act 2015 includes a fairness test with respect to the enforceability of terms and to consumer notices in contracts. The Act defines 'unfair' terms as those which put the consumer at a disadvantage, by limiting the consumer's rights or disproportionately increasing their obligations as compared to the trader's rights and obligations. This balance is made without reference to fault and seems to be made on the basis of shifting liability, arguably to excess, onto the trader to the benefit of the consumer. However, it can be argued that if, for example, goods sold are defective, then the supplier is at fault and should not be permitted to exclude that liability.

In human rights law, a state's margin of appreciation allows some exceptions to the idea of fault by a state (and therefore a society) from fulfilling its obligations under the ECHR. The term 'margin of appreciation' refers to the space for manoeuvre that the Strasbourg organs are willing to grant national authorities in fulfilling their obligations under the ECHR.

Summary

- Law plays three primary roles in society:
  - to protect people from harm
  - to ensure a common good
  - to settle arguments and disputes regarding finite resources.
- This can be seen in the effect of law on the balance between competing interests within society and the importance of fault as a basis for law in society.
- Different areas of law reflect this balance which is often unequal, particularly from the point of view of some communities and some sectors of society.
- The concept of fault plays a major role in both civil and criminal law.

2 Law and morality

After reading this chapter, you should be able to:
- Understand the distinction between law and morality and the diversity of moral views in a pluralist society
- Understand the relationship between law and morality and its importance
- Understand the legal enforcement of moral values

2.1 The distinction between law and morals

The nature of law has been considered in *AQA A-level Law for Year1/AS*, Chapters 1 and 2. The distinction between law and morality will now be discussed.

2.1.1 What is law?

As we have seen, rules exist in many contexts. A **rule** is something that determines the way in which we behave, whether because we submit ourselves to it voluntarily, as would be the case with moral rules, or because it is enforceable in some general way, as would be the case with laws.

> **Key term**
>
> **Rule** – this has been defined by Twining and Miers in *How to Do Things with Rules* (2014) as 'a general norm mandating or guiding conduct'.

Some rules are not based on law or morality, but are often referred to as laws. These might be the laws of football or the laws of chess. They are generally observed in the context in which they operate. If these laws are broken, there are sanctions in the context of the sport. Many would view any form of cheating in a sport or game as wrong and possibly as immoral.

Some laws are laws relating to the operation of the universe, such as the three laws of thermodynamics. These laws are immutable – they are unchanging and cannot be broken. The rules we are concerned with are English law. There are two main theories relating to the nature of law:

- **legal positivism**
- natural law.

Legal positivism

Legal positivists believe that laws are valid where they are made by the recognised legislative power in the state; they do not have to satisfy any higher authority.

> **Key term**
>
> **Legal positivism** – the theory of law that is based on the idea that laws are valid where they are made by the recognised legislative power in the state and do not have to satisfy any higher authority.

Each legal positivist has his own individual explanation of the theory. The nineteenth century philosophers are often referred to as classical legal positivists. Jeremy Bentham and John Austin are the best known of them.

Jeremy Bentham

Bentham was a utilitarian and law reformer. He made a distinction between what the law is, and commenting on its merits or otherwise. He believed that the philosophy of law should be concerned purely with what law is. He wrote: 'The existence of law is one thing, its merit or demerit is another. A law which exists is a law, though we happen to dislike it.'

So, as an individual or a group of individuals we might find a law offensive, but this does not affect its validity. In other words, morality is irrelevant to law.

John Austin

Austin developed the command theory of law. This has three main principles:

- Laws are commands issued by the uncommanded commander – the sovereign.
- Such commands are enforced by sanctions.
- A sovereign is one who is obeyed by the majority.

Austin recognised a sovereign as one whom society obeys habitually. This sovereign might be a single person (the king or queen or dictator) or a collective sovereign such as a Parliament, with a number of individuals, each having various authoritative powers. The authority is given by Parliament, for example to judges. Sanctions in criminal law are straightforward – disobey the law and suffer punishment (sanctions).

Other legal positivists: Hart, Raz and Kelsen

Criticisms of Austin and his rather simplistic view have been made by the modern legal positivists, in particular Professor H.L.A. Hart. Other modern legal positivists include Hans Kelsen and Joseph Raz. Kelsen argues that morality is no part of law. It is neither good nor bad. Raz argues that the identity and existence of a legal system may be tested by reference to three elements:

- efficacy
- institutional character
- sources.

Law is autonomous – we can identify its content without recourse to morality.

As a legal positivist, Hart insists on the separation of law and morality. His model of law is more sophisticated than that of Austin. He argues that there are two categories of rules, primary and secondary. These combine to form the basis of a workable legal system:

1 Primary rules either impose legal obligations or grant powers. Obligations include behaviour that is subject to the criminal law – such as not to kill or steal – and powers enable an individual to, for example, make a will.

2 Secondary rules are concerned with the operation of primary legal rules. Hart identifies three specific secondary rules:
   - The rule of recognition – this sets criteria for identifying primary rules.
   - Rules of change – these identify how legal rules are formed, amended or repealed.
   - Rules of adjudication – these enable the courts to settle disputes and interpret the law.

Figure 2.1 Key facts chart about legal philosophers who are utilitarian and legal positivists

Legal philosopher	Basic premise
Jeremy Bentham	A utilitarian who wrote about what the law is and a commentary on its merits or otherwise
	He believed that the philosophy of law should be concerned purely with what law is
John Austin	He developed the command theory of law with its three main principles
H.L.A. Hart	A legal positivist who believed in the separation of law and morality
	He argued that there are two categories of rules, primary and secondary
	These combine to form the basis of a workable legal system
Joseph Raz	A legal positivist who argues that the identity and existence of a legal system may be tested by reference to three elements
	Law is autonomous – we can identify its content without recourse to morality
Hans Kelsen	A legal positivist who argued that morality is no part of law

Natural law

Natural lawyers reject legal positivism. They believe that the validity of man-made laws depends upon the laws being compatible with a higher, moral authority. Where laws do not satisfy the requirements of this higher moral authority, the laws lack validity. There are different views on **natural law**, reflected in the work of Thomas Aquinas and Lon Fuller.

In ancient Athens, the philosopher Plato and his pupil Aristotle considered the question of how human beings should act. Both started by reflecting on the meaning of 'goodness'. For Aristotle, evil originates in naturally or morally failing to fulfil part or all of human nature and his definition of goodness. This is the basis for natural law. Ethics involves defining human nature, and from that definition deriving laws as principles of behaviour which either support or prevent human flourishing.

> **Key term**
>
> **Natural law** – a moral theory of jurisprudence, which maintains that law should be based on morality and ethics.

Thomas Aquinas

Thomas Aquinas combined the philosophy of Aristotle with Christian theology, including the Bible and the Ten Commandments, and Catholic Church tradition. He saw in Aristotle's philosophy a rational foundation for Christian doctrine. He sets out four kinds of law in his work, *Summa Theologica*:

- Eternal law: all things have a natural tendency to pursue their own God-given goals because all things are created by God. Human beings can have some understanding of the eternal law. This would include the laws of gravity.

- Natural law: the moral code which human beings are naturally inclined towards. What is good is that which we are naturally inclined towards. Man-made law must conform to this as it comes from a higher authority.
- Positive divine law is the commands of God – the Ten Commandments.
- Positive human law must be in accordance with natural law.

Aquinas also stated that there are three natural ends or goals from which we can work out moral principles:

1 Anything that exists has a natural tendency to go on existing. Natural law opposes death; therefore murder is wrong as it prevents human fulfilment.

2 All animals have a natural tendency to mate and bring up their young. Natural law commands we should follow this natural tendency. The right to life is paramount, as is the protection of children.

3 Humans have a rational nature which inclines us to know the truth about God and God's world and to live ordered lives in society. Natural law commands we should worship God (the ultimate purpose of humans), learn and live in harmony with others.

These goals help people work out our moral principles that should be reflected in man-made laws.

Lon Fuller

Fuller wrote *The Morality of Law* in 1964. He rejected legal positivism and also traditional religious forms of natural law theory. He argued that law serves a purpose. That purpose is 'to achieve social order through subjecting people's conduct to the guidance of general rules by which they may themselves orient their behaviour'.

If law is to achieve this purpose, it must satisfy eight principles which make up an inner morality of law. This is described by Fuller as a procedural version of natural law. Under the eight principles, laws should be:

- In existence – there must be rules which exist and not rules created for each specific case.

- Promulgated – that is, published, as law must be made public and not kept secret. Statutes and case law are all published in the UK, and statutes and delegated legislation have no effect until published.
- Prospective – set out in advance. It is illogical to govern conduct today by rules that will be enacted tomorrow. However, there can be exceptions where irregularities are remedied. This might bring into question case law generally, as exemplified by the case of *R v R* (1991).
- Clear and concise – so that they can be understood and obeyed by everyone. It is debatable whether modern legislation can be considered clear and concise given the volume of legislation and the size of some Acts of Parliament. The Cabinet Office and the Office of the Parliamentary Counsel published a paper in 2013 entitled 'When Laws Become Too Complex'. This recognised that there have been improvements since the 1970s but still found it necessary to launch a good law initiative.
- Not contradictory in nature – demanding competing actions gives no clear guidance as to what behaviour is expected by the law.
- Not require the impossible – must provide rules that humans are capable of fulfilling even if it is not always easy to draw the line between extreme difficulty and impossibility.
- Constant – this means that law must not keep changing rapidly if it is to produce stable expectations of what is required. However, this does not mean that law cannot change in order to meet the changing needs of society.
- Applied and administered as stated – what officials do must be in accordance with the law. People must not be subject to the arbitrary power and will of those in authority. This means that while officials can have discretion in coming to a decision, that discretion must be exercised for reasons within the law.

Hart criticises Fuller, not for the principles themselves but for calling them a morality.

Figure 2.2 Key facts chart on legal philosophers who are natural lawyers

Legal philosopher	Basic premise
Thomas Aquinas	Combined the philosophy of Aristotle with Christian theology, including the Bible and the Ten Commandments and Catholic church tradition He sets out four kinds of law
Lon Fuller	Argued that law serves the purpose 'to achieve social order through subjecting people's conduct to the guidance of general rules by which they may themselves orient their behaviour' If law is to achieve this purpose, it must satisfy eight principles which make up an inner morality of law

2.1.2 What is morality?

Hart's criticism of Fuller raises the question of what is morality. Morality is defined in the Oxford English Dictionary as 'a particular system of values and principles of conduct, especially one held by a specified person or society'.

Morality can be a personal morality or a collective morality of society as a whole.

Morality is 'normative' or prescriptive; that is, it specifies what ought to be done and delineates acceptable and unacceptable behaviour. In our society and in many others, morality has been influenced to a large extent by religious beliefs. The Bible provides a moral code for Christian communities, both in the very basic and strict rules of the Ten Commandments, and in the more advanced, socially aware teachings of Christ. In Islam, the Koran provides a very extensive moral code for Muslims.

Morality is the moral code that touches virtually every area of our lives – behaviour towards fellow human beings, money and property, and sexuality. There are 'core' moral beliefs such as issues surrounding birth, death and families.

Although morality is concerned with issues of 'right' and 'wrong', it is not at all black and white. Mary Warnock, an academic who has been predominantly concerned with moral issues, said:

> ❝ I do not believe that there is a neat way of marking off moral issues from all others; some people, at some time, may regard things as matters of moral right and moral wrong, which at another time or in another place are thought to be matters of taste, or of no importance at all. ❞

Moral attitudes change over time. This can be seen in attitudes to issues such as abortion, homosexuality, drugs and drink-driving. Morality was easy to see as a common morality when societies were insular, structured and not exposed to different beliefs and values. The customs of society formed the basis of a code of conduct that reflected that society, and members of the society accepted these customs in large measure. It was therefore part of the morality of that age. However, we now live in a multicultural society where there are a wide range of views.

Sociologist Emile Durkheim identified a range of factors as potentially contributing to the breakdown of a common morality. These included:

- the increasing specialisation of labour
- the growing ethnic diversity within society
- the fading influence of religious belief.

All of these factors are increasingly apparent in pluralist societies today. Under Durkheim's analysis, we should not be surprised to discover a parallel growth in the diversity of moral outlook and in norms of behaviour in modern Britain. There is, therefore, a more obvious difference between an individual's moral code and that of society as a whole.

The essential core of society is based on a shared morality; without a shared morality, society disintegrates. Law aims to prevent the disintegration of society, and so will reflect morality.

2.1.3 Characteristics of legal and moral rules

In order to discover the characteristics of legal and moral rules, it is useful to compare them under a number of headings:

- their origins
- their date of commencement
- their enforcement
- their ease of change
- their certainty of content
- the way the rules are applied.

These characteristics help to identify the rules and distinguish legal and moral rules.

Their origins

It is generally possible to trace legal rules back to a source. Originally this was the common law. The law of tort and contract have been developed incrementally by judges. Today, statutes have become an increasingly large source of law, together with delegated legislation. European Union law has become a major source of law making in the UK through treaties, directives, regulations and decisions.

Conventions that the UK subscribes to such as the ECHR also play their part in the origin of law in the UK today.

Moral rules are more difficult to trace back to a precise origin. The Bible and the Koran form the basis for many individuals of their moral outlook.

Codes such as these inform attitudes towards issues such as premarital sex, theft and how one treats fellow humans. For those who do not follow religious teaching, morality is based upon upbringing, education, peer views, or the leanings of their own consciences. For most people, their morality is based on a combination of all these influences.

Their date of commencement

Legal rules generally have a start date. Acts of Parliament come into force at a specific time. Precedents operate from the date of the decision, although it can be argued they have retrospective effect, as with the decision in R v R (1991).

Moral rules are less straightforward. For example, Western attitudes towards pre-marital sex have undergone significant change in the last 100 years. It is not possible to attach a date to this change, as it is part of a wider change in social attitudes towards matters of sexual morality. Similarly, it is not possible to fix a date when a person's particular morality came into being – it evolves over time.

Their enforcement

Legal rules can be enforced by the courts following a designated procedure and with appropriate sanctions such as criminal penalties or civil damages.

Sanctions may also be available for those who breach moral codes. Someone who uses offensive language may be excluded from a sports or social club. Moral rules are usually enforced through public disapproval through the media or privately through social ostracism rather than a formal sanction. Moral rules are less enforceable than legal rules, but it is often easier to show views about them.

Their ease of change

In theory, legal rules are relatively easy to change. Parliament has authority to pass a law whenever it wants. In practice, however, Parliament is often slow to respond to change.

As we have seen, courts also have the power to change legal rules but only when a case comes to court.

Moral rules tend to change gradually, perhaps over decades or centuries. It is often only in hindsight that we become aware of such change.

Sometimes the law leads morality, and sometimes the law follows the lead of morality.

Their certainty of content

It is normally possible to discover the precise content of legal rules through published statutes, delegated legislation and law reports.

The content of moral rules may also be clear. However, knowledge of the content of moral rules can often only be acquired informally through exposure to them in the setting where they are applied, such as the home.

Application of the rules

Legal rules generally apply to everyone in a situation covered by the law. The only difference is the ability of every individual to access the law.

Moral rules, on the other hand, range in application from enjoying almost universal adoption to having only marginal acceptance. Differing views are taken by different individuals and different sectors of society. This is particularly apparent in a pluralist society.

2.2 The diversity of moral views in a pluralist society

We have explored the distinction between law and morals and the views of legal positivists and natural lawyers. We have also considered the characteristics of legal and moral rules. This section now considers the fact that there is likely to be a variety of moral views in a **pluralist society**.

> ### Key term
>
> **Pluralist society** – a diverse society, where the people in it believe all kinds of different things and tolerate each other's beliefs even when they don't match their own.

2.2.1 Pluralism in the UK

Pluralism has been considered in the previous chapter. The UK has a multicultural society, with individuals having different or no religious beliefs. This leads to great variety in the moral values of the individuals in society. Often these individuals group together as a result of their moral views, whether as a collective view that binds them or because of common purpose in promoting their views. An individual's views are protected under the ECHR, as is his or her right to express his or her views and assemble with others to express the collective views.

The country in which we live plays a significant role in shaping our lives. Both other members of society and the laws of the country shape our views. The kinds of lives we can lead are constrained by the state, which has the right to punish individuals if they go beyond what the state deems to be appropriate limits.

One example is that of the conscientious objector who, when the country is at war, refuses to fight. The large majority of society accept that they must be prepared to fight and may not fully accept the views of those who will not. Conscientious objectors believe it to be completely wrong in any circumstance and accept that the state may punish them and much of society will shun them. Such a view is not necessarily a judgement about a government's policy but a moral judgement, drawn from personal beliefs. The difficulty arises when an individual changes his or her views.

In the news

Conscientious objection in the UK armed forces

Conscientious objection to military service is a subtle concept. Broadly speaking, it arises when a serving or prospective member of the armed forces finds that his or her work cannot/could not be done in good conscience. When the claim of conscience is sufficiently powerful for the person to seek to remove him- or herself from his or her work, then a conscientious objection can be said to exist. This could arise in relation either to specific orders or military operations, or to military service in all its aspects.

Source: 'Informed Choice? Armed Forces Recruitment Practice in the UK', David Gee (2007)

So how does this work in practice?

The case of *R v Lyons* (2011) shows that refusal of a lawful order even on the grounds of conscientious objection is a punishable offence in the UK armed forces under the Armed Forces Act 2006.

R v Lyons (2011)

Lyons, aged 18, had joined the Royal Navy and became a Leading Medical Assistant in submarines. Five years later, he was told that he would be deployed to Afghanistan. He applied for discharge from the Royal Navy on the basis that he objected to the UK's role in Afghanistan.

His application on grounds of conscientious objection was refused. Before his appeal against this refusal was decided, he was ordered to undertake a pre-deployment weapons training course, because of the risk all personnel faced in that theatre, combatant or not. On refusing to submit to this he was convicted of insubordination.

He argued that Article 9 ECHR (freedom of thought, conscience and religion) protected him from active service from the moment when he told his commanding officer of his objections, until his appeal on grounds of conscientious objection was finally determined.

The Court Martial Appeal Court ruled that moral objections to the UK's involvement in Afghanistan do not constitute a defence to an insubordination charge. The appellant was not entitled to disobey a lawful command on the ground of conscientious objection.

Similarly, there is the criminal who is prepared to steal but is not prepared to kill in order to steal. The majority of society and the state would agree with him or her that killing is wrong, but a small proportion would consider that stealing is not wrong.

2.2.2 Pluralism in Europe and the ECHR

The attempt to keep morality and religions out of politics and the law arises from the worry that, for example, religious fundamentalists will impose intolerant and coercive laws and practices on all of society. We have seen this in various countries with respect to attitudes towards abortion, stem-cell research on embryos and in-vitro fertilisation (IVF).

In Ireland, where abortion is illegal, the case of *Open Door Counselling and Dublin Woman Well Centre v Ireland* (1992) was heard by European Court of Human Rights (ECtHR). The court found that the Ireland Supreme Court's injunction restraining counselling agencies from providing pregnant women with information concerning abortion facilities abroad violated Article 10 ECHR (right to freedom of expression).

See Chapter 33 for more details about the case and the relationship between Article 10 and health and morals.

In *Evans v United Kingdom* (2007), the ECtHR stated that for the right to respect for the decision to become a parent in the genetic sense, the margin of appreciation to be afforded to the respondent state under Article 8 (right to respect for private and family life) has to be a wide one. This case involved the refusal of one partner to the destruction of frozen embryos following the ending of the parents' relationship.

2.2.3 Summary

John Stuart Mill said 'All silencing of discussion is an assumption of infallibility'.

When someone is silenced or coerced while wanting to express an opinion, they are often trying to voice positions that should be heard. In a democracy, minorities can become majorities. The tyranny of the majority can undermine the very nature of democracy and its search for the best way of living together. This is reflected in ECHR and should be reflected in UK law.

Freedom of thought and expression is frequently restricted as being contrary to the moral views of the majority. The difficulty is deciding when the greater good of society as a whole should prevent the individual's view which is not being considered acceptable, be it on the grounds of protection (anti-terrorism, online bullying), obscenity (likely to deprave or corrupt) or sexual matters (same-sex relationships, abortion, contraception).

2.3 The relationship between law and morality, and its importance

Law and morality often overlap, although there is often a period where one leads and the other follows. This relationship coincides for much of the time, and at other times the one influences the other.

This can be seen in the coincidence of legal and moral rules and the influences of law and morality on each other.

2.3.1 The coincidence of legal and moral rules

Legal and moral rules, though distinctive, share certain characteristics. They are both concerned with setting standards, which are essential for governing the behaviour of individuals within society. They both dictate the way in which people are expected to behave.

Legal and moral rules employ similar language: they distinguish between right and wrong, and they speak of duties, obligations and responsibilities.

Legal rules are strengthened when they are the same as moral rules, and their enforcement can more readily be justified and is accepted by society. Sometimes legal rules possess no obvious moral content. Parking a car on a double yellow line in an empty town centre at four o'clock in the morning does not seem to infringe any moral code (other than the act itself of breaking the law). Most would think it was immoral to impose a parking fine in that situation and merely a money-raising exercise on behalf of a local council.

In the news

Zealous parking wardens under attack

A publican was handed a fixed penalty notice for parking at 9.15pm in the loading bay outside his pub that he had used without any problems for 13 years, and a motorist was fined after breaking down on double yellow lines at 8.30pm.

Other instances of overly-zealous enforcement in the town, a Thirsk Town Council meeting heard, included a delivery driver being told he could not unload 11 boxes from his van, and another driver being fined for parking on yellow lines while getting change for a parking meter.

Members of North Yorkshire and Hambleton District Councils, which employ wardens hired by Scarborough Borough Council, said that, while motorists who block key access points need to be dealt with, the style of enforcement is not in keeping with market towns and is causing significant embarrassment.

Scarborough Council has carried out an investigation into the actions of one parking warden after receiving complaints, but found no wrongdoing.

Source: Adapted from an article in the Darlington and Stockton Times online, 25 November 2016

It is not surprising that the principle of strict liability is controversial as legal rules are given greater validity by their moral content.

There are many moral rules that are not part of the law. Most people would agree that adultery is immoral and indeed may be the basis of a divorce, but it is not illegal in the UK, even though it is in some other countries of the world.

Some acts that may be considered immoral are not criminal but may be sufficient to support a claim in civil law. The line between them is blurred, as might be seen in some cases of gross negligence manslaughter.

Tip

There are many areas of law and cases you have studied that show acts which are not criminal but are immoral, and where civil law provides a remedy.

2.3.2 The influences of law and morality on each other and the importance of morality

Changing moral values can lead to developments in the law. This can be seen in the historical development of the law relating to rape within marriage. It was ruled in 1736 that 'a man cannot rape his wife', yet in *R v R* (1991) Owen J stated: 'I find it hard to believe that it ever was common law that a husband was in effect entitled to beat his wife into submission to sexual intercourse.'

In this way, the law eventually caught up with perceived public morality.

Extension activity

Research and make a list of key developments in other areas of law that have changed to reflect changing morality. You could use abortion or homosexuality for this. Then perform the same research for areas of law where public morality has followed the lead of the law such as discrimination on the grounds of gender or race.

Ideally, the law and morality change in harmony with little lead or lag. For example, the Sexual Offences Act 1967 was passed following the Wolfenden Report. However, there were many more influences on the public's view at the time. There had been the famous case of *R v Penguin Books Ltd* (1961) which considered the novel *Lady Chatterley's Lover* by D.H. Lawrence not to be obscene under the Obscene Publications Act 1959. So-called underground magazines became available, such as *OZ* and *IT*; satirical magazines such as *Private Eye* developed a large circulation, reporting and commenting on current issues and scandals which many considered immoral and required action by the state and a change of the law.

2.4 The legal enforcement of moral values

As the UK is a multicultural society, it contains a diversity of moral views. This section explores the questions of whether, and to what extent, the law should seek to enforce any particular moral views. This is not just a subject of academic debate as judges are often forced to consider these questions before determining the law. There are two starting points for this debate:

- The law, as the guardian of public morals, should intervene to ensure the continuation of the dominant morality within the state.
- Individuals should be left free to decide their own morality.

These starting points appear to be diametrically opposite, but, in practice, both these positions are modified so that they tend towards convergence.

2.4.1 The influence of John Stuart Mill

In his book *On Liberty*, John Stuart Mill, a nineteenth-century philosopher, explored the nature and limits of the power which can be legitimately exercised by society over the individual.

He stated that there is a limit to the legitimate interference of collective opinion with individual independence. Nevertheless, Mill accepted that rules governing an individual's conduct must be imposed upon them. The problem, though, is identifying where society should or should not be permitted to interfere with individual liberty. Therefore, Mill developed the harm principle as the appropriate test to be used when considering this issue. He wrote:

> The only purpose for which power can be rightfully exercised over any member of a civilised community, against his will, is to prevent harm to others. His own good, either physical or moral, is not a sufficient warrant ... Over himself, his own body and mind, the individual is sovereign.

Under this principle, an individual should be allowed to harm him/herself and society can only intervene where his or her conduct harms others.

Mill does, however, limit the application of the harm principle in one significant way. He states it does not apply to those who are not in the maturity of their faculties. In other words, it does not apply to children, over whom society enjoys absolute power and presumably also those suffering a severe mental disability. They must be protected against their own actions as well as against the actions of others.

Mill recognised that others might refuse to admit this distinction between that part of a person's life which concerns only him- or herself and that which concerns others. One such objector was the nineteenth-century judge, Sir James Stephen, who opposed the liberalism of Mill. Stephen argued that there is no distinction between acts that harm others and acts that harm oneself. He wrote: 'There are acts of wickedness so gross and outrageous that they must be punished at any cost to the offender.'

He went on to argue that the prevention of wickedness and immorality is a proper end in itself and justifies state action. The law, Stephen argued, has a duty to proscribe behaviour condemned by society at large.

Mill answered such objections by making a distinction between the harmful act itself and its particular consequences.

In summary, Mill argued that society should not impose morality on individuals. Individuals should be free to choose how they behave, provided that no harm is caused to other members of society. If harm is done, he argued, this should not outweigh the harm that denying individual liberty would do.

Problems with Mill's approach

Mill's approach raised questions. It is not clear what constitutes 'harm', physical or otherwise; does it include, for example, pornography, drug-taking or sexual practices when carried out consensually or alone? Equally, it is not clear whether an embryo or a foetus falls within the definition of other members of society.

A logical extension of Mill's approach is that crimes without victims should not really be crimes at all. Edwin Schur and Hugo Bedau in their book, *Victimless Crimes: Two Sides of a Controversy*, argue that 'a victimless crime' is a term used to refer to actions that have been made illegal but which do not directly violate or threaten the rights of any other individual. It often involves consensual acts, or solitary acts in which no other person is involved. Such acts would not lead to any person calling for help from the police. This would include recreational drug use. The argument is that some of these laws produce secondary crime, and all create new criminals, many of whom are otherwise law-abiding citizens and people in authority. These victimless crimes that only do harm to the criminal should be decriminalised. They cite as examples drug use, homosexuality and abortion (these being illegal at the time of the book's publication). If such activities are criminalised, demand will still be there and the activities will be pushed underground.

2.4.2 The Hart–Devlin debate

This debate between an eminent Law Lord, Patrick Devlin, and the academic Professor H.L.A. Hart was sparked by the publication of the Wolfenden Report. The report concluded that the law has a role in preserving public order and decency, but:

> It is not, in our view, the function of the law to intervene in the private life of citizens, or to seek to enforce any particular pattern of behaviour ... [There] must remain a realm of private morality and immorality which is, in brief and crude terms, not the law's business.

In his book, *The Enforcement of Morals*, published in 1965, Lord Devlin wrote: 'Without shared ideas on politics, morals, and ethics, no society can exist.'

Society, therefore, is constituted in part by its morality. Lord Devlin argued that the fabric of society is dependent upon a shared or common morality. Where the bonds of that morality are loosened by private immoral conduct, the integrity of society will be lost and society will be liable to disintegrate. Society therefore has the right to defend itself against immorality. Even private wickedness and immorality may be punished because they are harmful to society. Lord Devlin stated: 'The suppression of vice is as much the law's business as the suppression of subversive activities.'

Lord Devlin also recognised that there are limits to the right of society to interfere with private immoral conduct. He believed that 'There must be toleration of the maximum individual freedom that is consistent with the integrity of society'. He accepted that personal preferences, or likes and dislikes, should not form the basis for decisions about what immoral conduct should be outlawed. He therefore developed an apparently objective test, that of the reasonable or ordinary man, to help decide where the boundaries are to be drawn. Only where immoral conduct is regarded by this ordinary man with 'intolerance, indignation or disgust', should it be prohibited by law.

Professor Hart proposed a more limited role for the law in the enforcement of morality. Whereas Lord Devlin started from the general principle that society has a duty to enforce its dominant morality, and then limited the application of this general principle to acts that the ordinary man regards with intolerance, Professor Hart started from the opposite end of the spectrum – that society should not interfere with private moral or immoral conduct. However, Hart then limited the application of this general principle by sanctioning the enforcement of morality in certain situations.

He accepted that enforcement is permitted when one of society's dominant moralities is being eroded by a true threat to the cohesion of society. Such a threat, though, has to be more than merely a challenge to society's code of conduct. There must be evidence that it creates a genuine public nuisance.

Issues reflecting the legal enforcement of moral values in contract law

Judges and Parliament are often forced to confront complex moral issues. Parliament can choose whether to legislate. Judges have no choice. If a case comes to court they have to make a decision, and of course if a case reaches the higher appeal courts, it becomes a precedent.

In civil law, the principle that promises should be kept lies beneath the law of contract. Much of the law of equity was historically founded upon principles of conscience, with maxims such as 'equity will not allow a statute to be used as a cloak for fraud' and 'he who comes to equity must come with clean hands'.

Historically, certain contracts can be declared void because of their association with immorality. For example:

- *Pearce v Brooks* (1866): a cab owner failed to enforce a contract with a prostitute who used his cabs for trade because the courts were not prepared to allow contracts for immoral purposes.
- *Parkinson v The College of Ambulance* (1925): the contract was void because its whole purpose was corruption in public life.

In more recent times, the courts have again stated their views on the relationship between law and morality. In *Otkritie International Investment Management Ltd v Urumov* (2013), the court specifically made the connection between morality and the law when it said:

> Public policy requires that the courts will not lend their aid to a man who founds his action upon an immoral or illegal act. The action will not be founded upon an immoral or illegal act, if it can be pleaded and proved without reliance upon such an act.

While other examples are raised in Chapter 17, the issue of economic duress will be considered here.

Economic duress, exclusion clauses and morality
In *Progress Bulk Carriers Ltd v Tube City* (2012), Lord Steyn stated:

> The aim of our commercial law ought to be to encourage fair dealing between parties. But it is a mistake for the law to set its sights too highly when the critical enquiry is not whether the conduct is lawful but whether it is morally or socially unacceptable. That is the enquiry in which we are engaged.

For there to be economic duress, the illegitimate pressure must be distinguished from the rough and tumble of the pressures of normal commercial bargaining. In other words, it must be something beyond the tough commercial world.

With respect to exclusion clauses, these can be seen as tough bargains. If you do not like the terms of a contract, do not enter it is commonly stated as being a justification. However, when exclusion clauses are oppressive and there are no realistic alternatives, the law steps in by protecting consumers either under the Consumer Rights Act 2015 or under the Unfair Contract Terms Act 1977. These, and related Acts of Parliament, have arguably swung the balance too far the other way. The decisions in cases such as *L'Estrange v Graucob* (1934) and *Thompson v LMS Railway* (1930) are unlikely to be replicated if the cases were heard today. However, it could be argued that these decisions are little different to successful claims against individuals at the hands of payday lenders or businesses selling products for what is effectively multiples of their cash price to those who have no access to mainstream lines of credit. Even if the businesses might be acting in an immoral way, the consumer is unlikely to be willing or able to complain even if he has been made aware that there was a possible case he could raise.

Issues reflecting the legal enforcement of moral values in the law of tort

In the law of negligence, Lord Atkin's famously Biblical description of the duty of care as one owed to one's fellow man as a 'neighbour' in *Donoghue v Stevenson* (1932) reworked the parable of the Good Samaritan. This can be applied in a way that perhaps does not reflect a moral view as seen in *McFarlane v Tayside Health Board* (1999) (a case where, despite a vasectomy, Mr MacFarlane fathered a child, and he and his wife sought damages for the cost of care among other claims). The claim for damages in respect of the rearing of the child was dismissed. Lord Steyn stated:

> It may be objected that the House must act like a court of law and not like a court of morals. That would only be partly right. The court must apply positive law. But a judge's sense of the moral answer to a question, or the justice of the case, has been one of the great shaping forces of the common law. What may count in a situation of difficulty and uncertainty is not the subjective view of the judge but what he reasonably believes that the ordinary citizen would regard as right. "

So the situation is conflicted. Whether one talks of 'morals' or 'values', judges have to apply themselves to real cases with real facts and real people and reflect the situation as they perceive it as to any moral or values issues.

The duty of care to trespassers

As we have seen in *AQA A-level Law for Year 1 and AS*, Chapter 25, owing a duty of care to a trespasser was traditionally absent, as in *Addie v Dumbreck* (1929). The change in the law in *British Railways Board v Herrington* (1972) brought in the concept of common humanity and the subsequent Law Commission report led to the Occupiers Liability Act 1984. The Act appears to have given trespassers a right to claim compensation when they have been injured while trespassing. However, there have been a number of court decisions which have restricted when a duty is owed to trespassers and, if a duty is owed, whether the occupier is liable.

The idea of allowing a claim by a trespasser demonstrates the changing morality of society. Children, in particular, should be able to claim for injuries caused by hidden dangers about which they are not expected to be aware, even if the child is a trespasser. This is not a huge move from the position where the child is in a public space, but is too young to read warning signs as in *Glasgow Corporation v Taylor* (1922). The difficulty arises where the injured person is trespassing, even though trespassing in that place is common. The Act sets out when there may be a legal duty in s 1(3). This reflected the morality of the time – over 30 years ago. The interpretation of the Act has been criticised for allowing too much discretion to the judiciary and too great a possibility of refusing a claim on the grounds of public policy and an attempt to reduce the compensation culture that has been growing in recent years.

Activity

Read the newspaper article below. Write down the arguments for and against there being a legal duty of care owed to the child and also whether there is a moral duty of care owed. Would the position be different if the child was a trespasser in the building?

In the news

Michael Sousa, 12, died after falling off banister at Jane Austen College, Norwich

A 12-year-old boy fell 20 feet to his death at school after sliding down the banisters despite being told to stop, an inquest heard yesterday.

Michael Sousa suffered severe head injuries when he fell over the stairwell from the third floor at Jane Austen College, a free school in Norfolk, a day after his birthday in January. He died eight days later in hospital when his life support machine was switched off.

The Year 7 pupil had attempted to slide down the banisters while wearing a heavy rucksack, Norfolk coroner's court was told. Pupils described seeing Michael 'leaning over with his stomach as if to slide', but thought that 'the backpack rides up his back as if to pull him over'.

He lost his balance, Jacqueline Lake, Norfolk's senior coroner said, recording a verdict of death by misadventure.

Staff saw the pupil fall past as they stood on the second floor. Peter Bloomfield, who was vice-principal at the time, said: 'I sensed what I thought was an object dropping past me. I looked down to see a pupil on the floor who was not moving. I shouted to the students to go back upstairs and get away from the scene and proceeded to clear the space. I identified the pupil as Michael Sousa and he appeared unresponsive although he was breathing.'

Michael was treated at the scene by a cover teacher trained in first aid. Paramedics arrived 15 minutes later and he was airlifted to Addenbrooke's Hospital in Cambridge. A post-mortem examination gave the cause of death as severe traumatic brain injury.

Rebecca Handley Kirk, who had been acting principal at the college, run by the Inspiration Trust, said that an investigation by the Education Funding Agency had made no recommendations, adding that teachers were 'meticulous' in keeping children safe.

Source: Adapted from an article by Fariha Karim in The Sunday Times online, 31 October 2017

The rule in Rylands v Fletcher

This was developed to give a remedy where a person's property is damaged or destroyed by the escape of non-naturally stored material onto adjoining property. It is arguable that this rule of strict liability reflects a person's moral responsibility for the consequences of an escape of something brought onto land. Originally this was almost always water. A reservoir was a valuable asset as it could drive a water wheel to power a mill. However, the water could seep out and flood an adjoining landowner's mine with disastrous consequences, including death of miners and financial ruin. Liability was made strict as otherwise the necessary proof for negligence or nuisance could be very difficult, meaning that the person with moral responsibility would be able to evade moral responsibility.

However it could be argued that the modern interpretation of the rule shows a more legalistic rather than a moral viewpoint in cases such as *Cambridge Water Co. v Eastern Counties Leather* (1994) and *Stannard (t/a Wyvern Tyres) v Gore* (2012).

It should also be remembered that the right of abatement allows someone who is suffering a nuisance to take action that would otherwise be illegal, such as cutting overhanging branches of a diseased tree to prevent possible injury or damage to property.

Issues reflecting the legal enforcement of moral values in human rights law

Human rights are based on the principle of respect for the individual. Their fundamental assumption is that each person is a moral and rational being who deserves to be treated with dignity. We can therefore expect morality to be the dominant feature of human rights law. The ECHR contains 14 Articles setting out different individual rights which are mainly civil and political in nature. Some, such as Articles 2 and 5, are absolute rights where a state cannot justify interfering with them. Others, such as Articles 8, 10 and 11 are qualified rights, so that if the state can justify a limitation of these rights which is in accordance with law and meet a legitimate aim, there will be no breach of the EHCR. So absolute rights are obviously based on morality, but qualified rights find a balance between law and morality dependent on the view we take on the morality of a state's legitimate aims and the legislation it creates to support that.

Example under Articles 5 and 8 ECHR

The case of *Mengesha v Commissioner of Police of the Metropolis* (2013) shows the interrelationship of the articles, an absolute right and a qualified right.

Mengesha v Commissioner of Police of the Metropolis (2013)

On 30 November 2011, among those attending a public sector trade union march was the claimant, acting, with others, as a legal observer. She was a law graduate and was a member of the 'Bar in the Community' scheme at the Bar Pro Bono Unit. In the afternoon the police authorised containment as they were entitled to do in the circumstances (also known as 'kettling'). About 100 people were contained, among whom was the claimant. Since containment is only lawful to prevent an imminent breach of the peace in circumstances where there are no other means by which that imminent breach can be obviated, the police must review and assess the grounds of containment and bring it to an end once an imminent breach of the peace is no longer anticipated. This is lawful under Article 5 – justified deprivation of liberty for lawful arrest or detention – as it was a 'procedure prescribed by law'.

As the law then stood, the police could search those detained and so organised a release of those kettled through a search funnel. The Chief Superintendent decided that those who were being released from the containment would be filmed and asked for their details. The claimant was held in a separate area, surrounded by police officers, and filmed. She was asked to give her name and address and date of birth. She attempted to ask what police power was relied upon authorising the police to film her and ask her details. Those questions were not answered and she was told she would not be released until she had been filmed and given her details. This is the potential breach of Article 8 – the right to respect for private and family life, home and correspondence. The qualification to this right is that any restriction must be for one of the specified reasons, such as the prevention of disorder or crime. The court decided that the images and personal details were unlawfully obtained so there was a breach of Article 8.

This case raises a number of issues with respect to morality. First, with respect to Article 5, clearly the unjustified deprivation of liberty is immoral. It does not matter whether this is temporary or permanent. However, in this case it was considered justified as it followed the commission of a number of offences by at least some of those kettled, and the kettling was done to prevent further offences being committed, which seemed likely. Therefore, there was no breach of Article 5 and the state acted in a moral manner to protect its citizens and their property against illegal and immoral activities.

With respect to Article 8, since the complainant was not suspected of any offence, it can be considered immoral to collect personal details and images without permission for police and security purposes. Equally, to make giving permission a condition of release is equally immoral as it is effectively blackmail of an entirely innocent purpose.

Summary

- There are two main theories relating to the nature of law: legal positivism and natural law.
- Legal positivists believe that laws are valid where they are made by the recognised legislative power in the state; they do not have to satisfy any higher authority.
- Natural law is a moral theory of jurisprudence, which maintains that law should be based on morality and ethics.
- Morality is 'normative' or prescriptive, that is, it specifies what ought to be done and delineates acceptable and unacceptable behaviour.
- There are six characteristics which help to identify the rules and distinguish legal and moral rules.
- Legal and moral rules, though distinctive, share a number of characteristics.
- Changing moral values can lead to developments in the law and vice versa.
- Judges and Parliament are often forced to confront complex moral issues. Parliament can choose whether to legislate. Judges have no choice.

3 Law and justice

Tip

Law and justice is largely considered in the context of criminal law and contract law or human rights law.

3.1 The meaning of justice

Justice is a concept that can be described simply by a synonym such as fairness, equality or even-handedness. We have a sense of justice from a very young age. The idea includes treating like cases in a like manner, showing impartiality and acting in good faith. However, the term 'justice' has occupied the minds of some of the greatest thinkers across the ages. As a result, there is a wide range of theories available to explain its meaning and application.

One of the earliest attempts to define justice was set out by the fourth century BC Greek philosopher Plato. He saw justice as being harmony between the different sectors or classes in society. He regarded justice as an overarching virtue of both individuals and societies, so that almost every issue he would classify as ethical comes in under the notion of justice. For example, it is unjust for a person to steal from someone else, or not to give them what he or she owes them; these concepts are reflected in both criminal and civil law today.

Plato's work was continued by his pupil, Aristotle, who stressed the need for proportionality and for achieving the middle way – a balance between extremes. This can be seen today in the law's efforts to balance competing interests, for example freedom of contract and protection of consumers or the individual's right to freedom of expression and protection of society from extreme views.

In the thirteenth century, Thomas Aquinas continued attempts to define justice. He described justice in language similar to that of Aristotle.

Aquinas considered justice as governing our relationships with other people. It is the constant willingness to deal with other people as they deserve. The end result of justice is the common good, for the individual and for the community (society).

From the eighteenth century onwards, legal philosophy developed quickly. We will consider these areas in the next section:

■ distributive justice, which is concerned with the fair allocation of the benefits (for example, money, property, family life) and responsibilities (for example, taxes, civic duties) of life
■ utilitarianism, where maximising happiness is the object of justice
■ social justice, which is concerned with equal justice, not just in the courts, but in all aspects of society.

Tip

Make sure you can explain the meaning of each type of justice and can link relevant philosophers to each.

3.2 Theories of justice

There are many theories relating to justice. Above, we have noted the Greek philosophers and the idea of justice as harmony. We will now consider the philosophies behind the following theories:

■ distributive justice
■ utilitarianism
■ social justice.

3.2.1 Distributive justice

Distributive justice is concerned with the fair allocation of the benefits (for example, money, property, family life) and responsibilities (for example, taxes, civic duties) of life. There are several philosophers who have expounded this view including:

■ Aristotle
■ Thomas Aquinas
■ Karl Marx
■ Chaim Perelman.

Aristotle

Aristotle was a pupil of Plato. He joined Plato's Academy in Athens in the fourth century BC. Like Plato, he described justice as referring to individuals in their dealings with each other, and to the state in making and enforcing laws. He often stressed the need for proportionality, and for achieving the middle way – a balance between extremes.

Aristotle identified particular examples of justice that apply to different situations. Among these is distributive justice. Aristotle argued that a just state will distribute its wealth on the basis of merit, giving to each according to his 'virtue' and to his contribution to society. This is a proportionate system where the worthiest, rather than the neediest, receive the greatest share.

To allocate resources on the basis of people's needs would be unjust, as it would reward the lazy at least as much as the hard-working. We might consider how this would apply today to paying for care for the elderly or by providing social security benefits to all without question.

Thomas Aquinas

Thomas Aquinas, the thirteenth-century theologian, described justice in language similar to that of Aristotle. In general terms, justice governs our relationships with other people. It is the willingness to deal with other people as they deserve. The end result of justice is the common good, for the individual and for society.

Aquinas identified particular forms of justice that govern our dealings with others, which help put into practice the general principle that people are given what is due to them. First of all, distributive justice concerns the fair allocation of goods and responsibilities throughout the community. This is governed by the principle of due proportion. This means that people receive what they are due in accordance with their merit, rank and need.

Concerning merit, it would be wrong to pay workers an equal amount for unequal work, or an unequal amount for equal work.

Aquinas based his doctrine on natural law.

> See Chapter 2, section 2.1.1 for more information on natural law.

Karl Marx

Karl Marx, regarded as the nineteenth-century founder of communism, developed a radically different model of distributive justice. This model was embodied in his slogan, 'from each according

to his ability, to each according to his need'. This enshrines two principles of the ideal of communism:

■ Each will maximise his or her contribution to the common wealth by making full use of his or her abilities.
■ Each will receive according to his or her need, irrespective of the personal contribution he or she has made to the production process.

Aristotle would have regarded this model of distribution as unjust in that it has the potential for giving the greatest rewards to the least productive, and therefore least deserving, members of society.

The main criticism of Marx's views is that no country has so far been able to put them into practice with sufficient success to bring about the just society envisaged by Marx. However, capitalist societies that follow principles of distributive justice, closer to those held by Aristotle and Aquinas, are also criticised for social injustice.

Chaim Perelman

The models of distributive justice described above are among those identified by Chaim Perelman. In 1944, Perelman produced a study of justice, entitled *De la Justice*. He concluded that justice cannot be studied logically, as each attempt to define it is based upon a person's subjective values.

In *De la Justice,* he discusses different understandings of justice:

1 'To each according to his merits': each person is treated in the manner he or she deserves. The good are rewarded, the bad deprived or punished. This view is consistent with the practice of the criminal courts, handing out punishment in the measure that is warranted by the offence committed. It is also consistent with many people's religious beliefs about life after death.

2 'To each according to his needs': this approach is consistent with social democracy, in which a welfare system allocates resources such as social housing, tax allowances and benefits payments according to a means-tested system. Those in greatest need receive a proportionately higher share of the common wealth that is set aside for alleviating the most acute states of poverty. This was the dominant philosophy behind the development of the welfare state in the UK.

3 'To each according to his works': a liberal, individualistic approach reflected in the enterprise culture as it measures an individual's rewards

according to the contributions he or she has made. Under this system, a highly skilled worker will receive considerably greater rewards than an unskilled worker. This approach is claimed to provide incentives for people to better themselves.

4 'To each equally': this has a superficial attraction, and in some situations will be the fairest system of allocating scarce resources. This can be seen in the use of rationing as occurred in times of great shortage, such as food during and after the Second World War and petrol in 1956. There were exceptions, for example pregnant women were issued with more food tokens and more petrol was permitted for those who had essential jobs and needed transport, such as a midwife in a rural area.

Petrol rationing ensured a fair (equal) allocation of scarce resources

5 'To each according to his rank': for example, the quarters of army officers are superior to those of their troops. It may also refer to age – people aged over 75 do not require a television licence, irrespective of the ability to pay.

6 'To each according to his legal entitlement': this is a rights-based system and is not dependent upon merit. Thus, even the worst offender in a prison is entitled to protection from attack by other prisoners.

Extension activity

Research each of the philosophers that have been discussed. How much do you think that their views were influenced by the times in which they lived? You can continue this process with other philosophers that will be studied later.

3.2.2 Utilitarianism

Utilitarianism is a philosophy that developed in the nineteenth century from the writings of Jeremy Bentham and John Stuart Mill.

Jeremy Bentham

Jeremy Bentham was a social reformer who developed the theory known today as utilitarianism. This philosophy is centred around this concept: the more an action increases overall happiness, the more valuable it is; and the more it decreases happiness, the more reprehensible. Utilitarians are only interested in the outcome of an act, regardless of what the act itself is. For a utilitarian, maximising happiness is the object of justice.

Figure 3.1 Key facts about legal philosophers concerned with distributive justice

Legal philosopher	Basic premise
Aristotle	An ancient Greek philosopher
	He described justice as referring to individuals in their dealings with each other, and to the state in making and enforcing laws
Thomas Aquinas	A thirteenth-century theologian
	He stated that justice governs our relationships with other people. It is the constant willingness to deal with other people as they deserve
	The end result of justice is the common good, for the individual and for the community
Karl Marx	Widely regarded as the founder of communism, he developed a radically different model of distributive justice
	This model was embodied in his slogan, 'from each according to his ability, to each according to his need'
Chaim Perelman	He produced a study of justice, entitled *De la Justice*
	He concluded that justice cannot be studied logically, as each attempt to define it is based upon a person's subjective values
	He saw six possible models of distributive justice

One of the criticisms of utilitarianism is that the interest of an individual may be sacrificed for greater community happiness. For example, if a drunk person announces that he or she is about to drive home to see his or her child who has suddenly fallen ill, would you be justified in stealing his or her car keys so he or she could not set off? Not having the car keys may well cause distress and inconvenience. Would it be different if the person was about to set off to take part in a demonstration or a terrorist attack? The greater happiness brought to the larger community by your action might outweigh the pain of the individual.

Consider this in the light of the Investigatory Powers Act 2016 which, according to the Government, aims to be:

> ...an Act to make provision about the interception of communications, equipment interference and the acquisition and retention of communications data, bulk personal datasets and other information; to make provision about the treatment of material held as a result of such interception, equipment interference or acquisition or retention; to establish the Investigatory Powers Commissioner and other Judicial Commissioners and make provision about them and other oversight arrangements; to make further provision about investigatory powers and national security; to amend sections 3 and 5 of the Intelligence Services Act 1994; and for connected purposes.

Another view of the Investigatory Powers Act 2016 can be seen from whistle-blower Edward Snowden's tweet: 'The UK has just legalised the most extreme surveillance in the history of western democracy. It goes further than many autocracies.'

John Stuart Mill

John Stuart Mill was a nineteenth-century liberal, whose pamphlet, *Utilitarianism*, published in 1861, supported the basic principles of utilitarianism put forward by Bentham.

Mill wrote that actions are right 'in proportion as they tend to promote happiness, wrong as they tend to produce the reverse of happiness'. However, he focused upon the quality of happiness rather than merely upon its quantity. He wrote: 'Better to be a human being dissatisfied than a pig satisfied.'

Mill also linked utilitarianism to justice. Justice, he explained, includes respect for people, for property and for rights, as well as the need for good faith and impartiality. All of these are consistent with the principle of utility, since their application brings the greatest happiness to the greatest number.

It could also be argued that punishing wrongdoers also brings happiness to the greatest number. However, Mill argued that punishment is in itself an evil as it involves inflicting harm or pain, and can only be justified where it brings a greater benefit, such as public order.

Act and rule utilitarianism

The theory of utilitarianism has developed since Bentham and Mill. Under act utilitarianism, the rightness of an act is judged in isolation to see whether it adds to, or subtracts from, the sum of human happiness. For example, when I drive my car at 130 m.p.h. on an empty motorway, I am increasing my own happiness and causing pain to nobody else: the sum of human happiness is increased.

According to rule utilitarianism, the rightness of an action is judged according to whether the sum of human happiness would be increased if everyone acted in the same way. Developing the example, if all car owners tried to drive along the same stretch of motorway at the same speed and at the same time, an accident might well occur, resulting in pain and misery: the sum of human happiness would decrease.

Figure 3.2 Key facts about legal philosophers concerned with utilitarianism

Legal philosopher	Basic premise
Jeremy Bentham	He developed the legal and moral principle of utility: what makes an action right or wrong is the usefulness, or value, of the consequence it brings The more an action increases overall happiness, the more valuable it is; and the more it decreases happiness, the more reprehensible
John Stuart Mill	Justice, he explained, includes respect for people, for property and for rights, as well as the need for good faith and impartiality All of these are consistent with the principle of utility, since their application brings the greatest happiness to the greatest number

3.2.3 Social justice

Social justice can be said to be the ability people have to realise their potential in the society where they live. It is concerned with equal justice, not just in the courts, but in all aspects of society. This concept demands that people have equal rights and opportunities; everyone, from the poorest person on the margins of society to the wealthiest, deserves an even playing field.

The Department for Work and Pensions published a paper on this topic in 2012. In the document the key expression was 'Social Justice is about making society function better – providing the support and tools to help turn lives around'.

Look online

Read the introduction to the document on pages 4 and 5 to gain an insight about social justice: www.gov.uk/government/uploads/system/uploads/attachment_data/file/49515/social-justice-transforming-lives.pdf.

This is not a new idea, as it has been expounded by philosophers including John Rawls and Robert Nozick.

John Rawls

John Rawls published A *Theory of Justice* in 1971, which set out the concept of social justice. Rawls described justice as fairness, and then presented a hypothetical society where each member would distribute its resources in a disinterested manner. To make this possible, nobody would know in advance what his or her position in that society would be, nor what stage of that society's development he or she would be born into. He or she would operate behind a 'veil of ignorance'. Rawls stated:

> No one knows his place in society, his class position or social status, nor does anyone know his fortune in the distribution of natural assets and abilities, his intelligence, strength, and the like.

Rawls believed that, on this basis, benefits and burdens would be distributed justly and therefore fairly.

He argued that two basic principles of justice would be evident within this society:

- Each person would have 'an equal right to the most extensive scheme of basic liberties compatible with a similar scheme of liberties for others'. This would include certain basic freedoms, such as the right to own property, freedom of speech, freedom of association, and freedom from arbitrary arrest, which we can see as many of the freedoms under the ECHR.
- Social and economic inequalities may exist, but only:
  - where they benefit the least advantaged members of society, and
  - provided all offices and positions are open to everyone.

This would mean that it is acceptable for a surgeon to earn several times the average wage, live in a large detached house and drive a luxury car, etc. because his work benefits disadvantaged members of society. In addition, his work would encourage others to imitate his example, further benefiting the disadvantaged. It is only acceptable provided that everyone with skills and abilities comparable to those of the neurosurgeon has a reasonable opportunity to pursue a similar path.

In employing the fiction of the 'veil of ignorance' to develop a society based upon consent, Rawls was promoting a rights-based system. So basic human rights such as freedom of speech and association are 'inalienable': they can never be sacrificed for the common good.

The state must always respect the autonomy of the individual. Rawls wrote:

> Each person possesses an inviolability founded on justice that even the welfare of society as a whole cannot override. Therefore, in a just society the rights secured by justice are not subject to political bargaining or to the calculus of social interests.

This distinguishes Rawls from Bentham and the utilitarians, against whom the final comment is directed, for utilitarians might allow individual freedoms to be sacrificed where this is considered necessary to promote wider benefits for the greater number.

Robert Nozick

Robert Nozick published *Anarchy, State and Utopia* in 1974, in which he developed an entitlement theory of justice, which consisted of three principles:

- a principle of justice in acquisition, dealing with how property is initially acquired

- a principle of justice in transfer, dealing with how property can change hands
- a principle of rectification of injustice, dealing with injustices arising from the acquisition or transfer of property under the two principles above; this third principle would not be required if the world was entirely just.

Where a person obtains property in accordance with the principles of acquisition or transfer, he or she is entitled to keep that property. Where a person obtains property by fraud or theft or other unjust means, the third principle provides a remedy.

This is different from Rawls, who argued that inequalities may exist only where they benefit the most disadvantaged members of society. Nozick places no limits upon private ownership. Property justly acquired may not be appropriated simply as a form of redistribution of wealth, to reduce inequalities. He wrote: 'No one has a right to something whose realisation requires certain uses of things and activities that other people have rights and entitlements over.'

This is a free-market, libertarian form of justice.

Nozick revives John Locke's theory of justice. He argues that state interference should be kept to a minimum to achieve a just society and that it should be restricted to the basic needs – protecting the individual against force, theft/fraud and enforcing contractual obligations. The emphasis is on protecting the individual's rights, particularly one's property rights. Nozick does not believe that property can be owned by the state, but by individuals.

Nozick's theory may be criticised, but many of the recent political moves in our society show this theory in practice:

- privatisation of state-owned facilities
- making the individual more responsible for his or her own welfare – this can be seen in the tightening of the welfare net in terms of social security and pension provision
- reducing the dependence of the individual on the state.

Figure 3.3 Key facts about legal philosophers concerned with social justice

Legal philosopher	Basic premise
John Rawls	He described justice as fairness He argued that two basic principles of justice would be evident within society
Robert Nozick	In his book, *Anarchy, State and Utopia*, he developed an entitlement theory of justice, which consisted of three principles This contrasts with Rawls who provided a philosophical basis for the welfare state and the redistribution of wealth to help the disadvantaged in his book, *A Theory of Justice*

3.3 The extent to which the law (civil and criminal) achieves justice

This section will try to address this question: 'Is the law, and the legal system, just?' We will need to consider **procedural justice** and **corrective justice**, as well as **substantive justice**.

A distinction is often made between procedural law and substantive law. Hart referred to justice 'according to law' and justice 'of the law'. The former term relates to how laws are made and how the legal system operates; the latter to the laws themselves. It is a useful distinction upon which to base this topic.

Key terms

Procedural justice – this is concerned with making and implementing decisions according to fair processes.

Corrective justice – this is sometimes known as restorative justice, and is when the law restores the imbalance that has occurred between two individuals or an individual and the state.

Substantive justice – the content of the law itself must be just.

3.3.1 Procedural justice

This can be considered from the aspect of legal aid availability. Legal aid is an important part of social justice. Everyone has a right to access justice, to receive a fair hearing and to understand their legal rights and obligations. Many people need help to access and use these rights. Legal aid should do this. In 2010 when introducing the Government's legal aid reforms, the then Justice Secretary Ken Clarke said, 'I genuinely believe access to justice is the hallmark of a civilised society'.

However, the effects of changes made by the Legal Aid Sentencing and Punishment of Offenders Act (LASPO) 2012 and subsequently have reduced the availability of legal aid. In April 2013, the Government cut £350 million from the relatively small £2.2 billion budget, lopping off entire areas of law. The bits that were removed included most of what is known as 'social welfare law' – advice on welfare benefits, employment, housing (except homeless cases), immigration (except asylum) and family (except in cases of domestic violence).

Legal aid is important because a person who cannot afford legal representation can be said to have no right to a fair trial. This right is protected under Article 6 ECHR enshrined in HRA 1998. The right of access to a court must be meaningful and practical, not theoretical.

Among the cases to be excluded from legal aid provision are most family cases, many immigration cases, education cases which do not involve special educational needs, most debt matters, most first instance welfare benefits cases and many cases involving employment and homelessness.

With respect to legal aid in criminal proceedings, anyone arrested and taken to a police station is entitled to free legal advice, whatever their means. After being charged or issued with a summons, a person's eligibility for further legal assistance becomes means-tested. This will cover the work that a solicitor will need to do to prepare the case and representation at the Magistrates' Court and the Crown Court. It must also be established that it is in the interests of justice for a person to be granted legal aid. If a person is found guilty, he or she may be required to repay his or her legal costs. The rules are constantly changing and it is important to take specialist advice from a solicitor who specialises in criminal law.

Legal aid deserts have therefore appeared, as firms can no longer afford to offer these services. Many firms have given up their criminal legal aid practices, raising serious concerns about increased risks of miscarriages of justice. Legal aid lawyers are not fat

cats – the average annual salary of a legal aid lawyer in 2013 was £25,000.

Thus justice requires access to the law. This is achieved as no one in the UK is specifically denied access to the law. *Effective* access to the law is a different matter, as those who are less able to act for themselves or to pay for someone to act for them may be denied justice.

3.3.2 Corrective justice – sanctions and damages

When judges or magistrates pass sentence upon an offender, they take into consideration a number of factors. These include the aim of the sentence: this may simply be to punish the offender for breaking the rules or to deter others from committing the same offence. Balanced against these may be the desire to rehabilitate the offender. The court will also consider aggravating and mitigating factors relating to the offence and to the offender and will have to follow sentencing guidelines. This can also be seen in the award of damages in civil law. In negligence, the aim of compensation is to restore the claimant to his pre-tort position, in so far as money can achieve this. To balance this, any contributory negligence on the part of the claimant will reduce his award.

For example, in *Jebson v Ministry of Defence* (2000) 75 per cent of the claimant's award was deducted for his contributory negligence. This reduction is just because it is proportionate: it reflects that the claimant was largely responsible for his own harm.

In contract law, the basis of assessment of damages is loss of bargain: the claimant is placed in the position he or she would have been in had the contract been performed. However, only losses that are reasonably within the contemplation of the parties may be recovered. This can be seen in *Victoria Laundry v Newman* (1949).

The judgments in the two cases above reflect the 'concept of proportionality' in that damages are awarded according to the merits of the claim, and not automatically in relation to the harm suffered. Under these tests, the awards of damages are just.

The criminal process

Trial by jury enables jury members to use their view of justice rather than adhere strictly to the rules of law and the evidence presented to them. In *Ponting* (1985), a civil servant was charged under the Official Secrets Act for releasing secret information about the sinking of the Argentinian warship *General Belgrano*. The judge told the jury that any public interest in the information did not provide a defence but the jury acquitted him. The rules of evidence adopted in criminal trials seek to balance the interests of the parties to the action.

For this reason, evidence of previous convictions is not generally admissible unless the facts are strikingly similar to those in the instant case.

On the other hand, even illegally obtained evidence may be admissible. In *Jeffrey v Black* (1978), the police arrested a student for the theft of a sandwich, and then conducted an illegal search of his flat, where they discovered some drugs. The magistrates threw out the case after ruling the evidence inadmissible. However, the Divisional Court ruled that the illegality of the search did not justify excluding the evidence it had exposed. This may at first seem to be unjust.

However, consider a situation where the police had discovered plans and materials to commit a terrorist attack. They would surely be justified in relying upon the material found in the 'illegal' search in court.

In general, justice is served by the criminal process, but individual cases may expose a lack of justice that is not always remedied at a later date.

Appeals in criminal cases

In criminal cases heard in the Magistrates' Court, the defendant may appeal against conviction or sentence or on a point of law.

Under the Criminal Justice Act 1998, the prosecution may appeal against 'unduly lenient' sentences. Convicted criminals appeal less frequently now that an appeal may result in a more severe sentence.

Under the Criminal Justice Act 1972, the Attorney-General may appeal on a point of law to the Court of Appeal where he or she wishes to question the judge's direction that has led to an acquittal. For example, in *Attorney-General's Reference (No. 2 of 1992)* the Court of Appeal considered the defence of automatism.

Appeals with respect to substantive law are always seen as achieving justice, but not necessarily for those who have been convicted under the 'old' law. In the interests of justice, today's sentencing guidelines are not applicable to offences committed before new guidelines came into force.

Miscarriages of justice in criminal cases

In spite of this system of appeals, injustices arise where people serve prison sentences for crimes they are not guilty of. Famous cases include the Birmingham Six and the Guildford Four. The publicity of these and other similar cases led to the establishment in 1997 of the Criminal Cases Review Commission (CCRC), whose role is to review the cases of those it feels have been wrongly convicted of criminal offences, or unfairly sentenced.

Look online

Look at cases that the CCRC have been involved with and their successes, at: www.ccrc.gov.uk/case-library/.

The CCRC does not consider innocence or guilt, but whether there is new evidence or argument that may cast doubt on the safety of the original decision. Derek Bentley and Sally Clark are among those who have had their convictions quashed by the Court of Appeal following reference from the CCRC.

The only comfort in terms of justice is the fact that systems exist to bring miscarriages of justice to the attention of the appeal courts, even if in some cases a considerable period of time can lapse before the miscarriage is put right, and in Bentley's case, many years after he had been hanged. Even then, compensation is unlikely to be paid unless it can be shown that their innocence was beyond all reasonable doubt as a result of fresh evidence.

Public funding for many aspects of this is limited. Procedural justice relies very heavily upon the integrity of those responsible for the investigation and prosecution of crime.

In the news

Birmingham pub bombings inquest: families to meet home secretary over funding

Relatives of victims of the IRA's 1974 Birmingham pub bombings are to meet the home secretary, Amber Rudd to request funding for legal representation at the resumed inquest.

The private discussions on Monday come amid mounting concern over the way police, prison officers and local authority staff are invariably provided with lawyers at coroners' courts whereas the families of those who died are repeatedly denied legal aid.

For the Hillsborough inquest, the Home Office did eventually provide discretionary payments for legal representation for families at the second inquest into the deaths of 96 men, women and children in the 1989 stadium disaster. The Birmingham families hope to persuade Rudd that a similar funding approach should be taken by the Home Office for their resumed inquest.

Source: Adapted from an article by Owen Bowcott in the Guardian online, 5 September 2016

Follow this link to read the complete article: **www.theguardian.com/uk-news/2016/sep/05/ birmingham-pub-bombings-inquest-families-to- ask-home-secretary-for-funding.**

3.3.3 Rules of natural justice

Natural justice is often described as containing two basic principles. The first is that the court must not only be impartial, but also seen to be so. Judges should have no personal interest in a case. In the *Pinochet* case (1998), the House of Lords ruled that General Pinochet, the former dictator of Chile, could be extradited to Spain to stand trial for his alleged involvement in the torture and death of Spanish citizens in Chile.

The House of Lords initially included Lord Hoffman. He was a director of one part of Amnesty International who had been given permission to take part in the appeal. Clearly this infringed the principle of impartiality.

The second principle is that each party to the dispute must have a fair opportunity to present his or her own case and to answer the case of his or her opponent. In *Ridge v Baldwin* (1964), the House of Lords ruled that the decision by a police authority to dismiss its chief constable without a personal hearing contravened natural justice.

The rules of natural justice are designed to protect the interests of individuals against arbitrary decisions. In both the *Pinochet* case and *Ridge v Baldwin*, the original decision may have been correct. However, each was unreliable because of the breach of the rules of natural justice.

The application of justice must be fair, and must be seen to be fair.

3.3.4 Substantive law – crime
The mandatory life sentence

The principle of proportionality generally governs the sentencing practice of judges and magistrates. This satisfies our expectations that the more serious the offence, the harsher the sanction that will be imposed.

Those convicted of murder are subject to a mandatory life sentence. The sentencing judge will then impose a tariff, this being the minimum term the murderer has to serve.

Many agree that imposing a life sentence on a killer is just. Public opinion polls regularly show strong support for the return of the death penalty, to provide a degree of retributive justice.

Some murderers are viewed as worse than others: the setting of a tariff does not allow for proportionality, and so may lead to harsh decisions. In *Cocker* (1989), the defendant suffocated his wife, at her insistence, with a pillow; she had been terminally ill and in much pain. The trial judge denied the defendant any partial defence that would reduce murder to manslaughter. Here a life sentence may seem a disproportionate punishment.

However, the judge may be inclined to provide a measure of justice by imposing a reduced tariff period; this was shown in *R v Inglis* (2010).

R v Inglis (2010)

The trial judge imposed a nine-year tariff period, reduced on appeal to five years, when D was found guilty of murdering her son. She killed him because she believed that she was acting in the best interests of her son and did not want him to suffer any further. Lord Judge said:

> ❝ Mercy killing is murder. Until Parliament decides otherwise, the law recognises a distinction between the withdrawal of treatment supporting life, which may be lawful, and the active termination of life, which is unlawful. ❞

Cases such as this show that, perhaps, justice is better served by allowing judges and magistrates to pass the sentence they feel to be most appropriate, rather than have a system of fixed sentences or a suggested tariff.

Defences

Not all premeditated killing is equally culpable. The partial defences of loss of control, diminished responsibility and for the survivor in a suicide pact were created to limit liability. The defences of self-defence and automatism excuse liability altogether.

One of the generally accepted characteristics of justice is that like cases are treated in like manner. However, the law gives more favourable treatment to those who kill while suffering diminished responsibility or with a loss of control, than it does to those whose free will is overpowered by an external threat. The decision of the House of Lords in *Howe* (1987) clearly established that the defence of duress is not available on a charge of murder or attempted murder. Yet one feels much more sympathy for the defendant in *R v Gotts* (1991), a boy whose life was threatened by his own father, than one does for the defendant in *Byrne* (1960). The Law Commission has proposed adding duress as a defence that would attract conviction for second degree murder. This would introduce parity of treatment under the law, and satisfy a basic requirement of justice that like cases are treated in like manner.

3.3.5 Contract law
Formation of contract
In *Reveille Independent LLC v Anotech International (UK) Ltd* (2016), the court had to consider if a contract has come into existence between commercial parties when they were apparently still in negotiation. In examining the rules on offer and acceptance by conduct, the court was keen to preserve certainty and give due attention to what it considered to be the reasonable expectations of honest, sensible business people. This was stressed in order to achieve justice in these business situations.

Exclusion clauses
Parties to a contract may try to limit their liability by relying upon exclusion clauses. The traditional rule of *caveat emptor* (let the buyer beware) can work against the interests of the weaker bargaining party or where there is a pre-printed standard form of contract. The courts try to achieve a more just result.

Olley v Marlborough Court Hotel (1949)

The exclusion clause was invalid as it had not been brought to Mrs Olley's attention when she booked in at reception.

Spurling v Bradshaw (1956)

Lord Denning observed that some exclusion clauses were written in 'regrettably small print', and stated that the more harsh or unusual the term was, the more it needed to be brought to the attention of the person signing it, for example by being 'printed in red ink, with a red hand pointing to it'.

The Unfair Contract Terms Act 1977 restricts the use of exclusion clauses. A person cannot exclude liability for death or personal injury resulting from his or her negligence, and other exclusion clauses are subjected to the test of reasonableness. This Act aims to prevent those with strong bargaining power from taking unfair advantage of weaker parties and provide a fairer balance between the bargaining parties.

Further protection is given to consumers by legislation such as the Consumer Rights Act 2015 which sets out both rights and remedies in consumer transactions.

Penalty clauses
The justice of penalty clauses depends on the view of how far a person can force someone else to comply with what he has promised. European and international law allow a court to modify an excessive penalty in a contract term. Under UK law, the penalty clause is either invalid or not.

Cavendish Square Holding BV v Talal El Makdessi (2015) and ParkingEye Ltd v Beavis (2015)

The Supreme Court decision widened the previously applied tests in relation to the enforceability of penalty clauses. Lord Hodge stated that:

> The correct test for a penalty is whether the sum or remedy stipulated as a consequence of a breach of contract is exorbitant or unconscionable when regard is had to the innocent party's interest in the performance of the contract.

This suggests an idea of justice being applied.

In *El Makdessi*, the court held that the provisions contained in the agreements were there to protect the legitimate interests of the buyer.

In *ParkingEye*, it was held that although £85 may have been perceived to be an unreasonably high sum, there were clear legitimate commercial interests that were to be protected by the fine.

Third-party rights

Traditionally, a person could not sue unless he or she was a party to the contract. However, in *Jackson v Horizon Holidays* (1975) the claimant succeeded in seeking damages for himself and for members of his family after a package holiday failed to match the advertised description, even though only he, and not his family members, had made the contract. This is not too surprising given the law of agency and the doctrine of the undisclosed principal.

In 1999, Parliament passed the Contract (Rights of Third Parties) Act, allowing third parties to make a claim where the contract expressly provided for this, or where the contract purported to confer a benefit on them. These provisions were designed to avoid the obvious injustices caused in cases such as *Tweddle v Atkinson* (1861), and the subterfuges that were necessary to obtain a just result which occurred in *Beswick v Beswick* (1967).

It does appear that the Contracts (Rights of Third Parties) Act 1999 would now allow the *Beswick* claim even if she had not been an executor of the will. However, if it appears the parties did not intend the term to benefit a third party then the Act will not apply. The parties to the contract have therefore the right to exclude the Act from benefiting a third party. Most commercial contracts now include such a term so the Act is not as useful as might be hoped.

Frustrated contracts

Parliament again was responsible for legislating to ensure that, where a contract is frustrated through no fault of either party, a just outcome can be reached. The Law Reform (Frustrated Contracts) Act 1943 enabled the courts to apportion the losses more fairly between the parties: the court may order 'a just sum' to be paid where either expenses have been incurred or a valuable benefit obtained.

However, the courts seem reluctant to find frustration of contract. This can be seen in the case of *Armchair Answercall v People in Mind* (2016), where the court made the inference that 'one or other party [had] assumed the risk of the occurrence of the event' and so there was no frustration of contract.

3.3.6 Human rights law

As we have seen, corrective justice is involved when the law restores the imbalance that has occurred between an individual and the state. Human rights law is concerned with this as a central theme.

Article 8 ECHR and its operation in the UK has again come under scrutiny with respect to the treatment of past convictions and other records of the individual with respect to job applications. Despite the progress made and the Law Commission proposals mentioned in Chapter 32, there remain many issues, which are highlighted in the case of R *(on the application of P) v Secretary of State for Home Department* (2017).

R *(on the application of P) v Secretary of State for Home Department* (2017)

This appeal consisted of four challenges. The three successful ones were as follows:

1 P committed two shoplifting offences in 1999 when suffering from undiagnosed schizophrenia. Fifteen years later, she wanted to be a care assistant. The Court of Appeal held that the multiple conviction rule was disproportionate in its current automatic form to the interference with P's life. It did not generate interests of public safety so as even to make it arguably necessary.

2 G, when aged 13, had had consensual anal intercourse with two boys aged 9 and 10 and was reprimanded in 2006 by the police. In 2011, he worked for an employment agency in a library of a local college. He was asked for an enhanced criminal record certificate ('ECRC') because his work involved contact with children. This challenge also succeeded: disclosure was not necessary, given G's age at the time of offending. If he sought an ECRC, it might be justifiable to include this as soft intelligence, but then he could potentially challenge it on the grounds of irrelevance.

3 W, when aged 16 in 1982, was convicted of actual bodily harm, for which he received a conditional discharge. At age 47, he wanted to teach English as a second language. Unsurprisingly, it was held to be disproportionate to have to disclose this conviction.

Clearly, the balance between state, society and the individual had swung too far in these instances meaning that the retention and disclosures were unjust and a breach of Article 8.

Justice can also be seen in the courts' attitude to Article 2 ECHR – the right to life. In *Smith v Ministry of Defence* (2013), several British soldiers had been killed either as a result of 'friendly fire' (when soldiers on the same side accidentally kill one another) or the inability to check for hidden explosives, through poor training or inadequate equipment. The Supreme Court said they were protected by human rights law, even though they were acting abroad. The positive obligations under Article 2 should be given effect where it is reasonable to expect the individual to be afforded protection. This is, however, a matter of judgment, determined in light of the facts of each case and therefore requires justice.

Summary

- Justice is a concept that can be described simply by a synonym such as fairness, equality or even-handedness.
- There are many theories and aspects of justice, including: justice as harmony; distributive justice; utilitarianism; social justice; procedural justice; corrective justice; natural justice; substantive justice.
- Justice is essential in the law. The extent to which it is achieved varies with respect to different aspects of procedural and substantive law.
- Examples can be seen in both civil and criminal law.
- Judges are increasingly aware of the concept of justice and use the law to achieve justice even if this means overruling a previous case or distinguishing previous decisions on surprising grounds.

Criminal law

4 Rules and theory in criminal law

After reading this chapter, you should be able to:
- Understand the idea of harm as the basis of criminalising conduct
- Understand the concepts of autonomy of the individual, fault and individual responsibility
- Understand principles in formulating rules of criminal law including fair labelling, correspondence, maximum certainty and no retrospective liability

4.1 Rules of criminal law

The main rules for all the criminal offences you have to study at AS and A-level Law are:
- the concept of the elements of *actus reus* and *mens rea* in crimes
- the standard of proof in criminal cases, and
- the burden of proof in criminal cases.

These rules are outlined in *AQA A-level Law for Year 1 and AS*, Chapter 18. The concept of *actus reus* is then explained in more detail in Chapter 19 and *mens rea* in more detail in Chapter 20.

4.2 Factors in criminalising conduct

When deciding what behaviour should be criminalised, a number of factors come into play including:
- what ought to be the basis for criminalising conduct?
- how far should individuals have autonomy to do what they wish, or should the welfare of the community as a whole take priority?
- what principles should be used when framing rules of criminal law?

These factors are explored in the sections that follow.

4.3 Harm as the basis for criminalising conduct

The starting point for having criminal law is that everyone in a community has the right to be free from harm. This idea can be seen by having offences which act against those who cause physical harm to others. This can be illustrated by having offences of murder, manslaughter and the non-fatal offences. Property offences such as theft and burglary are less disruptive to a community, but are still of serious concern and cause harm to the victim.

Harm can be caused to the wider community which may include harm to public security. There are offences dealing with terrorism as well as less serious public order offences.

Regulatory offences (usually offences of strict liability) deal with the risk of harm to the public by dealing with issues of pollution, selling food which is past its 'sell-by' date or by selling products to under-age children. Road traffic offences are also aimed at avoiding harm to other road users and pedestrians.

Strict liability offences are explained in *AQA A-level Law for Year 1 and AS*, Chapter 21.

4.3.1 Paternalistic law

There is also the view that some conduct should be criminalised in order to protect us from doing harm to ourselves. This is the idea of 'paternalistic' law. For example, the supply and use of certain drugs such as cocaine and heroin is illegal. The reason for this is that such drugs are addictive and, in the long term, deprive people of the control over their lives. They can also lead to drug users committing crime in order to feed their habit.

However, it is not a crime for an adult to buy or smoke cigarettes, even though nicotine is an addictive drug and can cause serious health problems. Laws have, however, been introduced in recent years to stop smoking in workplaces, certain public areas and in vehicles when children are being carried.

Activity

Discuss in groups how the possession or consumption of alcohol is treated by the law in this country. You could consider:

- age limits for buying and consuming alcohol
- licensing hours
- carrying bottles or cans in the street
- offences committed after excessive consumption
- driving offences.

Do you think there are other areas where new laws should be introduced?

Where potentially illegal conduct is carried out in private between consenting adults, the law is not consistent and even judges have differing views. In *R v Brown* (1994), the men's conduct was ruled to be criminal even though none complained to the police and the activities were carried out in private.

R v Brown (1994)

Five men in a group of consenting adult sado-masochists were convicted of offences of assault causing actual bodily harm (s 47 of the Offences Against the Person Act (OAPA) 1861) and malicious wounding (s 20 OAPA 1861). They had carried out various painful acts on each other for their own pleasure. All the victims had consented and none had needed medical attention. Their convictions were upheld by the House of Lords.

The majority of the Law Lords clearly made this decision as a matter of public policy. For example, Lord Templeman said:

> **The question whether the defence of consent should be extended to the consequences of sado-masochistic encounters can only be decided by consideration of policy and public interest ... Society is entitled and bound to protect itself against a cult of violence.**

On the other hand, Lord Slynn dissented saying 'it is not for the courts in the interests of paternalism or to protect people from themselves to introduce into statutory crimes concepts that do not properly fit there'.

The majority decision to convict is contrasted by the decision in *R v Wilson* (1997), in which the parties were a husband and wife.

R v Wilson (1997)

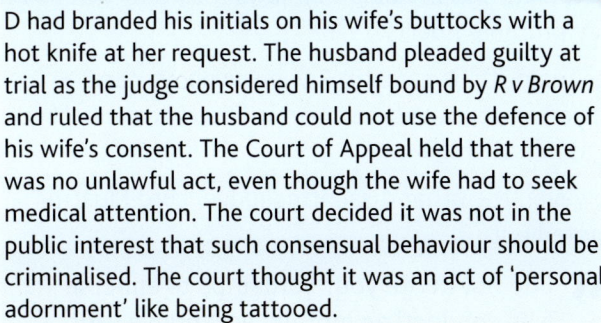

D had branded his initials on his wife's buttocks with a hot knife at her request. The husband pleaded guilty at trial as the judge considered himself bound by *R v Brown* and ruled that the husband could not use the defence of his wife's consent. The Court of Appeal held that there was no unlawful act, even though the wife had to seek medical attention. The court decided it was not in the public interest that such consensual behaviour should be criminalised. The court thought it was an act of 'personal adornment' like being tattooed.

The majority of the Law Lords were clearly taking a paternalistic approach in their decision making while the minority, and the Court of Appeal, were taking a more libertarian view. This was that acts between consenting adults in private, even those which cause injury, should not be the business of the law. An attempt to overturn the convictions in *Laskey, Jaggard and Brown v UK* (1997) in the European Court of Human Rights failed. The rationale for the decision was that whilst a person has a general right of free will, a state may, as a matter of public policy, restrict that in certain cases. This may include where it is for the general public good and for the protection of morals. As a result it was decided that this case fell within the scope of the UK Government's right to determine its legality.

One view of the decisions to convict is that it is paternalism by an unelected, unrepresentative group which uses, but fails to acknowledge, its power. The House of Lords failed to set a precise guide to decide where a defence of consent should succeed or where it should not. This failure could lead to laws being applied unequally to homosexuals or others whose practices are in the minority and who do not have the sympathy of judges. The opposite view is that because Parliament has failed to set laws in this area, someone or some body, the judges, had to set standards of behaviour. If Parliament then felt that the judges had taken a too paternalistic approach, then it could legislate.

4.3.2 Legal moralism

Rather than relying solely on the principle that harm should be the basis for criminalising conduct, there is another principle that conduct is wrongful if it is morally wrong. Legal moralism is a theory that laws may be used to prohibit or require behaviour based on society's collective judgement of whether the behaviour is moral or not. The opposite view is legal liberalism, which holds that laws may only be used if they promote liberty.

The majority decision in *R v Brown* above can be viewed as conduct being criminalised because of legal moralism.

However, the other dissenting judge, Lord Mustill, pointed out:

> ❝ I do not invite your Lordships to endorse [the conduct] as morally acceptable. Nor do I pronounce in favour of a libertine doctrine specifically related to sexual matters … What I do say is that these are questions of private morality; the standards by which they fall to be judged are not those of the criminal law. ❞

There are also other areas of law where the courts have ruled that conduct is criminal through legal moralism. The majority decision of the House of Lords in *R v Hinks* (2000) can be viewed in this way.

> This case is discussed in Chapter 8, section 8.2.2.

Lord Hobhouse said in his dissenting judgment:

> ❝ An essential function of the criminal law is to define the boundary between what conduct is criminal and what merely immoral. Both are the subject of the disapprobation of ordinary right-thinking citizens and the distinction is likely to be arbitrary or at least strongly influenced by considerations subjective to the individual members of the tribunal. To treat otherwise lawful conduct as criminal merely because it is open to such disapprobation would be contrary to principle. ❞

Another, older, example of legal moralism is from the 1960s, when senior judges considered themselves as guardians of public morality, particularly in sexual matters. This even went to the extent of creating new offences. In *Shaw v DPP* (1961), D published a booklet containing the names and addresses of prostitutes, their photographs, and details of the services they provided. He was charged with conspiracy to corrupt public morals, a supposed common law offence never

previously charged. The House of Lords (Lord Reid dissenting) upheld his conviction. Viscount Simonds said that:

> ❝ In the sphere of criminal law he had no doubt the courts retained a residual power to enforce the supreme and fundamental purpose of the law, namely, to conserve, not only the safety and order, but also the moral welfare of the State. It was their duty to guard against attacks which might be the more insidious because they were novel and unexpected. ❞

Viscount Simonds' statement was widely disapproved, but, as seen from the *Brown* case, judges can still allow their decisions to be influenced by moral factors.

4.4 Autonomy of the individual

This means that an individual should have freedom to do what he or she wants, where he or she wants and when he or she wants. Any attempt to limit autonomy should only be where it is necessary to limit harm. So where a person decides to attack another person, then the autonomy of that choice can be limited.

Looking again at *R v Brown* it can be argued that the acts should not have been criminalised as the men consented to the 'assaults' upon them, they were adults and the acts were carried out in private.

Autonomy also means that individuals should be treated as responsible for their own behaviour which links into the idea of fault; see section 4.5 below.

4.4.1 Limited autonomy

There are some groups of people whose ability to make choices is considered less than a competent adult. These include:

- those under 18
- those suffering from a mental disorder.

The criminal law is used to protect such groups as it is thought they are not in a position to make reasoned decisions about activities with significant consequences. Examples of the criminal law protecting such groups are seen by the prohibition of selling products to children below specified ages and prohibiting sexual activities with children under specified ages.

Another area where autonomy of the individual is an important issue is assisting in a suicide, where the person is so physically disabled that he or she cannot commit suicide without help. Committing suicide is not a crime, but assisting another to commit suicide is an offence. It is argued that this takes away the autonomy of a disabled person to choose to take his or her own life. The Director of Public Prosecutions has issued a Policy Guidance Statement about the factors to be considered when deciding in such cases whether to prosecute.

Look online

The Policy Guidance Statement can be found at: www.cps.gov.uk/publications/prosecution/assisted_suicide_policy.html.

4.5 Fault

In deciding whether a defendant is to be blamed for his or her conduct, the criminal law generally presumes that a defendant is responsible for his or her own actions and the consequences of his or her actions.

However, there are several occasions when the courts will recognise that a person is not wholly or partly to blame for the consequences of his or her actions:

1 Some groups are exempt from criminal prosecution, such as children under the age of criminal responsibility. In England and Wales, this is age ten.
2 A person may not be liable for an involuntary act, such as where a crime is committed when a person is pushed by another person. The push might result in a fatal or non-fatal offence as in *R v Mitchell* (1983) or perhaps damage to property

R v Mitchell (1983) is discussed in AQA *A-level Law for Year 1 and AS*, Chapter 19, section 19.1.4.

3 If a person commits an offence in a state of automatism or when he or she cannot form the required *mens rea* due to insanity or intoxication.

For the defences of automatism, insanity and intoxication, see Chapter 11.

4 If a person lacks the *mens rea* for an offence, he or she may not be to blame for his or her actions. For example, if a man takes a coat from a coat rack at a restaurant, genuinely, but mistakenly, believing that it is his own coat, he is not liable for theft as he does not have the necessary *mens rea*. He might be in control of his actions but does not have the required mental state for the offence.
5 There are some defences where, even though the defendant had the necessary mental state for an offence, he or she should not be blamed. These defences include self-defence or defence of another, and duress.

For the defences of self-defence and duress, see Chapter 12.

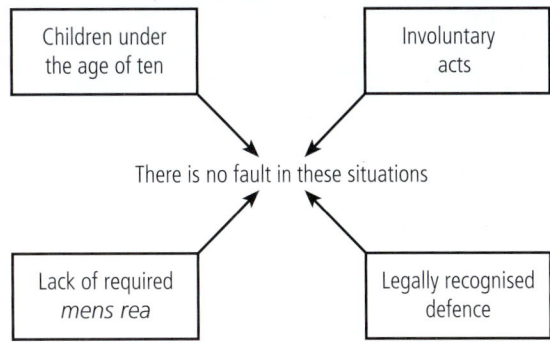

Figure 4.1 Situations where there is no fault

4.5.1 Strict liability or no fault offences

Although English law generally recognises that people are safeguarded from being found liable for an offence when their conduct has been without fault, there is one category of offence which appears to clash with this principle. These are offences of strict liability.

These offences are discussed in detail in AQA *A-level Law for Year 1 and AS*, Chapter 21.

As can be seen from cases discussed there, it could be said that, in strict liability offences, although all reasonable steps were taken to prevent the commission of an offence, criminal liability was still imposed. This was particularly shown in *Harrow LBC v Shah and Shah* (1999). In that case the Divisional Court held that the offence with which they were charged did not require any *mens rea* but the selling of the ticket to an under-age child was enough to make the defendants guilty. The defendant's arguments that they themselves did not sell the ticket and all necessary training had been given were not relevant to their conviction.

4.6 Individual responsibility

No one may be convicted of an offence except on the basis of his or her own individual criminal responsibility.

A person is not responsible for a crime committed by another person, unless he or she has contributed to the crime in some way. This may include attempting to commit a crime, or assisting in, or aiding or abetting the commission of a crime.

> For attempts and preliminary offences, see Chapter 10.

4.7 Principles in formulating rules of criminal law

There are also principles which should be followed when a new criminal offence is drafted. These include:

- fair-labelling
- correspondence between the *actus reus* and the *mens rea* of an offence
- the elements of the offence are clear and give maximum certainty
- the offence should not create retrospective liability.

4.7.1 Fair labelling

Fair labelling means that the offence of which a person is convicted must correctly describe the kind of crime that has been committed. The reason for this is that there may be a moral stigma attached to a conviction. So it is important that the crime should carry the correct 'label'.

The labelling must be fair in the description of the offence committed. It is argued that it is unfair to label a person a murderer when he or she did not intend to kill.

It is also important for the label to differentiate the offence committed from other offences. This can be

seen by comparing the offences of assault causing actual bodily harm (s 47 OAPA 1861) and inflicting grievous bodily harm (ss 18 and 20 OAPA 1861). The level of harm caused by each offence is clearly described and differentiated.

This fair labelling principle is linked to the correspondence principle.

4.7.2 Correspondence

The principle of correspondence is that where the *actus reus* and the *mens rea* do not correspond, the liability of the accused should not exceed the harm actually encompassed by his or her own *mens rea*.

This is easier to understand by considering the elements of an actual offence. For theft, the *actus reus* is that the defendant must appropriate property belonging to another person. The *mens rea* is that the defendant must intend to permanently deprive that other of the property and that the appropriation must be dishonest. It is clear that the mental element of theft directly relates to its *actus reus*.

However, there are offences which do not comply with the correspondence principle. One example is murder where the *mens rea* is an intent to kill or to commit grievous bodily harm. For the offence to comply with the correspondence principle a person should only be guilty if he or she intended to kill. The mental element would then correspond with the *actus reus* by referring to the consequence of death.

> See Chapter 5 for further details of the offence of murder.

Unlawful act manslaughter also fails to comply with the correspondence principle. The *mens rea* of the offence does not require any recognition on the part of the accused that his or her conduct was likely to cause harm. This is shown by *DPP v Newbury and Jones* (1976) when the House of Lords decided that it only had to be proved that the defendant had the *mens rea* for the unlawful act. It was not necessary for the defendant to realise that the act is unlawful or dangerous.

> See Chapter 7, section 7.2.5 for details of this case.

Sections 47 and 20 OAPA 1861 also fail to follow the correspondence principle. In both these offences, liability may be incurred where the harm intended or foreseen by the defendant was less than the harm caused. For s 47, the *mens rea* is that of the lesser offences of assault or battery which causes actual bodily harm. For s 20, the *mens rea* is an intent or recklessness to cause *some* harm, which may not necessarily be the wound or grievous bodily harm actually caused.

> These offences are discussed in detail in *AQA A-level Law for Year 1 and AS*, Chapter 22.

4.7.3 Maximum certainty

The law should be as certain as possible. If it is not known what elements constitute a crime, then it is not fair that a person could be convicted of that crime. Tony Honoré in his book, *About Law*, points out that:

> ❝ It is generally agreed that, as part of the rule of law, a person should not be punished by the state except for a crime defined by law in advance. But crimes can be very vaguely defined. In some countries there are crimes like 'bringing the state into disrepute', or 'corrupting public morals'. Can anyone be certain that what he or she does will not be held by the courts of his country to come under one of these headings? ❞

Offences are not often challenged for uncertainty. However, one case where there was such a challenge was *R v Misra and Srivastava* (2004), when the defendants were convicted of gross negligence manslaughter. They challenged their convictions on the basis that the elements of this offence were too uncertain and relied on a report published by the Law Commission, 'Legislating the Criminal Code: Involuntary Manslaughter' (Law Com No. 237). The report had identified that the test for gross negligence manslaughter was circular and this led to uncertainty. The report stated: 'It is possible that the law in this area failed to meet the standard of certainty required by the European Convention on Human Rights.'

However, the Court of Appeal rejected the challenge on the basis that the earlier case of *R v Adomako* (1995), decided by the House of Lords, had made the elements of the offence clear.

> These cases are discussed in detail in Chapter 7.

Other cases where the offence were uncertain or unknown until a final decision of the House of Lords are *DPP v Shaw* 1961 and *R v R* 1991 discussed in Chapter 19 of *AQA A-level Law for Year 1 and AS* at 19.1.2.

4.7.4 No retrospective liability

Where the particular conduct is not an offence at the time the defendant does the conduct, then it is clearly unfair to convict of the offence. This idea of not being liable retrospectively for a crime is set out in the European Convention on Human Rights at Article 7(1):

> ❝ No one shall be held guilty of any criminal offence on account of any act or omission which did not constitute a criminal offence under national or international law at the time when it was committed. ❞

This prevents a government from creating a law to make a person guilty even though the act was not an offence when it was done.

Retrospective legislation can be considered as legislation that operates on matters taking place before the legislation has been enacted. Its effect is to penalise behaviour that was lawful when it took place. There is a presumption that a statute is not intended to have retrospective effect – that it only applies to future conduct.

It is rare in English law for retrospective legislation to lead to a criminal prosecution against an individual for activities he or she had been involved in that had not been covered by an existing law at the time those activities were carried out.

However, one law which did create retrospective criminal liability was the War Crimes Act 1991. This provided that if a person was a British citizen or UK resident from 1990 onwards, he or she could be prosecuted for a war crime carried out in Germany during the Second World War, regardless of his or her nationality at that time.

When asked to outline the Government's position on introducing this retrospective legislation, former Solicitor General, Harriet Harman, replied that the state would have to consider whether the general public interest in the law not being changed retrospectively may be outweighed by any competing public interest.

Most judicial precedents will only take effect from the date of the judgment. However, one case in which it was argued that the judgment created retrospective effect was *CR v UK* (1995). A challenge was made in the European Court of Human Rights under Article 7 where the defendant had been convicted of raping his wife. The challenge to the conviction was on the grounds that the offence did not exist until the House of Lords decision that he was guilty of it. The challenge was unsuccessful on two grounds:

1 There had been earlier cases where the offence was beginning to be recognised.
2 The offence was one which supported fundamental objectives of the ECHR.

> This case (shown as *R v R* (1991)) is discussed in *AQA A-level Law for Year 1 and AS*, Chapter 6, section 6.1.3 and again in Chapter 18, section 18.1.2.

Summary

- Criminal law generally prohibits conduct which causes harm.
- Conduct may also be criminalised in order to protect us from ourselves – 'paternalistic'; or where it is wrong in the sense of legal moralism.
- Autonomy – the freedom of individuals to make their own choices and decisions – is important. It should only be limited where:
  - it is necessary to prevent harm
  - it interferes with the autonomy of other people
  - the people involved have weaker ability to make their own choice and need to be protected from potentially harmful activity.
- Fault should be the basis of criminal liability.
- It is recognised that there is no fault in the following situations:
  - children under the age of ten
  - involuntary acts
  - a lack of the required *mens rea*
  - a recognised legal defence.
- Strict liability offences are an exception to the requirement for fault.
- Individuals are only responsible for the crimes they commit.
- The principles to be followed in creating new criminal laws include:
  - fair labelling
  - correspondence
  - maximum certainty in the elements
  - no retrospective effect.

5 Murder

After reading this chapter, you should be able to:
- Understand the *actus reus* of murder
- Understand the *mens rea* of murder
- Apply the law of murder to scenario-based situations

5.1 Homicide

Homicide is a general term used to describe the unlawful killing of a human being. As can be seen in Figure 5.1 below, different offences can be charged, depending on the *mens rea* of the defendant or whether there is a special defence available. The most serious homicide offence is murder.

5.2 The offence of murder

Murder is a common law offence. This means that it is not defined by any Act of Parliament but has been defined by decisions of judges in different cases. The accepted definition is based on one given by a seventeenth-century judge, Lord Coke: 'Murder is the unlawful killing of a reasonable person in being and under the King's (or Queen's) Peace with malice aforethought, express or implied.'

The different elements of this definition are considered in detail under the *actus reus* and *mens rea* of murder below.

Key term

Murder – 'the unlawful killing of a reasonable person in being and under the King's (or Queen's) Peace with malice aforethought, express or implied.'

5.3 The *actus reus* of murder

The *actus reus* of murder is the unlawful killing of a reasonable creature in being and under the Queen's Peace. Breaking this down, it has to be proved that:
- the defendant killed
- a reasonable creature in being
- under the Queen's Peace and
- the killing was unlawful.

5.3.1 'Killed'
Act or omission
The *actus reus* of killing can be by an act or omission, but it must cause the death of the victim. Usually in murder cases, the *actus reus* is a positive act such as hitting or stabbing the victim. An omission or failure to act can make a person liable for an offence of murder as seen by the case of *R v Gibbins and Proctor* (1918).

> See AQA A-level Law for Year 1 and AS, Chapter 19, section 19.2.

Causation
As murder is a result crime, the defendant cannot be guilty unless his or her act or omission caused the

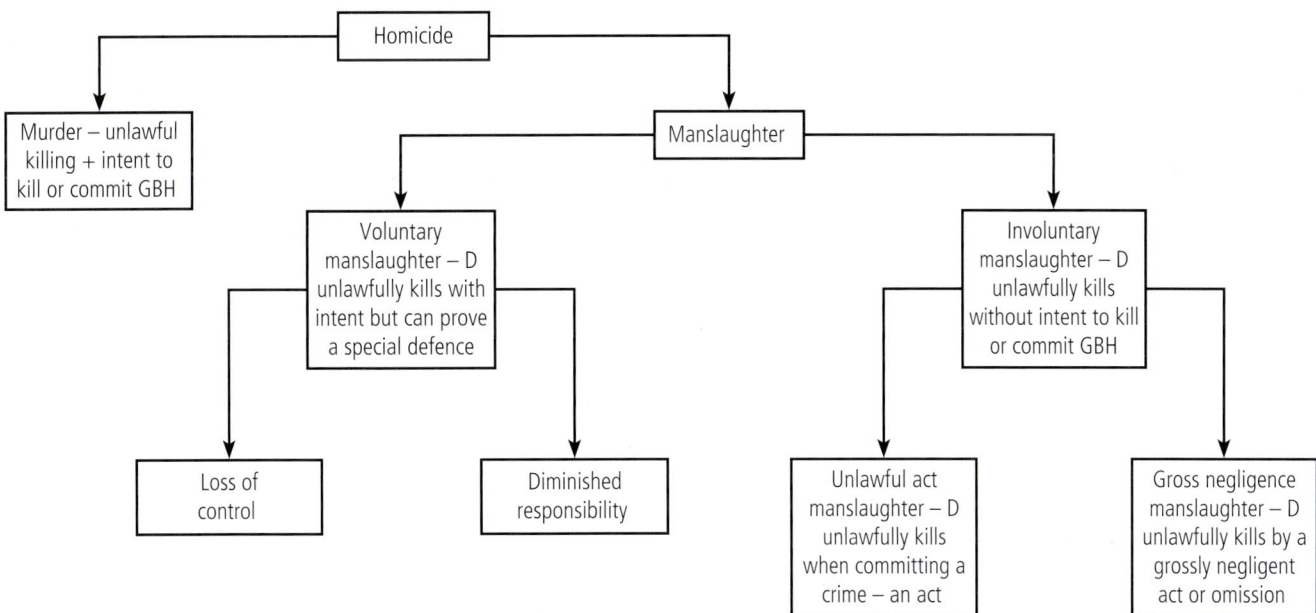

Figure 5.1 Overview of unlawful homicide offences

death. In most cases there is no problem with proving causation, for example if the defendant shoots the victim and the victim is killed instantly. However, in some cases there may be other causes contributing to the death which may raise a question of causation.

> The law on causation was considered fully in AQA A-level Law for Year 1 and AS, Chapter 19, section 19.3.

5.3.2 'Reasonable creature in being'

This phrase means 'a human being'. So, for murder, a person must be killed. Normally, this part of the definition does not cause any difficulties. The only two problem areas are:

- Is a foetus in the womb a 'reasonable creature in being'? A homicide offence cannot be charged in respect of the killing of a foetus. A child has to have an 'existence independent of the mother' for it to be considered a 'creature in being'.
- Is a victim still alive (and so a 'reasonable creature in being') if he or she is 'brain-dead' but being kept alive by a life-support machine? This was considered in *R v Malcherek* (1981) in *AQA A-level Law for Year 1 and AS*, Chapter 19, section 19.3.4. Doctors are allowed to switch off life-support machines without being criminally liable. This suggests that 'brain-death' is the recognised test for death.

'Year and a day' rule

There used to be a rule that death must have occurred within a year and a day. This rule was sensible when medical knowledge was not sufficient to prove that an attack had caused death after such a long time. However, with improvements in medical skill, the rule became out of date. In particular, it meant that, where a victim was in a coma and did not die until more than a year after the attack, the attacker could not be charged with his or her murder. The rule was abolished by the Law Reform (Year and a Day Rule) Act 1996 and there is now no time limit on when the death may occur after an unlawful act. However, where death occurs more than three years after an attack, the consent of the Attorney-General is needed for a prosecution.

5.3.3 'Queen's Peace'

This is unlikely to be an issue in most cases, but 'under the Queen's Peace' means that the killing of an enemy in the course of war is not murder.

5.3.4 'Unlawful'

The killing must be unlawful. If the killing is in self-defence or defence of another or in the prevention of crime and the defendant used reasonable force in the circumstances, then the killing is not unlawful.

> See Chapter 12 for the defence of self-defence.

If the defendant successfully argues the part defences of loss of control or diminished responsibility created by the Coroners and Justice Act 2009, the killing will still be unlawful but the defendant will be guilty of voluntary manslaughter and the judge will have greater discretion in sentencing.

> See Chapter 6 for an explanation of voluntary manslaughter.

Activity

Read the following situations and explain whether the *actus reus* for murder is present.

1 Anya is offered a lift home by Barnaby. After a few minutes, she realises he is driving away from her home. He then puts his hand on her thigh as he is driving and says that 'they can enjoy themselves'. Anya is so afraid that she jumps out of the car while it is travelling at 40 m.p.h. She is hit by another car and killed.

2 Lily decides to kill her partner, Kevin. She takes his shotgun and loads it. She waits for him to go to sleep, then she goes into his bedroom and shoots him in the head. Unknown to her, Kevin died from a heart attack 20 minutes before she shot him.

3 In a rage, James hits Valerie over the head. Valerie is taken to hospital and put on a life-support machine. Two months later the doctors decide that she will never recover and advise Valerie's family that the life-support system should be switched off.

5.4 The *mens rea* of murder

5.4.1 Intent to kill or commit grievous bodily harm

The *mens rea* for murder is 'malice aforethought, express or implied'. This means that there are two different intentions, either of which can be used to prove the defendant guilty of murder:

- express malice aforethought, which is an intention to kill, or

■ implied malice aforethought, which is intention to cause grievous bodily harm (GBH).

A defendant has the *mens rea* for murder if he or she has either of these intentions. This means that a person can be guilty of murder even though he or she did not intend to kill. This was decided in *R v Vickers* (1957).

R v Vickers (1957)

D broke into the cellar of a local sweet shop. He knew that the old lady who ran the shop was deaf. However, the old lady came into the cellar and saw D. He then hit her several times with his fists and kicked her once in the head. She died as a result of her injuries. The Court of Appeal upheld D's conviction for murder. It pointed out that where a defendant intends to inflict grievous bodily harm and the victim dies, that has always been sufficient in English law to imply malice aforethought.

The same point was considered by the House of Lords in *R v Cunningham* (1981) when it confirmed that an intention to cause grievous bodily harm was sufficient for the *mens rea* of murder.

R v Cunningham (1981)

D attacked V in a pub, attacking him repeatedly with a chair. V died from his injuries. The jury convicted D of murder, having found that he intended, really serious harm at the time of the attack. D appealed, arguing that the law of murder should be confined to those who intend to kill and the decision in *R v Vickers* was wrongly decided. The House of Lords dismissed his appeal and decided that the law was firmly established. An intention to cause GBH was sufficient for the *mens rea* of murder.

In this case, Lord Edmund Davies stated that he thought the *mens rea* for murder should be limited to an intention to kill. He said:

> 66 [It is] strange that a person can be convicted of murder if death results from, say, his intentional breaking of another's arm, an action which, while undoubtedly involving the infliction of 'really serious harm' and as such, calling for severe punishment, would in most cases be unlikely to kill. 99

Although he was very critical of the law, Lord Edmund Davies felt that any change to the law had to be made by Parliament. This was because the law has been the same for over 200 years and it would therefore be wrong for judges to change such a well-established law.

A further issue is what is meant by 'grievous bodily harm'? In *DPP v Smith* (1961), the House of Lords decided that 'grievous bodily harm' has the natural meaning of 'really serious harm'. However, even if the judge directed the jury leaving out the word 'really' and just said 'serious harm', this was not a misdirection.

5.4.2 Intention

The general rules on intention apply to murder. These were discussed in *AQA A-level Law for Year 1 and AS*, Chapter 20.

As was set out, there are two main forms of intent:

■ **Direct intent** where the defendant intends the consequence (in the case of murder, the death of the victim – in other words, a deliberate killing).

■ The second form is **oblique intent**, also known as indirect intent. This is where the defendant's aim or purpose was not to bring about the consequence (the death). The defendant does not have the *mens rea* for murder unless he or she foresaw that he or she would also cause death or serious injury as a result of his or her actions. This is known as foresight of consequences and was considered in detail in *AQA A-level Law for Year 1 and AS*, section 20.2.2. However, as the law in this area is complex and important, the main cases are set out again.

Key term

Direct intent – where the defendant intends the result – for murder, the death of the victim.

Oblique or indirect intent – where the defendant's aim or purpose was not to bring about the consequence (the death). It will be sufficient for a charge of murder if the defendant foresees death or serious injury as a result of his or her actions.

Foresight of consequences

The main rule is that foresight of consequences is not intention.

The main statutory provision is s 8 of the Criminal Justice Act 1967, which tried to make the law clear on this point. It states:

A court or jury in determining whether a person has committed an offence–

a shall not be bound in law to infer that he intended or foresaw a result of his actions by reason only of its being a natural and probable consequence of those actions; but

b shall decide whether he did intend or foresee that result by reference to all the evidence, drawing such inferences from the evidence as appear proper in the circumstances.

In addition, the House of Lords has tried in several cases to explain the effect of foresight of consequences. In *R v Moloney* (1985), where the defendant shot and killed his step-father in a drunken challenge to see who was quicker on the draw, it was held that foresight of consequences is only evidence from which intention may be inferred.

In *R v Nedrick* (1986), the defendant poured paraffin through the letter box of a house in order to frighten the woman who lived there. A child died in the fire. The Court of Appeal suggested that juries ask themselves two questions:

1 How probable was the consequence which resulted from the defendant's voluntary act?

2 Did the defendant foresee that consequence?

The Court of Appeal also said that members of the jury should be directed that they are not entitled to infer the necessary intention unless they feel sure that death or serious injury was a virtual certainty as a result of the defendant's actions, and that the defendant appreciated that such was the case.

In *R v Woollin* (1998), the House of Lords approved this direction but disapproved of the use of the two questions. They approved the direction given in *Nedrick*, provided that the word 'find' was used instead of 'infer'. So, in every case where it is suggested the defendant had oblique intent, members of the jury should be directed that they are not entitled to find the necessary intention unless they feel sure that death or serious injury was a virtual certainty as a result of the defendant's actions, and that the defendant appreciated that such was the case.

The decision in *R v Woollin* (1998), where the House of Lords speaks about intention being found from foresight of consequences, has made the law uncertain. It is not clear whether there is a substantive rule of criminal law that foresight of consequences is intention, or if there is only a rule of evidence that intention can be found from foresight of consequences. In *R v Matthews and Alleyne* (2003), the Court of Appeal even said that there was little to choose between a rule of evidence and one of substantive law, leaving it even more unclear.

I don't intend to hurt you.

R v Matthews and Alleyne (2003)

The two defendants had pushed V from a bridge over a deep wide river so that he fell 25 feet into the river and drowned. The defendants knew that V could not swim. The trial judge, in his summing up to the jury, said that foresight of virtual certainty of consequences *was* intention. The defendants appealed against their conviction for murder. The Court of Appeal accepted that the judge had gone further than was permitted by saying that foresight of virtual certainty of consequences was intention.

However, the Court of Appeal upheld the convictions. The court thought that if the jury was sure that the defendants had appreciated the virtual certainty of V's death when they threw him into the river, it was 'impossible' to see how the jury could not have drawn the inference that the defendants intended V's death.

In its report in 2006 entitled 'Murder, Manslaughter and Infanticide' (Law Com No. 304), the Law Commission identified problems about foresight of consequences and the piecemeal development of the law.

On the one hand, it could be argued that it is unfair for a defendant to be convicted of the most serious charge of murder if he or she does not have the *mens rea* of the offence. However, the opposite view is that if the defendant has the intent to cause serious harm to the victim he or she should accept the consequences if the victim dies, as there is a close relationship between causing serious harm and causing death.

Finally, it seems strange that there are uncertainties in proving aspects of the most serious of offences. As the Law Commission noted in its general comments in 'Murder, Manslaughter and Infanticide' (at paragraph 1.8):

> " The law governing homicide in England and Wales is a rickety structure set upon shaky foundations. Some of its rules have remained unaltered since the seventeenth century, even though it has long been acknowledged that they are in dire need of reform. Other rules are of uncertain content, often because they have been constantly changed to the point that they can no longer be stated with any certainty or clarity. "

5.4.3 Transferred malice

The general rule on transferred malice applies to murder. So, if the defendant fires a shot at victim 1 but misses, but hits and kills victim 2, the defendant is guilty of the murder of victim 2. It does not matter that he or she did not intend to kill victim 2. His or her intention to kill (or seriously injure) victim 1 is transferred.

Note that the defendant does not have to fail in his or her intention or recklessness against victim 1 before he or she can also be liable for the injury caused to victim 2. If, for example, the defendant intends to kill victim 1 by exploding a device at a time when he or she has no idea that victim 2 is also present, he or she will be guilty of murdering both victim 1 and victim 2, if both are killed, because the malice can be applied to the intended victim, victim 1, while also being transferred to the unanticipated victim, victim 2.

See AQA A-level Law for Year 1 and AS, Chapter 20, section 20.5 for more detail on transferred malice.

Activity

In each of the following situations, explain whether the defendant has the required intention for murder.

1 Jamie is annoyed because Harry has been trying to date his girlfriend. Jamie sees Harry in a local pub and goes over and punches him hard in the face, saying, 'Perhaps that will make you leave my girlfriend alone.' Harry has a thin skull and the punch causes a brain haemorrhage from which he dies.

2 Diana intends to kill Edward. She fixes an explosive booby trap to the front door of his house, so that when he opens it the explosive will go off. Unbeknown to Diana, Edward has given Felix the keys to his house and told him to collect some papers from there. Felix opens the door and is killed by the explosion.

3 Ravinder's business has been losing a lot of money. He decides to set fire to one of the smaller buildings in the unit so that he can claim insurance on it. Ravinder knows that there is no one in his building, so he sets it alight. Unfortunately, the fire spreads to another building on the site. Nancy, who is working in that building, is trapped by the fire and dies.

Figure 5.2 Key facts chart for murder

	Law	Source/case
Definition	Murder is the unlawful killing of a reasonable person in being under the Queen's (King's) Peace with malice aforethought, express or implied	Lord Coke (in the seventeenth century)
Actus reus	An unlawful killing within the Queen's Peace Killing can be by an act or omission Victim must be alive – not a foetus or already dead Causation – defendant must have caused victim's death	R v Gibbins and Proctor (1918)
Mens rea	Intention to kill or Intention to commit grievous bodily harm Intent can be direct or Indirect – death or GBH was a virtual certainty of defendant's actions and defendant appreciated this to be the case	R v Nedrick (1986) R v Woollin (1998)
Sentence	Judge has to impose mandatory life sentence Judge will decide the minimum term the defendant will serve in prison before release on licence	

5.5 The mandatory life sentence

If a defendant aged 18 or over is convicted of murder, the judge has to pass a sentence of life imprisonment. For offenders aged 10–17 who are found guilty of murder, the judge has to order that they be detained at Her Majesty's Pleasure. Because the judge has no discretion in what sentence to impose, this is known as a mandatory sentence. The judge cannot give a different sentence even if it is felt that the defendant is not as blameworthy as a deliberate killer. This contrasts with every other criminal offence when the judge can decide the most appropriate sentence up to the maximum permitted by law. It is because of the mandatory life sentence that the special defences of diminished responsibility and loss of control (leading to a conviction of voluntary manslaughter) exist to give the judge greater flexibility in sentencing.

5.5.1 Minimum term

Once the judge has imposed the mandatory life sentence, the minimum number of years the offender must serve in prison before any application can be made for release on licence will be decided.

The Criminal Justice Act 2003 laid down certain guidelines which give the following starting points for adult offenders:

- a whole life term for exceptionally serious cases, such as premeditated killings of two or more people, sexual or sadistic child murders or politically motivated murders (this means the offender will never be released from prison)
- thirty years' minimum for murders of police or prison officers, murders involving firearms, sexual or sadistic killings or killings aggravated by racial or sexual orientation
- fifteen years' minimum for murders not falling within the two higher categories.

The imposition of the mandatory life sentence reflects the need to show that justice has been done to a person convicted of murder. After all, this is the most serious crime that can be committed and the sentence reflects this. However it is accepted, as shown by the guidelines above, that there are different levels of fault within the crime and the minimum term can reflect that level of fault.

In the news

Consider the outlines of the following cases. You can carry out internet searches to find out more detail about each case. Do you think that justice has been done in each case? Does each sentence reflect the level of the offender's fault?

Case 1

Ryan Gibbons, 29, was found guilty of murdering Mike Samwell after breaking into his home in Chorlton, Manchester and stealing his car. The victim and his wife woke to the sound of burglars who took the keys to the car from the kitchen table. The victim ran downstairs in his boxer shorts to confront Gibbons as he drove off, shouting 'Get out of the car' but was run over twice. Gibbons received the mandatory life sentence with a minimum term of 27 years. (November 2017)

Case 2

Frances Inglis killed her son with a lethal injection of heroin as she believed she was performing an 'act of mercy' for him. Her son, Thomas, had suffered serious head injuries when he jumped from a moving ambulance. She decided that her son would not want to live the life he was leading with the injuries. She admitted administering the heroin but said that she did so with 'love in her heart'. Inglis was found guilty of murder and received the mandatory life sentence with a minimum term of 9 years, which was later reduced to 5 years on appeal. (January 2010)

Case 3

Stephen Port had a fetish for sex with unconscious, boyish-looking men. He killed four young gay men that he had drugged and raped before dumping their bodies near his flat. The judge found that the killings were committed as part of a persistent course of conduct, while a high degree of planning was used to obtain the drugs and in luring the victims to his flat. Port was found guilty of four murders and received the mandatory life sentence with a whole life term. (November 2016)

Tip

The offence of murder often requires discussion of issues of *mens rea* and/or causation, rather than general *actus reus* issues.

Activity

Ignoring possible defences at this stage, consider the possible liability for a charge of murder in the following situations (we can look at the scenarios again after covering the part-defences in the next chapter):

1 Greg was very particular about his appearance and had a complex about people looking at him. When he was in a club he saw Kate look at him and make a remark to her friends, at which they all laughed. As he was about to leave the club Greg noticed Kate at the top of a staircase. He immediately went over and pushed her violently. She fell awkwardly, broke her neck and died.
  Advise whether Greg would be liable for the murder of Kate.

2 Carlo went into a local shop, pointed a gun at the counter assistant and demanded that she gave him all the money in the till. At that moment a customer, Dean, entered the shop. Carlo panicked and hit Dean on the head with the gun. Carlo then ran away.

Dean suffered serious head injuries and was taken to hospital by ambulance. On the way to the hospital, the ambulance was involved in a collision. This caused Dean to suffer more injuries and delayed getting him to hospital. Dean died shortly after arriving at hospital.
  Advise whether Carlo would be liable for the murder of Dean.

3 Frank hated all skateboarders and when he saw Larry skateboarding in town, he began shouting at him. Larry laughed and told him not to be so stupid. Frank seized Larry's board and hit him over the head several times with it with some force. Larry later died from a brain haemorrhage, which was caused by a genetic weakness.
  Advise whether Frank would be liable for the murder of Larry.

Summary

- Murder is 'the unlawful killing of a reasonable person in being and under the Queen's (or King's) Peace with malice aforethought, express or implied'.
- For the *actus reus* of murder, it has to be proved that:
  - D killed
  - a reasonable creature in being
  - under the Queen's Peace and
  - the killing was unlawful.
- For the *mens rea* of murder, there must be
  - express malice aforethought, which is the intention to kill, or
  - implied malice aforethought, which is the intention to cause grievous bodily harm.

- Foresight of consequences is only evidence of intention so that:
  - members of a jury should be directed that they cannot find the necessary intention unless they feel sure that death or serious injury was a virtual certainty as a result of the defendant's actions, and that the defendant appreciated that such was the case.
- An offender convicted of murder will be given the mandatory life sentence. The judge will fix the minimum term that has to be served in prison before release on licence.

6 Voluntary manslaughter

After reading this chapter, you should be able to:
- Understand the partial defence of loss of control (s 54 of the Coroners and Justice Act 2009)
- Understand the partial defence of diminished responsibility (s 2 of the Homicide Act 1957)
- Apply the law of these two defences to scenario-based situations

6.1 Partial defences to murder

Provocation was originally a common law defence but it was given statutory recognition in the Homicide Act 1957, which also introduced the defence of diminished responsibility. The Coroners and Justice Act 2009 altered provocation into a new defence of loss of control, which is set out in s 54. Diminished responsibility is still contained in s 2 of the Homicide Act, but it has been amended by s 52 of the Coroners and Justice Act.

Both of these defences are available only to a charge of murder. They operate as partial defences, which means that the defendant is not completely acquitted. Instead, when one of these defences is successful, the offence of murder is reduced to **voluntary manslaughter**. The defendant will have committed the *actus reus* of an unlawful killing and had the necessary *mens rea* for murder but successfully puts forward a reason why the murder was committed and that the defendant should be treated more leniently than if he or she was convicted of murder.

This verdict of voluntary manslaughter instead of murder is important because it means that the judge has discretion in which sentence to impose. When a defendant is found guilty of murder, the judge has to pass a sentence of life imprisonment – the mandatory life sentence. However, for voluntary manslaughter the judge can impose a lesser sentence up to a *maximum* of life imprisonment.

Key term

Voluntary manslaughter – the verdict when the defendant has a partial defence to murder, where the killing was carried out when the defendant was suffering from diminished responsibility or loss of control.

6.2 Loss of control

Loss of control is a partial defence to a charge of murder. If it is successful, the defendant will be found guilty of voluntary manslaughter instead of murder.

Section 54 (1) of the Coroners and Justice Act 2009 states:

> (1) Where a person ('D') kills or is a party to the killing of another ('V'), D is not to be convicted of murder if:
> (a) D's acts and omissions in doing or being a party to the killing resulted from D's loss of self-control,
> (b) the loss of self-control had a qualifying trigger, and
> (c) a person of D's sex and age, with a normal degree of tolerance and self-restraint and in the circumstances of D, might have reacted in the same or in a similar way to D.

So, all of the following points have to be proved for the defence to be successful:

- the defendant must have lost self-control
- there must be a qualifying trigger
- a person of the same sex and age would have reacted in the same way as the defendant in the same circumstances.

Note that as this defence replaced the previous defence of provocation all cases decided before the Coroners and Justice Act came into force no longer represent the current law. However, some are included in this text as they are considered to be useful for discussion and comparison purposes.

If the defendant successfully argues this defence, a charge of murder will be reduced to voluntary manslaughter, which has a maximum sentence of life imprisonment. The judge will then be able to impose such sentence, usually a term of imprisonment, to reflect the defendant's fault. Even though the defendant has committed the *actus reus* and has the *mens rea* of murder, the level of fault is lower as there is a reason for the unlawful killing.

6.2.1 Burden of proof

Once the defendant has suggested the possibility of the defence, it is for the prosecution to disprove. The defendant must put forward sufficient evidence of the possibility of the defence. In *R v Jewell* (2014) below, it was stated that there must be more than the accused's 'bare assertion' of the defence.

6.2.2 Loss of self-control

The first matter to be proved is that the defendant had lost self-control when doing the act which caused death.

This will be a matter for the jury to decide and it will have to be a total loss of self-control – a partial loss will not be sufficient. The jurors are entitled to draw upon their life experiences when considering the evidence, to decide if this requirement is satisfied. Although there has been no statutory interpretation of the meaning of this term, the Court of Appeal in *R v Jewell* (2014) adopted a definition from the Smith and Hogan textbook which was challenged, but not rejected, in *R v Gurpinar* (2015) as 'has D lost his ability to maintain his actions in accordance with considered judgment or … [has he] … lost normal powers of reasoning.'

However, it could mean that the:

- defendant lost his or her ability to maintain his or her action in accordance with considered judgement
- defendant lost his or her normal powers of reasoning, or
- defendant's behaviour was atypical, or out of character, and normally he or she would not have acted in this way.

Temper or anger or a reaction out of character, or even acting spectacularly out of character, are not sufficient. The defendant must have really 'lost it' or 'snapped'. In *R v Jewell* (2014), the fact that the defendant was unwell, sleeping badly,

tired, depressed and 'unable to think straight' was insufficient to amount to a loss of control.

R v Jewell (2014)

D shot V at point blank range using a shotgun and fled the scene. He was subsequently arrested in his car, which contained weapons, ammunition and what was described as a 'survival kit', including spare clothes, a tent, a passport, a driving licence and a cheque book. At his trial, D told the jury that when he got out of his car outside V's house,

> I did it because I lost control. I could not control my actions. I could not think straight. My head was fucked up. It was like an injection in the head, an explosion in my head.

The judge considered that there was insufficient evidence of D having lost his self-control and this decision was supported by the Court of Appeal.

Under s 54(2), the loss of self-control does not have to be sudden. This is different from the previous defence of provocation, which required a sudden and temporary loss of self-control. This led to some defendants being unable to use the defence of provocation, as their loss of control was not sudden. This was seen in the case of *R v Ahluwalia* (1992). Mrs Ahluwalia had been physically abused over many years by her husband. One night he threatened her with violence and when he was asleep she poured petrol over him and set him alight. He died six days later and she was charged with murder. She could not use the defence of provocation, as her response to his threat was not sudden.

The case of *R v Ahluwalia* (1992) is referred to in Chapter 1.3.1.

The Law Commission, in its 2006 report 'Murder, Manslaughter and Infanticide' (Law Com No. 304), had proposed removing the loss of self-control criteria completely because it recognised that women in abusive relationships may kill from 'a combination of anger, fear, frustration and a sense of desperation'. The Government decided not to follow this proposal. The only concession given in the new law was that the loss of control need not be sudden. If a similar case came to court now, it is possible that someone in the same situation as Mrs Ahluwalia would be able to use the defence.

6.2.3 Qualifying trigger

There has to be a qualifying trigger for the loss of control to come within the defence. Section 55 sets out the qualifying triggers which are permitted. These are where the loss of control was attributable to:

- the defendant's fear of serious violence from the victim against the defendant or another identified person (s 55(3)), or
- a thing or things done or said (or both) which –
  a constituted circumstances of an extremely grave character, and
  b caused the defendant to have a justifiable sense of being seriously wronged (s 55(4)).

Alternatively, the qualifying trigger can be a combination of these two matters (s 55(5)).

Figure 6.1 Requirements of loss of control

Fear of serious violence

Under s 55(3), the defendant must fear violence from the victim against him- or herself or another identified person. This will be a subjective test and the defendant will need to show that he or she lost self-control because of a genuine fear of serious violence, whether or not the fear was in fact reasonable.

The fear of serious violence needs to be a fear of violence against the defendant or against another identified person. For example, the fear of serious violence could be in respect of a child or other relative of the defendant. However, a fear that the victim would, in the future, use serious violence against people generally is not sufficient.

Under s 55(6)(a), where the defendant has incited the violence in order to have an excuse to use force, he or she cannot rely on the qualifying trigger. This was emphasised in R v Dawes (2013).

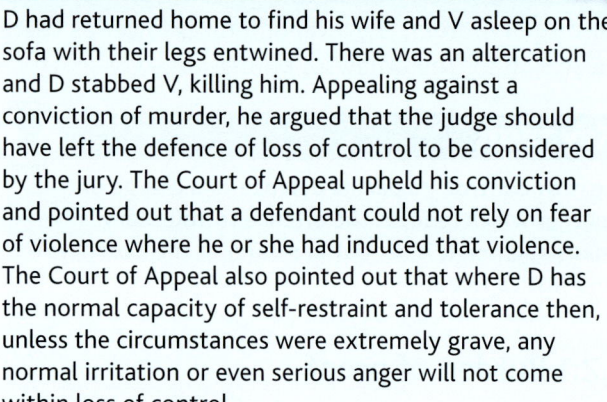

R v Dawes (2013)

D had returned home to find his wife and V asleep on the sofa with their legs entwined. There was an altercation and D stabbed V, killing him. Appealing against a conviction of murder, he argued that the judge should have left the defence of loss of control to be considered by the jury. The Court of Appeal upheld his conviction and pointed out that a defendant could not rely on fear of violence where he or she had induced that violence. The Court of Appeal also pointed out that where D has the normal capacity of self-restraint and tolerance then, unless the circumstances were extremely grave, any normal irritation or even serious anger will not come within loss of control.

Things done or said

Under s 55(4), there are two points which have to be shown if the defendant is relying on things done or said as a qualifying trigger. These are that they:

- were of an 'extremely grave character', and
- caused the defendant to have a justifiable sense of being seriously wronged.

The thing(s) done or said must amount to circumstances of an extremely grave character and cause the defendant to have a justifiable sense of being seriously wronged. Whether a defendant's sense of being seriously wronged is justifiable will be an objective question for a jury to decide (assuming that there is sufficient evidence of the defence to be considered by the jury).

Subsection (4) sets a very high threshold for the circumstances in which the defence is available where a person loses self-control in response to words or actions. The effect is to substantially narrow the potential availability of this defence in cases where a loss of control is attributable to things done or said compared to provocation (where no threshold existed in relation to the provoking circumstances). As a result, many cases where the defendant was able to use the former defence of provocation would not now come within loss of control.

This can be seen by comparing the cases of R v Doughty (1986) (where the defendant was able to use the defence of provocation) and R v Zebedee (2012) (where the defendant was not able to use the defence of loss of control).

Figure 6.2 Comparison of *R v Doughty* and *R v Zebedee*

R v Doughty (1986)	*R v Zebedee* (2012)
D killed his baby son aged 19 days because the child would not stop crying D put forward defence of provocation	D lost control when his 94-year-old father, who suffered from Alzheimer's and was doubly incontinent, repeatedly soiled himself D killed his father D put forward the defence of loss of control
D was convicted of murder, but the conviction was quashed as it should have been left to the jury to decide if the baby's crying was provocation by 'things done'	D was convicted of murder and his conviction was upheld on appeal
With loss of control, a jury might decide, on the objective test, that no reasonable person would have lost control in that situation	The jury must have considered D's defence and decided that neither of the qualifying trigger conditions (circumstances of an extremely grave character and D must have a justifiable sense of being seriously wronged) was present

In *Zebedee*, the judge could have refused to allow the defence to go before the jury on the grounds that it would not satisfy the objective trigger requirements, but he did not do so. Doughty argued that that he should have been allowed to put forward the defence, but even if he was allowed to do so, a jury might decide, on the objective test, that no reasonable person would have lost control in that situation.

Excluded matters

Under provocation, sexual infidelity was allowed as grounds for the defence, as the law had been developed over centuries to give a defence in cases involving murder based on sexual infidelity. When drafting the new rules, the Government considered that provocation allowed a defence to a jealous man who killed his wife or girlfriend because she was having an affair and that such male violence against women was not acceptable in the twenty-first century.

As a result, the Coroners and Justice Act states in s 55(6)(c) that, in deciding whether a loss of self-control has a qualifying trigger, the fact that a thing done or said amounted to sexual infidelity is to be disregarded.

So, if a thing done or said (as referred to in s 55(4)) amounts to sexual infidelity, that fact is disregarded in deciding whether the qualifying trigger in s 55(4) applies. The effect is that, if the defendant kills his or her spouse or partner because he or she has been unfaithful, the defendant will not be able to claim loss of control. It is the fact of sexual infidelity that is to be disregarded

under the provision, so the thing done or said can still potentially amount to a qualifying trigger if (ignoring the sexual infidelity) it still amounts to 'circumstances of an extremely grave character causing the defendant to have a justifiable sense of being seriously wronged'. This may arise only rarely, but an example of where it might be relevant is where the defendant discovers his or her spouse or partner (V) sexually abusing their young child (an act that amounts to sexual infidelity) and loses self-control and kills. The fact that V's act amounted to sexual infidelity must be discounted, but the abuse may still be claimed to amount to the qualifying trigger.

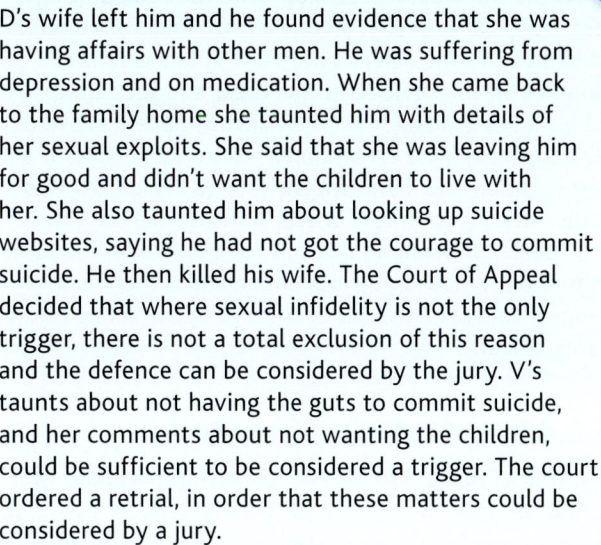

R v Clinton (2012)

D's wife left him and he found evidence that she was having affairs with other men. He was suffering from depression and on medication. When she came back to the family home she taunted him with details of her sexual exploits. She said that she was leaving him for good and didn't want the children to live with her. She also taunted him about looking up suicide websites, saying he had not got the courage to commit suicide. He then killed his wife. The Court of Appeal decided that where sexual infidelity is not the only trigger, there is not a total exclusion of this reason and the defence can be considered by the jury. V's taunts about not having the guts to commit suicide, and her comments about not wanting the children, could be sufficient to be considered a trigger. The court ordered a retrial, in order that these matters could be considered by a jury.

The point was made in *Clinton* that evidence of sexual infidelity is excluded only in relation to the qualifying trigger, not in relation to the 'circumstances' of the defendant to be taken into account when considering the requirement that a 'person of normal tolerance and self-restraint ...' So, if there is a trigger independent of the sexual infidelity, the sexual infidelity can then come into play when the final question is addressed.

Considered desire for revenge

Under s 54(4), the defence is not allowed if the defendant acted in a 'considered desire for revenge'. In this, it is similar to provocation. In provocation, there had to be a sudden loss of self-control.

So, if the defendant had time to consider revenge, then the defence was not available. This was seen in the case of *R v Ibrams and Gregory* (1981), where, following several incidents of threats and harassment, the two defendants made a plan to attack the person who had threatened them. They carried out this plan and killed him two days later. They were convicted of murder and their convictions were upheld, as there was no sudden loss of self-control.

However, if there was a sudden loss of self-control then provocation was available, even if there was also an element of a desire for revenge. This was illustrated in *R v Baillie* (1995).

R v Baillie (1995)

D learned that his son's drug dealer had threatened that the son would 'get a slap' if he tried to get drugs from any other dealer. D took a razor and a shotgun and drove to the dealer's house. D inflicted serious injuries on the dealer with the razor and then fired the shotgun, killing him. The Court of Appeal allowed D's appeal against conviction as there was evidence of provocation and it was for the jury to decide if D was still suffering from loss of self-control when he killed the dealer. It might be difficult for a person in the same situation to now argue loss of control as there would appear to be an element of revenge in the killing of the drug dealer.

6.2.4 Standard of self-control

Under s 54(1)(c), whichever 'qualifying trigger' is relied on, it is necessary for the defendant to show that 'a person of D's sex and age, with a normal degree of tolerance and self-restraint and in the circumstances of D, might have reacted in the same or similar way to D'. This is an objective test for the jury to consider.

Lady Justice Hallett, sitting in the Court of Appeal in *R v Rejmanski* (2017) analysed the wording of s 54(1)(c), saying:

> ...in assessing the third component, the defendant is to be judged against the standard of a person with a normal degree, and not an abnormal degree, of tolerance and self-restraint. If, and in so far as, a personality disorder reduced the defendant's general capacity for tolerance or self-restraint, that would not be a relevant consideration. Moreover, it would not be a relevant consideration even if the personality disorder was one of the 'circumstances' of the defendant because it was relevant to the gravity of the trigger ... Expert evidence about the impact of the disorder would be irrelevant and inadmissible on the issue of whether it would have reduced the capacity for tolerance and self-restraint of the hypothetical 'person of D's sex and age, with a normal degree of tolerance and self-restraint'.
>
> If a mental disorder has a relevance to the defendant's conduct other than a bearing on their general capacity for tolerance or self-restraint, it is not excluded by subsection (3), and the jury will be entitled to take it into account as one of the defendant's circumstances under s 54(1)(c). However, it is necessary to identify with some care how the mental disorder is said to be relevant as one of the defendant's circumstances. It must not be relied upon to undermine the principle that the conduct of the defendant is to be judged against 'normal' standards, rather than the abnormal standard of an individual defendant.

However, voluntary intoxication is not a matter to be considered as part of D's circumstances. This was confirmed in *R v Asmelash* (2013). The Court of Appeal said that if Parliament had meant that

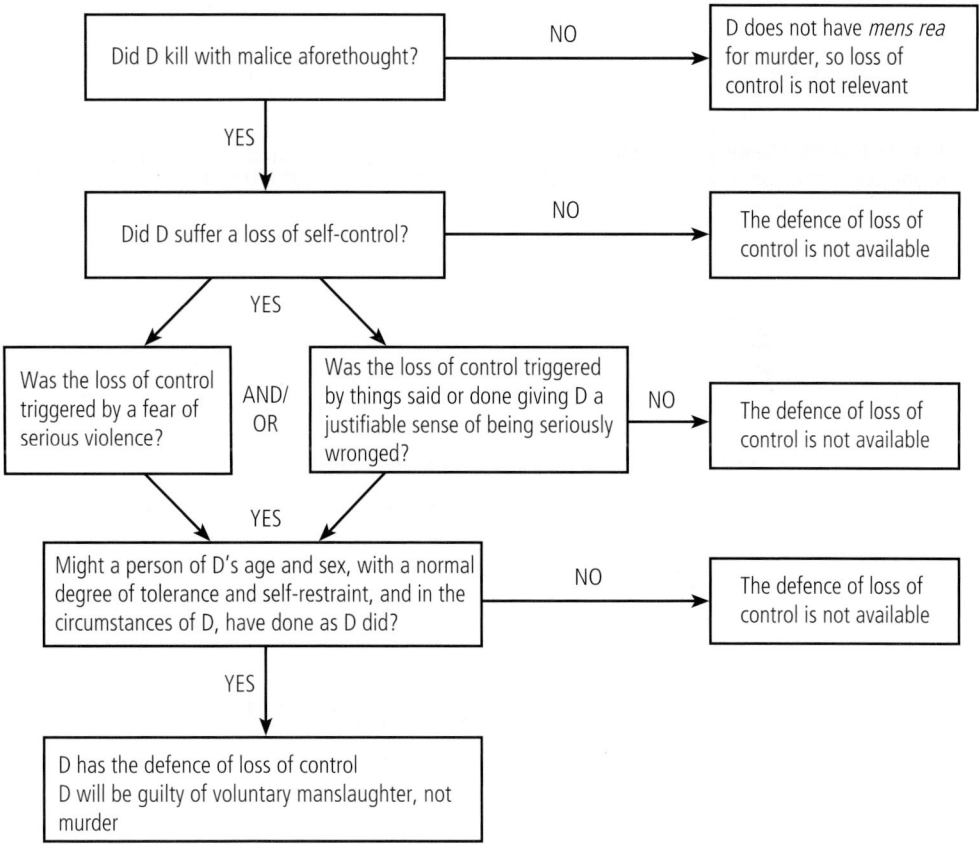

Figure 6.3 Flowchart on loss of control

to be the position, then it would have been clearly stated in the 2009 Act. They also pointed out that voluntary intoxication could not be used in diminished responsibility, and it was inconceivable that different criteria should govern the two defences.

Might have reacted in the same or a similar way to the defendant

The jury then has to consider whether the normal person in the circumstances of the defendant would have reacted as the defendant did. The defence will fail if the jury considers that the 'normal person' might have lost control but would not have reacted in the same way.

R v Van Dongen (2005), under the previous law of provocation, is an example of this. The jury was of

the opinion that the 'reasonable man' (the test at that time) would have lost self-control, but that he would not have reacted in the same way as the defendant who repeatedly kicked the victim about the head and body when the victim was lying curled up on the pavement.

In some ways, the defence of loss of control is wider than the defence of provocation. In particular, a loss of control does not have to be sudden and a fear of serious violence is an additional matter which can be considered.

In other ways, the defence of loss of control is narrower than the defence of provocation, particularly as sexual infidelity alone is not allowed as a qualifying trigger.

Figure 6.4 Key facts chart on loss of control

	Law
Main points of defence	■ D must have lost self-control ■ There must be a qualifying trigger ■ A person of the same sex and age would have reacted in the same or a similar way as D in the same circumstances
Loss of control	This need not be sudden
Qualifying triggers	Either or both of the following: ■ fear of serious violence ■ a thing or things done or said which constituted circumstances of an extremely grave character and caused D to have a justifiable sense of being seriously wronged
Standard of self-control	That of a person of D's sex and age, with a normal degree of tolerance and self-restraint
Circumstances of D	Circumstances of D (which do not have a bearing on capacity for self-control) can be taken into consideration in deciding whether a normal person might have reacted in the same way
Effect of defence	Reduces charge of murder to manslaughter

Figure 6.5 Key cases on loss of control

Case	Facts	Principle
R v Jewell (2014)	D shot and killed V at point-blank range and fled the scene When he was arrested, his car contained weapons, ammunition and a 'survival kit' D told the jury he could not control his actions or think straight	There needs to be sufficient evidence of D having lost his or her self-control for it to be considered by a jury
R v Dawes (2013)	D found his wife with another man, who D stabbed and killed	D cannot rely on fear of violence where he or she has induced that violence Where D has the normal capacity of self-restraint and tolerance then, unless the circumstances were extremely grave, any normal irritation or even serious anger will not come within loss of control
R v Clinton (2012)	D's wife taunted him with details of her sexual exploits She told him that he lacked the courage to commit suicide and that she was leaving him and didn't want the children to live with her D killed his wife	Where sexual infidelity is not the only trigger, there is not a total exclusion of this reason and the defence can be considered by the jury V's taunts about not having the guts to commit suicide, and her comments about not wanting the children, could be sufficient to be considered a trigger

In the news

Nightclub heir jailed for 13 years for killing abusive father

The heir to a multimillion-pound nightclub empire has been sentenced to 13 years in prison for stabbing his father to death following 'many years of verbal abuse'. A jury had failed to reach a verdict on a murder charge and he pleaded guilty to manslaughter by reason of loss of control.

David West Jr, 45, worked for his father, David West Sr, from the age of 14, and played a key role in the success and growth of the business. But after 'many years of abuse' from his father, who was an alcoholic, West Jr stabbed his 70-year-old father to death at his home off Jermyn Street after he found him in a drunken stupor. 'There was a toxic relationship between father and son,' said Orlando Pownall QC in mitigation. 'Although in latter years David West senior was frail he had an acerbic tongue that could reduce grown men to tears.'

He told the court that West junior was truly sorry for what he had done, adding: 'It was a momentary aberration born of a life experience.'

Employees of West described the business heir as 'his father's whipping boy'. His lawyer said he had suffered 'belittlement and contempt' from his father. West Jr dialled 999 after the stabbing and told police, 'I would like to admit to a murder. I've just killed my father.'

Source: Adapted from an article by Harry Readhead in Metro online, 9 November 2015

© MET POLICE HANDOUT

David West Jr

6.3 Diminished responsibility

This defence was originally introduced by the Homicide Act 1957.

6.3.1 Definition of diminished responsibility

The defence is set out in s 2 of the Homicide Act 1957, as amended by s 52 of the Coroners and Justice Act 2009. Section 2 now says:

> 1 A person ('D') who kills or is a party to the killing of another is not to be convicted of murder if D was suffering from an abnormality of mental functioning which–
>   (a) arose from a recognised medical condition,
>   (b) substantially impaired D's ability to do one or more of the things mentioned in subsection (1A), and
>   (c) provides an explanation for D's acts and omissions in doing or being a party to the killing.
>
> 1 A Those things are–
>   (a) to understand the nature of D's conduct;
>   (b) to form a rational judgement;
>   (c) to exercise self-control.
>
> 1 B For the purposes of subsection (1)(c), an abnormality of mental functioning provides an explanation for D's conduct if it causes, or is a significant contributory factor in causing, D to carry out that conduct.

6.3.2 Burden of proof

The burden of proving the defence is on the defendant, but the defendant need only prove it on the balance of probabilities. The defence accepts that the defendant is at fault, as he or she has committed the *actus reus* of murder and has the *mens rea,* but that he or she should not be considered wholly at fault as there is a medical reason for acting as he or she did.

It can be said to be unfair for the burden of proof of this defence to be on the defendant. For most other defences, the defendant only has to raise the issue and the prosecution has to disprove it. A defendant who pleads **diminished responsibility** is at a disadvantage by having to prove the defence, which is not faced by those raising loss of control as a defence.

It has also been argued that putting the burden of proof on the defendant could be a breach of Article 6(2) of the ECHR, which states that 'everyone charged with a criminal offence shall be presumed to be innocent until proven guilty according to law'. Making the defendant prove diminished responsibility could be considered a breach of this Article. However, this academic argument has not been accepted, as courts have consistently held that this requirement is not a breach of Article 6.

If the defendant successfully argues this defence, a charge of murder will be reduced to voluntary manslaughter, which has a maximum sentence of life imprisonment. The judge will then be able to impose such sentence as is considered appropriate to deal with the defendant's abnormality. This can be considered just, as the defendant will receive some punishment but may also receive treatment for his or her condition. If the abnormality is severe enough, a long-term hospital order can be made.

> **Key term**
>
> **Diminished responsibility** – a partial defence to a charge of murder which reduces the offence to one of voluntary manslaughter.

6.3.3 Abnormality of mental functioning

Until s 52 amended the definition of diminished responsibility, the phrase used to prove the defence was that the defendant was suffering from an 'abnormality of mind'. In *R v Byrne* (1960), the Court of Appeal considered that 'abnormality of mind' was wide enough to cover the mind's activities in all its aspects, including the ability to exercise will power to control physical acts in accordance with rational judgement. It means a state of mind so different from that of ordinary human beings that a reasonable person would term it abnormal.

R v Byrne (1960)

The defendant was a sexual psychopath who strangled a young woman and then mutilated her body. The medical evidence was that, because of his condition, he was unable to control his perverted desires. He was convicted of murder but the Court of Appeal quashed the conviction and substituted a conviction for voluntary manslaughter.

Although this case was decided on the 1957 definition, it is likely that the courts will continue to use the same test, which will be that the defendant's abnormality of mental functioning was so different from that of ordinary human beings that the reasonable person would term it abnormal.

6.3.4 Cause of the abnormality of mental functioning

The cause of the abnormality of mental functioning must arise from a 'recognised medical condition'. Most medical conditions are defined in the International Classification of Diseases prepared by the World Health Organization. This document is used internationally by health professionals to classify diseases and health problems. The current version is version 10. Chapter V covers mental and behavioural disorders. If the condition is recognised in this classification, it is likely to be accepted as an abnormality for the purposes of this defence.

Examples of accepted disorders include anxiety disorders, personality disorders, alcohol dependency and schizophrenia, as well as physical conditions which affect mental functioning such as epilepsy, sleep disorders or diabetes.

Medical evidence of the abnormality that the defendant is suffering from must be presented at the trial. It will be for the jury to decide if this evidence is sufficient for a finding of diminished responsibility.

Look online

Read more about the International Classification of Diseases and its classification of diseases and abnormalities at: www.who.int/classifications/icd/en/.

In its 2006 report, the Law Commission had recommended that developmental immaturity for defendants aged under 18 should also be included within diminished responsibility. Its reasoning for this was that there is evidence to show that frontal lobes of the brain, which play an important role in the development of self-control and in controlling impulsive behaviour, do not mature until the age of 14.

The Government took the view that there was no need to include 'developmental immaturity' as a specific cause of diminished responsibility. It thought that conditions such as learning disabilities and autism spectrum disorders were recognised medical conditions, and that these were particularly relevant in the context of juvenile offenders. This is true, but 'developmental immaturity' is not the same as learning disability.

If this condition cannot be accepted, children as young as ten could be convicted of murder when they are developmentally immature, as they cannot use the defence of diminished responsibility because they are not suffering from an abnormality of mental functioning.

6.3.5 Substantially impaired

The abnormality must have substantially impaired the defendant's ability to:

a understand the nature of the defendant's conduct

b form a rational judgement

c exercise self-control.

What amounts to 'substantial impairment' is not defined in the legislation. The definition of the word 'substantial' has been borrowed from the previous context in the cases mentioned below and imported into the new version of the defence.

In R v Byrne (1960), the Court of Appeal said that the question of whether the impairment was substantial was one of degree and that it was for the jury to decide whether the impairment was enough to be considered substantial.

In R v Lloyd (1967), it was held that 'substantial' does not mean total, nor does it mean trivial or minimal. It is something in between. It was repeated that it is for the jury to decide if the defendant's mental responsibility is impaired and, if so, whether it is substantially impaired. However, as it is a question of fact, the judge can withdraw the point from the jury if there is no evidence on which a reasonable jury could conclude that the defendant's mental responsibility was substantially impaired.

More recently, the Supreme Court considered the meaning of 'substantial' and the direction to be given to the jury in *R v Golds* (2016). It was pointed out that there is no indication in the 2009 Act that Parliament wished the word 'substantial' to carry a different meaning from the interpretations in *Byrne* and *Lloyd*.

R v Golds (2016)

D killed his partner and admitted the killing. The medical evidence was that he had an abnormality of mental functioning arising from a medical condition. The only issue was whether he was in a psychotic state at the time of the killing.

The Supreme Court upheld the conviction and said that the judge is not ordinarily required to define the meaning of 'substantially'. This should only be done where there is a risk that the jury will not understand the meaning of the word.

The court directed that 'substantially' in the context of this defence means an impairment which was of some importance, or was a serious degree of impairment. It needed to be something more than trivial. The reason for this meaning is that there must be an important reason to reduce murder to manslaughter, and not merely a reason which just passes a trivial level.

6.3.6 What must be substantially impaired?

The defendant's ability to do one of three things must be substantially impaired. They are to:

- understand the nature of his or her conduct
- form a rational judgement
- exercise self-control.

These three points were used in the case of *R v Byrne* (1960), above. In its judgment, the court said that 'abnormality of mind' (the then test for diminished responsibility) was wide enough:

> ❝ ...to cover the mind's activities in all its aspects, not only the perception of physical acts and matters, and the ability to form a rational judgement as to whether an act is right or wrong, but also the ability to exercise will power to control physical acts in accordance with that rational judgement. ❞

The amendments to the definition made by the Coroners and Justice Act 2009 have effectively put the decision in *Byrne* into statutory form.

So what do each of these three points mean?

Ability to understand the nature of his or her conduct

This covers situations such as where the defendant is in an automatic state and does not know what he or she is doing. It also covers situations where the defendant suffers from delusions and believes, for example, that he or she is killing the devil when in fact he or she is killing a person. In this situation, he or she does not understand the nature of what he or she is doing.

It could also cover people with severe learning difficulties whose mental age is so low that they do not understand the nature of what they are doing.

Ability to form a rational judgement

Even if the defendant does know the nature of his or her conduct, he or she may not be able to form a rational judgement about his or her acts or omissions. Those suffering from paranoia, schizophrenia or battered woman syndrome may not be able to form a rational judgement.

Ability to exercise self-control

This was the situation in *R v Byrne* (1960), where the defendant was a sexual psychopath. The medical evidence was that this condition meant he was unable to control his perverted desires.

6.3.7 Provides an explanation for the defendant's conduct

The amendment by the 2009 Act introduced a new principle, namely that the defendant has to prove that the abnormality of mental functioning provides an explanation for his or her conduct if it causes, or is a significant contributory factor in causing, the defendant to carry out that conduct. So, there must now be some causal connection between the defendant's abnormality of mental functioning and the killing.

So the abnormality of mental functioning need not be the only factor which caused the defendant to do or be involved in the killing. However, it must be a significant factor. This is particularly important where the defendant is intoxicated at the time of the killing.

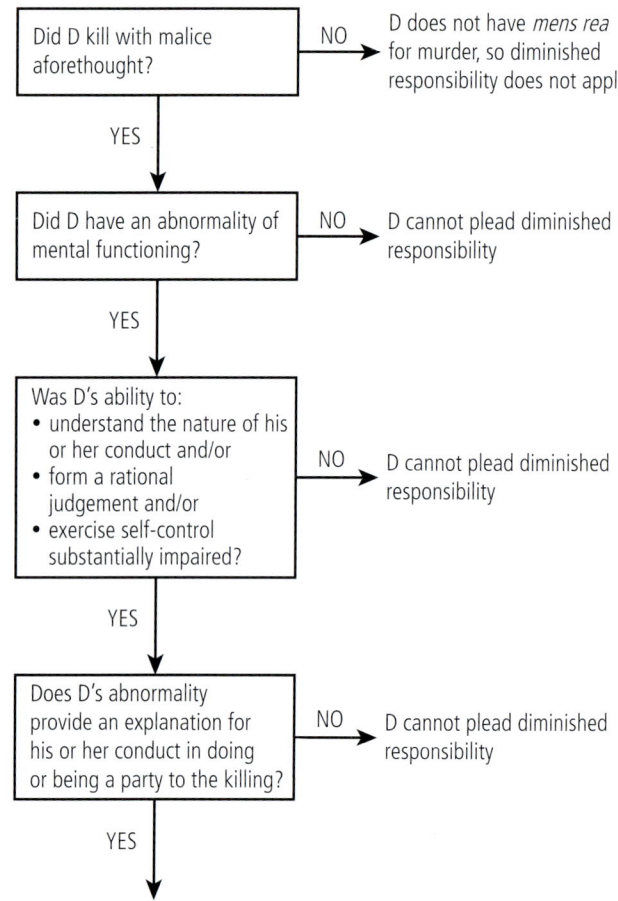

Figure 6.6 Flowchart on diminished responsibility

6.3.8 Diminished responsibility and intoxication

So the abnormality of mental functioning need not be the only factor which caused the defendant to do or be involved in the killing. However, it must be a significant contributory factor. This is particularly important where the defendant is intoxicated at the time of the killing.

There are three possibilities to consider:

- that the defendant was intoxicated at the time of the killing and tries to use the defence of diminished responsibility
- that the defendant was intoxicated and has a pre-existing abnormality of mental functioning
- that the intoxication is due to an addiction.

That the defendant was intoxicated at the time of the killing and tries to use the defence of diminished responsibility

Intoxication on its own cannot be used as the basis of a defence of diminished responsibility. The defence requires that the abnormality of mental functioning must be due to a recognised medical condition and intoxication does not fall within this. This was the position under the Homicide Act 1957 and is still the position after the Coroners and Justice Act 2009. This was confirmed in *R v Dowds* (2012), when the Court of Appeal stated that if Parliament had meant to change the law, then it would have introduced changes in the 2009 Act.

That the defendant was intoxicated and has a pre-existing abnormality of mental functioning

This was the situation in *R v Dietschmann* (2003).

R v Dietschmann (2003)

D was upset because, in his view, V was behaving in a way which was disrespectful to the memory of D's aunt who had just died. He killed V by repeatedly kicking him and stamping on him. The psychiatrists called by both the prosecution and the defence agreed D was suffering from an adjustment disorder in the form of depressed grief reaction to the death of his aunt. However, they disagreed on whether this had substantially impaired his mental responsibility for the killing. D had also drunk large amounts of alcohol before the killing. He was convicted and appealed.

Lord Hutton said, on his appeal to the House of Lords, that the question was not simply whether D would have killed had he not been intoxicated and he gave the following model direction to be given to juries: 'Has D satisfied you that, despite the drink, his mental abnormality substantially impaired his mental responsibility for his fatal acts, or has he failed to satisfy you of that?'

Lord Hutton also observed that if the jury decided that D would not have killed without taking the drink or drugs, it was unlikely it would find that the abnormality on its own was sufficient to impair his responsibility.

That the intoxication is due to an addiction

There is a recognised medical condition called alcohol dependence syndrome (ADS) which means that a person cannot control his or her drinking. This can amount to an abnormality of mental functioning and can be used as a basis for the defence of diminished responsibility. The leading case on this point is *R v Wood* (2008)

R v Wood (2008)

D was an alcoholic and, after drinking heavily, had gone to V's flat. D claimed he had fallen asleep there and been woken by V trying to perform oral sex on him. D repeatedly hit V with a meat cleaver, killing him. At the trial, medical experts agreed that D was suffering from ADS, but disagreed as to whether this had damaged his brain.

The judge directed the jury that if they found that D had suffered brain damage from his long-term abuse of alcohol then the defence of diminished responsibility was available to him. But if they found that he had not suffered brain damage, they then had to decide whether the drinking had been voluntary or not. If it was voluntary, D could not use the defence of diminished responsibility.

D was convicted of murder and appealed to the Court of Appeal, which reduced the conviction to voluntary manslaughter on the grounds of diminished responsibility.

In cases where the defendant has an addiction, the jury has to consider the effect of the alcohol consumed because of the addiction as this is classed as involuntary drinking.

If the consumption is not due to the addiction, it is classed as voluntary drinking and its effects cannot be considered.

If there is both voluntary and involuntary drinking, so not all the consumption is due to the addiction, the defence can still be pleaded but the jury can only consider the effects of the involuntary drinking, and it has to decide whether this substantially impaired the defendant's ability to do one or more of the things mentioned in subsection 1A.

The issue was considered again in *R v Stewart* (2009), when the Court of Appeal set out a three-stage test for juries in such cases to consider:

1 Was the defendant suffering from an 'abnormality of mental functioning'? The court pointed out that

Figure 6.7 Key facts chart on diminished responsibility

	Law	Act/Case

Definition	Suffering from an abnormality of mental functioning which:
	■ arose from a recognised medical condition
	■ substantially impaired D's ability to do one or more of the following:
	  ■ understand the nature of the conduct
	  ■ form a rational judgement
	  ■ exercise self-control, and
	■ provides an explanation for D's conduct
		Section 2(1) of the Homicide Act 1957 (as amended by the Coroners and Justice Act 2009)

Abnormality of mental functioning	A mental functioning so different from that of ordinary human beings that the reasonable person would term it abnormal	*R v Byrne* (1960)
Substantially impaired	A question of degree for the jury to decide 'Substantial' does not mean 'total' nor 'trivial' or 'minimal' but something in between	*R v Byrne* (1960) *R v Lloyd* (1967) *R v Golds* (2016)
Provides an explanation for D's conduct	The abnormality of mental functioning provides an explanation for D's conduct if it causes, or is a significant contributory factor in causing, D to carry out that conduct	Section 2(1B) of the Homicide Act 1957
Effect of intoxication	■ Transient effect of drink or drugs on brain cannot found the defence of diminished responsibility ■ Where the defendant has a pre-existing mental disorder, intoxication does not prevent him or her using the defence; the abnormality of mental functioning does not have to be the sole cause of the defendant doing the killing ■ Alcohol dependence syndrome can be an abnormality of mental functioning	*R v Dowds* (2012) *R v Dietschmann* (2003) *R v Wood* (2008) *R v Stewart* (2009)
Burden of proof	It is for the defence to prove on the balance of probabilities	Section 2(2) of the Homicide Act 1957
Effect of defence	The charge of murder is reduced to manslaughter	Section 2(3) of the Homicide Act 1957

Figure 6.8 Key cases chart on diminished responsibility

Case	Facts	Principle
R v Byrne (1960)	D was a sexual psychopath who strangled a young woman and then mutilated her body The medical evidence was that, because of his condition, he was unable to control his perverted desires	The test of whether D's mental functioning is impaired was whether it was so different from that of ordinary human beings that the reasonable person would term it abnormal
R v Golds (2016)	D killed his partner and admitted the killing Medical evidence showed that he had an abnormality of mental functioning arising from a medical condition but was he in a psychotic state at the time of the killing?	The meaning of 'substantially' means an impairment which was of some importance, or was a serious degree of impairment It needed to be something more than trivial
R v Dietschmann (2003)	D was upset as V was being disrespectful to the memory of his aunt He killed V by repeatedly kicking him and stamping on him The psychiatrists agreed D was suffering from an adjustment disorder in the form of depressed grief reaction to the death of his aunt but disagreed whether this had substantially impaired his mental responsibility for the killing D had also drunk large amounts of alcohol before the killing	A direction should be given to juries: 'Has D satisfied you that, despite the drink, his or her mental abnormality substantially impaired his or her mental responsibility for his or her fatal acts, or has he or she failed to satisfy you of that?' If the jury decided that D would not have killed without taking the drink or drugs, it was unlikely it would find that the abnormality on its own was sufficient to impair his or her responsibility
R v Wood (2008)	D was an alcoholic and after drinking heavily, had gone to V's flat where he had fallen asleep and woke to find V trying to perform oral sex on him D killed V with a meat cleaver At the trial medical experts agreed that D was suffering from ADS, but disagreed as to whether this had damaged his brain	Where D has an addiction, the jury has to consider the effect of the alcohol consumed because of the addiction as this is classed as involuntary drinking If the consumption is not due to the addiction, it is classed as voluntary drinking and its effects cannot be considered If there is both voluntary and involuntary drinking, so not all the consumption is due to the addiction, the defence can still be pleaded but the jury can only consider the effects of the involuntary drinking, and it has to decide whether this substantially impaired D's mental functioning

the mere fact that the defendant had ADS would not automatically amount to an abnormality. The nature and the extent of the ADS had to be considered.

2 If so, was the defendant's abnormality caused by the ADS?

3 If so, was the defendant's ability to do any of the things in subsection 1(A) substantially impaired? To decide this, all the evidence, including the medical evidence, should be considered. Relevant issues to be considered may include:

a the extent and seriousness of the defendant's dependency

b the extent to which the defendant's ability to control his or her drinking, or to choose whether to drink or not, was reduced

c whether the defendant was capable of abstinence from alcohol, and if so, for how long

d whether the defendant was choosing for a particular reason, such as a birthday celebration, to decide to get drunk, or to drink even more than usual

e the defendant's pattern of drinking preceding the killing, and

f the defendant's ability, if any, to make decisions about ordinary day-to-day matters.

In the news

Teenage girl gets life for manslaughter of Katie Rough

A teenager who killed a seven-year-old girl has been given a life sentence with a minimum detention of five years, after her own lawyer said there was no other clear means of protecting the public.

Katie Rough was playing in a field close to her home in Woodthorpe, York, when she was smothered to death by the 16-year-old girl, who cannot be named and was 15 at the time. The child was then slashed with a Stanley knife. Katie was found with deep cuts to her neck and chest after she and the teenager had gone to play together. After killing Katie, she was found standing in a cul-de-sac, covered in blood and carrying a Stanley knife, as she rang 999 to tell police what she had done.

The defendant, who denied murder but admitted manslaughter due to diminished responsibility at a previous hearing, appeared by video-link at Leeds Crown Court. Katie's family watched from the jury box as the girl sat clutching a soft toy, silent and with her head down throughout the hearing.

Mr Justice Soole said: 'The level of danger to the public is high. In the circumstances of your continuing silence, the critical question is whether there is any reliable estimate as to how long that danger will continue.' The judge told the girl that what happened on the field 'is known only to you. Further and most disturbing evidence points to this being planned and based on delusional thoughts. In this truly exceptional case, I have concluded that it is necessary to impose a sentence of detention for life.'

The court heard a full psychiatric assessment had been requested for the teenager, and the possibility of psychosis was flagged a month before the killing, yet no investigation was carried out. A friend told investigators the teenager self-harmed and liked to talk about death, and that she had said she dreamed of killing someone and heard voices in her head.

Two days before she killed Katie, she had posted a picture to Instagram of self-harm wounds to her arms made with pencil sharpener blades captioned: 'Mentally, seriously, not OK'. She was 'clearly crying out for help and support' said her barrister, Nicholas Johnson QC, He said his client had been telling people of 'delusional and bizarre thoughts' for many months before the killing, including the 'genuine belief in her head that her family and many others were not human and may be controlled by a higher and hostile force'.

The court had heard that experts could not agree a diagnosis of the girl's mental disorder, nor decide how long it would take before she could no longer be considered a danger because she had failed to engage with doctors. Psychiatrists have explored whether she was suffering from a depressive disorder and there has also been a concern she was suffering from an emerging schizo-type personality disorder.

Adapted from an article in the Guardian, 24 November 2017

Tip

When considering murder cases, look carefully at the facts. There are likely to be clear pointers. For example, the facts may include 'suffering from depression' or 'suffering from delusions' or that the defendant is 'suffering from an addiction' – these are pointers to diminished responsibility as a possible defence.

Activity

1 Ellie's husband, Glen, is an alcoholic and when drunk is often violent to her. Ellie has recently been suffering from depression for which she takes medication. One evening Glen comes home drunk and hits Ellie several times. He then goes to bed. Ellie stays up and after about four hours, in a sudden burst of rage, she gets a knife and stabs Glen, killing him.

Advise whether Ellie can avoid liability for murder by using the defences of loss of control or diminished responsibility.

2 Now, using possible defences, consider the possible liability for a charge of murder in the following situations:

a Greg was very particular about his appearance and had a complex about people looking at him. When he was in a club he saw Kate look at him and make a remark to her friends, at which they all laughed. As he was about to leave the club, Greg noticed Kate at the top of a staircase. He immediately went over and pushed her violently. She fell awkwardly, broke her neck and died.

Advise whether Greg would be liable for the murder of Kate.

b Carlo went into a local shop, pointed a gun at the counter assistant and demanded that she gave him all the money in the till. At that moment a customer, Dean, entered the shop. Carlo panicked and hit Dean on the head with the gun. Carlo then ran away.

Dean suffered serious head injuries and was taken to hospital by ambulance. On the way to the hospital, the ambulance was involved in a collision. This caused Dean to suffer more injuries and delayed getting him to hospital. Dean died shortly after arriving at hospital.

Advise whether Carlo would be liable for the murder of Dean.

c Frank hated all skateboarders and when he saw Larry skateboarding in town, he began shouting at him. Larry laughed and told him not to be so stupid. Frank seized Larry's board and hit him over the head several times with it with some force. Larry later died from a brain haemorrhage, which was caused by a genetic weakness.

Advise whether Frank would be liable for the murder of Larry.

Summary

- Loss of control and diminished responsibility are partial defences to a charge of murder – if successful they reduce the charge to one of manslaughter.

- For loss of control, there must be:
  - a loss of control
  - which must be due to a qualifying trigger, and
  - a person of the defendant's sex and age, with a normal degree of tolerance and self-restraint and in the circumstances of the defendant, might have reacted in the same or similar way.

- Once the defendant has suggested the possibility of the defence, it is for the prosecution to disprove. The defendant must put forward sufficient evidence of the possibility of the defence.

- A qualifying trigger is when the loss of control was attributable to:
  - the defendant's fear of serious violence from the victim against the defendant or another identified person (s 55(3)), or
  - a thing or things done or said (or both) which –
    a constituted circumstances of an extremely grave character, and
    b caused D to have a justifiable sense of being seriously wronged.

- Sexual infidelity alone is not a qualifying trigger, but it may be taken into account if other triggers are present.

- The defence is not allowed if the defendant acted in a 'considered desire for revenge'.

- The defendant must show that 'a person of D's sex and age, with a normal degree of tolerance and self-restraint and in the circumstances of D, might have reacted in the same or similar way to D' – an objective test.

- The jury cannot consider any circumstance of the defendant which might have made him or her have less self-control. The defendant's voluntary intoxication cannot be considered.

- If the defendant is successful, a conviction of voluntary manslaughter will result and the judge has a discretion on the sentence to impose.

- For diminished responsibility, the defendant must show that:
  - he or she was suffering from an abnormality of mental functioning and that this arose from a recognised medical condition
  - this substantially impaired the defendant's ability to—
    a understand the nature of his or her conduct
    b form a rational judgement, or
    c exercise self-control

    and the substantial impairment provides an explanation for the defendant's conduct.

- The burden of proof of the defence is on the defendant.

- If the defendant is successful, a conviction of voluntary manslaughter will result and the judge has a discretion on the sentence to impose.

7 Involuntary manslaughter

After reading this chapter, you should be able to:
- Understand the elements of unlawful act manslaughter
- Understand the elements of gross negligence manslaughter
- Apply the law on both types of involuntary manslaughter to scenario-based situations

7.1 Defining involuntary manslaughter

Involuntary manslaughter is an unlawful killing where the defendant does not have the *mens rea* for murder.

It is also important not to confuse involuntary manslaughter with voluntary manslaughter. For voluntary manslaughter, the defendant has the intention to kill or cause grievous bodily harm but the charge is reduced from murder because the defendant can use one of the special defences – either diminished responsibility or loss of control

The special defences to murder were explained in Chapter 6.

7.1.2 Ways of committing involuntary manslaughter

There are two main ways of committing involuntary manslaughter. These are:
- unlawful act manslaughter – this is when the defendant commits an unlawful act (a crime) in the course of which the victim dies
- gross negligence manslaughter – this is when the defendant owes some form of duty to the victim but the duty is broken and the victim dies as a result.

Examples of ways in which both forms of manslaughter may be committed are shown in the table below.

Figure 7.1 Examples of ways in which involuntary manslaughter may be committed

Unlawful act manslaughter	Gross negligence manslaughter
V is punched in a fight, falls, hits his or her head on the ground and dies	V dies as a result of a medical error
V tries to escape from an attack and runs into a road, is hit by a car or lorry and dies	V dies as a result of an accident in the workplace
V dies after jumping from a building while trying to escape from an attack	V dies when a relative or carer fails to look after him or her or call for medical help
V dies from a heart condition in the course of a robbery or burglary	V, a rescuer, dies in an explosion while trying to perform a rescue
	V dies from a drug overdose when a friend or relative is supposed to be looking after him or her

7.2 Unlawful act manslaughter

This is also known as constructive manslaughter because the liability for the death is built up, or constructed, from the liability for another crime. The defendant has committed an unlawful and dangerous act – which is a crime - which causes a death. This makes the defendant liable even though they did not realise that death or injury might occur.

The elements of **unlawful act manslaughter** are:
- the defendant has committed an unlawful act – a crime
- that act must be objectively dangerous
- the act must cause the death, and
- the defendant must have the required *mens rea* for the unlawful act – the crime.

Key term

Unlawful act manslaughter – where the defendant causes a death through doing an unlawful act that is objectively dangerous with the necessary *mens rea* for the unlawful act.

7.2.1 Range of involuntary manslaughter

Involuntary manslaughter covers a wide range of circumstances. At the top end of the range, the behaviour of the defendant which caused the death can be highly blameworthy, as there was a high risk of causing death or serious injury. At the bottom end of the range, the defendant's behaviour may verge on carelessness and only just enough to be considered blameworthy.

The maximum sentence for involuntary manslaughter is life imprisonment, so this gives the judge discretion to impose a sentence which is suitable for the particular circumstances of the offence, including, in some cases, even a non-custodial sentence.

7.2.2 Unlawful act

The death must be caused by an unlawful act. The unlawful act must be a criminal offence. A civil wrong (tort) is not enough. In *R v Franklin* (1883), the defendant threw a large box into the sea from the West Pier at Brighton. The box hit and killed a swimmer. It was held that this was a civil wrong which was not enough to create liability for unlawful act manslaughter. Another case illustrating that there must be a criminal unlawful act is *R v Lamb* (1967).

R v Lamb (1967)

Lamb and his friend were playing around with a revolver. They both knew that it was loaded with two bullets in a five-chamber cylinder but thought that it would not fire unless one of the bullets was opposite the barrel. They knew that there was no bullet in this position, but did not realise that the cylinder turned so that a bullet from the next chamber along would be fired. Lamb pointed the gun at his friend and pulled the trigger, killing him. It was held that the defendant had not committed an unlawful act. The pointing of the gun at the friend was not an assault as the friend did not fear any violence from Lamb.

There must be a positive act. An omission cannot create liability for unlawful act manslaughter – though it may lead to a charge of gross negligence manslaughter. In *R v Lowe* (1973), the Court of Appeal quashed a conviction for manslaughter when the defendant was convicted of wilfully neglecting his baby son, who later died. The trial judge had directed the jury that, if they found the defendant guilty of wilful neglect, he could also be guilty of manslaughter. However the appeal court decided that a finding of wilful neglect involved a failure

to act, which could not support a conviction for unlawful act manslaughter.

If the prosecution has doubts about which form of manslaughter applies they are likely to charge an accused with both forms of manslaughter, leaving it to the jury to decide which applies.

In many cases, the unlawful act will be some kind of assault, but any criminal offence can form the unlawful act, provided that it involves an act which is dangerous in the sense that it is likely to cause some injury. Examples of offences which have led to a finding of unlawful act manslaughter, when an unlawful killing has resulted, include:

- arson – *R v Goodfellow* (1986) (see section 7.2.3)
- criminal damage – *DPP v Newbury and Jones* (1976) (see section 7.2.5)
- burglary – *R v Watson* (1989) (see section 7.2.3).

7.2.3 Dangerous act

The unlawful act must be dangerous on an objective test. In *R v Church* (1965), it was held that the test was 'such as all sober and reasonable people would inevitably recognise must subject the other person to, at least, the risk of some harm resulting therefrom, albeit not serious harm'.

From this, it can be seen that the risk need only be of 'some harm'. The harm need not be serious. If a sober and reasonable person realises that the unlawful act might cause some injury, then this part of the test for unlawful act manslaughter is satisfied. It does not matter that the defendant him- or herself did not realise there was any risk of harm to someone else. The defendant can be convicted, even though he or she was unaware of the risk of any harm occurring.

In 1996 the Law Commission in their report, 'Legislating the Criminal Code: Involuntary Manslaughter' (Law Com No. 237) recommended the abolition of unlawful act manslaughter. The Commission criticised the concept of unlawful act manslaughter, pointing out:

> **66** It ... is inappropriate to convict a defendant for an offence of homicide where the most that can be said is that he or she ought to have realised that there was the risk of some, albeit not serious, harm to another resulting from his or her commission of an unlawful act. **99**

Unlawful act manslaughter is nearly always based on crimes involving injury to the person, a non-fatal offence, for which *mens rea* (intention or recklessness as to harm in some form) must be proved. Alternatively, it will be based on damage to property which involves a very obvious risk of injury to a person, often a very obvious risk of very serious injury.

The case of *R v Larkin* (1943) illustrates both the need for an unlawful act and for there to be, from an objective viewpoint, the risk of some harm.

R v Larkin (1943)

D threatened another man with an open cut-throat razor, in order to frighten him. The mistress of the other man tried to intervene and, because she was drunk, accidentally fell onto the open blade which cut her throat and killed her. On appeal, D's conviction for manslaughter was upheld. The act of threatening the other man with the razor was a technical assault. It was also an act which was dangerous because it was likely to injure someone.

Humphries J explained this in the judgment when he said:

> 66 Where the act which a person is engaged in performing is unlawful, then, if at the same time it is a dangerous act, that is, an act which is likely to injure another person, and quite inadvertently he causes the death of that other person by that act, then he is guilty of manslaughter. 99

The unlawful act need not be aimed at the victim. This was the situation in *Larkin* where the assault was against the man but the woman died. It is also shown by the case of *R v Mitchell* (1983) discussed in *AQA A-level Law for Year 1 and AS*, Chapter 19, section 19.1.4 and again earlier in this book in Chapter 4, section 4.5. It will be remembered that D tried to push his way into a queue at the post office and punched a man who had told him off for this. Due to the punch the man fell into an elderly woman who was injured and died a few days later. D was convicted of unlawful act manslaughter of the woman. He had committed an unlawful act by punching the man. This act was dangerous as it was an act which was likely to injure another person. Finally, the act caused the death of the woman.

I'm only playing dominoes.

It can be seen that all the elements set by Humphries J in his statement in *R v Larkin* (1943) are present. The defendants in both *Larkin* and *Mitchell* were guilty of unlawful act manslaughter, despite the fact that, in each case, the person threatened (or punched) was not the one who died.

Some harm

It is not necessary for the sober and reasonable person to foresee the particular type of harm that the victim suffers. It is enough that the sober and reasonable person would foresee some harm. This was stated in *R v J M and S M* (2012).

R v J M and S M (2012)

J M lit a cigarette inside a nightclub and was asked to leave. After some pushing, both J M and his brother S M left. Later they both returned and kicked a fire door. This led to a fight between the brothers and doormen. During the fight V, one of the doormen, collapsed and died shortly afterwards. The cause of death was loss of blood. V's renal artery had ruptured due to a weakness in the artery wall. The rupture was extremely unlikely to have occurred spontaneously and it was accepted that the fight was a substantial cause of V's death. However, at the trial, the judge ruled that the jury would have to be satisfied that 'the victim died as a result of the sort of physical harm that any reasonable and sober person would inevitably realise the unlawful act in question risked causing'. The judge stopped the trial as the rupture of the artery was a completely different form of harm from that foreseeable by the reasonable and sober person.

The prosecution appealed against this ruling and the Court of Appeal held that the sober and reasonable person only had to foresee some harm. They did not have to foresee any specific type of harm. Sober and reasonable people would 'readily have recognised that all the doormen ... were at risk of some harm'.

Act against property

The unlawful act does not have to be aimed at a person; it can be aimed at property, provided it is 'such that all sober and reasonable people would inevitably recognise must subject another person to, at least, the risk of some harm'. This can be illustrated in R v Goodfellow (1986).

R v Goodfellow (1986)

D decided to set fire to his council flat so that the council would have to rehouse him and his family. The fire got out of control and his wife, son and another woman died in the fire. He was convicted of manslaughter and appealed. The Court of Appeal upheld the conviction because all the elements of unlawful act manslaughter were present:

- The act was unlawful – it was arson, an offence under the Criminal Damage Act 1971.
- Reasonable people would recognise that setting fire to the flat might cause some harm to another person – there was an obvious risk that someone in the flat might be hurt.
- The act caused the deaths.
- D had the *mens rea* of arson – D intended to set the flat on fire.

Physical harm

The 'risk of harm' refers to physical harm. Something which causes fear and apprehension is not sufficient. It was acknowledged that fear can trigger 'shock', which is physical harm. Shock, of course, can trigger a heart attack in a victim with a heart condition. This was an issue in R v Dawson (1985).

R v Dawson (1985)

Three defendants attempted to rob a petrol station. They were masked and armed with pick-axe handles. The petrol station attendant managed to sound the alarm but died from a heart attack. The defendants were charged with unlawful act manslaughter.

The problem in this case was that it was decided that the risk of harm by shock was not reasonably

foreseeable on the facts known to the defendants or, perhaps, on the facts which ought to have been known. The defendants' knowledge, actual or constructive, would be the knowledge available to the reasonable person. The court took the view that it could only have been reasonably foreseeable if the victim's special condition would, or perhaps, 'should', have been known to the reasonable person. As a result, the defendants' convictions for manslaughter were quashed.

However, it was stated in R v Watson (1989) that where a sober and reasonable person would be aware of the victim's frailty and the risk of physical harm to him or her, then the defendant will be liable.

R v Watson (1989)

Two defendants threw a brick through the window of a house and entered it, intending to steal property. The occupier was a frail 87-year-old man who heard the noise and came to investigate what had happened. The two defendants physically abused him and then left. The man died of a heart attack 90 minutes later. Although the Court of Appeal quashed the convictions for manslaughter, the court stated that the act of burglary could be 'dangerous' in that it became dangerous as soon as the old man's condition would have been apparent to the sober and reasonable person as an elderly man could have suffered some harm from a confrontation.

Burglary is an unlawful act which is not normally dangerous under the *Church* definition with a risk of some harm resulting from it. However, a burglary may be carried out in such a way that the circumstances of the commission of the offence make it dangerous. This was the situation in R v Bristow, Dunn and Delay (2013).

R v Bristow, Dunn and Delay (2013)

The defendants were part of a gang of at least six men who had agreed to burgle V's workshop. The workshop was down a long drive so there was a risk of someone discovering the burglary and trying to prevent the burglars from escaping. At least two vehicles were used to get to the workshop. V was found dead near the workshop a few hours after the burglary. There was evidence that he had been hit by one or both of the vehicles. The defendants were convicted of V's manslaughter. The Court of Appeal upheld their convictions on the basis that the circumstances of the burglary meant that a reasonable and sober person would recognise the risk of some harm resulting from the burglary.

7.2.4 Causing the death

The unlawful act must cause the death.

> The rules on causation are the same as for murder and are set out in *AQA A-level Law for Year 1 and AS*, Chapter 19, section 19.3.

An important point to note is that if there is an intervening act which breaks the chain of causation, then the defendant cannot be liable for unlawful act manslaughter. An example of this is *R v Williams and Davis* (1992), where the defendants picked up a hitchhiker but he jumped out of the car when it was travelling at 30 m.p.h., hit his head on the road and died. The prosecution alleged that the defendants were in the course of robbing him when he jumped out and their actions amounted to unlawful act manslaughter. However, there was no evidence to support the prosecution allegation and the victim jumping out of the car amounted to a **novus actus interveniens** which broke the chain of causation.

Key term

Novus actus interveniens – an intervening act which breaks the chain of causation. See *AQA A-level Law for Year 1 and AS*, Chapter 19, section 19.3.3.

Proving causation has been an issue in cases where the defendant supplied the victim with an illegal drug and the victim subsequently dies. Some defendants had been found guilty of unlawful act manslaughter through the unlawful act of administering a noxious substance to the victim, contrary to s 23 OAPA 1861. It was settled in *R v Kennedy* (2007) by the House of Lords who ruled that there was no unlawful act by the defendant under s 23 if the defendant filled a syringe and handed it to the victim who then self-injected. The act of self-injection was a voluntary intervening act by V which broke the chain of causation.

R v Kennedy (2007)

D had prepared an injection of heroin and water for V to inject himself. He handed the syringe to V who injected himself and then handed the syringe back to D. V later died. Initially Kennedy was convicted and the Court of Appeal upheld his conviction. The case was then referred back to the Court of Appeal by the Criminal Case Review Commission. Again the Court of Appeal upheld

the conviction on the basis that filling the syringe and handing it to V was administering a noxious substance and an unlawful act.

The case was then appealed to the House of Lords who quashed the conviction as D had not done an unlawful act which caused the death. D had not administered a noxious substance for an offence under s 23 OAPA 1861. V's act in injecting the heroin himself was an intervening act which broke any chain of causation.

The House of Lords pointed out that the criminal law generally assumes the existence of free will. The victim had freely and voluntarily administered the injection to himself. The defendant could only be guilty if he was involved in administering the injection.

> See autonomy of the individual, Chapter 4, section 4.4.

Tip

Cases involving unlawful act manslaughter often also involve issues of causation. Make sure you are familiar with, and can apply, the rules of causation.

7.2.5 Mens rea

It must be proved that the defendant had the *mens rea* for the unlawful act – the crime – but it is not necessary for the defendant to realise that the act is unlawful or dangerous. This was made clear in the case of *DPP v Newbury and Jones* (1976).

DPP v Newbury and Jones (1976)

The defendants were two teenage boys who pushed a piece of paving stone from a bridge onto a railway line as a train was approaching. The stone hit the train and killed the guard. They were convicted of manslaughter and the House of Lords was asked to decide the question of whether a defendant could be convicted of unlawful act manslaughter if he did not foresee that his act might cause harm to another. The House of Lords confirmed it was not necessary to prove that the defendant foresaw any harm from his act. The boy's convictions were upheld.

So, a defendant can be convicted provided that the unlawful act – the crime – was dangerous and the defendant had the necessary *mens rea* for that act (the crime).

Figure 7.2 Key cases chart on unlawful act manslaughter

Case	Facts	Law
R v Lamb (1967)	D fired a gun at a friend; both thought it was safe because there was no bullet in the firing chamber	There must be an unlawful act for a charge of manslaughter; in this case there was no assault as the friend did not fear violence
R v Lowe (1973)	D failed to take proper care of a baby who died	There has to be an act; unlawful act manslaughter cannot be committed by an omission
R v Larkin (1943)	D threatened a man with a razor – a woman fell on it and died	The unlawful act need not be aimed at V but it must be objectively dangerous in the sense that it is likely to cause some harm
R v Goodfellow (1986)	D set fire to his flat causing three deaths	The unlawful act can be aimed at property. The test is whether it is objectively dangerous in the sense that it is likely to cause some harm
R v Dawson (1985)	A petrol station attendant died of a heart attack when his petrol station was robbed	The test is 'would sober and reasonable people have recognised that the attendant was likely to suffer some harm?' In this case the test was not satisfied
R v Watson (1989)	During a burglary the defendants physically abused the 87-year-old occupant. He later died of a heart attack	A reasonable person would have been aware of V's frailty and the risk of V suffering some harm
R v Kennedy (2007)	D supplied a drug to V who self-injected and later died	Self-injection broke the chain of causation and D was not guilty of manslaughter
DPP v Newbury and Jones (1976)	The defendants pushed a paving stone onto a passing train, killing the guard	D need only have the *mens rea* to do the unlawful act; there is no need for D to foresee that it might cause some harm

Figure 7.3 Key facts chart on unlawful act manslaughter

Part of offence	Comment	Cases
Unlawful act	Must be unlawful A civil wrong is not enough It must be an act; an omission is not sufficient	*R v Lamb* (1967) *R v Franklin* (1883) *R v Lowe* (1973)
Dangerous act	Objective test – would a sober and reasonable person realise the risk of some harm? No need to realise serious harm or the specific harm suffered An act does not have to be aimed at a person – it can be aimed at property There must be a risk of physical harm – fear is not enough	*R v Church* (1965) *R v Larkin* (1943) *R v Goodfellow* (1986) *R v J M and S M* (2012) *R v Dawson* (1985)
Causation	The normal rules of causation apply – D's act must be the cause of V's death An intervening act, e.g. V self-injecting, or V's own action will break the chain of causation	 *R v Kennedy* (2007)
Mens rea	D must have *mens rea* of the offence; it is not necessary to prove that D foresaw any harm from his or her act	*DPP v Newbury and Jones* (1976)

7.3 Gross negligence manslaughter

Gross negligence manslaughter is another way of committing manslaughter. It is completely different from unlawful act manslaughter. It is committed where the defendant owes the victim a duty of care but breaches that duty in a very negligent way, causing the death of the victim. It can be committed by an act or an omission, neither of which has to be unlawful. The leading case on gross negligence manslaughter is *R v Adomako* (1994).

R v Adomako (1994)

D was the hospital anaesthetist for a patient who was having an operation on a detached retina. During the operation, D failed to notice that one of the tubes supplying oxygen to the patient had become disconnected. As a result the patient suffered a heart attack caused by the lack of oxygen. In addition the patient suffered brain damage and subsequently died. Doctors giving evidence in the trial said that a competent anaesthetist would have noticed the disconnection of the tube within seconds and that D's failure to react was 'abysmal'. D was convicted and the conviction was upheld by the House of Lords which set out the following elements of the offence:

- the existence of a duty of care by the defendant towards the victim
- an act or omission (conduct) in breach of that duty
- which creates a serious and obvious risk of death
- and which causes death
- the whole must amount to *gross* negligence – conduct so bad in all the circumstances as to be criminal conduct.

If the defendant is convicted, the judge can impose any appropriate sentence up to a maximum of life imprisonment.

Key term

Gross negligence manslaughter – a form of involuntary manslaughter committed where D is grossly negligent in the breach of a duty of care towards V, which results in V's death.

7.3.1 Duty of care

In *R v Adomako* (1994), Lord Mackay said that the ordinary principles of negligence in civil law applied to decide whether a duty of care was owed. These come from the case of *Caparo v Dickman* (1990)

(see *AQA A-level Law for Year 1 and AS*, Chapter 24.1) and are likely to be applied where the death results from an omission. However, if death results from an act which creates an obvious and serious risk of death, this almost inevitably carries with it a duty of care not to endanger life and it is barely necessary to consider the *Caparo* principles at all.

Note that an act *or* an omission can form the basis of negligence in civil law. It will be the same for a charge of gross negligence manslaughter.

Case examples of duty of care

There have been a number of cases where it has clearly been established that medical professionals owe a duty of care to their patients. In addition it has been decided that a duty of care exists in very different situations including:

- *R v Singh* (1999), where D was the landlord of a property in which a faulty gas fire caused the deaths of tenants. D owed a duty to manage and maintain the property properly.
- *R v Litchfield* (1997), where D was the owner and master of a sailing ship. He sailed, knowing that the engines might fail because of contamination to the fuel. The ship was blown onto rocks and three crew members died. D owed a duty for the safety of the crew.
- *R v Khan and Khan* (1998), where the defendants supplied heroin to V and then left her alone. She died. The defendants' conviction for unlawful act manslaughter was quashed but the Court of Appeal stated *obiter* that duty situations could be extended to this type of area.
- *R v Finlay* (2001), where a scoutmaster took a group of scouts climbing on a mountain, but one of the scouts fell and died. In this case, the defendant's omission was considered by the jury not so bad as to be criminal.
- *R v Edwards* (2001), when parents allowed their children to play on a railway and the children were killed by a train. The parents owed a duty of care to their children.

An extension of the type of duty recognised by the courts occurred in *R v Wacker* (2002).

R v Wacker (2002)

D agreed to bring 60 illegal immigrants into England. They were put in the back of his lorry for a cross-channel ferry crossing. The only air into the lorry was through a small vent and it was agreed that this vent should be closed at certain times to prevent the immigrants from being discovered. D closed the vent before boarding the ferry. The crossing took longer than usual and at Dover customs officers found that 58 of the immigrants had died. D argued that it was impossible to determine the extent of his duty, but the Court of Appeal held that D knew that the safety of the immigrants depended on his own actions in relation to the vent and he clearly assumed a duty of care.

An interesting point in *Wacker* was that the victims were parties to an illegal act. In civil negligence this would have meant that the victims (or their dependants) could not have made a claim for compensation. However, the Court of Appeal held that for the criminal law, it was irrelevant that the victims were parties to an illegal act. It pointed out that the purposes of civil and criminal law were different and public policy demanded that defendants in this type of situation were liable under the criminal law.

This case suggests that this area of the law may be extended in the future, and it is difficult to predict what duties may be recognised.

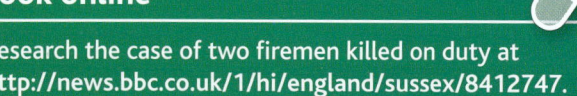

Look online

Research the case of two firemen killed on duty at http://news.bbc.co.uk/1/hi/england/sussex/8412747.stm. Who owed a duty to them and what was the duty owed?

D has created a state of affairs

In *R v Evans* (2009) (see *AQA A-level Law for Year 1 and AS*, Chapter 19.2.1), the defendant half-sister of the victim appealed against her conviction, claiming she did not owe a duty of care to her half-sister.

One view of the Court of Appeal's approach is that it applied an extended version of the creation of a dangerous situation as in *R v Miller* (1983) (also referred to in *AQA A-level Law for Year 1 and AS*, Chapter 19.2.1) by causing or contributing (by supplying drugs) to a state of affairs allegedly threatening life. This was the consequence of self-injecting the drugs. A problem with this approach is that what threatened life was not the supply, but the injection, which seems to break the chain of causation. As a result, a conclusion could be drawn that a duty now arises if the defendant was aware, or ought to have been aware, that the victim's life was at risk and any one of the following applies:

1 the defendant contributed by supply, or
2 the defendant was in a relationship such as parent/child, or
3 the defendant and victim were engaged in a dangerous joint enterprise which went wrong, or
4 the defendant voluntarily assumed a duty of care.

An alternative view is that something in addition to the supply of the drugs was required, such as some kind of aftercare or responsibility which, though not enough to be a 'voluntary assumption of responsibility' in itself, nevertheless amounted to some acknowledgement of responsibility on the part of the defendant.

According to this decision:

- although the jury must be left to decide the facts – including questions such as did the defendant supply the drugs and did he or she feel that he or she was responsible for aftercare
- whether or not on those facts a duty arises is for the judge to decide.

In directing the jury, the judge must say, 'If you find w and x proved, the defendant will have been under a duty. If you find y and z proved, D will not have been under a duty.'

> Many of the cases relating to gross negligence manslaughter involve a failure or omission on the part of the defendants. Remind yourself about when an omission can amount to a criminal offence in *AQA A-level Law for Year 1 and AS*, Chapter 19, section 19.2.

7.3.2 Breach of duty causing death

Once a duty of care has been shown to exist, it must be proved that the defendant was in breach of that duty of care and that this breach caused the death of the victim.

Lord Mackay in *R v Adomako* (1994) said:

> ❝ On this basis in my opinion the ordinary principles of the law of negligence apply to ascertain whether or not the defendant has been in breach of a duty of care towards the victim who has died. If such breach of duty is established the next question is whether that breach of duty caused the death of the victim. If so, the jury must go on to consider whether that breach of duty should be characterised as gross

negligence and therefore as a crime. This will depend on the seriousness of the breach of duty committed by the defendant in all the circumstances in which the defendant was placed when it occurred. The jury will have to consider whether the extent to which the defendant's conduct departed from the proper standard of care incumbent upon him, involving as it must have done a risk of death to the patient, was such that it should be judged criminal. **"**

So whether there is a breach of duty is a factual matter for the jury to decide. Did the defendant negligently do or fail to do something?

Causation is important; it must be proved that the breach of duty caused the death. The general rules on causation apply.

> Rules on causation are covered in detail in *AQA A-level Law for Year 1 and AS*, Chapter 19, section 19.3.

7.3.3 Gross negligence

The fact that a defendant has been negligent is not enough to convict him or her of gross negligence manslaughter. The negligence has to be 'gross'. This was first explained in *R v Bateman* (1925), which involved negligent treatment of a patient by a doctor.

R v Bateman (1925)

D was a doctor who attended a woman for the birth of her child at her home. During the childbirth, part of the woman's uterus came away. D did not send V to hospital for five days, and she later died. D's conviction was quashed on the basis that he had carried out the normal procedures that any competent doctor would have done. He had not been grossly negligent.

In his judgment, Lord Hewart said:

" The facts must be such that, in the opinion of the jury, the negligence of the accused went beyond a mere matter of compensation between subjects and showed such disregard for the life and safety of others as to amount to a crime against the State and conduct deserving of punishment. **"**

In *R v Adomako* (1994), Lord Mackay in the House of Lords approved this test and stressed that it

was a matter for the jury. The jury had to decide whether, having regard to the risk of death involved, the conduct of the defendant was so bad in all the circumstances as to amount, in its judgement, to a criminal act or omission.

The jury has to consider the seriousness of the breach of duty in all the circumstances in which the defendant was placed when it occurred and whether it was so bad as to be criminal. This is an increased role for this offence; one which a jury may not be capable of carrying out. For most offences, the judge will decide if the defendant's conduct is capable of being a crime and the jury then decide on the facts whether the defendant has committed the alleged crime.

This could mean that jury verdicts are inconsistent as, in some cases such as *R v Finlay* (2001) above, the jury found the defendant not guilty, presumably deciding that his failure to care for the victim did not meet the criminal standard. In many other reported cases juries have been satisfied that the defendants have been criminally negligent. There is a contrast between the role of the jury in this offence and for most other offences.

Risk of death

In *R v Adomako* (1994), it was not totally clear whether there has to be a risk of death through the defendant's conduct or whether the risk need only be to 'health and welfare' of the victim. Earlier, in *R v Stone and Dobinson* (1977), where the defendants had undertaken the care of Stone's sister, the test was expressed as the risk being to the 'health and welfare' of the sister who died.

When Lord Mackay gave judgment in *Adomako*, he approved this way of explaining the matter. However, Lord Mackay also approved the test in *Bateman* (1925) where the test is 'disregard for the life and safety of others'. In addition, Lord Mackay specifically mentioned 'a risk of death' on two occasions in his judgment.

The matter has now been resolved in *R v Misra and Srivastava* (2004).

R v Misra and Srivastava (2004)

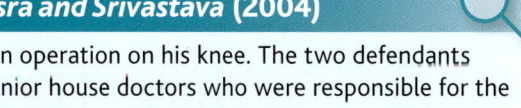

V had an operation on his knee. The two defendants were senior house doctors who were responsible for the post-operative care of V. They failed to identify and treat V for an infection which occurred after the operation and V later died. The defendants were convicted of gross negligence manslaughter and appealed on the basis that the elements of the offence were uncertain and so breached Article 7 of the European Convention on Human Rights which says that no one shall be guilty of a crime if it was not an offence at the time it was committed.

The Court of Appeal held that *Adomako* had clearly laid down the elements, so there was no breach of Article 7. The test in gross negligence manslaughter involves consideration of the risk of death. It is not sufficient to show a risk of bodily injury or injury to health. The defendants' conviction for manslaughter was upheld.

For this offence there must be an obvious risk of death, judged objectively. As a matter of policy, the Crown Prosecution Service will not prosecute for anything less.

Supply of illegal drugs

It is possible that in situations where the defendant has supplied a drug to the victim who self-injects but then dies, the defendant could be liable for gross negligence manslaughter. This view was put forward in R v Dias (2002).

R v Dias (2002)

D was a heroin addict used to injecting heroin. The victim was also a drug user but was not known to inject heroin. They were living rough and went into the stairway of a block of flats where D prepared a syringe of heroin and gave it to the victim who injected himself. D then injected himself. When D had recovered from the effects of the heroin he realised that the victim was very ill. He asked a passer-by to call an ambulance and then left the scene. The victim was taken to hospital but died. D's conviction for manslaughter on the basis of an unlawful act was quashed.

Although the conviction for unlawful act manslaughter was quashed, the Court of Appeal suggested that a conviction for gross negligent manslaughter might be possible where a duty of care could be established. This might possibly be through a duty not to supply and prepare drugs.

There have been convictions on this basis where there has been a close relationship between the defendant and the victim. In these cases, it is possible to show that the defendant owed the victim a duty of care. It may also be possible to rely on gross negligence manslaughter if the drug user is either particularly vulnerable, for example a young first-time user, or the defendant is aware of problems following the victim's self-injection. But it is clear following the House of Lords' decision in R v Kennedy (2007) that unlawful act manslaughter cannot be proved if the victim dies after self-injecting.

7.3.4 Mens rea

The defendant will be judged by their behaviour rather than their state of mind. There must be an obvious risk of death, but this is judged objectively, so it does not matter that the defendant did not see the risk.

Figure 7.4 Key facts chart on gross negligence manslaughter

Part of offence	Comment	Cases
Duty of care	D must owe V a duty of care – civil test of negligence will apply	*R v Adomako* (1994)
	Not relevant that V is a party to an illegal act	*R v Wacker* (2003)
Breach of duty	Can be act or omission – usually an omission	
Gross negligence	This is beyond a matter of mere compensation and shows such disregard for the life and safety of others that it amounts to a crime	*R v Bateman* (1925)
	Conduct which is so bad in all the circumstances as to be criminal	*R v Adomako* (1994)
Risk of death	Is the risk only to the health and welfare of victim? OR	*R v Stone and Dobinson* (1977)
	Is there disregard for the life and safety of another? OR	*R v Bateman* (1925)
	Is there an obvious risk of death judged objectively?	*R v Adomako* (1994)
Mens rea	As the risk of death is judged objectively, it does not matter that defendant did not see the risk	

Activity

Explain whether the following situations could be unlawful act manslaughter and/or gross negligence manslaughter.

1 Asif is throwing stones at passing cars. One of the stones goes through the open side window in Dawn's car and hits her on the side of the head. She loses control of the car and hits a pedestrian, Keith, who is killed.

2 Justine and Oliver have spent the evening at Justine's flat, drinking heavily. Oliver has not taken any drugs but he knows that Justine has taken an Ecstasy tablet. Justine passes out and Oliver, who is afraid he may get into trouble, decides to leave and go home. The next morning, Justine is discovered dead.

3 Liam is very angry with Sam and kicks out at him. This causes Sam to trip and fall down some steps, breaking his neck. Liam does not call for help or help Sam in any way – he goes off to the pub. Sam is eventually found but dies in hospital.

4 Patsy has been caring for her elderly aunt who is very frail and unable to walk without assistance. Patsy goes away on a fortnight's holiday, leaving her aunt on her own. The aunt dies through cold and lack of food.

Look online

Research the case of Honey Rose who, at trial, was convicted of gross negligence manslaughter but whose conviction was then overturned on appeal: www.aop.org.uk/ot/professional-support/clinical-and-regulatory/2017/07/31/appeal-court-quashes-conviction-of-optometrist-honey-rose. Consider the reasons for the appeal court decision.

Look online

In its 2006 report, 'Murder, Manslaughter and Infanticide' (Law Com No. 304), the Law Commission made recommendations to improve the law of gross negligence manslaughter. Research the recommendations at www.lawcom.gov.uk and consider whether they would improve the law.

Tip

Make sure you are clear on the law for both types of involuntary manslaughter. Be prepared to consider any relevant defences, especially to an unlawful act manslaughter charge.

Activity

In the street, Francesca snatches a bicycle from 14-year-old Jordan. In an attempt to keep his bicycle Jordan begins punching Francesca and trying to wrestle the bicycle away from her. Francesca kicks out hard at Jordan, striking him in the face. Jordan stumbles and falls, and fractures his skull on the kerb. Kevin sees Jordan fall and immediately telephones for an ambulance. Kevin gives the wrong location as he is a stranger to the area. As a result, the ambulance takes an hour to reach Jordan, who dies in hospital later that day.

Assess whether Francesca and/or Kevin can be criminally liable for the involuntary manslaughter of Jordan.

Summary

- There are two types of involuntary manslaughter:
  - unlawful act manslaughter
  - gross negligence manslaughter.
- For unlawful act manslaughter, the following conditions must exist:
  - there must be an unlawful act
  - that act must be dangerous on an objective test
  - the act must cause the death
  - the defendant must have the required *mens rea* for the unlawful act.

- For gross negligence manslaughter, there must be:
  - the existence of a duty of care by the defendant towards the victim
  - a breach of that duty of care which causes death
  - gross negligence which the jury considers to be criminal
  - the *mens rea* of gross negligence.

8 Property offences: theft

8.1 Definition of theft

Everyone knows that theft, or stealing, is wrong and a crime. The definition in the Theft Act 1968 attempts to put the meaning of theft in legal terms so that there are rules to decide in cases where theft is not so obvious. As we shall see, there are occasions where the application of the Act results in decisions that may be considered unjust.

When the Theft Act 1968 was passed, the definition of 'theft' was meant to be in simple everyday language that ordinary people could understand. However, there have been some case decisions on the elements of theft which show that is not always the case.

Theft is defined in s 1 of the Theft Act 1968: 'A person is guilty of theft if he dishonestly appropriates property belonging to another with the intention of permanently depriving the other of it.'

Sections 2–6 of the Act help with the meaning of the words or phrases in the definition. This is done in the order that the words or phrases appear in the definition, making it easy to remember the section numbers. They are:

- s 2 – dishonestly (part of the *mens rea*)
- s 3 – appropriates (part of the *actus reus*)
- s 4 – property (part of the *actus reus*)
- s 5 – belonging to another (part of the *actus reus*)
- s 6 – with the intention of permanently depriving the other of it (part of the *mens rea*).

Remember that the offence is in s 1. A person charged with theft is always charged with stealing 'contrary to s 1 of the Theft Act 1968'. Sections 2–6 are definition sections explaining s 1. They do not themselves create any offence.

The *actus reus* of theft is made up of the three elements in the phrase 'appropriates property belonging to another'. So, to prove the *actus reus* it has to be shown that there was appropriation by the defendant of something which is property within the definition of the Act and which, at the time of the appropriation, belonged to another.

There are two elements which must be proved for the *mens rea* of theft. These are that the appropriation of the property must be done 'dishonestly' and there must be the intention of permanently depriving the other person of it. All the elements of the *actus reus* and *mens rea* must be proved for there to be theft. This chapter covers the *actus reus* elements first and then the *mens rea*.

Key term

Theft – A person is guilty of theft if he or she dishonestly appropriates property belonging to another with the intention of permanently depriving the other of it.

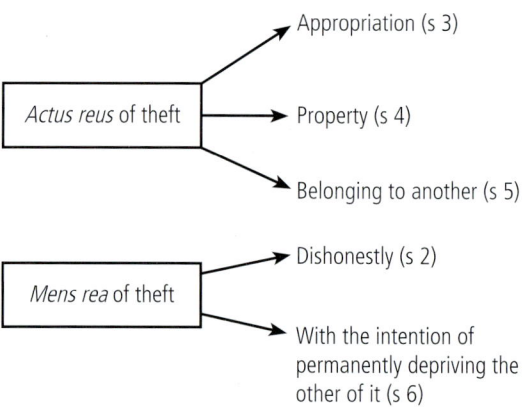

Figure 8.1 The elements of theft

8.2 'Appropriation'

Appropriation is the act of taking something. The more obvious situations of appropriation in theft involve a physical taking, for example a pickpocket taking a wallet from someone's pocket. A wide variety of acts can be considered as appropriation. They include the physical picking up of an item, destroying property, throwing items away, selling property, switching price labels on items, giving worthless cheques in payment for goods, receiving a gift and deciding to keep an item.

Section 3(1) states that:

❝ Any assumption by a person of the rights of an owner amounts to an appropriation, and this includes, where he has come by the property (innocently or not) without stealing it, any later assumption of a right to it by keeping or dealing with it as owner. 🙶

Taking goods from a shelf in a supermarket and placing them in one's pocket or own shopping bag is an example of an appropriation. This is clearly assuming the rights of an owner. It has been decided that the action of taking the goods from a shelf in a supermarket is of itself an appropriation. The issue of the shop's consent to this normal action of shopping is discussed at section 8.2.1 below.

The important words are 'any assumption by a person of the rights of an owner amounts to appropriation'. Under s 3(1), the word 'appropriation' is significant because it replaces the word 'taking' in the old law prior to the Act. Appropriation can apply to any of the rights of an owner, rather than necessarily taking all the rights of an owner. The question in any case revolves around what are the rights of the owner and have they been taken. As any of an owner's rights can be appropriated, the courts have been able to take a very wide interpretation of appropriation.

Tip

Remember appropriation alone does not constitute theft. It is only one of the five elements that must be proved for there to be theft.

The rights of the owner include selling the property or destroying it as well as possessing it, consuming it, using it, lending it or hiring it out. So for there to be appropriation, the thief must do something which assumes (takes over) at least one of the owner's rights. This can be seen clearly in the case of *R v Vinall* (2011), a robbery case.

R v Vinall (2011)

Two young men were out cycling when they encountered the defendants, who subjected them to verbal abuse and then punched one from his bike, made other threats and then chased them for a short distance. The defendants walked away, one of them having picked up the bike. The bike was left by a bus shelter some 15 metres further on and the police stopped them about half a mile away. The appeal against conviction raised issues of appropriation, intention permanently to deprive, and the time at which, and the purpose for which, force was used in determining whether robbery had been committed.

With respect to appropriation, the Court of Appeal stated either of two actions could be regarded as a sufficient assumption of the rights of owner:

- the initial taking of the bike
- the subsequent act of abandoning the bike.

The rights of an owner also include the right to sell property. An appropriation by assuming the right to sell is demonstrated by the case of *R v Pitham and Hehl* (1977).

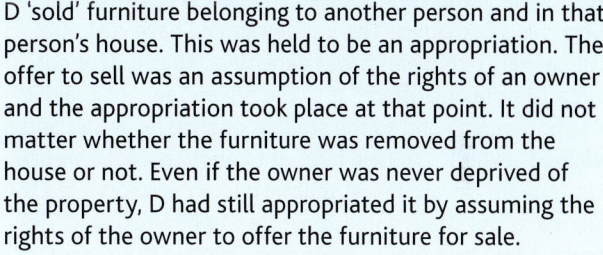

R v Pitham and Hehl (1977)

D 'sold' furniture belonging to another person and in that person's house. This was held to be an appropriation. The offer to sell was an assumption of the rights of an owner and the appropriation took place at that point. It did not matter whether the furniture was removed from the house or not. Even if the owner was never deprived of the property, D had still appropriated it by assuming the rights of the owner to offer the furniture for sale.

The right to destroy property is also an owner's right. This means that if D destroys property belonging to another person, D can be charged with theft, although D has also, of course, committed the separate offence of criminal damage. Similarly, if the property is not destroyed but merely thrown away, there is an infringement of the owner's rights.

The wording in s 3(1) is 'any assumption by a person of the rights of an owner'. Does the assumption have to be of all of the rights or can it just be of any of the rights? This was considered in *R v Morris* (1983).

R v Morris (1983)

D had switched the price labels of two items on the shelf in a supermarket. He had then put one of the items, which now had a lower price on it, into a basket provided by the store for shoppers and taken the item to the checkout, but had not gone through the checkout when he was arrested. His conviction for theft was upheld as the owner's right to put a price label on the goods was a right that had been assumed.

So it is clear that there does not have to be an assumption of all the rights of an owner.

8.2.1 Consent to the appropriation

Can a defendant appropriate an item when it has been given to him or her by the owner? The Theft Act 1968 does not state that the appropriation has to be without the consent of the owner, even though the previous law was that theft could only occur where owners did not consent to the taking. So, what is the position where the owner has allowed the defendant to take something because the owner thought that the defendant was taking what was owed to him or her? This point was considered in *Lawrence v Commissioner for Metropolitan Police* (1972) where the court stated appropriation was an assumption of any of an owner's rights, taking place regardless of whether the owner consents.

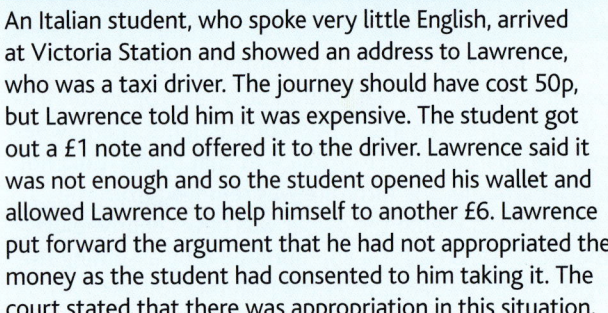

Lawrence v Commissioner for Metropolitan Police (1972)

An Italian student, who spoke very little English, arrived at Victoria Station and showed an address to Lawrence, who was a taxi driver. The journey should have cost 50p, but Lawrence told him it was expensive. The student got out a £1 note and offered it to the driver. Lawrence said it was not enough and so the student opened his wallet and allowed Lawrence to help himself to another £6. Lawrence put forward the argument that he had not appropriated the money as the student had consented to him taking it. The court stated that there was appropriation in this situation.

In *R v Morris*, the whole system of supermarket shopping is shown to rely on the customer taking goods from shelves and the idea of the 'honest shopper'. This means that there is an implied consent from shops operating a self-service style of shopping to customers removing items from shelves or petrol from a pump for the purpose of purchasing the goods at the price stated. Switching labels involves an interference with the goods that is not consented to. We would all consider this a dishonest

action so whether there was an appropriation seems a curious defence, but perhaps the key point is that a different offence, such as fraud, may have been more appropriate.

The point was considered again in the case of *R v Gomez* (1993), from which it can be seen that any removal of goods from a shelf in a shop is an appropriation.

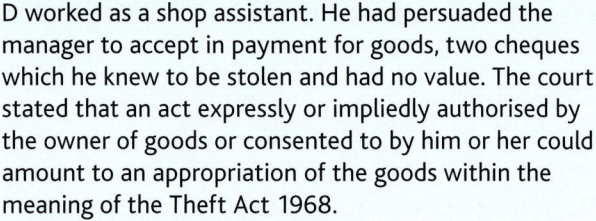

R v Gomez (1993)

D worked as a shop assistant. He had persuaded the manager to accept in payment for goods, two cheques which he knew to be stolen and had no value. The court stated that an act expressly or impliedly authorised by the owner of goods or consented to by him or her could amount to an appropriation of the goods within the meaning of the Theft Act 1968.

So, to have committed an *appropriation*, the defendant need not do anything contrary to the owner's *apparent* wishes. The issue of theft will still depend on, for example, dishonesty, and usually what the defendant is doing is not consistent with the victim's actual wishes (because V does not usually know the facts behind D's actions).

8.2.2 Consent without deception – the problem of gifts

So does the decision in *Gomez* (1993) extend to situations where a person has given property to another without any deception being made? This was the problem raised in the case of *R v Hinks* (2000).

R v Hinks (2000)

D, aged 38, was friendly with John Dolphin, aged 53, who was of limited intelligence, but understood the concept of ownership of property and making a valid gift. D described herself as Mr Dolphin's main carer. In the period April to November 1996 Mr Dolphin withdrew sums totalling around £60,000 from his building society account and deposited them in D's account. Mr Dolphin also gave D a television set. During the summer of that year Mr Dolphin made withdrawals of the maximum permissible sum of £300 every day so that he lost most of his savings and moneys inherited from his father. The House of Lords decided that even though there was a valid gift, there was an appropriation. The question remained as to whether an ordinary member of the public would see the act as dishonest for there to be theft.

A major argument against the ruling in *Hinks* is that in civil law the gift was valid, and the £60,000 and the television set belonged to the defendant. Lord

Steyn, in the leading judgment, accepted that this was the situation but he considered it to be irrelevant to the decision.

8.2.3 When does appropriation take place?

Another effect of the decision in *Gomez* is that the appropriation is viewed as occurring at one specific point in time. We have already seen that in the case of *R v Vinall* (2011). The reason that this is important is that criminal law has a basic principle of coincidence of *actus reus* and *mens rea*. The later act, in a case such as *Vinall*, might be the relevant one if, for example, it was impossible to prove an intention permanently to deprive at the time of the initial taking of the bike.

This is further illustrated by the case of *R v Atakpu and Abrahams* (1994), where it can be seen that appropriation occurs the first time a person assumes the rights of the owner. The defendants were still assuming the right of an owner by continuing to drive the cars and by bringing them into this country. However, the court did not say that the appropriation was a continuing act.

R v Atakpu and Abrahams (1994)

The defendants hired cars in Germany and Belgium using false driving licences and passports. They were arrested at Dover and charged with theft. The Court of Appeal quashed their convictions because the moment of appropriation under the law in *Gomez* was when they obtained the cars. So the thefts had occurred outside the jurisdiction of the English courts and as the defendants had already stolen the cars in Germany and Belgium, keeping and driving them in England was not a new appropriation – a later assumption of the right of an owner or a continuing act.

8.2.4 A later assumption of a right

Section 3(1) makes it clear that there can also be an appropriation where the defendant acquires property without stealing it, but then later decides to keep or deal with the property as owner. The appropriation in this type of situation takes place at the point of 'keeping' or 'dealing'.

This could occur where the defendant hires a drill from a tool hire shop, but instead of returning it decides to keep it. He or she is acting as though he or she is the owner with the right to keep the drill.

Dealing in the property could occur where the defendant borrows a cycle (or other property) but then sells it or gives it away. This can also happen where the defendant hires a car. If he or she sells it

instead of returning it, then he or she has dealt with it as an owner.

The effect of the interpretations of appropriation are that there can be seen to be a just result, even though the practical applications can appear to be inconsistent and not reflect the idea of contemporaneity of *actus reus* and *mens rea*.

Activity

Discuss whether there has been an appropriation in each of the following situations:

1 Jake has had an argument with his neighbour. When his neighbour is out, Jake holds an auction of the neighbour's garden tools. The neighbour returns before any of the tools are taken away.

2 Saskia goes shopping at the local supermarket and takes her five-year-old son, Tom, with her. While at the checkout Tom takes some bars of chocolate from a shelf and puts them in his pocket. Saskia does not realise Tom has done this until she finds the chocolate when they get home. Saskia decides she will not take the chocolate back to the supermarket.

3 The owner of a shop asks Parvati, who is a lorry driver, to pick up a load of computer equipment and take it to a warehouse. Parvati agrees to do this but, after collecting the equipment, she decides not to take it to the warehouse but to sell it for cash.

4 Otto, aged 18, is infatuated with Harriet, a married woman aged 32. Otto uses his student loan to buy expensive presents for Harriet. She knows he is a student and has very little money but she accepts the gifts from him.

8.3 'Property'

For there to be theft, the defendant must have appropriated 'property'. Section 4 gives a very comprehensive definition of property, which means that almost anything can be stolen. The definition is in s 4(1) of the Theft Act 1968: '"Property" includes money and all other property real or personal, including things in action and other intangible property.'

Section 4 lists five types of items which are included in the definition of 'property'. These are:

- money
- real property
- personal property
- things in action
- other intangible property.

In this list, 'money' means coins and banknotes of any currency.

'Personal property' covers all moveable items such as books, jewellery, clothes and cars, as well as trivial items such as a sheet of paper.

It was even held in *R v Kelly and Lindsay* (1998) that dead bodies and body parts can be personal property for the purposes of theft. The law has also recognised that regenerative body materials, such as hair (*R v Herbert* (1961)), blood (*R v Rothery* (1976)) and urine (*R v Welsh* (1974)), can be the subject of property rights and are capable of being stolen in certain circumstances.

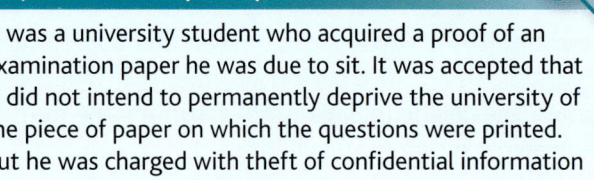

R v Kelly and Lindsay (1998)

Kelly was a sculptor who asked Lindsay to take body parts from the Royal College of Surgeons where he worked as a laboratory assistant. Kelly made casts of the parts. They were convicted of theft and appealed on the point of law that body parts were not property. The Court of Appeal held that, though a dead body was not normally property within the definition of the Theft Act 1968, the body parts were property as they had acquired 'different attributes by virtue of the application of skill, such as dissection or preservation techniques, for exhibition or teaching purposes'.

8.3.1 Real property

Real property is the legal term for land and buildings. Under s 4(1), land can be stolen, but s 4(2) states that this can only be done in three particular circumstances, for example where someone not in possession of the land severs anything forming part of the land from the land. So, it is theft to dig up turf from someone's lawn or to dismantle a wall and take the bricks. In 1972, a man was prosecuted for stealing Cleckheaton railway station by dismantling it and removing it – he was in fact acquitted, but there was no doubt that the station could be property under the Theft Act 1968 definition.

8.3.2 Things in action

A thing in action is a right which can be enforced against another person by an action in law. The right itself is property under the definition in s 4. An example is a bank account. The customer has a right to demand the actual money equivalent to the extent of the credit in the account or to the extent of any agreed unexceeded overdraft limit. So, if the defendant causes the bank to debit another person's account, he or she has appropriated a thing in action. Similarly, a credit card account holder also has a thing in action to the unexceeded limit of the card/account. This can be appropriated too, by unauthorised use.

A cheque itself is a thing in action, but it is also a piece of paper – this is property which can be stolen, and it is a 'valuable security' which can also be stolen under the definition of property.

8.3.3 Other intangible property

This refers to other rights which have no physical presence but can be stolen under the Theft Act 1968. For example, the Act creates a separate offence with respect to electricity. The courts have accepted that confidential information cannot be stolen, as seen in *Oxford v Moss* (1979), where knowledge of the questions on an examination paper was held not to be property.

Oxford v Moss (1979)

D was a university student who acquired a proof of an examination paper he was due to sit. It was accepted that D did not intend to permanently deprive the university of the piece of paper on which the questions were printed. But he was charged with theft of confidential information (the knowledge of the questions). He was found not guilty.

8.3.4 Things which cannot be stolen

There are some things which cannot be stolen except in specific circumstances. These are set out in ss 4(3) and 4(4) of the Theft Act 1968. These include plants, but only those growing wild, so it is possible to steal cultivated plants. Taking apples from trees in a farmer's orchard would be theft, but picking blackberries growing wild in the hedgerow around the field would not be theft unless it was done for sale or reward or other commercial purpose.

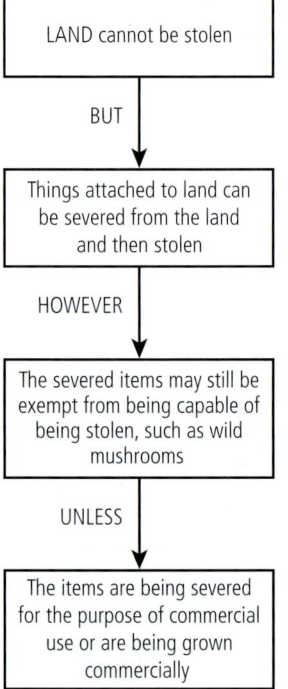

Figure 8.2 Theft of and from land

Activity

Explain whether the items in each of the following situations would be property for the purposes of theft.

1 Arnie runs a market stall selling flowers. Just before Christmas, he picks a lot of holly from a wood, intending to sell it on his stall. He then digs up a small fir tree for his own use. On his way home, he sees some late flowering roses in a garden and picks them to give to his girlfriend.

2 Della discovers the examination papers she is to sit next week in the next-door office. She writes out the questions from the first paper on her own notepad. The second paper is very long, so she uses the office photocopier to take a copy, using paper already in the machine.

8.4 'Belonging to another'

In order for there to be a theft of the property, that property must 'belong to another'. However, s 5(1) of the Theft Act 1968 gives a very wide definition of what is meant by 'belonging to another' so that possession or control of the property or any proprietary interest in it is sufficient. One reason for making it wide ranging is so that the prosecution does not have to prove who the legal owner is.

8.4.1 Possession or control

Obviously, the owner of property normally has possession and control of it, but there are many other situations in which a person can have either possession or control of property. Someone who hires a car has both possession and control during the period of hire. If the car is stolen during this time then the thief can be charged with stealing it from the hirer. Equally, as the car-hire firm still owns the car (a proprietary right), the thief could be charged with stealing it from them.

The possession or control of the item does not have to be lawful. Where B has stolen jewellery from A and subsequently C steals it from B, B is in possession or control of that jewellery and C can be charged with stealing it from B. This is useful where it is not known who the original owner is, as C can still be guilty of theft. This wide definition of 'belonging to' has led to the situation in which an owner was convicted of stealing his own car, in R v Turner (No. 2) (1971).

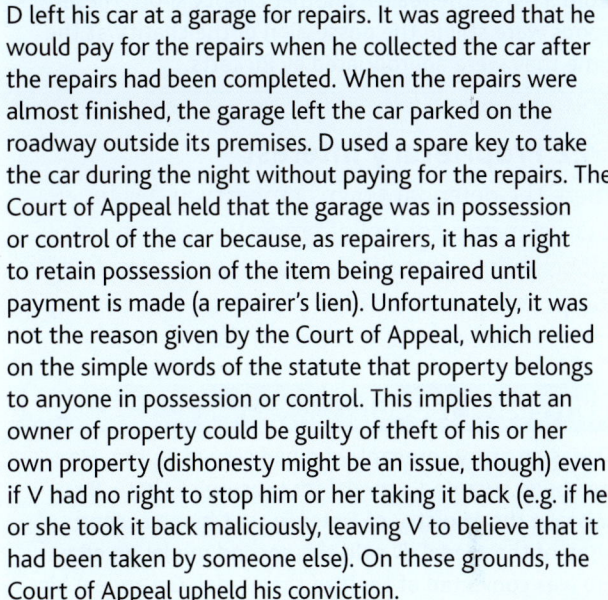

R v Turner (No. 2) (1971)

D left his car at a garage for repairs. It was agreed that he would pay for the repairs when he collected the car after the repairs had been completed. When the repairs were almost finished, the garage left the car parked on the roadway outside its premises. D used a spare key to take the car during the night without paying for the repairs. The Court of Appeal held that the garage was in possession or control of the car because, as repairers, it has a right to retain possession of the item being repaired until payment is made (a repairer's lien). Unfortunately, it was not the reason given by the Court of Appeal, which relied on the simple words of the statute that property belongs to anyone in possession or control. This implies that an owner of property could be guilty of theft of his or her own property (dishonesty might be an issue, though) even if V had no right to stop him or her taking it back (e.g. if he or she took it back maliciously, leaving V to believe that it had been taken by someone else). On these grounds, the Court of Appeal upheld his conviction.

It is possible for someone to be in possession or control of property even though he or she does not know it is there. This happened in R v Woodman (1974).

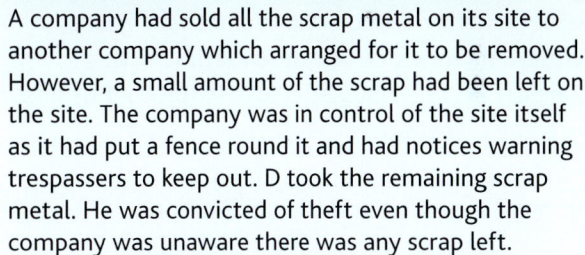

R v Woodman (1974)

A company had sold all the scrap metal on its site to another company which arranged for it to be removed. However, a small amount of the scrap had been left on the site. The company was in control of the site itself as it had put a fence round it and had notices warning trespassers to keep out. D took the remaining scrap metal. He was convicted of theft even though the company was unaware there was any scrap left.

Where goods are left for someone, the goods belong to the original owner until the new owner takes possession of them. This occurred in a case involving items left for collection outside the door of a charity shop in R (on the application of Ricketts) v Basildon Magistrates' Court (2010).

R (on the application of Ricketts) v Basildon Magistrates' Court (2010)

In the first offence, Ricketts had taken bags containing items of property from outside a charity shop. He argued that the original owner had abandoned the property and, therefore, it did not belong to another. The court ruled that the goods had not been abandoned – the giver had attempted to deliver them to the charity and delivery would only be complete when the charity took possession. Until then, they were the property of the giver.

In the second offence, Ricketts had taken bags of goods from a bin at the rear of another charity shop. These goods were still in the possession of the charity at the time they were appropriated by Ricketts.

8.4.2 Proprietary interest

Where the defendant owns property and is in possession and control of property, he or she can still be guilty of stealing it if another person has a proprietary interest in it. This point was the key matter in the case of *R v Webster* (2006).

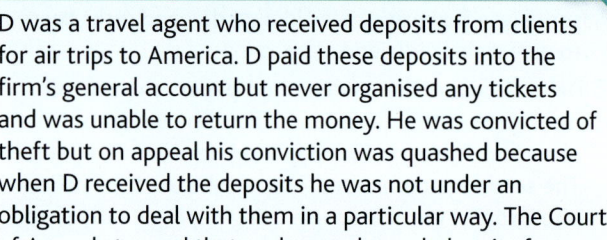

R v Webster (2006)

D was an army sergeant who had served in Iraq. He had been awarded a medal for his service there. By mistake the Ministry of Defence sent him a second copy of the medal. D sold this second medal on eBay. He was convicted of theft of the medal. On appeal his conviction was upheld on the basis that the Ministry of Defence had retained an equitable interest in the medal. In other words, the Ministry still had a proprietary interest in the medal.

Section 5 makes it clear that in certain situations a defendant can be guilty of theft even though the property may not 'belong to another'. These are situations in which the defendant is acting dishonestly and has caused a loss to another or has made a gain. These are:

- trust property, where a trustee can steal it
- property received under an obligation
- property received by another's mistake.

8.4.3 Property received under an obligation

There are many situations in which property (usually money) is handed over to the defendant on the basis that he or she will keep it for the owner or will deal with it in a particular way. Subsection 5(3) of the Theft Act 1968 tries to make sure that such property is still considered to 'belong to the other' for the purposes of the law of theft.

Under this subsection, there must be an obligation to retain and deal with the property in a particular way. So, where money is paid as a deposit to a business, the prosecution must prove that there was an obligation to retain and deal with those deposits in a particular way. If the person paying the deposit only expects it to be paid into the bank account of the business, then if that is what happens, there cannot be theft, even if all the money from the

account is used for other business expenses and the client does not receive the goods or service for which he or she paid the deposit. The key aspect of this is then the question of dishonesty if an offence is to be established. An example can be seen in *R v Hall* (1972).

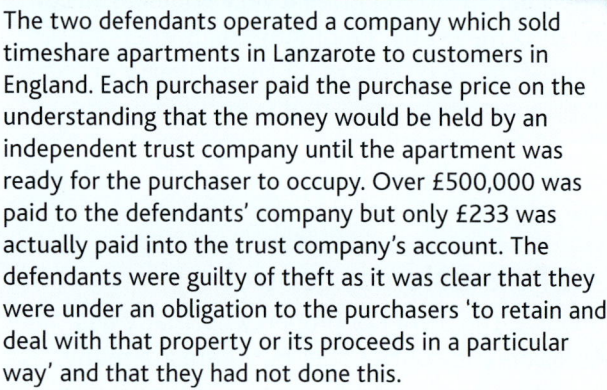

R v Hall (1972)

D was a travel agent who received deposits from clients for air trips to America. D paid these deposits into the firm's general account but never organised any tickets and was unable to return the money. He was convicted of theft but on appeal his conviction was quashed because when D received the deposits he was not under an obligation to deal with them in a particular way. The Court of Appeal stressed that each case depended on its facts.

In *R v Klineberg and Marsden* (1999), there was a clear obligation to deal with deposits in a particular way.

R v Klineberg and Marsden (1999)

The two defendants operated a company which sold timeshare apartments in Lanzarote to customers in England. Each purchaser paid the purchase price on the understanding that the money would be held by an independent trust company until the apartment was ready for the purchaser to occupy. Over £500,000 was paid to the defendants' company but only £233 was actually paid into the trust company's account. The defendants were guilty of theft as it was clear that they were under an obligation to the purchasers 'to retain and deal with that property or its proceeds in a particular way' and that they had not done this.

There can be an obligation in less formal situations, such as paying a shared bill. This was shown by *Davidge v Bunnett* (1984).

Davidge v Bunnett (1984)

D was given money by her flatmates to pay the gas bill but instead she used it to buy Christmas presents. There was a legal obligation to deal with the money in a particular way and, as she had not fulfilled that obligation, she was guilty of theft.

8.4.4 Property received by a mistake

Section 5 also provides for situations where property has been handed over to D by another's mistake and so has become D's property. If there were no special provision in the Act then this could not be 'property belonging to another' for the purposes of the law of theft.

This section was considered in *Attorney-General's Reference (No. 1 of 1983) (1985)*.

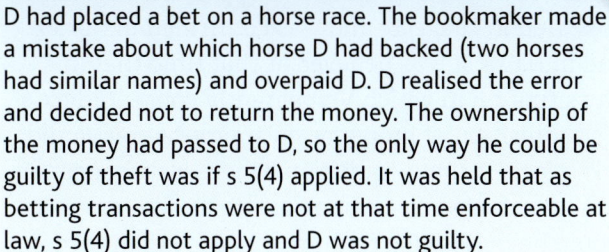

Attorney-General's Reference (No. 1 of 1983) (1985)

D, a police woman, had received an overpayment of wages when her pay went into her bank account. She recognised it was an overpayment. She did not withdraw any part of the money, but did not return it. She was convicted of theft of the property (a thing in action) as she was under an obligation to return it.

There must be a legal obligation to restore the property. In some situations there is no legal obligation to restore money. This is shown by *R v Gilks* (1972).

R v Gilks (1972)

D had placed a bet on a horse race. The bookmaker made a mistake about which horse D had backed (two horses had similar names) and overpaid D. D realised the error and decided not to return the money. The ownership of the money had passed to D, so the only way he could be guilty of theft was if s 5(4) applied. It was held that as betting transactions were not at that time enforceable at law, s 5(4) did not apply and D was not guilty.

Figure 8.3 Key cases chart on belonging to another

Case	Facts	Law
R v Turner (No. 2) (1971)	D left his car for repair at a garage He agreed he would pay for the repairs when he collected the car He used a spare key to take the car from the garage without paying	An owner can steal his or her own property if another has possession of it
R v Woodman (1974)	Site owners had arranged for all scrap metal on the site to be removed Unknown to them a small amount was left and this was stolen by D	A person or business can be in possession or control of property even though they do not know the property is on their land
R v Webster (2006)	An army sergeant was sent a duplicate medal by mistake He sold it	The Ministry of Defence retained an equitable interest in the medal so D was guilty of theft
R v Hall (1972)	A travel agent received travel deposits from customers He paid the money into the firm's general account and did not arrange tickets for the customers	D was not under an obligation to deal with the deposits in a particular way under s 5(3) and so was not guilty of theft
R v Klineberg and Marsden (1999)	Money was paid for timeshare apartments on the understanding that the money would be held in an independent trust The money was instead paid into the company's general account	Where there was a clear obligation to deal with property in a particular way, D was guilty of theft if that property was dealt with in a different way
Davidge v Bunnett (1994)	D was given money by her flatmates to pay the gas bill She did not pay the bill but used the money to buy Christmas presents	Even though this was an informal arrangement, there was a clear obligation to deal with property in a particular way D was guilty of theft when the money was dealt with in another way
Attorney-General's Reference (No. 1 of 1983) (1985)	An overpayment was made by D's employers into her bank account	By s 5(4), D was under an 'obligation to make restoration' If she did not then there was an appropriation of the property Whether D was guilty of theft would depend on whether or not she acted dishonestly
R v Gilks (1972)	D was overpaid for winnings on a bet He realised the error and decided not to make repayment	There was no legal obligation to restore the money as betting transactions were not at that time enforceable at law This meant that s 5(4) did not apply and D was not guilty of theft

8.4.5 The operation of s 5(3) and s 5(4) today

These sections were enacted at a time when it was not appreciated that the courts would adopt the extensive interpretation of appropriation that appeared in *Lawrence* and was confirmed in *Gomez* and in *Hinks*. It was believed at that time that in any situation in which V apparently consented to D's acquisition of property, no appropriation would take place. If that acquisition (whether dishonest or not) transferred ownership (not just possession), it would be impossible for him or her to commit theft by anything that he or she subsequently did with the property, of which he or she was now owner. In these circumstances, either s 5(3) or s 5(4) might have some relevance. If the requirements for either were met, then it would restore the possibility of theft by continuing to regard the original owner as still the owner (notionally) – or s 5(3) the intended recipient of the property as now the owner (notionally) – so that there could be a later appropriation of property 'belonging to another' by D.

However, under the law as now interpreted, those subsections will often be unnecessary. D will appropriate property from V as soon as he or she assumes the rights of an owner, even with consent (e.g. just laying hands on the money) and if he or she was dishonest at that point and intended permanently to deprive, he or she would be guilty of theft. For example, in *Gilks* now, if he knew he was getting an overpayment as he took it, and if he could be regarded as dishonest in those circumstances, he would be guilty of theft immediately, and without need to resort to s 5(4).

8.5 'Dishonestly'

The first point which needs to be proved for the *mens rea* of theft is that when the defendant appropriated the property he or she did it dishonestly. Because of the problems arising from making appropriation so wide, proof of dishonesty is now the main distinguishing point between theft and an honest appropriation.

There is no definition of what is meant by dishonesty in the Act. Section 1(2) states that 'it is immaterial whether the appropriation is made with a view to gain, or is made for the thief's own benefit'.

In other words, if all the elements of theft are present, the motive of the defendant is not relevant. This means that a modern-day Robin Hood stealing to give to the poor would be guilty of theft. The defendant does not have to gain anything from the theft.

The Act does set out behaviour which is *not* dishonest, despite the difficulty of proving something through a negative.

8.5.1 Behaviour which is not dishonest

The Theft Act 1968 gives three situations in which the defendant's behaviour is not considered dishonest.

Section 2(1) provides that a person's appropriation of property belonging to another is not to be regarded as dishonest if he or she appropriates the property in the belief that:

- he or she has in law the right to deprive the other of it, on behalf of him- or herself or of a third person (s 2(1)(a))
- he or she would have the other's consent if the other knew of the appropriation and the circumstances of it (s 2(1)(b)), or
- the person to whom the property belongs cannot be discovered by taking reasonable steps (s 2(1)(c)).

All these three situations depend on the defendant's belief. It does not matter whether it is a correct belief or even whether it is a reasonable belief. If the defendant has a genuine belief in one of these three, then he or she is not guilty of theft.

The first exception requires an honest, but not necessarily reasonable, belief by the defendant of his or her right to take the item. This is a subjective test, so the sole concern is for the defendant to convince a jury that he or she reasonably held that belief. An example of this is where an employee is instructed to collect goods from a third party. The employee honestly believes he or she has the legal right to do so (having been told to so by his or her boss) and therefore will not be dishonest in taking the goods even if, in fact, there is no such right to do so.

An example of this can be seen in the case of *R v Small* (1987), where the defendant noticed an old car parked in the road for some time with the key in the ignition. Parts were missing, and there was no petrol in it. The defendant thought the car had been dumped and therefore decided to get it going and drive it. His defence to stealing the car was that he believed it had been abandoned by its owner and therefore he had a legal right to take it. However, the owner could have been found from the registration number (this is why this case is different to one falling within the third exception). In fact, this was not the case; nevertheless, he was not guilty of theft.

The second exception requires an honest belief that the owner of the goods would consent if he or she knew of the circumstances. An example of this is borrowing your friend's ruler without asking, using it and then returning it, or continuing a habitual practice of borrowing tools and machinery between neighbours.

The third exception most usually applies in situations of finding items and then keeping them. This requires an honest belief by the defendant that the owner cannot be found by taking reasonable steps. An example would be finding a £1 coin in the street. Here, there is usually an honest belief that the owner could not reasonably be found, but that would not be so if the defendant had just seen someone pull the coin out of their pocket along with a handkerchief. Clearly, the more valuable the item, the less likely the owner cannot reasonably be found.

Where these exceptions do not apply, the courts have developed a test for what amounts to dishonesty. There is usually little argument about whether an act is dishonest – for example, shoplifting is obviously dishonest and a jury would have little difficulty with that.

However, defendants from time to time claimed that they had not been dishonest and there was no standard test that should be applied. Examples include borrowing from the petty cash at work without permission and contrary to the company rules but intending to replace the money the next day, or borrowing from the till and leaving an IOU. This test is discussed in 8.5.3 below.

What is an unreasonable belief?

It has been held in *R v Small* (1987) that the fact that the belief was an unreasonable one does not prevent the defendant from relying on these sections. If the jury decides that the defendant did have a genuine belief, even though an unreasonable one, in one of the three situations then he or she must be found not guilty.

R v Small (1987)

D took a car. He said he believed it to be abandoned as it had been left for two weeks in the same place. It was unlocked with the keys in the ignition. There was no petrol in the tank and the battery and tyres were flat. D put petrol in the tank and drove it off. As he was driving away he saw police flashing their lights at him. He panicked and ran away. He said it was not until he saw the police that he thought the car might have been stolen. He was convicted of theft.

The conviction was quashed because the question to consider was whether D had an honest belief that the owner could not be found.

A person will not be considered dishonest where he or she believes he or she has in law the right to deprive the other of the property. *R v Holden* (1991) and *R v Robinson* (1977) illustrate this 'claim of right' defence.

R v Holden (1991)

D was charged with the theft of scrap tyres from Kwik Fit where he worked. He claimed that other people had taken tyres with the permission of the supervisor. However, taking tyres was a sackable offence. The Court of Appeal quashed his conviction. As the test is subjective, a person was not dishonest if he or she believed, reasonably or not, that he or she had a legal right to the property, providing that belief is genuinely held.

R v Robinson (1977)

D was owed £7 by the victim's wife. When D went to collect the money, a fight developed between D and her husband, during which a £5 note dropped out of the husband's pocket. D kept the £5 note. His conviction for robbery was quashed by the Court of Appeal as there was no theft (an underlying part of robbery) because he had an honest belief that he was entitled to the money.

8.5.2 Willing to pay

In some situations, the defendant may say that he or she is willing to pay for the property or may, on taking property, leave money to pay for it. This does not prevent the defendant's conduct from being dishonest, as s 2(2) states that 'a person's appropriation of property belonging to another may be dishonest notwithstanding that he is willing to pay for the property'.

This prevents the defendant taking what he or she likes, regardless of the owner's wishes.

8.5.3 The *Ghosh* test for dishonesty

The case of *R v Ghosh* (1982) is the leading case on what is meant by 'dishonestly'. In this case, the Court of Appeal set out the tests to be used.

Tip

You need to know the *Ghosh* test precisely, as it is used for both theft and robbery (among other offences).

R v Ghosh (1982)

D was a doctor acting as a locum consultant in a hospital. He claimed fees for an operation he had not carried out. He said that he was not dishonest as he was owed the same amount for consultation fees. The Court of Appeal decided that the test for dishonesty has both an objective and a subjective element to it:

- Was what was done dishonest according to the ordinary standards of reasonable and honest people?
- Did the defendant realise that what he or she was doing was dishonest by those standards?

The first stage of the *Ghosh* test requires the jury to consider whether what was done was dishonest according to the ordinary standards of reasonable and honest people. This has the odd effect that if the jury thinks it is not dishonest, then the defendant will be found not guilty, even though he or she may have thought he or she was being (and intended to be) dishonest.

The second part of the test is not totally subjective, as the defendant is judged by what he or she realised ordinary standards were. This prevents a defendant from saying that, although he or she knew that ordinary people would regard his or her actions as dishonest, he or she did not think that those standards applied to him or her.

In a trial, the judge will use the *Ghosh* test to direct the jury only where there is an issue about dishonesty.

However, the second part of the *Ghosh* test is now in doubt following the unanimous decision of the Supreme Court in the civil case of *Ivey v Genting Casinos Ltd t/a Crockfords* (2017).

Lord Hughes (with whom Lord Neuberger, Lady Hale, Lord Kerr and Lord Thomas agreed) stated in paragraph 74:

" [There are] ... convincing grounds for holding that the second leg of the test propounded in *Ghosh* does not correctly represent the law and that directions based upon it ought no longer to be given. The test of dishonesty is as set out by Lord Nicholls in *Royal Brunei Airlines Sdn Bhd v Tan* and by Lord Hoffmann in *Barlow Clowes* ... When dishonesty is in question the fact-finding tribunal must first ascertain (subjectively) the actual state of the individual's knowledge or belief as to the facts. The reasonableness or otherwise of his belief is a matter of evidence (often in practice determinative) going to whether he held the belief, but it is not an additional requirement that his belief must be reasonable; the question is whether it is genuinely held. When once his actual state of mind as to knowledge or belief as to facts is established, the question whether his conduct was honest or dishonest is to be determined by the fact-finder by applying the (objective) standards of ordinary decent people. There is no requirement that the defendant must appreciate that what he has done is, by those standards, dishonest. "

As this is a civil case, the decision is only *obiter* with respect to the criminal law, although it is likely that it will eventually become a criminal law precedent. The Supreme Court did away with the second limb of the *Ghosh* test, thus making what the defendant thought about how others would regard his or her actions irrelevant.

The problems of applying the *Ghosh* test of dishonesty were shown in the case of *DPP v Gohill* (2007).

DPP v Gohill (2007)

The defendants were manager and assistant manager of an outlet hiring plant and equipment to customers. They had allowed some customers to borrow equipment for periods of less than two hours without charge. These hirings were recorded by the defendants on the computer. However, when the customer returned the item within two hours, the defendants had either recorded that it had been returned as faulty or incorrectly chosen (for which no charge was made under the company's rules) or, in some cases, they altered the computer records to show that the item had only been reserved and not actually borrowed.

The defendants stated that they regarded this as good customer service which kept customers who frequently hired happy. It was not done for personal gain and they did not ask for any money for doing this. Sometimes the customer would tip them £5 or £10 but at other times they were not given any money by the customer.

The magistrates acquitted the defendants of theft and false accounting on the basis stating that they 'were not satisfied beyond reasonable doubt that by the ordinary standards of reasonable and honest people [they] had acted dishonestly'.

The Divisional Court allowed the prosecution's appeal against the acquittal. The court held that the behaviour of the defendants was dishonest by the ordinary standards of reasonable and honest people and they sent the case back for retrial by a new bench of magistrates.

This case shows that even magistrates and judges cannot agree on what is dishonest, so it is even more likely that juries will have very different views on what is dishonest.

8.6 'Intention of permanently depriving'

The final element that has to be proved for theft is that the defendant had the intention permanently to deprive the other of the property. In many situations there is no doubt that the defendant had such an intention, for example where an item is taken and sold to another person or where cash is taken and spent by the defendant. This last example is true even if the defendant intends to replace the money later, as was shown in *R v Velumyl* (1989).

R v Velumyl (1989)

D, a company manager, took £1050 from the office safe. He said that he was owed money by a friend and he was going to replace the money when that friend repaid him. The Court of Appeal upheld his conviction for theft as he had the intention of permanently depriving the company of the banknotes which he had taken from the safe, even if he intended replacing them with other banknotes to the same value later.

Another situation where there is a clear intention to permanently deprive is where the defendant destroys property belonging to another. This can be charged as theft, although it is also criminal damage.

There are, however, situations where it is not so clear and, to help in these, s 6 of the Theft Act 1968 explains and expands the meaning of the phrase. It provides that, even though a person appropriating property belonging to another does not mean the other permanently to lose the thing itself, he or she can be regarded as having the intention to permanently deprive the other of it if his or her intention is to treat the thing as his or her own to dispose of, regardless of the other's rights.

In *DPP v Lavender* (1994), the court ruled that the dictionary definition of 'dispose of' was too narrow, as a disposal could include 'dealing with' property.

DPP v Lavender (1994)

D took doors from a council property which was being repaired and used them to replace damaged doors in his girlfriend's council flat.

The doors were still in the possession of the council but had been transferred without permission from one council property to another. Here D was dealing with the doors as his own by moving them from one property to another without permission.

8.6.1 Borrowing or lending

Another difficulty with s 6 is the point at which 'borrowing or lending' comes within the definition. Normally borrowing would not be an intention to permanently deprive, such as where a student takes a textbook from a fellow student's bag in order to read one small section and then replaces the book.

Section 6 states that borrowing is not theft unless it is for a period and in circumstances making it equivalent to an outright taking or disposal. In *R v Lloyd* (1985), it was held that this meant borrowing the property and keeping it until 'the goodness, the virtue, the practical value … has gone out of the article'.

R v Lloyd (1985)

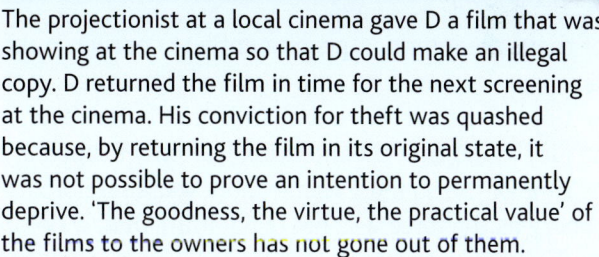

The projectionist at a local cinema gave D a film that was showing at the cinema so that D could make an illegal copy. D returned the film in time for the next screening at the cinema. His conviction for theft was quashed because, by returning the film in its original state, it was not possible to prove an intention to permanently deprive. 'The goodness, the virtue, the practical value' of the films to the owners has not gone out of them.

From this it appears that, in the example of the data usage, it can be argued that there would be an intention to permanently deprive if all the data allowance had been used up, but not otherwise.

If someone dishonestly takes property belonging to another, does it matter whether he or she intends permanently to deprive that person of the property? This would make it possible to convict of theft in situations such as *R v Lloyd* (1985) above, where a film was copied and then returned. On the present law, Lloyd was not guilty, yet he had appropriated property belonging to another, was being dishonest, as the only reason for the appropriation was to take an illegal copy, and temporarily deprived the other of his property.

Conditional intent

Another difficulty is where the defendant examines property to see if there is anything worth stealing. What is the position if he or she decides it is not worth stealing and returns it? This is what happened in *R v Easom* (1971).

R v Easom (1971)

D picked up a handbag in a cinema, rummaged through the contents and then replaced the handbag without having taken anything. His conviction for theft of the handbag and its contents was quashed. There was no evidence that the defendant had intended to permanently deprive the owner of the bag or items in it so he could not be guilty of theft.

See Chapter 10, section 10.3 on the point of whether a defendant in the situation of *Easom* can be guilty of attempted theft.

8.6.2 Intent permanently to deprive and throwing things away

We have seen this in the case of *R v Vinall* (2011) (see 8.2 above).

For theft, the intention permanently to deprive could have been formed when the bike was first taken or at the time of the subsequent abandonment. However, if the jury found that the intention was only formed at the time of the abandonment, there was therefore no robbery as the force was not used 'immediately before' the theft, and nor was it used 'in order to' steal.

Vinall can be compared with *Easom*, in which the handbag was replaced approximately in the position from which it had been removed.

Pitchford LJ explained the situation as follows:

> If the prosecution is unable to establish an intent permanently to deprive at the moment of taking it, it may nevertheless establish that the defendant exercised such a dominion over the property that it can be inferred that at the time of the taking he intended to treat the property as his own to dispose of regardless of the owner's rights.)

Subsequent 'disposal' of the property may be evidence either of an intention at the time of the taking or evidence of an intention at the time of the disposal. When the allegation is theft, a later appropriation will suffice; when the allegation is robbery, it almost certainly will not. The manner in which the property was disposed of is evidence supporting the inference of the section 6(1) intention. In *The Chief Constable of Avon and Somerset Constabulary v Smith* (1984), the defendants broke into a parked car and removed two cases. Having searched them they concealed the cases, one in a nearby hedge and the other in a public lavatory cubicle. The court stated that there plainly was evidence capable of establishing intent, at the time the cases were taken from the car, permanently to deprive the owner of them. There was clearly evidence capable of amounting to an intention, at that moment, to treat the briefcases as the respondent's own, to dispose of regardless of the true owner's rights. They were in fact so disposed of. They were not taken back to the car. In *Easom* the replacement of the handbag, could not support the inference.

Figure 8.4 Key facts chart on theft

Section of Theft Act 1968	Definition	Comment/cases
s 1	A person is guilty of theft if he or she dishonestly appropriates property belonging to another with the intention of permanently depriving the other of it	Full definition of theft D is charged under this section
s 2	Dishonesty 1 Not dishonest if D believes: ■ he or she has a right in law (s 2(1)(a)) ■ he or she would have the other's consent (s 2(1)(b)) ■ the owner cannot be discovered (s 2(1)(c)) 2 Can be dishonest even if D intends to pay for property	No definition of 'dishonesty' in the Act *Ghosh* (1982) two-part test: ■ Is it dishonest by ordinary standards? ■ If so, did D know it was dishonest by those standards?
s 3	Appropriation 'Any assumption of the rights of an owner' Includes a later assumption of rights	Held to be assumption of any of the rights of an owner: *Gomez* (1993) Given 'neutral' meaning, so consent irrelevant: *Lawrence* (1972), *Hinks* (2000)
s 4	Property Includes money and all other property real or personal, including things in action and other intangible property Land cannot be stolen except by trustee or tenant or by severing property from land Wild mushrooms, fruit, flowers and foliage cannot be stolen unless done for commercial purpose Wild animals cannot be stolen unless tamed or in captivity	
s 5	Belonging to another Property is regarded as belonging to any person having possession or control or any proprietary right Property belongs to the other where it is received under an obligation to retain and deal with it in a particular way Property received by a mistake where there is a legal obligation to make restoration belongs to the other	Not limited to owner: *Turner (No. 2)* (1972) stole his own car *Hall* (1972), *Klineberg and Marsden* (1999) *Attorney-General's Reference (No. 1 of 1983)* (1985) Must be a legal obligation: *Gilks* (1972)
s 6	Intention to permanently deprive Treat the thing as his or her own to dispose of regardless of the other's rights Dispose of includes 'dealing with' property	The 'goodness' or practical value must have gone from the property: *Lloyd* (1985) *DPP v Lavender* (1994)

Activity

In each of the following situations, explain whether all the elements of theft are present.

1 Roland works in a small factory where there are only 20 employees. One day he finds a small purse in the washroom. He opens it. It contains a £10 note and some coins. There is no name or other identification in it. Roland decides to keep the money as he does not think he can find the owner.

2 Venus comes from a country where property placed outside a shop is meant for people to take free of charge. She sees a rack of clothes on the pavement outside a shop and takes a pair of jeans from it.

3 Natalie is given a Christmas cash bonus in a sealed envelope. She has been told by her boss that the bonus would be £50. When she gets home and opens the envelope she finds there is £60 in it. She thinks her employer decided to be more generous and so keeps the money. Would your answer be different if:

   ■ Natalie realised there had been a mistake but did not return the money, or
   ■ the amount in the envelope was £200?

4 Errol is given permission by his employer to borrow some decorative lights for use at a party. Errol also takes some candles without asking permission. When putting up the lights Errol smashes one of them. He lights two of the candles so that by the end of the evening they are partly burnt down. One of the guests admires the remaining lights and asks if he can have

them to use at a disco at the weekend. Errol agrees to let him take the lights.

5 Jabez is late for work one day so he takes his neighbour's bicycle to get to work on time. His neighbour is away, but Jabez has used the bicycle on previous occasions. He intends returning it that evening when he comes home from work. Jabez parks the bicycle at the back of the shop where he works. When he leaves work in the evening he finds that the lamp and the pump have been taken from the bicycle and it has been damaged. He is frightened to return the bicycle in this state so he throws it into the local canal.

6 Advise whether Conrad is liable for theft in respect of the following situations:

Conrad works in an electronics shop. At the end of his shift he takes £100 out of the till as he is going on a night out. He plans to replace the money in the morning before the shop opens. On his way home, Conrad goes into a clothes shop and finds a pair of designer jeans he likes. They cost £120 but Conrad swaps the label with that on another pair of jeans, which cost £65.

Conrad then goes into a supermarket where he puts some small items into his trolley. On the way round he takes and eats a chocolate bar from a display. At the till, Conrad pays for the items in his trolley. Conrad then goes home. On the way he picks some flowers from a garden to give to his girlfriend.

7 Discuss the problems caused by the word 'appropriation' in the definition of theft.

Summary

■ Theft is defined by s 1 of the Theft Act 1968.
■ In order to prove theft there must be:
   – appropriation
   – of property
   – belonging to another
   – with the intention of permanently depriving that other of it, and
   – dishonesty.
■ Appropriation occurs where there is an assumption of the rights of an owner.
■ Property includes money and all other property real or personal.
■ Things which cannot be stolen include:
   – knowledge
   – mushrooms, flowers, fruit and foliage growing wild (unless taken for commercial purposes)
   – wild creatures who are not in captivity
   – electricity.
■ Property belongs to another if he or she has possession of control of it or any proprietary interest in it or it has been received under an obligation or by mistake.
■ Dishonesty is not defined in the Theft Act 1968. The *Ghosh* test states that the defendant is dishonest if:
   – what was done was dishonest according to the ordinary standards of reasonable and honest people, and
   – D realised that what he or she was doing was dishonest by those standards.
■ D is regarded as having the intention to permanently deprive if it is his or her intention to treat the thing as his or her own to dispose of.

9 Robbery

After reading this chapter, you should be able to:
- Understand the *actus reus* of robbery under s 8 of the Theft Act 1968
- Understand the *mens rea* of robbery under s 8 of the Theft Act 1968
- Apply the law on robbery to scenario-based situations

9.1 Defining robbery

A robber is often depicted in cartoons as running away with a bag of swag. The robber is not distinguished from the thief or the burglar. However, **robbery** can be seen as theft with violence, such as in the Great Train Robbery where the train driver suffered severe head injuries at the hands of the robbers.

The three men arrested in connection with the Great Train Robbery leaving Linslade Court

Robbery is an offence under s 8 of the Theft Act 1968. It is a theft which is aggravated by the use or threat of force. Section 8 states:

> A person is guilty of robbery if he steals, and immediately before or at the time of doing so, and in order to do so, he uses force on any person or puts or seeks to put any person in fear of being then and there subjected to force.

So the elements which must be proved for robbery are for the *actus reus*:
- theft
- force or putting or seeking to put any person in fear of force.

In addition, there are two conditions on the force: it must be immediately before or at the time of the theft, and it must be in order to steal.

For the *mens rea* of robbery it must be proved that the defendant:
- had the *mens rea* for theft, and
- intended to use force to steal.

Key term

Robbery – theft with the use or threat of force.

9.1.1 Completed theft

There must be a completed theft for a robbery to have been committed. This means that all the elements of theft have to be present. If any one of them is missing then, just as there would be no theft, there is no robbery. For example, there is no theft in the situation where the defendant takes a car, drives it a mile and abandons it because he or she has no intention permanently to deprive. Equally, there is no robbery where the defendant uses force to take that car. There is no offence of theft, so using force cannot make it into robbery, as in *R v Zerei* (2012).

R v Zerei (2012)

D and another man approached V, whom they knew, and told him that they were going to take his car. D then pulled a knife, punched V and took his car keys. D drove the car off. The car was found abandoned (but undamaged) about one kilometre away. D was convicted of robbery (which requires a theft) but the conviction was quashed on appeal. The Court of Appeal held that the trial judge had misdirected the jury on the issue of intention to permanently deprive. The judge had given the jury the impression that a forcible taking was enough to show an intention to permanently deprive and this is not the law. Also the judge had failed to deal with the fact that D had abandoned the car not far away.

Another case on this point is *R v Waters* (2015).

R v Waters (2015)

D snatched V's phone from her and told her that she could have it back if one of her friends would speak to D. The police were immediately called to the scene and D was charged and convicted of robbery. The Court of Appeal quashed the conviction because the evidence did not establish an intention to permanently deprive V of her phone. D's condition for returning the phone could have been 'fulfilled in the near future'. This meant that there was no theft and, therefore, no robbery.

The case of *R v Robinson* (1977), seen in Chapter 8, section 8.5.1, also demonstrates that if the elements of theft are not complete, then there cannot be robbery.

Where force is used to steal, then the moment the theft is complete there is a robbery. This is demonstrated by the case of *Corcoran v Anderton* (1980).

Corcoran v Anderton (1980)

One of the defendants hit a woman in the back and tugged at her bag. She let go of the bag and it fell to the ground. The defendants ran off without the bag (because the woman was screaming and attracting attention). It was held that the theft was complete so the defendants were guilty of robbery.

However, if the theft is not completed, for instance if the woman in the case of *Corcoran v Anderton* had not let go of the bag, then there is an attempted theft and the defendant could be charged with attempted robbery.

9.1.2 Force or threat of force

As well as theft, the prosecution must prove force or the threat of force. The amount of force can be small. This is clearly shown by the case of *R v Dawson and James* (1976).

R v Dawson and James (1976)

One of the defendants pushed the victim, causing him to lose his balance which enabled the other defendant to take his wallet. They were convicted of robbery. The Court of Appeal held that 'force' was an ordinary word and it was for the jury to decide if there had been force.

This decision was confirmed in *R v Clouden* (1987).

R v Clouden (1987)

The Court of Appeal held that D was guilty of robbery when he had wrenched a shopping basket from the victim's hand. The Court of Appeal held that the trial judge was right to leave the question of whether D had used force on a person to the jury.

It can be argued that using force on the bag was effectively using force on the victim as the bag was wrenched from her hand. However, if a thief pulls a shoulder bag so that it slides off the victim's shoulder, would this be considered force? Probably not. It would certainly not be force if a thief snatched a bag which was resting (not being held) on the lap of someone sitting on a park bench.

This view is supported by *P v DPP* (2012).

P v DPP (2012)

D snatched a cigarette from V's hand without touching V in any way. It was held that as there had been no direct contact between D and V, it could not be said that force had been used 'on a person'; therefore D was not guilty of robbery.

The situation in *P v DPP* is similar to pickpocketing, where the victim is unaware of any contact. However, where the pickpocket (or accomplice) jostles the victim to distract him or her while the theft is taking place, there is force which could support a charge of robbery rather than theft.

The definition of robbery makes clear that robbery is committed if the defendant puts or seeks to put a person in fear of force. It is not necessary that the force be applied. Putting the victim 'in fear of being there and then subjected to force' is sufficient for robbery. This covers threatening words, such as 'I have a knife and I'll use it unless you give me your wallet', and threatening gestures, such as holding a knife in front of the victim.

Robbery is also committed even if the victim is not actually frightened by the defendant's actions or words. If the defendant seeks to put the victim in fear of being then and there subjected to force, this element of robbery is present. So if the victim is a plain-clothes policeman put there to trap the defendant and is not frightened, the fact that the defendant sought to put the victim in fear is enough.

A case illustrating the fact that the victim does not have to be frightened and also that the amount of force does not have to be great is *B and R v DPP* (2007).

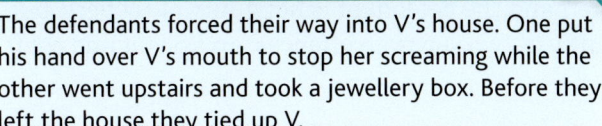

B and R v DPP (2007)

V, a schoolboy aged 16, was stopped by five other school boys. They asked for his mobile phone and money. As this was happening, another five or six boys joined the first five and surrounded the victim. No serious violence was used against V, but he was pushed and his arms were held while he was searched.

The defendants appealed against their convictions for robbery on the basis that no force had been used and V had not felt threatened. The Divisional Court upheld the convictions for robbery on the grounds that:

- there was no need to show that V felt threatened; the defendant only has to seek to put any person in fear of being then and there subjected to force
- there could be an implied threat of force; in this case, surrounding V by so many created an implied threat
- in any event, there was some limited force used by holding V's arms and pushing him.

'On any person'

This means that the person threatened does not have to be the person from whom the theft occurs. An obvious example is an armed robber who enters a bank, seizes a customer and threatens to shoot that customer unless a bank official gets money out of the safe. This is putting a person in fear of being then and there subjected to force. The fact that it is not the customer's property which is being stolen does not matter.

9.1.3 Force immediately before or at the time of the theft

The force must be immediately before or at the time of stealing. This raises two problems. First, how immediate does 'immediately before' have to be? Consider the situation where a bank official is attacked at his or her home by a gang in order to steal keys and security codes. The gang then drives to the bank and steals money. The theft has taken place an hour after the use of force. Is this 'immediately before'? It would seem sensible that the gang should be convicted of robbery. But what if the time delay were longer, as could happen if the attack on the manager was on Saturday evening and the theft of the money not until 24 hours later. Does this still come within 'immediately before'? There have been no decided cases on this point.

The second problem has come in deciding the point at which a theft is completed, so that the force is not 'at the time of stealing'. This was considered in *R v Hale* (1979).

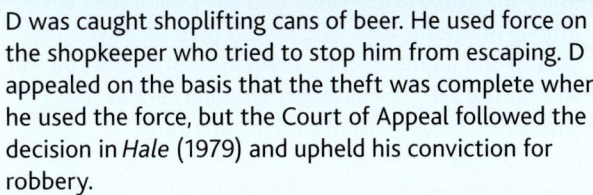

R v Hale (1979)

The defendants forced their way into V's house. One put his hand over V's mouth to stop her screaming while the other went upstairs and took a jewellery box. Before they left the house they tied up V.

Here there was force immediately before the theft when one of the defendants put his hand over V's mouth. Tying up V could also be force in order to steal, as the theft was still ongoing.

The decision in *Hale* was followed in *R v Lockley* (1995).

R v Lockley (1995)

D was caught shoplifting cans of beer. He used force on the shopkeeper who tried to stop him from escaping. D appealed on the basis that the theft was complete when he used the force, but the Court of Appeal followed the decision in *Hale* (1979) and upheld his conviction for robbery.

As shown in the cases of *Hale* (1979) and *Lockley* (1995), the courts have been prepared to view appropriation as a continuing act. In *Lockley*, the defendant used force to escape after he had stolen. Despite the fact that the appropriation for the theft occurred before the force, the Court of Appeal still held that the defendant was guilty of robbery. This conflicts with the courts' approach in theft cases, particularly *R v Atakpu and Abrahams* (1994) (see Chapter 8, section 8.2.3).

But there must be a point when the theft is complete and so any force used after this point does not make it robbery. What if in *Lockley* the defendant had left the shop and was running down the road when a passer by (alerted by the shouts of the shopkeeper) tried to stop him, and the defendant then used force on the passer-by to escape? Surely the theft is completed before this use of force. The force used is a separate act to the theft and does not make the theft a robbery. The force will, of course, be a separate offence of assault.

9.1.4 Force in order to steal

The force must be used in order to steal. So if the force was not used for this purpose, then any later theft will not make it into robbery. Take the situation where the defendant has an argument with the victim and punches him or her, knocking him or her out. The defendant then sees that some money has fallen out of the victim's pocket and decides to take it. The force was not used for the purpose of that theft and the defendant is not guilty of robbery, but guilty of two separate offences: an assault and theft.

9.1.5 *Mens rea* for robbery

The defendant must have the *mens rea* for theft: this means he or she must be dishonest and he or she must intend to permanently deprive the other of the property. He or she must also intend to use force to steal.

Activity

Explain whether or not a robbery has occurred in each of the following situations.

1 Albert holds a knife to the throat of a three-year-old girl and orders the child's mother to hand over her purse or he will 'slit the child's throat'. The mother hands over her purse.

2 Brendan threatens staff in a post office with an imitation gun. He demands that they hand over the money in the till. One of the staff presses a security button and a grille comes down in front of the counter so that the staff are safe and Brendan cannot reach the till. He leaves without taking anything.

3 Carla snatches a handbag from Delia. Delia is so surprised that she lets go of the bag and Carla runs off with it.

4 Ellie breaks into a car in a car park and takes a briefcase out of it. As she is walking away from the car, the owner arrives, realises what has happened and starts to chase after Ellie. The owner catches hold of Ellie, but she pushes him over and makes her escape.

5 Freya tells Harmid to hand over his Rolex watch and, that if he does not, Freya will send her boyfriend, Grant, round to beat Harmid up. Harmid knows that Grant is a very violent man. Harmid takes his watch off and gives it to Freya.

Figure 9.1 Key facts chart for robbery

Element	Law	Case
Theft	There must be a completed theft; if any element is missing there is no theft and therefore no robbery	*R v Robinson* (1977)
	The moment the theft is completed (with the relevant force) there is robbery	*Corcoran v Anderton* (1980)
Force or threat of force	The jury decides whether the acts amounted to force, using the ordinary meaning of the word	*R v Dawson and James* (1976)
	It includes wrenching a bag from V's hand	*R v Clouden* (1987)
On any person	The force can be against any person	
	It does not have to be against the victim of the theft	
Immediately before or at the time of the theft	For robbery, theft has been held to be a continuing act	*R v Hale* (1979)
	Using force to escape can still be at the time of the theft	*R v Lockley* (1995)
In order to steal	The force must be in order to steal	
	Force used for another purpose does not become robbery if D later decides to steal	
Mens rea	*Mens rea* for theft plus an intention to use force to steal	

Activity

1 Blake is angry with Conroy. Blake lies in wait and attacks Conroy, knocking him unconscious. When Conroy is unconscious, Blake notices that Conroy is wearing a very expensive watch and decides to steal the watch. Discuss whether Blake is liable for the offence of robbery.

2 Explain the need for there to be a theft in order for the offence of robbery to be committed.

Summary

- Robbery is defined by s 8 of the Theft Act 1968 as stealing and using or threatening force immediately before or at the time.
- There must a completed theft.
- The defendant must use force or put or seek to put any person in fear of force.
- The force must be immediately before or at the time of the theft.
- The amount of force can be small.
- The defendant must intend to steal and intend to use force to steal.

10 Preliminary offence: attempt

10.1 What is meant by 'an attempt'?

An attempt is where a person tries to commit an offence but, for some reason, fails to complete it. For example, the defendant fires a gun at the victim, intending to kill the victim. Just as the defendant pulls the trigger, the victim stoops to tie her shoelace. The bullet misses the victim and goes over her head. The defendant intended to kill the victim but has not succeeded, so the defendant cannot be charged with murder as the victim is still alive. However, it is obvious that the defendant ought to be criminally liable for some offence. It would be ridiculous if he were just allowed to go free. The defendant is clearly a dangerous person and should be liable under the criminal law. In this type of situation the defendant can be charged with attempted murder.

A case example of an attempt to commit murder is *R v White* (1910).

R v White (1910)

D put cyanide in his mother's drink, intending to kill her. She died of a heart attack before she could drink it. He tried to commit murder but did not actually kill his mother. He was convicted of attempted murder.

10.1.1 Definition of 'attempt'

'Attempt' is now defined by s 1(1) of the Criminal Attempts Act 1981 which states:

> If, with intent to commit an offence to which this section applies, a person does an act which is more than merely preparatory to the commission of the offence, he is guilty of attempting to commit the offence.

A charge of attempting to commit an offence can only be brought if the full offence is one which is triable on indictment including an either way offence charged via an indictment. In general, offences which are triable summarily only cannot be the subject of an attempt.

As with all offences, the prosecution must prove the *actus reus* and the *mens rea*. The definition above sets these out. They are:

■ *Actus reus* – a person does an act which is more than merely preparatory to the commission of the offence
■ *Mens rea* – with intent to commit that offence.

Key term

Attempt – in criminal law, an attempt occurs where a person with the relevant *mens rea* does an act which is more than merely preparatory to the commission of an offence.

10.2 *Actus reus* of attempt

The act that the defendant commits has to be more than merely preparation for the main crime. Some acts are obviously mere preparation, but other acts are more difficult to categorise.

Let's take the example where the defendant decides to rob a bank. First, he buys himself a shotgun and converts it into a sawn-off shotgun. Both the buying and the converting are 'merely preparatory'. Next, he drives around the area, checking escape routes. Again, this is 'merely preparatory'.

On the day of the robbery, the defendant steals a car ('merely preparatory') and drives to the bank (still 'merely preparatory'). He stands on the pavement outside the bank, carrying the sawn-off shotgun in a bag. This is getting nearer, but, according to the case of *R v Campbell* (1990) (see below), is still only 'merely preparatory'. Then he walks into the bank. Has he now gone beyond mere preparation and can he be charged with attempted robbery?

There have been many cases on the meaning of 'merely preparatory'. It is difficult to draw any general principle from them. In *Attorney-General's*

Reference (No. 1 of 1992) (1993), it was decided that the defendant need not have performed the last act before the crime proper, nor need he or she have reached the 'point of no return'.

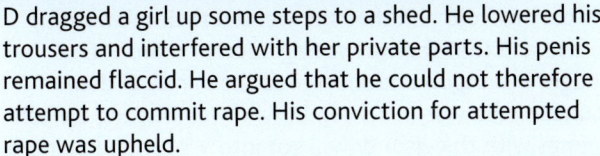

Attorney-General's Reference (No. 1 of 1992) (1993)

D dragged a girl up some steps to a shed. He lowered his trousers and interfered with her private parts. His penis remained flaccid. He argued that he could not therefore attempt to commit rape. His conviction for attempted rape was upheld.

Looking at the whole of D's acts, this seems a sensible decision. However, if he had been stopped immediately after he had dragged the girl to the shed, and before he lowered his trousers or interfered with her, then it is unlikely that he could have been convicted. His act of dragging her was probably 'merely preparatory'.

In *R v Gullefer* (1987), the Court of Appeal held that 'more than merely preparatory' means that the defendant must have gone beyond purely preparatory acts and be 'embarked on the crime proper'.

R v Gullefer (1987)

D jumped onto a race track in order to have the race declared void and so enable him to reclaim money he had bet on the race. His conviction for attempting to steal was quashed because his action was merely preparatory to committing the offence.

10.2.1 Cases showing mere preparation

The case of *R v Gullefer* (above) illustrates a situation in which D's acts were mere preparation. Although D had tried to interfere with the race, he had several other acts to do before the theft (the point at which he would get his betting money back). He had to go to one of the betting points and ask for his money back. Even just going towards the point would not be sufficient. However, asking for the money would change his actions into 'more than merely preparatory'. He would be guilty of attempted theft. It is worth noting that when the money was handed to him, he would then be guilty of the main offence of theft.

The Court of Appeal stated that an attempt begins when 'the merely preparatory acts have come to an end and the defendant embarks upon the crime proper'. It also pointed out that when this moment occurs will depend on the facts in any particular case.

The case of *R v Geddes* (1996) also illustrates acts which were only preparatory.

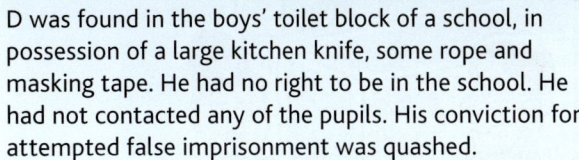

R v Geddes (1996)

D was found in the boys' toilet block of a school, in possession of a large kitchen knife, some rope and masking tape. He had no right to be in the school. He had not contacted any of the pupils. His conviction for attempted false imprisonment was quashed.

This case is difficult to justify. The defendant had no right to be on the premises. He had entered the school with all the equipment for falsely imprisoning a student. The next step would be for him to approach one of the students. If the law of attempt is to be effective in protecting people from the main offence, then surely he should have been guilty of an attempt at that point. Is it sensible to wait until he approaches one of the students?

However, the Court of Appeal thought that attempts should be considered by asking two questions:

■ Had the accused moved from planning or preparation to execution or implementation?
■ Had the accused done an act showing that he was actually trying to commit the full offence, or had he got only as far as getting ready, or putting himself in a position, or equipping himself, to do so?

Using these two questions, it can be seen that *Geddes* had not quite moved from planning or preparation to execution. Also, it can be argued that he had got only as far as getting ready, or putting himself in a position, to commit the full offence.

Another case which is perhaps even more difficult to justify is *R v Campbell* (1990).

R v Campbell (1990)

D, who had an imitation gun, sunglasses and a threatening note in his pocket, was in the street outside a post office. His conviction for attempted robbery was quashed.

The next step in this case would have been for D to enter the post office. Again, if the law of attempt is to be effective in protecting people from the main offence, surely he should have been guilty of an attempt at that point? Is it sensible to wait until he enters the post office? If the gun had been real then customers and staff in the post office would have been put at risk.

No, I'm not attempting to rob the bank.

10.2.2 Cases in which there was an attempt

The following three cases show situations where the defendant had gone beyond mere preparation. In each case, the defendants were held to be guilty of an attempt to commit the full offence.

R v Boyle and Boyle (1987)

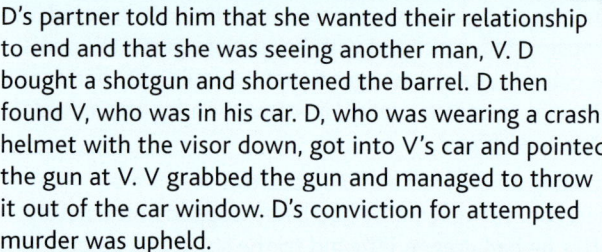

The defendants were found standing by a door of which the lock and one hinge were broken. Their conviction for attempted burglary was upheld.

The Court of Appeal held that the test to use was whether the defendant was embarking on the crime proper. In this case, once the defendants had entered they would be committing burglary, so trying to gain entry was an attempt.

R v Tosti (1997)

D intended to burgle premises. He took metal cutting equipment with him and hid it behind a hedge near to the premises. He then examined the padlock on the door. He did not damage the padlock. He was found guilty of attempted burglary.

The difference from *Campbell* for both these cases is that burglary is committed at the moment D enters as a trespasser with intent to steal (or do certain other offences). Robbery is not committed until D actually steals, in the course of which, and for which,

he uses force. Walking into a building still leaves another step before the crime proper is committed.

In the next case, *R v Jones* (1990), the defendant had done almost everything he could before committing the full offence.

R v Jones (1990)

D's partner told him that she wanted their relationship to end and that she was seeing another man, V. D bought a shotgun and shortened the barrel. D then found V, who was in his car. D, who was wearing a crash helmet with the visor down, got into V's car and pointed the gun at V. V grabbed the gun and managed to throw it out of the car window. D's conviction for attempted murder was upheld.

D tried to argue that, as the safety catch was still on, he had not done the last act before the crime proper. The Court of Appeal said that buying the gun, shortening it, loading it and disguising himself with the visor were all preparatory acts. But once D got into V's car and pointed the gun at V, then there was sufficient evidence to leave to the jury the question of whether there was an attempt.

It is not always easy to follow the reasoning in these decisions. The term 'more than merely preparatory' does not make it clear how one is to distinguish between acts which are 'merely preparatory' and those which are *more than* merely preparatory'. A good way to consider this is to start with the situation suggested by the facts as if they occur. At that point the offence would be committed and not just attempted. One can then work backwards to decide the point at which it can be said that an act has occurred that is more than just preparation for the offence.

Let us take the case of *Campbell* (1990) above:

1 If he entered the post office and showed the gun and the note to the person behind the counter and thus obtained money, there is clearly robbery.

2 If, having shown the gun and note, he did not obtain any money or changed his mind at that point, then there is no theft, so no robbery, but the acts are more than preparatory – attempted robbery.

3 If he went into the post office with his note and gun hidden, this is more problematic, although it would almost certainly be burglary. Burglary is not part of the AQA specification, but can be committed by someone entering a building as a trespasser (consider this as without permission for the purpose of the entry) and with the intention to steal something. The intention to

steal must be at the time of entry. With respect to attempted robbery, this would appear to be still merely preparatory

4 If he does not enter the post office, there should be no offence of robbery or burglary as the carrying of the note and the gun are merely preparatory to a robbery, and he has not entered the building for there to be a possible burglary.

Figure 10.1 Key cases chart on 'merely preparatory' in attempts

Case	Facts	Offence attempted	Law
Cases where there was sufficient evidence for an attempt			
Attorney-General's Reference (No. 1 of 1992) (1993)	D tried to rape a girl but could not get an erection	Rape	Need not have performed the last act
R v Boyle and Boyle (1987)	Standing by door with broken lock	Burglary	Had done part of a series of acts
R v Jones (1990)	Gun safety catch was left on	Murder	Sufficient evidence to leave the question of whether there was an attempt to the jury
Cases which were merely preparatory			
R v Gullefer (1987)	Disrupted race intending to reclaim bet	Theft	Has D 'embarked upon the crime proper'?
R v Geddes (1996)	In school with knife, rope and tape	False imprisonment	Has D 'actually tried to commit the offence in question'?
R v Campbell (1990)	Outside post office with imitation gun and threatening note	Robbery	Merely preparatory

10.3 *Mens rea* of attempt

For an attempt, the defendant must normally have the same intention as would be required for the full offence. If the prosecution cannot prove that the defendant had that intention then he or she is not guilty of the attempt. This was shown by the case of *R v Easom* (1971).

R v Easom (1971)

D picked up a woman's handbag in a cinema, rummaged through it, then put it back on the floor without removing anything from it. His conviction for theft of the bag and its contents was quashed. The Court of Appeal also refused to substitute a conviction for attempted theft of the bag and specific contents (including a purse and a pen), as there was no evidence that D intended to steal the items.

In this case, there was no evidence that D had intended permanently to deprive the owner of the bag or items in it (part of the required *mens rea* for theft). As a result, he could not be guilty of attempted theft.

A similar decision was made in the case of *R v Husseyn* (1977).

R v Husseyn (1977)

D and another man were seen loitering near the back of a van. When the police approached, they ran off. D was convicted of attempting to steal some sub-aqua equipment that was in the van. The Court of Appeal quashed his conviction.

The decisions by the Court of Appeal in both these cases can be criticised. Surely the defendant did intend to steal something? The fact that Easom did not do so (presumably because there was nothing really worth stealing) should not make him not guilty of attempting to steal. Equally, in the case of Husseyn, the fact that he ran off because the police arrived does not mean that he was not trying to steal.

These problems were resolved in *Attorney-General's Reference (Nos 1 and 2 of 1979) (1979)* where the Court of Appeal decided that if D had a conditional intent

(D intended stealing if there was anything worth stealing), D could be charged with an attempt to steal some or all of the contents. This is a technical procedural way around the problem.

So, Easom would now be charged with attempting to steal some or all of the contents of the bag, rather than the bag itself and specific items in it. Husseyn would be charged with attempting to steal some or all of the contents of the van. In this way they could be found guilty of attempted theft.

10.3.1 *Mens rea* of attempted murder

The *mens rea* for attempted murder involves proving a higher level of intention than for the full offence of murder. The full offence requires that the prosecution proves the defendant had the intention either to kill or to cause grievous bodily harm (GBH). However, for attempted murder, the prosecution must prove an intention to kill. An intention to cause serious harm is not enough. This means that the prosecution always has to prove the higher level of intention for attempted murder. This was shown by the case of *R v Whybrow* (1951).

> ### *R v Whybrow* (1951)
>
> The defendant wired up his wife's bath and caused her an electric shock. He was convicted of attempted murder. When he appealed, the court, although upholding his conviction, criticised the trial judge's summing up and stressed that only an intention to kill was sufficient for the *mens rea* of attempted murder.

The justification for this rule is on grounds of public policy and that a defendant should not be permitted to escape a conviction for murder if the evidence shows that death occurred as a direct result of their assault intended to result in GBH.

However, if no death occurs and there is evidence that the accused intended really serious harm, then this is a s 18 offence rather than attempted murder. In reality the effective sentence on conviction may not be very dissimilar and can be said to achieve justice.

10.3.2 Is recklessness enough for the *mens rea*?

What if it can be proved that the defendant was reckless? Is this sufficient for him or her to be guilty of an attempt? In *R v Millard and Vernon* (1987), it was decided that it was not sufficient.

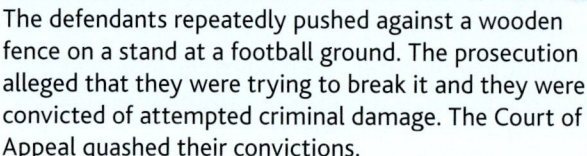

> ### *R v Millard and Vernon* (1987)
>
> The defendants repeatedly pushed against a wooden fence on a stand at a football ground. The prosecution alleged that they were trying to break it and they were convicted of attempted criminal damage. The Court of Appeal quashed their convictions.

Recklessness is not normally sufficient *mens rea* for an attempt. This is so even where recklessness would suffice for the completed offence. However, there appears to be an exception in that recklessness as to one part of the offence can be sufficient. This is illustrated by *Attorney-General's Reference (No. 3 of 1992)* (1994).

> ### *Attorney-General's Reference (No. 3 of 1992)* (1994)
>
> D threw a petrol bomb towards a car containing four men. The bomb missed the car and smashed harmlessly against a wall. D was charged with attempting to commit arson with intent to endanger life. The trial judge ruled that it had to be proved that D intended to damage property and to endanger life. D was acquitted.
>
> The Court of Appeal held that the trial judge was wrong. It was necessary to prove that D intended to damage property, but it was only necessary to prove that he was reckless as to whether life would be endangered.

However, this case has been criticised, not least by the Court of Appeal in *R v Pace and Rogers* (2014) where Davies LJ ruled 'that as a matter of ordinary language', the expression 'with intent to commit an offence' contained in s 1(1) 'connotes an intent to commit all the elements of the offence'.

There are some offences where recklessness is sufficient *mens rea* for the full offence. However, for an attempt of such offences, the prosecution must prove that the defendant had the *intent* to commit the offence.

10.4 Impossibility

In some situations, a person may intend to commit an offence and may do everything he or she possibly can to commit it, but in fact the offence is impossible to commit.

An example of this would be where the defendant goes to the victim's room and stabs the victim as he or she lies in bed. In fact, the victim died of a heart attack two hours before the defendant stabbed him or her. The defendant has merely stabbed a dead body. Murdering the victim is physically impossible so the defendant cannot be guilty of his or her murder, but can the defendant be guilty of attempting to murder the victim?

Under the common law before 1981, the House of Lords had held that where a crime was legally or physically impossible to commit, the defendant could not be guilty of attempting to commit it. When the Criminal Attempts Act 1981 was passed, it contained a subsection (s 1(2)) which was intended to close this loophole and make defendants guilty of an attempt even though the full offence was impossible.

Section 1(2) of the Criminal Attempts Act 1981 states: 'A person may be guilty of attempting to commit an offence … even though the facts are such that the commission of the offence is impossible.'

After the Act was passed, the House of Lords had to consider this section and the problem of attempting the impossible in the case of *Anderton v Ryan* (1985).

Anderton v Ryan (1985)

Mrs Ryan bought a video recorder very cheaply. She thought it was stolen. Later she admitted this to police who were investigating a burglary at her home. Her conviction was quashed because the video recorder was not in fact stolen.

The House of Lords held that even though Mrs Ryan had gone beyond merely preparatory acts, in fact all her acts were innocent. The video recorder was not stolen. On this basis, they thought that s 1(2) did not make her guilty.

However, less than a year later, the House of Lords overruled this decision in *R v Shivpuri* (1986).

R v Shivpuri (1986)

D agreed to receive a suitcase which he thought contained prohibited drugs. The suitcase was delivered to him, but it contained only snuff and harmless vegetable matter. D was convicted of attempting to be knowingly concerned in dealing with prohibited drugs.

This time, the House of Lords said that both ss 1(2) and 1(3) were relevant. Subsection 1(3) states:

In any case where–

a apart from this subsection a person's intention would not be regarded as having amounted to an intent to commit an offence; but

b if the facts of the case had been as he believed them to be, his intention would be so regarded, then, for the purpose of subsection (1) he shall be regarded as having an intent to commit that offence.

The combined effect of ss 1(2) and 1(3) of the Criminal Attempts Act 1981 meant that a person could be guilty of an attempt even if the commission of the full offence was impossible. In *R v Shivpuri* the facts as he believed them to be were that the suitcase contained prohibited drugs. He intended dealing in drugs so his intention, under s 1(3), was regarded as being an intention to commit that offence.

The House of Lords accepted that its decision in *Anderton v Ryan* (1985) had been wrong and they used the 1966 Practice Statement to overrule that decision.

Activity

Explain whether in each of the following scenarios there is an attempt to commit an offence.

1 Amir knows his girlfriend has been going out with Blake. Amir plans to disfigure Blake. He buys some acid which he intends to throw in Blake's face and then drives to Blake's house. As he is about to get out of the car, he sees a police car nearby. Amir immediately drives off.

2 Connor puts some poison in Donna's drink, intending to kill her. The amount he puts in the drink is insufficient to kill and Donna survives.

3 Faye sees a handbag in the ladies' cloakroom. She hopes there will be some money in it, so she opens it. In fact, the bag contains only make-up and tissues. Faye closes the bag and replaces it.

4 Greg and Hans are found in the garden of a house with masks, a torch and screwdrivers in their pockets. They admit they intended to burgle the house.

5 Ian fires a shot at Jani but misses her. He admits he intended to kill her.

Figure 10.2 Key facts chart on attempts

	Attempt	Case or statute
Definition of 'attempt'	With intent to commit an offence, a person does an act which is more than merely preparatory to the commission of the offence	s 1(1) of the Criminal Attempts Act 1981
'More than merely preparatory'	D must have embarked on the crime proper OR D must be trying to commit the full offence	*R v Gullefer* (1987) *R v Geddes* (1996)
Mens rea of attempt	D must have intention for the full offence A conditional intention is sufficient Recklessness is not normally sufficient BUT recklessness as to part of the offence may be sufficient.	*R v Easom* (1971) *Attorney-General's Reference (Nos 1 and 2 of 1979)* (1979) *R v Millard and Vernon* (1987) *Attorney-General's Reference (No. 3 of 1992)* (1994)
Attempting the impossible	ss 1(2) and 1(3) of the Criminal Attempts Act 1981 mean that D is guilty even if the full offence is legally or physically impossible	*R v Shivpuri* (1986)

Figure 10.3 AQA specification offences and the law on attempts

Offence	Indictable or either way charged as indictable offence	Can there be a charge of the attempted offence?
Murder	Yes	Yes
Involuntary manslaughter	Yes	Yes*
Unlawful and malicious wounding or infliction of GBH (s 18 OAPA 1861)	Yes	Yes
Unlawful and malicious wounding or causing of GBH (s 20 OAPA 1861)	No	No
Assault (as assault or battery) occasioning actual bodily harm (s 47 OAPA 1861)	Yes	Yes
Assault	No	No
Battery	No	No
Robbery	Yes	Yes
Theft	Yes	Yes

* With respect to involuntary manslaughter, the *actus reus* requires proof that D caused V's death, so the intention required for the attempt must be an intention to cause V's death. This is the *mens rea* for murder, so it would seem that there is no scope for a charge of attempted involuntary manslaughter, despite current practice.

Activity

1 Dan is very annoyed that Wayne has got a promotion at work instead of Dan. He decides to make life difficult for Wayne. He sets a booby trap on the door to Wayne's office, so that a book will fall when the door is opened. However, when Wayne tries to open the door it jams and the booby trap does not work.

Next Dan obtains what he believes is cocaine. In fact it is a harmless powder. He puts some in Wayne's coffee and Wayne drinks it.

Discuss whether Dan is liable for an attempt to cause actual bodily harm in these two situations.

2 Discuss the problems in the law on attempting the impossible.

Summary

Attempt is defined by s 1(1) of the Criminal Attempts Act 1981.

- The *actus reus* of attempt is doing an act which is more than merely preparatory to the commission of the offence.
- Prior to the 1981 Act, the courts had used several different tests of the *actus reus*. These tests are no longer law: the only test is the more than merely preparatory test.
- The *mens rea* of attempt is that the defendant must have the *mens rea* required for the full offence.
- For murder there must be an intention to kill.
- There can be a conditional intent – where the defendant intends to steal if there is something worth stealing.
- Recklessness is not normally sufficient for the *mens rea* of attempt.

Impossibility

- Originally the courts held that if the full offence was impossible to commit, then the defendant could not be guilty of an attempt.
- In *R v Shivpuri*, the courts overruled their previous decision and held that a person could be guilty of an attempt even though the commission of the full offence was impossible.

Points to note

- The courts have not been very clear in deciding the dividing line between what is 'merely preparatory' and what is an attempt.
- An attempt cannot be committed by an omission.
- Is only direct intention sufficient for the *mens rea* of attempt?
- The early decisions on *mens rea* left a loophole where the defendant intended to steal if he or she could find anything worth stealing.
- Should the defendant be guilty because of his or her intention, although it is impossible for him or her to commit the full offence?

11 Capacity defences

11.1 Insanity

The defence of insanity is a special defence. The defendant has to prove that he or she comes within the legal rules of insanity. If the defendant proves this, then there is a special verdict of 'not guilty by reason of insanity'.

11.1.1 The *M'Naghten* Rules

The rules on **insanity** are based on the *M'Naghten* Rules, set as a result of the decision in the case of 1843.

M'Naghten (1843)

D suffered from extreme paranoia. He thought he was being persecuted by the 'Tories' (the then Government). He tried to kill a member of the Government, Sir Robert Peel, but instead killed his secretary. Because of his mental state D was found not guilty of murder. In fact, he was committed to a mental hospital because of his mental state, but this was not as a result of the verdict. The fact that he could be found not guilty and need not have been sent to a mental hospital caused a public outcry, leading the judges in the House of Lords to answer a series of questions in order to clarify the law in respect of insanity. The answers to those questions have created the rules on insanity which are used in legal cases today.

The rules are that:
- 'in all cases every man is presumed to be sane and to possess a sufficient degree of reason to be responsible for his crimes.'
- the defendant must be 'labouring under such a defect of reason, from disease of the mind, as not to know the nature and quality of the act he was doing, or if he did know it, that he did not know he was doing what was wrong.'

From this it can be seen that three elements need to be proved. These are that the defendant was suffering from:
- a defect of reason,
- which must be the result of a disease of the mind
- which caused the defendant not to know the nature and quality of his or her act, or not to know he or she was doing wrong.

At the time of this case, medical knowledge of mental disorders was very limited and there is much greater knowledge about mental disorders today. It is suggested that a more modern definition of the defence should be used which agrees with medical opinions.

Key term

Insanity – a special defence to a criminal offence. The defendant must be labouring under such a defect of reason, from disease of the mind, as not to know the nature and quality of the act he or she was doing, or if he or she did know it, that he or she did not know he or she was doing what was wrong.

The burden of proving insanity is on the defence, and it must be proved on the balance of probabilities. Where a defendant is found to be insane, the verdict is 'not guilty by reason of insanity'. It is possible that this reverse burden of proof is in breach of Article 6 of the ECHR, which states that the defendant is innocent until proven guilty.

The jury has to decide if the defendant is insane or not. It is considered that this is not an appropriate function for a jury but should be decided by medical experts. Where there is dispute, the jury has to listen to medical evidence and try to understand technical and complex psychiatric issues. There is the possibility that jurors may be so revolted by the crimes committed that they will refuse to return the verdict of not guilty by reason of insanity. Especially in murder cases, jurors may disregard the medical evidence and, instead of returning the special verdict, find the defendant guilty of murder.

It used to be thought that insanity was a defence to all offences. However, in *DPP v H* (1997), where the defendant was charged with driving with excess alcohol, it was held that insanity is not a defence to offences of strict liability as no mental element is required to be proved.

11.1.2 Defect of reason

This means that the defendant's powers of reasoning must be impaired. If the defendant is capable of reasoning but has failed to use those powers, then this is not a defect of reason. This was decided in *R v Clarke* (1972), where it was held that the defect of reason must be more than absent-mindedness or confusion.

R v Clarke (1972)

D went into a supermarket, picked up three items including a jar of mincemeat, put them into her own bag and then left the store without paying. She was charged with theft but claimed in her defence that she lacked the *mens rea* for theft as she had no recollection of putting the items into her bag. Indeed, she did not even want the mincemeat as neither she nor her husband ate it. She said she was suffering from absent-mindedness caused by diabetes and depression. The trial judge ruled that this amounted to a plea of insanity, so she pleaded guilty to the theft but later appealed.

The Court of Appeal quashed the conviction and held that the phrase 'defect of reason' in the *M'Naghten* Rules applied only to 'persons who by reason of a "disease of the mind" are deprived of the power of reasoning'. The Court of Appeal also said that the rules of insanity do not apply to people who simply have moments of confusion or absent-mindedness. It might be appreciated now that confusion or absent-mindedness may be a precursor of something much more serious such as dementia, though there was no evidence of this in Clarke's case.

11.1.3 Disease of the mind

The defect of reason must be due to a disease of the mind. This is a legal term, not a medical one. The disease can be a mental disease or a physical disease which affects the mind. An example of this is seen in *R v Kemp* (1956).

R v Kemp (1956)

D was suffering from hardening of the arteries which caused a problem with supply of the blood to his brain which caused D to have moments of temporary loss of consciousness. During one of these moments he attacked his wife with a hammer causing her serious injury. He was charged with inflicting grievous bodily harm under s 20 OAPA 1861.

At his trial the question arose as to whether this condition came within the rules on insanity. D admitted that he was suffering from a 'defect of reason' but said that this was not due to a 'disease of the mind' as it was a physical illness causing the problem and not a mental illness. He was found 'not guilty by reason of insanity' and appealed. The Court of Appeal upheld this finding, stating that the law was not concerned with the brain but with the mind. Kemp's ordinary mental faculties of reason, memory and understanding had been affected and so his condition came within the rules on insanity.

In *R v Sullivan* (1984), the House of Lords was asked to decide whether epilepsy came within the rules of insanity.

R v Sullivan (1984)

D, aged 51, had suffered from epilepsy since childhood. He was known to have fits and had shown aggression to those trying to help him during a fit. He injured an 80-year-old man during a visit to a neighbour's flat. The trial judge ruled that he would be directing the jury to return a verdict of 'not guilty by reason of insanity'. Due to this, D pleaded guilty to assault occasioning actual bodily harm (s 47 OAPA 1861) but then appealed. Both the Court of Appeal and the House of Lords confirmed the conviction.

The House of Lords ruled that the source of the disease was irrelevant. It could be 'organic, as in epilepsy, or functional', and it did not matter whether the impairment was 'permanent or transient and intermittent', provided that it existed at the time at which the defendant did the act.

Organic insanity is when the brain has been damaged by a physical cause such as epilepsy or a degenerative disease like Alzheimer's. Functional insanity is when there is no organic reason for the damage to the brain.

This ruling means that, for the purpose of the *M'Naghten* Rules, the disease can be of any part of the body provided it has an effect on the mind. In *R v Hennessy* (1989), high blood sugar levels because of diabetes was classed as insanity because the sugar levels affected his mind.

R v Hennessy (1989)

D was a diabetic who had not taken his insulin for three days. He was seen driving a car which had been reported as stolen. He was charged with taking a motor vehicle without consent and driving while disqualified. He had no recollection of taking or driving the car. The judge ruled that D was putting forward a defence of insanity (and not non-insane automatism which

D suffering from defect of reason	+	Defect is due to disease of the mind	+	D does not know nature and quality of his or her action, or if he or she does know it, does not know it is wrong

Figure 11.1 The *M'Naghten* Rules

the defendant wanted to use as a defence (see section 11.2 below)). D then pleaded guilty and appealed on the grounds that he should have been allowed to put forward the defence of non-insane automatism. The Court of Appeal held that the correct defence was insanity as the diabetes was affecting his mind. As a result diabetes was brought within the definition of insanity.

Another case in which a condition amounted to insanity was *R v Burgess* (1991). In this case, it was decided that, in some instances, sleep-walking was within the legal definition of insanity.

R v Burgess (1991)

D and his girlfriend had been watching videos. They both fell asleep and, in his sleep, D attacked her. There was no evidence of any external cause for this sleep-walking and evidence was given that, in this case, it was due to an internal cause – a sleep disorder. The judge ruled that this was evidence of insanity and the defendant was found 'not guilty by reason of insanity'. The Court of Appeal agreed with this finding. However in some countries such as Canada, sleepwalking has been accepted as being within the defence of automatism, as argued by *Burgess*, rather than automatism and this would be more acceptable to the medical profession.

External factors

This is where the defendant is in a state where he or she does not know what he or she is doing due to an external cause. It does not amount to a disease of the mind and the defence of insanity does not apply. This can be shown in *R v Quick* (1973), where the defence of automatism applied.

R v Quick (1973)

D was a diabetic who had taken his insulin but had not eaten enough food. This caused him to have low blood sugar levels which affected his brain. D was a nurse at a mental hospital and assaulted a patient there. The Court of Appeal ruled that his condition did not come within the definition of insanity. It was caused by an external factor, the insulin, which meant that the correct defence was automatism (see section 11.2).

The decisions in *Hennessy* (1989) and *Quick* (1973) highlight the problems with the law. People with diabetes can go into an automatic state in which they do not know what they are doing. This state can be caused by:

- the disease itself, which causes high levels of blood sugar (hyperglycaemia), or
- taking insulin, which is used to control blood sugar levels. If, after taking insulin, the defendant fails to eat, the blood sugar level will become too low (hypoglycaemia).

If it is the disease which causes the automatic state then, as shown in *Hennessy* (1989), the correct defence is insanity as it is an internal cause. If it is the drug which causes the automatic state then, as shown in *Quick* (1973), it does not come within the rules on insanity but can rely on the defence of automatism.

It seems inconsistent that a physical disease such as diabetes should be classed as a condition of insanity, and that a diabetic has to rely on a different defence depending on whether it was the drug or the disease itself which caused the automatic state.

Voluntary intoxication and insanity

Where the defendant voluntarily takes an intoxicating substance and this causes a temporary psychotic episode, the defendant cannot use the defence of insanity. This is because the intoxicating substance is an external factor. The case of *R v Coley* (2013) illustrates this.

R v Coley (2013)

D, aged 17, was a regular user of cannabis and one evening watched a violent video game. Later that night he entered a neighbour's house and attacked her and her partner with a knife. When arrested he was calling for his mother and threatening suicide. He said he had blacked out and had no recollection of what had happened. The psychiatric evidence was that he could have suffered a brief psychotic episode induced by the taking of cannabis and that he might have been acting out the role of a character in the video game he had been playing.

The judge refused to leave the defence of insanity to the jury and D was convicted of attempted murder. The Court of Appeal upheld the conviction as they considered his state of mind was caused by voluntary intoxication and it was not a case of insanity. (See section 11.2.2 for further discussion of this case and self-induced automatism.)

11.1.4 Not knowing the nature and quality of the act

Nature and quality refer to the physical character of the act. There are two ways in which the defendant may not know the nature and quality of the act. These are:

- because he or she is in a state of unconsciousness or impaired consciousness, or
- when he or she is conscious but due to his or her mental condition he or she does not understand or know what he or she is doing.

If the defendant can show that either of these states applied to him or her at the time of the act, then he or she satisfies this part of the *M'Naghten* Rules.

An example of not knowing the nature and quality of the act could be where a nurse throws a baby onto a fire believing it to be piece of wood. A case of a defendant not knowing the nature and quality of his act was *R v Oye* (2013).

R v Oye (2013)

The police were called to a café where D was behaving oddly. He threw crockery at the police and was arrested and taken to a police station. At the police station D continued to behave oddly including drinking water out of a lavatory cistern. When the police moved D to the custody suite he became aggressive and punched a woman officer, breaking her jaw. D was charged with assault occasioning actual bodily harm and two charges of affray.

D's defence was that he believed the police had demonic faces and were agents of evil spirits. Medical evidence at the trial was that D had had a psychotic episode and that he had not known what he was doing and/or that he was doing wrong. Despite this evidence and the judge pointing out the defence of insanity, the jury convicted D. On appeal the Court of Appeal substituted a verdict of not guilty by reason of insanity.

This case also raised issues regarding the defence of self-defence that are dealt with in Chapter 12, section 12.1.

Where the defendant knows the nature and quality of the act, he or she still can use the defence of insanity if he or she does not know that what he or she did was wrong. Wrong, in this sense, means legally wrong not morally wrong. If the defendant knows the nature and quality of the act and that it is legally wrong, he or she cannot use the defence of insanity. This is so even if the defendant is suffering from a mental illness as shown by *R v Windle* (1952).

R v Windle (1952)

D's wife constantly spoke of committing suicide. One day the defendant killed her by giving her 100 aspirins. He gave himself up to the police and said, 'I suppose they will hang me for this.' He was suffering from mental illness, but these words showed that he knew what he had done was legally wrong. As a result he could not use the defence of insanity and was found guilty of murder.

Note that this case was in 1952 when the special defence of diminished responsibility to a charge of murder did not exist. The decision in *Windle* was followed in *R v Johnson* (2007).

R v Johnson (2007)

D forced his way into a neighbour's flat and stabbed him. D was charged with wounding with intent (s 18 OAPA 1861). At his trial two psychiatrists gave evidence that he was suffering from paranoid schizophrenia and suffering from hallucinations. However, they both agreed that, despite this, D knew the nature and quality of his acts and that they were legally wrong. One psychiatrist was of the view that D did not consider that what he had done was wrong in the moral sense. The judge ruled that the defence of insanity was not available to D and D was convicted of wounding with intent. The Court of Appeal upheld the judge's ruling that insanity was not available as D knew the nature and quality of his acts and that they were legally wrong. They followed the decision in *Windle* (1952) where the court had held that the word 'wrong' meant knowing that the act was contrary to law.

In its judgment in *Johnson*, the Court of Appeal pointed out that there had been an Australian case in which the Australian courts had refused to follow

Figure 11.2 Key facts chart on insanity

	Law	Case(s)
Definition	D must be labouring under a defect of reason from disease of the mind AND must either not know the nature and quality of the act he or she is doing OR not know he or she is doing wrong	*M'Naghten* (1843)
Defect of reason	D's powers of reasoning must be impaired Absent-mindedness is not enough	*R v Clarke* (1972)
Disease of the mind	This is a legal term NOT a medical one There must be an internal cause It need not be permanent: it can be 'transient and intermittent' An external cause is not sufficient	*R v Kemp* (1956) *R v Sullivan* (1984) *R v Quick* (1973) *R v Coley* (2013)
Not know nature and quality of act OR **Not know he is doing wrong**	This can be because D is in a state of unconsciousness or impaired consciousness OR D is conscious but does not understand or know what he or she is doing D must not know it is legally wrong: if he or she does, he or she cannot rely on the defence of insanity	*R v Oye* (2013) *R v Windle* (1952) *R v Johnson* (2007)
Special verdict	Not guilty by reason of insanity	

Windle (1952). The view of the Australian court was that if a defendant believed his or her act to be right according to the ordinary standard of a reasonable person, then he or she was entitled to be acquitted even if he or she knew that it was legally wrong.

The Court of Appeal felt it was obliged to follow *Windle* (1952), but it did express the opinion that the Australian case contained 'illuminating passages indicating the difficulties and internal inconsistencies which can arise from the application of the *M'Naghten* Rules if the decision in *Windle* is correct'.

11.1.5 The special verdict

When a defendant successfully proves insanity, then the jury must return a verdict of 'not guilty by reason of insanity'. The judge can then impose:

- a hospital order (with or without restrictions as to when the defendant may be released)
- a supervision order
- an absolute discharge.

At least this wider range of options has stopped the injustice of epileptics and diabetics having to be sent to a mental hospital. Before the Criminal Procedure (Insanity and Unfitness to Plead) Act 1991, the only course available to a judge was to send the defendant to a mental hospital. Judges have now a much greater discretion when sentencing.

However, if the defendant is charged with murder, and there is a finding of insanity, then the judge must impose an indefinite hospital order. This means that the hospital can only release the defendant from the hospital if the Home Secretary gives consent.

The overlap with automatism

There is an overlap between insanity and automatism. It will have to be decided whether the defendant's condition is due to a mental illness or due to external factors. The courts have decided that those suffering from any illness, mental or physical, which affects their mind amounts to insanity. This means that the defence of non-insane automatism has been removed from such people as epileptics and diabetics.

This has consequences, as those successfully using the defence of automatism are entitled to a complete acquittal. Whereas, on a finding of 'not guilty by

Figure 11.3 Key cases on insanity

Case	Facts	Law
M'Naghten (1843)	Suffering from paranoia, D shot Sir Robert Peel's secretary	House of Lords clarified the law on insanity D must be labouring under a defect of reason, from disease of the mind AND must either not know the nature and quality of the act he or she was doing OR not know he or she was doing wrong
R v Clarke (1972)	Absent-mindedly D took items from a supermarket	Mere absent-mindedness or confusion is not insanity
R v Kemp (1956)	D suffering from hardening of the arteries which caused blackouts	Within the rules of insanity as his condition affected his mental reasoning, memory and understanding
R v Sullivan (1984)	Injured friend during epileptic fit	Insanity included any organic or functional disease It also applied even where it was temporary
R v Hennessy (1989)	Diabetic took a car after failing to take his insulin	If the disease affects the mind then it is within the definition of insanity
R v Burgess (1991)	Injured girlfriend while sleepwalking	If the cause of sleepwalking is internal, it is a disease within the definition of insanity
R v Quick (1973)	Diabetic who failed to eat after taking his insulin assaulted patient	This was an external cause (the effect of the drug) and not insanity
R v Windle (1952)	D was suffering from a mental disorder and killed his wife, who had constantly spoken of committing suicide	Because D knew what he had done was legally wrong, he was not insane by the M'Naghten Rules
R v Johnson (2007)	D stabbed his neighbour. when suffering from paranoid schizophrenia and hallucinations	Because D knew what he had done was legally wrong, he was not insane by the M'Naghten Rules

reason of insanity', the judge is likely to impose some form of order on the defendant.

It may be argued that the reason there is a reluctance to allow defendants to use the full defence of automatism is because it will lead to an acquittal and the defendant will be free from any order or supervision. There is the argument that, even though the cause of the erratic behaviour may be a physical illness, there is still the risk that such a person may commit further offences. Extending insanity to cover those who commit an offence because of a physical illness means that these people can be supervised.

Extension activity

In 2013, the Law Commission published a Discussion Paper, 'Criminal Liability: Insanity and Automatism'. This sets out the current law and discusses the problems with the defence. Research the Law Commission's discussion paper on their website, at http://lawcom.gov.uk. The problems with the law on insanity are given in more detail in Chapter 1, sections 1.30–1.77 of the Discussion Paper. These problems include the social stigma of the word 'insanity'. It is suggested that a new defence of 'Not criminally responsible by reason of a medical condition' should replace the defence of insanity. From this report, research why this defence would be more appropriate for those suffering from a physical condition affecting the mind.

11.2 Automatism

In *Bratty v Attorney-General for Northern Ireland* (1963), **automatism** was defined as:

> An act done by the muscles without any control by the mind, such as a spasm, a reflex action or a convulsion; or an act done by a person who is not conscious of what he is doing such as an act done whilst suffering from concussion or whilst sleep-walking.

This definition can cover two types of automatism:

1 **Insane automatism**

   This is where the cause of the automatism is a disease of the mind within the *M'Naghten* Rules. In such a case, the defence is insanity and the verdict not guilty by reason of insanity.

2 **Non-insane automatism**

   This is where the cause of the lack of control is external. Where such a defence succeeds, it is a complete defence and the defendant is not guilty.

Key terms

Automatism – a defence to a criminal offence. It is an act done by the muscles without any control by the mind, such as a spasm, a reflex action or a convulsion; or an act done by a person who is not conscious of what he or she is doing such as an act done while suffering from concussion or while sleepwalking.

Insane automatism – where the cause of the automatism is a disease of the mind within the *M'Naghten* Rules and comes within the defence of insanity.

Non-insane automatism – a complete defence where the cause of the automatism is external.

11.2.1 Non-insane automatism

This is a defence because the *actus reus* of a crime committed by the defendant is not a voluntary action and because of the automatism the defendant does not have the required *mens rea*. As a result, the defendant is not at fault for his or her uncontrolled actions.

The cause of the automatism must be generally external to the defendant. Examples of external causes which have been accepted as conditions of automatism include:

- a blow to the head
- an attack by a swarm of bees
- a sneezing fit
- hypnotism
- the effect of taking a drug, which might raise issues of self-induced automatism.

This concept of no fault when the defendant was in an automatic state through an external cause was approved in *Hill v Baxter* (1958).

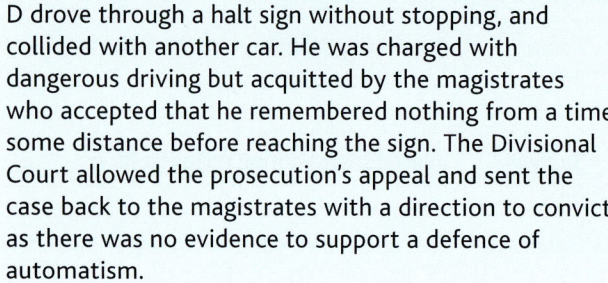

Hill v Baxter (1958)

D drove through a halt sign without stopping, and collided with another car. He was charged with dangerous driving but acquitted by the magistrates who accepted that he remembered nothing from a time some distance before reaching the sign. The Divisional Court allowed the prosecution's appeal and sent the case back to the magistrates with a direction to convict as there was no evidence to support a defence of automatism.

The court approved the judgment in the earlier case of *Kay v Butterworth* (1945) where the judge said:

> A person should not be made liable at the criminal law who, through no fault of his own, becomes unconscious when driving, as, for example, a person who has been struck by a stone or overcome by a sudden illness, or when the car has been put temporarily out of his control owing to his being attacked by a swarm of bees.

In *R v T* (1990), it was accepted that exceptional stress can be an external factor which may cause automatism.

R v T (1990)

D was raped. Three days later she took part in a robbery and an assault. She claimed that at the time she was suffering from post-traumatic stress disorder as a result of the rape and that during the robbery she had acted in a dream-like state. The trial judge allowed the defence of automatism to go to the jury, but D was convicted.

There has to be a total loss of voluntary control as set out in *Attorney-General's Reference (No. 2 of 1992)* (1993). A reduced or partial control of one's actions is not sufficient to amount to automatism.

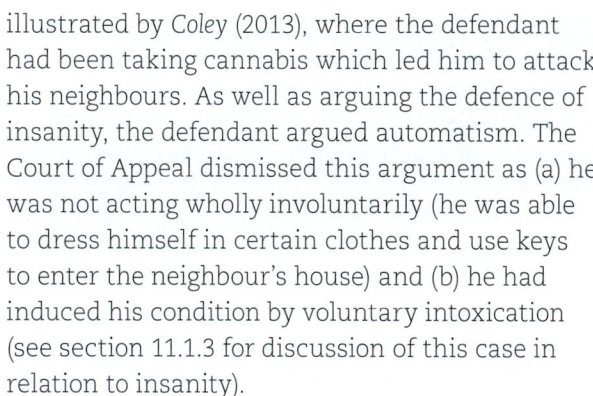

Attorney-General's Reference (No. 2 of 1992) (1993)

D was a lorry driver, who after driving for several hours, drove along the hard shoulder of a motorway for about half a mile. He hit a stationary broken-down car, killing two people. He said that he was suffering from a condition of 'driving without awareness' which puts a driver into a trance-like state. This could be brought on by driving for long distances on featureless motorways. He was acquitted. The Attorney-General referred a point of law to the Court of Appeal who ruled that, because this condition only causes partial loss of control, it does not amount to automatism. Even in this state, a driver has still enough awareness to drive a vehicle.

11.2.2 Self-induced automatism

This is where the defendant knows that his or her conduct is likely to bring on an automatic state. Examples include a diabetic, who knows the risk of failing to eat after taking insulin, or a person who drinks after taking medication when he or she has been told by his or her doctor that he or she must not take alcohol while on that medication.

How the defence works depends on whether the offence committed is one of **specific intent** or **basic intent**.

Key terms

Specific intent offences – offences for which the *mens rea* required is only intent. These offences include murder and s 18 OAPA 1861. For both these offences the *mens rea* is intent only.

Basic intent offences – offences where recklessness is part of the *mens rea*. This includes manslaughter, ss 20 and 47 OAPA 1861 and some property offences such as criminal damage.

> The same distinction between specific and basic intent offences is made in the defence of intoxication below.

When the state of automatism comes about from the defendant's own voluntary conduct, the effect will then be as follows:

- If it results from voluntary intoxication, the intoxication rules in section 11.3 operate. Whether the defence can apply will depend on whether the offence is one of specific or basic intent. This is illustrated by *Coley* (2013), where the defendant had been taking cannabis which led him to attack his neighbours. As well as arguing the defence of insanity, the defendant argued automatism. The Court of Appeal dismissed this argument as (a) he was not acting wholly involuntarily (he was able to dress himself in certain clothes and use keys to enter the neighbour's house) and (b) he had induced his condition by voluntary intoxication (see section 11.1.3 for discussion of this case in relation to insanity).

- The same approach was taken in the case of *R v McGhee* (2013) heard at the same time as *Coley*. The defendant, suffering from tinnitus, took temazepam and drank alcohol. He was charged with s 47 and s 18 offences against shopkeepers but claimed he had no recollection of the assaults. The court ruled that even if he had been in a state of automatism, the defence would have failed on the grounds that he induced it through his voluntary fault. He had voluntarily drunk himself into a state of intoxication which was worsened by the combination of temazepam with alcohol, and he was well aware of the dangers of taking them together.

- If it results from some perfectly appropriate action but with unanticipated consequences, automatism will be a defence to offences of both specific and basic intent. This could occur, for example, from a wholly unexpected adverse reaction to taking a legitimate prescription drug.

- If the automotive state results from some kind of improper action or failure by the defendant, for example if a diabetic took an excessive dose of insulin or failed to eat sufficient food having taken insulin, automatism will be a defence to specific intent offences because D cannot be in a worse position than he or she would be in if his or her state resulted from intoxication. However, automatism will not be a defence to a basic intent offence if D knew, or knew of the risk, that if he or she did become an automaton, he or she might engage in dangerous or aggressive conduct. This is similar to the position with the defence of voluntary intoxication below.

Illustrations of the operation of these rules are in the cases of *R v Bailey* (1983) and *R v Hardie* (1984).

R v Bailey (1983)

D was a diabetic who had failed to eat enough after taking his insulin to control his diabetes. He became aggressive and hit the victim over the head with an iron bar. He was charged with s 18 OAPA 1861 – a specific intent offence. The trial judge ruled that the defence of automatism was not available. The Court of Appeal decided that the judge's decision to deny the defence to a specific intent offence was wrong (and would have been in the case of the basic intent offence unless D knew or knew of the risk that he might engage in dangerous or aggressive behaviour) but the result was not affected because there was no significant evidence of automatism.

R v Hardie (1984)

D was depressed because his girlfriend had told him to move out of their flat. He took some Valium tablets which he had not been prescribed. The girlfriend encouraged him to take the tablets, saying that it would calm him down. He then set fire to a wardrobe in the flat. His defence was automatism as he said he did not know what he was doing because of the Valium. The trial judge directed the jury to ignore the effect of the tablets and he was convicted of arson (part of criminal damage – a basic intent offence).

The Court of Appeal quashed his conviction as the defendant had taken the drug because he thought it would calm him down. This is the normal effect of Valium. So the defendant had not been reckless and the defence of automatism should have been left to the jury to consider.

The issue in this case was whether the defendant was reckless as to the possible effects of falling into a state of automatism.

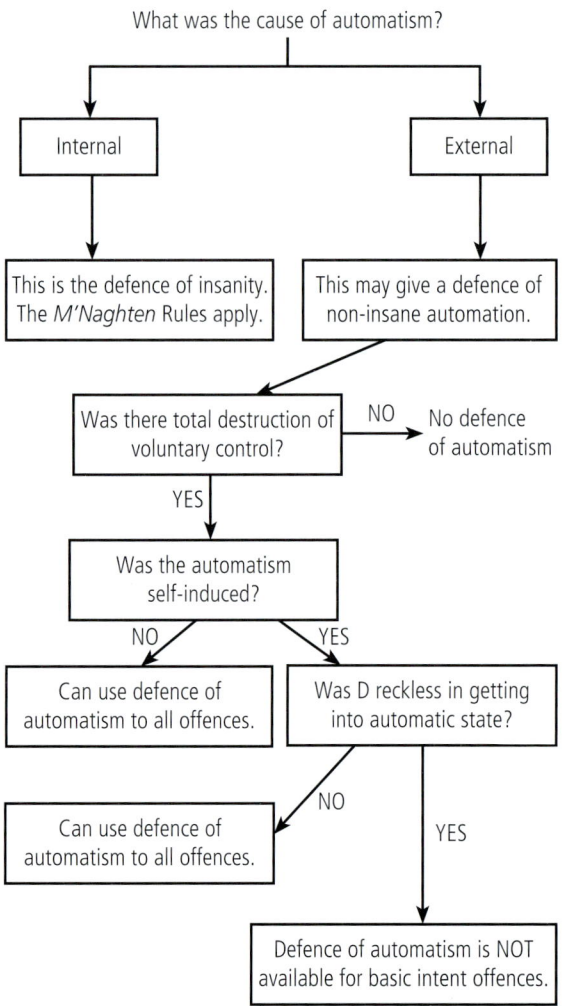

Figure 11.4 Flowchart on automatism

The main problem when automatism is raised is whether it should be treated as insane automatism or non-insane automatism. This is very important as the effect of these two types of automatism as a defence is so different, as seen in Figure 11.4.

Figure 11.5 Comparison of insanity and automatism as defences

Insanity	Automatism
This defence has to be proved, with medical evidence, by the defence on the balance of probabilities	Defence is raised by the defendant and must be disproved by the prosecution
M'Naghten Rules apply – D must be suffering from a defect of reason due to a disease of the mind so as not to know the nature and quality of what he or she was doing, or if he or she did know it, that he or she did not know he or she was doing what was wrong	D must be suffering from a total loss of voluntary control
D suffering from internal factor	Caused by an external factor
Successful use of defence – not guilty by reason of insanity	Successful use of defence is an acquittal
Judge can impose whatever sentence he or she considers appropriate up to a hospital order	No sentence required

Figure 11.6 Key cases on automatism

Case	Facts	Legal principle
R v T (1990)	Three days after being raped, D was involved in a robbery She claimed automatism due to PTSD	She was suffering from an external factor which could be considered by the jury
Attorney-General's Reference (No. 2 of 1992) (1993)	A lorry driver crashed on a motorway killing two people He said that he was suffering from a condition of 'driving without awareness' which puts a driver into a trance-like state	Automatism not available as there has to be a total loss of voluntary control
R v Bailey (1983)	A diabetic failed to eat enough after taking insulin He hit V with iron bar He was charged with s 18 OAPA 1861 – a specific intent offence	The jury should be able to consider automatism as a defence to specific intent offence
R v Hardie (1984)	D took some Valium tablets because he was depressed He set fire to a wardrobe in the flat – a basic intent offence He said he did not know what he was doing because of the drug	D had not been reckless and the jury should have been able to consider his defence of automatism

11.3 Intoxication

This covers intoxication by alcohol, drugs or taking other substances such as sniffing glue. To consider this defence, it has to be shown that the defendant was so intoxicated by the drink, drug or other substance that he or she was incapable of forming the *mens rea* of the offence. This will usually require evidence that the defendant had more than just a drink or two or a small amount of a drug.

The law on intoxication as a defence is largely policy-based for two main reasons:

1 Intoxication is a major factor in the commission of many crimes; many offences are committed when the defendant is in an intoxicated state. Statistics suggest that one half of all violent crimes are committed by a defendant who is intoxicated through drink and/or drugs.

2 There is a need to balance the rights of the defendant and the victim; if intoxication were always to be a defence, then victims' rights would not be protected.

As a result, there is conflict between public policy and legal principles. Public policy is based on public protection and the encouragement of good behaviour. Legal principles impose liability where there is fault. The fault must be voluntarily assumed or there must be the deliberate taking of a risk.

The law on intoxication has endeavoured to balance these opposing points of view, but over the past 30 or so years it can be argued that public policy has become the main theme.

Changes in public policy can be clearly seen in the law of self-defence, particularly in relation to householders (see Chapter 12, section 12.1.1). In relation to intoxication, Parliament has enacted s 76(5) of the Criminal Justice and Immigration Act 2008, which provides that the defendant cannot rely on 'any mistaken belief attributable to intoxication that was voluntarily induced' when claiming any of these defences (see section 11.3.3 below).

Whether the defendant is guilty or not depends on:

- whether the intoxication was voluntary or involuntary, and
- whether the offence charged is one of specific or basic intent.

> The same distinction applied with specific and basic intent offences as was set out for automatism in section 11.2.

Specific intent offences	Basic intent offences
• these have intent only as the *mens rea*, e.g. murder, s 18 OAPA 1861	• these have recklessness as part of the *mens rea*, e.g. manslaughter, ss 20 and 47 OAPA 1861, assault, battery, criminal damage

Figure 11.7 Specific and basic intent offences

Tip

In relation to the defence of intoxication, references to the defendant's consumption of alcohol, for example 'he drank 5 pints of beer' or 'half a bottle of whisky' or even 'he had a lot to drink', do not show in themselves that the defendant was intoxicated. You still have to make the point that the defendant could not form the *mens rea* of the offence.

11.3.1 Voluntary intoxication

Voluntary intoxication is where the defendant has chosen to take an intoxicating substance. It can also occur where the defendant knows that the effect of taking a prescribed drug will be to make him or her intoxicated.

Voluntary intoxication and specific intent offences

If the defendant is voluntarily intoxicated, this could mean he or she did not form the *mens rea* of the offence due to the intoxication.

Originally, the test set by Lord Birkenhead in *DPP v Beard* (1920) was: 'If he [the defendant] was so drunk that he was incapable of forming the intent required, he could not be convicted of a crime which was committed only if the intent was proved.'

More modern authority, such as *R v Sheehan and Moore* (1975), says that the true test is whether, because of intoxication, the defendant did not form the intent, irrespective of whether he or she was incapable of doing so. Inevitably, the best evidence that he or she did not will be evidence that he or she *could* not, but the 'could not' test from *DPP v Beard* was considered too high a test.

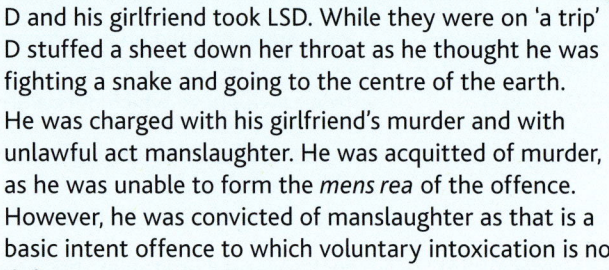

R v Sheehan and Moore (1975)

The defendants, in a drunken state, poured petrol over a homeless man and set light to it, causing his death. It was decided that the relevant question was not whether the defendants were capable of forming the *mens rea*, it was whether they had in fact formed the *mens rea* – a drunken intent is still an intent.

It is for the prosecution to prove that the defendant had the intent. In this case, they were unable to do so and the defendants were convicted of unlawful act manslaughter.

So, where there is an alternative basic intent offence, the defendant may be charged with both a specific intent offence and a basic intent offence, and it can be left to the jury to decide whether the defendant had the *mens rea* for the specific intent offence. For example, a defendant could be charged with both murder (specific intent) and manslaughter (basic intent). In this case, the prosecution will know that they will at least get a conviction for the lesser

offence if the jury finds that the defendant did not form the *mens rea* of murder.

This was seen in *R v Lipman* (1970).

R v Lipman (1970)

D and his girlfriend took LSD. While they were on 'a trip' D stuffed a sheet down her throat as he thought he was fighting a snake and going to the centre of the earth.

He was charged with his girlfriend's murder and with unlawful act manslaughter. He was acquitted of murder, as he was unable to form the *mens rea* of the offence. However, he was convicted of manslaughter as that is a basic intent offence to which voluntary intoxication is no defence.

As can be seen from the above, murder has an alternative (fallback) offence of manslaughter. Section 18 OAPA has an alternative (fallback) offence of s 20 OAPA. One difficulty is that not every offence has a 'fallback' option. If, for example, a defendant is charged with theft and successfully claims that he or she did not form the *mens rea* because he or she was too intoxicated, there is no fallback option and therefore no conviction.

Where the defendant has the necessary *mens rea* despite his or her intoxicated state, then he or she is still guilty of an offence, as a drunken intent is still intent. This can be shown by *Attorney-General for Northern Ireland v Gallagher* (1963).

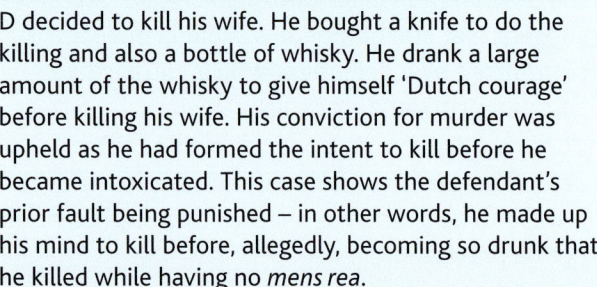

Attorney-General for Northern Ireland v Gallagher (1963)

D decided to kill his wife. He bought a knife to do the killing and also a bottle of whisky. He drank a large amount of the whisky to give himself 'Dutch courage' before killing his wife. His conviction for murder was upheld as he had formed the intent to kill before he became intoxicated. This case shows the defendant's prior fault being punished – in other words, he made up his mind to kill before, allegedly, becoming so drunk that he killed while having no *mens rea*.

Voluntary intoxication and basic intent offences

Where the offence charged is one of basic intent, then voluntary intoxication is not a defence. This is because becoming intoxicated voluntarily is considered a reckless course of conduct and recklessness is enough to constitute the necessary *mens rea*. The leading case on this is *DPP v Majewski* (1977).

DPP v Majewski (1977)

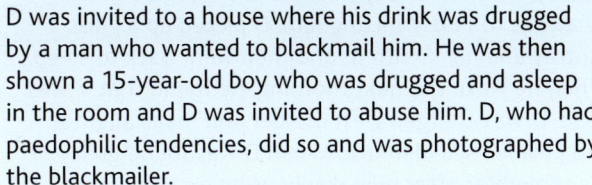

D had consumed large quantities of alcohol and drugs and then attacked the landlord of the public house where he was drinking. The landlord called the police and D also attacked the police officers who tried to arrest him. D also damaged the pub and the police station where he was taken. All the offences he was charged with were basic intent offences. D claimed that he had no memory of what he had done due to the drink and drugs he had consumed. The Law Lords held that becoming intoxicated by drink and/or drugs was a reckless course of conduct, and recklessness was enough to constitute the necessary *mens rea* in the offences with which he was charged, so he could not use the defence of intoxication.

If the defendant does not realise the strength of the intoxicant, this could still be a defence. In *R v Allen* (1988), D drank some home-made wine which had a much greater effect on him than he expected. While under the influence of this wine he committed sexual assaults. He claimed he was so drunk he did not know what he was doing and that he had not voluntarily put himself in that condition as the wine was much stronger than he realised.

It was decided that his intoxication was still voluntary, even though he had not realised the strength of it. However, sexual assault is a crime of basic intent and therefore D was unable to rely on his intoxicated state to negate the *mens rea*.

11.3.2 Involuntary intoxication

Involuntary intoxication covers situations where the defendant did not know he or she was taking an intoxicating substance. This may be where, for example, a soft drink has been 'laced' or 'spiked' with alcohol or drugs. It also covers situations where a prescribed drug has the unexpected effect of making the defendant intoxicated and the defendant does not realise its effect.

If the defendant was intoxicated through no fault of his or her own:

- he or she is allowed to argue that he or she did not form the *mens rea* whether the offence is of specific or basic intent, but that
- if the prosecution can prove that he or she did form the *mens rea*, he or she will be guilty of the offence whether specific or basic intent, even if he or she would not have committed it had he or she not been involuntarily intoxicated.

This was decided in *R v Kingston* (1994).

R v Kingston (1994)

D was invited to a house where his drink was drugged by a man who wanted to blackmail him. He was then shown a 15-year-old boy who was drugged and asleep in the room and D was invited to abuse him. D, who had paedophilic tendencies, did so and was photographed by the blackmailer.

The House of Lords upheld his conviction for indecent assault. They decided that if a defendant had formed the *mens rea* for an offence before becoming intoxicated then involuntary intoxication could not be a defence.

The decision in this case ignores the fact that the defendant was not to blame for his intoxication. Such a defendant would be not guilty of a basic intent offence where the prosecution relied on recklessness (as in *Hardie* (1984), see below). This appears to be unfair to a defendant in Kingston's situation.

Where, however, the defendant did not have the necessary intent or has not been reckless in getting intoxicated he will be not guilty. He has no *mens rea* and so cannot be guilty of a specific or basic intent offence. An example of this is *Hardie* (1985) (see section 11.2.2), where the defendant took Valium tablets, not knowing they could make his behaviour unpredictable, but he was not reckless in taking the tablets.

11.3.3 Intoxicated mistake

If the defendant is mistaken about a key fact because he or she is intoxicated, then it depends on what the mistake was about as to whether he or she has a defence or not.

Where the mistake is about something which means that the defendant did not have the necessary *mens rea* for the offence, then for a specific intent offence he or she has a defence. However, where the offence is one of basic intent then the defendant has no defence.

If the mistake is about another aspect, for example the amount of force needed in self-defence, the defendant will not have a defence. This was stated in *R v O'Grady* (1987) and confirmed in *R v Hatton* (2005).

R v O'Grady (1987)

After D and V, who were friends, had been drinking heavily, they fell asleep in D's flat. D claimed that he awoke to find V hitting him. D picked up a glass ashtray and hit V with it, and then went back to sleep. When he woke the next morning, he found that V was dead. D was charged with murder and manslaughter and pleaded self-defence. When D was found guilty of manslaughter after mistakenly using excessive force against his friend, the mistaken belief was not allowed to be used for self-defence and he was convicted of manslaughter. The Court of Appeal upheld this conviction saying that a defendant is not entitled to rely, so far as self-defence is concerned, upon a mistake of fact which has been induced by voluntary intoxication.

Lord Lane CJ said:

> There are two competing interests. On the one hand the interest of the defendant who has only acted according to what he believed to be necessary to protect himself, and on the other hand that of the public in general and the victim in particular who, probably through no fault of his own, has been injured or perhaps killed because of the defendant's drunken mistake. Reason recoils from the conclusion that in such circumstances a defendant is entitled to leave the Court without a stain on his character.

O'Grady was convicted of manslaughter which is a basic intent offence. This is clearly in line with the decision in DPP v Majewski (1977), as getting drunk is a 'reckless course of conduct' and recklessness is sufficient for a basic intent offence such as manslaughter.

Lord Lane's comments that an intoxicated mistake as to the amount of force needed in self-defence was not a defence to a specific intent offence has been confirmed in R v Hatton (2005).

R v Hatton (2005)

D had drunk over 20 pints of beer. He and another man (V) went back to D's flat. In the morning D claimed he found V dead from injuries caused by a sledgehammer. D said he could not really remember what had happened but thought V had hit him with a five-foot-long stick and he had defended himself. D was convicted of murder. The

Court of Appeal held that the decision in O'Grady (1987) was not limited to basic intent offences, but also applied to specific intent offences. A drunken mistake about the amount of force required in self-defence was not a defence.

It could be said that the decisions in *Majewski*, *O'Grady* and *Hatton* are contrary to the normal rules of coincidence of *mens rea* and *actus reus*. For example in *Majewski*, the decision that the defendant was guilty of basic intent offences because getting drunk is a 'reckless course of conduct' ignores the principle that *mens rea* and *actus reus* must coincide. A defendant's decision to drink or take drugs may be several hours before he or she commits the *actus reus* of any offence. For example, in *O'Grady* the defendant had fallen asleep after becoming intoxicated and only committed the act of hitting his friend some hours afterwards.

In addition, the recklessness in becoming intoxicated means that the defendant takes a general risk of doing something 'stupid' when drunk. At the time of becoming intoxicated the defendant has no idea that he or she will actually commit an offence. Normally, for offences where recklessness is sufficient for the *mens rea*, it has to be shown that the defendant knew there was a risk of the actual offence being committed.

Shorry, I thought you were a martian.

Criminal Justice and Immigration Act 2008

Statute law now makes it clear that a mistaken belief caused through the defendant's voluntary intoxication cannot give a defence of self-defence, defence of another or prevention of crime.

Section 76 of the Criminal Justice and Immigration Act 2008 states that reasonable force may be used for the purposes of self-defence, defence of another or prevention of crime. However, s 76(5) says that this 'does not enable the defendant to rely on any mistaken belief attributable to intoxication that was voluntarily induced'.

Exception

An exception to the rule on intoxicated mistake is *Jaggard v Dickinson* (1980).

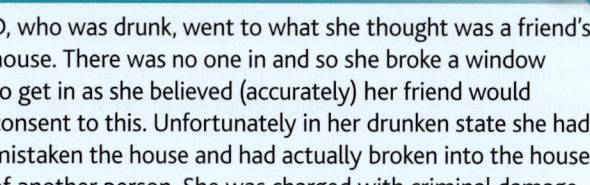

Jaggard v Dickinson (1980)

D, who was drunk, went to what she thought was a friend's house. There was no one in and so she broke a window to get in as she believed (accurately) her friend would consent to this. Unfortunately in her drunken state she had mistaken the house and had actually broken into the house of another person. She was charged with criminal damage.

The Divisional Court quashed her conviction holding that she could rely on her intoxicated belief as Parliament had 'specifically required the court to consider the defendant's actual state of belief, not the state of belief which ought to have existed'.

This exception is because s 5 of the Criminal Damage Act 1971 allows an honest belief that the person to whom the property belonged would have consented to the damage or destruction as a lawful excuse to a charge of criminal damage, whether or not the belief is justified. This has been interpreted as giving a defendant a defence even where the mistake was made through intoxication.

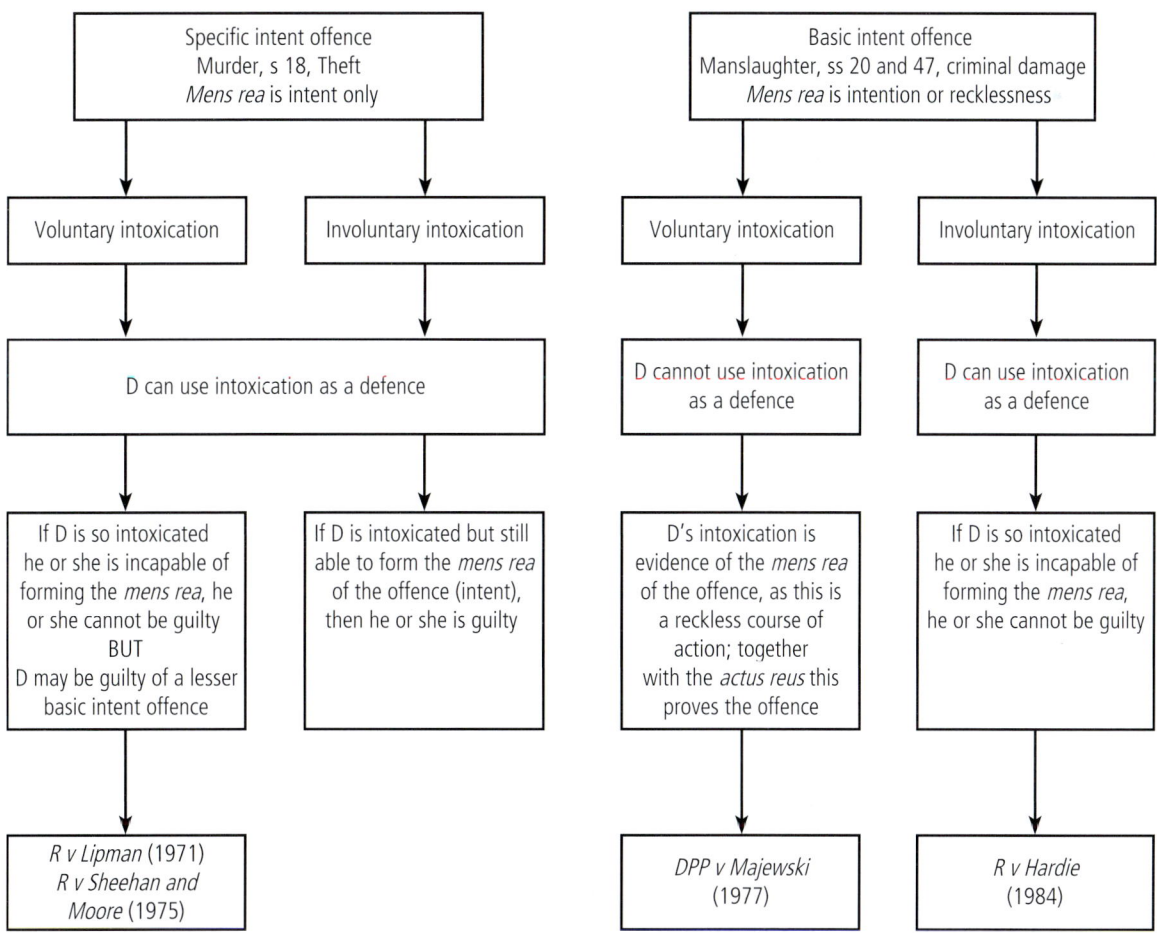

Figure 11.8 Intoxication flowchart

Figure 11.9 Key cases on intoxication as a defence

Case	Facts	Legal principle
R v Lipman (1970)	D and his girlfriend took an LSD trip and he stuffed a sheet down her throat	As he was unable to form the *mens rea* of the offence, he was not guilty of murder (a specific intent crime) but instead was convicted of manslaughter as that is a basic intent offence to which intoxication is no defence
Attorney-General for Northern Ireland v Gallagher (1963)	D decided to kill his wife and drank whisky to give himself 'Dutch courage'	He was convicted of murder as he had formed the intent to kill before he became intoxicated
DPP v Majewski (1977)	D consumed large quantities of alcohol and drugs and then assaulted the landlord of the pub and the police and damaged property – all basic intent offences	Becoming intoxicated by drink and/or drugs was reckless and recklessness was enough to constitute the necessary *mens rea* in the offences with which he was charged, so he could not use the defence of intoxication
R v Kingston (1994)	D had paedophilic tendencies, was invited to a house where his drink was drugged by a man who wanted to blackmail him He was filmed abusing a boy	He was guilty of indecent assault as he had formed the *mens rea* for an offence before becoming intoxicated and involuntary intoxication could not be a defence
R v O'Grady (1987)	A man killed his friend after a drinking session claiming he did so in mistaken self-defence	D is not entitled to rely, so far as self-defence is concerned, upon a mistake of fact which has been induced by voluntary intoxication
R v Hatton (2005)	D had drunk a lot of beer D found V dead D thought he had acted in self-defence but could not remember what had happened	The decision in *O'Grady* applied to both specific and basic intent offences A drunken mistake about the amount of force required in self-defence was not a defence
Jaggard v Dickinson (1980)	D, who was drunk, broke into the wrong house believing that, if it was the correct house, she had permission to do so She was charged with criminal damage	A statutory exception to the general rule applied in criminal damage cases

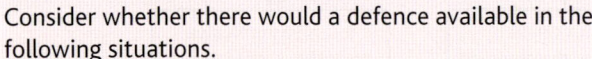

Activity

Consider whether there would a defence available in the following situations.

1. Alice took some illegal drugs. She is told that while she was under the influence of the drugs, witnesses saw her hit Peter in the face with a saucepan, breaking his jaw. Alice cannot remember doing this. What defence(s) might be available to her if she is charged with offences under ss 18 and 20 OAPA 1861?

2. Courtney is a diabetic. One morning he gets up late and in his rush to get to work he forgets to take his insulin. As a result he becomes violent later in the day and punches Jemima in the face. What defence(s) might be available to him if he is charged with an offence under s 47 OAPA 1861?

3. Zahir is hit on the head by a slate which accidentally falls off a building. He loses consciousness briefly but is then able to walk home. Later that day he attacks his partner, Lynne, causing serious injuries to her. He has no recollection of doing this. What defence(s) might be available to him if he is charged with offences under ss 18 and 20 OAPA 1861?

4. Jameela suffered from paranoid schizophrenia, which caused her to believe that people were intending to harm her. When she found herself in a large crowd in town, she began to panic and lash out at anyone nearby. In doing so, she knocked down Ken, an elderly man. In his fall, Ken broke his hip. What defence(s) might be available to her if she is charged with offences under ss 18 and 20 OAPA 1861?

5. Michael was driving to work when he realised that he had forgotten to bring an important document that he needed. Without thinking, he suddenly tried to swing

his car round to go back in the opposite direction. However, he lost control of the car, struck a kerb and injured Nick, a passing cyclist. Michael himself suffered a head injury in the collision and he staggered away from the car with little idea of what was happening. When Tina tried to help him, he punched her, cutting her lip.

What defence(s) might be available to him if he is charged with offences under ss 20 and 47 OAPA 1861?

Tip

When considering the appropriateness of various defences, look for potential indicators in the facts, such as alcohol (intoxication), drugs (intoxication or perhaps automatism) or some form of condition (insanity). This should help you to decide which defences are relevant.

Summary

Insanity

- The definition of insanity is based on the *M'Naghten* Rules.
- The defendant must prove that he or she was 'labouring under such a defect of reason, from disease of the mind, as not to know the nature and quality of the act he was doing, or if he did know it, that he did not know he was doing what was wrong'.
- Disease of the mind includes physical diseases which affect the mind: it does not include the effect of an external factor.
- If the defendant knows the act is legally wrong, then he or she cannot use the defence of insanity.
- If the defence is successful, the verdict is not guilty by reason of insanity.
- A judge now has a discretion to impose whatever sentence is considered appropriate.

Automatism

- This is an act done by the muscles without any control by the mind.
- Automatism can be categorised as insane (covered by the defence of insanity) or non-insane.
- If the defendant's automatism is caused by an external factor then there is defence and the defendant is not guilty.

- The external factor has to cause a total loss of voluntary control
- If the automatism is self-induced, the defendant will be able to use the defence for a specific intent offence.
- If the automatism is self-induced because of the defendant's recklessness, he or she will have no defence for a basic intent offence.

Intoxication

- Voluntary intoxication can only be a defence to a specific intent offence where the defendant is so intoxicated that he or she does not have the necessary *mens rea* for the offence.
- Voluntary intoxication is not a defence to a basic intent offence, as becoming intoxicated is a reckless course of conduct.
- Involuntary intoxication is a defence to a specific intent offence where the defendant did not have the necessary *mens rea* for the offence.
- Involuntary intoxication can be a defence to a basic intent offence, as the defendant has not been reckless in becoming intoxicated.
- Where the defendant makes a mistake because he or she is intoxicated, then if the mistake means that the defendant did not have the necessary *mens rea* for the offence, he or she can use intoxication as a defence.

12 Necessity defences

After reading this chapter, you should be able to:
- Understand the defence of self-defence/prevention of crime
- Understand the defence of duress
- Understand the defence of duress of circumstances
- Apply the defences to scenario-based situations

12.1 Self-defence/prevention of crime

This is a complete defence in criminal law and, if successful, the defendant will be found not guilty. It covers not only actions needed to defend oneself from an attack, but also actions taken to defend another person, or one's property. The defence is now set out in both common law and statute.

The basic idea is that:

- the common law defences of self-defence (including defence of another) and defence of property, as amended by the Criminal Justice and Immigration Act 2008, and
- the statutory defence in s 3(1) of the Criminal Law Act 1967 of self-defence in the prevention of crime or effecting or assisting in a lawful arrest

permit the use of 'such force as is reasonable in the circumstances'. As a result, they are all governed by much the same rules.

The defence of self-defence continues to exist by virtue of common law and other statutes including, most recently, by s 76 of the Criminal Justice and Immigration Act 2008. This section confirms the rules when 'the question arises whether the degree of force used by D against a person ("V") was reasonable in the circumstances' (s 76(1)(b)).

It follows that there are two questions to be asked in answering the question whether D used such force as was reasonable in the circumstances in self-defence:

- Was it necessary to use any degree of force?
- If so, was the degree of force actually used proportionate or reasonable (to the harm threatened or the risk to be averted)?

Following on from this, if the use of some force was unnecessary, then the question of proportion never arises and the use of force cannot be reasonable. If the use of some force was necessary, the first hurdle is overcome but the second – proportionate force – must then be overcome. If this hurdle is not overcome, the force used will not have been reasonable in the circumstances. The defence applies to all fatal and non-fatal offences and, if accepted by the jury, is a complete defence.

Was it necessary to use force? Subjective test	+	Was the force used reasonable? Objective test

Figure 12.1 Requirements of self-defence

12.1.1 Was it necessary to use some force?

The defendant will be judged according to the facts as he or she genuinely believed them to be (a subjective test).

In the following cases, the defendants had genuinely mistaken views of the facts so the courts had to decide how they should be judged.

> #### *R v Gladstone Williams* (1987)
>
> D was on a bus when he saw what he thought was a man assaulting a youth. In fact, the man was trying to arrest the youth for mugging an old lady. D got off the bus and asked what was happening. The man said that he was a police officer arresting the youth, but when D asked him to show his police ID card he could not do so. There was then a struggle between D and the man in which the man was injured. D was convicted of ABH s 47 OAPA 1861 after the judge directed the jury that D only had a defence if his mistake was a reasonable one.
>
> The Court of Appeal quashed his conviction because the jury should have been told that if they thought the mistake was genuine they should judge the defendant according to his genuine, mistaken, view of the facts, regardless of whether this mistake was reasonable or unreasonable.

The honesty of the defendant's belief was also the issue in *Beckford v The Queen* (1988).

Beckford v The Queen (1988)

D was a police officer in Jamaica and was issued with a gun and ammunition and sent with other armed officers to a house. According to D, a report had been received from a woman that her brother was terrorising her mother with a gun. D said that on arriving at the house, he saw a man run from the back door with an object which appeared to be a firearm. D stated that the man fired at the police and, in response to this, he fired back, killing the man. No gun was found. The trial judge directed the jury as follows:

> A man who is attacked in circumstances where he reasonably believes his life to be in danger or that is in danger of serious bodily injury may use such force as on reasonable grounds he thinks necessary in order to resist the attack and if in using such force he kills his assailant he is not guilty of any crime even if the killing is intentional.

D was convicted of murder (which carries the death penalty in Jamaica). He appealed, arguing the judge was wrong to direct that the mistake needed to be reasonably held.

His appeal was allowed and the conviction was quashed. The Privy Council decided that the test to be applied for self-defence is that a person may use such force as is reasonable in the circumstances as he honestly believes them to be in the defence of himself or another.

Section 76 of the Criminal Justice and Immigration Act 2008 puts the decisions in *Gladstone Williams* and *Beckford* onto a statutory footing. It states:

(3) The question whether the degree of force used by D was reasonable in the circumstances is to be decided by reference to the circumstances as D believed them to be …

(4) If D claims to have held a particular belief as regards the existence of any circumstances –

  (a) the reasonableness or otherwise of that belief is relevant to the question whether D genuinely held it; but

  (b) if it is determined that D did genuinely hold it, D is entitled to rely on it for the purposes of subsection (3), whether or not –

    (i) it was mistaken, or

    (ii) (if it was mistaken) the mistake was a reasonable one to have made.

So, in each situation, the important point is to establish the facts as the defendant genuinely believed them to be. If the defendant genuinely made a mistake then he or she is to be judged on the facts as he or she believed them to be. This is so, even if the mistake was unreasonable.

Section 76(5) makes it clear that if a defendant made the mistake because he or she had voluntarily got drunk or taken drugs, and made a mistake because of his or her intoxicated state, then he or she cannot rely on his or her mistaken belief. An example would be where a defendant had taken drugs which caused hallucinations causing him or her to believe that he or she was being attacked by snakes. If he or she then assaults someone believing that that person is a snake, then he or she cannot use the defence of self-defence. He or she genuinely believes he or she is being attacked by a snake, but this mistake has been caused by his or her voluntary intoxication.

Is the defendant suffering from delusions?

The defendant's genuine belief can include delusions resulting from a psychiatric condition or another condition such as PTSD. This had to be considered in *R v Seun Oye* (2013).

R v Seun Oye (2013)

D, who had no previous convictions, spontaneously attacked police in the staff area of a coffee shop and later in the cells. He was charged with s 20 OAPA 1861 and two counts of affray contrary to s 3 of the Public Order Act 1986. In his defence he relied on insanity and self-defence, claiming that he was being threatened and 'rushed' by evil spirits and had to defend himself. Two psychiatric experts agreed that D was legally insane. However, as set out in Chapter 11, insanity is a matter for the jury to decide, and they rejected it leaving self-defence, which again the jury rejected.

The Crown accepted at trial that the first, subjective limb of self-defence (D's belief that circumstances exist that justify force) was satisfied, meaning there was no issue that D believed he felt threatened by evil spirits. The problems were in relation to the second, objective, limb. D argued that the objective limb – whether the force used was proportionate to the threat – must have been satisfied, given the nature of the threat. He was, he claimed, justified in attacking the police officers.

The Court of Appeal was not impressed by this argument, because 'it could mean that the more insanely deluded a person may be in using violence in purported self-defence, the more likely that an entire acquittal may result' and the courts would be unable to impose any hospital or supervision order on a dangerous individual.

As a result of this decision, where a defendant has delusions, his or her mental illness is not to be taken into account. If it were to be, it could mean that the more insanely deluded a person is, the more likely he or she is to be acquitted. The court, in this case, pointed out that there are 'strong policy objections' to this view. The public could be put at risk of further violence. Also a court would not be able to make a hospital order where it was appropriate.

Likewise, in *R v Press and Thompson* (2013) the Court of Appeal applied the same principles to post traumatic stress disorder (PTSD) suffered by the defendants who were both serving solders. It was alleged they had launched an unprovoked and vicious assault on an innocent victim in a fast food shop. While the PTSD might cause them to misapprehend whether defensive action is necessary, the reasonableness or otherwise in the degree of force used must remain objective and cannot be influenced by or replaced with a lesser form of reasonableness within the disorder itself. Parliament, when enacting s 76 of the Criminal Justice and Immigration Act 2008, had sought to give statutory effect to an already existing principle and had not intended to modify the objective criteria for reasonable force.

Is a pre-emptive strike allowable?

In other words, does a person have to wait until he or she is attacked before he or she can use force? This can be illustrated by *R v Bird* (1986).

R v Bird (1986)

D's ex-boyfriend turned up at her birthday party with his new girlfriend. There was an argument and D asked him to leave. He did so but later returned and there was another argument. D poured a drink over him and he slapped her and pinned her against a wall. D punched him in the face, claiming that she had forgotten that she had a glass in her hand. The glass broke, causing him to lose an eye. She was charged with wounding under s 20 OAPA 1861 but she argued she acted in self-defence. The Court of Appeal quashed her conviction. It ruled that while withdrawing or showing an unwillingness to fight is good evidence that the defendant is acting reasonably and in good faith, there is no requirement to show an unwillingness to retreat. This principle is now set out in s 76(6A) of the Criminal Justice and Immigration Act 2008.

Is there a duty to retreat?

There is no duty to retreat; it is a factor to be taken into account. Section 76(6A) makes it clear that a person is not under a duty to retreat when acting for a legitimate purpose. But the possibility that the person could have retreated is to be considered as a relevant factor in deciding whether the degree of force was necessary.

What if the defendant is the aggressor?

Even if he or she is the initial aggressor, the defendant may use force if the victim's response is wholly disproportionate and so seriously threatens the defendant, provided that this was not, in truth, the defendant's aim all along – in other words to give himself an excuse to use much more serious violence. This was the issue in *R v Rashford* (2005).

R v Rashford (2005)

D sought out V, intending to attack him in revenge for an earlier dispute, but V and his friends responded out of proportion to D's aggression. At this point, D had to switch from aggression to defence. The Court of Appeal held that a defendant will only lose the defence by being the aggressor throughout the situation. The question of when a defendant is entitled to rely on self-defence depends on whether he or she feared that he or she was in immediate danger from which he or she had no other means of escape, and if the violence he or she used was no more than appeared necessary to preserve his or her own life or protect him- or herself from serious injury. On the facts, the jury's decision to convict was not unsafe.

Generally, a person who starts a fight, the aggressor, cannot rely upon self-defence to render his or her actions lawful, as such actions are not lawful; they are unlawful acts of violence. Subsequently, during a fight, a person will not only strike blows, but will defend him/herself by warding off blows from his or her opponent, but if he or she started the fight or if he or she volunteered for it, the defence will not be available. On the other hand, a person who is attacked or believes that he or she is about to be attacked may use such force as is both necessary and reasonable in order to defend him- or herself. If that is what he or she does, then he or she acts lawfully.

12.1.2 Was the force used proportionate?

The reasonableness of the force used is considered on the facts as they were or, if the defendant made a mistake, on the facts as the defendant genuinely believed them to be.

The basic rule is set out in s 76(6) of the Criminal Justice and Immigration Act 2008 which states that, except in a 'householder case', force which is disproportionate will not be reasonable.

- The test is objective as referred to in *R v Seun Oye* (2013) and *R v Press and Thompson* (2013) above.
- It invites consideration of a balance between the risk of harm to the defendant and the risk of harm to the victim, but taking into account that:
  - a person acting for a legitimate purpose may not be able to weigh to a nicety the exact measure of any necessary action (s 76(7)(a)), and
  - evidence of a person's having only done what the person honestly and instinctively thought was necessary for a legitimate purpose constitutes strong evidence that only reasonable action was taken by that person for that purpose (s 76(7)(b)).

The following points may be taken into account:

- There is no simple reckoning of equality. It will not be the case that, for example, a fight of 'fists has to be with fists'. It may be proportionate in some cases that a weapon may be used in extreme cases where the defendant is attacked without the use of a weapon.
- Initially proportionate force may develop into disproportionate force, for example if the defendant does not stop after the danger has been removed or passed.
- The defence is lost entirely when the force used is disproportionate (excessive).

These points can be illustrated by considering two cases where the defendants were both charged with murder but both pleaded the defence of self-defence. These were both well-known and, at the time, controversial. The cases are *R v Clegg* (1995) and *R v Martin* (2002).

R v Clegg (1995)

D was a soldier on duty at a checkpoint in Northern Ireland with a small group of other soldiers. D's orders had been to stop joyriders. A car came towards the checkpoint at speed and with its headlights full on. One of the soldiers shouted for it to stop but it did not. D fired three shots at the windscreen of the car and one as it had passed. This final shot hit a passenger in the back and killed her. As the evidence showed that the fatal shot had been fired as the car had gone past, D could not use the defence of self-defence. The danger had passed when the fatal shot was fired and excessive force had been used.

R v Martin (Anthony) (2002)

Two burglars broke into D's isolated farmhouse. D fired several shots at them; one of the intruders died and the other suffered serious injuries. D claimed he had shot in self-defence but the evidence showed that they were leaving when D shot them. D's defence was rejected as the danger had passed.

The decisions in these two trials were felt by the public to be unfair and that justice was not being done. In Clegg's case, he was on active service and following orders. In Martin's case, he was defending his property against intruders. The decision in the *Martin* case caused such an outcry that the Government had to consider reviewing the law, especially for householders using self-defence to protect themselves in their homes. As a result, a rule was introduced in householder cases by s 76(5A) of the Criminal Justice and Immigration Act 2008, which states that, in a 'householder case', force which is *grossly disproportionate* will not be reasonable. It means that a householder can use reasonable force, and now disproportionate force, to protect himself and others in the house, but not grossly disproportionate force. The terms 'reasonable', 'disproportionate' and 'grossly disproportionate' have not been defined in statute so will require judicial interpretation when cases come to court.

To be a householder case:

- the force must be used by the defendant while in or partly in a building that is a dwelling
- the defendant must not be a trespasser
- the defendant must have believed the victim to be a trespasser.

This is intended to cover situations where a burglar, or other intruder, enters the defendant's house. It also applies where a building has a dual purpose as a place of residence and of work and there is an internal means of access between the two parts. For example, where a shopkeeper is confronted by an intruder in the shop area, there could be a risk to his or her family in the adjoining residential part. But this extended defence does not apply to customers who happen to be in the shop who use force against an intruder. The normal rules of self-defence apply to them.

In a householder case, and assuming that the defendant genuinely believed that it was necessary to use force to defend him- or herself, the tests to be considered are:

1 Was the degree of force the defendant used grossly disproportionate in the circumstances as he or she believed them to be? If the answer is 'yes', he or she cannot use the defence of self-defence. If 'no', then

2 Was the degree of force the defendant used nevertheless reasonable in the circumstances he or she believed them to be? If it was reasonable, he or she has a defence. If it was unreasonable, he or she does not.

One case considering these rules has come to the appeal court to date: *R v Ray* (2017).

R v Ray (2017)

D and V's former partner were in a relationship and spending time in the former shared home. V arrived at the house in an angry mood. In the course of a fight, and fearing that V would use a knife against him, D fatally stabbed V.

The Court of Appeal confirmed the interpretation of the defence given in a previous case of *R (Denby Collins) v Secretary of State for Justice* (2016) that, in householder cases, the law is as follows:

1 Whether the degree of force used in any case is reasonable is to be considered by reference to the circumstances as the defendant believed them to be (this is contained in the common law and s 76(3)).

2 A householder is not regarded as having acted reasonably in the circumstances if the degree of force used was grossly disproportionate (s 76(5A)).

3 A degree of force that went completely over the top would, on the face of it, be grossly disproportionate.

4 However, a householder may or may not be regarded as having acted reasonably in the circumstances if the degree of force used was disproportionate. This will be a matter for the jury to decide.

The jury might have to consider matters such as:

■ the shock of coming across an intruder in the house
■ the time of day
■ the presence and vulnerability of others in the house, especially any children

■ if any weapon or object was being used or picked up
■ the conduct (or previous conduct, if known) of the intruder.

Figure 12.2 The amount of force that can be used in self-defence

Basic rule	In householder cases
D can use reasonable force to protect him- or herself, others or property	D can use reasonable force to protect him- or herself or others in the home BUT D can use disproportionate force if it is honestly and instinctively thought to be required
D cannot use disproportionate (excessive) force	D cannot use grossly disproportionate force

12.1.3 The statutory defence – also known as the public defence

Section 3(1) of the Criminal Law Act 1967 states that:

> A person may use such force as is reasonable in the circumstances in the prevention of crime, or in effecting or assisting in the lawful arrest of offenders or suspected offenders or of persons unlawfully at large.

So, reasonable force can be used by an individual in the prevention of any crime or in making an arrest to:

■ allow a person to defend him- or herself from any form of attack, so long as the attack is criminal
■ prevent an attack on another person, or
■ defend his or her property – this can include possessions such as a watch, bag or wallet demanded by a mugger, where there might also be physical danger to the owner.

It is a subjective test as to whether the defendant believed that force was necessary in the prevention of crime or in effecting or assisting in a lawful arrest, and whether the force used was reasonable is governed by an objective test. So, generally, the same tests apply to both the private defence and the public defence – a person may use such force as is (objectively) reasonable in the circumstances as he or she (subjectively) believes them to be.

Figure 12.3 Key cases on the defence of self-defence

Case	Facts	Legal principle
R v Gladstone Williams (1987)	D witnessed what he thought was a fight, intervened and injured a man	D should be judged according to his or her genuine, mistaken, view of the facts, regardless of whether this mistake was reasonable or unreasonable
Beckford v The Queen (1988)	D was an armed police officer who fired and killed a suspect leaving a house, believing the suspect to be armed	The test for self-defence is that a person may use such force as is reasonable in the circumstances as he or she honestly believes them to be in the defence of him- or herself or another
R v Seun Oye (2013)	D attacked police in the staff area of a coffee shop and later in the cells He claimed that he was being threatened and 'rushed' by evil spirits and had to defend himself	Where D has delusions, his or her mental illness is not to be taken into account in the objective test, unless the reference is to s 76(7)
R v Bird (1986)	D hit her ex-boyfriend but argued she acted in self-defence as she hit him before he hit her	Withdrawing or showing an unwillingness to fight is good evidence that D is acting reasonably and in good faith There is no requirement to show an unwillingness to retreat
R v Rashford (2005)	D sought out V, intending to attack him in revenge for an earlier dispute, but V and his friends responded out of proportion to D's aggression D switched from aggression to defence	D will lose the defence if he or she is the aggressor throughout the situation D can use the defence if he or she feared that he or she was in immediate danger from which he or she had no other means of escape, and if the violence he or she used was no more than appeared necessary to preserve his or her own life or protect him- or herself from serious injury
R v Ray (2017)	D stabbed V during a fight in V's former home	In householder cases D can use reasonable force to protect him- or herself or others in the home and disproportionate force if it is honestly and instinctively thought to be required Grossly disproportionate force cannot be used

12.2 Duress

The starting point of the common law in criminal law is that an adult of sound mind is responsible for any crime he or she commits. There is a limited exception to this if the defendant has been forced to commit a crime against his or her will or because of threats that have been made to him or her. It is a common law defence and, if successful, it is a full defence so that the defendant will be found not guilty. It is not available as a defence for the crimes of:

- murder
- attempted murder, or
- possibly the offence of treason.

In *R v Howe* (1987), the House of Lords ruled that the defence was not available to anyone charged with murder, even if he or she was only a secondary party and had not done the killing him- or herself.

R v Howe (1987)

With others, D took part in torturing and abusing a man who was then strangled by one of the others. On a second occasion another man was tortured, abused and then strangled by D. D claimed that he took part in the killings because of threats that had been made against him. The trial judge ruled that duress was available to D for the first killing where D was a secondary party to the killing, but that it was not available for the second killing where D had carried out the killing. The House of Lords decided that duress was not available as a defence in either case.

Lord Hailsham said:

> I do not at all accept in relation to the defence of murder it is either good morals, good policy or good law to suggest ... that the ordinary man of reasonable fortitude is not to be supposed to be capable of heroism if he is asked to take an innocent life rather than sacrifice his own.

The Court of Appeal confirmed in *R v Wilson* (2007) that this rule applies even if the defendant is young (in this case he was 13) and less able to resist pressure. The Court of Appeal accepted that there might be grounds for criticising a principle of law that did not allow a 13-year-old any defence to a charge of murder, even though he was only doing what his father told him as he was too frightened to refuse to obey his father.

In *R v Howe* (1987), the House of Lords said *obiter* that it thought the defence should not be available on a charge of attempted murder, and this was confirmed in *R v Gotts* (1992) by the Court of Appeal.

The ruling in *R v Howe* (1987) that **duress** is not available on a charge of murder ignores a situation such as a motorist being hijacked and forced to act as getaway driver. Lord Griffiths simply dismissed such examples as being inconceivable that such a person would be prosecuted. However, this cannot be guaranteed.

Another situation could be if a mother's car is hijacked by terrorists and she is told that her two young children will be killed unless she helps plant a bomb. Lord Hailsham thought that the ordinary person should be capable of heroism if he or she is asked to take an innocent life rather than sacrifice his or her own. But, in this situation, the mother is being asked to sacrifice her two children, yet she would have no defence.

There is an anomaly in that duress is not available for murder but is available for a charge under s 18 OAPA 1861 where the *mens rea* of intention to cause grievous bodily harm can be the same as for murder.

There is an additional problem where a defendant is charged with murder which carries a mandatory life sentence. The judge has to sentence the defendant to prison for life, though any duress can be taken into account when fixing the tariff. Where the defendant is charged with attempted murder, the judge has some discretion in sentencing. For example, in the case of the 16-year-old defendant in *R v Gotts* (1992), the judge placed him on probation.

In *R v Hasan* (2005), Lord Bingham set out the following tests, all of which have to be satisfied for the defence to succeed:

1 There must be a threat to cause death or serious injury.

2 The threat must be directed against the defendant or his or her immediate family or someone close to him or her.

3 Whether the defendant acted reasonably in the light of the threats will be judged objectively.

4 The threats relate directly to the crime committed by the defendant.

5 There was no evasive action the defendant could have taken.

6 The defendant cannot use the defence if he or she has voluntarily laid him- or herself open to the threats.

There are two possible defences of duress – the defence of duress itself and a separate defence of duress of circumstances. For both defences, the defendant can be considered to be so terrified that he ceases 'to be an independent actor' and commits the *actus reus* for the offence and has the required *mens rea*. So, if the law did not allow the defence, he would be liable for the offence. Where the defendant raises the possibility of a duress defence, it will be for the prosecution to prove beyond reasonable doubt that the defendant was not acting under duress. This may prove to be a difficult task for the prosecution, as the defence is likely to be based on claims which may be difficult to disprove, especially when they are only raised at trial.

Key term

Duress – a defence in criminal law based on the fact that the defendant has been effectively forced to commit the crime.

12.2.1 The threat

The threat has to be of death or serious injury. Serious injury will be given its normal meaning, so the victim will have to be subject to injury equivalent to grievous bodily harm. A lesser threat, such as a threat to disclose a previous conviction, is not sufficient. However, provided there are serious threats, the cumulative effect of the threats can be considered, as in *R v Valderrama-Vega* (1985).

R v Valderrama-Vega (1985)

The defendant illegally imported cocaine. He claimed he had done this because of death threats made by a mafia-type organisation involved in drug-smuggling and also because of threats to disclose his homosexuality and because of financial pressures. The trial judge said that the defence was only available to him if the death threats were the sole reason for his committing the offence. The Court of Appeal quashed his conviction as the jury was entitled to look at the cumulative effects of all the threats made against him.

If there had not been a threat of death, then the other threats in this case would not be enough on which to base a defence of duress. But as there had been a threat of death, the jury was entitled to consider all the threats.

The threat must be effective at the moment the crime is committed, but this does not mean that the threats need to be able to be carried out immediately. In *R v Hudson and Taylor* (1971), the trial judge in a perjury case ruled that the defence of duress was not available because the threat could not be put into effect while the girls were giving evidence, so there was no reason for them not to have given truthful evidence.

The Court of Appeal said that the threat had to be a 'present' threat but that this was in the sense that it was effective to neutralise the will of the defendant at the time of committing the offence. If the threat is hanging over the defendant at the time he or she commits the offence, then the defence of duress is available.

12.2.2 Against whom must the threat be made?

The threat must be directed against:

- the defendant, or
- his or her immediate family, or
- someone close to him or her, or
- a person for whose safety the defendant would reasonably regard him- or herself responsible.

12.2.3 Did the defendant act reasonably?

In deciding if the defence should succeed, the jury must consider a two-stage test:

1 Was the defendant compelled to act as he or she did because he or she reasonably believed he or she had good cause to fear serious injury or death? The defendant must genuinely believe in the effectiveness of the threat – but also reasonably believe in it, too. He or she must *reasonably* believe he or she had *good cause*. After some doubts, this has been re-asserted as a test of an objective nature.

2 If the first test is satisfied, would a sober person of reasonable firmness, sharing the characteristics of the accused, have responded in the same way?

The jury is allowed to take certain of the defendant's characteristics into account, as the reasonable person is regarded as sharing the relevant characteristics of the defendant.

The characteristics that can be taken into account were decided in *R v Bowen* (1996). In this case, the defendant had a low IQ of 68 and he obtained goods by deception for two men who had told him they would petrol-bomb him and his family unless he carried out this offence. It was held that this was irrelevant in deciding whether the defendant found it more difficult to resist any threats. The relevant characteristics must go to the ability to resist pressure and threats. This test was laid down by the Court of Appeal in *R v Graham* (1982) and approved by the House of Lords in *Howe* (1987) and again in *R v Hasan* (*formerly Z*) (2005).

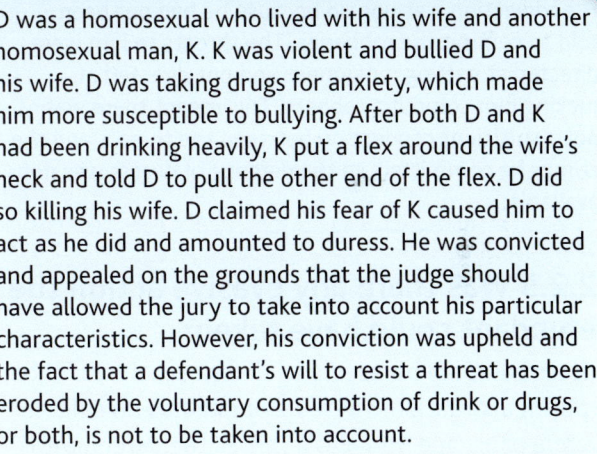

R v Graham (1982)

D was a homosexual who lived with his wife and another homosexual man, K. K was violent and bullied D and his wife. D was taking drugs for anxiety, which made him more susceptible to bullying. After both D and K had been drinking heavily, K put a flex around the wife's neck and told D to pull the other end of the flex. D did so killing his wife. D claimed his fear of K caused him to act as he did and amounted to duress. He was convicted and appealed on the grounds that the judge should have allowed the jury to take into account his particular characteristics. However, his conviction was upheld and the fact that a defendant's will to resist a threat has been eroded by the voluntary consumption of drink or drugs, or both, is not to be taken into account.

In *Bowen*, it was accepted that the following could be relevant:

- Age: very young people and the very old could be more susceptible to threats.
- Pregnancy: there is the additional fear for the safety of the unborn child.
- Serious physical disability: this could make it more difficult for the defendant to protect himself.
- Recognised mental illness or psychiatric disorder: this could include post-traumatic stress disorder or any other disorder which meant that a person might be more susceptible to threats. This does not include a low IQ, which may be seen as harsh as it can mean that the defendant fails to understand the true nature of matters.

■ Gender: although the Court of Appeal thought that many women might have as much moral courage as men.

12.2.4 Did the threats relate directly to the crime committed by the defendant?

The defendant can only use the defence if the threats are made in order to make him or her commit a specific offence. This can be illustrated by the case of *R v Cole* (1994).

R v Cole (1994)

D claimed that he and his girlfriend and child had been threatened (and he had been actually hit with a baseball bat) in order to make him repay money he owed. As he did not have the money, D carried out two robberies at building societies to get sufficient money to repay the debt. D said he only did this because of the threats of violence to him and his family.

His conviction was upheld because he had not been told to commit the robberies. The threats to him were directed at getting repayment and not directed at making him commit a robbery. This meant there was not a sufficient connection between the threats and the crimes he committed, so the defence of duress was not available.

12.2.5 Was there any evasive action the defendant could have taken?

Duress can only be used as a defence if the defendant is put in a situation where he or she has no safe avenue of escape. In *R v Gill* (1963), the defendant claimed that he and his wife had been threatened unless he stole a lorry. However, there was a period of time during which he was left alone and so could have raised the alarm. As he had the possibility of a 'safe avenue of escape', he could not rely on the defence of duress. If police protection is possible, then the defendant cannot rely on duress. It should be made clear to a jury that if the threat is not likely to be carried out almost immediately, there may be little room for doubt that the defendant could have taken evasive action, either by going to the police or in some other way, to avoid committing the crime. In *R v Hudson and Taylor* (1971), the Court of Appeal accepted that police protection could not be completely fool-proof. Even where a defendant had the opportunity to go to the police and tell them of the duress, he or she might be so afraid of the consequences that he or she would not go to the police.

12.2.6 Did the defendant lay him- or herself open to the threats?

The defendant cannot use the defence if he or she has voluntarily laid him- or herself open to the threats.

The Court of Appeal in *R v Sharp* (1987) commented that:

> 66 Where a person has voluntarily, and with knowledge of its nature, joined a criminal organisation or gang which he knew might bring pressure on him to commit an offence and was an active member when he was put under such pressure, he cannot avail himself of the defence of duress. 99

R v Hasan (formerly Z) (2005)

D came into contact with a violent drug dealer. The dealer told D to burgle a house in order to steal a large amount of money that was in a safe there. The dealer threatened D that if he did not do this then D and his family would be harmed. D, carrying a knife, broke into the house but was unable to open the safe. D claimed the defence of duress but was convicted of aggravated burglary. The House of Lords upheld his conviction. Lord Bingham said:

> 66 The policy of the law must be to discourage association with known criminals, and it should be slow to excuse the criminal conduct of those who do so. If a person voluntarily becomes or remains associated with others engaged in criminal activity in a situation where he knows or ought reasonably to know that he may be the subject of compulsion by them or their associates, he cannot rely on the defence of duress to excuse any act which he is thereafter compelled to do by them. 99

He also said at paragraph 39:

> 66 the defence of duress is excluded when as a result of the accused's voluntary association with others engaged in criminal activity he foresaw, or ought reasonably to have foreseen, the risk of being subjected to any compulsion by threats of violence. 99

In *R v Ali* (2008), Dyson LJ slightly modified Lord Bingham's statement when he said:

> It is true that Lord Bingham refers at paragraph 39 to a voluntary association with others 'engaged in criminal activity'. That is not surprising because in most cases where A subjects B to compulsion by threats of violence, A is engaged in criminal activity. But, as the Judicial Studies Board specimen directions make clear, the core question is whether the defendant voluntarily put himself in the position in which he foresaw or ought reasonably to have foreseen the risk of being subjected to any compulsion by threats of violence. As a matter of fact, threats of violence will almost always be made by persons engaged in a criminal activity; but in our judgment it is the risk of being subjected to compulsion by threats of violence that must be foreseen or foreseeable that is relevant, rather than the nature of the activity in which the threatener is engaged.

If this modification is accepted, then the general rule will be that:

> ...the defence of duress is excluded when as a result of the accused's voluntary association with others ... he foresaw or ought reasonably to have foreseen the risk of being subjected to any compulsion by threats of violence.

Figure 12.4 Key cases on duress

Case	Facts	Legal principle
R v Howe (1987)	D took part in two killings, one as principal, the other as secondary party	Duress not available as a defence to murder or attempted murder (*R v Gotts* (1992))
R v Valderrama-Vega (1985)	D illegally imported cocaine He claimed he received death threats, threats to disclose his homosexuality and financial pressures	The cumulative effects of all the threats should be considered by the jury
R v Bowen (1996)	D had a low IQ and obtained goods by deception for two men who had told him they would petrol-bomb him and his family unless he carried out the offence	Low IQ was irrelevant in deciding whether D found it difficult to resist any threats The relevant characteristics must go to the ability to resist pressure and threats
R v Graham (1982)	D lived with his wife and another violent man, K K told D to kill his wife D, who was taking drugs to deal with anxiety, claimed his fear of K caused him to act as he did	The fact that a defendant's will to resist a threat has been eroded by the voluntary consumption of drink or drugs, or both, is not to be taken into account
R v Cole (1994)	D carried out two robberies to get money to repay a debt; he and his family had been threatened if he did not repay the debt	There was insufficient connection between the threats and the crimes committed, so the defence was not available
R v Hasan (2005)	D was charged with aggravated burglary He claimed he was forced to commit the offence because of threats made to him	The tests for the defence to succeed: ■ There must be a threat to cause death or serious injury ■ The threat must be directed against D or his or her immediate family or someone close to him or her ■ Whether D acted reasonably in the light of the threats will be judged objectively ■ The threats relate directly to the crime committed by D ■ There was no evasive action D could have taken ■ D cannot use the defence if he or she has voluntarily laid him- or herself open to the threats

12.3 Duress of circumstances

Duress of circumstances differs from duress in that the circumstances dictate the crime rather than a person. An example of the use of this defence is *R v Willer* (1986).

R v Willer (1986)

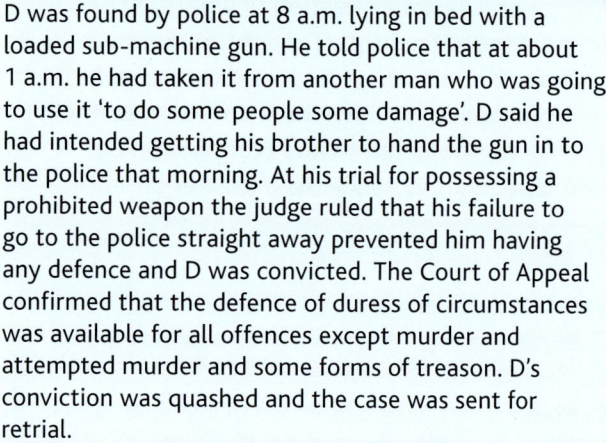

D and a passenger were driving down a narrow alley when their car was surrounded by a gang of youths who threatened them. D realised that the only way to get away from the gang was by driving on the pavement. He did this quite slowly (about 10 m.p.h.) and having made his escape he drove to the police station to report the gang.

He was charged and convicted of reckless driving for having driven on the pavement.

The Court of Appeal allowed his appeal and said that the jury should have been allowed to consider whether the defendant drove 'under that form of compulsion, that is, under duress'.

In *R v Conway* (1988), the threats were to a passenger, P, rather than the driver, D.

R v Conway (1988)

P had been shot at by two men a few weeks earlier. D's car was stationary when P saw two men running towards the car. He thought they were the two men who were after him (in fact they were plain-clothes policemen). He yelled at D to drive off. D did so very fast and was charged with reckless driving. The trial judge refused to leave duress for the jury to consider and D was convicted. On appeal the Court of Appeal quashed his conviction and ruled that a defence of duress of circumstances was available if, on an objective standpoint, the defendant was acting in order to avoid a threat of death or serious injury.

A final example is *R v Martin* (1989).

R v Martin (1989)

D's wife became hysterical and threatened suicide unless D drove her son (who was late and at risk of losing his job) to work. D had been disqualified from driving but he eventually agreed to drive the boy to work. He was convicted of driving while disqualified. On appeal it was ruled that duress of circumstances could be available. The same two-stage test put forward in *Graham* (1982) applied. So the tests were:

- Was the defendant compelled to act as he did because he reasonably believed he had good cause to fear serious injury or death?

- If so, would a sober person of reasonable firmness, sharing the characteristics of the accused have responded in the same way?

The decision in *R v Pommell* (1995) confirmed that duress of circumstances could be a defence to all crimes except murder, attempted murder and treason, the same as duress.

R v Pommell (1995)

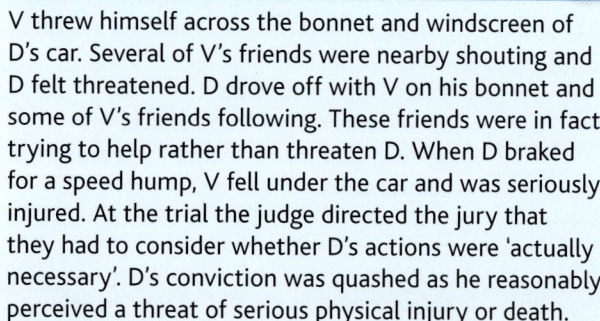

D was found by police at 8 a.m. lying in bed with a loaded sub-machine gun. He told police that at about 1 a.m. he had taken it from another man who was going to use it 'to do some people some damage'. D said he had intended getting his brother to hand the gun in to the police that morning. At his trial for possessing a prohibited weapon the judge ruled that his failure to go to the police straight away prevented him having any defence and D was convicted. The Court of Appeal confirmed that the defence of duress of circumstances was available for all offences except murder and attempted murder and some forms of treason. D's conviction was quashed and the case was sent for retrial.

In *R v Cairns* (1999), the court had to consider whether there had to be a real threat to the defendant or whether the defence was available where the defendant reasonably perceived a threat of serious physical injury or death, even though there was no actual threat.

R v Cairns (1999)

V threw himself across the bonnet and windscreen of D's car. Several of V's friends were nearby shouting and D felt threatened. D drove off with V on his bonnet and some of V's friends following. These friends were in fact trying to help rather than threaten D. When D braked for a speed hump, V fell under the car and was seriously injured. At the trial the judge directed the jury that they had to consider whether D's actions were 'actually necessary'. D's conviction was quashed as he reasonably perceived a threat of serious physical injury or death.

It is sufficient for the defendant to show that he or she acted as he or she did because he or she reasonably perceived a threat of serious physical injury or death. He or she is not required to prove that the threat was an actual or real threat. This is shown in *R v Abdul-Hussain* (1999).

R v Abdul-Hussain (1999)

The defendants, who were Shi'ite Muslims, had fled to Sudan from Iraq because of their religion and the risk of punishment and execution. They feared that, when they landed, they would be sent back to Iraq. They hijacked the plane which eventually landed in the UK. The defendants were charged with hijacking and pleaded duress of circumstances. The trial judge decided that the danger they were in was not sufficiently 'close and immediate' as to give rise to a 'virtually spontaneous reaction' and he ruled that the defence could not be considered by the jury. The defendants were convicted and appealed. The Court of Appeal quashed their convictions, holding that the threat need not be immediate but it had to be imminent in the sense that it was hanging over them.

The Court of Appeal in *Abdul-Hussain* ruled that:

- There must be immediate peril of death or serious injury to the defendant, or to those for whom he or she has responsibility.
- The peril must operate on the defendant's mind at the time of committing the otherwise criminal act, so as to overbear his or her will; this is a matter for the jury.
- Execution of the threat need not be immediately in prospect.
- There is no avenue of escape.

In duress of circumstances, the defence may be used for any offence which is an appropriate response to the danger posed by the circumstances. As seen in *Abdul-Hussain*, the danger was of torture and execution, and the offence committed was hijacking which enabled them to get to a safe venue.

Figure 12.5 Key facts chart on duress of circumstances

	Law	Case
Availability	All offences EXCEPT: ■ murder ■ attempted murder ■ treason (possibly)	*R v Howe* (1987) *R v Gotts* (1992)
Seriousness of threat	Must be of death or serious injury BUT can consider cumulative effect of other threats with threat of injury	*R v Valderrama-Vega* (1985)
Subjective and objective tests	There are two tests: ■ Was D compelled to act because he or she feared serious injury or death (subjective)? ■ Would a sober person of reasonable firmness have responded in the same way (objective)?	*R v Graham* (1982)
	Some of D's characteristics can be taken into account, especially: ■ age ■ pregnancy ■ serious physical disability ■ recognised mental illness	*R v Bowen* (1996)
Avenue of escape	Duress is NOT available as a defence if there is a safe avenue of escape	*R v Gill* (1963)
Imminence of threat	The threat need not be immediate but it must be imminent	*R v Hudson and Taylor* (1971), *R v Abdul-Hussain* (1999)
Self-induced duress	Duress is NOT available where: ■ D joins a criminal gang which he or she knows is violent ■ D puts him- or herself in a position where he or she foresaw (or should have foreseen) the risk of being subjected to compulsion	*R v Sharp* (1987) *R v Hasan* (2005)

Did the defendant perceive a real threat of death or serious injury?

+

Was the threat or peril operating on the defendant's mind?

+

The threat does not have to be immediate but imminent

Figure 12.6 Principles of duress

Figure 12.7 Key cases on duress

Case	Facts	Legal principle
R v Pommell (1995)	D was found with a gun, which he said he intended to hand in to the police	The defence was available for all offences except murder and attempted murder and some forms of treason
R v Abdul-Hussain (1999)	Ds hijacked a plane as they feared for their safety if they returned to their own country	■ There must be imminent peril of death or serious injury ■ The peril must operate on the defendant's mind at the time of committing the act, so as to overbear his or her will ■ Execution of the threat need not be immediately in prospect but should be imminent

Activity

Consider whether a defence of duress would be available in the following situations.

1. Clancy is threatened by Neil, a fellow employee, who tells Clancy that he will tell their boss about Clancy's previous convictions for theft. Neil says that Clancy has to help him shoplift from a small corner shop by distracting the counter-staff while Neil does the stealing. Clancy feels obliged to do this as he does not want to lose his job.

2. Joseph, who is of a timid nature and low intelligence, is told by Katya that she will beat him up unless he obtains goods for her from a shop using a stolen credit card. He does this and obtains a DVD player for her.

3. Natasha's boyfriend, Ross, is a drug dealer. She also knows that he has convictions for violence. He threatens to beat her 'senseless' unless she agrees to take some drugs to one of his 'customers'. She is caught by the police and charged with possessing drugs with intent to supply.

4. Sanjeet's wife has tried to commit suicide previously. She is very depressed because they are heavily in debt. She tells Sanjeet that she will throw herself under a train unless he can get the money to pay off their debts. Sanjeet obtains the money by robbing a local off-licence.

5. Tamara is due to give evidence against Alexia's boyfriend who is facing a trial for attempted murder. A week before the trial is due to take place, Alexia sends Tamara a text message saying that Tamara will be killed if she gives evidence. Tamara attends the court but lies in evidence saying, untruthfully, that the man she saw was much shorter than Alexia's boyfriend.

Summary

Self-defence

■ A complete defence when needing to defend oneself, another or property.

■ Common law rules have been codified by s 76 of the Criminal Justice and Immigration Act 2008.

■ It has to be considered whether force was required (subjective test) and whether force used was reasonable (objective test).

■ The subjective test looks at the facts as the defendant believed them to be, even if he or she is mistaken, as long as the mistaken belief is honestly and genuinely held. The defendant cannot have any delusions taken into account.

■ The defendant can strike pre-emptively. There is no duty to retreat – it is a factor to be taken into account.

■ Objective test is whether the degree of force was reasonable and not disproportionate.

■ In householder cases the degree of force can be disproportionate but cannot be 'grossly disproportionate'. The jury will consider a number of factors in deciding whether force used was disproportionate or grossly disproportionate.

■ The statutory defence allows the defendant to use such force as is reasonable to prevent crime or assist in a lawful arrest.

Duress: this is where the defendant is forced by threats to commit an offence.

- It is not available for murder, attempted murder and, possibly, treason.
- The threat must be of death or serious injury – but cumulative effect of threats can be considered.
- The threat must be to the defendant or his or her family, or someone close to him or her.
- There are two tests:
  a subjective: was the defendant compelled to act as he or she did because he or she reasonably believed that he or she had good cause to fear death or serious injury?
  b objective: if (a) is satisfied, would a sober person of reasonable fitness, sharing the same characteristics as the defendant, have responded in the same way?

- Relevant characteristics include age, pregnancy, gender, serious physical disability, recognised mental illness or psychiatric disorder (low IQ is not included).
- The threats relate directly to the crime committed by the defendant and are imminent.
- There was no evasive action the defendant could have taken.
- The defendant cannot use the defence if he or she has voluntarily laid him- or herself open to the threats.

Duress of circumstances: this is where the defendant is forced to act because of circumstances.

- The defence is not available for murder or attempted murder or, possibly, treason.
- All tests for duress by threats are relevant.
- The circumstances must mean that there is a threat of death or serious injury.

Tort law

13 The rules and theory of tort law

After reading this chapter, you should be able to:

■ Understand rules and principles covering liability and fault in actions for negligence, occupiers' liability, nuisance and vicarious liability
■ Have a basic understanding of:
  – the public policy factors governing the imposition of a duty of care in negligence
  – the policy factors governing imposition of liability for pure economic loss and psychiatric injury
  – the factors governing the grant of an injunction as a remedy, and the way in which conflicting interests are balanced
  – the factors granting an injunction as a remedy and the way that conflicting interests are balanced
  – the nature and purpose of vicarious liability

13.1 The rules of tort law

In *AQA A-level Law for Year 1 and AS*, Chapter 23 there is an introduction to the rules of tort law with specific emphasis on liability in the torts of negligence and occupiers' liability and of remedies in tort.

In this chapter, you will be introduced to the general rules of some other torts that you will need to learn at A-level. These other torts are:

■ Economic or financial loss – this covers the areas of pure economic loss and negligent misstatement. Detailed coverage of the rules of this action are contained in Chapter 14.
■ Where the victim has suffered psychiatric injury (as opposed to physical injury) – this is also known as 'nervous shock'. Again, detailed coverage of the rules of this action are contained in Chapter 14.
■ Private nuisance and the associated tort of *Rylands v Fletcher* which deals with the escape of dangerous things from one property and which damages an adjoining property. Detailed coverage of the rules of these actions are contained in Chapter 15.

■ Vicarious liability, which is not a tort in itself, but which imposes liability on a person for the actions of another. Principally, it will be seen that an employer is vicariously liable for the wrongful actions of an employee if they are committed in the course of employment. Detailed coverage of the rules of this form of liability are contained in Chapter 16.

13.1.1 Fault

Torts based on negligence require the claimant to prove that the defendant was at fault. Fault means that there is some wrongdoing by the defendant and he or she is to blame for the loss or injury suffered by the claimant.

Negligence

As we saw in *AQA A-level Law for Year 1 and AS*, Chapter 24, in an accident claim based on negligence, the evidence will have to show how and why the accident happened and that it was due to the wrongdoing, or fault, of the defendant. This will be when the defendant has broken his or her duty of care towards the claimant. This proving of fault may be difficult for the claimant as expert evidence will have to be obtained and this may be expensive and take a long time to produce. Expert evidence will also have to be obtained by the defendant to prove that the claimant was at fault to establish the defences of consent and/or contributory negligence. If the claimant cannot present sufficient evidence to prove fault, he or she will be left without compensation, even if he or she is suffering physical injury or damage to his or her property.

Occupiers' liability

As we saw in *AQA A-level Law for Year 1 and AS*, Chapter 25, a claim in this tort is similar to a claim in negligence. The occupier owes a visitor, whether a lawful visitor or a trespasser, a duty of care when the visitor comes onto the occupier's property. If this duty is broken and the visitor is injured, this will be because the occupier is at fault and has broken his or her duty of care. Again, evidence will have to be produced by the claimant to show how the defendant occupier broke his or her duty causing injury to the visitor.

Economic loss and negligent misstatement

This is a claim based on negligence so the claimant will firstly have to show the defendant was negligent – in other words at fault. Usually this will be where the defendant gives negligent advice which results in a loss of money to the claimant. There will usually be no contract between the parties. In addition to proving negligence, the claimant will be required to show the existence of a 'special relationship'. This requirement is in place to prevent the floodgates opening to too many claims. More detail on the requirements of this liability are contained in Chapter 14.

Psychiatric injury or nervous shock

Again, this is a claim based on negligence, so the claimant will first have to show the defendant was negligent – in other words at fault. The claimant will have suffered mental injury instead of, or as well as, physical injury. This injury has to be severe enough to cause loss. The usual loss will be loss of earnings as the claimant will be unable to work for a period of time as a result of suffering the injury. Again we will see in Chapter 14 there are special rules in place to prevent the floodgates opening to too many claims.

13.1.2 Strict liability

Some torts do not require fault to be proved, and they are known as strict liability actions. They will usually be cheaper and simpler for the claimant to prove as they do not require detailed evidence to be produced to show how and why the accident, injury or loss happened. In this specification strict liability applies to the torts of nuisance and *Rylands v Fletcher*. It also applies to vicarious liability.

Private nuisance

This is an action to stop the unreasonable use of neighbouring land and which causes loss of enjoyment of the claimant's property. In most claims, it will not be necessary to show that the neighbour causing the interference was at fault, as the court will consider factors such as the length of the nuisance, the time of day and the character of the neighbourhood. However, if malice of the neighbour is alleged, this will involve fault of the neighbour, as the action will be deliberately aimed at the claimant.

Rylands v Fletcher

This is an action for damage to the claimant's land caused by material escaping from neighbouring land. The claimant will not have to show that the neighbour was at fault, merely that the offending material was stored on the neighbour's land, it escaped and caused damage to the claimant's land.

Vicarious liability

This liability is seen most frequently when an employee commits a tort in the course of employment causing loss or injury to the claimant. The claimant can take action against both the employee and the employer. It will usually be more beneficial to take action against the employer as the employer will have more money than the employee to pay compensation and the employer should be insured against liability to third parties. There can be an element of fault here, but it will be the fault of the employee who caused the loss or injury. The fault of the employer does not have to be explicitly proved to make the employer liable. However, it could be said that the employer is implicitly at fault as the employer should have supervised the employee more effectively and/or chose the wrong person to employ in the first place.

> **Tip**
>
> Be clear on which torts are fault-based and which torts are strict liability.

13.1.3 Associated defences and remedies

Defences

As was shown in AQA *A-level Law for Year 1 and AS*, Chapters 24 and 25, there are few defences available in tort law. The defences that may apply are:

- *Volenti* or consent of the claimant to suffer the injury – this is a complete defence.
- Contributory negligence where the claimant is partly at fault for the injuries that have been suffered – if this defence is successful the amount of compensation will be reduced by the amount of the claimant's fault.
- Warning notices – these will only be a defence to a claim of occupiers' liability. If successful they will be a complete defence to a claim.
- In *Rylands v Fletcher* actions there are some specific defences, and these are dealt with in Chapter 15.

Remedies

> See AQA *A-level Law for Year 1 and AS*, Chapter 26 for information on the remedy of compensatory damages.

If the defendant is at fault, he or she will usually be ordered to pay compensation to the claimant. It can be said that it is morally right that if the defendant is at fault, he or she should pay compensation to the injured victim.

The purpose of the award of damages in tort is to put the claimant back in the position he or she was in before the accident, so far as money can do so. The amount of compensation will not necessarily reflect the fault of the defendant, but will reflect the injury suffered by the claimant. The defendant may have only been at fault in a small way, but have caused significant loss to the claimant. In this case, the compensation payable will not reflect the fault of the defendant. This can be said to be morally unfair as there is a view that a person should only be required to pay compensation up to the level of his or her fault.

13.2. Theories of tort law

13.2.1 The public policy factors governing the imposition of a duty of care in negligence

In *AQA A-level Law for Year 1 and AS*, Chapter 24, we discovered that the purpose of establishing a duty of care in the tort of negligence is to show a legal relationship between the claimant and the defendant, thereby allowing the claimant to provide evidence that the defendant fell below a certain standard and breached their duty of care.

An explanation of the factors used by the court in a negligence action to decide, in novel situations, whether a duty of care is owed in negligence is contained in *AQA A-level Law for Year 1 and AS*, section 24.1. Originally, the neighbour test set out by Lord Atkin in *Donoghue v Stevenson* (1932) was used to decide whether a duty of care was established. In more recent times the courts have been required to use the *Caparo* three-stage test (from *Caparo v Dickman* (1990)) of:

- proximity of relationship
- whether the loss or injury is reasonably foreseeable, and
- if it is fair just and reasonable to impose a duty of care.

In the majority of negligence claims that come before the court, the question whether a duty of care exists will not be an issue. This three-stage test provides a broad framework and will only be required to consider novel situations. It allows courts in these situations to follow a step-by-step approach by analogy with previous situations. The reason for this approach is to prevent the floodgates opening to too many claims. However, it is still recognised that the categories of negligence are never closed, and that, provided the three-stage test can be satisfied, a duty of care can be established in a situation which has never previously arisen. An example of the use of this three-stage approach can be seen in *Watson v British Boxing Board of Control* (2000). In this case, the boxer Michael Watson was injured in a fight and suffered severe brain injuries. He claimed from the Board, arguing that if proper medical facilities had been provided at ringside, his injuries would have been less severe. The Court of Appeal decided, using the *Caparo* three-stage test, that the Board owed him a duty of care as it was the responsible body for licensing professional boxing.

On the other hand, using the third element of the *Caparo* test, decisions have been made that a duty of care does not exist. This is when it is not fair, just and reasonable for a duty of care to exist, even if the other two elements are satisfied. Decisions of this type are based on public policy.

This public policy reasoning was seen in the case of *Hill v Chief Constable of West Yorkshire* (1990) (see *AQA A-level Law for Year 1 and AS*, Chapter 24, section 24.1.3), which appeared to give the police blanket immunity from being sued. The reasoning for this protection was that if the police could be sued, it could lead to defensive policing and take them away from their prime roles of public protection and the prevention of crime. However, the recent case of *Robinson v Chief Constable of West Yorkshire* (2018) appears to have overruled *Hill*. *Robinson* was a decision of the Supreme Court and involved two policemen who had a violent struggle with a suspect they were trying to arrest. This struggle resulted in them knocking over the claimant who was an elderly lady. She claimed damages from the police for her foreseeable personal injury caused by their negligence. The judgments of the Supreme Court Justices analyse in detail the earlier authorities, including *Hill*, but the fundamental aspect of the case is that the court rejected the argument of the police that they have, since *Hill*, enjoyed a complete immunity from liability to the public in the tort of negligence. The decision confirms that they still retain that immunity in respect of harm caused by their negligent investigation of crime but they do have a duty of care under the normal rules of negligence not to cause, by positive action, physical harm or damage to property which ought reasonably to be avoided.

This approach was followed in cases involving the fire service, another public service. It seems to be established that an emergency call to the fire service does not establish proximity of relationship, as there is no guarantee that if they attended they would successfully put out the fire. It is also clear that the fire service will not owe a duty of care if they fail to attend a fire if they get lost and cannot find the fire, or are called to deal with another, more serious, situation while on the way to an emergency call. The only time the fire service will be liable is if they have taken positive action at a fire which fails to deal with the situation. This was established in *Capital and Counties plc v Hampshire County Council* (1997), when the fire service turned off a sprinkler system allowing a fire to get out of control.

As is seen in *Kent v Griffiths* (2000) (see AQA *A-level Law for Year 1 and AS*, Chapter 24, section 24.1.1), the ambulance service is not in the same position as the other emergency services. In that case, they did owe a duty to a patient after they had accepted an emergency call. It was said that this was analogous to a patient turning up at an A & E department of a hospital and failing to receive treatment.

This analysis shows that the courts are, in certain situations and for certain services, prepared to set rules, to provide protection from civil claims. Whether this protection is morally justified is doubtful, as the claimant will have suffered loss or injury and will be unable to claim compensation.

13.2.2 The policy factors governing imposition of liability in negligence for pure economic loss and psychiatric injury

Pure economic loss

Many claims in tort, and negligence in particular, will include some form of financial loss and can be described as being economic. These claims could include where property has been damaged or there is loss of earnings, and it is well established that damages can be awarded to compensate for these losses.

'Pure economic loss' in tort has a different meaning. This is where a claimant suffers financial loss that does not come from personal injury or damage to property. It can include loss of profit due to the

defendant's negligence. Tort law has been reluctant to compensate for this financial loss.

The rules covering claims for pure economic loss are explained in Chapter 14. A leading case is *Spartan Steel v Martin* (1972), where claims were made for:

- Damaged metal that was on the production line at the time of the power cut: this claim was allowed, as it was property damaged as a result of negligence.
- Loss of profit on that damaged metal: this again was allowed, as it was financial or economic loss arising from the damaged property.
- Loss of profit while the factory was closed due to the power cut: this claim was not allowed, as the majority in the Court of Appeal considered that it was 'pure economic loss', which is not recoverable in tort.

The court's decision was based on the ground that while a duty of care was owed to the claimants not to damage their property (and to pay for any loss arising from such damage), there was no duty to compensate for loss of profit. There were two main reasons for this approach:

1 Financial or economic loss would traditionally be compensated through the law of contract. This law offers certainty, as a defendant could be liable for a loss caused by his or her failure to complete a freely undertaken agreement, and this has been widely accepted in the commercial field.

2 There was a fear that by allowing the third part of the claim, it would lead to the 'floodgates' opening to many similar claims. The possible loss from those claims could be astronomical. It was said that the validity of such claims may be difficult or impossible to check. While this reasoning was not helpful to the claimant in *Spartan Steel v Martin*, or for others in similar situations, one of the roles of the law is to provide business with a framework within which it can plan its activities and future liabilities. Preventing claims for pure economic loss helps this approach.

The counter to this argument is that it should be no more difficult to check claims for loss of profit than any other claim, as evidence could be produced in support in the same way as it would be needed for a personal injury claim. Again, it can be argued that it is morally justified to compensate the claimant who has lost money through no fault of his or her own. However these artificial rules prevent such compensation being awarded.

Psychiatric injury

The rules covering claims for psychiatric injury will be explained in detail in Chapter 14. As will be seen there, a claimant has first to show whether they are a primary victim or a secondary victim. Primary victims are involved in an accident and can suffer either physical or mental injury or both. They have to prove negligence on the part of the defendant. Secondary victims are not directly involved in an accident, and they have more hurdles to negotiate in order to claim. They have to prove that:

- the defendant was negligent
- there is recognisable mental injury (with medical evidence)
- the claimant has close ties of love and affection with the victim
- the injury was suffered at the scene of the accident or at its immediate aftermath
- the claimant suffered the injury through his or her own unaided senses and not by third-party means, and
- a reasonable person would have suffered in the same way as the claimant.

The first point to make is that for a victim who is suffering from a severe mental injury, having to prove all these points will be quite a task. The reason for imposing all these hurdles is to prevent the floodgates opening to too many claims. This argument could be supported if we consider the number of potential claimants at the Hillsborough football stadium disaster in 1989, the subject of the *Alcock v Chief Constable of South Yorkshire* (1991) and *White v Chief Constable of South Yorkshire* (1999) claimants. If there were no restrictions in place, the number of potential claimants would be enormous. They could include those injured, the players, officials and support staff, other spectators at the ground (50,000+), stewards and emergency services, not to mention the families of the victims at home and elsewhere, and those watching on television and listening to radio commentaries (potentially millions of people). If all these were able to claim as a result of a disaster, the cost of the initial negligence would be enormous. In the case of Hillsborough, the cost would have fallen on the police and possibly their insurers, but ultimately it could fall upon the state.

On the other hand, it seems for genuine claimants that there are too many difficulties placed to prevent them making a claim and it is morally indefensible

for an injured victim not to receive compensation. The following criteria have to be established:

1. The first criteria is having a close relationship with the victim. This will be a matter of fact for the judge to decide, and it will be for the claimant to prove a close relationship. Only those friends or relatives who can pass this test will be able to claim. Merely being a friend or a relative is not sufficient. A close relationship has to be proved. Many friends or relations of the victim may suffer distress knowing that the victim has been involved in an accident, but only those who can prove a close relationship will be able to claim.

2. The next criteria to satisfy is that of proximity in time and space to the accident. This criteria was set in *McLoughlin v O'Brian* (1982), where Mrs McLoughlin saw her family covered in blood and dirt from the accident and she suffered shock as a result of seeing them in that state. It could be said that the sight of something shocking is not the only cause of psychiatric injury. Hearing about a traumatic event, especially when not knowing who might be involved or the outcome, could be equally shocking. Watching the aftermath unfold on television is likely to cause shock to those who know their family members are present, yet the courts in *Alcock* (1991) were clear that this did not give sufficient proximity. The time limit for suffering the shock is not easy to justify either. Among the claimants in *Alcock* was a man who knew his brother was at the game and who searched all night for him before finding that he had died. It is difficult to explain why all those hours searching and worrying would be less likely to cause shock than someone who saw a dead or injured loved one immediately after the accident.

3. The third criteria has the requirement for the shock to have been suffered as a result of a sudden event. It is difficult to justify why this is necessary, as a family member who has been caring for a seriously injured or dying relative over a period of time is likely to suffer similar effects and feelings to a person who has witnessed a sudden event. A line has to be drawn somewhere, but the justification for making the shock due to a sudden event is hard to justify.

4. A final point concerns rescuers. In *White* (1999), a requirement was introduced by the House of Lords that a rescuer could claim only if he or she feared for his or her own safety. This could create unjust distinctions. An example given by Lord Goff in

that case illustrates the distinction. Imagine two rescuers from a train crash subsequently suffering mental injury as a result of their experiences. One had been helping at the front end of the train, where there was an element of danger, and could claim; but the other had been helping at the rear, where there was no danger, and would *not* be able to claim. This seems illogical and morally indefensible, as both were helping rescue others and it is pure chance whether danger was present or not.

13.2.3 The factors governing the objective standard of care in a negligence action

> An explanation of the standard of care required to be shown in a negligence action is contained in AQA A-level Law for Year 1 and AS, Chapter 24, section 24.2.

A defendant's conduct is judged against what a reasonable person would have done in the same situation. This is consistent with the rest of negligence and tort law, which is concerned with what is reasonable in the circumstances. This differs from criminal law which often considers what the defendant was doing or thinking at the time of the offence. In relation to negligence, what the defendant was thinking, for example whether his or her conduct seemed reasonable to him or her or whether he or she was trying to achieve a high standard, is irrelevant.

The court will ignore the defendant's own characteristics, such as the level of his or her experience. So, for example, in *Nettleship v Weston* (1971), the fact that Mrs Weston was a very inexperienced driver was irrelevant; she was judged at the same standard as the ordinary experienced motorist. This was harsh on her and other learner drivers but, for the courts, it is a simpler task to judge and standard for them to set. This approach can be justified by the existence of compulsory insurance cover for all motorists, no matter how experienced they are. Those at greater risk will pay higher premiums to reflect the level of risk.

The risk of harm and the precautions taken against the risk can also lead to unfairness; see for example, *Bolton v Stone* (1951) discussed at *AQA A-level Law for Year 1 and AS*, Chapter 24, section 24.2.2.

In this case, it was unfair on the claimant, who had done nothing wrong, for her claim to be disallowed,

as the cricket club had done everything reasonable bearing in mind the risk. This shows that the owners or occupiers of property do not have to make their premises completely safe, or do everything possible to prevent harm – only to do what is reasonable in the circumstances. This was further illustrated in *Latimer v AEG* (1952), when the factory owners were not required to make the factory completely safe for their employees.

On the other hand, in some cases, special characteristics may be taken into account. Examples include:

- the age of the participants, as in *Mullen v Richards* (1998) where the girls were judged as 15-year-olds and not as adults
- any special characteristics of the claimant, such as in *Paris v Stepney Borough Council* (1951) where the claimant was injured by the defendant's failure to provide protective goggles
- if the defendant is acting for the public benefit, as in *Watt v Hertfordshire County Council* (1954) where the claimant fireman was injured on the way to an emergency; the court observed that if this had happened in a commercial situation where the defendant was gaining a profit, the claimant would not have been successful
- where the defendant is exercising a special skill, for example medicine, as in *Bolam v Friern Barnet Hospital Management Committee* (1957) which established that a doctor's actions or omissions will be judged according to the standards in the profession at the time.

Tip

You need to understand the policy reasons used by the courts to deny liability in claims of negligence, psychiatric injury and purely financial loss.

13.2.4 The grant of injunctions and balancing conflicting interests

> An explanation of the use of injunctions in a tort action is given in AQA A-level Law for Year 1 and AS, Chapter 26, section 26.4. See Chapter 15 of this book for the use of injunctions in private nuisance actions.

Injunctions

An injunction is a form of court order that requires one of the parties to an action to do something, or not to do something. If the order is not complied with, the party will face further penalties, which may include imprisonment.

An injunction is an equitable remedy, which was originally ordered by the courts of equity. Common law courts could only order an award of damages. Like other equitable remedies, it was traditionally granted when a wrong could not be effectively remedied by the award of money. Since 1865 it can be granted by any court. Injunctions are intended to make whole again someone whose rights have been violated and which cannot be adequately remedied by money.

An injunction is a discretionary remedy – in other words, the court will consider whether it is right in each particular case to grant the order. When deciding whether to grant an injunction, the court will give special attention to questions of fairness, good faith, delay or 'coming to court with clean hands' – in other words, contributing to the problem. If any of these apply, the court is less likely to grant an injunction.

Balancing conflicting interests

Legal scholar Rudolf von Jhering analysed law in the broad context of society. In his view, the purpose of law is to secure the conditions of social life, and this determines the content of law. The conditions of social life include both physical existence and ideal values, but these are relative to the social order of the time and place. He developed the idea of a scheme of interests and designated them as individual, state and public, the last two of which he tended to treat as one.

However, he did not develop a successful means of 'evaluation' of the interests as against each other. This theory was developed further by Roscoe Pound, who identified public and private interests, claiming that a just result in every case could be achieved if those interests could be balanced. However, in his view the interests could only be balanced if they were on the same level – public and public or private and private. If there was a conflict then the public interest would prevail.

An illustration of both the theory of balancing interests and the granting of an injunction can be seen in the private nuisance case of *Miller v Jackson* (1977), when Mr and Mrs Miller complained about cricket balls being hit into their garden. The public interest was represented by the local community and the cricket club, using the cricket field for their matches and for recreation generally. The private interest was that of Mr and Mrs Miller who complained they were unable to use their garden because of cricket balls being hit into it during matches. The Court of Appeal decided in favour of the public interest and refused the Millers an injunction to stop games being played. This illustrates Pound's theories that, as the interests were on different levels, the public interest would prevail.

The decision also illustrates equitable principles behind the decision of whether to grant an injunction. One of the judges, Lord Justice Cumming Bruce, particularly relied on equitable principles to decide that it would be unfair to grant an injunction to the Millers. He took into account these factors:

- The cricket club had been in existence, and the ground had been used by the local community, for a long time.
- Stopping the playing of sport would be a loss to the whole community.
- The Millers received the benefit of living adjacent to an open space.

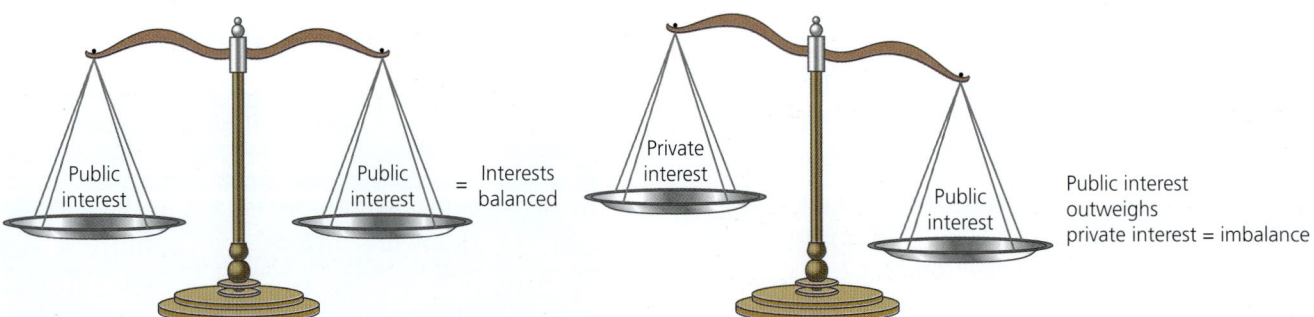

Figure 13.1 Balancing interests

- They should have considered the possibility of balls coming into their garden before they bought the house.
- Mrs Miller, in particular, showed a very hostile attitude to the club and players.

Considering these factors, Cumming Bruce decided it would not be equitable to grant the Millers an injunction. One of the other judges, Lord Denning, using his discretion, weighed up the public versus private interest issue to decide that an injunction should not be granted. The other judge considered that he was bound by judicial precedent and that an injunction should be awarded.

13.3 The nature and purpose of vicarious liability

As will be explained in Chapter 16, this is not a tort as such, but is a way of ensuring that the claimant receives compensation for the injury, loss or damage he or she has suffered. It will most often apply in an employment relationship, though it could also be relevant in a parent/child relationship.

The defendant who causes the loss, injury or damage will be primarily liable but there may be reasons why he or she will not be able to pay compensation. For example, an employee may not be insured or financially able to pay the compensation ordered. If the employer is vicariously liable, they will be accepting some responsibility for the actions or omissions of their employee and they are likely to be insured or will, financially, be able to pay the compensation.

There are two conditions in an employment situation for vicarious liability to apply:

- the employee is employed and is not an independent contractor, and
- he or she is acting in the course of employment.

The liability of the employer is said to be strict as the employer may have played no part in causing the injury, loss or damage. However, the liability can be justified as an employer may have had, or perhaps should have had, a degree of control over the activities of the employees. In some cases, the tort may have happened because the employee has followed the direct instructions of the employer, which led to the tort. In this case, it is only fair that the employer should bear the cost of the employee's actions.

The employer can be said to be receiving a benefit from the employee's work, so it is only fair that they accept the burden of the employee's actions.

In addition, employers are responsible for the initial hiring and subsequent firing or disciplining their staff. An employer may have been careless in selecting an employee, and, if employees are either careless or likely to cause harm, and the employer is aware of this, the employer has the ability to do something about it. Internal disciplinary systems allow the employer to ensure that lapses of behaviour are not repeated. There is, of course, the ultimate sanction of dismissing a member of staff who refuses to, or is unable to, follow set procedures or legitimate orders.

Finally, an employer is responsible for making sure that all their employees are trained so that work is done safely and that safe procedures are followed.

The rule can be criticised for applying liability unfairly as an apparently innocent party, the employer, is liable for something which they have not done or failed to do. The employer may not be directly at fault for causing the loss, injury or damage. However, this argument is overwhelmed by the reasons for the existence of the liability and it seems to be an accepted consequence of being an employer especially as the consequence can be covered by public liability insurance cover.

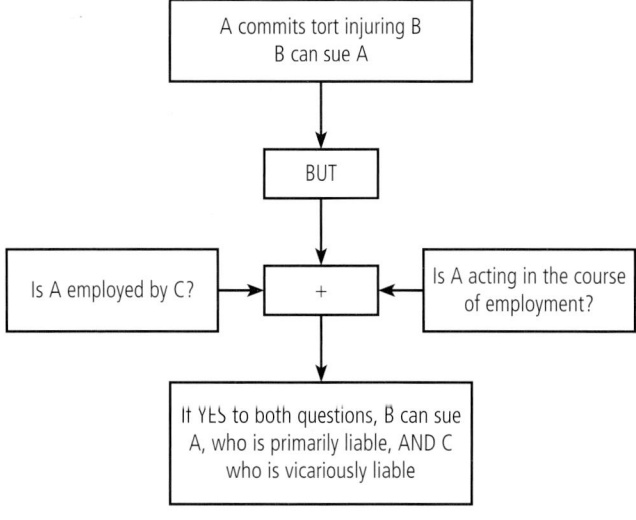

Figure 13.2 Vicarious liability

Figure 13.3 Key cases for rules and theory of tort law

Case	Facts	Legal principle
Watson v British Boxing Board of Control (2000)	Michael Watson was left severely brain damaged when, due to the negligence of the BBBC, there were inadequate medical facilities at a boxing match organised by them	BBBC owed Watson and all other fighters in matches organised by them a duty of care to ensure appropriate medical facilities were present
Hill v Chief Constable of West Yorkshire (1990)	The police were sued by the mother of the last victim of the Yorkshire Ripper for their failure to catch him before he killed the victim	For public policy reasons, the police do not owe a duty of care to ordinary members of the public, as this would result in defensive policing
Swinney v Chief Constable of Northumbria (1999)	The police failed to protect the claimant after she had given evidence about a criminal to them and, as a result, she suffered severe mental injuries and lost her business	The police do owe a duty of care where they have accepted responsibility for the safety of a specific person
Capital and Counties plc v Hampshire County Council (1997)	The fire service turned off a sprinkler system in a building they attended, allowing a fire to get out of control and destroy the building and its contents	The fire service will owe a duty of care where they take negligent but positive action
Kent v Griffiths (2000)	Due to an unexplained delay by the ambulance service in attending an emergency call, a patient suffered more severe injuries	The ambulance service were subject to a duty of care when they accepted an emergency call
Spartan Steel v Martin (1972)	Due to workmen's negligence an electricity cable was severed causing a factory to stop production	A claim could be made for goods damaged on the production line and loss of profit on those goods but not for loss of profit while the factory was closed, as this was 'pure' economic loss
McLoughlin v O'Brian (1982)	A mother suffered shock when she saw her family in hospital in the aftermath of an accident	A claim for nervous shock could be made by a person who had close ties of love and affection with the victim of an accident and who saw the aftermath of the accident
Alcock v Chief Constable of South Yorkshire (1991)	Families of the Hillsborough victims suffered shock after learning that family members died in the tragedy	A claim for nervous shock could be made by a person who had close ties of love and affection with the victim of an accident, who saw the accident or its immediate aftermath and who suffered shock through his or her own unaided senses
White v Chief Constable of South Yorkshire (1999)	Claims for nervous shock were made by police officers on duty at the Hillsborough ground	Rescuers could only claim for nervous shock if they feared for their own safety
Nettleship v Weston (1971)	Due to the negligence of a learner driver, her instructor was injured	A learner is treated at the same standard as an experienced person
Bolton v Stone (1951)	A woman was injured by a cricket ball hit out of the ground	The cricket club had taken all necessary precautions bearing in mind the risk and had not breached its duty of care
Latimer v AEG (1952)	After a flood, factory owners spread sawdust on the floor and required their workers to return to work	The owners had taken all necessary precautions to make the factory safe taking into account the risk, and they had not breached their duty of care
Mullen v Richards (1998)	In a play fight, a girl was injured when a plastic ruler split and damaged her eye	Children are to be treated as children and not as adults

Case	Facts	Legal principle
Paris v Stepney Borough Council (1951)	A workman was blinded when his employers failed to provide him with goggles when welding	The claimant was particularly vulnerable and the employers should have provided him with extra protection
Watt v Hertfordshire County Council (1954)	The claimant fireman was injured when on the way to an emergency	Greater risks can be taken when dealing with emergencies
Bolam v Friern Barnet Hospital Management Committee (1957)	The claimant was injured when receiving ECT for treating mental illness	There was no breach of duty by the doctor, who should be judged according to the standard of what others in the profession would have done
Miller v Jackson (1977)	A family claimed that cricket balls hit into their garden from an adjoining ground amounted to a nuisance	The public benefit of using the cricket ground outweighed the disadvantage to the individual householders

Summary

- A tort is a civil wrong which causes loss or injury to the claimant.

- The claimant will take a tort action to claim compensation for the loss or damage he or she has suffered.

- Damages in tort are awarded to put the claimant back in the position he or she was in before the tort happened as far as money can do so.

- Torts based on negligence require the claimant to show the fault of the defendant in causing the loss, injury or damage.

- Other torts such as nuisance and *Rylands v Fletcher* are strict liability and do not need to show the fault of the defendant.

- In vicarious liability, the claimant does not have to show the fault of the third party to make him or her liable.

- A duty of care in negligence establishes a legal relationship between the parties.

- The *Caparo* three-stage test is used to decide if a duty of care exists in novel cases.

- The courts use public policy reasons to decide that some emergency services do not owe a duty of care where there is no previous contact between the parties.

- 'Pure economic loss' is where a claimant suffers financial loss that does not come from personal injury or damage to property.

- The floodgates argument has been used to restrict possible claims as courts consider claims should be made in contract law rather than tort.

- The 'floodgates' argument is also in place for psychiatric injury to prevent too many claims being made, but this does lead to injustice.
  - The requirements for proving close relationship and the way and time limits for suffering shock seem unnecessarily harsh.
  - The objective requirement for rescuers can result in unfairness.

- In negligence, a defendant's conduct is judged against what a reasonable person would have done in the same situation.

- The defendant's own characteristics will be ignored but some special characteristics can be taken into account when deciding if the defendant has breached the duty of care.

- An injunction is a discretionary order of the court to do or not to do something. It will only be granted if it is equitable to do so.

- Rudolph von Jhering identified a scheme of interests which could be designated as individual on the one hand and state and public on the other.

- Roscoe Pound developed the theory further, identifying public and private interests and that a just result could be achieved if those interests could be balanced.

- Vicarious liability requires that an employer accepts financial responsibility for the tortious actions of employees.
- It is justified because the employer has control over employees, they have employed and trained them and are taking a benefit from their work.
- This liability is criticised as the employer may not be directly at fault in causing the accident.

14 Liability in negligence for economic loss and psychiatric injury

14.1 Liability for pure economic loss caused by negligent acts and negligent misstatements

If a claimant successfully proves a negligent act or omission by another (the defendant), they will be able to claim damages for:

■ any physical injury suffered, and/or
■ any damage to their property.

So, if the defendant causes a car accident by negligent driving and, as a result, the claimant is injured and their vehicle is damaged, the claimant will be able to claim damages for their injuries and for the cost of repair to or replacement of their vehicle. The claimant will also be able to recover damages for any consequential economic (financial) loss which arises directly from the physical damage. This will cover, for example, the cost of hiring a replacement vehicle while repairs are being carried out and any loss of clothing or loss of earnings.

A claimant will not be able to claim for what is called 'pure economic loss'. This is considered as being economic or financial loss which is not caused by physical injury or damage. So this will cover, for example, any loss of profit suffered by a business while it is unable to operate.

One exception to the pure economic loss rule is that a claimant who suffers a financial loss as a result of acting on a negligent misstatement will be able

to claim for the loss if they can establish a 'special relationship' with the defendant who gave the advice. This is a result of the *Hedley Byrne* case explained at 14.1.2 below.

14.1.1 Loss caused by negligent acts

Decisions by the courts were clear – there was no liability for a 'pure economic loss'. This approach was based on policy and the idea that 'economic loss', which is likely to be a loss of profit, was more an issue of contract law rather than tort. The approach has been clearly stated and can be illustrated in a case such as *Spartan Steel v Martin and Co. (Contractors) Ltd* (1973).

Spartan Steel v Martin and Co. (Contractors) Ltd (1973)

An electric power cable outside the claimant's factory was negligently cut by the defendant's workmen. This led to a loss of power for several hours to the factory which made steel alloys. A 'melt' in the furnace at the time of the power cut had to be destroyed to stop it from solidifying and wrecking the furnace. There were three parts to the claim:

■ For the damage to the melts on the production line and the furnace – this could be claimed as it was physical damage.
■ For the loss of profit on those melts – this could be claimed as it amounted to consequential economic loss from the physical damage.
■ For the loss of profit while the factory was out of action – it was decided by the Court of Appeal that this part of the claim should not be allowed as it amounted to pure economic loss. This was a financial loss which was not caused by physical damage to the claimant. Lord Denning decided that a line must be drawn as a matter of policy, and that this loss of profit was better borne by insurers than by the defendants alone.

The idea of pure economic loss being a loss of profit can also be seen in the case of *Weller v Foot and Mouth Disease Research Institute* (1966).

Weller v Foot and Mouth Disease Research Institute (1966)

The foot and mouth virus was negligently allowed to escape from the defendant's premises. It infected cattle, rendering them unsaleable and causing many to be destroyed. Restrictions were placed on the movement of all animals for some time to prevent the spread of the disease. The claimant was an auctioneer and brought an action claiming the loss of profit he would have made had he been able to continue his normal sales. His claim failed as the court decided that pure economic loss is not recoverable under tort law.

A similar result came in the case of *D Pride and Partners v Institute for Animal Health* (2009), when again foot and mouth disease escaped from a research institute in 2007 and restrictions were placed on the movement of cattle. Farmers suffered significant losses, including lost income, as a result of their inability to sell or export animals, loss of milk production and the extra costs of feeding and keeping animals on their farms. The judge decided that these losses were all pure economic losses and because of the 'exclusionary rule', which excludes such losses from the scope of any duty of care, the claim failed. It was also commented that the claim was rejected for policy reasons as, if it was allowed, it would create limitless liability on the defendants to farmers across the country.

These cases show that the courts draw what appear to be artificial distinctions, created for policy reasons, purely for the purpose of restricting liability. The distinction has the obvious potential to create unfair anomalies in the law as there is no doubt that the factory, the auctioneer and the farmers lost money due to negligence. In *Spartan Steel v Martin and Co.*, the distinction between the three types of financial loss was very small, and it should have been foreseeable to the contractors that if they negligently cut the electricity cable the factory would be without power for a period, affecting production and profit. The failure to make an award against the defendants could be seen as allowing a negligent defendant to 'get away' with his or her behaviour. It could also be considered morally unfair not to compensate a claimant who suffered loss through no fault of his or her own.

On the other hand, it could be argued that the loss of profit is really a failure to make a gain. The aim of tort law is to compensate the victim of a tort for his or her loss, so allowing a claim for loss of profit goes against the point of tort law. Drawing on the *Caparo* three-stage test, it was not fair, just or reasonable to impose a duty of care for loss of profit on the defendants in each case.

14.1.2 Loss caused by negligent misstatements

The rules on claiming for a loss suffered due to a negligent misstatement can apply in two situations:

- Two-party liability – this can be when A gives advice or makes a statement to B and B suffers loss in relying on it. In this case, if there is a contract between A and B such as for professional advice given for a fee, for example by a solicitor or accountant, if the advice is negligent and B suffers financial loss by relying on it, then B can claim damages for breach of contract. If there is no contract between A and B, because B has not paid for the advice, then B cannot use the law of contract to claim for any financial loss he or she suffers through A's negligent advice. The question here is whether B can bring a claim against A in the tort of negligence? Does A owe a duty of care to B regarding the advice?

- Three-party liability – this is where A makes a statement to B, and B communicates it to C. C then suffers loss in relying on the statement. In this case, there is no contractual relationship between A and C. Will A owe a duty of care to C, so as to become liable to C in the tort of negligence for negligent advice or a negligent misstatement?

Figure 14.1 Key cases for pure economic loss caused by negligent acts

Case	Facts	Legal principle
Spartan Steel v Martin and Co. (Contractors) Ltd (1973)	Power cables to a factory were negligently cut, causing steel melts on the production line to be destroyed Property destroyed and loss of profit on it could be claimed for as they were foreseeable consequences; loss of profit was not allowed	Pure economic loss, being a loss of profit while the factory was out of action, was not allowed for policy reasons
Weller v Foot and Mouth Disease Research Institute (1966)	Foot and mouth virus escaped from the defendant's premises which led to restrictions on the movement of animals The claimant suffered loss of income and profit as he was unable to hold cattle auctions	Loss of income and profit was pure economic loss and not recoverable under tort law

The requirements for making a claim by establishing a special relationship are the same for both two-party liability and three-party liability, but the first form (two-party liability) will be the most common situation.

Traditionally, a claim for financial loss due to reliance on a statement was only available in the tort of deceit, and only when the defendant had made a fraudulent statement. This view remained until *Candler v Crane Christmas and Co.* (1951). In this case, Lord Denning, dissenting with the majority in the Court of Appeal, felt that a duty of care should be owed to an investor who lost money relying on advice, and also to:

> **❝** ...any third party to whom they themselves show the accounts, or to whom they know their employer is going to show the accounts so as to induce them to invest money. **❞**

Subsequently, as a result of the *Hedley Byrne* case (below), the rule was set that a claim may be made by those who suffer financial loss as a result of relying on a statement. However, it has to be established that:

- the statement was made negligently, and
- there is a 'special relationship' between the parties.

Hedley Byrne v Heller and Partners (1964)

An advertising company, Hedley Byrne, was approached by Easipower to place adverts in newspapers and magazines. It had not previously dealt with Easipower so it requested a reference from Easipower's bank. The bank gave a favourable reference and Hedley Byrne went ahead with the campaign. However, Easipower went into liquidation without paying for the campaign. Hedley Byrne sued Easipower's bankers for the loss it suffered as a result of its reliance on the reference.

The House of Lords decided that, in principle, a claim could be made for a negligent misstatement if a special relationship between the parties could be proved. In this case, there was a special relationship but the reference contained a disclaimer of liability. This amounted to a defence, which meant that Hedley Byrne could not succeed.

In the House of Lords, Lord Denning's dissenting judgment in *Candler v Crane Christmas and Co.* (1951) was approved. The interesting point of the court's approval of the principle is that they were agreeing that a duty could apply despite there being no contractual relationship between the parties, and despite the fact that, in effect, they were accepting that they could impose liability for an economic loss.

The precise meaning of what amounts to a 'special relationship' was never really examined in *Hedley Byrne* (1964). It was not until the case of *Caparo v Dickman* (1990) that the House of Lords set out the features of a special relationship, which in effect means that the person giving the advice owes a duty of care to the claimant.

> See AQA A-*level Law for Year 1 and AS*, section 24.1 for details of the *Caparo* test in negligence.

Caparo Industries v Dickman (1990)

Caparo Industries were shareholders in a company called Fidelity Ltd. Caparo considered the annual books of audit of Fidelity, prepared by Dickman. These books showed a profit and Caparo decided to launch a takeover to completely own Fidelity. When they had completed the deal, Caparo found that Fidelity was almost worthless and it sued Dickman for its loss. The preparation of the annual books of audit was a statutory requirement.

The House of Lords decided that the books of audit were not designed as a guide for new investors, or for existing investors to increase their shares and, as a result, Dickman did not owe a duty of care to Caparo.

The House of Lords set out in more detail what is needed to prove a special relationship for the purposes of negligent misstatement. A special relationship requires all of the following to be proved:

- The possession of a special skill or expertise on the part of the person giving the advice. This can be having a recognised qualification but can also be when a person is holding him- or herself out, or representing him- or herself, as having some special skill or knowledge in the field in which advice is being given. The advisor does not have to be a 'professional advisor'.
- A reliance by the claimant on the advice – in other words, the advice is used and acted on by the claimant. The real test is whether there is sufficient proximity between the parties for there to be reasonable reliance on the advice. In *Raja v Gray* (2002), the Court of Appeal held that there was insufficient proximity between valuers appointed by receivers and parties with an interest in mortgaged property generally. It will not be foreseeable reliance if the claimant belongs to a group of potential claimants that is too large,

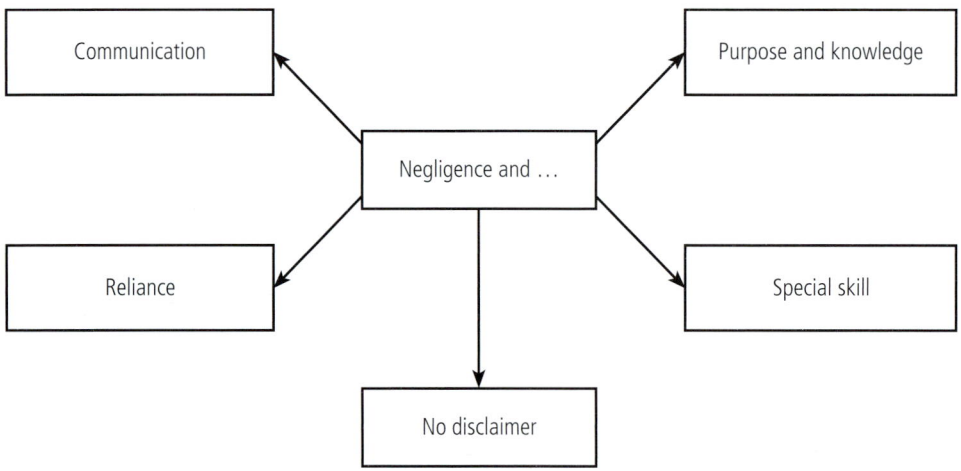

Figure 14.2 The requirements of a special relationship

such as readers of a newspaper. The claimant must show actual reliance and consequent detriment (loss) suffered.

■ The advice is communicated directly to the claimant and not through a third party or by third-party means such as a newspaper, television or radio.

■ The person giving the advice knows that it is being required for a purpose described at the time to the defendant, at least in general terms, and that it is being used for that purpose. He or she must know that the advice will be acted upon by the claimant without taking any further independent advice.

■ There is no **disclaimer** to act as a defence. Including a disclaimer is standard practice when, for example, a professional is giving a reference.

Key term

Disclaimer – a statement informing the claimant that the company does not accept responsibility for the advice being given.

If all these requirements are present and the claimant loses money, the loss can be claimed from the person giving the advice.

Normally, the advice will be given in a quasi-business situation. However, it has been decided in *Chaudhry v Prabhakar* (1988) that a special relationship can exist even if the advice was given in a social situation or in the course of a social relationship.

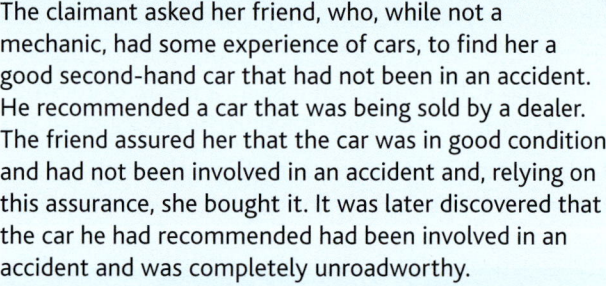

Chaudhry v Prabhakar (1988)

The claimant asked her friend, who, while not a mechanic, had some experience of cars, to find her a good second-hand car that had not been in an accident. He recommended a car that was being sold by a dealer. The friend assured her that the car was in good condition and had not been involved in an accident and, relying on this assurance, she bought it. It was later discovered that the car he had recommended had been involved in an accident and was completely unroadworthy.

The claimant recovered the cost of the vehicle from the dealer under contract law but also successfully sued her friend for his negligent misstatement.

One view of this decision is that the defendant was unfortunate in being liable, as he was not an expert in the true sense or someone with special knowledge. However, the result can be justified since he had much more knowledge about cars than the claimant, he had recommended the vehicle to her, and he should have applied the same caution in advising her that he would have taken if he had been buying the car himself.

As the law on claiming losses for negligent misstatement has been developed by judicial precedent, and only in cases that have come before the courts, it is complicated. The courts have been restrictive in their approach and have been anxious to avoid opening the floodgates to too many claims. This led at one time to the unfair situation that surveyors or architects who advise on the construction of a building which turns out to be defective could be sued (probably as they had indemnity insurance cover), whereas builders who

Figure 14.3 Key cases on loss caused by negligent misstatement

Case	Facts	Legal principle
Hedley Byrne v Heller and Partners (1964)	The claimants relied on a bank reference to give credit to a company The company went into liquidation owing the claimants money They sued the bank for their loss	A claim for negligent misstatement can be made when there is a special relationship between the parties
Caparo Industries v Dickman (1990)	Caparo relied on statutory audit books to buy a company It later found the company to be worthless and sued for its loss	A special relationship requires skill or knowledge of the person giving advice, reliance on advice, knowledge of reliance, communication, and no disclaimer
Chaudhry v Prabhakar (1988)	The claimant relied on a friend's recommendation when buying a car that turned out to be unroadworthy	Negligent misstatement can be claimed even if the advice is given in a social situation

were negligent in the construction of a building were not liable (as they were less likely to have insurance cover).

The general approach is that negligent advice given in an informal setting, such as a party or social gathering, cannot be claimed for. However, the decision in *Chaudhry v Prabhakar* seems to conflict with this general approach. This could be because of the claimant's complete reliance on her friend and his strong recommendation to her to buy the car. It seems fair to restrict claims of negligent misstatement to those to whom advice is given directly. This means that advice given through newspaper columns or in radio and television programmes can still be given without fear of being sued.

14.2 Liability for psychiatric injury sustained by primary and secondary victims

It is common to find that the victim of an accident (a primary victim) suffers physical and/or mental injury. A person who witnesses an accident or tragic event but who is not directly involved in it (a secondary victim) may suffer mental injury as a result of what he or she has seen.

Claims for **psychiatric injury** are a development of the law of negligence that was covered in AQA

Key term

Psychiatric injury – also known as nervous shock. A severe, long-term mental injury which is more than shock or grief.

A-level Law for Year 1 and AS, Chapter 24. They are sometimes called claims for 'nervous shock'. The law on these claims has been developed solely by judges by their decisions in court. Just as with claims for pure economic loss and negligent misstatement covered previously, judges have developed policy reasons to restrict the number of claims, especially by secondary victims. The loss suffered by a claimant will often be loss of earnings, as the extent of the mental injury will be so severe that the claimant will be unable to work, or be unable to do the work he or she was involved in before the accident.

Primary victims (those involved in the accident) have to prove negligence on the part of the defendant. Judges have not placed restrictions on these claims. However, restrictions have been placed on claims by secondary victims (those not directly involved in an accident). To be successful, a secondary victim has to prove:

- there was an accident or sudden event where someone (the defendant) was negligent which caused the injury
- some form of mental injury
- the claimant passes certain criteria (known as the *Alcock* criteria, after the case of that name) to allow them to claim, and
- that a person of reasonable fortitude would have suffered the same injury in the circumstances.

14.2.1 Negligence by the defendant has initially to be proved

This means, as with a claim for physical injury, that the defendant owed the claimant a duty of care, the duty was breached and loss or damage was caused. In nervous shock claims, it will be a mental injury.

14.2.2 A mental injury

The claim will have to be supported by medical evidence and the injury will have to be sufficiently serious that the claimant is badly affected by it. It must be more than mere shock or grief – it must be a long-term injury that, for example, prevents the claimant from working. The claim can therefore include loss of earnings, both past and future, while suffering from the condition. Examples of injuries covered by these types of claims include post-traumatic stress, reactive depression and acute anxiety. The mental injury must come from a sudden event: if the claimant has, for example, nursed a loved one over a period of time and then suffered mental injuries following death, this cannot be claimed for. Proving a long-term serious mental injury will need medical evidence which may be difficult and expensive. In addition, the claimant will have to show loss of past and future earnings at a time when he or she is struggling with his or her illness.

Early development of the rules

Initially, judges were suspicious of claimants with mental injuries, and a claim could be made only if the claimant suffered mental injury as a result of fearing for his or her own safety. This was as a result of *Dulieu v White* (1901).

Dulieu v White (1901)

The claimant was working in a bar when, as a result of an accident in the street outside, a coach and horses crashed into the bar. She suffered fear for her own safety. Her claim was allowed as it was foreseeable that, in the event of an accident, someone could suffer real and immediate fear of personal danger. This was probably the first successful claim for mental injuries.

The next development was in *Hambrook v Stokes* (1925), when the rule from *Dulieu v White* was extended.

Hambrook v Stokes (1925)

A mother was walking with her children along a pavement when a runaway lorry passed her. She heard a crash ahead of her and also that the lorry was involved in an accident involving a child. She suffered severe shock as she feared for the safety of her children. Her claim was allowed and, as a result, a claim could be made by those suffering shock due to fearing for the safety of a family member.

The next important case was a claim made by someone who witnessed the immediate aftermath of a fatal accident.

Bourhill v Young (1943)

A pregnant fishwife heard an accident involving a motorbike as she was getting off a tram. She went to look at the scene and, when she saw blood on the road, suffered such shock that she miscarried. Her claim against the estate of the dead motorcyclist who had caused the accident failed, as she was not related to him and she was not within the range of people who could be foreseen as suffering shock. There was no proximity of relationship between her and the motorcyclist.

This decision confirmed the previous cases that, in order to claim, a mental injury had to be suffered due to injury to oneself or a member of family and the persons able to claim must fall within a foreseeable range of people who could be affected by the negligence.

The next claim developed the law to deal with a mental injury suffered a short time after an accident. Before this case, a claim could only be made by someone at the scene of the accident.

McLoughlin v O'Brien (1982)

Mrs McLoughlin's husband and children were involved in a car accident due to the negligence of a lorry driver. She was at home and was informed of the accident. She went to the hospital where her family were being treated. She suffered shock when she saw them there and learned of the death of one of her children.

Two principles were set by the House of Lords which extended the rules for claiming nervous shock further:

1 A claim could be made by someone who had close ties of love and affection with a victim of the accident.

2 The shock could be suffered either at the scene of the accident or within its immediate aftermath. No time was set for this, but Mrs McLoughlin arrived at the hospital within two hours of the accident.

The phrase 'close ties of love and affection' was not defined but could be considered to include blood relatives of the victim. It was sufficiently open to allow more distant relatives to qualify and could include close friends or those in a relationship with the victim. Whatever the relationship, the courts would require proof of the close ties of love and affection requirement. This decision extended the period in which a claimant could suffer the shock and it could occur up to two hours after the accident as a result of what was seen at the scene of the accident or in an ambulance or at hospital.

14.2.2 Primary and secondary victims

The House of Lords, in the case of *Page v Smith* (1995), made a distinction in claims for psychiatric injury between primary and secondary victims.

Primary victims were those who were involved in the accident and suffered either physical injuries, mental injuries or both. They are required to prove the defendant was negligent and can claim for both his or her physical and mental injuries.

Secondary victims were not involved in the accident but suffered mental injury as a result of what they saw or heard at the scene of the accident or its immediate aftermath. For this type of victim, there are additional hurdles to pass in order to restrict the number of potential claims. These hurdles include the need to prove negligence, as with primary victims, but also certain criteria (the *Alcock* criteria, see below) and a threshold test, which means that they can only succeed if a reasonable person in that position would have suffered the shock.

> ### Key terms
>
> **Primary victim** – a victim of an accident who suffers physical or mental injuries, or both.
>
> **Secondary victim** – a person who suffers mental injury after witnessing an accident or its immediate aftermath.

Page v Smith (1995)

The claimant had suffered from ME before the accident. He was in recovery when he was involved in a minor car accident due to the defendant's negligence. He was not physically injured but the accident triggered his ME which became chronic and permanent. As a result he was unable to return to his job as a teacher. The House of Lords decided that provided some kind of personal injury was foreseeable, it did not matter whether the injury was physical or psychiatric and so the distinction was made between primary and secondary victims.

In addition, it was said that the fact that an ordinary person would not have suffered the injury incurred by the claimant was irrelevant, as defendants must take their victims as they find them under the thin skull rule.

In addition to proving negligence, secondary victims have to prove the *Alcock* criteria.

The *Alcock* criteria

These were established by the House of Lords in a case brought by a representative group of people who suffered mental injuries as a result of their family members dying at the Hillsborough football ground in 1989.

Alcock v Chief Constable of South Yorkshire (1992)

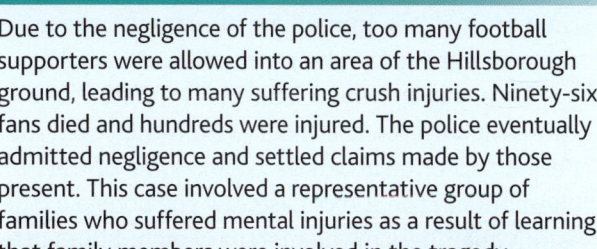

Due to the negligence of the police, too many football supporters were allowed into an area of the Hillsborough ground, leading to many suffering crush injuries. Ninety-six fans died and hundreds were injured. The police eventually admitted negligence and settled claims made by those present. This case involved a representative group of families who suffered mental injuries as a result of learning that family members were involved in the tragedy.

Fans are pulled to safety at Hillsborough

The House of Lords developed the following criteria that had to be satisfied for claimants in this case. They laid down the precedent that the criteria had to be satisfied by secondary victims in future cases. The criteria are as follows:

- The claimant had to have close ties of love and affection with the victim. This means that:
  - the relationship is a close type of relationship, and
  - the relationship is close in fact.

  A close type of relationship means that the claimant was related by blood or in a relationship with the victim. However, it could also include a claim by a close friend. Closeness in fact has to be proved whether or not the claimant was a family member.

As we have seen, this was a requirement originally set out in *McLoughlin v O'Brien*. Claimants are likely to be suffering from the effects of a mental injury when they are required to bring a case. Proving close ties of love and affection may be difficult, as it can require gathering evidence of previous contacts, visits and phone calls at a time when claimants are struggling with their illness and the grief of losing their loved one.

■ The claimant suffered mental injuries at the scene of the accident or in its immediate aftermath. This time limit of 'the immediate aftermath' was not defined, but the two-hour period in *McLoughlin v O'Brien* was approved. This meant that if the claimant suffered the shock within the two hour period this criteria was satisfied. Some of the claimants in the *Alcock* case saw the bodies of their family members in the mortuary eight hours after the events and suffered shock at this point. These claims were not allowed, as it was considered too distant in time from the incident. It appears that if claimants suffer the shock nearer two hours than eight hours, they will be able to pass this criterion. These do seem to be rather artificial time limits. Whatever the length of time, a claimant will be suffering a mental injury and it would seem to be morally fair to award compensation.

■ The claimant suffered shock through his or her own unaided senses – in other words, he or she saw or heard the accident or its aftermath. If the claimant suffered the shock through watching television, listening to the radio or hearing about the accident by a phone call or on social media, this criteria would not be satisfied.

Tip

All three of the '*Alcock*' criteria have to be satisfied for a claim to succeed. It will be unfair for a claimant who cannot prove all the *Alcock* criteria as he or she will still be suffering from his or her mental injuries and is likely to have suffered, and will continue to suffer, financially. The claimant will be left without compensation for the losses he or she has suffered. This unfairness is due to the *Alcock* threshold tests which act as control mechanisms to limit the number of possible claims.

Finally, remember that there is a threshold test to be satisfied – that a person of reasonable fortitude would have suffered the same reaction and injury as the claimant.

Look online

You can investigate in more detail the background of the Hillsborough disaster by reading the independent report at https://assets.publishing.service.gov.uk/government/uploads/system/uploads/attachment_data/file/229038/0581.pdf

14.2.3 Other categories of claimants
Rescuers

Rescuers will have been actively involved in helping victims of the accident. The courts do not wish to discourage rescuing, and it is likely that a claim for mental injuries suffered in the act of rescuing will be allowed. This rule was set in *Chadwick v British Rail* (1967).

Chadwick v British Rail (1967)

The claimant helped victims of the Lewisham train crash, which occurred close to his home. Because of his small size, he was encouraged to crawl into the wreckage to give injections and comfort to trapped passengers. As a result of his experience, he suffered mental injuries. His claim against the negligent railway authority was successful, as the court considered he was a primary victim, at risk to himself, and it did not want to discourage members of the public from rescuing, if required.

Usually these days, only professional rescuers who put themselves at risk will be able to claim. This was the case in *Hale v London Underground* (1992), when a fireman attending the Kings Cross station fire successfully claimed for the post-traumatic stress disorder he suffered as a result of his experience in the rescue attempts. This is because rescuers who put themselves in danger are classified as primary victims. However, if the rescuers do not put themselves physically at risk, they are secondary victims and will have to satisfy the *Alcock* criteria.

White v Chief Constable of South Yorkshire (1998)

Police officers who took part in the rescue operation at Hillsborough claimed to have suffered post-traumatic stress disorder as a result of their experiences. Their claims were denied as they did not put themselves at risk. A further reason was that the judges considered that public policy prevented them from recovering compensation when the relatives of the victims could not recover.

Police line up on the pitch at Hillsborough after the match was stopped

The reasoning in *White*, that the officers did not put themselves at risk, was followed in *French v Chief Constable of Sussex Police* (2006) in respect of police officers who claimed to suffer nervous shock after being investigated for the shooting of an innocent man.

As an alternative, a rescuer could potentially claim as a secondary victim if he or she can satisfy all the *Alcock* criteria.

Bystanders

Bystanders are witnesses to an accident, or its aftermath, and who do nothing to help. If they suffer mental injuries, they will not be able to claim unless they can satisfy the *Alcock* criteria. This was decided in *McFarlane v E E Caledonia* (1994)

McFarlane v E E Caledonia (1994)

The claimant was on board a supply ship when the Piper Alpha oilrig exploded in the North Sea. He witnessed the explosions and the rescue of survivors and suffered psychiatric injury as a result of what he saw. He did not help in the rescue.

McFarlane failed in his claim because he was classed as a bystander rather than a rescuer, and he did not satisfy all the *Alcock* criteria.

As a result of this case, the court will not extend a duty of care to mere bystanders of horrific events nor to a rescuer lacking ordinary courage. Whether a person is to be regarded as a rescuer is a question of fact to be decided on the facts of the case. If trivial or peripheral assistance is given, this will not usually be sufficient.

Property owners

One successful claim for psychiatric injury has been made by a woman who did not witness an accident but who suffered shock when she saw her house burning down.

Attia v British Gas (1987)

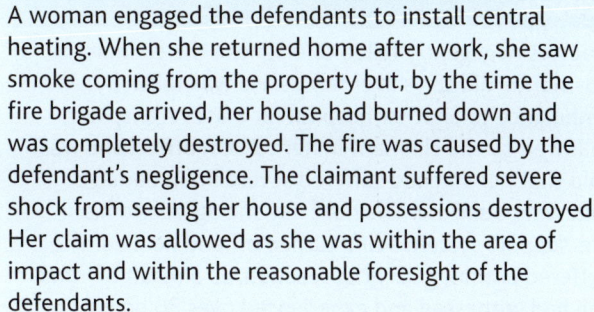

A woman engaged the defendants to install central heating. When she returned home after work, she saw smoke coming from the property but, by the time the fire brigade arrived, her house had burned down and was completely destroyed. The fire was caused by the defendant's negligence. The claimant suffered severe shock from seeing her house and possessions destroyed. Her claim was allowed as she was within the area of impact and within the reasonable foresight of the defendants.

This seems to be a fair decision as the defendants were at fault and it was morally right that they should be required to compensate the claimant.

'Near missers'

These are people who were close to the scene of the accident and may have suffered physical or mental injuries. They are regarded as primary victims and can claim for their injuries if they can prove the defendant who caused the accident was negligent. A 'near misser' does not have to be related to the victim of the accident.

Those suffering gradual rather than sudden shock

The usual claimant will be a victim who has suffered mental injury as the result of witnessing a sudden event. There have been attempts to extend the boundaries of claims to those who suffer mental injury as a result of a gradual appreciation of events rather than a sudden shock. In *Sion v Hampstead Health Authority* (1994), a claim was not allowed.

Sion v Hampstead Health Authority (1994)

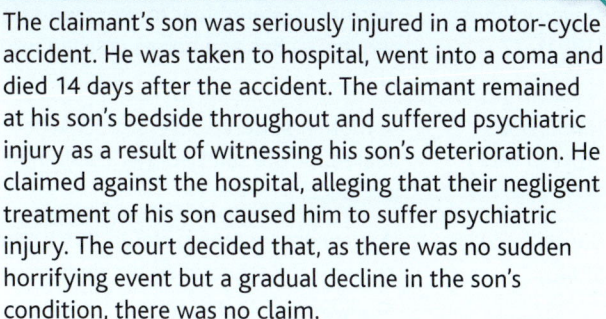

The claimant's son was seriously injured in a motor-cycle accident. He was taken to hospital, went into a coma and died 14 days after the accident. The claimant remained at his son's bedside throughout and suffered psychiatric injury as a result of witnessing his son's deterioration. He claimed against the hospital, alleging that their negligent treatment of his son caused him to suffer psychiatric injury. The court decided that, as there was no sudden horrifying event but a gradual decline in the son's condition, there was no claim.

On the other hand, where there is a shorter period of decline in the patient's condition, a claim may be allowed, as in *North Glamorgan NHS Trust v Walters* (2002).

North Glamorgan NHS Trust v Walters (2002)

Doctors negligently failed to diagnose the claimant's 10-month-old son's liver failure. He was taken by ambulance to another hospital for a liver transplant, followed by the claimant in her car. On arrival she was told that her son had suffered severe brain damage following a seizure. The next day she agreed to his life-support system being turned off and he died. She suffered pathological grief reaction, as a result of what she had witnessed and experienced over 36 hours. The Court of Appeal decided this could amount to a sudden appreciation of a horrifying event, even though the time was made up of discrete events.

This case was then referred to in *Galli-Atkinson v Seghal* (2003), where the claimant's 16-year-old daughter was killed in a crash. She arrived at the scene of the accident after her daughter had been removed. Hysterical, she was taken to the mortuary and saw her daughter's body, which was badly disfigured, and suffered severe shock. The Court of Appeal decided that, in this case, the immediate aftermath was an uninterrupted series of events from the time of the accident until the claimant left the mortuary. It was different from the victims in *Alcock* whose visits to the mortuary were eight hours after the events, and when the claimants knew of the events that had taken place.

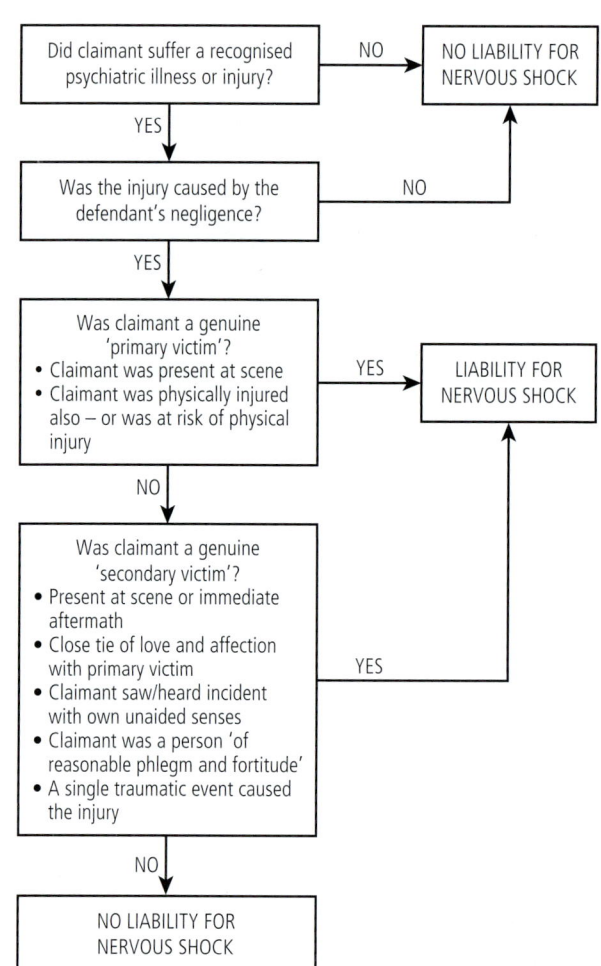

Figure 14.4 The means of deciding liability for psychiatric injury

Figure 14.5 Key cases for claiming psychiatric injury

Case	Facts	Legal principle
Dulieu v White (1901)	Barmaid suffered fear for her own safety when coaches and horses crashed into the bar	A claim for nervous shock can be made when the claimant suffers real and immediate fear of personal danger
Hambrook v Stokes (1925)	A mother suffered severe shock when she feared for the safety of her children in an accident	A claim can be made if the claimant suffered nervous shock fearing for the safety of a family member
Bourhill v Young (1943)	A pregnant woman suffered shock when she saw the scene of an accident She was not related to anyone involved in the accident	No claim can be made if the person suffering shock is outside the range of people who could be foreseen as being affected
McLoughlin v O'Brien (1982)	Claimant suffered shock at hospital when she saw her family being treated after being involved in an accident	Claim for nervous shock can be made by someone not involved in an accident if: 1 he or she has close ties of love and affection with a victim of the accident, and 2 the shock is suffered at the scene of the accident or within its immediate aftermath

Case	Facts	Legal principle
Page v Smith (1995)	The claimant's ME was triggered when he was involved in a minor car accident	Distinction is made between primary and secondary victims Primary victims are involved in the accident and have to prove negligence to claim for physical or mental injuries Secondary victims are not involved in the accident but suffer mental injuries
Alcock v Chief Constable of South Yorkshire (1992)	Families of Hillsborough victims claimed for mental injuries after learning that family members were involved in the tragedy which was due to police negligence	Claim for nervous shock can be made by a secondary victim if the *Alcock* criteria are satisfied: 1 he or she has close ties of love and affection with a victim of the accident 2 the shock is suffered at the scene of the accident or within its immediate aftermath, and 3 shock is suffered with the claimant's own unaided senses
Chadwick v British Rail (1967)	The claimant suffered nervous shock after he helped survivors after a train crash	Rescuers are primary victims and can claim for nervous shock if they assist at an accident Rescuers should not be discouraged
White v Chief Constable of South Yorkshire (1998)	Police officers helping at Hillsborough suffered PTSD from what they witnessed	Rescuers are secondary victims unless they are in the range of foreseeable physical injury and have to prove the *Alcock* criteria Public policy reasons prevented them from recovering compensation when the families of the victims were unable to recover
McFarlane v E E Caledonia (1994)	The claimant suffered psychiatric injury when witnessing explosions and the rescuing of survivors on the Piper Alpha oil rig	Bystanders are not rescuers and have to satisfy all the *Alcock* criteria to claim as secondary victims
Attia v British Gas (1987)	A woman witnessed her property being destroyed by fire due to the defendant's negligence and suffered severe shock	A claim for nervous shock can be made if caused by witnessing the destruction of your own property
Sion v Hampstead Health Authority (1994)	The claimant suffered psychiatric injury as a result of witnessing his son's deterioration in hospital over 14 days	No claim in nervous shock as there was no sudden horrifying event
North Glamorgan NHS Trust v Walters (2002)	The claimant suffered a pathological grief reaction from witnessing the treatment and ultimate death of her child over 36 hours	This could amount to a sudden appreciation of a horrifying event and a claim can be allowed

Summary

Economic loss

- The courts will not allow claims for 'pure economic' loss for policy reasons, as it is felt that loss of profit is more to do with contract law.

- A claim for negligent misstatement requires a statement to be given negligently and the existence of a special relationship between the claimant and the defendant.

- A special relationship requires special skill of the person giving the statement, reliance on the statement and knowledge of such reliance, communication of the statement, acting on the statement and suffering a loss. If there is a disclaimer present, this can act as a defence.

- Negligent advice given in a social situation can be claimed for only if the claimant completely relies on the advice to the knowledge of the person giving the advice.

- The remedy for negligent misstatement is damages for the loss suffered.

Psychiatric injury

- A person has to suffer a recognised psychiatric injury to make a claim following an accident.
- Primary victims can suffer physical and/or mental injury and have to prove negligence.
- Secondary victims have to prove negligence, the *Alcock* criteria and that a person of reasonable fortitude would have suffered in the same way.
- The *Alcock* criteria are close ties of love and affection with the victim, the shock is suffered at the scene of the accident or its immediate aftermath, and is suffered through the claimant's own unaided senses.
- The psychiatric injury has to be suffered through a sudden event.
- Rescuers are secondary victims unless they are in the range of foreseeable physical injury and have to prove the *Alcock* criteria.
- Bystanders are secondary victims and have to prove the *Alcock* criteria.
- A claim can be made if psychiatric injury is suffered due to seeing your property destroyed.

15 Nuisance and the escape of dangerous things

After reading this chapter, you should be able to:
- Understand the rules of private nuisance
- Understand the rule in *Rylands v Fletcher*

Private nuisance concerns people living in proximity to one another. It will almost always involve the competing claims of people to do as they wish on their own land. It is not unreasonable to expect to be able to do what you like on your own land. Problems only arise when this affects a neighbour's ability to enjoy his or her land and when the use is termed unreasonable. What is reasonable depends not so much on the conduct of the defendant, but whether the interference caused by that conduct is sufficient to give rise to a legal action. Not every intentional interference with the enjoyment of land will be classed as a nuisance, only that which is classed as unreasonable.

Key term

Private nuisance – a tort claim where someone's use or enjoyment of their property is affected by the unreasonable behaviour of a neighbour.

Activity

Discuss with others in your class whether your neighbours have complained about any behaviour of you or your family.

- Have you or your family had reason to complain to your neighbours about their behaviour?
- What was the complaint about?
- How was the complaint resolved?
- How was the neighbour relationship affected by the complaint?

15.1 The rules of private nuisance

Private nuisance can be defined as 'an unlawful indirect interference with a person's use or enjoyment of land coming from neighbouring land'.

There are two main types of private nuisance:

- loss of amenity nuisance when caused by noise, smell or smoke, and

- material damage nuisance, when a dangerous state of affairs on the defendant's land causes significant physical damage to the claimant's land, such as tree roots causing subsidence.

It may be easier for a claimant to establish a claim based on material damage than loss of amenity, as factors such as locality are irrelevant where there is physical damage.

15.1.1 The parties to an action

Since nuisance involves the competing rights of neighbours to use their land how they wish, the basic rule is that anyone who uses or enjoys land and is affected by an interference may claim. It is important to note that the claimant must have an interest in the land. This will include being an owner or a tenant but not a member of the owner's family, such as a child who has no legal interest in the property.

The person who is causing, or allowing, the nuisance can be sued. For example, in *Tetley v Chitty* (1986) a local authority who allowed go-kart racing on its land was held liable for a nuisance. Where the occupier is not responsible him- or herself for creating the nuisance, he or she might still be liable as a result of 'adopting' the nuisance – in other words, failing to deal with the problem, even if it was caused by a previous owner or a trespasser. This can be seen by the case of *Sedleigh Denfield v O'Callaghan* (1940).

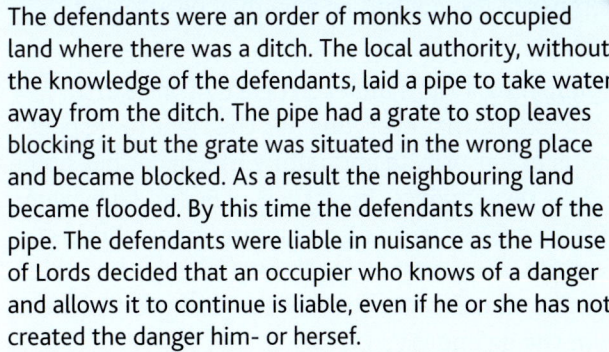

Sedleigh Denfield v O'Callaghan (1940)

The defendants were an order of monks who occupied land where there was a ditch. The local authority, without the knowledge of the defendants, laid a pipe to take water away from the ditch. The pipe had a grate to stop leaves blocking it but the grate was situated in the wrong place and became blocked. As a result the neighbouring land became flooded. By this time the defendants knew of the pipe. The defendants were liable in nuisance as the House of Lords decided that an occupier who knows of a danger and allows it to continue is liable, even if he or she has not created the danger him- or herself.

A defendant can also be liable where the nuisance is the result of natural causes which he or she is aware of but fails to deal with. This was shown in both the following cases.

Leakey v National Trust (1980)

The defendants owned land on which there was a large natural mound on a hillside. They were aware that it could slip, and following a hot summer it did slip, damaging the claimant's cottage. The defendants were held liable as they knew that a slippage might happen and they failed to prevent it.

Anthony v The Coal Authority (2005)

The defendant took over responsibility for land from a former colliery. The land was later landscaped and sold as common land. A fire started through spontaneous combustion which lasted for three years, causing fume and smoke interference to people living in the area. The defendant was liable because it was aware of the problem while the tip was still under its control and failed to prevent the nuisance.

Note that the defendant who is causing the nuisance does not have to have an interest in the land from which the nuisance is coming.

| Complaining neighbour – has to have an interest in the land affected | v | Neighbour who receives complaint – does not have to have an interest in the land – can be liable if he or she allowed the nuisance to continue |

Figure 15.1 The parties to a nuisance action

In *Hunter v Canary Wharf Ltd* (1997) below, the House of Lords confirmed that members of a household who do not have an interest in the land cannot claim. More people now work or study from home and hours of work are more flexible. It seems unfair to restrict claims only to those who have an interest in the land affected and not to extend the ability to claim to any member of the household who may be affected.

However, this restriction may be overtaken by establishing a right under Article 8 of the ECHR, which states that everyone has the right to respect for his or her private and family life, his or her home and correspondence. In *McKenna v British Aluminium* (2002), over 30 claimants, including some children, who had no interest in the land affected, were able to claim in nuisance for the noise and fumes that came from the defendant's factory.

15.1.2 The elements of private nuisance

We will now look more closely at the different parts of the definition of private nuisance.

'Unlawful'

Mere interference on its own is insufficient for an action. The claimant must prove that the defendant's activity amounts to an unlawful use of land. 'Unlawful' here does not mean illegal, but rather means that the court accepts that the defendant's use of land is unreasonable in the way that it affects the claimant.

The court will attempt to balance the conflicting interests of the neighbours in a nuisance action. They will expect neighbours to experience a certain amount of 'give and take' and consider whether it is reasonable for the claimant to have to suffer the particular interference and whether the interference is excessive. There will be a certain amount of fault involved by the defendant by not having regard for his or her neighbour. However, fault, in the sense of how and why the interference occurred, does not have to be proved.

'Indirect interference'

Over the years, a variety of actions have been decided as amounting to a nuisance. The following could be considered as amounting to a loss of amenity:

■ fumes drifting over neighbouring land
■ smell from farm animals
■ noise – from a children's playground, due to gunfire and from a speedway and motor racing circuit.

The following could be considered as amounting to material damage:

■ vibrations from industrial machinery
■ hot air rising into other premises
■ oily smuts from chimneys
■ fire
■ cricket balls being hit into a garden.

However, some forms of interference will not be protected or be allowed to be claimed for. A claimant cannot take action to protect a right to a view of the surrounding countryside, or the right to light, and nor can interference to television reception be protected – as shown in the case of *Hunter v Canary Wharf Ltd* (1997).

Hunter v Canary Wharf Ltd (1997)

The claimants were a number of people who were living in the Docklands area of East London when the Canary Wharf office tower was being built. They claimed that the building affected their television reception. The House of Lords decided that the loss of this kind of recreational facility was not sufficient interference to give rise to an action in nuisance. This was partly because other forms of reception such as cable and satellite were available.

The court also confirmed the rule that only those with an interest in the land, and not members of families, had the right to bring an action.

Buildings in Canary Wharf, London

On the other hand, the courts are prepared to protect feelings of emotional distress. For example:

- *Thompson-Schwab v Costaki* (1956) – the Court of Appeal decided that the running of a brothel in a respectable residential area of London amounted to a nuisance.
- *Laws v Florinplace Ltd* (1981) – an injunction was awarded where a shop in an area of shops, restaurants and some housing was converted into a sex shop.

15.1.3 Factors of reasonableness

Because the tort is all about balancing competing interests of the claimant and the defendant, the court will take into account any relevant factors to decide whether the use of land by the defendant is unreasonable.

Locality

Nuisance is all about the use of land in the area it is situated, so the character of the neighbourhood has to be considered. The court will consider questions such as whether the area is purely residential, if it is partly residential and partly commercial or industrial, if it is situated in the town or country, or whether the character of the area has changed over time. As Thesiger LJ stated in *Sturges v Bridgman* (1879), 'what would be a nuisance in Belgrave Square would not necessarily be so in Bermondsey'.

The duration of the interference

To be actionable, the interference is likely to be continuous and carried on at unreasonable hours of the day. A noisy one-off party to celebrate a special occasion may not be a nuisance, but if regular, noisy, late-night parties are held, this may amount to a nuisance. However, in one case, an event lasting for a maximum of 20 minutes was held to be a nuisance.

Crown River Cruises Ltd v Kimbolton Fireworks Ltd (1996)

A river barge was set alight by flammable debris, resulting from a firework display lasting only 20 minutes. It was said that the short-term display amounted to an actionable nuisance.

De Keyser's Royal Hotel v Spicer Bros (1914)

An injunction was granted to prevent building work taking place at night, despite the fact the work was only temporary in nature. The work was considered unreasonable as it interfered with the claimant's sleep.

If the interference is only temporary, this is not a sufficient reason to avoid a claim if it is of a kind, and at times, when it is an unreasonable interference.

The sensitivity of the claimant

If it can be shown the claimant is particularly sensitive, then the action may not be a nuisance.

Robinson v Kilvert (1889)

The claimant stored brown paper on the ground floor of a building. The defendant stored paper boxes in the basement. He needed the conditions to be hot and dry. The heat in the basement caused the brown paper to dry out and the claimant sued for its loss in value. The court decided that the brown paper was particularly delicate and the heat from the basement would not have dried out normal paper. The court did not grant an injunction or damages.

The law on nuisance is moving away now from the idea of 'abnormal sensitivity' to a general test of foreseeability as shown in the case of *Network Rail Infrastructure v Morris* (2004).

Network Rail Infrastructure v Morris (2004)

The claimant ran a recording studio near the main London to Brighton rail line. The railway company installed new track circuits which interfered with the amplification of electric guitars causing the claimant to lose business. The Court of Appeal considered that the use of amplified electric guitars was abnormally sensitive equipment and, as the interference was not foreseeable, the defendants were not liable.

Malice

A deliberately harmful act will normally be unreasonable behaviour and considered a nuisance.

Hollywood Silver Fox Farm v Emmett (1936)

The claimant bred mink on his farm. The defendant had a disagreement with the claimant and told his son to shoot his guns near to the property to frighten the animals so they would not breed. This was a deliberate and unreasonable act, and amounted to a nuisance.

Christie v Davey (1893)

The claimant was a music teacher and held musical parties and lessons in his house. The defendant became annoyed by the noise and responded by banging on the walls with his hands and with trays, blowing whistles and shouting. An injunction was granted against him due to his deliberate and malicious behaviour.

Social benefit

If it is considered that the defendant is providing a benefit to the community, the court may consider the actions reasonable.

Miller v Jackson (1977)

The claimants' use of their garden was disrupted by cricket balls being hit into it from the adjoining recreation ground. The cricket club tried to compromise with the claimants by erecting high fencing and instructing batsmen to hit the ball on the ground. However, the claimants continued with their action to stop cricket being played. The court weighed up the use of the ground and the benefit of sport to the community against the claimant's use of their garden. They decided that the community use of the ground outweighed the private use and refused an injunction.

Supporting the benefit to the public was certainly behind the decision of the Court of Appeal not to grant an injunction to Mr and Mrs Miller to stop the playing of cricket on the adjoining recreation ground. The decision of the majority judges was to provide justice and equity, rather than to decide the outcome on strict legal grounds. The decision perhaps also reflected the behaviour of the parties. Mrs Miller, in particular, had been confrontational and unwilling to compromise. The cricket club had tried many approaches to deal with the problem and it was perhaps rewarded for its conciliatory approach.

In *Adams v Ursell* (1913), it was decided that a well-used fish and chip shop was causing a nuisance to local residents due to smells coming from it and it was forced to close. It is unlikely that a similar decision would be reached today, as the court could make a positive order against a restaurant or takeaway to fit extractors to remove excessive smells.

The court in *Dennis v Ministry of Defence* (2003) considered that the benefit to the public should be a reason to award compensation to the claimants rather than an injunction. The claimants brought an action because of fighter jets constantly flying low over their property. The Ministry of Defence defended on the basis that the training of pilots was for the benefit of the public and the country. The court awarded substantial compensation without limiting the flying.

This decision perhaps was a forerunner to the decision in *Coventry v Lawrence* (2014) below, when comments were made by one of the judges that an injunction should not automatically be ordered in a nuisance case. Many claimants will take court action as a last resort to stop a nuisance continuing, and will not be looking for compensation. However, in the light of this decision, this cannot now be guaranteed for a successful applicant.

The court will not be looking for a number of factors in each case. It will be assessing the strength of arguments on each side and each case will be decided on its merits. If one factor is particularly important, for example malice, this may be sufficient to bring a finding of unreasonable behaviour. If the court makes such a finding, it will show that a neighbour has been at fault by not respecting people affected by his or her activity.

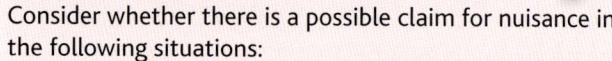

Activity

Consider whether there is a possible claim for nuisance in the following situations:

1 Raj and Jas recently received successful A-level results and held a very noisy party that lasted till 3 a.m. Ada and Florence who live next door were kept awake and were quite annoyed.

2 Tara lives next door to Albert, an amateur shortwave radio enthusiast. When he is using his equipment, it causes interference to both sound and vision on Tara's television.

3 Ricky, a music promoter, proposes to hold an open-air pop concert lasting one week, in parkland at the head of a residential cul-de-sac.

4 Norris is annoyed because Rita's cat regularly comes into his garden and makes a mess on his flowers, some of which have died.

5 Residents in a private home for the elderly object to the noise from junior football matches played on local authority playing fields near to the home.

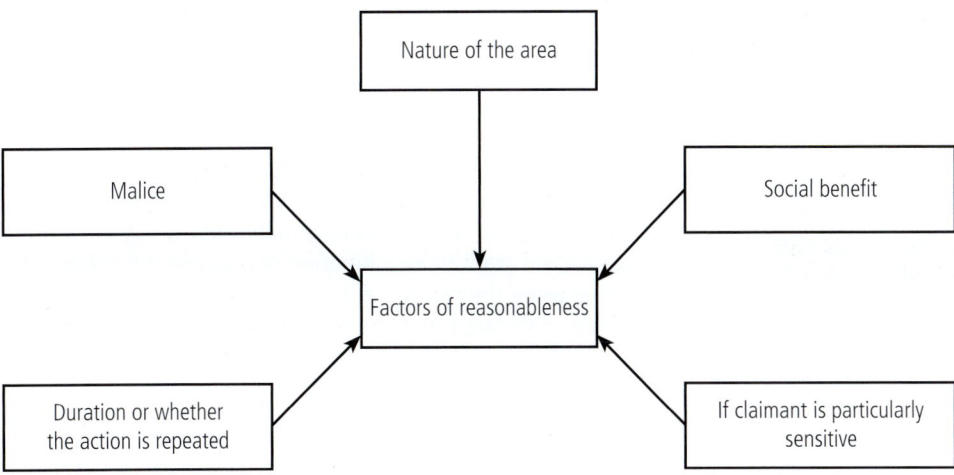

Figure 15.2 Factors of reasonableness

15.1.4 Defences

Unlike some other torts, the defendant can argue a number of defences.

Prescription

This is a defence that is unique to private nuisance. Prescription may be a defence to a nuisance action if the action has been carrying on for at least 20 years and there has been no complaint between the parties in that time. If this is the case, the defendant may be said to have a prescriptive right to continue. This was shown in *Sturges v Bridgman* (1879).

Sturges v Bridgman (1879)

The claimant, a doctor, had lived and worked next to the defendant's confectionary factory. The claimant then built a consulting room in his garden on the boundary to the factory. He complained of a nuisance due to vibrations from the defendant's machinery. The defendant argued that he had a prescriptive right to continue as he had been using the factory without complaint for a number of years. The court decided that the defence of prescription failed as the nuisance began when the consulting room was built.

The operation of this defence has been considered in the case of *Coventry v Lawrence* (2014), below. The Supreme Court confirmed that the defence only applied to an activity that was an actionable nuisance for at least 20 years – not just that an activity had been carried on for that time without complaint.

Linked to this, the defence of *volenti non fit injuria* – consent by the claimant to the nuisance – can apply.

Moving to the nuisance

The defendant may argue that the claimant is only suffering the nuisance as he or she has moved closer to the alleged problem (as in *Sturges v Bridgman*), or moved into the area (*Miller v Jackson*), and that there was no issue previously. This argument will not give a defence to the defendant.

Statutory authority

Since many of the activities that can amount to a nuisance are now regulated or licensed by environmental or other laws, statutory authority is likely to be one of the most effective defences. The operation of this defence is shown in the following cases.

Allen v Gulf Oil Refining (1981)

Residents in the area where the defendants were operating an oil refinery brought an action in private and public nuisance. The defendants had been given statutory authority to acquire the site and build a refinery, but not express permission to operate it. The House of Lords said that it must have been Parliament's intention, when it gave permission for the defendants to operate a refinery. As the nuisance was an inevitable consequence of operating the refinery, the defence of statutory authority succeeded.

If a statute provides the only possible remedy, an action in nuisance may not be possible as an alternative.

Marcic v Thames Water plc (2003)

Through the failures of the defendants, the claimant's home became flooded with sewage on many occasions. The Water Industry Act 1991, which governed the conduct of the defendants, provided appropriate remedies and procedures and excluded a private action in nuisance. The House of Lords decided that, as there were clear statutory procedures, there could be no nuisance action. If such action was allowed, it would conflict with the intentions of Parliament.

Local authority planning permission can, in some circumstances, act in the same way as lawful justification for a nuisance.

Gillingham Borough Council v Medway (Chatham) Dock Co. (1993)

Planning permission was granted to use part of a dockyard as a commercial port. Access was only available by residential roads, which caused residents noise disturbance from heavy lorries. The court decided that as the character of the neighbourhood had been changed by the planning permission, what could have previously been a nuisance could now be considered reasonable. It was held not to be an actionable nuisance because of the grant of planning permission changing the character of the neighbourhood.

However, if the planning permission does not change the character of the neighbourhood, it will not operate as a defence.

Wheeler v Saunders (1996)

A pig farmer was granted planning permission to expand by building two more pig houses, each containing 400 pigs. One pig house was only 11 metres from the cottage of a neighbour who then took action in nuisance due to the strong smells he experienced. The Court of Appeal confirmed that the grant of planning permission could only be a defence if its effect was to change the character of the neighbourhood so that the nuisance was not unreasonable. This had not been the case here and the planning permission was not a defence.

This principle has been confirmed again in *Watson v Croft Promo-Sport* (2009), which was a case about a sporting venue.

Watson v Croft Promo-Sport (2009)

Planning permission was granted in 1963 to use a former aerodrome as a motor racing track and it was then used as a track for 16 years. Racing then ceased but in 1995 new owners reopened the track and it became a very popular circuit. The new owners reapplied for planning permission for 210 days per year and following a public inquiry this was granted. The claimant, who lived about 300 metres from the circuit, brought an action in private nuisance claiming noise disturbance, an injunction and damages. The defendant argued that the planning permission had changed the character of the area and so the use of the circuit was reasonable. However, the Court of Appeal granted an injunction restraining the defendant from using the race track for more than 40 days per year. They considered that the area remained essentially rural and that there was an actionable nuisance.

The Supreme Court has considered the law of nuisance and possible remedies in the more recent case of *Coventry v Lawrence* (2014).

Coventry v Lawrence (2014)

The claimant bought a house in 2006, 864 metres from the defendant's motor sport stadium. Planning permission had originally been granted in 1975 for speedway use and subsequently for other motor sport use including stock cars, bangers and motorcross. The claimant brought an action based on noise nuisance requiring an injunction limiting the use of the track. The Supreme Court confirmed the existence of a noise nuisance and granted an injunction limiting the use of the track. They decided that the rule in *Sturges v Bridgman* (1879) – about considering the character of the neighbourhood – still applies. Further, that provided the claimant uses his or her property for the same purposes as his or her predecessor, the defendant cannot use the defence of coming to the nuisance, but:

- where a claimant builds on his or her property or changes the use of his or her property after the defendant has started his or her use of the activity complained of, then the defence of coming to the nuisance may fail, and

- damages may be considered as a remedy more often in nuisance cases, especially where planning permission has been awarded to the defendant for the use of his or her land, or where the public interest is involved, such as employees losing their jobs if an injunction is awarded.

Motor racing in Denmark

Look online

Research to find a report of a neighbour dispute. What was the cause of the dispute? If it is an ongoing dispute how do you think it can be resolved? If the dispute is over, do you think it has been resolved to the satisfaction of both parties?

15.1.5 Remedies

Until the case of *Coventry v Lawrence* (2014), the most common remedy for a nuisance claim, and the point of bringing an action, was an injunction. This would generally be prohibitory, ordering the defendant to stop causing the nuisance. An injunction could also be positive in nature – for example to order the defendant to install a filter to prevent the escape of smell or smuts. The injunction could be linked to the award of damages where a loss has occurred.

This approach followed the *Shelfer* test (from *Shelfer v City of London Electric Lighting Co.* (1895)), which set out that damages should be awarded over an injunction when the injury to the claimant's rights was small, the claimant can be compensated by money, a small payment is adequate and it would be unfair on the defendant to grant an injunction.

Now, in *Coventry v Lawrence* (2014), the Supreme Court laid down guidance as to the future use of injunctions and the award of damages in nuisance. It considered that:

- an injunction could be the default order in a nuisance claim, but
- it is open to the defendant to argue that an award of damages would be a suitable alternative
- the *Shelfer* test should not be applied rigidly, and
- an injunction will not automatically be granted, even if the *Shelfer* test is satisfied.

One of the judges in the Supreme Court, Lord Sumption, suggested that damages would ordinarily be an appropriate remedy in nuisance.

For the future, following this guidance, the courts may award fewer injunctions in nuisance claims and be prepared to award damages instead. Whichever remedy they decide to grant, the court is likely to take into account matters of social benefit, as outlined at 15.1.3 above.

A further remedy available to a claimant in nuisance is 'abatement'. This could involve entering the defendant's premises in order to prevent further nuisance. For example, a claimant could enter a defendant's land in order to chop down overhanging branches, although these would need to be returned to the defendant.

15.1.6 Nuisance and fault

For fault-based torts, the claimant has to prove how and why the accident happened. Nuisance is not considered to be a fault-based tort in the same way as negligence, as the claimant does not have to show why the neighbour has interfered with his or her use or enjoyment of land. However, the claimant will have to show there is unreasonable interference and some element of fault in showing the presence of one of the factors. The presence of malice is obviously showing fault by a neighbour as it will be a deliberate annoyance. Also, causing a noise at an unreasonable time or for an unreasonable duration are other signs of fault, as little or no thought is being given to the neighbours.

Disputes between neighbours can lead to very strained relations, and indeed a number of television programmes have been made about neighbour disputes that have got out of hand. The courts in recent times have encouraged the use of alternative dispute resolution (ADR) in general in civil disputes. Negotiation and mediation are especially useful in dealing with neighbour disputes. They allow both parties to put their case and the parties themselves come to a resolution. This is a better way of neighbours approaching and dealing with the problem than resorting to court actions. A court case will often lead to confrontation between the parties who still have to live alongside each other when the court case is finished.

Figure 15.3 Key cases on nuisance

Case	Facts	Legal principle
Sedleigh Denfield v O'Callaghan (1940)	A pipe laid by the local authority but on the defendant's land was blocked, flooding the neighbouring land	An occupier who knows of a danger and allows it to continue is liable in nuisance, even if he or she has not created the danger him- or herself
Leakey v National Trust (1980)	There was a large natural mound on a hillside on the defendant's land The defendant was aware that it could slip and following a hot summer it did slip, damaging the claimant's cottage	A landowner could be liable in nuisance if he or she knew a slippage might happen and he or she failed to prevent it
Hunter v Canary Wharf Ltd (1997)	Residents in Docklands complained of interference with television reception when Canary Wharf was being built	The loss of a recreational facility is not sufficient interference to give rise to an action in nuisance
Crown River Cruises Ltd v Kimbolton Fireworks Ltd (1996)	A river barge was set alight by flammable debris, from a 20-minute firework display	Even a short-term activity can amount to a nuisance
De Keyser's Royal Hotel Ltd v Spicer Bros Ltd (1914)	Building work was carried out at night and interfered with the claimant's sleep	Even temporary building work can amount to a nuisance
Robinson v Kilvert (1889)	Paper boxes were stored in hot and dry conditions which caused paper stored above them to dry out	If the claimant is unduly sensitive, a nuisance will not be found
Christie v Davey (1893)	The defendant was annoyed by his neighbour's music and deliberately banged on the walls, banging trays, blew whistles and shouted to disturb the neighbours	The defendant's deliberate and malicious behaviour amounted to a nuisance
Miller v Jackson (1977)	The claimants' use of their garden was disrupted by cricket balls being hit into it from the adjoining recreation ground	The use of a sports ground and its benefit to the community outweighed the private use of the claimant's garden
Sturges v Bridgman (1879)	A doctor complained that his new consulting rooms were affected by vibrations from a neighbouring factory The defendant argued that he had a prescriptive right to continue	The defence of prescription failed as the nuisance began when the consulting room was built The period before the building was erected did not count
Allen v Gulf Oil Refining (1981)	Residents near an oil refinery brought a nuisance action The defendants had statutory authority to acquire the site and build a refinery, but not express permission to operate it	It must have been Parliament's intention when giving permission for development to also operate a refinery
Gillingham Borough Council v Medway (Chatham) Dock Co. (1993)	Planning permission was granted to use a dockyard as a commercial port but nuisance was caused when lorries accessed the port	As the character of the neighbourhood had been changed by planning permission, what could have previously been a nuisance could now be considered reasonable
Coventry v Lawrence (2014)	Planning permission had been given for motor sports near the claimant's house A claim of noise nuisance was made, limiting the use of the track	The rule in *Sturges v Bridgman* still applies Damages may be considered as a remedy more often in nuisance, especially where planning permission has been awarded or where public interest is involved

Activity

Consider whether any defence to a claim for nuisance is possible in the following situations:

1 The noise from a busy railway line distresses homeowners living in houses next to the railway line.
2 Burglars break into Ravinder's home while he is spending six months in India and leave his radio, television, and music equipment playing on maximum volume, causing considerable annoyance to neighbours.
3 Anna lives in a block of flats in the flat beneath Roger. Anna is very distressed because she has to get up at 6 a.m. to go to work, and when Roger returns from his work at around 1 a.m. she can hear his footsteps walking around for hours.
4 Residents of a small estate want a nearby local authority playground to be shut down because of the noise from children playing.
5 For more than 15 years, Archie has kept pigs in his backyard. His neighbour Reggie eventually objects to the smell.

15.2 The rule in *Rylands v Fletcher*

If the use or enjoyment of land is affected by something intangible coming from a neighbour's land, an action in private nuisance can be taken. If, however, property is destroyed or damaged by something that comes from a neighbouring property, then a different type of action has to be used. This will be a claim in the tort of **Rylands v Fletcher** (see section 15.2.1 for the case facts). Mr Justice Blackburn said in the Court of Exchequer Chamber in that case:

> We think that the true rule of law is, that the person who, for purposes of his own, brings on his land and keeps there anything likely to do mischief if it escapes, must keep it in at his peril, and, if he does not do so, he is *prima facie* answerable for all the damage which is the natural consequence of its escape.

This definition contains the major requirements of the tort. Lord Cairns then added in the appeal to the House of Lords the further requirement that for the claimant to succeed, the thing brought onto the land must amount to a 'non-natural' use of land.

Traditionally, it could be said that the liability was strict because there was no particular requirement to show fault, and the defendant could be made liable even if he or she had taken care to avoid the escape. The tort was

also originally distinguished from nuisance because of the requirement in nuisance that harm of the type caused by the nuisance should be foreseeable, but no such requirement is apparent in *Rylands v Fletcher* (1868).

This is not now the case since the House of Lords in *Cambridge Water Co. v Eastern Counties Leather plc* (1994) identified the tort as a type of nuisance, and subject to the same test of foreseeability.

Key term

Rylands v Fletcher – where a person's property is damaged or destroyed by the escape of non-naturally stored material onto adjoining property.

15.2.1 Essential elements of the tort

There are essentially four elements that must be proved in order for there to be a successful claim under the tort of *Rylands v Fletcher* (1868):

- the bringing onto the land and an accumulation (or storage)
- of a thing likely to cause mischief if it escapes
- which amounts to a non-natural use of the land, and
- which does escape and causes reasonably foreseeable damage to adjoining property.

In the case of *Rylands v Fletcher*, all the elements were present and the defendants were liable.

Rylands v Fletcher (1868)

The defendant, a mill owner, hired contractors to create a reservoir on his land to act as a water supply to the mill. The contractors negligently failed to block off disused mineshafts that they came across during their excavations. Unknown to the contractors, these shafts were connected to other mine works on adjoining land. When the reservoir was filled, water then flooded the neighbouring mines.

There was a bringing onto land and storage of water, a large volume of water could do damage if it escaped, this storage amounted to a non-natural use of land and the water did escape through the mineshafts, causing considerable damage to the claimant.

The parties to an action

It has traditionally been thought that a person who can take an action has to have an interest in the land affected. This means that he or she must own the land or rent it or have some sort of property interest in it.

According to Viscount Simon's test in *Read v Lyons* (1947), a defendant to an action in *Rylands v Fletcher* (1868) will be either the owner or occupier of land who satisfies the four ingredients of the tort, all of which must be present for liability. It is assumed that they must have some control over the land on which the material is stored.

The bringing onto the land

There must be a bringing onto land of a substance which is not naturally present on the land. If the thing in question is already naturally present on the land, then there can be no liability. So in *Giles v Walker* (1890), there was no liability when weeds spread onto neighbouring land as they were naturally growing.

There cannot be liability for a thing that naturally accumulates on the land. In *Ellison v Ministry of Defence* (1997), rainwater that accumulated naturally on an airfield at Greenham Common did not lead to liability when it escaped and caused flooding on neighbouring land.

The thing is likely to do mischief if it escapes

The thing which the defendant brings onto his or her land must be likely to do damage if it escapes. This is a test of foreseeability. It is not the escape that must be foreseeable – only that damage is foreseeable, if the thing brought onto land does escape.

Examples of things which courts have decided can do mischief are:

- gas and electricity
- poisonous fumes
- a flag pole
- tree branches
- an occupied chair from a chair-o-plane ride in the case of *Hale v Jennings Bros* (1938).

Hale v Jennings Bros (1938)

A 'chair-o-plane' car on a fairground ride became detached from the main assembly while in motion and injured a stallholder as it crashed to the ground. The owner of the ride was liable as the risk of injury was foreseeable if the car came loose. This is one of the few cases where a claim for personal injury using *Rylands v Fletcher* was successful. Note that in *Transco plc v Stockport Metropolitan Borough Council* (2003), the House of Lords commented, *obiter*, that it is not now possible to claim for personal injury under the tort.

A non-natural use of land

Lord Cairns in the House of Lords in *Rylands v Fletcher* (1868) indicated the requirement of a non-natural use of land. He said:

> If the defendants, not stopping at the natural use of their close, had desired to use it for any purpose which I may term a non-natural use ... and in consequence of doing so ... the water came to escape ... then it appears to me that which the defendants were doing they were doing at their own peril.

This concept of non-natural use was developed and explained by Lord Moulton in *Rickards v Lothian* (1913):

> It is not every use of land which brings into play this principle. It must be some special use bringing with it increased danger to others, and not merely by the ordinary use of land or such a use as is proper for the general benefit of the community.

Non-natural use of land is clearly a complex concept, and one which inevitably changes to take into account technological change and changes in lifestyle. It is inconceivable, for instance, that leaving a car garaged with petrol in the tank could be seen as a non-natural use of land today, though it was seen as such in 1919 at the time of *Musgrove v Pandelis* (1919).

Case law suggests that 'non-natural' refers to some extraordinary or some unusual use of land. In general, storage of things associated with the domestic use of land will not normally be classified as non-natural even though they may be potentially hazardous. The following have been decided by courts as being a natural use of land:

- a fire in a grate which spread to the claimant's premises
- defective electric wiring that caused a fire which spread to the claimant's premises
- a domestic water supply.

Rickards v Lothian (1913)

An unknown person turned on water taps and blocked plugholes on the defendant's premises, so that damage was caused in the flat below. The defendant was not liable as the use of water in domestic pipes was a natural use of land.

British Celanese v A H Hunt Ltd (1969)

The defendants stored strips of metal foil, which were used in the manufacturing of electrical components. Some of these strips of foil blew off the defendant's land onto an electricity substation, causing a power failure. The court held that the use of land was natural because of the benefit obtained by the local population.

However, courts have been prepared to accept that certain activities may always lead to a potential level of danger, which amount to a non-natural use of land whatever the benefit to the public of the activities. However, in *Cambridge Water Co. v Eastern Counties Leather plc* (1994) the storage of chemicals in a factory was a classic example of a non-natural use of land. Just because the activity was an important source of local employment did not make the storage a natural use of land.

The thing stored must escape and cause foreseeable damage

The stored item must escape from one property onto an adjoining property so that if the substance did not move from one property onto another property there can be no liability. This was the case in *Read v J Lyons and Co. Ltd* (1947).

Read v J Lyons and Co. Ltd (1947)

A munitions inspector was inspecting the interior of a munitions factory and was injured, along with a number of employees, when a shell exploded. The House of Lords held that the rule did not apply because there was 'no escape at all of the relevant kind'. Viscount Simon explained that an escape in *Rylands v Fletcher* (1868) means 'an escape from a place where the defendant has occupation or control over land to a place which is outside his occupation or control.'

Note that this rule is not always strictly applied – in *Hale v Jennings Bros* (1938) both stalls operated on the same piece of land and neither stallholder owned the land. Yet liability was imposed.

The House of Lords in *Transco plc v Stockport Metropolitan Borough Council* (2003) (see below for the facts) reviewed the past case law on the issue of escape and approved the line taken in *Read v Lyons*. This was on the basis that the court felt that the tort, being a specific form of nuisance, required a proprietary interest in land by the claimant. The House of Lords introduced in *Cambridge Water Co. v Eastern Counties Leather* (1994) a requirement that the damage to adjoining property must be reasonably foreseeable.

Cambridge Water Co. v Eastern Counties Leather (1994)

The defendants stored chemicals to do with its leather tanning. There were frequent spillages over the years and the chemicals seeped through the concrete floor and into the soil below. It polluted an area where the claimants extracted water for the local population and involved the water company spending over a million pounds in moving its operations. The water company claimed these expenses from the owners of the factory but the House of Lords decided that the damage was not reasonably foreseeable and too remote from the site of the spillage.

There are two recent examples of *Rylands v Fletcher* actions based on damage caused by fire. The first is *LMS International Ltd v Styrene Packaging and Insulation Ltd* (2005), where the claimant was successful. The second is *Stannard (t/a Wyvern Tyres) v Gore* (2012), where the claimant was successful at trial but the decision was reversed on appeal.

LMS International Ltd v Styrene Packaging and Insulation Ltd (2005)

The defendant's factory contained a large quantity of flammable material which was stored close to hot wire-cutting machines. A fire broke out, and spread to the claimant's adjoining property, although the fire services arrived within five minutes of being called. The claimant brought an action based on *Rylands v Fletcher*, nuisance and negligence for damage to its property.

It was held that as the defendant had accumulated things which were a known fire risk, it was liable in *Rylands v Fletcher*. Storage of the flammable items represented a recognisable risk to the claimant and a non-natural user of the land. The defendant was also liable in negligence and nuisance.

Stannard (t/a Wyvern Tyres) v Gore (2012)

The defendant stored tyres in relation to his tyre fitting business. A fire broke out and spread rapidly, causing damage to the claimant's adjoining premises. The trial judge found that the defendant was not negligent, but was strictly liable to the claimant in *Rylands v Fletcher*.

The judge found that tyres are not in themselves normally flammable, but they did have a special fire risk so that if a fire did develop the tyres might ignite; and if they did they may burn rapidly and intensely. Further, the tyres were stored in a haphazard manner and in a large quantity (approximately 3000) for the size of the premises. In this case the storage of tyres, in this particular situation, presented an exceptionally high risk of danger, and was a non-natural use of land.

However, the Court of Appeal disagreed. The majority reasoning was that in light of *Transco plc v Stockport Metropolitan Borough Council* (2003), it was not possible for a *Rylands v Fletcher* claim here. In their view it is an essential requirement of the tort that the defendant has brought some exceptionally dangerous 'thing' onto his land, and that thing must escape causing damage. In this case, where the fire had escaped but not the tyres, a claim based on *Rylands v Fletcher* must fail. In any event the tyres were not exceptionally dangerous or mischievous.

Further, the commercial activity carried on by the defendant as a motor tyre supplier was a perfectly ordinary and reasonable activity to be carried on in a light industrial estate, and was not therefore a non-natural use of the land for the purposes of the rule in *Rylands v Fletcher*.

In *Wyvern*, Ward LJ concluded that in an appropriate case, damage caused by fire moving from an adjoining property can fall within a *Rylands v Fletcher* claim, but the appropriate case is likely to be very rare, because:

1 It is the 'thing' which had been brought onto the land which must escape, not the fire which was started or increased by the 'thing'.

2 While fire may be a dangerous thing, the occasions when fire as such is brought onto the land may be limited to cases where the fire has been deliberately or negligently started by the occupier or one for whom he is responsible.

3 In any event, starting a fire on one's land may well be an ordinary use of the land.

This case will have significant consequences for claims in *Rylands v Fletcher* for fire damage as it will now be very difficult for claimants to succeed in such cases without proof of negligence.

Fire engines at the scene of a fire in Leicestershire

15.2.2 Defences

Despite the tort being described as strict liability, many defences are possible in the event of a claim.

- *Volenti non fit injuria* (consent) – there will be no liability where the claimant has consented to the thing that is accumulated by the defendant.
- Act of a stranger – if a stranger over whom the defendant has no control has been the cause of the escape causing the damage, then the defendant may not be liable, as in *Perry v Kendricks Transport Ltd* (1956).

Perry v Kendricks Transport Ltd (1956)

The defendants parked their bus on their parking space, having drained the tank of petrol. A stranger removed the petrol cap and a child was injured when another child threw a match into the tank which ignited fumes. A claim was made in *Rylands v Fletcher*. There was a valid defence of an act of a stranger and no liability.

- Act of God – this defence may succeed where there are extreme weather conditions that 'no human foresight can provide against'. It is only likely to succeed if there are unforeseeable weather conditions, as in *Nichols v Marsland* (1876).

Nichols v Marsland (1876)

The defendant made three artificial ornamental lakes by damming a natural stream. Freak thunderstorms accompanied by torrential rain broke the banks of the artificial lakes, which caused the destruction of bridges on the claimant's land. There was no liability because the weather conditions were so extreme and amounted to an Act of God.

- Statutory authority – if the terms of an Act of Parliament authorise the defendant's action, this may amount to a defence.
- Contributory negligence – where the claimant is partly responsible for the escape of the thing, then the Law Reform (Contributory Negligence) Act 1945 applies and damages may be reduced according to the amount of the claimant's fault.

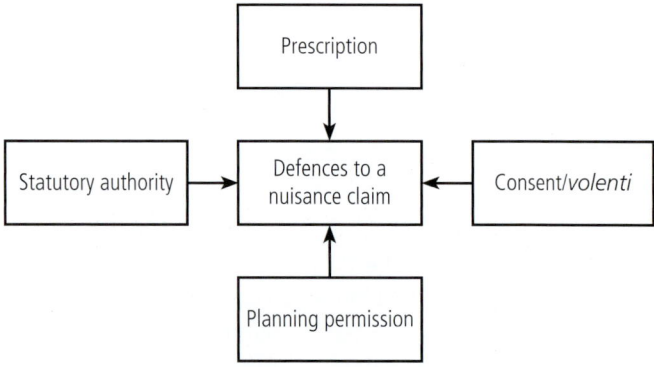

Figure 15.4 Defences to a nuisance claim

15.2.3 Remedies

A claimant must show damage to, or destruction of, his or her property in order to succeed in a claim for damages. The level of damages will be the cost of repair or replacement of the property damaged or destroyed.

15.2.4 *Rylands v Fletcher* and fault

Rylands v Fletcher is considered to be a true no-fault tort. The claimant has to prove the storage of a non-natural substance, which escaped and which caused reasonably foreseeable damage to his or her property. The reason for or how the escape occurred does not have to be proved – it merely needs to be shown that the substance did escape. To this extent, it should prove to be an easier tort to prove than the alternative of negligence, where the reason for the escape would have to be proved.

15.2.5 Developments in *Rylands v Fletcher*

When *Rylands v Fletcher* was first decided, there was a view that it was a broad, strict liability, action covering both damage to property and personal injury. However as time went by, the courts, as seen in a case such as *Rickards v Lothian*, took a restrictive approach and claimants were encouraged to use the tort of negligence, even though it required the proof of fault. As a strict liability tort, where fault does not have to be proved, it should have been easier for a claimant to prove *Rylands v Fletcher* action than use the alternative action of negligence. However, unlike some other strict liability actions, it allowed a number of defences available which limited its usefulness.

There were other factors which make the tort difficult to prove. Lord Cairns added the requirement that there be a non-natural use of land. So the simplest way to defeat a claim is to show that the use of land in question is a natural use.

Moreover, judges have shown hostility to the general principle of strict liability in the tort and have restricted the application of the rule still further:

1 According to *Read v Lyons* (1947), there can only be liability if the thing brought onto the defendant's land escapes from that land.
2 According to *Rickards v Lothian* (1913), there must be a 'special use of land bringing with it increased danger to others'.

3 The return to foreseeability of type of damage, as in *Cambridge Water Co. v Eastern Counties Leather plc* (1994).

There were calls for *Rylands v Fletcher* to be abolished as an action altogether. For example, the Pearson Commission report in 1978 recommended it should be replaced with a statutory scheme for injuries suffered in hazardous activities and required those who engaged in them to pay compensation for injuries caused in true strict liability fashion. This approach has been developed by Parliament into a number of specific, true strict liability actions, which may reflect the increasing technology present in today's society. These actions include the Reservoirs Act 1975 when water has been accumulated, the Nuclear Installations Acts 1965 and 1969, which cover the escape of radioactive substances, and even the Health and Safety at Work Act 1974. A claimant would be encouraged to use a specific action under one of these statutes rather than a *Rylands v Fletcher* action.

The House of Lords took the opportunity to review the tort in the case of *Transco plc v Stockport Metropolitan Borough Council* (2003). They expressed the view that a *Rylands v Fletcher* action is a form of nuisance. In the nuisance case of *Hunter v Canary Wharf Ltd* (1997), it was doubted whether personal injury was recoverable in nuisance and so it is unlikely now to be possible in *Rylands v Fletcher*.

Transco plc v Stockport Metropolitan Borough Council (2003)

The council was responsible for a high pressure water pipe supplying multi-storey flats. The pipe had leaked over time and caused an embankment to collapse, exposing the claimant's gas pipeline and leaving it in a dangerous condition. The claimant sought the cost of repairs from the council. The House of Lords held that there was no accumulation of a thing likely to cause mischief if it escaped, and that also the use of land by the council was a normal use. Lord Bingham felt that a *Rylands v Fletcher* action involved a defendant doing something that he ought to realise would give rise to a high risk of danger if material escaped, however unlikely the escape. He also considered that a test of 'ordinary' use was preferable to one of 'natural' or 'non-natural' use.

Figure 15.5 Key cases for *Rylands v Fletcher*

Case	Facts	Legal principle
Rylands v Fletcher (1868)	The defendant made a reservoir as a water supply for his mill Mineshafts were not blocked off causing flooding to a mine	A claim could be made if material was brought onto land and stored, it was likely to cause mischief if it escapes, which amounted to a non-natural use of the land, and which escaped
Rickards v Lothian (1913)	An unknown person turned on water taps and blocked plugholes causing damage to the flat below	There has to be a non-natural use of the land – not present in this case as domestic pipes were a natural use of land
Read v Lyons (1947)	An explosion took place in a munitions factory causing injury	The material has to escape from one property onto adjoining property – no liability here as there was no escape
Cambridge Water Co. v Eastern Counties Leather (1994)	Stored chemicals seeped through the concrete floor of a factory into the soil below, polluting an area where water was extracted	Damage has to be reasonably foreseeable and not too remote from the escape
LMS International Ltd v Styrene Packaging and Insulation Ltd (2005)	A fire started in the defendant's factory containing flammable material The fire spread to the adjoining property causing damage	The defendant was liable in *Rylands v Fletcher* as it had accumulated materials which were a known fire risk The storage was a recognisable risk to the adjoining property and a non-natural use of the land
Stannard (t/a Wyvern Tyres) v Gore (2012)	A fire spread from the defendant's tyre fitting business damaging the claimant's adjoining property	The Court of Appeal's view was that tyres were not exceptionally dangerous or mischievous The defendant was not carrying on any non-natural use of land on a light industrial estate

So, as a result of this case, the tort only applies when the defendant's use of land is extraordinary or unusual in the particular circumstances and at the particular point in time. An interest in the land affected by the escaping material is needed and personal injury is not within the scope of a claim. The House rejected the idea of abandoning the tort or that it should be treated as having been absorbed within the general law of negligence.

Activity

Jayden stores cooking oil in containers near to the boundary fence between his factory and Mina's garden. The oil was used in the production process of Jayden's food processing factory. On one occasion oil leaks from the containers. As a result, Mina's garden flowers and vegetables are ruined and the soil in her garden is contaminated.

Assess whether Mina has any rights and remedies against Jayden.

Tip

Make sure that you can identify and explain all four elements of the *Rylands v Fletcher* tort.

Summary

Nuisance

- Private nuisance is 'an unlawful interference with a person's use or enjoyment of land coming from neighbouring land'.

- Any person with an interest in the land affected can claim.

- The defendant will be the person who caused the nuisance or who allowed it to continue.

- The court will take various factors into account when considering if the defendant's activities are reasonable; they include the character of the neighbourhood, duration, sensitivity of the claimant, malice and social benefit.

- Defendants can argue defences such as prescription and statutory permission, but moving to the nuisance is not an arguable defence.

- Courts have wider discretion in the remedy to order. Damages may be considered more widely than in the past as an appropriate remedy.

Rylands v Fletcher

- The tort of *Rylands v Fletcher* was developed in the case of the same name.

- It was a strict liability tort providing that a claim could be made if material was brought onto land and stored, it was likely to cause mischief if it escapes, which amounted to a non-natural use of the land, and which escaped causing damage to adjoining land.

- A person who can take an action has to have an interest in the land affected.

- A defendant will be the owner or occupier who satisfies the four ingredients of the tort and he or she must have some control over the land on which the material is stored.

- The damage caused to the adjoining property has to be reasonably foreseeable.

- Various defences are available, including act of a stranger, act of God, statutory authority to storage, consent and contributory negligence.

- The claimant can claim damages for the cost of repairing his or her property.

16 Vicarious liability

After reading this chapter, you should be able to:
- Understand the nature and purpose of vicarious liability
- Understand the testing of employment status
- Understand other areas of vicarious liability

16.1 The nature and purpose of vicarious liability

Vicarious liability is not an individual tort claim in the same way as negligence or nuisance. It is a way of imposing liability for a tort onto someone who did not commit the tort.

Key term

Vicarious liability – where a third person has legal responsibility for the unlawful actions of another. It is commonly seen in the workplace where the employer is responsible for the actions of his or her employee, who acted in the course of his or her employment.

It was originally based on the idea that an employer has control over his or her employees at work, and should therefore be responsible for any torts committed by the employee at work.

In a less sophisticated society, with traditional methods of work, control by an employer was more possible. Modern methods of employment, and where work is carried out, make employers' control of their employees less clear. For example, the work done by a surgeon at a hospital cannot be said to be under the control of a manager who has no medical expertise. Also, should an employer be responsible for the actions of an employee who is working from home?

The rule can be criticised for applying liability unfairly as an apparently innocent party is liable for something which he or she has not personally done or failed to do. It also imposes liability when the employer has not been directly at fault and is an example of strict (or no fault) liability.

However, the liability is justified for the reason that the victim of a tort is able to receive compensation for the injury or damage suffered. In addition:

- An employer may traditionally have had a degree of control over the activities of employees in the workplace. Indeed, it may well be that an employee has carried out the instructions of the employer which led to the tort. In this case, it is only fair that the employer should bear the cost of the employee's actions.
- Employers are responsible for hiring, firing and disciplining their staff. An employer may have been careless in selecting staff and, if employees are either careless or likely to cause harm and the employer is aware of this, the employer has the ability to do something about it. Internal disciplinary systems allow the employer to ensure that lapses of behaviour are not repeated. There is the ultimate sanction of dismissing a member of staff who refuses to, or is unable to, follow set procedures.
- An employer is responsible for making sure that all employees are trained so that work is done safely and that safe procedures are followed. The employer may be at fault for providing inadequate or inappropriate training and should accept responsibility for this.
- An employer should have supervised the employee more effectively. However, on this point, employers are likely to want to allow employees, especially more experienced ones, greater freedom to do their work as otherwise an army of supervisors will have to be employed to closely monitor every employee for every minute of work.
- The major concern of a victim is whether he or she will receive compensation and whether the defendant is worth suing. An employer will usually be in a better financial position to pay compensation than one of its employees. In addition, an employer is required to take out public liability insurance to cover injuries in the workplace so that it is likely the victim will receive compensation.

An accident at work can involve compensation

There are two main tests required to prove vicarious liability:

- Was the person alleged to have committed the tort an employee? Generally there will be no vicarious liability for the tort committed by an independent contractor who will be legally responsible for his or her own actions.
- Did the employee commit the alleged tort 'during the course of his or her employment'?

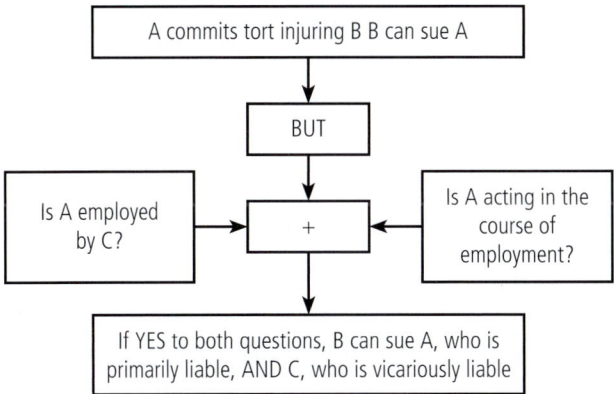

Figure 16.1 The operation of vicarious liability

16.2 Testing employment status

The old test of employment was whether a person was providing:

- a contract of service – he or she would be an employee, or
- a contract for services – he or she would be an independent contractor.

The distinction is important, because an employer can be vicariously liable for the actions of its employees, but an independent contractor, otherwise known as a self-employed person, is legally responsible for his or her own actions and can be sued by the victim of a tort which is committed by him or her. An independent contractor should therefore have his or her own liability insurance cover.

It is not always possible to easily decide whether a person is employed or is an independent contractor. Different tests may be used according to who is doing the testing. For example, the only concern of HM Revenue and Customs is to decide liability for payment of tax and not for any other purpose. So the fact that a person is paying Schedule D tax, or is subject to self-assessment, is not necessarily a legal test of self-employed status.

Various different forms of working relationships have developed in recent times which may not fit into traditional definitions. Full-time and part-time work will often indicate employment, but what of casual, temporary or seasonal work or 'zero hours' contracts? And what of workers carrying out internships or volunteering? Should an employer be legally responsible then?

Over the years the courts have developed several methods of testing employee status.

16.2.1 The control test

The oldest of these is the 'control test'. In *Yewens v Noakes* (1880), the test was whether the master (the employer) had the right to control what the employee did and the way in which it was done. According to McArdie J in *Performing Rights Society v Mitchell and Booker* (1924), the test concerns 'the nature and degree of detailed control'.

Lord Thankerton in *Short v J W Henderson Ltd* (1946) identified many key features which would show that the master had control over the servant. These included the power to select the servant, the right to control the method of working, the right to suspend and dismiss, and the payment of wages.

Such a test is virtually impossible to apply accurately today. Nevertheless, there are circumstances in which a test of control is still useful, as seen in the case below regarding borrowed workers.

Mersey Docks and Harbour Board v Coggins and Griffiths (Liverpool) Ltd (1947)

A crane driver had been hired out by his employers, the Harbour Board, to stevedores who loaded and unloaded ships. By his negligence the driver injured a person in the course of his work. His employers, the Harbour Board, had made a contract which set out that he was the employee of Coggins but the Harbour Board paid his wages and kept the power to sack him. When deciding who was vicariously liable the House of Lords decided that:

- the terms in any hire contract of an employee are not decisive
- the permanent employer is presumed liable unless the contrary can be proved, and
- if an employee alone is hired out there can be an inference that the hirer becomes the employer. If the employee is hired out with equipment (as in this case with the crane), the inference is not as strong as the hirer may not have any control over how the equipment can be used.

A more recent development of the control test concerns the activities of bouncers operating outside clubs. Should a club be vicariously liable for the bouncer's actions outside its premises?

Hawley v Luminar Leisure Ltd (2006)

A bouncer, who was supplied to nightclubs by a firm of specialist suppliers, assaulted a customer outside the defendant's club. The suppliers went into liquidation so the injured claimant sued the club. The court decided that, as the club exercised so much control over the bouncer in how he should do his work, they employed him and were vicariously liable for his actions.

Can more than one employer be vicariously liable for the actions of a worker? This was a question for the Court of Appeal in *Viasystems (Tyneside) Ltd v Thermal Transfer (Northern) Ltd* (2005).

Viasystems (Tyneside) Ltd v Thermal Transfer (Northern) Ltd (2005)

The claimants contracted with D1 to install air conditioning in their factory. D1 subcontracted some work to D2. D2 agreed with D3 to provide fitters and fitters' mates on a labour-only basis. S was a fitter's mate. He damaged some ducting that came into contact with a sprinkler which fractured, causing a flood.

It had to be decided whether D2 or D3 or both were vicariously liable for S's negligence.

The leading authority was *Mersey Docks and Harbour Board v Coggins and Griffith (Liverpool) Ltd* (1946), above. That case was authority for the principle that decisions as to employment depended on the particular facts but certain considerations might be relevant.

There was a long-standing assumption, which was not a legal principle, that a finding of dual vicarious liability was not possible. The reason for this was that in order to find a temporary employer vicariously liable there would have to be a transfer of employment. The question for the court was: 'Who was entitled and in theory obliged to control the employee's negligent act in order to prevent it?' There could be some cases in which the sensible answer would be each of two 'employers', so D2 and D3 were both liable.

Where there was dual vicarious liability arising out of the negligence of a single employee, it followed that the responsibility of each employer for the purposes of contribution must be equal, and D2 and D3 should each contribute 50 per cent to the claimant.

16.2.2 The integration or organisation test

Lord Denning in *Stevenson Jordan and Harrison Ltd v MacDonald and Evans* (1952) established this test. It provides that a worker will be an employee if his or her work is fully integrated into the business. If a person's work is only accessory to the business, that person is not an employee.

According to this test, the master of a ship, a chauffeur and a staff newspaper reporter are all employees. On the other hand the pilot bringing a ship into port, a taxi driver and a freelance writer are not employees.

The test can work well in some cases but there are still problems. Teachers who are examiners for exam boards may be classed as employed persons as tax and pension contributions may be deducted from their earnings, but the contract will specify that examiners are not to be considered as employees and there are no rights to dismissal or redundancy pay when their services are no longer required.

16.2.3 The economic reality or multiple test

In view of problems with the above tests, courts have recognised that a single test of employment status is not satisfactory and may produce confusing results. This economic reality test considers various factors which may indicate employment or self-employment. It was established in *Ready Mixed Concrete (South East) Ltd v Minister of Pensions and National Insurance* (1968).

Ready Mixed Concrete (South East) Ltd v Minister of Pensions and National Insurance (1968)

The case involved the payment of National Insurance contributions. Vehicles were bought by drivers on hire-purchase from the company and they had to be painted in the company colours and showing the company logo. Drivers had to maintain the vehicles and were only allowed to use them on company business. Working hours were flexible and pay was subject to an annual minimum rate according to the amount of concrete hauled. In the event of an accident should the company be liable or should a driver? McKenna J developed a test which set three conditions which had to be met before an employment relationship was identified:

1 The employee agrees to provide work or skill in return for a wage.

2   The employee expressly or impliedly accepts that the work will be subject to the control of the employer.

3   All other considerations in the contract are consistent with there being a contract of employment rather than any other relationship.

Taking these tests into account, the result was that the drivers were not employees.

More recently, the test has been updated so that all factors in the relationship should be considered and weighed according to their significance. Relevant factors might include:

■   the ownership of any tools, plant or equipment – an employee is less likely to own the plant and equipment used at work

■   the method of payment – a self-employed person is likely to take a payment for completing a whole job where an employee will usually receive regular payments (salary) for the period of employment

■   if tax, National Insurance and pension contributions are deducted from employees' wages – a self-employed person will have to submit self-assessments and pay tax annually

■   any job description – a person may describe him- or herself as an employee or as self-employed; this will usually, but not always, be an accurate description

■   any independence in doing a job – probably one of the most important tests of self-employed status is the amount of independence and flexibility in being able to take work from different sources, and when and how to do it.

All of these factors are useful in identifying the status of the worker, but none are an absolute test or are definitive on their own. There can still be conflicting decisions. For example, in *Carmichael v National Power* (2001) tour guides employed on a casual basis were not employees as there was no formal contractual arrangement between the parties. In *Ferguson v Dawson* (1976), a contract stated that a building labourer was self-employed but the court decided he was employed and the employers were required to protect him under safety laws.

16.2.4 Recent developments

A number of cases have reached the appeal courts in recent years that test whether or not the tortfeasor was an employee. There was often no traditional employment relationship and it had to be decided whether 'the employer' should be vicariously liable. Several cases involved claims of historic abuse.

E v English Province of Our Lady of Charity (2012)

The question in this case was whether a nun in charge of a children's home and a visiting priest were employees and whether the Bishop of the diocese could be vicariously liable for sexual abuse carried out on the claimant.

The Court of Appeal stated that the court was required to look for:

1   a relationship akin (or similar) to employment

2   which was established by a connection between a putative defendant and an 'actor' which was sufficiently close so that

3   it was fair and just to impose liability on the defendant.

Several questions could be considered which might point to vicarious liability:

a   control by the 'employer' of the 'employee'

b   control by the contractor of him- or herself

c   the organisation test (how central was the activity to the organisation?)

d   the integration test (whether the activity was integrated into the organisational structure of the enterprise)

e   the entrepreneur test (whether the person was in business on his or her own account).

Applying such tests, the majority of the court decided that the priest was more like an employee than an independent contractor. As his relationship with the bishop was close enough and similar to that of employer/employee it made it just and fair to impose vicarious liability.

JGE v Trustees of the Portsmouth Roman Catholic Diocesan Trust (2012)

The claimant alleged that, when she was very young, she was sexually abused and raped by a Roman Catholic priest while living in a children's home. She brought an action against the church for the acts of the priest. The church argued that it was not liable for the acts of the priest as he was not an employee, only an office holder following his vocation and not subject to the level of control required to demonstrate an employment relationship.

The Court of Appeal held that, even though the priest was not an employee of the church, his relationship with the church was sufficiently close to one of employment that it was fair and just to hold the church vicariously liable for damages as a result of his conduct. Factors such as the level of control and supervision exercised by the church and the role of the priest within the structure of the church were considered to be important.

The Catholic Child Welfare Society v Various Claimants (FC) and The Institute of the Brothers of the Christian Schools (2012)

A group of 170 men alleged that they were physically and sexually abused by their teachers while living at a school for boys in need of care. The teachers were members of the Brothers of the Christian Schools (the 'Institute'), a religious organisation which sent its members to the School as part of its mission to 'teach children, especially poor children, those things which pertain to a good and Christian life'. The members had contracts of employment with the school. The Supreme Court had to decide whether the Institute could be held liable for abuse carried out by its members. The school argued that the Institute should share responsibility for the acts of its members. The Institute responded that only a body managing a school and employing a brother in that school as a teacher should be vicariously liable for his wrongdoing.

The court held that the Institute could be held liable for the alleged sexual abuse committed by its members because the relationship between the Institute and its members was sufficiently akin to one of employer and employee, and there was a close connection between that relationship and the sexual abuse allegedly committed by the brothers while teaching in the school.

The court examined the school's claim against the Institute under a two-part test:

1 whether the relationship between the Institute and its members was capable of giving rise to vicarious liability, and

2 whether the alleged acts of sexual abuse were connected to that relationship in such a way as to give rise to vicarious liability.

The court held that the first element of vicarious liability can be based on a relationship that, while not arising under a formal contract of employment, is sufficiently 'akin to that between an employer and an employee'. The court explained that the Institute's relationship with its members was sufficiently close to one of employment based on the hierarchical structure of the Institute, the ability of the Institute to direct where its members taught, the importance of teaching activity in the organisation's mission, and the manner in which its members were bound by its rules. The second element was also satisfied based on the close connection between the Institute's relationship with

its members, and the alleged sexual abuse its members committed while pursuing their mission to provide an education to vulnerable students living on the premises of the school.

As a result, the court decided that the Institute should be responsible for the acts of its members even though they were employees of the school.

In *Mohamud v WM Morrison Supermarkets plc* (2016), Lord Toulson in the Supreme Court restated the test of whether the tortfeasor is employed or not.

Mohamud v WM Morrison Supermarkets plc (2016)

A man employed at the defendant's petrol station assaulted a customer, causing him serious injuries. The Supreme Court considered the job that had been given to the employee and whether there was a sufficient connection between the employee's job and what he did to the customer. They decided that as the employee was acting within the field of his employment – it was at work and within working hours, and there was a close connection between what he did and what he was required to do in his job – the employer was vicariously liable to pay compensation to the victim.

Per Lord Toulson:

> 44. In the simplest terms, the court has to consider two matters. The first question is what functions or 'field of activities' have been entrusted by the employer to the employee, or, in everyday language, what was the nature of his job. As has been emphasised in several cases, this question must be addressed broadly ...

> 45. Secondly, the court must decide whether there was sufficient connection between the position in which he was employed and his wrongful conduct to make it right for the employer to be held liable under the principle of social justice.

The case of *Cox v Ministry of Justice* (2016) was heard alongside *Mohamud*.

Cox v Ministry of Justice (2016)

The claimant was employed in a prison as a catering manager. She was injured by a prisoner who negligently dropped a sack of rice on her back. She claimed compensation from the Ministry of Justice. The Court of Appeal stated that the relationship between the prisoner and the prison service was similar to that of employer and employee. The Supreme Court agreed, noting that:

> A relationship other than one of employment is in principle capable of giving rise to vicarious liability where harm is wrongfully done by an individual who carries on activities as an integral part of the business activities carried on by a defendant and for its benefit (rather than his activities being entirely attributable to the conduct of a recognisably independent business of his own or of a third party).

In other words, the Supreme Court recognised that today many workers, in reality, are part of the workforce of an organisation without having a contract of employment with that organisation. Further, the word 'business' did not necessarily require the carrying out of commercial activities, nor the pursuit of profit. It was enough here that the prison carried on activities in the furtherance of its own interests; here, rehabilitating prisoners.

On the other hand a case which did not impose vicarious liability was *Fletcher v Chancery Supplies Ltd* (2017).

Fletcher v Chancery Supplies Ltd (2017)

The claimant, who was a police officer, was riding his police-issue mountain bike on a cycle lane alongside a busy main road. A man, T, suddenly emerged from behind a stationary van and collided with the claimant in the cycle lane. The claimant fell to the floor and suffered severe leg injuries.

T had been working that morning, was wearing a work polo shirt and work boots, and told officers attending the scene, 'I have attempted to cross the road to where my shop is'. He gave the shop as his home address. At trial the judge found T's employer vicariously liable.

Applying the questions in *Mohamud*, the Court of Appeal decided that as there was no explanation why T had previously left the shop, there was no sufficient connection between his work and him causing the accident to make T's employer vicariously liable.

The principles from these cases that will apply when it is not obvious that the tortfeasor is an employee or not are summarised in Figure 16.2.

Figure 16.2 Key cases when it is not obvious that the tortfeasor is an employee

Case	Principle
E v English Province of Our Lady of Charity (2012)	The court has to look for: 1 a relationship akin (or similar) to employment 2 which was established by a sufficiently close connection so that 3 it was fair and just to impose liability on the defendant
JGE v Trustees of the Portsmouth Roman Catholic Diocesan Trust (2012)	Being an office holder, as opposed to an employee, could make the church vicariously liable for the actions of a priest as the priest's relationship with the church was sufficiently akin (close) to one of employment and it was fair and just to hold the church vicariously liable
The Catholic Child Welfare Society v Various Claimants (FC) and The Institute of the Brothers of the Christian Schools (2012)	The relationship between the Institute and its members was akin to an employer and employee relationship, and the sexual abuse connected to that relationship gave rise to vicarious liability
Mohamud v WM Morrison Supermarkets plc (2016)	As the employee was acting within the field of his employment – it was at work and within working hours, and there was a close connection between what he did and what he was required to do in his job – the employer was vicariously liable
Cox v Ministry of Justice (2016)	If a person is carrying on activities as an integral part of the business activities carried on by a defendant and for its benefit, then the business will be vicariously liable

Complete a table of two columns showing whether the following characteristics are of being employed or being an independent contractor (self-employed):

- the worker has set hours of work
- the worker uses his or her own tools or equipment in work
- a regular salary is paid
- holiday can be taken at a time of the worker's choice
- a manager directs how work should be done
- the worker keeps his or her own financial records
- health and safety training is provided
- tax and pension contributions are deducted
- invoices are sent out for work completed
- maternity/paternity leave is available
- additional workers can be employed when required
- a uniform is provided
- the worker has his or her own liability insurance policy
- the worker has dismissal and redundancy rights
- the worker provides a contract for services
- the worker enters into a contract of service.

In the news

Uber to take appeal over ruling on drivers' status to UK Supreme Court

Uber plans to appeal to the UK's Supreme Court against a ruling that drivers should be classed as workers, setting the scene for a landmark legal battle with major implications for the gig economy.

The taxi app lost a tribunal case brought by two drivers last year and tasted defeat for a second time earlier this month when the employment appeal tribunal upheld the original decision.

Uber hopes the Supreme Court will grant it permission to leapfrog the court of appeal and take its case directly to the highest court in the country as soon as February.

'We have this afternoon requested permission to appeal directly to the Supreme Court in order that this case can be resolved sooner rather than later,' said a spokesperson.

The case hinges on the employment status of Uber drivers, who the taxi app claims are self-employed contractors. Uber says the majority of its 50,000

drivers prefer their self-employed status, pointing out that the two drivers who brought the case no longer drive for the company.

It could also have ramifications for a host of gig economy firms, which operate by inviting workers to accept small jobs at short notice, often via smartphone apps.

Source: Adapted from an article by Rob Davies in the Guardian online, 24 November 2017

Look online

Although not involving vicarious liability, tribunals have had to consider whether Uber drivers are employees and entitled to the benefits of being employed. Follow the weblink for a full report of this decision: www.theguardian.com/technology/2017/nov/24/uber-to-take-appeal-over-ruling-on-drivers-status-to-uk-supreme-court.

- What employment rights does this ruling give Uber drivers?
- What does this ruling mean if a driver has an accident while carrying a passenger?

Extension activity

Identify some of the reasons given for the decision.

Activity

L is a private hire driver working for a business providing a 24-hour service at an airport. The business has an exclusive contract with the airport to provide a taxi service. L owns and is responsible for his own vehicle, has to obtain an operating licence and pays his own tax and National Insurance. He collects fares from passengers, but pays a percentage of each fare to the business. L can work as and when he wishes.

- Is L an employee of the business or an independent contractor?
- What similarities and differences can you see with the Uber case?

Tip

For vicarious liability, the starting point is to consider whether the person who caused the injury is an employee. Only then should you consider the second part of liability – whether the employee is acting in the course of employment.

16.3 Acting in the course of employment

In order for the employer to be liable, the employee has to commit the tort 'in the course of the employment'.

Whether an action is carried out in the course of employment or not is a question of fact for the court to decide in each case. It is often difficult to see consistency in the judgments, and recent judgments appear to be weighted in favour of claimants.

Regardless of the reasoning applied in them, there are two lines of cases:

- where there is vicarious liability because the employee is acting in the course of the employment
- where there is *no* vicarious liability because the employee is said not to be acting in the course of employment.

16.3.1 Torts committed in the course of employment

There are various ways the court has to decide whether an act is carried out in the course of employment.

Acting against orders

If the employee is doing his or her job but acts against orders in the way he or she does it, the employer can be liable for any tort committed by him or her. This can be illustrated by the cases of *Limpus v London General* (1862) and *Rose v Plenty* (1976).

Limpus v London General (1862)

The employer instructed its bus drivers not to race other drivers when collecting passengers. One driver caused an accident when racing. The employer was liable to the injured claimant as the driver was doing what he was employed to do – even though it was against orders.

Rose v Plenty (1976)

A dairy instructed its milkmen not to use child helpers on their milk rounds. One milkman did use a boy to help him but the boy was injured on the round due to the milkman's negligent driving. The dairy was vicariously liable for the milkman's negligence, as the milkman was doing his job, even though disobeying orders.

However if the employee gives the claimant an unauthorised lift, the employer will not be liable.

Twine v Beans Express (1946)

The claimant's husband was killed through the negligence of a driver who had been forbidden by his employer to give lifts. This instruction was supported by notices on the side of the van stating who could be carried in it. The employers were not liable as the driver was doing an unauthorised act and the employers were gaining no benefit from it.

If the employee causes injury by doing something outside what he was employed to do, the employer will not be liable. This is shown in *Beard v London General Omnibus Co.* (1900).

Beard v London General Omnibus Co. (1900)

A bus conductor, employed to collect fares, drove a bus, without the authority of his employer, injuring the claimant. The employer was not liable, as the conductor was doing something outside the course of his employment.

Employee committing a criminal act

If the employee commits a crime during his or her work, the employer may be liable to the victim of the crime if there is a 'close connection' between the crime and what the employee was employed to do. This test was established by the House of Lords in *Lister v Hesley Hall* (2001)

Lister v Hesley Hall (2001)

The warden of a school for children with emotional difficulties sexually assaulted some of the children. He was convicted of criminal offences. The House of Lords decided there was a close connection between his job and what he did as the assaults were carried out on the school premises when he was looking after the children.

On the other hand, the fact that a police officer uses his uniform to gain the trust of a victim will not necessarily give rise to vicarious liability if the officer commits a crime.

N v Chief Constable of Merseyside Police (2006)

Two hours after he had gone off duty, D was parked outside a nightclub still in uniform. A first aider from the club was worried because a young woman was very drunk and had taken the drug ecstasy. D offered to take her to a police station. D took the woman to his house where he committed various sexual assaults on her including rape. The court held that there was no close connection between D's employment and the assaults. D had merely made use of his uniform to gain trust and abuse it.

Mattis v Pollock (2003)

A bouncer was employed to keep order outside a nightclub. The bouncer inflicted serious injuries on a customer and was jailed for committing serious criminal offences. The nightclub was held vicariously liable for the bouncer's actions as he was encouraged to use force, to be violent and intimidating and his criminal actions were closely connected to his work

This principle has been looked at again in *Mohamud v WM Morrison Supermarkets plc* (2016) by the Supreme Court; see section 16.2.4 for case details.

It is obviously fair on victims of crimes committed at work that they should receive compensation for the injuries suffered as they would be unlikely to obtain compensation from the person who inflicted those injuries, especially if they are serving prison sentences. On the one hand, in cases such as *Mohamud v WM Morrison Supermarkets plc* (2016) it could be said to be unfair on the employers as they had no knowledge of what their employee was doing when committing the assault. On the other hand it could be said to be fair that the employer is liable as it should have been supervising the employee more carefully.

Employee committing a negligent act

If the employee does a job badly, the employer can be liable for his actions which cause injury to another. This was shown in *Century Insurance Co. Ltd v Northern Ireland Road Transport Board* (1942).

Century Insurance Co. Ltd v Northern Ireland Road Transport Board (1942)

A petrol tanker driver was delivering petrol to a petrol station when he lit a cigarette and threw a lighted match on the ground. This caused an explosion which destroyed several cars and damaged some houses. The employer was liable to pay compensation as the driver was doing his job, even though negligently.

The principle of vicarious liability should encourage employers to take greater care when selecting their employees and on providing suitable training and supervision in the workplace. The decision in the *Century Insurance* case is an example of this as the employer should have made it totally clear to its employees that smoking while delivering petrol was dangerous. It shows that employers have a social

responsibility for their position and a business should see 'in the course of business' responsibility as one of the underlying costs of being an employer. However, modern methods of working from home or working flexibly mean that it is not always possible for employers to closely supervise their workforce and it could be said to be unfair on them to accept liability for an employee's actions when he or she is working away from the employer's eyes.

Employee acting on a 'frolic' of his or her own

On the other hand, if the employee causes injury or damage to another while doing something, or at a time, outside the area or time of his or her work, the employer will not be liable. It is said in this case that the employee is acting on 'a frolic of his or her own'. This is illustrated in the case of *Hilton v Thomas Burton (Rhodes) Ltd* (1961), below. However the opposite result was reached in *Smith v Stages* (1989), as the employee was doing something he was supposed to be doing. These appear to be inconsistent and unfair decisions and the victim, or the victim's relatives, will be unsuccessful in claiming compensation. This is obviously unfair as someone such as Mrs Hilton clearly suffered a loss and although her husband was killed in his work time and in the employer's van, she was unsuccessful in proving vicarious liability. This contrasts with *Smith v Stages* (1989), below, where, on similar facts, the victim was able to prove vicarious liability. The difference in the decisions was merely related to the purpose of the employee's journey. Again in *Beard v London General Omnibus Co.* (1900), the injured victim would not have been aware that the employee was not authorised to drive the bus and, as result, was not able to prove vicarious liability. This was unfair as he was injured as a result of another's fault.

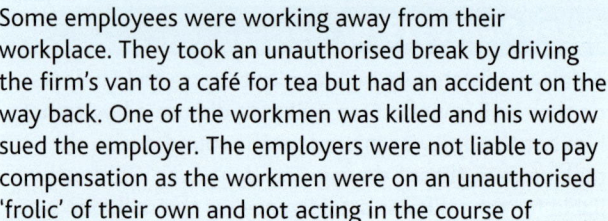

Hilton v Thomas Burton (Rhodes) Ltd (1961)

Some employees were working away from their workplace. They took an unauthorised break by driving the firm's van to a café for tea but had an accident on the way back. One of the workmen was killed and his widow sued the employer. The employers were not liable to pay compensation as the workmen were on an unauthorised 'frolic' of their own and not acting in the course of employment.

Smith v Stages (1989)

The employee was driving back to his place of work after working elsewhere and caused an accident. The employer was vicariously liable because the court decided that he was acting in the course of employment as he was being paid during his travelling time.

16.3.2 Payment of compensation

The employee will be primarily liable and can be ordered to pay compensation. However, there may be a question whether the employee is financially able to pay. If the tort is committed by an employee acting in the course of employment, the employer will be vicariously liable and ordered to pay compensation to the injured victim. The victim will only receive one payment.

By the Civil Liability (Contribution) Act 1978, the employer can recover any compensation paid out by it from the employee by, for example, deduction from wages. If this message was more widely known, it could act as a deterrent to committing wrongs in the workplace and during working time. However, this right of recovery is unlikely to be effective in practice. The employee is unlikely to be earning a sufficient amount to make it worth the employer pursuing him or her for large amounts of money. Also, the employee could leave the employment, or be dismissed, and the employer's rights of recovery would be difficult, or impossible, to enforce. This would certainly be the case if the employee has committed a crime during the employment and is serving a sentence of imprisonment. Rogue employees will know that there is little chance of them being sued or financially penalised by their employer so they may have limited incentive to take care at work.

Workmen stop for lunch at a roadside cafe in East London

Activity

Decide whether each of the following workers is employed or self-employed, giving reasons for your answers:

- X is a caddie at a golf club. The club provide him with a number, a uniform and a clothes locker. Caddying work is allocated according to a strict rotation and at set rates. Caddies can choose when they work and there is no guarantee of work. The club charges members and passes payment to the caddies.
- Y is a lap dancer performing for guests at a private member's club. She pays the club a fee for each night that she performs. In return, she decides for whom she dances, for how long and the fee.
- Z is a driver who owns his own car. He pays a mini-cab operator a weekly fee and in return has a radio installed and access to the computer system, which allocates customers to drivers. He is required to wear a uniform and is prohibited from working for any other operator. He can choose when to work and for how long, and he keeps all the fares he collects.

16.4 Other areas of vicarious liability

As has been said, the typical operation of vicarious liability is seen in the workplace when an employer will be vicariously liable for the actions of its employees who were acting in the course of employment.

Another situation where it may apply is when a parent may be vicariously liable for the actions of his or her child which cause injury to a third party. For example, if a child runs out into the road and causes an accident, the parent who failed to supervise the child may be vicariously liable for the damage and injury caused.

As set out previously in section 16.2.4, the following have been considered to be vicariously liable:

- the bishop of a church diocese for sexual abuse carried out by a priest – *E v English Province of Our Lady of Charity* (2012) and *JGE v Trustees of the Portsmouth Roman Catholic Diocesan Trust* (2012)
- a religious organisation whose members taught in a school and who abused children taught there – *The Catholic Child Welfare Society v Various Claimants (FC) and The Institute of the Brothers of the Christian Schools* (2012)
- an employer whose employee assaulted a customer – *Mohamud v WM Morrison Supermarkets plc* (2016)

- the prison service when a prisoner negligently injured a catering manager – *Cox v Ministry of Justice* (2016)

In a recent case heard by the Supreme Court, the boundaries of vicarious liability have been extended further. In *Armes v Nottinghamshire County Council* (2017), it was decided that the council was vicariously liable for the physical and sexual abuse carried out by a succession of foster carers on the claimant. It was said that as the council exercised powers of approval, inspection, supervision and ultimately removal, it had a significant degree of control over what the foster carers did and how they did it and had to accept liability.

Figure 16.3 Key cases for vicarious liability (see also Figure 16.2)

Case	Facts	Legal principle
Mersey Docks and Harbour Board v Coggins and Griffiths (Liverpool) Ltd (1947)	A hired crane driver negligently injured a person Who was vicariously liable for his negligence?	Look at terms of the hiring contract If the worker and the equipment is hired out, there is a presumption that the original employer is liable If the worker only is hired out, the presumption is that the hirer is liable
Hawley v Luminar Leisure Ltd (2006)	A bouncer assaulted a customer outside the club He was employed by specialist suppliers	As the club exercised so much control over how the bouncer should work, it employed him and was vicariously liable for his actions
Ready Mixed Concrete (South East) Ltd v Minister of Pensions and National Insurance (1968)	Should the company or a driver be liable for the payment of National Insurance contributions?	Three conditions are to be met to show an employment relationship: 1 a relationship similar to employment 2 which was established by a close connection 3 it was fair and just to impose liability on the employer
Viasystems (Tyneside) Ltd v Thermal Transfer (Northern) Ltd (2005)	The claimants contracted with D1 to install air conditioning in their factory D1 subcontracted some work to D2 D2 agreed with D3 to provide fitters and fitters' mates S was a fitters' mate who caused damage through negligence	More than one 'employer' could be vicariously liable Here D2 and D3 were each 50% liable
Limpus v London General (1862)	A bus driver caused an accident when racing, despite being told not to race by his employer	The employer was liable to the injured claimant as the driver was doing what he was employed to do – even against orders
Rose v Plenty (1976)	A dairy instructed its milkmen not to use child helpers on their milk rounds One milkman did use a boy to help him but the boy was injured on the round	The dairy was vicariously liable for the milkman's negligence as the dairy was benefiting from the work done by the boy
Twine v Beans Express (1946)	The claimant's husband was killed through the negligence of a driver who had been forbidden to give lifts	The employers were not liable as the driver was doing an unauthorised act and the employers were gaining no benefit from it
Beard v London General Omnibus Co. (1900)	A bus conductor, employed to collect fares, drove a bus without the authority of his employer, injuring the claimant	The employer was not liable as the conductor was doing something outside the course of his employment

Case	Facts	Legal principle
Lister v Hesley Hall (2001)	The warden of a school for children with emotional difficulties sexually assaulted some of the children He was convicted of criminal offences	The House of Lords decided there was a close connection between his job and what he did as the assaults were carried out on the school premises when he was looking after the children
N v Chief Constable of Merseyside Police (2006)	After he had gone off duty, the defendant in police uniform offered to take a woman to the police station The defendant committed sexual assaults on her including rape	There was no close connection between the employment and the assaults The defendant had merely made use of his uniform to gain trust and abuse it
Mattis v Pollock (2003)	A bouncer inflicted serious injuries on a customer and was jailed for committing serious criminal offences	The nightclub was vicariously liable for the bouncer's actions as he was encouraged to use force, to be violent and intimidating and his criminal actions were closely connected to his work
Century Insurance Co. Ltd v Northern Ireland Road Transport Board (1942)	A petrol tanker driver threw a lighted match in a petrol station This caused an explosion which destroyed several cars and damaged some houses	The employer was liable to pay compensation as the driver was doing his job, even though negligently
Hilton v Thomas Burton (Rhodes) Ltd (1961)	Some employees took an unauthorised break by driving the firm's van but had an accident on the way back One was killed and his widow sued the employer	The employers were not liable to pay compensation to the victim of the accident as the workmen were on an unauthorised 'frolic' of their own and not acting in the course of employment

Activity

Jamie is a lorry driver employed by Larry. Larry instructs all of his drivers, including Jamie, not to use their mobile phones while they are driving. One day, while on his way to make a delivery, Jamie drives on a motorway. While he is sending a text on his mobile, Jamie loses control of his lorry, which swerves and collides with Mary's car. Mary is seriously injured and the car is badly damaged.

Assess whether Mary has any rights to claim compensation against Jamie and against Larry.

Summary

- Vicarious liability means that someone other than the person who committed the tort is responsible for his or her actions, and for paying compensation.
- It usually applies where an employer has to pay for a tort committed by an employee.
- Strict liability is imposed on the employer.
- Two conditions have to be satisfied:
  - the person who committed the tort is an employee as opposed to an independent contractor, and
  - he or she was acting in the course of his or her employment.
- Whether a person is employed or is self-employed is a legal test which may involve:
  - the control test – how much control the employer had over the employee in what the employee did and how it was done, and/or
  - the integration test – if a person's work is fully integrated into the business he or she will be considered an employee, and/or
  - the economic reality or multiple test – looks at the whole situation between the worker and the employer including ownership of tools, equipment or uniform, payment of wages, deductions from wages, job description, taking of orders and hours to be worked.
- Where there is no traditional employment relationship, the court will consider whether the tortfeasor had a relationship akin to an employment relationship. This will involve looking at the nature of the work and whether there is a sufficient connection between the work and the wrongful action to make it right to hold the employer vicariously liable.
- An employer can be liable if an employee acts against orders, works negligently or commits a crime.
- An employer will not be liable if an employee commits 'a frolic of his or her own'.
- An employer can recover any compensation paid out from the employee under the Civil Liability (Contribution) Act 1978.

Contract law

17 The rules and theory of contract law

After reading this chapter, you should be able to:
- Understand the rules and principles of contract law concerning formation, terms, vitiating factors, discharge of a contract and associated remedies
- Have a basic understanding of the theory of the law of contract
- Analyse and evaluate the voluntary nature of a contract and of principles governing contract law

17.1 Rules and principles of contract law

A contract can be defined as an agreement that the law will enforce. There are the following areas that need to be studied for the AQA specification Paper 3, The Law of Contract:

- Formation of contract: this is all about making an agreement to do something, for example buy a car. This area of the specification must be evaluated as well as known, understood and applied.
- The terms of the contract: the terms are the obligations and rights of each party to the contract. At its simplest, it would be to pay the agreed price for the car and to hand over legal ownership of the car to the buyer. However, some terms are specifically *agreed* by the parties while others are *implied*, that is they are part of the contract whether or not the parties have thought about it. This area of the specification must be evaluated as well as known, understood and applied.
- Vitiating factors: this area of law covers factors that may make a contract invalid. Here we are considering the law of misrepresentation and economic duress. Misrepresentation might be where the seller of the car stated its mileage was 20,000 when in fact it was 80,000.
- Discharge of contract: this involves examining exactly what amounts to performance of a

contract, when there is breach of contract through non- or part-performance, and what happens when performance of the contract is prevented by events outside the control of the parties to the contract.
- Remedies: this is all about what legal remedies a party to the contract can seek when the contract has been breached (broken) or the contract has been affected by a vitiating factor.

Contract law is largely derived from the common law – case law. The principles have been developed over many years – we will consider *Pinnel's case* (1602) in Chapter 19. Originally, itinerant justices travelled the land making judgments to settle disputes. Cases involving the buying and selling of goods were often decided according to local rules or customs. These rules were gradually extended over wider areas, eventually becoming the common law of the land. These were developed and refined into the modern law of contract.

Equity provides some ways of overcoming aspects of inherent unfairness in the common law. We can see this, for example, with equitable remedies available for breach of contract.

There are some Acts of Parliament that have been passed to deal with problems that have arisen in the common law. The Sale of Goods Act 1979 is a modern incarnation of the Sale of Goods Act 1893. This first Act was created by Parliament to reflect the then current law on Sale of Goods as part of the Victorian idea to codify commercial law so that it could easily be used throughout the world. It therefore reflected the case law on sale of goods that existed at that time.

European law has influenced today's contract law by making regulations that are often designed to help consumers. The Unfair Terms in Consumer Contract Regulations 1999 are one example. These regulations are not subsumed in the Consumer Rights Act 2015.

17.2 The theory of the law of contract

The usual principle of the common law is freedom of contract and the sanctity of contracts. The nineteenth century definition of a contract is 'a promise or set of promises which the law will enforce', that is there are mutual promises between the promisor and the promisee. The rights and obligations or duties are created by the agreement between the parties to the contract.

Under this theory, contract law is based on promising. To promise is to assume an obligation to the promisee by means of a communication to the promisee to that effect. An agreement is taken to entail the making of a promise in return for a promise (or for performance), and if an agreement is recognised as a contract in law, the law recognises a contracting party as having incurred a legal obligation to perform his or her promise.

The argument against allowing past consideration as a valid form of consideration is made to prevent opening the floodgates to dubious cases. This would seem a poor argument, as few minor cases would ever go to court given the cost of litigation. Bigger cases tend to be resolved on the basis of commercial reality and the expectation of payment of a reasonable sum on the basis of *quantum meruit*, which might well be agreed after the event. It is interesting to compare *Re McArdle* with an implied promise to pay, as in *Lampleigh v Braithwait* (see Chapter 19, section 19.1.1).

There is also a reliance theory: an agreement states the performance required of a contracting party, but that party does not promise the performance and does not incur an obligation to provide it. Contract is not based on promising it, but on what is described as the 'assumption of responsibility'. A contracting party assumes responsibility for reliance incurred by the other party on the assumption that the specified performance will be provided.

Whichever theory is considered, the agreed terms must be certain, which is a principle in contract law. An offer must be certain before it can be accepted, so in the case of *Guthing v Lynn* (1831) the offer to pay £5 more for a horse if it was 'lucky' was too vague and not an offer. This leads to problems where two businesses try to deal with each other, but both businesses have their own conditions of trading. If there is no certainty, then there would appear to be no contract, but the parties have gone on with the deal without formally agreeing whose terms are the contract terms.

This can be seen in *Butler Machine Tool Co. Ltd v Ex-Cell-O Corporation* (1977), where Lord Denning said:

> I have much sympathy with the judge's approach to this case. In many of these cases our traditional analysis of offer, counter-offer, rejection, acceptance and so forth is out of date. This was observed by Lord Wilberforce in *New Zealand Shipping*

Co. Ltd v AM Satterthwaite (1975). The better way is to look at all the documents passing between the parties and glean from them, or from the conduct of the parties, whether they have reached agreement on all material points, even though there may be differences between the forms and conditions printed on the back of them. [Applying *Brogden v Metropolitan Railway Co.* (1877)] it will be found that in most cases when there is a 'battle of forms' there is a contract as soon as the last of the forms is sent and received without objection being taken to it. Therefore, judgment was entered for the buyers.

Lord Denning is suggesting that the subjective view of the contract terms that the parties to the contract have is replaced by an objective view that the parties must have agreed, as is the case with implied terms in a contract. *Reveille Independent LLC v Anotech International (UK) Ltd* (2016) is another example of the courts concluding what the terms of a contract actually were from the dealings between the parties.

Implied terms are also placed in a contract that neither party may have agreed. In *Marks and Spencer plc v BNP Paribas Securities Services Trust Company (Jersey) Ltd* (2015), Lord Neuberger emphasised that construing the express words of a contract is a different exercise from implying words which are not there to be construed. So, for example, reasonableness is to be judged objectively – in considering what the parties would have agreed. Here,

> one is not strictly concerned with the hypothetical answer of the actual parties, but with that of notional reasonable people in the position of the parties at the time at which they were contracting.

This is moving away from the idea that a contract is a freely negotiated deal under the freedom of contract theory.

The courts will be very careful when departing from the common law principle of freedom of contract. They will therefore be reluctant to imply terms into a contract, especially in cases where this would set a general implication of a term into all contracts of a similar nature.

It could be argued that the courts try to avoid this because of the long-debated criticism of judge-made law, and the argument that Parliament should make changes to the law. However, when Parliament changes the law, we tend to get a confusing situation where the clarity and extension of rights in one situation, for example the Consumer Rights Act 2015, are balanced by areas which lack clarity. For example, what protection is afforded by the law, if any, for the purchaser of goods in a private sale? Is a sale on eBay a private sale?

Freedom of contract is eroded when Parliament creates an Act that implies terms in a contract. At one extreme is the Consumer Rights Act 2015 that inserts terms, rights and remedies that cannot be excluded by a business. Even the Sale of Goods Act did this, although most of the terms implied could be excluded by the parties to a contract. That right to exclude the implied terms became less likely under the Unfair Contract Terms Act 1977.

The traditional use of conditions and warranties promotes certainty. If a condition is breached and the contract has not been fully performed then it may be terminated. But if it is a warranty, there is no right to terminate. This approach is inflexible and can lead to unfair results, as it does not consider the consequences of a breach.

A minor breach of a condition gives the right to terminate the contract. This is always the case except when there is a contract for the sale of goods when s 15A of the Sale of Goods Act 1979 applies. This is where the buyer has the right to reject the goods because the seller breached one of the implied terms in ss 13–15 of the Act, but the breach is so slight that it would be unreasonable for him or her to reject them. In this case the breach is not to be treated as a breach of condition, but may be treated as a breach of warranty.

There is, however, an exception to this exception. This section applies unless a contrary intention appears in, or is to be implied from, the contract. Presumably this means that a term of a contract stating that all terms, express or implied, are to be treated as conditions would then nullify this section of the Sale of Goods Act 1979. Of course that term may be an unfair contract term and be found to be ineffective on that basis.

A similar effect is produced as a result of s 5A of the Supply of Goods and Services Act 1982. However, if an innocent party suffers a major breach of a warranty, no termination is possible.

The innominate terms approach is less certain. It can be difficult to decide if the effect of the breach is sufficiency serious to justify termination. This is important in relation to remedies available and may mean that if a party purports to terminate when he or she is not entitled to do so, he or she will be in breach of the contract.

Despite the problems that could be caused, it is possible to see that the innominate terms approach of considering the effect of the breach is more flexible. This is particularly true as many terms are put in contracts to protect the party with the stronger bargaining power. There would be one fewer hurdle for the weaker party if all terms were innominate terms.

17.2.1 Implied terms are default terms

In contracts for the sale of goods and the supply of services, both for businesses and consumers, there are a number of implied terms. Examples include goods corresponding with description, care and skill in carrying out a service and the inability to exclude liability for death of personal injury.

We can make sense of the emphasis that the House of Lords placed in *Liverpool City Council v Irwin* (1977) on the courts only implying a term by law into a contract when it is necessary to do so. However, 'necessary' here is not the same as 'necessary to give business efficacy' to the contract.

The Supreme Court has apparently clarified the law on when the court can imply a term in a contract. It has endorsed the traditional approach that the term either must be so obvious as to go without saying, or must be necessary to give business efficacy to the contract. But which test is favoured?

In *Marks and Spencer plc v BNP Paribas Securities Services Trust Company (Jersey) Ltd* (2015), the court considered the Privy Council's decision in *Attorney General of Belize v Belize Telecom* (2009), which had generally been accepted as the leading modern case on the implication of terms.

In *Belize*, Lord Hoffmann suggested that in the process of implying terms, the only question was whether a reasonable reader of the contract, with the relevant background knowledge, would understand the term to be implied. That decision led to a great deal of academic debate as to whether it had changed the law, so that reasonableness could now be seen as a sufficient ground for implying a term.

In the *Marks and Spencer* case, the Supreme Court is unanimous in emphasising that *Belize* should not be taken as having watered down the traditional, highly restrictive approach to the implication of terms. The upshot of the decision is that reasonableness in itself is not sufficient; the tests of obviousness or business efficacy must be met. There still remains an alternative.

There are two different approaches to the purpose of exclusion clauses

- One approach would use the whole of the contract, including any exclusion clauses, to define the obligations set out in it.
- The other approach would be to define the obligations set out in the contract without reference to the exclusion clauses. The exclusion clauses would then be used as defences when necessary.

Cheshire, Fifoot and Furmston's Law of Contract suggests that the approach usually depends upon the wording of the exclusion clause being considered. However, exclusion clauses are more commonly viewed as a defence.

The argument is that there is still freedom of contract. If you do not like the terms of a contract, then do not enter the contract. You may have no choice but to agree to the terms (as in a music streaming contract), but you still have freedom of choice.

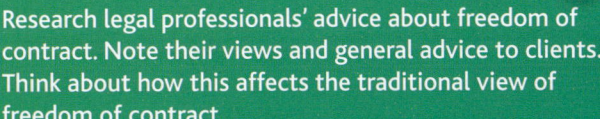

Look online

Research legal professionals' advice about freedom of contract. Note their views and general advice to clients. Think about how this affects the traditional view of freedom of contract.

Search for UK websites, such as www.shoosmiths.co.uk/client-resources/legal-updates/guidance-freedom-contract-not-open-interpretation-11014.aspx.

17.2.2 Freedom of contract and the competing need to protect the consumer

As we have seen, the Consumer Rights Act 2015 inserts terms, rights and remedies that cannot be excluded by a business in order to protect consumers. The right to exclude terms has become less frequently available under legislation and as the courts attempt to limit the efficacy of exclusion clauses.

The argument is that there is still freedom of contract. If you do not like the terms of a contract, do not enter the contract. The difficulty is in establishing which terms will be in the contract and which will be disallowed by the law. While the Consumer Rights Act 2015 applies in many contracts, there are still other contracts, such as contracts to rent a flat, which are in effect consumer contracts but do not appear to fall within the scope of the Consumer Rights Act 2015.

17.2.3 The distinction between offers, offers in unilateral contract and invitation to treat

The law distinguishes between an offer and an invitation to treat. An invitation to treat is not an offer and therefore it cannot be accepted to make a contract. However, this distinction can become blurred in some situations. For example, as we shall see in Chapter 18, an advertisement is generally not considered to be an offer, but an invitation to treat, as in *Partridge v Crittenden* (1968). However in reward cases, such as *Carlill v The Carbolic Smoke Ball Co. Ltd* (1893), the advertisement became the offer in a unilateral contract where acceptance takes place by conduct.

There is much legislation about misleading advertisements which suggests that these advertisements only have legal significance if they lead to a contract; while the legislation leads to criminal sanctions, the individual affected by the advertisement is usually only left with a claim for misrepresentation unless some part of the advertisement has become a term of the contract or there is protection under the Consumer Rights Act 2015. The only remaining value of *Carlill* appears to be in genuine reward cases – the missing cat advertisement!

The distinction between an offer and an invitation to treat is confusing to both parties to a contract. The differences between an invitation to treat and an offer are often very slight.

In *Fisher v Bell* (1961) (see Chapter 18, section 18.1.1), the justification for the decision is based on the traditional view of freedom of contract. If the shop window display was an offer, this would remove the shop owner's right to decide whether to contract with that particular customer or not. The customer could enter the shop and accept the offer and create a legally binding contract. The shop owner may then be liable for selling prohibited goods to a person who is under a particular age, for example a knife.

In a self-service shop, people generally believe the goods can be bought there and then, or at least when brought from a store room. If the goods are not in stock, the customer believes the seller will be able to provide them at a later date but recognises that both sides have the option to decline the contract. It has been suggested that all invitations to treat should be treated as offers, so the law would mirror the public's belief in the situation. However, this would again cause problems with respect to age-restricted goods.

If the item on the shelf had the status of an offer then once the item is placed in the customer's basket, a contract, arguably, would be made and the customer would then be bound to pay for the item or possibly charged with theft. This would also prevent a customer changing his or her mind without being in breach of contract. If there was a pricing error, neither party could rectify the situation.

It appears that the word 'offer' is generally used to encompass invitations to treat. This is not just in the general public's mind, but can be seen in most guidance given to retailers by local authorities. It would seem that the term 'invitation to treat' is redundant except to lawyers.

17.2.4 Acceptances including the rationale for the postal rule and its relationship to electronic communications

Acceptance by conduct is not the only issue with acceptance of an offer. The posting rules relate back to a time when post was the only realistic method of long-distance communication and developed to such an extent that many towns had several deliveries each day. More modern, electronic methods of communication have raised new issues for the law. The law has lagged on these and still struggles with the rules, despite case law and legislation.

The postal rule appears to be unfair on an offeror who may never receive the letter of acceptance or it is late. The offeror is a party to a legally binding contract without realising so. The offeror may have contracted with another party in the meantime, so the courts have to make a decision that is only satisfactory to one of the offerees.

A further problem with the postal rule is whether it applies to any other method of communication. The *Entores* and *Brinkibon* cases, discussed in Chapter 18, indicate the courts' unwillingness to expand the rule to more modern methods of communication. This unwillingness may be due the courts' belief that an offeree should take reasonable steps to ensure the acceptance is received and that the postal rule is outdated in any event and should therefore be restricted.

If the obligations with respect to providing key information to the consumer are omitted, then, under the Consumer Rights Act 2015, no contract is formed. However, the seller may still have received payment and it may be difficult to regain the payment made under the non-existent contract.

17.2.5 The rationale for consideration, and the relationships between consideration and privity, and between consideration and economic duress

Consideration reflects the idea that the law is concerned with bargains and not gifts. The rule of consideration that it must be sufficient, as in *Chappell v Nestlé Co. Ltd* (1960) (see Chapter 19, section 19.1.1), may be viewed by a member of the public as ridiculous as the chocolate wrapper has no value in the real world. The justification for this rule is often said to be the courts' willingness to validate an agreement.

If a party wishes to give something to another party and this is to form the basis of the agreement, then the court will always attempt to allow the agreement to exist and be enforceable. This means that anyone who understands the courts' attitude need not use a deed of gift, but can merely agree to sell something at a gross undervalue to achieve the objective. This was the case in *Thomas v Thomas*. This may then conflict with the criminal law of fraud, or be evidence of coercion on the part of the beneficiary that may be more difficult to prove where there is a deed.

So long as there is something of some value, however small, there is consideration given so that there is a bargain, a contract. The assumption is that this is freely negotiated, yet this is not always the case. We have noted that consumers, and to a lesser extent businesses, often have no choice but to accept terms stated or implied in a contract. This is all very well when the terms protect the weaker party, such as the consumer, but it is more difficult to justify where there is a great disparity of bargaining power such as when a small business deals with a large business.

This is not the only problem. The rationale for freedom of contract presupposes that the benefits of a contract will only be to the contracting party. This is reflected in the concept of privity of contract where only a party to a contract can take legal action on it and thus ensure that the terms are fulfilled. The Contracts (Rights of Third Parties) Act 1999 allows someone who is not a party to a contract (a 'third party') to enforce the contract in certain circumstances. However, this right can be excluded by a contract term and frequently is excluded, so the purpose of the law of protecting people can be negated under so-called freedom of contract.

Similarly, pressure can be put on one party to enter the contract. It is clearly not a freely entered contract when it is made with a gun to your head. The law is rather belatedly looking at an economic 'gun' where there is economic duress. Economic duress occurs where the threat is made to damage a business or person financially. However, the court will consider each case involving economic duress according to its individual circumstances, so it is not clear when such a claim will be successful in vitiating the contract.

It has always been a commercial reality that some customers will be unable to pay their debts as they fall due. The idea of bankruptcy and company insolvency rules recognise this and provide a means of distributing assets in the event of insolvency. The development of rules to combat agreements made near to the date of insolvency such as those on fraudulent preference reflect this. Many businesses accept a part payment in settlement of a debt, as they will have to wait longer and possibly receive less if there is an insolvency.

The strict legal position would appear to be modified only by the very special circumstances in *Central London Property Trust Ltd v High Trees House Ltd* (1947) (see Chapter 19, section 19.1.1). The doctrine of promissory estoppel only applies when it is inequitable for the creditor to insist on his full rights. Practical considerations mean that, subject to the principle of fraud and duress, the reality reflects the principle of freedom of contract. There is a conflict between the morality of breaking a promise and the strict rule of law that consideration is required for a valid contract.

17.2.6 The nature and effectiveness of exemption clauses

Exclusion clauses are terms in a contract that exclude or limit liability for a breach of the contract. Freedom of contract is often reflected during negotiations where one party is in a much stronger position than another.

For example, as an individual or even as a business, you have little opportunity to negotiate the terms of a contract for a rail ticket or a mobile phone contract. The courts and Parliament have tried to find ways of limiting the effectiveness of an exclusion clause.

However the idea of incorporation of terms in a contract can be helpful to those suffering exclusion clauses, even though decisions such as *Hollier v Ramler Motors* (1972) and *McCutcheon v David MacBrayne Ltd* (1964) seem contradictory. Similarly, modern commercial cases seem to have reduced the role of the *contra proferentem* rule – see, for example, *Transocean Drilling UK Ltd v Providence Resources plc* (2016), *Persimmon Homes Ltd v Ove Arup and Partners Ltd* (2017) and *Oliver Nobahar-Cookson v The Hut Group* (2016).

On the other hand, the Consumer Rights Act 2015 has made incorporation clear and also assists interpretation – s 69 states that if a term or consumer notice 'could have different meanings', the meaning that is most favourable to the consumer is to prevail.

A dispute arises when one party to the contract argues that a term of the contract has one particular meaning and the other party disagrees. With respect to exclusion clauses, this is particularly important as an exclusion clause is usually put in a contract by someone in a stronger bargaining position. You can see this when you look at the terms and conditions of everyday contracts such as a mobile phone contract or a streaming contract. Most people agree to the terms without reading them or enquiring about the meaning of the terms. It is only when there is a problem with the contract that the meaning of the terms is considered.

In the context of terms excluding or limiting liability, suppose that there are two possible meanings of the term. The first is a narrow one which would reduce the scope of the exclusion or limitation of liability. The second is a broader one which would leave the scope of the exclusion or limitation correspondingly broad. Obviously, the party seeking to rely on the exclusion will argue for the broad meaning, but the *contra proferentem* rule will point towards the narrow meaning.

While there are cases that illustrate the ability to curb the worst excesses of exclusion clauses such as *Curtis v Chemical Cleaning and Dyeing Co. Ltd* (1951), cases such as *L'Estrange v Graucob* (1934) do not fill one with confidence in the courts' approach. Legislation has been slow in coming, and still does not protect businesses. Even the Consumer Rights Act 2015 does not fully protect consumers, as putting an exclusion or limitation clause in a standard form, non-negotiable contract is not illegal. The term may be ineffective, but only where the affected party has the will (and means) to challenge big business. The effectiveness of these terms remains as few will challenge them, and they are routinely relied on by big businesses until someone dares to challenge them.

With respect to the law on consideration and the rights of third parties, it will be seen that the decision in *Tweddle v Atkinson* (1861) (see Chapter 19, section 19.1.1) does not give effect to the arrangement made by the families. It would appear to be more than just a social arrangement yet fails to be enforced on the basis that the young couple were not a party to the agreement. A similar result was the outcome in *Beswick v Beswick* (1967) (see Chapter 19, section 19.2.4). In that case, the aunt did in fact succeed as she could carry out her late husband's contracts in her capacity of the executor of his estate.

The Contract (Rights of Third Parties) Act 1999 would apply in the situations in *Tweddle v Atkinson* and *Beswick v Beswick*. However, the parties to the contract may specifically exclude the Act's application so that a carefully drafted contract will not allow a third party to obtain the benefit of the contract. Many commercial contracts contain such an exclusion. The question remains as to whether these exclusions are unfair contract terms under the Unfair Contract Terms Act 1977 (for business-to-business contracts) or under the Consumer Rights Act 2015 for consumers.

> **Tip**
>
> Look at the terms and conditions related to a contract you are likely to make. Note any exclusion clauses and consider whether you consider they should be valid. You can analyse their actual validity when you have studied the material on exclusion clauses later in this book.

17.2.7 The nature and effectiveness of remedies, including specifically consumer remedies

Remedies in contract law may be legal, equitable or as a result of legislation. While legal remedies for breach of contract are a right, equitable remedies are discretionary. These are effective remedies, although

the way in which equitable remedies are awarded may be seen to be somewhat arcane. Few, apart from lawyers, are likely to be familiar with the operation of the maxims of equity and the ways in which these maxims may allow or disallow a remedy.

Remedies under the Consumer Rights Act 2015 can be seen as an improvement, as they readily address the problem in a manner that is sensible and should reflect good business practice, particularly where businesses are given a second chance. For example, the Consumer Rights Act 2015 covers contracts between traders and consumers and includes a 'fairness test' for enforceability of terms and consumer notices and a 'grey list' of potentially unfair clauses in consumer contracts.

17.2.8 Good faith

The ideas of reliance and responsibility are also present in English contract law. For contracts and commerce to work, there must be an expectation that both parties will do what they said they will do. If they do not do so, then the law will settle the dispute. Criminal sanctions are reserved for the worst cases (fraud) but even these are extended by Parliament with respect to many aspects of trading.

Corrective justice can be seen to be applied in contract law. The basis of assessment of damages is loss of bargain: the claimant is placed in the position he or she would have been in had the contract been performed. In other words, responsibility for the losses is taken by the person at fault, and both parties entered the contract relying on each other to perform their obligations.

However, only losses that are reasonably within the contemplation of the parties may be recovered, as can be seen in *Victoria Laundry v Newman* (1949).

> #### Victoria Laundry v Newman (1949)
>
> The defendant had been late in fitting a boiler. As a result, the claimant had suffered not only normal business losses, but also exceptional losses through losing a special contract with the Ministry of Supply. As the latter were not within the contemplation of the parties at the time of the contract, they were not recoverable.

In *Wellesley Partners LLP v Withers LLP* (2015), the basic rule in contract was summarised:

> " A contract breaker is liable for damage resulting from his breach, if at the time of making the contract, a reasonable person

in his shoes would have had damage of that kind in mind as not unlikely to result from a breach. **"**

This is another objective test that may not, therefore, reflect the freedom of contract principle. This would seem to indicate that contracts are expected to be made between the parties in good faith.

Good faith is incorporated as an underlying principle in contracts of insurance, where all material facts must be disclosed if there is not to be a misrepresentation. However, imposing a duty of good faith in all contracts would run contrary to the general principle of contract law. Businesses enter into contracts and their aim is to make as much profit as possible within a competitive market, subject to the law as it stands at the time. However, contract parties are involved in a competitive situation and cannot be expected to disclose every aspect of their business deal. What the law does is to attempt to balance the interests of the parties to a contract by legislation, interpretation of the contract and the common law with a smattering of equity. The results of this, however, lack certainty.

Article 7 of the United Nations Convention on Contracts for the International Sale of Goods (1980) states:

" In the interpretation of this Convention, regard is to be had to its international character and to the need to promote uniformity in its application and the observance of good faith in international trade. **"**

Interestingly, most international commercial contracts state as a term of the contract that English law will apply and disputes will be settled in accordance with English law in London. So much for good faith.

17.2.9 Balancing interests and justice

We have seen that judges often have to balance competing interests in their judgments. This can lead to unusual results. Parliament also sets out to balance rights between contracting parties, which seems to go against the theory of freedom of contract. As we have seen, parties to a contract may try to limit their liability by relying upon exclusion clauses. The traditional rule of *caveat emptor* (let the buyer beware) could operate harshly against the interests of the weaker bargaining party.

There are apparently conflicting decisions such as:

- *Olley v Marlborough Court Hotel* (1949) – the exclusion clause was invalid as it had not been brought to Mrs Olley's attention when she made the contract.
- *Thompson v LMS Railway* (1930) – an exclusion clause was implied even though she could not read the printed terms which referred to another document she would have had to locate.

However, if we are aware of a risk and take it, why should death and personal injury not be excluded from a voluntary contract?

Only a party to a contract can take legal action on it. This could lead to injustice, despite the legal position of an **agent**.

Key term

Agent – a person who is authorised to act for another (the principal) in the making of a contract with third parties. The resulting contract is made between the principal and the third party, and not with the agent.

In *Jackson v Horizon Holidays* (1975), the claimant succeeded in seeking damages for himself and for members of his family after a package holiday failed to match the advertised description, even though only he, and not his family members, had signed the contract.

The Contract (Rights of Third Parties) Act 1999 modified the law by allowing third parties to make a claim where the contract expressly provided for it, or where the contract purported to confer a benefit on them. Obvious injustices such as *Tweddle v Atkinson* (1861) are remedied, but the provisions of the Act are frequently excluded in standard form contracts and so the benefit of the Act is largely negated for consumers.

The law with respect to frustration of contract has also been modified by Parliament. The Law Reform (Frustrated Contracts) Act 1943 enabled the courts to apportion the losses more fairly between the parties: the court may order 'a just sum' to be paid where either expenses have been incurred or a valuable benefit obtained.

17.2.10 The principle of fault

The principle of fault has two distinct elements:

- the degree of responsibility for actions
- the liability under the law.

Responsibility is seen as one theory in contract law.

A misrepresentation is an untrue statement of fact made by one party to the contract which induces the other party to enter into the contract. It is a vitiating factor in a contract and the remedies vary in accordance with the type of misrepresentation. These are categorised as innocent, negligent or fraudulent; in other words, by the perceived amount of blameworthiness or fault. Sometimes statements are recognised as no more than advertising slogans and so do not create liability.

Smith v Land and House Property (1884)

A tenant was described by the defendant as 'most desirable'. In fact, the tenant was completely unreliable. As this misrepresentation was relied upon by the other party, the maker of the statement could be sued – at fault for the statement and therefore for the loss it caused.

Generally, silence will not amount to misrepresentation. After all, there is freedom of contract, and if you do not ask about something, there is no obligation to be told about it unless it is a contract where good faith is required, such as one of insurance. This was shown in *Fletcher v Krell* (1873). However, where there is a deliberate attempt to conceal an important fact, there will be liability. This occurred in *With v O'Flanagan* (1936).

See Chapter 22, section 22.2.1 for full details of these cases.

Breach of contract depends on the level of blameworthiness to determine the injured party's rights. This will determine whether a person can end the contract or must continue it but claim some compensation. The cases of *Poussard v Spiers and Pond* (1876) and *Bettini v Gye* (1876) illustrate this point.

See Chapter 20, sections 20.2.1 and 20.2.2 for full details of these cases.

In 1995, the Law Commission reported on damages which considered the situation where there could be punitive damages. The recommendation was that punitive damages must not be awarded for breach of contract. However, the law on penalty clauses in contract seems to allow what might appear to be punitive damages, subject to the judicial view as to what is commercially justifiable.

In *ParkingEye v Beavis* (2015), Mr Beavis parked in the car park, but overstayed the two-hour limit by almost an hour and the charge of £85 was upheld by the court. Lords Sumption and Neuberger placed some emphasis on the context in which the contract was made in reaching their decision:

> **The penalty rule is an interference with freedom of contract. In a negotiated contract between properly advised parties of comparable bargaining power, the strong initial presumption must be that the parties themselves are the best judges of what is legitimate in a provision dealing with the consequences of breach.**

17.2.11 Morality

A rule is something that influences the way in which we behave, either because we submit ourselves to it voluntarily, as with moral rules, or because it is enforceable by some authority, as with laws.

Many rules are neither morally binding, nor do they ultimately have the force of law attached to them. They are kept because of the context in which they operate. For example, rules, sometimes called laws, define a sport and how it is played. These have evolved to cope with new situations, improve the sport and protect participants. There are sanctions here too, and some of the sanctions may be the result of a legal contract when taking out membership of a sporting body or club.

Rules might also come about through custom or practice, and involve the disapproval of the community rather than any legal sanction if such a rule is broken.

Morality is generally to do with beliefs, so may be affected by religion. We all have a moral code of some kind which defines what we think is and is not acceptable behaviour. Morality can differ from culture to culture and from individual to individual, although some behaviour is universally unacceptable. Morality is most obviously intertwined with criminal law, but aspects of contract law are also affected by morality.

Contracts can be declared void because of their association with immorality. In *Pearce v Brooks* (1866), a cab owner's contract with a prostitute to use his cabs for her trade was void because it was a contract for immoral purposes.

Other examples of contracts being void because of illegality include:

- *Parkinson v The College of Ambulance* (1925), where the whole purpose of the contract was to buy an honour (knighthood, OBE, etc.) – that is, corruption in public life.
- *Dann v Curzon* (1910) – the courts were not prepared to enforce a contract to commit a tort or a crime.
- *Napier v National Business Agency* (1951) – the courts will not allow parties to take advantage of contracts that set out to defraud.

Today, there are frequent press reports about contracts obtained as a result of bribery and contracts made to hide the true situation with respect to tax. These contracts may be viewed as immoral, but are only illegal if involving tax evasion rather than tax avoidance. The same may be said for methods to avoid contractual obligations with respect to wages and minimum wage regulation.

Economic duress may be considered immoral (as would physical duress). Equity reflects morality when the principle of equitable estoppel is applied. This can be seen in:

- *Central London Property Trust Ltd v High Trees House Ltd* (1947) – a morally correct response to the situation that became the legal principle
- *D and C Builders v Rees* (1965) – Mrs Rees' behaviour may be seen as immoral and certainly had no legal effect.

Equitable remedies are a reflection of morality and justice in contract law.

The area of fraudulent misrepresentation developed in *Derry v Peek* (1889), while based on the tort of deceit, still reflects the view in contract law that it would be wrong to allow a contract to be obtained by fraud.

Freedom of contract allows, subject to illegality, any contract to be made. It may, however, be viewed that some contracts are so outrageous that they are immoral, but they are rarely illegal. Under the Victorian Moneylenders Acts, any contract to lend money with a rate of interest above 50 per cent was unenforceable in a court of law. Today we allow much higher rates of interest to be used and enforced, despite most religions taking a strong view about charging interest to lend money. Is this a changing view of morality in business?

Summary

- Contracts have a number of elements that can be considered as a whole or individually.
- Contract law is largely based on common law, so most of the law comes from decided cases.
- The elements that come from Acts of Parliament are mostly to do with consumer protection.
- The main theory of contract law is freedom of contract. This means that a person can make any contract he or she likes, even if it is disadvantageous to him or her. There is, however, some statutory protection.
- The principle of good faith is an underlying principle; a person assumes that the other party will fulfil his or her promise and that the law will help when he or she does not.
- The law tries to balance interests between parties, particularly where exclusion clauses are concerned.
- The concept of fault applies particularly to the law on misrepresentation in contracts.
- Morality is present in contract law, particularly with illegal contracts, economic duress, terms imposed in contracts and equitable remedies.

18 Essential requirements of contract (1): offer and acceptance

After studying this chapter, you should be able to:
- Understand offer and acceptance, including the rules of communication and revocation

18.1 The offer

This chapter deals with the idea of agreement in formation of a contract. This requires an offer and acceptance. These, and the relevant rules, are explored in this section of the chapter and evaluated in the next section.

An **offer** is the starting point for a contract. Contract law sets out what amounts to an offer, when the offer comes into existence and when it comes to an end. Once an offer is communicated to the offeree by the **offeror**, the **offeree** can choose whether to accept that offer or not until such time as the offer ends.

Key terms

Offer – a proposal (or promise) showing a willingness to contract on firm and definite terms.

Offeror – the person who makes the offer.

Offeree – the person to whom an offer is made.

The offer must be definite in its terms. Words such as 'might be prepared to' or 'may be able to' indicate uncertainty. Therefore, it is likely that the statement will be an invitation rather than an offer. This can be seen in the case of *Gibson v Manchester City Council* (1979).

Gibson v Manchester City Council (1979)

Mr Gibson was a council tenant. The council wrote to him stating:

> " The Corporation may be prepared to sell the house to you ... If you would like to make formal application to buy your Council house, please complete the enclosed application form. "

He completed the application but the council refused to accept his application.

It was decided that the council's letter was not an offer. The reason was that it was not a firm and definite proposal, as it stated that the council 'may be prepared to sell the house', but not that it definitely would. His formal application was the offer that the council could accept or reject.

An acceptance of the offer forms the basis of a valid contract. The difficulty is in deciding whether a statement amounts to an offer or whether it is just a statement preparatory to an offer which is known as an invitation to treat.

18.1.1 An offer or an invitation to treat?

Key term

Invitation to treat – an indication that one person is willing to negotiate a contract with another, but that he or she is not yet willing to make a legal offer.

The law distinguishes between an offer and an **invitation to treat**. An invitation to treat is not an offer and therefore it cannot be accepted to make a contract. It is an invitation by one party to another to make an offer, for example the invitation by the council in the *Gibson* case to the council tenant to make an application to buy his council house. This means that a firm proposal made in response to an invitation to treat amounts only to an offer and cannot be an acceptance so as to create a contract. There are a number of examples of invitations to treat.

Advertisements

Generally, an advertisement cannot be an offer, and is thus only an invitation to treat. This can be seen in the case of *Partridge v Crittenden* (1968).

Partridge v Crittenden (1968)

Crittenden placed an advertisement stating 'Bramblefinch cocks, bramblefinch hens, 25s [£1.25] each'. He was prosecuted for 'offering for sale' a wild bird under the Protection of Birds Act 1954. He was not guilty as the advertisement was not an offer but an invitation to treat. Any offer leading to a contract would be made by the person responding to the advertisement

Exceptionally, if an advertisement contains a clear indication that there is an 'offer' because it is expected to be taken seriously, then the court may well decide it is an offer. This usually occurs in a unilateral rather than a **bilateral contract**.

In a **unilateral contract,** the offeror makes a promise in exchange for an act by another party. If the offeree acts on the offeror's promise, the offeror is legally obligated to perform his or her side of the contract, but an offeree cannot be forced to act because no return promise has been made to the offeror. After an offeree has performed his or her act, only one enforceable promise exists, that of the offeror. A unilateral contract arises only when the offeree completely performs the required act. This is typical in reward cases where, for example, there is a reward offered for someone finding and returning a missing pet. The offer, for example, contained in a reward poster for finding the missing pet is accepted by the person finding it and at that point there is a legal obligation to pay the reward to the finder. There is no obligation to look for the missing pet.

In a bilateral contract, there is an exchange of mutual promises. An example is a contract to buy a loaf of bread for £1. Both parties have an obligation – to provide the bread on one party, to pay £1 on the other party.

Key terms

Bilateral contract – this requires both offeror and offeree to do something. Both parties have obligations.

Unilateral contract – an agreement to pay in exchange for performance, if the potential performer chooses to act. There is no obligation to perform the act.

A unilateral contract can be seen in the case of *Carlill v Carbolic Smokeball Co.* (1893).

Carlill v Carbolic Smoke Ball Co. (1893)

The company advertised a patent medicine, the smoke ball. The advertisement stated that if someone (not necessarily the person who bought the product) used it correctly and still got flu, then the company would pay him or her £100. Mrs Carlill did get flu after using the smoke ball as instructed. The court awarded her the £100. The promise was an offer that could be accepted by anyone who used the smoke ball correctly and still contracted the flu as the advertisement was a unilateral offer.

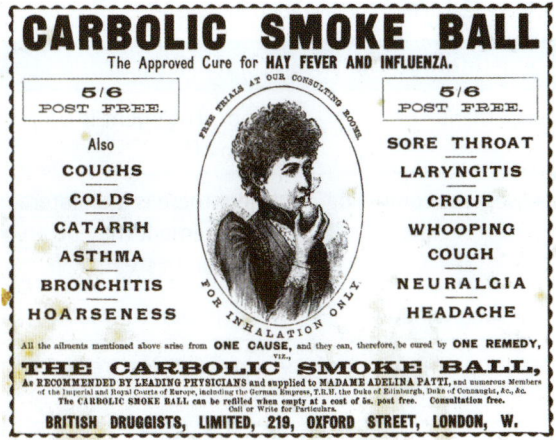

Advertisement from 1897

Goods in a shop window or on a shop shelf

The goods on the shelf are an invitation to treat and remain so when put in the customer's basket. The contents of the basket become an offer when the customer presents them to the checkout operator (or self-service scanner). The shop then accepts or declines the customer's offer through their checkout operator or assistant at the self-service scanner.

Fisher v Bell (1961)

A shopkeeper displayed a flick-knife with a price tag in his window for sale. He was charged with 'offering it for sale', an offence under the Offensive Weapons Act 1959. The display of the knife in the window was an invitation to treat so the knife had not been offered for sale. He was therefore not guilty of the offence.

Lord Justice Parker said:

> ❝ It is perfectly clear that according to the ordinary law of contract the display of an article with a price on it in a shop window is merely an invitation to treat. It is in no sense an offer for sale the acceptance of which constitutes a contract. ❞

Pharmaceutical Society of Great Britain v Boots Cash Chemists (1953)

Boots were charged with selling controlled pharmaceutical products other than under the supervision of a pharmacist. The shop was a self-service shop where the items that had to be sold by a pharmacist were on a shelf for customers to select. They were found not guilty as the offer was made by the customer at the till where there was a pharmacist present to approve the acceptance of the offer. The approval by a pharmacist was required by the Act controlling such sales.

Figure 18.1 Key facts chart for invitation to treat

Offer or invitation to treat?	Brief legal rule	Case example
An advertisement	An advertisement is usually an invitation to treat, not an offer	*Partridge v Crittenden* (1968)
An advertisement containing an offer	Where there is a unilateral contract, the advertisement may be an offer rather than invitation to treat	*Carlill v Carbolic Smokeball Co.* (1893)
Goods in a shop window	An invitation to treat	*Fisher v Bell* (1961)
Goods on a supermarket shelf	An invitation to treat	*Pharmaceutical Society of Great Britain v Boots Cash Chemists* (1953)
Goods at an auction	Each lot is an invitation to treat; offer made by the bidder	*British Car Auctions v Wright* (1972)
Request for information and reply to the request	An invitation to treat	*Harvey v Facey* (1893)

This principle makes good sense. A seller of goods is not obliged to sell the goods to you. The goods might be a display item (that is, the actual item itself is not for sale), even with a price ticket on the item. There may be none left to sell or there may be legal restrictions on the sale of the goods. Examples include the cases of *Fisher v Bell* (1961) and *Pharmaceutical Society of Great Britain v Boots Cash Chemists* (1953).

Lots at an auction

At an auction the bidder makes the offer that the auctioneer then accepts by banging his or her hammer. This means that the lots available at an auction are an invitation to treat. This can be seen in the case of *British Car Auctions v Wright* (1972).

British Car Auctions v Wright (1972)

In this case, the auctioneers were prosecuted for offering to sell an unfit vehicle at an auction. However, the prosecution failed because there was no offer, only an invitation to treat.

A request for information

A request for information and a reply to such a request is not an offer. This might be just a general enquiry such as when an item displayed for sale does not have a price in it. An example of this is where a person enquires about the price of an item – 'How much is the red dress?' This can be seen in the case of *Harvey v Facey* (1893).

Harvey v Facey (1893)

Harvey wanted to buy Facey's farm and sent a message: 'Will you sell me Bumper Hall Pen [the farm]? State lowest price.'

Facey replied: 'Lowest price acceptable £900.'

Harvey tried to buy the farm for £900 but could not as the reply was merely a reply to the request for information, not an offer.

18.1.2 Who can make an offer?

An offer can be made by anyone. This can be by an individual, a partnership, limited company or other organisation. An offer made other than by an individual is made by an employee of the business or an agent. It can also be made through a notice or a machine as in *Thornton v Shoe Lane Parking* (1971).

Thornton v Shoe Lane Parking (1971)

Mr Thornton put money into a machine and was given a ticket at the entrance to a car park. The offer was made by the machine on behalf of the company owning the car park. The acceptance was made by putting the money into the machine. This was where the contract was made which dictated what terms were in the contract – the terms displayed by the machine.

18.1.3 To whom can an offer be made?

An offer can be made to a named individual as in *Gibson v Manchester City Council* (1979), to a group of people as at an auction, or to the world at large as in *Carlill v Carbolic Smokeball Co.* (1893). An offer can be targeted at particular individuals and may be conditional on another contract being made. An example of this which had disastrous consequences was the Hoover free flights fiasco.

Here was an offer to give a free flight if you bought a Hoover product costing more than £100. Inevitably, the offer was taken up by many people who realised that this was effectively a flight to the US for £100 with a free hoover product thrown in! Hoover nearly went bankrupt as a result – it sold £30 million worth of its products but had to pay £50 million for the flights!

Hoover's offer of free flights nearly bankrupted the company

18.1.4 How long does an offer last?

An offer can only be accepted while it is open. Once an offer has ended, it cannot be accepted and cannot form the basis of a contract. It is therefore essential to establish when an offer starts and when it ends.

An offer comes into existence when it is communicated to the offeree. Communication requires the offeree to know of the existence of the offer. This can be seen in the case of *Taylor v Laird* (1856).

Taylor v Laird (1856)

Taylor gave up the captaincy of a ship overseas. He needed to get back to England. He worked as an ordinary crew member on the ship in order to get back to England, but received no wages. The ship owner had not received any communication of his offer to work as an ordinary crew member. Therefore no contract could exist for the payment of wages on this voyage.

Exact timing can be critical – this can be seen in the case of *Stevenson v McLean* (1880).

Stevenson v McLean (1880)

On Saturday, the offeror offered to sell iron to the offeree. The offer was stated to be open until Monday. On Monday at 10 a.m., the offeree sent a telegram asking if he could have credit terms, but got no reply. At 1.34 p.m. the offeree sent a telegram accepting the offer, but at 1.25 p.m. the offeror had sent a telegram, 'Sold iron to third party', arriving at 1.46 p.m. The offeree sued for the breach of contract but the offeror argued that the query about credit was a counter offer so there could be no acceptance. It was decided that the query about credit was only an enquiry, so a binding contract was made at 1.34 p.m.

18.1.5 How an offer can end

An offer can come to an end in the following ways:

- revocation
- rejection
- lapse of time
- death
- acceptance.

Revocation

An offer can be revoked (withdrawn) at any time before acceptance. The offeror must communicate the revocation to the offeree before the revocation can take effect, as in *Routledge v Grant* (1828). This can have implication/s where there is an offer to the whole world – the *Carlill v Carbolic Smokeball* type of offer. In these circumstances, the offer can end in three ways:

- by setting a time limit in the offer such as by stating the 'reward' will only be available to be paid until a particular date
- by the expiry of a reasonable time as is discussed later
- by publishing revocation of the offer in the same way as the original offer was made.

Routledge v Grant (1828)

Grant had offered his house for sale, stating that the offer would remain open for six weeks. When he told Routledge that he no longer wished to sell the house, this was effective revocation of the offer, even though it was within the six-week period. Routledge could no longer accept the offer as it had ended.

Tip

Note that an offer is revoked as soon as the revocation is communicated to the offeree. You can exemplify this from *Stevenson v McLean* (1880) as well as *Routledge v Grant* (1828).

However, an offeree can make a separate contract with the offeror to keep the offer open, or only to sell to him or her. This is known as a collateral contract which can be enforced if the offeror refuses to sell within the agreed period or sells the item to someone else.

Communication of revocation does not have to be from the offeror directly if the person communicating the revocation is reliable. There are no particular categories of 'reliable person' but evidence could be given that the communication took place and could be expected to be taken seriously:

- In *Routledge v Grant* (1828), it was the offeror who communicated the revocation of the offer to the offeree.
- In *Dickinson v Dodds* (1876), the offeree heard about the revocation of the offer from a reliable source. This was effective communication of revocation.

Dickinson v Dodds (1876)

Dodds had offered to sell houses to Dickinson. When a reliable person known to both of them told Dickinson that Dodds had withdrawn the offer, this was effective revocation.

Rejection

Once an offer is rejected, it cannot be accepted by the person rejecting the offer as the rejection ends the offer. If the offer is made to more than one person, rejection by one person does not mean the other offerees can no longer accept the offer. The rejection must be communicated to the offeror before it takes effect as in revocation.

One way is specifically responding to the offer by saying 'No'.

The next way is when a **counter offer** is made. A counter offer is not just a price negotiation but anything else that makes a significant difference to the terms of the contract, such as a different delivery date. A counter offer is a rejection of an offer. An example of rejection through a counter offer occurs in *Hyde v Wrench* (1840).

Key term

Counter offer – a response to an offer which makes a firm proposal that materially alters the terms of the offer.

Hyde v Wrench (1840)

Wrench offered to sell his farm for £1000 to Hyde. Hyde replied with a counter offer of £950. Wrench rejected this counter offer. Hyde then replied that he accepted Wrench's earlier offer to sell for £1000. However, the counter offer ended Wrench's original offer, so Hyde could not accept it. Wrench could have accepted Hyde's offer of £1000 but did not do so.

Sometimes there are enquiries during negotiations. As has been seen in *Stevenson v McLean*, these are generally treated as requests for information and not counter offers. Whereas a counter offer operates as a rejection of the offer, a request for information does not. Thus, the offeree can accept the offer following the request for information.

Tip

It is not always easy to decide whether there has been a request for information or a counter offer. One perspective is that a request for information does not seem to imply a rejection of the offer made. A further point is that a request for information is drafted as a question whereas a counter offer is not. Thus, a request for information is not a firm proposal which rejects the offer, whereas a counter offer is. A counter offer ends the original offer, but it isn't always clear when there is a counter offer and when there is just a request for information. This confusion can be seen from the status of an enquiry about credit in *Stevenson v McLean*.

Lapse of time

An offer can come to end by lapse of time. If a fixed period for the duration of the offer is stated, then as soon as that expires there is no offer to accept. The problem arises when no time is set. In this situation the time is a reasonable time. This is clearly going to vary depending on the nature of the offer. You would expect a longer time for the duration of an offer to buy a metal tank than an offer to buy a specific cake. An example is *Ramsgate Victoria Hotel v Montefiore* (1866).

Ramsgate Victoria Hotel v Montefiore (1866)

On 8 June, Montefiore offered to buy shares at a fixed price in the hotel. On 23 November, his offer was accepted but he no longer wanted them as the share price had fallen so he refused to pay. It was held that the long delay between the offer and the acceptance meant the offer had lapsed and could no longer be accepted.

Death

The effect of the death of either the offeror or the offeree depends on which party died and the type of contract involved. If the offeree dies then the offer ends and those dealing with his estate cannot accept on his behalf. The executors or administrators of his estate can make a new offer as can the offeror.

When an offeror dies, acceptance can still take place until the offeree learns of the offeror's death. However, this is obviously not the case where the

Figure 18.2 Key facts chart for duration of an offer

	Brief legal rule	Case example
Offer not communicated to offeree	No offer exists	*Taylor v Laird* (1856)
Offer must exist to be open for existence	The exact timing of the duration of the offer is critical	*Stevenson v McLean* (1880)
Revocation of offer	Can be made at any time	*Routledge v Grant* (1828)
Communication of revocation of offer	Must be effectively communicated, not necessarily by the offeror	*Dickinson v Dodds* (1876)
Offer rejected	Once rejected, the offer ends and cannot be accepted	*Hyde v Wrench* (1840)
Offer lapsed	Lapses after end of fixed time, or if no time, after a reasonable time	*Ramsgate Victoria Hotel v Montefiore* (1866)
Death of one party	Ends the offer when known or if the offer is for personal services by the deceased	

offer is to perform some personal service such as to provide personal tuition.

Points to consider about the ending of an offer

The law can be confusing as to what exactly forms the offer and how long it remains open. There are many ways an offer can come to an end. A counter offer ends the original offer, but it is not clear when there is a counter offer and when there is just a request for information. This confusion can be seen from the status of an enquiry about credit in *Stevenson v McLean*.

If you state the length of time the offer will be open, you can still change your mind, as in *Routledge v Grant*. If you do not state the length of time it will be open, it is for a reasonable time as in *Ramsgate Victoria Hotel v Montefiore*. How long is a reasonable time? The answer is that it depends on the circumstances. This leads to confusion. The balance is between doing what is morally right and losing money or arguing the point and losing goodwill. This seems to be a poor choice for a business.

A counter offer ends the original offer and this may take place on several occasions during negotiations. This seems a perfectly fair rule as an attempt to go back to the original offer is rarely refused during negotiations – the price rarely goes up during negotiations.

Acceptance

Once an offer has been accepted there is agreement, and assuming that the other essential features of a contract have been fulfilled, there is a legally binding contract.

18.2 Acceptance

Acceptance must be positive and unqualified. It must be acceptance of the whole offer and all the terms in it. There is no acceptance if the response to the offer is 'Yes, if …' or Yes, but …'. Where there is a 'Yes, if …' or 'Yes, but …', this is a counter offer unless it can be seen as just a request for information.

Key term

Acceptance – a final and unconditional agreement to all the terms of the offer.

Acceptance of all the terms in a contract can be seen when you tap on 'I agree' to accept the contract on your phone or computer. This then incorporates all the terms and conditions that you have indicated you have read, whatever they might be.

18.2.1 How do you accept an offer?

Usually, acceptance can be in any form, provided it is unequivocal and communicated to the offeror. It does not have to be in the same format, so an email can be responded to by a text, letter, telephone call, etc. However, acceptance cannot be by silence; there must be some positive act for acceptance. This can be seen in the case of *Felthouse v Bindley* (1863).

Felthouse v Bindley (1863)

There were discussions about the purchase of a horse. The final letter from the offeror stated: 'If I hear no more, I consider the horse mine.' There was no further response, but the court decided there was no contract as an offer could not be accepted by silence or inactivity on the part of the offeree.

Although there can be any form of acceptance, providing it is effectively communicated, the offeror can require a specific method for acceptance. For example, the acceptance must be made personally. If the offer requires a particular manner of acceptance, that must usually be complied with if there is to be a valid acceptance. There can sometimes be a waiver of the requirement stated. This can be seen in the case of *Yates v Pulleyn* (1975).

Yates v Pulleyn (1975)

An option to purchase land was required to be agreed by notice in writing 'sent by registered or recorded delivery post'. When a letter was sent by ordinary post it was argued that there was no acceptance. This argument was rejected as it was a convenience for the offeree, sent by registered post to ensure certainty that the acceptance had arrived. Lord Denning made the distinction between the requirement being mandatory and being directory. A mandatory instruction would have to be followed exactly (acceptance must be registered post). A directory instruction only requires completion within the time frame set – so any form of post would do.

18.2.2 When does acceptance take place?

As we have seen in *Stevenson v McLean*, the actual time of revocation of an offer is critical. This is equally important with acceptance. The general rule is that acceptance takes place when the acceptance is communicated to the offeror. There are three ways of accepting an offer that need special attention. These are:

- acceptance by conduct
- acceptance by use of the post – the postal rules
- electronic methods of communication.

Acceptance by conduct

This has been seen in *Carlill v Carbolic Smokeball Co*. The case of *Reveille Independent LLC v Anotech International (UK) Ltd* (2016) reflects what occurs quite often in business contracts – the job proceeds before the formal contract is agreed in all its detail, with numerous offers and counter offers.

Reveille Independent LLC v Anotech International (UK) Ltd (2016)

In common with many potential contracts, there was a written offer document which stated that it was not binding until signed by both parties. The offeree made some alterations and signed the document but the alterations amounted to a counter offer and the document remained unsigned by the offeror. However, there was performance by one party of the 'contract' in accordance with its terms. The dispute concerned whether a binding contract came into existence. It was claimed that Reveille agreed to integrate and promote products in three episodes of Season 2 of MasterChef US, as well as other matters. The promotions took place but the document remained unsigned.

The counter offer had been accepted by conduct, because the prescribed mode of acceptance was said to have been waived by the original offeror. Acceptance was by the conduct of the offeree, as, objectively, it was intended to be acceptance.

Acceptance by use of the post – the postal rules

The postal rules were developed in the nineteenth century to deal with the problem of when a contract came into existence and, should a letter not be delivered correctly, where the loss should fall. The rule also adapted the idea that once you have posted a letter you cannot get it back.

The rules only apply to letters of acceptance, not to offers or counter offers.

The rules are:

1. The rules only apply if post is the usual or expected means of communication.
2. The letter must be properly addressed and stamped.
3. The offeree must be able to prove the letter was posted.

If the rules apply, acceptance takes place at the moment the letter is properly posted.

The rules were set out in the case of *Adams v Lindsell* (1818).

Adams v Lindsell (1818)

Lindsell wrote to Adams offering to sell them some wool and asking for a reply 'in the course of post'. The letter was delayed in the post. On receiving the letter Adams posted a letter of acceptance the same day. However, because of the delay Lindsell assumed Adams did not want the wool and sold it to someone else. However there was a valid contract because acceptance took place as soon as the letter was placed in the post box and there had been no communication about revoking the offer.

Electronic methods of communication

The law has struggled to deal with the issues arising from modern methods of communication. The principle is that acceptance, apart from the postal rules, occurs when the offeror is aware of the acceptance. This can be seen in the statement of Lord Denning in *Entores v Miles Far East* (1955):

> If a man shouts an offer to a man across a river but the reply is not heard because of a plane flying overhead, there is no contract. The offeree must wait and then shout back his acceptance so that the offeror can hear it.

The case of *Brinkibon Ltd v Stahag Stahl* (1983) dealt with the problem of out-of-hours messages. These are only effective once the office is reopened. Fax, text and email are more modern forms of communication and the same problems and the same principles very often apply.

The Consumer Protection (Distance Selling) Regulations 2000 give consumers a number of rights in addition to those within the Consumer Rights Act 2015. If the obligations with respect to providing key information to the consumer are omitted, then no contract is formed. The Regulations apply to telephone, fax, internet shopping, mail order, email and television shopping.

Article 11 of the Electronic Commerce (EC Directive) Regulations 2002 states that where a buyer is required to give his or her consent through technological means (such as clicking on an icon), the contract is made when the buyer has received from the service provider electronically an acknowledgement of receipt of the acceptance. Thus many online businesses state, 'Your order has been received and is now being processed' or words to that effect, rather than 'Your order has been accepted'. This ensures that online sellers are not required to accept the order at this point.

In *Bernuth Lines Ltd v High Seas Shipping Ltd* (2006), it was stated that clicking on the 'send' icon still raised questions of there being effective acceptance. For example, the email must be sent to the email address of the intended recipient. It must not be rejected by the system or otherwise delayed. If the sender does not require confirmation of receipt he or she may not be able to show that receipt has occurred. There may be circumstances where, for instance, there are several email addresses for a recipient, or different devices will only receive emails to particular addresses. Even if it is received, is the device being used by the intended recipient or a colleague or merely a family member?

The law continues to fail to address the problems with respect to modern communications methods. The case of *Thomas and Gander v BPE Solicitors* (2010) demonstrates this. Here the question was whether an email acceptance is effective when it arrives, or at the time when the offeror could reasonably be expected to have read it, which was not straightforward.

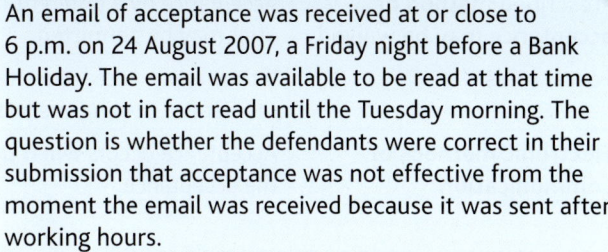

Thomas and Gander v BPE Solicitors (2010)

An email of acceptance was received at or close to 6 p.m. on 24 August 2007, a Friday night before a Bank Holiday. The email was available to be read at that time but was not in fact read until the Tuesday morning. The question is whether the defendants were correct in their submission that acceptance was not effective from the moment the email was received because it was sent after working hours.

The court stated that it must be resolved 'by reference to the intentions of the parties, by sound business practice and in some cases by a judgment where the risks should lie' as had been stated in the case in *Brinkibon*. In the context in which the 6 p.m. email was sent – this was a transaction that could have been completed that evening – the court did not consider that 6 p.m. was outside working hours. The email was available to be read on a portable device within working hours, despite the fact that the recipient had in fact gone home. So there was a valid acceptance.

The effect of *Thomas and Gander* is that each case is decided on its particular facts. Given the prevalence of mobile phones with email capabilities being a normal part of business communications today and the use or otherwise of automated messages indicating an email or text has been read, it appears that the courts will look at each case on the basis of its particular facts and the business practices that have been in use in the negotiations. Thus the result might be different for booking a restaurant table, buying a car or selling a business.

Silence and acceptance

The courts claim the law on formation of contracts will consider what the parties intended to do. This is a subjective approach. In practice, an objective test is often applied disguised as a subjective judgment. In *Felthouse v Bindley* both parties wanted there to be a contract. The court said that from an objective viewpoint there was no evidence of an acceptance from the nephew. In fact the nephew had contacted the auctioneer holding the horse to remove it from the auction which might contradict that view.

However, for the court to decide there is a valid contract, there should be clear and identifiable evidence. The offer has to be communicated and so, logically, must the acceptance.

Figure 18.3 Key facts chart for acceptance of an offer

	Brief legal rule	Case example
Acceptance by conduct	Valid Particularly in unilateral contracts	*Carlill v Carbolic Smokeball Co.* (1893)
Prescribed method of acceptance may be waived	Acceptance by a different method to that in the offer may be permitted	*Reveille Independent LLC v Anotech International (UK) Ltd* (2016)
Postal rules	If they apply, acceptance takes place at the moment of posting the letter	*Adams v Lindsell* (1818)
Electronic methods of communication	Acceptance occurs when the offeror is aware of the acceptance	Electronic Commerce (EC Directive) Regulations 2002), Article 11

The Unsolicited Goods and Services Act 1971 states that, for example, where goods are received without request there can be no contract unless the acceptance is communicated to the sender. So the individual may benefit and the business may lose out and be prosecuted, but is it moral to keep the goods?

Of course, the need to communicate an acceptance may be said to have been waived, as in *Carlill* and *Reveille*.

Tip

When considering offer and acceptance cases, you need to adopt a logical and precise approach. Consider and reference authority – usually decided cases. See Figure 18.4.

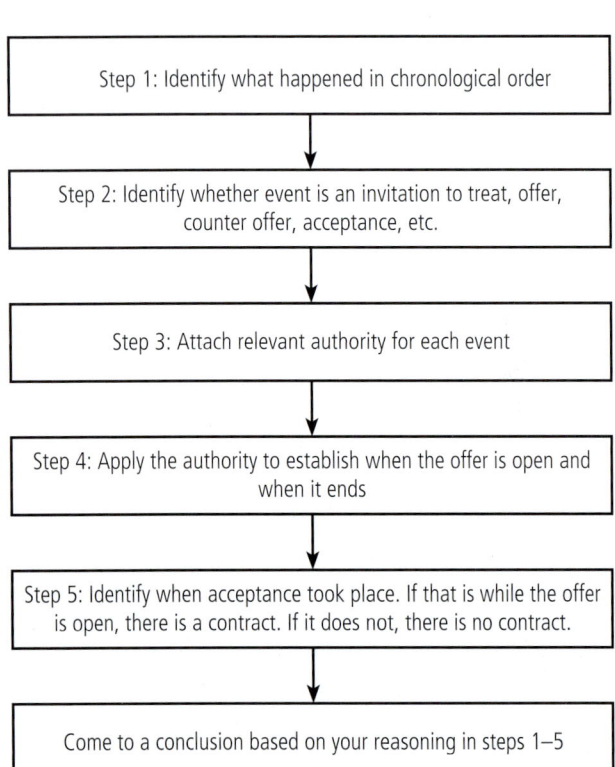

Step 1: Identify what happened in chronological order

↓

Step 2: Identify whether event is an invitation to treat, offer, counter offer, acceptance, etc.

↓

Step 3: Attach relevant authority for each event

↓

Step 4: Apply the authority to establish when the offer is open and when it ends

↓

Step 5: Identify when acceptance took place. If that is while the offer is open, there is a contract. If it does not, there is no contract.

↓

Come to a conclusion based on your reasoning in steps 1–5

Figure 18.4 Steps to take to decide whether an offer has been accepted

Tip

How to work out an offer and acceptance problem in order to establish whether there is a contract or not

Consider the facts of *Adams v Lindsell* (1818). Assume that A found out (from L or a reliable source) that L had sold the wool on 9 September:

2 Sept   L wrote to A offering to sell wool

5 Sept   A received the letter

5 Sept   A sent a letter of acceptance

8 Sept   L sold the goods to X

9 Sept   L received the letter of acceptance

The offer opened when A received the letter. The offer ended when A learned the wool had been sold (9 September). The acceptance took place when the letter of acceptance was posted. The contract was therefore made on 5 September between A and L.

A slightly more complicated case is *Byrne v Van Tienhoven* (1880):

1 Oct   V T posted a letter offering goods for sale

7 Oct   Letter of 1 Oct arrived with B

8 Oct   V T revoked the offer in a letter

11 Oct   B accepted the offer by telegram

15 Oct   B posted a letter confirming acceptance

20 Oct   Letter of revocation arrived with B

Here, the revocation was not effective until it was received on 20 October. This was too late, as the contract was made on 15 October when the letter of acceptance was posted or when the telegram arrived, whichever is earlier.

Activity

Look at the case of *Stevenson v McLean* (1880) and follow the same techniques as shown in Figure 18.4 to decide when the contract was made.

Figure 18.5 Key cases chart for offer and acceptance in contract law

Case	Judgment
Gibson v Manchester City Council (1979)	An offer must have definite terms, not vague such as 'may be prepared to'
Partridge v Crittenden (1968)	An advertisement is usually an invitation to treat and not an offer
Carlill v Carbolic Smoke Ball Co. (1893)	Here the advertisement contained promises that were intended to be taken seriously so it was an offer leading to a unilateral contract
Fisher v Bell (1961)	Goods in a shop window are an invitation to treat
Pharmaceutical Society of Great Britain v Boots Cash Chemists (1953)	Goods in a self-service shop are an invitation to treat
British Car Auctions v Wright (1972)	The bidder makes the offer at an auction; the auctioneer accepts it
Harvey v Facey (1893)	A request for information and the response to the request are not an offer
Thornton v Shoe Lane Parking (1971)	In a vending machine or ticket machine the offer is made by the person inserting the coin
Taylor v Laird (1856)	An offer only comes into existence when it is communicated to the offeree
Stevenson v McLean (1880)	Exact timing of the offer and acceptance are critical in deciding when a contract comes into existence
Routledge v Grant (1828)	An offer can be revoked at any time, providing revocation is communicated to the offeree
Dickinson v Dodds (1876)	Revocation can be via a reliable source rather than directly communicated
Hyde v Wrench (1840)	Once an offer is rejected it cannot be accepted
Ramsgate Victoria Hotel v Montefiore (1866)	An offer ends through lapse of time when a reasonable time has elapsed
Felthouse v Bindley (1863)	Acceptance cannot be made through silence
Yates v Pulleyn (1975)	A mandatory method of acceptance by a particular method must be complied with
Reveille Independent LLC v Anotech International (UK) Ltd (2016)	A directory method of acceptance by a particular method does not have to be complied with
Adams v Lindsell (1818)	If the posting rules apply, acceptance takes place at the moment of posting
Entores v Miles Far East (1955)	With non-postal acceptance, acceptance takes place when the offeror is aware of the acceptance
Brinkibon Ltd v Stahag Stahl (1983)	Acceptance takes place when a message is opened
Byrne v Van Tienhoven (1880)	An example of the working of offer and acceptance issues in negotiations

Summary

- Agreement in the formation of contract requires an offer to be accepted while it is open.
- An offer is a statement of the terms upon which a person is prepared to be bound by a contract.
- An offer differs from an invitation to treat, as only an offer can form the basis of a contract.
- An advertisement is an invitation to treat. It can only be an offer when there is a unilateral contract.
- Other invitations to treat include goods in a shop window or on a shop shelf, lots at an auction and requests for information.
- It is essential to know when an offer has been communicated so that it is open and when it ends.
- An offer can end through revocation, rejection, lapse of time, death and when accepted.
- Acceptance must be communicated to be effective; there are special rules in some circumstances where there is acceptance using the post.

19 Essential requirements of contract (2): consideration and privity, intention to create legal relations

After studying this chapter, you should be able to:
- Understand consideration (including privity of contract)
- Understand intention to create legal relations: domestic and commercial, presumptions and rebuttals

19.1 Consideration

Consideration is essential for every valid contract because contract law requires a bargain and not a gift. This means that both parties to a contract will give something to the other by way of exchange. Consideration is defined in *Currie v Misa* (1875) as 'some right, interest, profit or benefit accruing to one party or some forbearance, detriment, loss or responsibility given, suffered or undertaken by the other'.

The definition given by Sir Frederick Pollock and approved by Lord Dunedin in *Dunlop v Selfridge Ltd* (1915) is:

> **❝** An act or forbearance of one party, or the promise thereof, is the price for which the promise of the other is bought, and the promise thus given for value is enforceable. **❞**

In our everyday contracts this might be paying money for a newspaper. When the consideration has been performed it is said to be **executed**; if it is yet to be performed, it is said to be **executory**.

Key terms

Executed consideration – an act in return for a promise.
Executory consideration – a promise for a promise.

19.1.1 The rules of consideration

Over time, a number of rules have been developed that are applied to the principle of consideration and to which there are some exceptions. These rules are:
- Consideration need not be adequate but must be sufficient.
- Past consideration is not good consideration.
- Consideration must move from the promisee.
- Performing an existing duty cannot be the consideration for a new contract.
- A promise to accept part payment of a pre-existing debt in place of the whole debt is not consideration.

Consideration need not be adequate but must be sufficient

Adequacy

Consideration confirms that the law is concerned with bargains and not gifts. This can be seen in cases such as *Chappell v Nestlé Co. Ltd* (1960) (see below) and *Esso Petroleum Co. Ltd v Commissioners of Customs and Excise* (1976) (see section 19.3.1).

The idea of adequacy is that the parties to the contract themselves agree that the value of things being exchanged is acceptable. The law does not concern itself with the equivalence of consideration between the parties. This can be seen in the cases of *Thomas v Thomas* (1842) and *Chappell v Nestlé Co. Ltd* (1960).

Thomas v Thomas (1842)

Before he died, a man expressed the wish that his wife should be allowed to remain in the house after he died. This wish was not stated in his will. The executors carried out this wish and charged the widow a nominal rent of £1 per year. When they later tried to evict her they failed because consideration was provided by the £1 per year rent.

Chappell v Nestlé Co. Ltd (1960)

Nestlé's customers were able to claim a recording of a song at a fraction of the normal cost if they sent in some of their chocolate bar wrappers. The total consideration was the payment and the chocolate bar wrappers. The House of Lords stressed that even if the contract had been to supply the record merely for the wrappers alone, without any money, the wrappers would have constituted consideration, even though they were of only nominal value.

Paying a sum of money to abandon a claim is valid consideration, even though the claim had little chance of success (but was not fraudulent). This makes an agreement to settle a claim, for example for alleged defective goods, enforceable as a contract, whether or not the original claim would have succeeded.

Sufficiency

Sufficiency means the consideration must be real, and have some value. Real means the consideration must exist. Consideration must be definite and having some value means it has at least a nominal amount of value (as in *Chappell v Nestlé Co. Ltd*).

However, there is little consistency in approach – *White v Bluett* (1853) and *Ward v Byham* (1956) show conflicting decisions.

White v Bluett (1853)

A son owed his father money and had given him a promissory note (a written promise to pay a sum of money) to cover the debt. The father died with the promissory note unpaid. The father's executors sued for the money. The son claimed that his father had promised to write off the debt if he stopped complaining about the way his father was handing out his assets, which he had done. There was no consideration as he had no legal right to complain and natural love and affection were not consideration, so he still had to pay the debt.

Ward v Byham (1956)

The parties were the parents of an illegitimate daughter. The child lived with the father at first, but the mother asked for the child to live with her. The father agreed subject to a letter saying:

> Mildred, I am prepared to let you have Carol and pay you up to £1 per week allowance for her providing you can prove that she will be well looked after and happy and also that she is allowed to decide for herself whether or not she wishes to come and live with you.

The father eventually stopped making the payments. As there was no legal obligation to keep the child happy, the court considered this to be consideration.

Past consideration is no consideration

'Past consideration is no consideration' means that consideration has no value where it has already been done at the time the agreement is made. It is clearly not the price for which the promise is bought as it had been completed before the agreement was made. This can be seen in *Re McArdle* (1951).

Re McArdle (1951)

Mrs McArdle had carried out work on the bungalow in which she lived with her husband and his mother. The bungalow was part of the estate of her husband's father. After the work had been carried out, those inheriting the bungalow signed a document stating 'in consideration of you carrying out the repairs we agree that the executors pay you £488 from the estate'. As the promise to make payment came after the work had been done, it was past consideration. There was, therefore, no contract to pay her the £488.

There is an exception to this rule when there is the **promisor**'s express or implied request for a particular task and there must be an implied understanding that the task should be paid for. This is often the case in commercial agreements such as *Re Casey's Patent* (1892) and occasionally can be seen in other 'important' matters such as in the case of *Lampleigh v Braithwait* (1615).

Key term

Promisor – in contract law, a person who makes a promise to another.

Re Casey's Patent (1892)

The claimant worked on patents for a company. The company later promised him a one-third share in the patents. The company then refused to hand over the share of the patents on the basis that there was no contract as the consideration was past consideration. The court decided the claimant was entitled to the share as it was implied that when he worked on the patents he would receive some payment.

Lampleigh v Braithwait (1615)

Braithwait had been convicted of murder and was to be hanged. Lampleigh agreed to do what he could to obtain a royal pardon (the only way to avoid being executed). Lampleigh negotiated the pardon, and Braithwait then promised to pay him £100, but did not do so. Braithwait's argument was that the gaining of the pardon was past consideration so there was no obligation to pay the

£100. The court decided that although the consideration had preceded the promise, the actions taken were at the defendant's request and were so important that a fee must have been implied.

Thus there must be all of the following for these exceptions to apply:
- an express or implied request by the promisor to the promisee to perform a task
- an implied promise inherent in the request that the promisor will pay the promisee a reasonable sum for performing the task
- the performance of the task, and
- the payment of money by the promisor to the promisee for that performance.

While it is sometimes said that this is an exception to 'past consideration is no consideration', it is not – the performance of the task occurs after the implied promise to pay by the promisor.

Consideration must move from the promisee

Consideration moving from the **promisee** means that a person cannot sue or be sued under a contract unless he or she has provided consideration for it. In a bilateral contract each person is a promisor and a promisee but in a unilateral contract one party makes the promise and the other does the act rather than make a promise. Central to this idea is privity of contract, which is dealt with later in this chapter (see section 19.2.1).

Key term

Promisee – this is the person to whom the promise is made.

An example can be seen in *Tweddle v Atkinson* (1861).

Tweddle v Atkinson (1861)

Both fathers of a young couple who intended to marry agreed in writing to each give a sum of money to the couple. The woman's father died before giving over the money and the husband then sued the executors of the estate when they refused to pay the money. Even though the husband was named in the agreement, his claim failed because he had given no consideration and was not a party to the agreement himself.

Performing a pre-existing duty cannot be the consideration for a new contract

A pre-existing duty is something that you are already legally required to do. This can occur in three ways:
- a duty imposed under a public duty to act, such as the police doing what they are required to do under their public duty

- a duty imposed under an existing contract with the promisor, such as in a contract of employment, merely doing one's job
- a promise to make payment of an already existing debt, such as repaying a loan.

Examples include a public duty, as in the case of *Collins v Godefroy* (1831), or an obligation under an existing contract, as in *Stilk v Myrick* (1809).

Collins v Godefroy (1831)

A policeman was under a court order to attend and give evidence at a trial. It was important to the defendant that the policeman attended, so the defendant promised to pay the policeman some money to make sure he did. There was no consideration as the policeman was already under a duty to be in court.

Stilk v Myrick (1809)

Stilk agreed to sail as crew with Myrick for £5 per month. Part way through the voyage, two of the crew deserted and the captain asked the remaining crew to do the extra work, sharing the wages saved. The claim for the additional wages failed as there was no consideration as crew agree to do everything possible in the event of emergencies.

However, if there is an extra element required for the new payment, there is consideration. This was demonstrated in *Glasbrook Bros v Glamorgan County Council* (1925) and in *Hartley v Ponsonby* (1857).

Glasbrook Bros v Glamorgan County Council (1925)

During a strike, a pit-owner asked for extra protection from the police by having police officers live on site. For this there would be a payment. When the strike was over, the pit-owner refused to pay, arguing that the police were in any case bound to protect his pit. As the police had provided more men and in a different way than they would normally have done, there was consideration for the promise.

Hartley v Ponsonby (1857)

This case involved similar facts to *Stilk v Myrick* (1809). However, after desertion only 19 members of a crew of 36 remained. A similar promise to pay more money to the remaining crew was enforceable because the reduction in numbers made the voyage much more dangerous, so there was an extra element amounting to good consideration.

More modern examples can be seen in which the courts give commercial effect to arrangements that might appear to have no consideration. The current situation can be seen in *Williams v Roffey Bros and Nicholls (Contractors) Ltd* (1990).

Williams v Roffey Bros and Nicholls (Contractors) Ltd (1990)

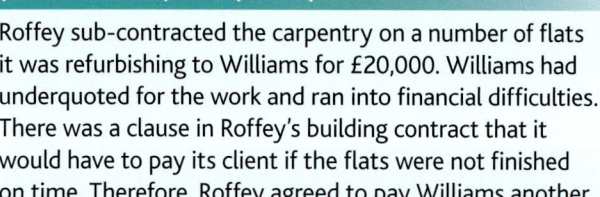

Roffey sub-contracted the carpentry on a number of flats it was refurbishing to Williams for £20,000. Williams had underquoted for the work and ran into financial difficulties. There was a clause in Roffey's building contract that it would have to pay its client if the flats were not finished on time. Therefore, Roffey agreed to pay Williams another £10,300 if he would complete the carpentry on time.

Williams completed the work on time but Roffey failed to pay the extra £10,300. Even though Williams was only doing what he was already contractually bound to do, Roffey was gaining the extra benefit of not having to pay the money for delay to its client. Williams was thus providing consideration for Roffey's promise to pay him more for the work merely by completing his existing obligations on time. The reason why Roffey refused to pay Williams the additional sum was that, in completing the work on time, W was merely performing his pre-existing contractual duty.

It is not easy to reconcile these decisions. However, in *Stilk v Myrick* the crew members did not receive the extra payment as they were only carrying out an existing duty – an interpretation of the terms. The same could be said in *Hartley v Ponsonby* except for the greater number of crew members who had deserted, so there was a variation of the terms of the contract or possibly a new contract.

- In *Stilk*, there was a hint of pressure from the crew on the captain for the extra payment or they would all desert.
- In *Hartley*, the remaining crew had to get the ship to its destination under the possible threat of desertion if they did not.
- In *Williams v Roffey*, there was no pressure as it was the defendant builder who offered the extra payment to the claimant roofer.

Today's courts appear to take the view that there is a commercial reality in applying the strict rules of consideration.

A promise to accept part payment of an existing debt in place of the whole debt is not consideration

This rule arises from *Pinnel's case* (1602). In that case the judge said that the payment of a lesser sum on the day a debt is due cannot be in satisfaction of the greater debt.

This means that a creditor is able to claim the remainder of a debt even if he or she has agreed with the debtor that a part payment will clear the debt, unless there is early repayment or something additional given. This rule was confirmed in the case of *Foakes v Beer* (1884), where an agreement to pay a debt by instalments was no consideration for not claiming the whole debt at once.

Foakes v Beer (1884)

Dr Foakes owed Mrs Beer £2090 after a court gave judgment in favour of Mrs Beer. The two reached an agreement for Foakes to pay in instalments, with Mrs Beer agreeing that no further action would be taken if the debt was paid off by an agreed date. Later Mrs Beer demanded the interest to which she was entitled under a judgment debt and sued when Foakes refused to pay. She was successful following the rule in *Pinnel's case*.

The law in *Pinnel's case* is harsh, so two exceptions to the rule have developed:

1. The principle of accord and satisfaction – where there is agreement (accord) to end a contract and satisfaction (consideration) that has been acted upon voluntarily. Thus accepting something other than money for the whole debt is good consideration, even if it is not of equal value to the debt. This must be done at the request of the creditor, not the debtor. An example of this is if A owed B £1000 and A suggested that B gives him £200 and B's car (even if the car was not worth £800) and B agrees to that arrangement.

2. The doctrine of **promissory estoppel** – if one party to an existing contract agrees to vary the contract and the other party relies on that promise, the promisor cannot go back on the agreement as he or she is estopped (prevented) from breaking the promise. This developed with respect to part payment, but it is really about adjustment of rights under a contract, not just money.

There is a line of authority outlined below based on *High Trees* which undermines the rule in *Pinnel's case/ Foakes v Beer* but which is outside the scope of the AQA specification. It does, however, inform some aspects of economic duress discussed later.

Key terms

Estoppel – being prevented from making assertions that contradict what has previously been said to be a fact.

Promissory estoppel – an equitable doctrine which can prevent a person going back on a promise which is not supported by consideration.

Promissory estoppel was seen in *Central London Property Trust Ltd v High Trees House Ltd* (1947).

Central London Property Trust Ltd v High Trees House Ltd (1947)

The owner of a block of flats agreed with the company to which he leased the block that only half rent was to be paid during the Second World War. The agreement was made because finding individual tenants for the flats in London was very difficult. After the war finding tenants was easy so the landlord claimed the full rent for the period after the war had ended. The owner was entitled to the full rent after the war.

Even though there was no consideration from the tenant for the reduction in rent, he had relied on and acted on the owner's promise. The owner had accepted the reduced rent without question, so both parties had acted voluntarily on the agreement and so the agreement was valid. However, the owner would not have been entitled to the foregone half rent accrued during the war.

This appears to be in direct conflict with the decision in *Foakes v Beer*. If Mrs Beer could break her promise not to sue for more, how and why is the landlord in the *High Trees* case not allowed to break his promise? The decision seems to indicate that consideration was not a crucial element of a contract and the courts have been reluctant to develop this idea. An example is *Re Selectmove Ltd* (1995).

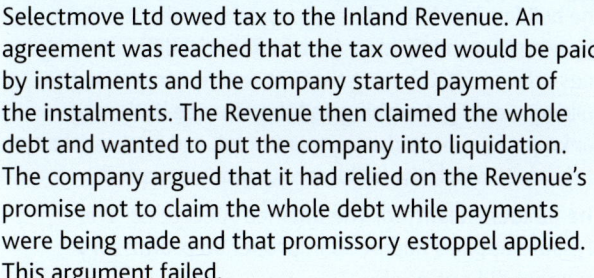

Re Selectmove Ltd (1995)

Selectmove Ltd owed tax to the Inland Revenue. An agreement was reached that the tax owed would be paid by instalments and the company started payment of the instalments. The Revenue then claimed the whole debt and wanted to put the company into liquidation. The company argued that it had relied on the Revenue's promise not to claim the whole debt while payments were being made and that promissory estoppel applied. This argument failed.

Despite doubts, there have been a number of cases in which promissory estoppel have been used.

Limitations to the doctrine are:

- It operates to modify existing obligations in a contract – it cannot be used to found a new contract, only defend an existing claim.
- The promisee must have relied to his or her detriment on the promise.
- It may only suspend rights but not extinguish the rights of the promisor – as seen in *Central London Property Trust Ltd v High Trees House Ltd* (1947).
- Since promissory estoppel is an equitable principle, anyone seeking to rely on the principle must show he or she behaved equitably – as seen in *D and C Builders v Rees* (1965). In that case, the full debt was recoverable because the agreement to accept less was made under pressure, which would not be equitable.

Figure 19.1 Key facts chart for consideration

	Brief legal rule	Case example
Consideration must be sufficient	Sufficiency means the consideration must be real, and have some value	*Chappell v Nestlé Co. Ltd* (1960) *White v Bluett* (1853)
Past consideration is no consideration	Consideration has no value where it has already been done at the time the agreement is made	*Re McArdle* (1951)
Consideration must move from the promisee	A person cannot sue or be sued under a contract unless he or she has provided consideration for it	*Tweddle v Atkinson* (1861)
Performing an existing duty is not consideration	Performing an existing duty cannot be the consideration for a new contract	*Stilk v Myrick* (1809)
Where there is acceptance of part payment of a debt	Payment of a lesser sum on the day a debt is due cannot be in satisfaction of the greater debt	*Foakes v Beer* (1884)
Promissory (equitable) estoppel	An equitable doctrine which can prevent a person going back on a promise which is not supported by consideration	*Central London Property Trust Ltd v High Trees House Ltd* (1947)

D and C Builders v Rees (1965)

The builders had been chasing payment of about £480. Knowing that the builders were in financial difficulties, Mrs Rees offered £300, saying that if it was not accepted, the builders would get nothing and therefore be likely to go bankrupt. She made the payment in full and final satisfaction of the debt which the builders reluctantly accepted.

The builders' claim for the balance succeeded. The pressure applied had been improper so promissory estoppel did not apply.

Tip

When considering a situation involving payment of a lesser sum than what is due, look for something which can amount to good consideration for the creditor abandoning the rest. If there is nothing, consider equitable estoppel, but remember that it only applies when it is inequitable for the creditor to insist on his or her full rights.

Figure 19.2 Key cases chart for consideration

Case	Judgment
Thomas v Thomas (1842)	Payment of the very small rent was consideration, not the moral obligation to carry out the dead man's wishes
Chappell v Nestlé Co. Ltd (1960)	The chocolate bar wrappers amounted to consideration for the record
White v Bluett (1853)	An intangible benefit is not consideration
Ward v Byham (1956)	Going beyond one's existing legal duty can amount to consideration
Re McArdle (1951)	The promise to make payment came after the work had been done, so it was past consideration and of no value
Re Casey's Patent (1892)	The court can find an implied term as to make some payment to circumvent the past consideration rule
Lampleigh v Braithwait (1615)	The matter was so important that some payment could be implied as intended by the parties
Tweddle v Atkinson (1861)	The claim failed because he had given no consideration and was not a party to the agreement himself
Collins v Godefroy (1831)	There was no consideration for it as the policeman was already under a duty to be in court
Stilk v Myrick (1809)	A pre-existing contractual obligation was not sufficient consideration to create a contract
Glasbrook Bros v Glamorgan County Council (1925)	The police had provided more men and in a different way than they would normally have done, so there was consideration for the promise
Hartley v Ponsonby (1857)	A great change in circumstances and workload amounted to consideration
Williams v Roffey Bros and Nicholls (Contractors) Ltd (1990)	The extra benefit of not having to pay a sum for delay to a client is consideration
Pinnel's case (1602)	Payment of a lesser sum on the day a debt is due cannot be in satisfaction of the greater debt
Foakes v Beer (1884)	Pinnel's case was applied
Central London Property Trust Ltd v High Trees House Ltd (1947)	Both parties had acted voluntarily on the agreement. The agreement was valid as equitable estoppel applied
Re Selectmove Ltd (1995)	No additional consideration had been given so the agreement to pay by instalments was invalid
D and C Builders v Rees (1965)	Mrs Rees had not acted equitably, so the principle of equitable estoppel could not apply

19.2 Privity

19.2.1 The general principle of privity of contract

The principle of **privity of contract** means that a contract cannot confer rights nor impose obligations on someone who is not a party to the contract. So a contract between A and B cannot result in C claiming rights (or having obligations imposed) under the contract.

> **Key term**
>
> **Privity of contract** – only those who are parties to a contract are bound by it and can benefit from it.

The rule of privity can be seen in *Dunlop Pneumatic Tyre Co. Ltd v Selfridge* (1915).

> **Dunlop Pneumatic Tyre Co. Ltd v Selfridge (1915)**
>
> Dunlop manufactured tyres and sold some to Dew, who agreed not to resell them below a certain price. Dew resold to Selfridge on the basis of the same term not to resell below a certain price. Selfridge then resold below this price. As Dew refused to sue Selfridge, Dunlop sued them. Because Dunlop was not a party to the contract between Dew and Selfridge, it could not sue Selfridge for selling below the agreed price.

19.2.2 The relationship between privity and consideration

The rule of privity can be seen as based on the rule that consideration must move from the promisee, as in *Tweddle v Atkinson* (1861).

The privity rule is seen as causing injustice, and the courts have tried to find ways of avoiding the rule. In *Jackson v Horizon Holidays Ltd* (1975), the rule would prevent all members of a family party claiming as the claimant had made the booking for everyone.

> **Jackson v Horizon Holidays Ltd (1975)**
>
> Mr Jackson booked a holiday for himself and his family. The holiday was very disappointing. He sued for damages for himself and his family. The court decided that it would be unfair to limit the award of damages to Mr Jackson. Damages awarded reflected the loss suffered by all the members of the holiday party.

> **Extension activity**
>
> Research and look for legal justifications in other cases such as those discussed in this article about *Jackson v Horizon Holidays*: www.lawgazette.co.uk/law/claiming-damages-for-a-ruined-holiday/55929.article.

19.2.3 General exceptions

There are some exceptions when the rule of privity does not apply.

Agency

An agency arises when one person, the agent, is authorised to make a contract on behalf of another person, the principal. The effect is that the principal will be bound by the terms of the contract even though he or she did not make the contract him- or herself. The principal and the agent are treated as being the same person so the principal is a party to the contract. This occurs, for example, when an employee makes a contract on behalf of a company.

Collateral contracts

The court may be able to avoid the strict rule of privity by finding a second contract alongside the main agreement, as in the case of *Shanklin Pier Ltd v Detel Products Ltd* (1951).

> **Shanklin Pier Ltd v Detel Products Ltd (1951)**
>
> Contractors employed to paint the pier were told by the pier company to use paint manufactured by Detel. The paint was bought by the contractors from Detel. Detel made a representation to the pier company that the paint would last for seven years. The paint only lasted three months.
>
> There was no privity of contract between the pier company and the defendant paint manufacturer, but the court found that there was a collateral contract between them to the effect that the paint would last for seven years, the consideration for which was the instruction given by the pier company to its contractors to order the paint from the defendant.

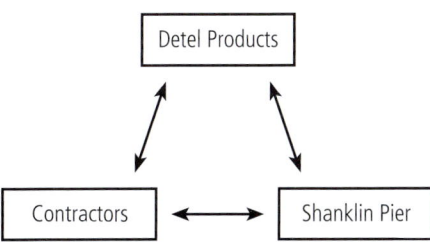

Figure 19.3 *Shanklin Pier Ltd v Detel Products Ltd* (1951)

19.2.4 Contracts (Rights of Third Parties) Act 1999

Under s 1 of the Contracts (Rights of Third Parties) Act 1999, someone who is not a party to a contract (a 'third party') may enforce the contract against either or both of the actual parties to the contract if:

- the third party is expressly identified by name, or as a member of a class or as answering a particular description, and
- the contract expressly provides that the third party may enforce the contract, or
- the contract term is an attempt to confer the benefit of the term on the third party.

This seems to get round the difficulty that occurred in *Beswick v Beswick* (1967).

Beswick v Beswick (1967)

Mr Beswick made a contract with his nephew to sell his coal merchant's business, in exchange for weekly payments to the uncle for life and, after his death, to his wife, the nephew's aunt. After the death of the uncle the nephew refused to pay the weekly payments to his aunt. The court decided that the aunt was not a party to the contract and so there was no privity of contract.

The reason why the aunt would now be able to claim under the Contracts (Rights of Third Parties) Act 1999 is that she was named in the contract and the contract intended to confer a benefit on her.

The parties to the contract have the right to exclude the Act from benefiting a third party.

Where the Act applies, under s 3 if the contract is being enforced by a third party, the person who made the contract can rely on any defence or valid exclusion clause that was available to the original contracting party. Thus, if A books a holiday with B and the list given to A of those going on that holiday includes another, C, C will be able to claim rights under the contract. A will, however, be able to rely on

Figure 19.4 Key facts chart for privity of contract

	Brief legal rule	Case example
The rule of privity of contract	Only those who are parties to a contract are bound by it and can benefit from it	*Dunlop Pneumatic Tyre Co. Ltd v Selfridge* (1915)
Relationship with consideration	In certain circumstances the courts try to avoid the strict rule of privity by allowing for damages for distress	*Jackson v Horizon Holidays Ltd* (1975)
Agency provides an exception to privity	An agent is authorised to make a contract on behalf of another person, the principal	
Collateral contracts can provide an exception to privity	The court may be able to avoid the strict rule of privity by finding a second contract alongside the main agreement	*Shanklin Pier Ltd v Detel Products Ltd* (1951)
Contracts (Rights of Third Parties) Act 1999	The Act allows someone who is not a party to a contract (a 'third party'), in some circumstances, to enforce the contract against either or both of the actual parties to the contract	*Beswick v Beswick* (1967)

Figure 19.5 Key cases chart for privity of contract

Case	Judgment
Dunlop Pneumatic Tyre Co. Ltd v Selfridge (1915)	As Dunlop was not a party to the contract between Dew and Selfridge it could not sue Selfridge for selling below the agreed price
Jackson v Horizon Holidays Ltd (1975)	It would be unfair to limit the award of damages to Mr Jackson The claims of his family were allowed even though, strictly, they were not parties to the holiday contract
Shanklin Pier Ltd v Detel Products Ltd (1951)	There was found to be a collateral contract between them to the effect that the paint would last for seven years
Beswick v Beswick (1967)	The aunt was not a party to the contract, so there was no privity of contract

any defence he or she might have including reliance on any valid term of the contract limiting his or her liability for any breach of that contract.

In consumer contracts, there are often rights where goods are bought for someone else, such as when a gift receipt is obtained. However, the parties to the contract have the right to exclude the Act from benefiting a third party. Most commercial contracts now include such a term, so the Act is not as useful as might be hoped.

19.3 Intention to create legal relations

Once offer and acceptance have taken place and an agreement is formed, it would appear that there is a contract. However, as a contract is an agreement that the law will recognise, there must be an **intention to create legal relations** and make the contract legally binding. This is presumed in a business agreement and is presumed not to exist where the agreement is purely of a social and domestic nature.

This means that where an agreement is made between a business and someone else (whether another business or a consumer), the law presumes that the agreement is intended to be legally binding and a contract. There can, however, be evidence that the agreement is not intended to be legally binding and then it will not be a contract. This is when the presumption is rebutted, as seen in *Jones v Vernons Pools* (1938).

Similarly, where the agreement is merely a social agreement, the presumption is that it is not legally binding, although, as we shall see, this presumption may also be rebutted.

Key term

Intention to create legal relations – the parties to a contract expressly or impliedly agree that the contract is legally binding and therefore enforceable in court.

19.3.1 Business agreements

Business agreements are presumed to be legally binding. This is quite logical but does not take into account the fact that the presumption can be rebutted by showing the opposite is the case. This can be seen in a so-called gentlemen's agreement which is usually discovered by a term that states the

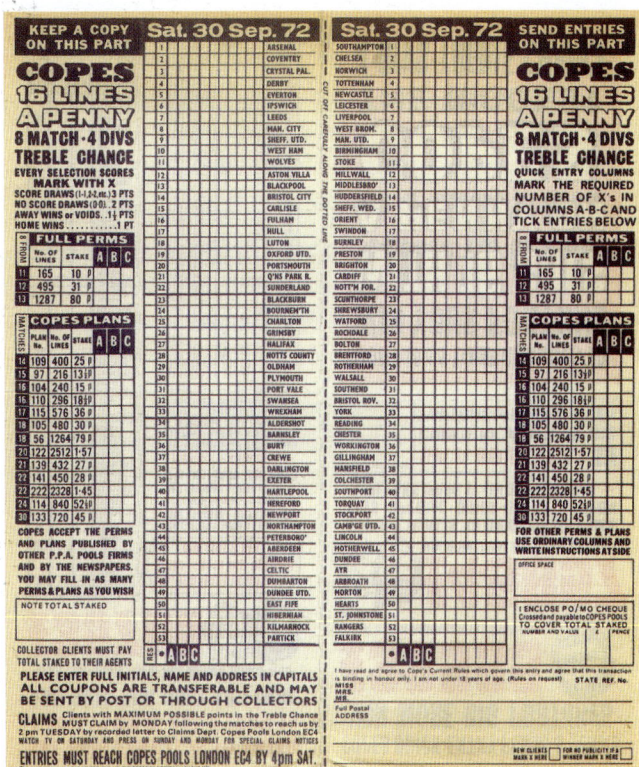

A pools coupon from the 1970s

contract is binding in honour only, as in the case of *Jones v Vernons Pools* (1938).

Jones v Vernons Pools (1938)

Mr Jones claimed that he had a winning football pool coupon. The coupon, which he signed, stated that the transaction was 'binding in honour only'. As the agreement was based on the honour of the parties and not legally binding, there was no intent to create legal relations and no legal contract.

The burden of proof is on the person seeking to establish there is no legal intention, that is, that the presumption has been rebutted.

An example of this is seen in *Edwards v Skyways Ltd* (1969).

Edwards v Skyways Ltd (1969)

Negotiations had taken place about rights and payments to redundant airline pilots. Skyways tried to avoid making the agreed *ex gratia* (without admitting the payment was a legal requirement) payment in Edwards' redundancy. This failed because, while *ex gratia* suggests a voluntary payment with no liability to make it, the agreement here was seen as a business agreement and therefore there was a presumption the agreement was intended to be legally binding, which the claimant had failed to rebut.

In *Edmunds v Lawson* (2000), a case about a pupillage contract with a barrister and minimum wage regulations, the court stated 'Whether the parties intended to enter into legally binding relations ... is an issue to be determined objectively'. This means that each case will be decided on its own facts.

The offer of a free gift also creates problems. Where this is to promote a business it can still be held to be legally binding, as in *Esso Petroleum Co. Ltd v Commissioners of Customs and Excise* (1976).

Esso Petroleum Co. Ltd v Commissioners of Customs and Excise (1976)

Esso gave a World Cup coin with every four gallons of petrol purchased. Should this free gift attract tax? As Esso was clearly trying to gain more business from the promotion, there was held to be intention to be bound by the arrangement, so tax was payable.

Another situation is where prizes are offered in competitions. Just as the free gift is designed to promote the company offering it, the same occurs where a company offers a competition prize as in *McGowan v Radio Buxton* (2001).

McGowan v Radio Buxton (2001)

The claimant entered a radio competition. The prize was stated to be a Renault Clio car. The winner was given a four-inch scale model of a Renault Clio. Radio Buxton argued that there was no intention to create legal relations. The court decided that there was legal intention in line with previous cases.

The same problem arises with a **letter of comfort** which is not usually intended to be legally binding.

Key term

Letter of comfort – a written assurance usually provided by a parent company in respect of its subsidiary's financial obligations to a bank. It is usually where the parent company wishes to give some assurance to the lender in respect of the subsidiary's ability to repay the loan but has no obligation to pay on its behalf.

This can be seen in *Kleinwort Benson Ltd v Malaysian Mining Corporation* (1989), where the courts found that there is no legal contractual obligation, only a moral obligation. The Court of Appeal decided that, as a matter of construction of the letter of comfort, MMC had not made a promise to do anything but represented a fact that it was their present intention to ensure that Metals Ltd would be able to meet its liabilities. As a result, intention to create legal relations was irrelevant.

Kleinwort Benson Ltd v Malaysian Mining Corporation (1989)

Kleinwort lent £10 million to Metals Ltd, a subsidiary of the Malaysian Mining Corporation (MMC). MMC would not guarantee this loan but issued a comfort letter stating its intention to ensure Metals had sufficient funds for repayment. When Metals went out of business without repaying Kleinwort, a claim based on the comfort letter failed as there was no legal intention. If Kleinwort had required a guarantee it should have insisted on one.

19.3.2 Business or domestic agreement?

It has been suggested in *Sadler v Reynolds* (2005) that there may be situations which fall into a sort of 'halfway house' between domestic and commercial, and that in this case the burden of overturning the presumption may be affected.

Sadler v Reynolds (2005)

The alleged contract was between a journalist and a businessman who were friends. The journalist wanted to ghost-write the autobiography of the businessman. The judge suggested that the agreement fell 'somewhere between an obviously commercial transaction and a social exchange'.

The burden was on the journalist to prove that there was an intention to create legal relations, that it was a business agreement and not a social one.

19.3.3 Social and domestic arrangements

These are presumed not to be legally binding, but the presumption can be rebutted. The most usual distinction can be seen in *Balfour v Balfour* (1919) and *Merritt v Merritt* (1970).

Balfour v Balfour (1919)

A husband worked abroad. His wife stayed in England. He promised her an income of £30 per month. Later the marriage failed and she petitioned for divorce and claimed her £30 per month. As the agreement had been made at an amicable point in their relationship, not in contemplation of divorce, it was a purely domestic arrangement and not legally enforceable.

However, where husband and wife are already separated, an agreement between them may be taken as intended to be legally binding.

Merritt v Merritt (1970)

Mr Merritt had left his wife. An agreement to pay the wife an income if she paid the outstanding mortgage was held to be intended to create legally binding obligations and was enforced by the court.

Sometimes families make arrangements that appear to be business arrangements because of the nature of what they are doing. In such cases, the court must examine the real purpose of the arrangement – was it purely a social matter or something with much more legal intent?

Jones v Padavatton (1969)

A mother had persuaded her daughter to come to England to study for the Bar, promising to allow her to stay in her house. Several years later, the daughter had still not passed any Bar examinations. They fell out and the mother wanted to evict her. The daughter said that there had been a contract for her to stay there.

At the time when the first arrangement was made, the mother and daughter were very close, so the court was satisfied that neither party at that time intended to enter into a legally binding contract.

If money has changed hands, then even if the arrangement is made socially, it is more likely to be a business arrangement and therefore legally binding, as in *Simpkins v Pays* (1955).

This is usually the case with arrangements such as lottery ticket syndicates. It is, of course, wise to make some record of the agreement, as it is difficult to decide whether an agreement has been made or is merely social chatter with insufficient evidence of a binding agreement, as in *Wilson v Burnett* (2007).

Simpkins v Pays (1955)

A lodger and two members of the household entered competitions. The lodger filled in the form in the landlady's name. One of the entries won. The claim was made by the lodger on the basis there was understanding that they would share any winnings. Their action succeeded as this was more than just a social arrangement.

In *Wilson v Burnett* (2007), there was a similar situation, which was tested objectively.

Wilson v Burnett (2007)

Three young women worked together. They decided to attend a bingo session, at which one of them had won a local prize of £153 and then a national prize of over £100,000. The question was whether there was a contract between them to share any winnings over £10. The suggestion of a prior agreement was undermined by the fact that when one of them had won the local prize of £153 and they were waiting to hear the national result, others repeatedly asked if she was 'going to share'. This suggested to the court that an intention to create a legal relationship did not exist at that time so the claim for a share failed.

However, if parties put their financial security at risk for an agreement, then it must have been intended that the agreement should be legally binding.

Parker v Clarke (1960)

A young couple were persuaded by an older couple to sell their house to move in with them, with the promise also that they would inherit the property on their death. Later, the couples fell out and the young couple was asked to leave. The young couple successfully argued that they had a legally binding agreement. Giving up their security indicated that the arrangement was intended to be legally binding.

19.3.4 Summary of the law of intention to create legal relations

The first issue is whether the parties intend to form a contract at all. In *Kleinwort Benson Ltd v Malaysian Mining Corporation* (1989), the courts had to decide whether or not the document was in fact intended to be legally binding. Courts can view individual letters of comfort as a contract or not, depending on all the evidence in the case.

Whether the contract is commercial or social is a question that also has to be resolved. It has been suggested in *Sadler v Reynolds* (2005) that there may be situations which fall into a sort of 'halfway house' between domestic and commercial. If that is the case, the presumption will vary depending on which side the decision is made.

The two presumptions created by the courts have proved helpful when deciding if an agreement has legal validity or not. However, the court will always consider all the circumstances surrounding the case and, particularly in respect of social and domestic arrangements, the final decision will not always be obvious:

■ The case of *Jones v Padvatton* (1968) divided the Court of Appeal as to the existence of legal intent.

- In *Ellis v Chief Adjudication Officer* (1997), there was not a legally binding contract as the court found that the parties did not intend that to be the case. However, in *Hardwick v Johnson* (1978) the agreement had legal intent on somewhat similar facts.

The presumption against legal intent for social and domestic arrangements is understandable but, by considering the surrounding circumstances, the courts reach inconsistent decisions.

This is also the case in business situations. In *Esso Petroleum Co. Ltd v Commissioners of Customs and Excise* (1976), the court, by a majority, considered that the offer of the free coin was enough to allow the presumption for legal intent to remain as it was inextricably linked to the purchase of fuel.

It can also be argued that there should be no need to prove legal intent. Offer, acceptance and consideration are the foundations on which a contract is made. If these elements are all present and there is no clear statement that the agreement is not to be legally binding, then it should be a valid contract. Indeed, it has been argued that this should be the case even where there is no consideration. A straightforward objective test might be a satisfactory solution to the issue.

Figure 19.6 Key facts chart for intention to create legal relations

	Brief legal rule	Case example
The presumption with business contracts	Business agreements are presumed to be legally binding	*Edwards v Skyways Ltd* (1969)
Rebutting the presumption in business contracts	The presumption can be rebutted by showing the opposite is the case	*Jones v Vernons Pools* (1938)
The position of letters of comfort	A letter of comfort is not usually intended to be a legally binding document but, confusingly, it may give rise to a legally binding obligation depending on the wording	*Kleinwort Benson Ltd v Malaysian Mining Corporation* (1989)
The presumption with social and domestic arrangements	Social and domestic arrangements are presumed not to be legally binding	*Balfour v Balfour* (1919)
Rebutting the presumption in social and domestic arrangements	The presumption can be rebutted by showing the opposite is the case	*Merritt v Merritt* (1971)
Social arrangements can be like business arrangements	If money has changed hands, then even if the arrangement is made socially, it is more likely to be a commercial arrangement and therefore legally binding	*Simpkins v Pays* (1955)

Figure 19.7 Key cases chart for intention to create legal relations

Case	Judgment
Edwards v Skyways Ltd (1969)	The agreement to actually pay a redundancy package is binding even though it is described as *ex gratia*
Jones v Vernons Pools (1938)	The football pool coupon, which he signed, stated that the transaction was 'binding in honour only' This rebutted the presumption in the business contract
Esso Petroleum Co. Ltd v Commissioners of Customs and Excise (1976)	As Esso were clearly trying to gain more business from the promotion, there was held to be legal intention in the arrangement
McGowan v Radio Buxton (2001)	A prize in a competition is part of a legally binding contract
Kleinwort Benson Ltd v Malaysian Mining Corporation (1989)	The claim based on the comfort letter failed as there was no legal intention If Kleinwort had required a legally binding guarantee it should have insisted on one

Case	Judgment
Sadler v Reynolds (2005)	There may be situations which fall into a sort of 'halfway house' between domestic and commercial The person alleging it is legally binding must show that is the case
Balfour v Balfour (1919)	The agreement was not binding as it was a domestic arrangement between an amicable married couple
Merritt v Merritt (1971)	The agreement was binding as it was an arrangement between a separated married couple about future maintenance payments
Jones v Padavatton (1969)	There is a presumption that cohabitants would not intend to create enforceable contractual obligations between themselves
Simpkins v Pays (1955)	If money has changed hands, then even if the arrangement is made socially, it is more likely to be a commercial arrangement and therefore legally binding
Parker v Clarke (1960)	If parties put their financial security at risk for an agreement, then it must have been intended that the agreement should be legally binding

Activity

Here are two short scenarios. In each case write down the arguments for and against there being a valid contract on the basis of intention to create legal relations. Discuss your arguments with a group of fellow students and come to a justified conclusion.

1 Three students share a flat. They take it in turns to buy milk for the fridge. As people often forget to do this, they have instituted a fine system of 50p each time someone forgets their turn, all money collected to go towards an end-of-term meal out. One member of the flat refuses to pay the 50p 'fine'.

2 Anna's Uncle Paul said he would let her have his car if she got into a degree course at a top university. She has now achieved this but he refuses to give her his car as he has just spent most of his savings on a brand new Ferrari.

Summary

- There must be an intention to create legal relations for there to be a valid contract.
- There is a distinction between business or commercial contracts and those that are of a social and domestic nature.
- Consideration involves each party to a contract giving something of value to the other.
- There are five rules with respect to what amounts to consideration.
- Privity of contract means that only a party to the contract can take legal action on it.
- There are exceptions to the doctrine of privity, both from case law and statute.

20 Contract terms: general and specific to consumer contracts

After reading this chapter, you should be able to:

- Understand general terms of contract: express and implied
- Understand types of term: conditions, warranties, innominate terms
- Understand specific terms implied by statute law in relation to consumer contracts
- Understand the provisions of the Consumer Rights Act 2015: terms for supply of goods and services and remedies for breach

20.1 Express and implied terms

The terms of a contract are what the parties to the contract have agreed. These terms can either be:

- specifically agreed between the parties, known as express terms, or
- implied in the contract.

Terms define the obligations of each party to the contract. For example, if I buy a cup of coffee for £1, the stated terms are coffee and £1 which represent the consideration in the contract. Other terms may be implied in the contract, for example that the coffee will be hot.

Express and implied terms may be of different types which, if not complied with, have different consequences.

20.2 Types of term

Terms in a contract can be categorised as:

- a condition
- a warranty
- an innominate term.

The type of each individual term depends on the evidence, particularly on any description of the term in a contract. Any term that is not clearly a condition or a warranty is an innominate term.

20.2.1 Condition

A condition is a term in a contract so important that a failure to perform the obligation would destroy the main purpose of the contract. For example, if I make a contract to buy a phone, it is central to the contract that it can make and receive calls when attached to a phone network. The reason this is important is that if a condition is broken, the person suffering the failure is entitled to end the contract. This ending of the contract is known as repudiation.

Tip

It is easy to confuse repudiation with rescission. Repudiation is done by the party to the contract bringing it to a premature end. This can be done for a breach of condition but not a breach of warranty.

Key terms

Condition – a term in a contract that is central to the contract, breach of which may allow the contract to be repudiated.

Repudiation – the ending of the contract.

Rescission – this is an equitable remedy that is made at the discretion of the judge. The purpose of rescission is to place the parties back in their pre-contractual position.

A condition is said to go to the root of a contract. This can be seen in the case of *Poussard v Spiers and Pond* (1876).

Poussard v Spiers and Pond (1876)

An actress agreed to perform the lead role in a production. She failed to attend the first few performances. Her role was given to an understudy. When she did attend, she was not allowed to take up the role. She had in fact broken her contract by not turning up for the performances. As the lead, her presence was central. It was therefore a condition in the contract so the contract could be repudiated.

The whole discussion of rescission and repudiation is explored in more detail in Chapter 22.

20.2.2 Warranty

A warranty is a minor term of the contract. Only damages can be claimed for a breach of warranty – the contract is not ended and the main purpose of the contract can continue to be performed despite the breach. For example, for a phone, it is not central to the contract if the phone will only store 99 contacts rather than the 100 stated in the contract.

There is no right of the injured party to repudiate the contract. An example is *Bettini v Gye* (1876).

Key term

Warranty – a minor term in a contract, breach of which does not end the contract but allows a claim for damages only.

Bettini v Gye (1876)

A singer was contracted to perform at a series of concerts and six days of rehearsal. He failed to attend the first three days of rehearsals. He was replaced as the singer for his failure to turn up to these rehearsals. When he did turn up, he was not permitted to continue the contract.

This was a breach of warranty, so the concert organiser could not repudiate his contract which continued. The singer was, therefore, awarded damages for loss of earnings for the breach of his contract.

20.2.3 Innominate term

An **innominate term** is a term in a contract that is not clearly a condition or a warranty. Indeed, the essence of innominate terms is that they are neither conditions nor warranties, i.e. they are 'intermediate or indeterminate terms'. Rather the consequences of the breach of an innominate term can be those of a condition or a warranty, depending on the gravity or otherwise of the breach.

Key term

Innominate term – a term in a contract that is not defined as a condition or a warranty. Whether it is regarded as a condition or a warranty depends on the severity of the consequences of any breach of the term. Instead of insisting at the outset of the contract, the parties wait until the effect of the breach makes it a condition or warranty.

Many terms in contracts are not clearly either a condition or a warranty until the breach of that term has occurred, as in *Hong Kong Fir Shipping Co. Ltd v Kawasaki Kisen Kaisha Ltd* (1962).

Hong Kong Fir Shipping Co. Ltd v Kawasaki Kisen Kaisha Ltd (1962)

The defendants chartered a cargo ship from the claimants for two years. A term in the contract required that the ship should be 'in every way fitted for ordinary cargo service'. In fact there were problems with the ship's engine and the ship was not fully seaworthy. Eighteen weeks' use of the ship was lost while the ship was being repaired. The defendants repudiated the contract. Was the term a condition or a warranty?

The court said that not all contract terms could be simply divided into conditions and warranties; many contracts are more complex and

> *some breaches will, and others will not, give rise to an event which will deprive the party not in default of substantially the whole benefit which it was intended that he should obtain from the contract.*

Unless expressly provided for in the contract, the classification depends on the consequences of the breach. These are known as innominate terms. In fact the court decided this was only a breach of warranty so only damages could be awarded.

This is a straightforward solution to the problem where general terms can have a variety of breaches. The proper remedy is only discovered after the consequences of the breach have been identified. However, there is an element of uncertainty to the innominate term. The outcome of a particular breach is uncertain until the term has been construed taking into account the severity of the breach that has occurred.

Figure 20.1 Key facts chart for terms in a contract

	Brief legal rule	Case example
Condition in a contract	A term in a contract that is central to the contract, breach of which may allow the contract to be repudiated	*Poussard v Spiers and Pond* (1876)
Warranty in a contract	A minor term in a contract, breach of which does not end the contract but allows a claim for damages only	*Bettini v Gye* (1876)
Innominate term in a contract	A term in a contract that is not defined as a condition or a warranty. Whether it is treated as a condition or a warranty depends on the consequences of any breach of the term	*Hong Kong Fir Shipping Co. Ltd v Kawasaki Kisen Kaisha Ltd* (1962)

Figure 20.2 Key cases chart for terms in a contract

Case	Judgment
Poussard v Spiers and Pond (1876)	Her presence was central to the production; it was a condition entitling the producers to repudiate her contract for her non-attendance
Bettini v Gye (1876)	The rehearsals were not central to the contract to sing, so the concert organiser could not repudiate his contract
	He had not broken a condition in the contract
Hong Kong Fir Shipping Co. Ltd v Kawasaki Kisen Kaisha Ltd (1962)	Not all contracts could be simply divided into terms that are conditions and terms that are warranties
	Many contracts are more complex

20.3 Is a statement a mere representation or a term of the contract?

The distinction between a term and a mere representation is important in relation to remedies – if a term is not observed, this gives rise to a claim for breach of contract, whereas if a representation is untrue, the remedy is for misrepresentation. When negotiations are taking place, many things are discussed so that the terms of the contract are agreed. If what is said is a mere representation, then if it is untrue it will be a mere misrepresentation as we will see in Chapter 22. The difficulty is deciding whether what is said is a *term* or remains a mere *representation*.

The courts will take into account the following factors:

- the importance attached to the representation
- special knowledge or skill of the person making the statement
- any time lag between making the statement and making the contract
- whether there is a written contract.

20.3.1 The importance attached to the representation

Where the statement is obviously important to the contract, it will be seen as a term of the contract. This was demonstrated in *Couchman v Hill* (1947).

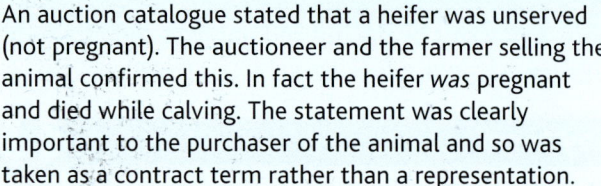

Couchman v Hill (1947)

An auction catalogue stated that a heifer was unserved (not pregnant). The auctioneer and the farmer selling the animal confirmed this. In fact the heifer *was* pregnant and died while calving. The statement was clearly important to the purchaser of the animal and so was taken as a contract term rather than a representation.

20.3.2 Special knowledge or skill of the person making the statement

There are two contrasting cases which show the importance of the skill expected of a person making a statement. The private seller of a car is not expected to have the same level of understanding about cars as a car dealer:

Oscar Chess v Williams (1957)

The private seller of a car believed it to be a 1948 model but it was actually much older. This statement was not a term of the contract.

Dick Bentley v Harold Smith Motors (1965)

The car dealer stated the car had done 20,000 miles when in fact it had done 100,000 miles. Even though that statement was not written in the contract, it was taken to be a term of the contract rather than a mere representation.

This distinction is important as the purchaser of the car could take action for breach of contract rather than for misrepresentation. In the *Dick Bentley* case it is crucial because the purchaser of the car would have lost his or her rights under misrepresentation – the law at the time would only have allowed a claim for rescission, which was not available in this case.

20.3.3 The time lag between the making of the statement and the making of the contract

Where a contract is made some time after negotiations and does not refer to the statement that has been made during negotiations, it is likely that the statement does not become a term of the contract. This can be seen in *Routledge v Mackay* (1954).

Figure 20.3 Key facts chart for term or representation in a contract

	Brief legal rule	Case example
The importance attached to the representation	Where the statement is obviously important to the contract it will be seen as a term of the contract	*Couchman v Hill* (1947)
Special knowledge or skill of the person making the statement	Where there is special knowledge or skill, the statement is more likely to be a term of the contract	*Oscar Chess v Williams* (1957) *Dick Bentley v Harold Smith Motors* (1965)
The time lag between making the statement and making the contract	Where a contract is made later and does not refer to the statement, it is likely that the statement does not become a term of the contract	*Routledge v Mackay* (1954)
Whether there is a written contract	The court tends to presume that everything the parties wanted to include as a term of the contract is put in the written contract	*Routledge v Mackay* (1954)

Figure 20.4 Key cases chart for term or representation in a contract

Case	Judgment
Couchman v Hill (1947)	The statement was clearly important to the purchaser of the animal and so was taken as a contract term rather than a representation
Oscar Chess v Williams (1957)	A private seller of a car believed it to be a 1948 model but was actually much older This statement was not a term of the contract, just a representation
Dick Bentley v Harold Smith Motors (1965)	The misleading mileage of a car was a term of the contract rather than a mere statement
Routledge v Mackay (1954)	It was presumed that the actual date of manufacture of the vehicle was not seen as important as it was not in the written contract

Routledge v Mackay (1954)

Both parties were private individuals and relied on the registration documents. The contract was made later and did not refer to the date of the vehicle. The time lag was seven days before it was written down. The actual date of manufacture was misstated by 12 years. The date of manufacture of the vehicle was not included in the written contract and the time gap between negotiations and the written contract was important, so the statement was a mere representation and not a term of the contract.

20.3.4 Whether there is a written contract

As we have seen in *Routledge v Mackay*, the court tends to presume that everything the parties wanted to include as a term of the contract is put in the written contract.

20.4 Terms implied by common law or statute

Terms can be implied into the contract by the common law or by statute. Statutory implied terms are seen in different Acts depending, for example, on whether the contract is business-to-business or business-to-consumer:

- In business-to-business contracts, terms may be implied by Acts such as the Sale of Goods Act 1979 and the Sale of Goods and Services Act 1982.
- In a contract between a business (trader) and a consumer, terms are implied by the Consumer Rights Act 2015.

However, as the Consumer Rights Act 2015 has similar provisions to the Sale of Goods Act 1979 and the Supply of Goods and Services Act 1982, interpretation of the earlier Acts will inform the meaning of many of the provisions of the Consumer Rights Act 2015.

20.4.1 Terms implied by common law

Terms can be implied by common law in two ways:

- through business efficacy and the officious bystander test
- by custom or prior dealings between the parties.

Terms implied through business efficacy and the officious bystander test

The courts will imply a term into a contract if the term is necessary to make sure that the contract works on a business-like basis. There is a two-part test for this:

- Is the term necessary to make the contract effective?
- If the parties to the contract had thought about it, would they have agreed that the suggested term was obviously going to be in the contract?

Business efficacy

An example of this can be seen in the case of *The Moorcock* (1889).

The Moorcock (1889)

The defendants owned a wharf with a jetty on the River Thames. They agreed to dock a ship and unload cargoes at the wharf. Both parties were aware at the time of contracting that this could involve the vessel being there at low tide, and that then the ship would rest on the bottom. When the ship grounded it broke up on a ridge of rock. The defendants stated there was no term covering this. The court implied a term that the ship would be at a safe mooring and that the ship would not be damaged when it settled at low tide.

The officious bystander test

The test can be seen in *Shirlaw v Southern Foundries Ltd* (1939), where it was stated:

> *Prima facie* that which in any contract is left to be implied and need not be expressed is something so obvious that it goes without saying; so that if, while the parties were making their bargain, an officious bystander were to suggest some express provision for it in their agreement, they would testily suppress him with a common 'Oh, of course!'

In *Hollier v Rambler Motors* (1972), the court accepted that a failure to sign a document on one occasion did not prevent the terms in that document being present in the contract if it was merely an oversight in not signing the document on that particular occasion.

Terms will not be implied if the parties would never have agreed to it had they thought about it. This was shown in *Shell UK Ltd v Lostock Garage Ltd* (1977).

Shell UK Ltd v Lostock Garage Ltd (1977)

In the contract, Shell supplied petrol and oil to Lostock who in return agreed to buy these products only from Shell. Shell later supplied petrol to other garages at lower prices as part of a price war. This forced Lostock to sell at a loss. Lostock argued there was a term in the contract that Shell would not abnormally discriminate against it. This argument failed as Shell would never have agreed to such a term.

Genuinely implied terms are what a reasonable person would have understood to be the intention of both parties in the context of the contract. *Egan v Static Control Components (Europe) Ltd* (2004) is a good example.

Egan v Static Control Components (Europe) Ltd (2004)

Static Control Components supplied Egan's company with components. Before 1999, Egan had signed three guarantees making him personally liable for the company's debts up to £75,000. In 1999, with the debt rising Egan was asked to repay in six weekly instalments and to sign a new guarantee for up to £150,000 in the same form as the previous guarantees. When the company went into liquidation Egan tried to argue that the 1999 guarantee only applied to goods supplied after it was signed. The court decided that a reasonable person would assume that the guarantee applied to both existing and future debts.

In a recent case, *Marks and Spencer plc v BNP Paribas Securities Services Trust Company (Jersey) Ltd* (2015), the Supreme Court has clarified the law relating to implied terms in contracts:

- Reasonableness is to be judged objectively – in considering what the parties would have agreed, 'one is not strictly concerned with the hypothetical answer of the actual parties, but with that of notional reasonable people in the position of the parties at the time at which they were contracting'.
- Fairness and acceptability to the parties are not enough – the fact that a term appears fair or that one considers that the parties would have agreed to it if it had been suggested are necessary but not sufficient grounds for implying it.
- The requirement for reasonableness and equitableness will usually add nothing to the other tests – 'if a term satisfies the other requirements, it is hard to think that it would not be reasonable and equitable'.

- The business efficacy and officious bystander tests are not cumulative – they can be alternatives in that only one needs to be satisfied, 'though it would be a rare case where only one of those two requirements would be met'.
- The officious bystander test may not be straightforward – it is important to formulate the question to be posed by the officious bystander 'with the utmost care'.
- The test of necessity for business efficacy involves a value judgement – it is not a test of absolute necessity, because the necessity is judged by reference to business efficacy. Lord Sumption suggested that it may be more helpful to say that 'a term can only be implied if, without the term, the contract would lack commercial or practical coherence'.

Terms implied by custom

Much of English law is founded on the law of custom. Some local customs survive, such as the one in the case of *Hutton v Warren* (1836).

Hutton v Warren (1836)

Local custom meant that at the end of an agricultural lease, a tenant farmer was entitled to an allowance for seed and labour on the land. The court decided that the terms of the lease must be viewed in the light of the custom.

Terms implied by prior dealings between the parties

The prior conduct of the parties may indicate terms to be implied, as shown in *Hillas v Arcos* (1932).

Hillas v Arcos (1932)

A contract drawn up in 1930 between the two parties included an option clause, allowing the claimants to buy a further 100,000 lengths of timber during 1931. The agreement for 1931 was otherwise quite vague as to the type of timber, etc. The 1930 timber contract was fulfilled.

In 1931, the claimants then wanted the further 100,000 lengths of timber but the defendants refused to deliver them. Their argument was that since the 1931 agreement was vague in many major aspects, it was therefore no more than a basis for further negotiations.

The court decided that, while the option clause lacked specific detail, it was implied that it would be on the same terms as the previous contract.

Figure 20.5 Key facts chart for implied terms in a contract

	Brief legal rule	Case example
Business efficacy and the officious bystander test	Is the term necessary to make the contract effective?	*The Moorcock* (1889)
Terms can be implied by custom	The terms of the lease must be viewed in the light of the custom	*Hutton v Warren* (1836)
Terms can be implied by a course of dealing between the parties	The court may imply a term that reflects the previous dealings between the parties	*Hillas v Arcos* (1932)
Terms will not be implied if the parties would never have agreed to them had they thought about them	Terms will not be implied if the parties would never have agreed to them had they thought about them	*Shell UK Ltd v Lostock Garage Ltd* (1977)
The implied terms reflect the clear intention of the parties	Genuinely implied terms are what a reasonable person would have understood to be the intention of both parties in the context of the contract	*Egan v Static Control Components (Europe) Ltd* (2004)
Reasonableness is to be judged objectively	It is not strictly concerned with the hypothetical answer of the actual parties, but with that of notional reasonable people in the position of the parties at the time at which they were contracting	*Marks and Spencer plc v BNP Paribas Securities Services Trust Company (Jersey) Ltd* (2015)

Figure 20.6 Key cases chart for implied terms in a contract

Case	Judgment
The Moorcock (1889)	There was an implied undertaking that the ship would be at a safe mooring that would not damage the ship
Hutton v Warren (1836)	Local custom meant that at the end of an agricultural lease, a tenant farmer was entitled to an allowance for seed and labour on the land
Hillas v Arcos (1932)	While the option clause lacked specific detail, nevertheless it was in the same terms as the contract of sale that had been completed if the option were to be taken up
Hollier v Rambler Motors (1972)	A failure to sign a document on one occasion did not prevent the terms in that document being present in the contract if it was merely an oversight in not signing the document on that particular occasion
Shell UK Ltd v Lostock Garage Ltd (1977)	Lostock argued there was a term in the contract that Shell would not abnormally discriminate against it This argument failed as Shell would never have agreed to such a term
Egan v Static Control Components (Europe) Ltd (2004)	The court decided that a reasonable person would assume that the guarantee applied to both existing and future debts
Marks and Spencer plc v BNP Paribas Securities Services Trust Company (Jersey) Ltd (2015)	The court set out the current position with respect to when terms may be implied in a contract

20.5 Specific terms implied by statute in relation to consumer contracts

20.5.1 The Consumer Rights Act 2015

The Consumer Rights Act 2015 brings together rights and remedies available to consumers when making a contract with a business. These contracts are defined as being between consumer and trader in the Act, with both 'consumer' and 'trader' being defined. With these contracts, terms are implied in the contract and 'rights' are given to the consumer and therefore impose a corresponding duty on the trader.

The Act also reforms and consolidates the law relating to unfair terms in consumer contracts and sets out specific remedies available to consumers in contracts to which the Act applies.

To whom does the Consumer Rights Act 2015 apply?

The Act applies to contracts and notices between a **consumer** and a **trader**.

> **Key term**
>
> **Consumer** – described in the Consumer Rights Act 2015 as 'an individual acting for purposes that are wholly or mainly outside that individual's trade, business, craft or profession'. Note that a company cannot be a 'consumer', as it is not an 'individual'.

This definition is wider than existing definitions, as it includes individuals who enter into contracts for a mixture of business and personal reasons, so long as the contracts are mainly for personal reasons. This means that if an author of a textbook, who is otherwise retired from work, buys computer software for his home computer and then uses the software to write part of the book, he will still be classified as a consumer. It is the trader who has to prove that an individual is not a consumer in the circumstances.

> **Key term**
>
> **Trader** – described in the Consumer Rights Act 2015 as 'a person acting for purposes relating to that person's trade, business, craft or profession, whether acting personally or through another person acting in the trader's name or on the trader's behalf'. Note that a trader can be a sole trader or a company or business partnership or any other form of business organisation.

This expressly provides that traders remain liable when dealing through a third party, as, for example, when dealing through an agent.

20.5.2 Terms implied into a contract to supply goods

The Consumer Rights Act 2015 applies to contracts of:

- sale
- hire

- hire-purchase
- other contracts for the transfer of goods.

Section 9 – the right of satisfactory quality

Section 9 of the Consumer Rights Act 2015 states, 'Every contract to supply goods is to be treated as including a term that the quality of the goods is satisfactory'.

Satisfactory quality is defined as being where the goods meet the standard that a reasonable person would consider satisfactory, taking account of:

- any description of the goods
- the price or other consideration for the goods (if relevant)
- all the other relevant circumstances.

The Act goes on to explain that the quality of goods includes their state and condition and takes into account:

- the fitness for all the purposes for which goods of that kind are usually supplied and their durability
- appearance and finish of the goods
- freedom from minor defects of the goods
- the safety of the goods.

However, this will not apply:

- with respect to defects specifically drawn to the consumer's attention before the contract is made
- where the consumer examines the goods before the contract is made in relation to any defect that the examination would have revealed, or
- where the goods have been sold after inspection of a sample and the defect would have been apparent on a reasonable examination of the sample.

Whether the goods are of satisfactory quality is an objective test based on the views of a 'reasonable person' rather than those of the trader/supplier or of the consumer.

In *Rogers v Parish (Scarborough) Ltd* (1987), a case involving the sale of a new Range Rover car, Lord Mustill stated:

> To identify the relevant expectation one must look at the factors listed in the subsection. The first is the description applied to the goods. In the present case the vehicle was sold as new. Deficiencies which might be acceptable in a second-hand vehicle were not to be expected in one purchased as new. Next, the description 'Range Rover' would conjure up a particular

set of expectations, not the same as those relating to an ordinary saloon car, as to the balance between performance, handling, comfort and resilience. The factor of price was also significant. At more than £14,000 this vehicle was, if not at the top end of the scale, well above the level of the ordinary family saloon. The buyer was entitled to value for his money.

> With these factors in mind, can it be said that the Range Rover as delivered was as fit for the purpose as the buyer could reasonably expect? The point does not admit of elaborate discussion. I can only say that to my mind the defects in engine, gearbox and bodywork, the existence of which is no longer in dispute, clearly demand a negative answer.'

This is very similar to the law under the Sale of Goods Act 1979, and we can assume that the case law under that Act will continue to apply. There are many examples of this relating to second-hand cars which can be explored in the following link: **www.newlawjournal.co.uk/content/risky-business-5**.

Activity
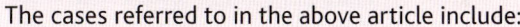

The cases referred to in the above article include:

- *Bartlett v Sidney Marcus Ltd* (1965)
- *Crowther v Shannon Motor Co.* (1975)
- *Lee v York Coach and Marine* (1977)
- *Keeley v Guy McDonald* (1984)
- *Lutton v Saville Tractors (Belfast) Ltd* (1986)
- *Shine v General Guarantee Corp. Ltd* (1988)
- *Business Applications Specialists Ltd v Nationwide Credit Corp. Ltd* (1988)

Select two cases and write down some brief facts and the decisions. Compare your cases with others in a group and debate whether there is a consistent approach in the cases.

Section 10 – the right of fitness for particular purpose

This section applies to a contract to supply goods if, before the contract is made, the consumer makes known to the trader (expressly or by implication) any particular purpose for which the consumer is contracting for the goods. In these circumstances there is an *implied* term that the goods are reasonably fit for that purpose, whether or not that is a purpose for which goods of that kind are usually supplied.

This term is again much the same as the provision in the Sale of Goods Act 1979.

Therefore, if the buyer is relying on the skill and judgement of the seller in buying the goods and has expressed a particular purpose for which the goods are required, the implied condition will be in the contract. This can be seen in *Baldry v Marshall* (1925).

Baldry v Marshall (1925)

The buyer had asked the seller to supply him with a fast, flexible and easily-managed car that would be comfortable and suitable for ordinary touring purposes. He then claimed that a Bugatti car sold to him was not fit for the purpose. The court agreed.

There is no need to state a purpose where the goods are being bought for their normal use, as in *Grant v Australian Knitting Mills Ltd* (1936) which involved underwear. There was no need to state that they were for wearing for the section to apply.

Where, however, the purchaser has a particular sensitivity that is not known to the seller, then so long as the goods are fit for the normal purpose to most people, there will be no breach of the requirement. This can be seen in the case of *Griffiths v Peter Conway Ltd* (1939), where the purchaser bought a coat specially made for her. The coat was fit for its purpose except that, because the purchaser had abnormally sensitive skin, the wearing of the coat caused her to contract dermatitis. Few people would have suffered in this way. Since she had not made the seller aware of this, the seller was not in breach of the implied term as to fitness for purpose.

Section 11 – the right relating to description

Section 11 of the Consumer Rights Act 2015 states, 'Every contract to supply goods by description is to be treated as including a term that the goods will match the description'.

This is again much the same as the equivalent in the Sale of Goods Act 1979. The description can be an implied description, for example when the goods are on a display. The description also includes relevant information that must be included in any statutory information relating to goods as set out in the Consumer Contracts (Information, Cancellation and Additional Charges) Regulations 2013.

There is also a provision that where the supply of goods is by reference to a model seen or examined by the consumer, then the goods supplied must match the model.

This has been seen to include the way in which goods are packaged.

The result can be harsh, as in *Re Moore and Co. Ltd and Landauer and Co.'s Arbitration* (1921), and also very sensible, as in *Beale v Taylor* (1967).

Re Moore and Co. Ltd and Landauer and Co.'s Arbitration (1921)

The contract was for tinned peaches packed in cartons of 30 tins. When the goods were delivered, many of the cartons contained 24 tins, although the total number of the tins was correct.

Beale v Taylor (1967)

The purchaser bought a car advertised as a 1961 Triumph Herald convertible. The rear half of the car was part of a 1961 Herald convertible car, but the front half was part of an earlier model, the two halves having been welded together. The rear of the car had a badge on it – '1200', which was first applied to the 1961 model. The front half had a smaller engine in it, not a 1200. The badge amounted to the description. The buyer was entitled to damages for breach of the then current Sale of Goods Act because, although the description of the car was not wholly false, the seller was selling a car of that description but it was not truly of that description.

Tip

Remember *Re Moore and Co.* when you look at the idea that performance must be complete and exact in Chapter 23.

20.5.3 Remedies for the breach of a term implied into a contract to supply goods

If the goods do not conform to the contract because of a breach of any of the rights we have studied, then there are new rights available to the consumer. These rights are cumulative, and are in addition to the usual contract remedies such as damages. The rights are:

- the short-term right to reject under s 20 of the Consumer Rights Act 2015
- the right to repair or replacement under s 23 of the Consumer Rights Act 2015
- the right to a price reduction or the final right to reject under s 24 of the Consumer Rights Act 2015.

Section 20 – the short-term right to reject

The short-term right to reject under s 20 must be exercised within 30 days of the delivery of the goods. Obviously the period will be shorter where the goods are perishable. Exercise of this right must be made clear to the trader by the consumer indicating to the trader that he or she is rejecting the goods and terminating the contract. The consumer is then entitled to a full refund.

The trader must bear any reasonable costs of returning the goods, other than any costs incurred by the consumer in returning the goods in person to the place where the consumer took physical possession of them. This is particularly important with respect to distance selling.

A refund must be given without undue delay, and in any event within 14 days, beginning with the day on which the trader agrees that the consumer is entitled to a refund. The refund must be given using the same means of payment as the consumer used, unless the consumer expressly agrees otherwise and the trader must not impose any fee on the consumer for making the refund.

Section 23 – the right to repair or replacement

If the s 20 right is not exercised by the consumer, he or she will have the right to repair or replacement under s 23. It would be impossible, for example, to replace faulty goods if they were unique. A replacement would also have to be identical, so that if the same make and model was no longer available, replacement would be impossible. A major factor determining whether either repair or replacement is disproportionate is if it would impose an unreasonable cost on the trader compared with the alternative remedy. If the consumer requires the trader to repair or replace the goods, the trader must do so within a reasonable time and without significant inconvenience to the consumer, and bear any necessary costs incurred in doing so. This includes the cost of any labour, materials or postage relating to the exercise of this right.

The consumer cannot require the trader to repair or replace the goods if it would be impossible, or disproportionate compared to other remedies. The trader must carry out any repairs within a reasonable time. This takes into account the nature of the goods and the purpose for which the goods were acquired. The fault complained of must have been present at the time of the original delivery.

Section 24 – the right to a price reduction or the final right to reject

If s 23 does not bring satisfaction, the consumer has the right to a price reduction or a final right to reject the goods and claim a refund under s 24. The trader can have only one attempt at repair or replacement for the consumer to have this right. Any refund is subject to a deduction for use. During the first six months any deduction for use is, at present, limited to motor vehicles.

Summary of remedies

Consumer remedies under the Consumer Rights Act 2015 for the implied terms are sometimes said to be sequential and tiered:

- a short-term right to reject and claim a refund within 30 days, which if not exercised leads to
- the right to repair or replacement and if this is unsatisfactory then
- the right to a price reduction or a final right to reject (and claim a refund) with a possible reduction for use of the item.

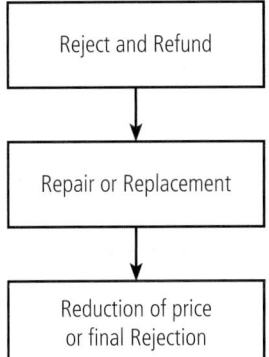

Figure 20.7 Remember the Rs!

Who has to show the non-conformity at time of supply for a breach of ss 9–11 (apart from short-term right to reject)?

Under s 19(14) and (15) of the Consumer Rights Act 2015, if a breach of the statutory rights, for example a fault in the goods supplied, arises in the first six months from delivery, it is presumed to have been present at the time of delivery. Therefore, if a fault is discovered within the first six months after buying the product, it is presumed to have been there since the time of purchase – unless the trader can prove otherwise. This applies where the consumer exercises his or her right to a repair or replacement or his or her right to a price reduction or the final right to reject. This does not apply where the consumer exercises the short-term right to reject.

If a fault develops after the first six months, the burden is on the consumer to prove that the product was faulty at the time of delivery.

20.5.4 Terms implied into a contract to supply services

Section 49 – reasonable care and skill

This section states that a contract to supply a service is to be treated as including a term that the trader must perform the service with reasonable care and skill. A contract to supply a service might be a contract to carry out building work, or to repair a bicycle. Such contracts often include both goods and services. The service element would include deciding what needed repair and the fitting of the parts to the bicycle. The parts themselves are a supply of goods. This is equivalent to the relevant section of the Supply of Goods and Services Act 1982, which the Consumer Rights Act 2015 replaced. Here the standard of care is equivalent to the standard of care expected in a claim in the tort of negligence. This is decided on a case-by-case basis and can be seen in the cases of *Thake v Maurice* (1986) and *Wilson v Best Travel* (1993).

Thake v Maurice (1986)

Mr and Mrs Thake already had five children so they decided that the husband should have a vasectomy. However, after the operation Mrs Thake became pregnant again and sued for breach of contract. There was an implied term that the surgeon would perform the operation to the standard of care and skill of a competent surgeon. The evidence was that he had reached that level of care and skill so the claim was unsuccessful.

Wilson v Best Travel (1993)

While on holiday in Greece, the claimant fell through a glass door and suffered injuries. The glass conformed to Greek but not British safety requirements. The court stated that, as the tour company had checked the premises to ensure the local safety regulations had been complied with and the danger posed by the glass would not cause 'reasonable holidaymakers' to decline to stay there, they had not breached the implied term.

Section 52 – performance within a reasonable time

This section states that the service has to be performed within a reasonable time where the contract does not expressly fix the time for the service to be performed, and does not say how it is to be fixed. This again is equivalent to the relevant section of the Supply of Goods and Services Act 1982, which the Consumer Rights Act 2015 replaced. This term applies where the contract does not have a term with respect to time and the service has not been completed or has taken longer than expected. What is a reasonable time is a question of fact which will depend on the circumstances.

The rights under ss 49 and 52 and the right of the trader to be paid a reasonable sum where no price is agreed, are subject to the possibility of pre-contract statements being incorporated into the contract. These are more likely to be quite detailed, particularly where the contract is for building work.

20.5.5 Remedies for the breach of a term implied into a contract to supply services

If the service does not conform to the contract, the consumer's rights are:

- the right to require repeat performance (s 55)
- the right to a price reduction (s 56).

Section 55 – the right to require repeat performance

This right requires the trader to perform the service again, to the extent necessary to complete its performance in accordance with the contract. If the right is demanded, and assuming that performance is not impossible, the trader must then provide it within a reasonable time and without significant inconvenience to the consumer. The trader must also bear any necessary costs incurred in doing so such as the cost of any labour or materials.

Section 56 – the right to a price reduction

This right is to reduce the price to the consumer by an appropriate amount for the trader's failure to perform the contract. This may result in the trader giving a refund, up to the full contract price.

This remedy is available only in two situations:

■ where completion by repeat performance is impossible, or

■ if the consumer has asked for repeat performance but the trader is in breach of the requirement to do it within a reasonable time and without significant interference to the consumer.

Activity

Read this scenario:

You have just bought a cup of coffee at a café. You have a loyalty card with the café, and as you have enough points on the card you get given a free toy.

The coffee makes you ill.

You give the toy to your niece but when she opens the box, the toy is broken.

1 List the express and implied terms or rights in each part of the scenario.

2 What rights do you have, and what rights does your niece have?

Summary

■ Terms are of three types:
  - conditions
  - warranties
  - innominate terms.

■ The courts have to decide whether a statement is a representation or a term.

■ Terms can be implied in a contract by the common law and/or by statute.

■ Breach of a term gives rise to different possible remedies.

■ The Consumer Rights Act 2015 uses the nomenclature of terms which provide 'rights' of consumers and duties of traders.

■ The Consumer Rights Act 2015 applies to contracts and notices between a 'consumer' and a 'trader'.

■ The Consumer Rights Act 2015 applies to contracts of sale, hire, hire-purchase and other contracts for the transfer of goods.

■ Terms implied into a contract to supply goods under the Consumer Rights Act 2015 are with respect to satisfactory quality, fitness for particular purpose and description.

■ Rights under the Consumer Rights Act 2015 include:
  - the short-term right to reject
  - the right to repair or replacement
  - the right to a price reduction
  - the final right to reject.

■ Terms implied into a contract to supply services under the Consumer Rights Act 2015 are to provide the service with reasonable care and skill and for performance within a reasonable time.

■ Remedies for the breach of a term implied into a contract to supply services under the Consumer Rights Act 2015 are a right to repeat performance and a right to a price reduction.

21 Contract terms: exclusion clauses

After reading this chapter, you should be able to:

■ Have a basic understanding of exclusion and limitation clauses
■ Understand common law control of exclusion clauses: rules relating to incorporation and construction
■ Understand statutory control of exclusion clauses: the Unfair Contract Terms Act 1977 and the Consumer Rights Act 2015

21.1 The nature of exclusion and limitation clauses

Exclusion clauses are terms in a contract that exclude or limit liability for a breach of the contract. They may also attempt to exclude liability in other areas of law, for example under the tort of negligence. Exclusion clauses also include terms in a contract that limit liability for a breach of contract or other loss. They are often found in standard form contracts and on notices.

There are many ways that a term of the contract tries to limit or exclude liability. For example, a term may attempt to restrict the value of any claim to the purchase price of the goods. Similarly it may try to exclude any claim for a defect to 14 days from the date of the contract. We have already seen that many contracts attempt to exclude the operation of the Contract (Rights of Third Parties) Act 1999.

Courts generally accept that the parties to a contract can agree any terms they like under the principle of freedom of contract. However, this view is balanced by the idea that often, during negotiations, one party is in a much stronger position than another. For example, as an individual or even as a business, you have little opportunity to negotiate the terms of a contract for a rail ticket or a mobile phone contract. The courts and Parliament have tried to find ways of limiting the effectiveness of an exclusion clause.

> **Tip**
>
> When considering exclusion clauses, first look at the common law approach through case law and see the result. If the clause is effective to exclude or limit liability, then look at the statutory provisions and see whether they reduce its effectiveness.

> **Key term**
>
> **Exclusion clause** – a term in a contract that prevents one party being liable for a breach of contract.

21.1.1 Rules relating to construction and interpretation of contracts

Many disputes are about the meaning of contracts and the terms that are in the contracts. The assumption is that each party to the contract understands that the terms agreed accurately recorded the contract. A dispute arises when one party to the contract argues that a term of the contract has one particular meaning and the other party disagrees. With respect to exclusion clauses, this is particularly important as an exclusion clause is usually put in a contract by someone in a stronger bargaining position. You can see this when you look at the terms and conditions of everyday contracts such as a mobile phone contract or a streaming contract. Most people agree to the terms without reading them or enquiring about the meaning of the terms. It is only when there is a problem that the contract and the meaning of the terms are considered. This is known as interpretation of the contract and there are a number of key principles in English law that guide the interpretation of the terms in a contract. We will consider this in detail later when we look at the *contra proferentem* rule in section 21.1.4 below.

The whole contract needs to be considered, rather than individual terms in isolation. The purpose is to establish the intention of the parties in making the contract.

Lord Halsbury, in *Glynn v Margetson* (1893), said:

> « Looking at the whole of the instrument and seeing what one must regard ... as its main purpose, one must reject words, indeed whole provisions, if they are inconsistent with what one assumes to be the main purpose of the contract. »

Contract interpretation is not an exact science. The rules of contract interpretation have developed over many years and there is no strictly defined approach. The cases suggest there are only guidelines, which does not help certainty. As with statutory interpretation, in recent years the general trend has been to move away from a literal approach to a purposive approach.

The starting point for analysis is the use of language in the contract. In *Pink Floyd Music Ltd v EMI Records Ltd* (2010), it was stated that ordinary English words will mean what they say. So if the words of the contract are clear and unambiguous, then it is assumed that is what the parties intended.

If the words are not clear and unambiguous, an objective test should be applied. In *Investors Compensation Scheme Ltd v West Bromwich Building Society* (1998), Lord Hoffman set out an objective test – what would a reasonable man interpret to be the meaning of the contract?

This is wider than just the words in the contract and can include relevant background information and contextual information. Thus the key issue is what the parties' understanding and intention were at the time the contract was made. In *M T Højgaard v E.ON Climate and Renewables UK Robin Rigg East Ltd* (2014), the court said that post-contract conduct is not usually a guide to interpretation.

It is possible to add a commercial, common sense angle to contract interpretation. This is obviously very wide but does allow common sense in business to be a relevant consideration when the actual meaning of the words is unclear and ambiguous.

21.1.2 Common law controls

A clause in a contract that seeks either to limit or exclude liability for breaches of the contract, is subject to all of the normal rules regarding terms, particularly those concerning incorporation of the term. Such terms are likely to seriously limit a party's rights under the contract. The first question to be considered by the court is whether the term is part of the contract. There are three matters to consider:

- whether the agreement is signed
- whether any notice with the term in it is incorporated in the contract
- whether the term is incorporated as a result of the previous dealings of the parties.

Whether the agreement is signed

Where a party has signed a written agreement, he or she is bound by that agreement, as in *L'Estrange v Graucob* (1934).

L'Estrange v Graucob (1934)

Mrs L'Estrange bought a cigarette vending machine from the defendant for use in her café. She signed a contract including a clause which excluded all implied conditions and warranties. The machine did not work properly and Mrs L'Estrange relied on the implied term that it was fit for purpose. However, she was bound by the exclusion clause in the contract, even though she had not read the contract.

However, if a party relying on an exclusion clause in a written document asks the other to sign it and, in response to a query from the other, misrepresents the effect of the clause, the clause will be interpreted in accordance with the misrepresentation and not with the written document. This is so even if the document is signed by the other. This was shown in *Curtis v Chemical Cleaning and Dyeing Co. Ltd* (1951).

Curtis v Chemical Cleaning and Dyeing Co. Ltd (1951)

Mrs Curtis took her wedding dress to be cleaned and was asked to sign a document that exempted the cleaners from liability for any damage 'howsoever arising'. Before signing the document, she asked what she was signing. She was told that it only referred to the fact that the cleaners would not accept liability for beads or sequins attached to the dress.

When the dress was returned, it had a large stain on it. The cleaners could not rely on the exclusion clause because of the oral assurances made to Mrs Curtis that they were only excluding liability for damage to beads and sequins.

Whether any notice with the term in it is incorporated in the contract by reasonable notice

This involves incorporating notices and forms into a contract, typically an unwritten contract. Incorporation can only happen if, at the time the contract was made, the unsigned document was brought to the attention of the person suffering the exclusion clause.

Any attempt to introduce new terms to the contract after acceptance will fail unless there is a new contract varying the original one or the original contract allows for variation of the terms. An example of price variation can be seen in most mobile phone contracts.

The problem of incorporation arises when the terms are not made clear when the contract is made. This can be seen in *Olley v Marlborough Court Hotel* (1949).

Olley v Marlborough Court Hotel (1949)

The claimants booked into the hotel at its reception desk. At this point a contract was formed. They later went out, leaving the key at reception as required. In their absence, someone took the key, entered their room and stole some of their belongings. The hotel claimed that they were not liable because of an exclusion clause. However, the clause was not incorporated in the contract since it was on a notice inside the Olleys' bedroom in the hotel and could not have been known about when they made the contract. This was the case even though they had the opportunity to read the notice before they left the room and their belongings and handed the key to reception as they went out.

The key point is whether it was brought to the attention of the other party before the contract was made. In *Olley v Marlborough Court*, it had not. The combination of notices, tickets and other documents may make it difficult for someone trying to rely on an exclusion clause to prove it was brought to the attention of the other party.

Activity

1 Compare the three ticket cases below and decide whether the exclusion clause in each case has been incorporated. You will need to justify your decision.
2 Find full reports of these cases online, and discover the decisions made by the courts.

Chapelton v Barry Urban District Council (1940)

Mr Chapelton hired two deckchairs on the beach at Barry Island, and received two tickets from the council's beach attendant on paying the hire charge for the chairs. Next to the deckchairs was a sign which gave the price and time limit, but did not refer to any exclusion clauses. However, on the back of the tickets it stated, 'The council will not be liable for any accident or damage arising from the hire of the chair'.

Mr Chapelton did not read the ticket as he thought it was merely a receipt so he would not be asked to pay again during the day. The canvas on one chair was defective and the chair collapsed, injuring him. The council tried to rely on their exclusion clause as a defence to a claim for his injuries.

Thompson v LMS Railway (1930)

Mrs Thompson was illiterate and could not read. She went on a railway excursion, and was given a ticket with the words, 'Excursion: for conditions see back'.

On the back of the ticket was a notice referring customers to the conditions printed in the company's timetables. These conditions excluded liability for any injury. She was injured on the journey and claimed for damages.

Thornton v Shoe Lane Parking Ltd (1971)

The claimant was injured in a car park owned by the defendants. At the entrance to the car park by the barrier where a ticket was issued by a machine, there was a notice that, as well as giving the charges, stated that parking was at the owner's risk. On the ticket was printed the words, 'This ticket is issued subject to the conditions of issue as displayed on the premises'.

Notices inside the car park then listed the conditions of the contract including an exclusion clause covering both damage and personal injury.

On this basis, an exclusion clause will only be incorporated into a contract when on an objective analysis it is contained in a document that has contractual significance. Lord Denning stated in the Thornton case:

> The customer is bound by the exempting condition if he knows that the ticket is issued subject to it; or, if the company did what was reasonably sufficient to give him notice of it. … it is so wide and so destructive of rights that the Court should not hold any man bound by it unless it is drawn to his attention in the most explicit way. … In order to give sufficient notice, it

would need to be printed in red ink with a red hand pointing to it – or something equally startling. "

Figure 21.1 Summary of the working of the reasonable notice cases

1 There must be a contractual document, with reference to the distinction between such a document and a receipt, as illustrated by *Chapelton v Barry*
2 There must be reasonable steps to draw the exclusion clause to the other party's attention, with reference to cases such as *Parker v SE Railway Co.*
3 The reasonable notice must be given before conclusion of a contract by acceptance of an offer – *Olley*, *Thornton* etc.

Whether the term is incorporated as a result of the previous dealings of the parties

If the parties have dealt on the same terms in the past, it is possible to imply knowledge of the clause from the past dealings provided that there has been a consistent course of dealing. In *Hollier v Rambler Motors* (1972), the court accepted that a failure to sign a document on one occasion did not prevent the terms in that document being present in the contract if it was merely an oversight in not signing the document on that particular occasion. It could be argued that the court was trying to avoid an exclusion clause in a standard form contract. Hollier had been to this garage on three or four occasions in the past five years before, and he had usually signed an invoice which said, 'the company is not responsible for damage caused by fire to customers' cars on the premises'. Had he taken the car to the garage on the occasion in question, he would no doubt have signed the document with the exclusion clause in it.

Hollier v Rambler Motors (1972)

Mr Hollier telephoned Rambler and spoke to the manager. He told him that he wanted some repair work done to the car. The manager said that the defendants could not do anything about it for the moment, but if the plaintiff would have it towed or sent in they would attend to the defects and put them in order. Mr Hollier agreed. Those were the only terms of the agreement, expressed over the telephone. Salmom LJ said:

" There would, however, obviously be an implied term that the defendants would carry out the repairs and look after his car with reasonable skill and care; and there would also be an implied term that the plaintiff would pay a fair and reasonable price for the repairs. "

The car was taken to the garage. While it was at the garage a fire broke out, as a result of which substantial damage was done to the car. Mr Hollier had been to this garage on three or four occasions in the past five years before, and he had usually signed an invoice which said, among other terms, 'The company is not responsible for damage caused by fire to customers' cars on the premises'.

The court decided that it was possible that the terms would be implied, but there was insufficient frequency in making the contract to justify that conclusion in this case.

However, the courts are reluctant to find that to be the case, for example in *McCutcheon v David MacBrayne Ltd* (1964).

McCutcheon v David MacBrayne Ltd (1964)

The claimant had often used the defendants' ferries. Sometimes, but not always, he was asked to sign a document (a risk note) including an exclusion clause. On this occasion, one of his relatives took the car to the ferry. The relative received a receipt which referred to notices containing conditions displayed on the ferry company premises. He did not read the receipt and was not asked to sign it. The ferry sank and the car was destroyed. The court decided there was no consistent course of action that allowed it to assume that the claimant knew that the exclusion clause was always present, so it was not incorporated in the contract.

21.1.3 The effect of exclusion clauses on third parties to the contract

As we have seen, the doctrine of privity usually prevents a third party from relying on the terms of a contract. This means an exclusion clause in a contract may not offer protection to parties other than the parties to the contract.

In *Scruttons Ltd v Midland Silicones Ltd* (1961), the claimant was the owner of goods which were shipped for it by a carrier. The contract limited the liability of the carrier for damage caused to the goods to $500. The carrier contracted with the defendant to unload the goods. When doing so, the defendant negligently damaged them. The defendant was not party to the contract between the owner and the carrier and so the doctrine of privity of contract prevented the defendant from taking the benefit of the limitation of liability to $500.

One success among many attempts to evade the consequences of the privity rule in this context is found in *New Zealand Shipping Co. v Satterthwaite* (1974). The facts were very similar to those in *Scruttons Ltd v Midland*

Silicones Ltd, but the exclusion clause between the owner and the carrier was expressly stated to cover anyone engaged by the carrier to assist in dealing with the goods, even though not party to the contract between owner and carrier. The Privy Council got round the privity of contract difficulty by holding that, when the owner entered into the contract with the carrier, the owner was in effect also making an offer (promise) to anyone who would assist the carrier that the exclusion clause would extend to that person. The act of assisting the carrier, performed by the defendant in unloading the goods, was both the acceptance of the owner's offer and the consideration for the owner's promise. So, it created a separate unilateral contract between the owner and the defendant and is an example also of consideration being the performance of an existing duty owed to a third person, since the defendant was already bound by contract with the carrier to unload the goods (see the discussion of consideration in Chapter 19).

Much of the difficulty encountered in such cases may now be eliminated by the provisions of s 1(6) of the Contracts (Rights of Third Parties) Act 1999, which permit the third party to enforce any terms which would exclude or limit liability. In *New Zealand Shipping Co. v Satterthwaite,* for instance, the contract between the owner and the carrier 'expressly identified the defendant … as a member of a class or as answering a particular description' (s 1(3)) and expressly provided that the defendant 'may in his own right enforce a term of the contract' (s 1(2)) by extending the cover provided by the exclusion clause to the defendant.

21.1.4 The *contra proferentem* rule

The *contra proferentem* 'rule' is a principle designed to assist in the interpretation of the meaning of the terms in a contract. It is not confined to terms which exclude or limit liability but its more general application to terms of any kind, especially in commercial contracts, is now very questionable. Consequently, it is of interest mainly in the discussion of exclusion and limitation of liability. The rule asserts that, where there is ambiguity or uncertainty in the meaning or scope of a term, it should be interpreted against the person who introduced it, and who seeks to rely on it. After all, that person has broken the contract in some way and is now trying to avoid some or all of the liability for doing so.

In the context of terms excluding or limiting liability, suppose that there are two possible meanings of the term. The first is a narrow one which would reduce the scope of the exclusion or limitation of liability. The second is a broader one which would leave the scope of the exclusion or limitation correspondingly broad. Obviously, the party seeking to rely on the exclusion will argue for the broad meaning but the *contra proferentem* rule will point towards the narrow meaning. So, in *Hollier v Rambler Motors* (1972), the term excluding liability for damage caused by fire to customers' cars on the premises could have covered damage caused only without negligence (narrow meaning) or caused in any way, including negligently (broad meaning). Using the *contra proferentem* rule, the court opted for the narrow meaning, arguing that much clearer words would have been required to exclude liability for negligence in such circumstances.

Key term

Contra proferentem – where there is doubt about the meaning of a term in a contract, the words will be construed against the person who put them in the contract.

It is clear from recent cases (*Transocean Drilling UK Ltd v Providence Resources plc* (2016), *Persimmon Homes Ltd v Ove Arup and Partners Ltd* (2017)) that, even in the context of terms excluding and limiting liability, the *contra proferentem* rule now has little application to commercial contracts where the parties bargain on equal terms, allocating potential losses between each other (with scope to insure against the losses), and doing so in words which are clear and unambiguous. Yet even in the commercial context, there are cases which indicate that the rule, or at least the notion of construing the term narrowly, continues to have some significance.

Transocean Drilling UK Ltd v Providence Resources plc (2016)

This case involved a claim for loss of use by Providence of oil exploration rigs off the coast of Ireland. Normally, it is assumed that exclusion clauses should be construed *contra proferentem*. However, the agreement in this case was a sophisticated arrangement which was drawn up for parties of equal bargaining power. The exclusion clause benefited both parties, and was part of a scheme for allocating losses between the parties.

The court stated that the *contra proferentem* principle is an approach to be used where the term is both one-sided and ambiguous. If the meaning of the words is clear, then the rule is not to be used.

Persimmon Homes Ltd v Ove Arup and Partners Ltd (2017)

Ove Arup were a firm of engineers engaged by Persimmon Homes, which was part of a consortium, to provide a variety of services in relation to the development of a large site at Barry Quays in South Wales. The consortium considered that the quantity of asbestos contaminating the site was substantially more than had been expected from Arup's report. If Arup had been negligent in failing to identify and report more accurately upon the asbestos, would an exclusion clause in the contract exempt Arup from all liability in relation to any asbestos-related losses?

The Court of Appeal decided that the meaning of the clauses was clear and unambiguous and should be given effect, so the *contra proferentem* rule was not relevant.

In *Oliver Nobahar-Cookson v The Hut Group* (2016), the Court of Appeal confirmed that, if necessary to resolve ambiguity, exclusion clauses should be narrowly construed.

Oliver Nobahar-Cookson v The Hut Group (2016)

The claimant company bought the defendant company. The defendant gave undertakings about many matters, such as its accounts, business and assets. The contract provided that any claim for breach of those undertakings must be served on the defendant as soon as reasonably practicable and, in any event, within 20 business days

'after becoming aware of the matter'. The ambiguity lay in that phrase since it could have meant:

1 aware of the facts giving rise to the claim even if unaware that those facts did give rise to a claim

2 aware that there might be a claim, or

3 aware of the claim and the proper basis for it.

The narrowest construction was (3) and the broadest was (1). Arguing that, if 'linguistic, contextual and purposive analysis' (the normal process of interpretation) could not resolve the ambiguity, then a narrow interpretation should be adopted, Briggs LJ adopted construction (3) and found for the claimant, who had acted within 20 days from becoming aware that there was a well-founded basis for a claim. In doing so, Briggs LJ said that, in contrast with the trial judge, who had rejected any application of *contra proferentem*, he had found that he was greatly assisted by the notion of adopting a narrow construction, though he also said that this had nothing to do with issues of who introduced the term into the contract and who sought to rely on it (both aspects of the *contra proferentem* rule as traditionally understood).

Note that in a 'consumer contract' (a contract between a trader and a consumer), s 69 of the Consumer Rights Act 2015 states that if a term or consumer notice 'could have different meanings', the meaning that is most favourable to the consumer is to prevail.

Figure 21.2 Key facts chart for exclusion clauses

	Brief legal rule	Case example
Exclusion clause definition	Exclusion clauses are terms in a contract that exclude or limit liability for a breach of the contract	
Is the term incorporated in the contract (1)	Where a party has signed a written agreement, he or she is bound by that agreement	*L'Estrange v Graucob* (1934)
Is the term incorporated in the contract (2)	Whether exclusion clauses are only incorporated into a contract requires the party subject to the clause to know of the clause at the time the contract was made	*Olley v Marlborough Court Hotel* (1949)
Is the term incorporated in the contract – the ticket cases	The combination of notices, tickets and other documents may make it difficult for someone trying to rely on an exclusion clause to prove it was brought to the attention of the other party	*Chapelton v Barry Urban District Council* (1940) *Thompson v LMS Railway* (1930) *Thornton v Shoe Lane Parking Ltd* (1971)
Is the term incorporated in the contract (3)	Is the term incorporated as a result of the previous dealings of the parties?	*McCutcheon v David MacBrayne Ltd* (1964)
The *contra proferentem* rule	The *contra proferentem* principle is an approach to be used only where the term is both one-sided and ambiguous	*Transocean Drilling UK Ltd v Providence Resources plc* (2016) *Persimmon Homes Ltd v Ove Arup and Partners Ltd* (2017) *Oliver Nobahar-Cookson v The Hut Group* (2016)

Figure 21.3 Key cases chart for exclusion clauses

Case	Judgment
L'Estrange v Graucob (1934)	Mrs L'Estrange was bound by the exclusion clause in the contract for the cigarette vending machine, regardless of the fact that she had not read it
Curtis v Chemical Cleaning and Dyeing Co. Ltd (1951)	The cleaners could not rely on the exclusion clause because of the oral explanation made to Mrs Curtis that they were only excluding liability for damage to beads and sequins
Olley v Marlborough Court Hotel (1949)	The clause was not incorporated in the contract since it was on a notice on a wall inside the Olleys' bedroom in the hotel and could not have been known about when they made the contract
Chapelton v Barry Urban District Council (1940)	It was unreasonable to assume that Mr Chapelton would automatically understand that the ticket was a contractual document, and the council was liable for his injuries
Thompson v LMS Railway (1930)	It was common knowledge that railway journeys were contracts and that there were terms of carriage involved The fact that Mrs Thompson was illiterate and could not read the ticket did not alter the legal position
Thornton v Shoe Lane Parking Ltd (1971)	The customer is bound by the terms of the contract as he can assume that all the terms are set out in the first notice as in *Chapelton v Barry Urban District Council* (1940)
McCutcheon v David MacBrayne Ltd (1964)	Previous dealings are only relevant if they prove knowledge of the terms and actual, not constructive, assent to them
Transocean Drilling UK Ltd v Providence Resources plc (2016)	If the exclusion clause is clear, *contra proferentem* has no application
Persimmon Homes Ltd v Ove Arup and Partners Ltd (2017)	Where the meaning of the clauses are clear and unambiguous they should be given effect, so the *contra proferentem* rule was not relevant
Oliver Nobahar-Cookson v The Hut Group (2016)	If necessary to resolve ambiguity, exclusion clauses should be narrowly construed

21.2 Statutory control of exclusion clauses

Where an exclusion clause is incorporated as part of a contract, there are statutory provisions that may make the clause invalid and of no effect. Statutory controls exist to deal with an imbalance between the parties to a contract. As we have seen, exclusion clauses are put in a contract by the party with the stronger bargaining position. In most consumer contracts, there is no opportunity to negotiate most of the terms of the contract.

However, there are two principal provisions provided by Parliament:

■ the Unfair Contract Terms Act 1977 – applies to exclusions for liability in tort as well as contractual breaches
■ the Consumer Rights Act 2015 – applies to contracts between traders and consumers.

The current state of play can be seen in Figure 21.4.

Figure 21.4 Summary of implied terms statutory provisions

Contractual relationship	Description of term(s)	Method of incorporation	Exclusion/limitation of liability for breach
Trader/Consumer	Title, description, satisfactory quality, fitness for purpose	Consumer Rights Act 2015	Prohibited by Consumer Rights Act 2015
	Reasonable care and skill Reasonable time for performance	Consumer Rights Act 2015	Prohibited by Consumer Rights Act 2015
	Other	Express or implied	Permitted if 'fair'
Business/Business	Title, description	Sale of Goods Act 1979 Supply of Goods and Services Act 1982	Prohibited by Unfair Contract Terms Act 1977
	Satisfactory quality, fitness for purpose	Sale of Goods Act 1979 Supply of Goods and Services Act 1982	Permitted by Unfair Contract Terms Act 1977 subject to 'reasonableness'
	Reasonable care and skill Reasonable time for performance	Supply of Goods and Services Act 1982	Permitted, but if one party deals on the other's written standard terms of business, it must satisfy 'reasonableness'
	Other	Express or implied	Permitted, but if one party deals on the other's written standard terms of business, it must satisfy 'reasonableness'
Private	Title, description	Sale of Goods Act 1979 Supply of Goods and Services Act 1982	Prohibited by Unfair Contract Terms Act 1977
	Other	Express or implied	Permitted

21.2.1 The Unfair Contract Terms Act 1977

The Unfair Contract Terms Act 1977 provides the main protection against exclusion clauses in non-consumer contracts.

It contains a test of reasonableness to be applied to exclusion clauses.

Exclusions and limitations made void by the Act

Certain types of exclusion clauses are invalidated by the Act and will therefore be unenforceable:

■ Under s 2(1), a person cannot exclude liability for death or personal injury caused by negligence.
■ Under s 6(1), the implied condition as to title (the Sale of Goods Act 1979 and s 7 of the Supply of Goods and Services Act 1982) cannot be excluded.

Section 3 – exclusions depending for their validity on a test of reasonableness

Section 3 imposes a reasonableness test to contracts where one party is subject to the other's standard written terms of business.

The test of reasonableness

Guidelines on what is reasonable are contained in both s 11 and Sch 2 of the Act. As these are only guidelines, the test is one that depends on all the circumstances of the case, and ultimately is for judges to interpret.

Section 11(5) requires the party who inserts the clause in the contract, and who seeks to rely on it, to show that it is reasonable in all the circumstances. An example is *Warren v Truprint Ltd* (1986).

Warren v Truprint Ltd (1986)

This case involved the development and printing of photographs. The contract contained a limitation clause where the defendants were responsible only for a replacement film in the event of failure to develop and print the photographs. Truprint were unable to show that this clause was reasonable when it lost a couple's silver wedding photos.

There are three tests of reasonableness:

1 Section 11(1) concerns exclusion clauses in general. The test is whether the insertion of the term in the contract is reasonable in the light of what was known to the parties at the time when the contract was made. This is sometimes called the knowledge test. This can be seen in the case of *Smith v Eric S Bush* (1990).

Smith v Eric S Bush (1990)

Surveyors negligently carried out a paid-for valuation on a building and a defect was missed which later resulted in loss to the purchaser. The surveyors and the mortgage application contained clauses excluding liability for the accuracy of the valuation report. The inclusion of the exclusion clause was not reasonable.

2 Section 11(2) covers exclusion clauses involving breaches of the implied conditions in the Sale of Goods Act 1979 and Supply of Goods and Service, Act 1982 in business-to-business dealings. The criteria are set out in schedule 2 of the Unfair Contract Terms Act 1977:

  - the strength of the bargaining position of the parties relative to each other, taking into account (among other things) alternative means of meeting the customer's requirements
  - whether the customer received an inducement to agree to the term, or in accepting it had an opportunity of entering into a similar contract with other persons, but without having to accept a similar term
  - whether the customer knew of the existence and extent of the term (knowing, among other things, any custom of the trade and any previous dealing between the parties)
  - where the term excludes or restricts any relevant liability if some condition is not complied with, whether it was reasonable at the time of the contract to expect that

compliance with that condition would be practicable
  - whether the goods were manufactured, processed or adapted to the special order of the customer.

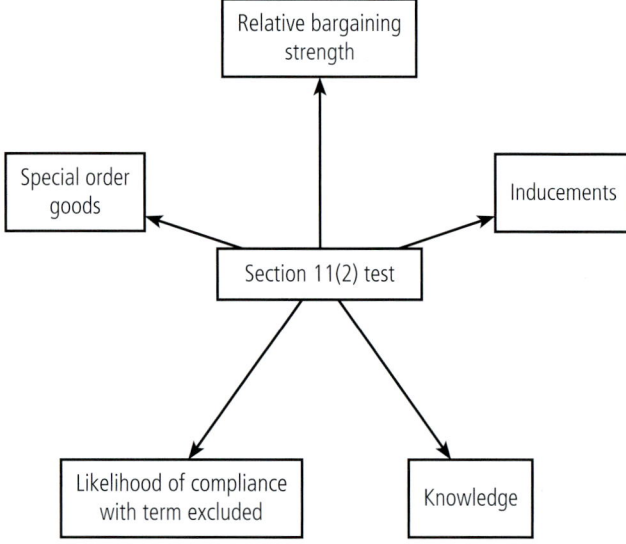

Figure 21.5 The s 11(2) test

An example of an exclusion clause being found to be reasonable can be seen in *Watford Electronics Ltd v Sanderson CFL Ltd* (2001).

Watford Electronics Ltd v Sanderson CFL Ltd (2001)

The claimant bought software from the defendant. The system failed to perform. In the defendant's standard terms there was a clause limiting any liability to the price of the goods supplied. The court said that it was a reasonable term since the parties were of equal bargaining power and the limitation clause was subject to negotiation when the contract was made.

3 Section 11(4) specifically relates to **limitation clauses**. There are two criteria:
  - the resources which the defendant could expect to be available for meeting his or her liability, should it arise
  - how far it was open to the defendant to cover him- or herself by insurance against any successful claim.

Key term

Limitation clause – a term in a contract that sets an upper limit on liability for breach of contract.

An example is *George Mitchell Ltd v Finney Lock Seeds Ltd* (1983).

George Mitchell Ltd v Finney Lock Seeds Ltd (1983)

The claimant ordered winter cabbage seed from the defendant at a cost of £201.60. The seed did not match the description and produced plants that were unfit for resale. The entire crop was lost, at a cost of £61,000.

The contract limited liability to replacement of the goods or a refund in price. The court stated the clause was not reasonable because:

- the breach arose from the seller's negligence
- the seller could have insured against crop failure at a modest cost
- in the past the seller had settled claims which exceeded the limitation sum – this showed that the seller himself did not always consider the clause fair and reasonable.

Figure 21.6 Key cases chart for statutory controls of exclusion clauses

Case	Judgment
Warren v Truprint Ltd (1986)	Section 11(5) of the Unfair Contract Terms Act 1977 requires the party who inserts the clause in the contract, and who seeks to rely on it, to show that it is reasonable in all the circumstances
Smith v Eric S Bush (1990)	The test is whether the insertion of the term in the contract is reasonable in the light of what was known to the parties at the time when the contract was made This is sometimes called the knowledge test
Watford Electronics Ltd v Sanderson CFL Ltd (2001)	The exclusion clause was a reasonable term since the parties were of equal bargaining power and the limitation clause was subject to negotiation when the contract was made
George Mitchell Ltd v Finney Lock Seeds Ltd (1983)	Section 11(4) of the Unfair Contract Terms Act 1977 specifically relates to limitation clauses and not exclusion clauses, as in this case

21.2.2 The Consumer Rights Act 2015

The Consumer Rights Act 2015 covers contracts between traders and consumers. It includes:

- a 'fairness test' for enforceability of terms and of consumer notices
- a provision that the main subject matter of the contract or terms that set the price are only exempt from the test of fairness if they are 'transparent and prominent'
- a 'grey list' of potentially unfair clauses in consumer contracts.

There are three main sections of the Act which set out the bars on exclusion clauses – ss 31, 57 and 65.

Section 31

Section 31 prohibits a term excluding or limiting liability, including for the following sections of the Act with respect to sale of goods:

- s 9 (goods to be of satisfactory quality)
- s 10 (goods to be fit for particular purpose)
- s 11 (goods to be as described)
- s 14 (goods to match a model seen or examined)
- s 15 (installation as part of conformity of the goods with the contract).

Section 57

Section 57 prohibits a term excluding or limiting liability, for the supply of services under the following sections of the Act:

- s 49 (service to be performed with reasonable care and skill)
- s 50 (information about trader or service to be binding)
- s 51 (reasonable price)
- s 52 (reasonable time).

Section 65

Section 65 prohibits exclusion or restriction of liability for death or personal injury resulting from negligence.

General fairness of terms

Under s 62, there is a requirement for all consumer contract terms and notices to be fair. The Act defines 'unfair' terms as those which put the consumer at a disadvantage, by limiting the consumer's rights or disproportionately increasing his or her obligations as compared to the trader's rights and obligations. However, a court should take into account the specific circumstances existing when the term was agreed, other terms in the contract and the nature of the subject matter of the contract.

This fairness test is supplemented by a so-called 'grey list' of terms. This is a non-exhaustive list of terms that may be unfair.

In particular, terms relating to the main subject matter of the contract or terms that set the price are not subject to the test of fairness, if they are both:

- transparent – in plain and intelligible language and, if in writing, legible, and
- prominent – brought to the consumer's attention in such a way that the average consumer would be aware of the term.

Written terms in consumer notices must also be transparent. So this could be in any communication or announcement, as long as it is reasonable to assume it can be seen or heard by a consumer.

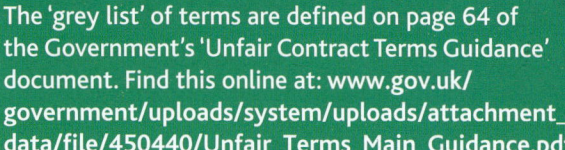

Look online

The 'grey list' of terms are defined on page 64 of the Government's 'Unfair Contract Terms Guidance' document. Find this online at: www.gov.uk/government/uploads/system/uploads/attachment_data/file/450440/Unfair_Terms_Main_Guidance.pdf.

Activity

Using the scenario in Chapter 20, you discover that the cafe limits liability for its food and drink to the price paid for the food and drink. Additionally, the loyalty card specifically excludes the Contracts (Rights of Third Parties) Act 1999. How would this change your answers to that scenario?

Summary

- Exclusion clauses are sometimes excluded from a contract by the operation of the common law.
- Judges have done their best to make the exclusion clauses ineffective.
- Statutory protection is more geared to consumers than to businesses.
- Different statutes cover different types of contract, which can lead to confusion.

- The Consumer Rights Act 2015 may need to be interpreted by reference to cases on legislation such as the Sale of Goods Act 1979.
- The combined effect of terms and restrictions on their use is beneficial to consumers, but goes against the principle of freedom of contract.

22 Vitiating factors

After reading this chapter, you should be able to:
- Understand the concept of a vitiating factor in a contract
- Understand misrepresentation, including omission in consumer contexts, and remedies
- Understand economic duress and its remedies
- Apply the law to factual situations.

22.1 What is a vitiating factor?

A **vitiating factor** makes a contract **void** or **voidable**. A contract is void if it has no legal standing.

Key terms

Vitiating factor – something that makes a contract void or voidable.

Void – a void contract is one that is declared to be a nullity, in other words, it never had legal effect. A void contract is said to be void *ab initio* (from the beginning).

Voidable – a voidable contract can be made void in certain circumstances. If the right to make it void is not exercised then the contract remains valid.

In this chapter, we will consider two vitiating factors that make a contract voidable:
- misrepresentation
- economic duress.

22.2 The nature of misrepresentation

In Chapter 20, section 20.3 we considered whether a statement is a mere representation or a term of the contract.

A **misrepresentation** only occurs during the formation of a contract: representations are statements that influence a decision on whether or not to make a contract, and are misrepresentations when false.

The effect of misrepresentation is to make the contract voidable. This means that the contract is valid unless a party to the contract who has suffered the misrepresentation takes action to seek to end the contract. This is known as rescission of the contract and is a discretionary remedy of the court. Rescission

treats the contract as if it had never existed. This means the parties would be put back in the positions they were in before the contract was made. This is known as *restitutio in integrum*.

Key term

Misrepresentation – a false statement of material fact made by a party to the contract that induces the other party to enter the contract.

We need to explore the following elements of this definition:
- a false statement
- of material fact
- made by a party to the contract
- that induces the other party to enter the contract.

22.2.1 False statement

A statement is usually written or verbal, although it does not have to be written or verbal. It could be anything that would influence the other's decision, as in *Spice Girls Ltd v Aprilia World Service BV* (2000).

Spice Girls Ltd v Aprilia World Service BV (2000)

The Spice Girls had signed a sponsorship agreement with Aprilia. While the agreement was being negotiated, unknown to Aprilia, a member of the group, Geri Halliwell, had given notice to leave the group. Filming of promotional material took place with all the girls together, but when one left it made the films worthless for promotional purposes. The court decided that by all of them attending, the group represented that none of them intended to leave the group and none of them was aware that one member intended to. This was a misrepresentation.

To be a misrepresentation, the statement made must be false, meaning it is not true or accurate. The extent of the person's knowledge of the accuracy of the statement when it is made defines the type of misrepresentation it might be.

Because there must be a statement to be a misrepresentation, silence cannot be a misrepresentation. There is no obligation on a person wishing to enter a contract to make any statement about what is being offered – but anything said in that respect must be true, as in *Fletcher v Krell* (1873).

Fletcher v Krell (1873)

A woman applied for a job of governess. She was not asked and she did not state that she was divorced. In Victorian times this would mean she would not be offered the job. The court decided that there was no misrepresentation as she was under no duty to disclose her marital status and she had not been asked about it.

There are, however, the following qualifications on this principle:

- change of circumstances
- the making of a half-truth
- confidential relationships.

Once a statement has been made, even if it is true when made, it can become a misrepresentation if it becomes false before the contract is made. This was shown in *With v O'Flanagan* (1936).

With v O'Flanagan (1936)

A doctor accurately stated the profits of his medical practice with a view to inducing purchasers to buy the practice. However, between the statement and the contract being made, the doctor fell ill and many of the patients left the practice. This made the original statement inaccurate. The court decided he had to tell the purchaser of the changed situation.

Therefore, a person must correct information where the situation has changed between making the representation and the acceptance of the offer.

Similarly, silence can be a misrepresentation where a statement made is a half-truth. What is not said is a non-disclosure, and may be a misrepresentation as the maker of the statement has a duty to reveal the whole truth of the situation. This can be seen in the case of *Dimmock v Hallett* (1866).

Dimmock v Hallett (1866)

A seller of land told the purchaser truthfully that there were tenants on the land. This was exactly what the purchaser wanted. However, he did not complete the statement by telling the purchaser that all the tenants were leaving. The court decided that this part-truth was a misrepresentation.

Where the relationship between the parties is based on trust then silence may be a misrepresentation. This was shown in *Tate v Williamson* (1866).

Tate v Williamson (1866)

A financial adviser advised his client to sell some land for less than half its value so that his client could clear his debts. The adviser then purchased the land himself but did not tell his client that he had done so. The court decided that the adviser's failure to disclose that he was intending to buy the land personally was a breach of trust and was therefore a misrepresentation.

Where a contract is a contract of 'utmost good faith' (*uberrimae fidei*) then all material facts must be disclosed whether asked about or not. This is most commonly seen in contracts of insurance, for example in *Lambert v Co-operative Insurance Society* (1975).

Lambert v Co-operative Insurance Society (1975)

A woman renewed her jewellery insurance policy. She did not tell the insurance company that her husband had recently been convicted of conspiracy to steal. This was an important fact which would have affected the insurance's decision whether to renew the insurance and, if so, at what premium. Her silence about the conviction was a misrepresentation. The company was entitled to avoid the policy and refuse to pay her claim.

22.2.2 Material fact

The misrepresentation must be of a material fact. This means that it would have led a person to make the contract and did in fact influence the mind of the person making the contract.

It must be a statement of fact rather than a statement of opinion. A statement of future intention can be seen as a 'fact' if at the time of making the statement it is what the person intends to do. If he or she does not really intend to do something, he or she misrepresents his or her state of mind, which is a fact.

Statements of opinion

In general, a statement of opinion which is honestly believed by the maker of the statement is not a statement of fact and, therefore, if the opinion proves to be false, it will not support a claim for misrepresentation. This is illustrated by *Bisset v Wilkinson* (1927) and *Edgington v Fitzmaurice* (1885).

But if the opinion was not honestly held by the person stating it, it is regarded as a statement of fact rather than one of opinion.

Bisset v Wilkinson (1927)

The seller of farmland that had never had sheep on it was asked by the buyer how many sheep it could take. Although not a sheep farmer, he stated that he thought it would support about 2000. This turned out to be false. However, as he genuinely believed his opinion to be accurate, it was not a misrepresentation.

Edgington v Fitzmaurice (1885)

The claimant invested in a company. The directors of the company falsely stated that the investment was to be used to complete alterations to the buildings of the company and other developments. In fact it was used to pay off existing debts. The representation was seen as a statement of fact rather than just future intention, as the directors did not have the intention to make alterations, etc. This was a misrepresentation.

Smith v Land and House Property Corporation (1884)

The seller of a property described it as 'let to Mr Frederick Fleck (a most desirable tenant) ... thus offering a first class investment'. The purchaser contracted to buy it, but before completion of the purchase refused to complete when he discovered that the tenant owed rent to the owner. It was held that the statement that Fleck was a 'most desirable tenant' was not one of opinion but of fact as, given that the seller knew that it was false, he had misrepresented the fact that he held that opinion.

Statements of intention

A statement of intention – a promise to do something in the future – is generally not one of fact, since a fact relates to a past event or something in existence. However, a statement of intention will amount to a statement of fact if the maker of the statement has no intention of carrying it out, as he or she is then misrepresenting the fact that he or she possesses the intention in question. As the court stated in *Edgington v Fitzmaurice* (1885), 'The state of a man's mind is as much a fact as the state of his digestion.'

22.2.3 Made by a party to the contract

This means that a person is not liable for statements made by others unless they are his or her agent. This means, for example, that a newspaper review of an item cannot be a misrepresentation. It should be noted that this limitation does not apply in the law of tort and negligent misstatements such as in the case of *Hedley Byrne and Co. Ltd v Heller and Partners Ltd* (1964), discussed in Chapter 14, section 14.1.2.

22.2.4 Induces the other party to enter the contract

This means that the statement must lead the other into making the contract, and must be a critical part of making the decision. The statement must be important to the person making the contract, and he or she must have relied on the statement made rather than his or her own judgement or information he or she obtained elsewhere for there to be a misrepresentation. This was shown in *Attwood v Small* (1838).

Attwood v Small (1838)

The seller of a mine made a false statement to the purchaser about the earnings from a mine. The buyer instructed a surveyor to confirm this statement, which he did (incorrectly). The purchaser bought the mine and then discovered the statement to be untrue. There was no misrepresentation as the purchaser relied on the survey report and not the seller's statement.

It does not matter if the victim could have discovered the truth by taking reasonable steps or it was unreasonable to rely on the untrue statement. The fact that the untrue statement was relied upon is enough to make it amount to a misrepresentation, as in *Redgrave v Hurd* (1881).

Redgrave v Hurd (1881)

The purchaser of a solicitor's practice was given a set of accounts to look at. The seller verbally misled the purchaser as to the true earnings. He relied on the statement and did not look at the accounts. Had he done so, he would have seen that the seller's statement was false. He was entitled to rely on the seller's statement, which, as it was untrue, was a misrepresentation.

In *Museprime Properties Ltd v Adhill Properties Ltd* (1990), it was decided that what the reasonable person would, or would not, have done is irrelevant.

Museprime Properties Ltd v Adhill Properties Ltd (1990)

The purchaser of property relied on inaccurate statements about rents made in auction particulars. The defendant argued that no 'reasonable' purchaser would have relied on these statements and would have made other enquiries. However, as the purchaser had relied on the statements, there was reliance and could be a misrepresentation.

22.2.5 Misrepresentation – omissions in consumer context

Section 12 of the Consumer Rights Act 2015 covers pre-contract information included in a contract to supply goods. The trader has to provide certain information to the consumer before the contract becomes binding. A change to any of that information, made before entering into the contract or later, is not effective unless expressly agreed between the consumer and the trader.

Under the Consumer Protection (Amendment) Regulations 2014, a misleading omission is where a trader deliberately misses out key information that the consumer might need to make an informed decision about the purchase of goods or services. All consumer information must be displayed clearly. For the purposes of the Regulations, it is considered misleading if a trader does any of the following:

- omits material information that the average consumer needs, according to the context, to make an informed transactional decision
- hides or provides material information in an unclear, unintelligible, ambiguous or untimely manner
- fails to identify the commercial intent of the commercial practice if not already apparent from the context.

In effect, the obscure presentation of consumer information will be treated as a misleading omission.

Figure 22.1 Key facts chart for the nature of misrepresentation

	Brief legal rule	Case example
Misrepresentation definition	Misrepresentation is a false statement of material fact made by a party to the contract that induces the other party to enter the contract	
There must be a false statement	If nothing is said or asked it cannot be a statement and, if false, misrepresentation	*Fletcher v Krell* (1873)
Silence is not usually a misrepresentation unless there are changed facts	A statement which is true when made but becomes false before the contract is made must be corrected	*With v O'Flanagan* (1936)
The statement does not have to be written or verbal	The statement can be made pictorially or by appearance	*Spice Girls Ltd v Aprilia World Service BV* (2000)
The misrepresentation must be of a material fact	It must be a statement of fact rather than a statement of opinion.	*Bisset v Wilkinson* (1927)
It must induce the other party to enter the contract	The statement must be important to the person making the contract and he or she must have relied on the statement made rather than his or her own judgement	*Redgrave v Hurd* (1881)

Figure 22.2 Key cases chart for the nature of misrepresentation

Case	Judgment
Fletcher v Krell (1873)	There was no misrepresentation as she was under no duty to disclose her marital status and she had not been asked about it
With v O'Flanagan (1936)	There was a continuing representation; he had to tell any prospective purchaser of changes to the situation
Dimmock v Hallett (1866)	A part-truth was a misrepresentation
Tate v Williamson (1866)	The adviser's failure to disclose that he was intending to buy the land personally was a breach of trust and was therefore a misrepresentation
Lambert v Co-operative Insurance Society (1975)	Where a contract is a contract of 'utmost good faith' (*uberrimae fidei*) then all material facts must be disclosed whether asked about or not An example is a contract of insurance
Spice Girls Ltd v Aprilia World Service BV (2000)	By all the Spice Girls attending photos for an advertising campaign, the group represented that none of them intended to leave the group and none of them was aware that one member intended to
Bisset v Wilkinson (1927)	An expression of the seller's honestly held opinions was not a misrepresentation
Edgington v Fitzmaurice (1885)	A statement of future intention can be seen as a statement of fact if it was proved that the maker had no such intention and therefore it is a misrepresentation
Attwood v Small (1838)	A person must have relied on the statement made rather than his or her own judgement or information he or she obtained elsewhere for there to be a misrepresentation
Redgrave v Hurd (1881)	The fact that the untrue statement was relied upon is enough to make it amount to a misrepresentation even if he could easily have found out the truth
Museprime Properties Ltd v Adhill Properties Ltd (1990)	What the reasonable person would, or would not, have done is irrelevant; if there is reliance on the false statement, it can be a misrepresentation

22.3 Different types of misrepresentation

There are three possible types of misrepresentation:

- innocent
- negligent
- fraudulent.

Each has different possible remedies.

22.3.1 Innocent misrepresentation

The Misrepresentation Act 1967 clarifies the definition of innocent misrepresentation as one which is genuinely held on reasonable grounds. This is a false statement made honestly – the person making the statement always believed it to be true and there is no element of negligence in that belief. The remedy is either rescission or damages instead of rescission. This is under the courts' discretion, as stated in the Misrepresentation Act 1967.

Rescission and damages are not both available for innocent misrepresentation (as for fraudulent and negligent misrepresentation) but only as alternative remedies.

22.3.2 Negligent misrepresentation

Historically, any misrepresentation that was not fraudulent was an innocent misrepresentation, and the only possible outcome was if the court was minded to award rescission. The law on negligent misrepresentation started with the case of *Hedley Byrne v Heller* (1964) with the possibility of a claim in the law of tort.

Negligent misrepresentation is a false statement made by a person who believed the statement was true, but who had no reasonable grounds for believing it to be true.

There are two types of negligent misrepresentation:

- under the common law tort of negligence
- under the Misrepresentation Act 1967.

Under the common law tort of negligence

In the case of *Hedley Byrne v Heller* (1964), the court suggested that a claim for a misrepresentation based on negligence would be allowed. This is discussed in more detail in Chapter 14, section 14.1.2.

Under the Misrepresentation Act 1967

Section 2(1) of the Misrepresentation Act created a statutory liability for negligent misrepresentation which does not require there to be a special relationship between the parties. All that is needed is for there to be a misrepresentation which results in a contract and the victim suffers loss. This is much broader than any of the previous possible claims. It is particularly appropriate where the claimant is unable to prove fraud.

Under the Act, once the victim has proved there was a misrepresentation the burden of proof is then on the person making the statement that there were reasonable grounds to believe the statement was true. This reverses the usual burden of proof in civil cases when it is for the victim to prove the case. This means it is preferable for the victim to use the Act rather than the *Hedley Byrne* principle. There may, of course, be other factors that may influence the finding of negligent misrepresentation. An example can be seen in the case of *Howard Marine v Ogden and Sons* (1978).

Howard Marine v Ogden and Sons (1978)

Ogden hired two dredgers from Howard Marine for £1800 per week to carry out works for Northumbrian Water Authority. So as to complete a tender for the work, Ogden asked Howard for the capacity of the barge. Howard checked Lloyds Register which stated the capacity was 850 cubic metres. In fact the entry was incorrect and the capacity was much lower. Therefore the work carried out by Ogden took much longer and cost a great deal more to perform.

Howard argued that they had reasonable grounds for believing the statement to be true as they had checked Lloyds Register. However, as they had the registration document of the barge, which stated the correct capacity, this argument failed.

If the misrepresentation is negligently made, the claimant has the choice of suing under the Misrepresentation Act 1967 or under the law of tort following the principles set out in *Hedley Byrne v Heller*. If the Act is chosen, then the relationship required for a claim using *Hedley Byrne v Heller* does not need to be established.

22.3.3 Fraudulent misrepresentation

Fraudulent misrepresentation has its origins in the tort of deceit. *Derry v Peek* (1889) set this out and stated that fraudulent misrepresentation is when there is a statement made without belief in the truth. This includes where the person making the representation knows it to be untrue, or is reckless as to whether or not it is true. To avoid being found to have made a fraudulent misrepresentation, the person who made the statement must believe it is true.

Derry v Peek (1889)

A tram company used horses to pull its trams. The directors of the company believed that under a recent Act of Parliament, the Board of Trade would consent to the company using motor-driven trams and that this consent was a formality, but did not check.

The use of powered trams would make the company more profitable and the directors advertised for investors for the company on this basis. The company did not obtain the consent and the company shares dropped in value. The purchasers of the shares sued for their losses.

There was no fraudulent misrepresentation because the issuers of the prospectus had applied for permission and reasonably expected it to be granted. The directors were only careless as to whether what they said was true (possibly either innocent or negligent misrepresentation).

In the news

Developer loses £5 million lawsuit

Richard Butler-Creagh hoped to make millions by acting as an intermediary in the sale of Fawley Court near Henley-on-Thames in Buckinghamshire. He went to court to sue the company involved for the disputed £5 million fee. But Mr Justice Eady threw out the legal action against Aida Hersham and her company Cherrilow Ltd after he found that Mr Butler-Creagh had constructed an elaborate scheme to convince the defendants to pay him millions for doing 'effectively nothing'.

Mr Butler-Creagh had acquired the contract for the grand house from the Marian Fathers, a Roman Catholic order, for £22.5 million in 2008. He claimed Ms Hersham owed him a £5 million 'facilitating fee' after he agreed to let her 'step into his shoes' and buy the impressive property. Ms Hersham denied that there had been any such agreement.

Cherrilow eventually bought the property for £13 million.

Mr Justice Eady threw out the action after finding Mr Butler-Creagh had failed to establish his case, adding that it was clear the developer had a scheme in mind. He said, 'In truth, and in law, he had no other role than as an officious bystander.' Mr Butler-Creagh, added the judge, 'told lie after lie' in his dealings with the Marian Fathers and Ms Hersham.

The judge concluded that Cherrilow did rely, as always intended by Mr Butler-Creagh, on false misrepresentations of fact and had it not done so, the purchase would not have been made. The company claims it has lost £9,864,940 from the transaction.

Source: Adapted from an article by Damien Gayle in the Daily Mail online, 7 October 2011

A fraudulent misrepresentation includes not only an out-and-out incorrect answer to an inquiry but can also be an overly optimistic view of the position. This was shown in *Greenridge Luton One Ltd v Kempton Investments Ltd* (2016).

Greenridge Luton One Ltd v Kempton Investments Ltd (2016)

The High Court considered a claim for fraudulent misrepresentation and held that a buyer of a commercial property was entitled to have its deposit returned because of an untrue representation made recklessly or fraudulently by the seller that there were no service charge arrears, when in fact there were such arrears. The buyer was also entitled to damages for deceit in the sum of £395,948.

The damages seek to put the claimant into the position he or she was in before the misrepresentation was made. On the facts of this case, the judge had no difficulty in finding reliance on the statement and that the buyer was induced to enter the contract by the misrepresentation.

22.4 Remedies for misrepresentation

22.4.1 Innocent misrepresentation

The remedy of rescission

Rescission is an equitable remedy. All equitable remedies are discretionary, which means that the court will only award it if it is fair to do so in all the circumstances. The idea of rescission means the parties are returned to the positions they were in before the contract was made. It is then as if the contract had never existed. The justification for this rule is that the misrepresentation induced the contract, and had the misrepresented party known the truth there would have been no contract.

However, the remedy of rescission will not be available in the following situations:

- restitution to the original pre-contract position is impossible
- the contract is affirmed
- delay
- a third party has gained rights over the property.

Restitution to the original pre-contract position is impossible

This was shown in *Clarke v Dickson* (1858).

Clarke v Dickson (1858)

The claimant was misled into becoming a partner. Rescission was not available – he could not return the partnership as the firm had become a limited company.

The contract is affirmed

Affirmation is where the innocent party decides to carry on with the contract despite being aware of the misrepresentation. The right to seek to rescind the contract is then lost, as demonstrated in *Long v Lloyd* (1958).

Long v Lloyd (1958)

The claimant was told by the seller that a lorry was in excellent condition, but shortly after the sale it broke down. The claimant noticed faults with the lorry and contacted the defendant who offered to pay half the repairs, which he agreed to.

The lorry broke down again shortly afterwards and the claimant wanted to rescind the contract. The court refused to grant rescission because by persevering with the lorry after the first breakdown and agreeing the share of the cost of repairs, he had indicated his willingness to continue with the contract and so affirmed the contract.

Delay

One maxim of equity is that delay defeats equity. The idea behind this is that once a contract has been completed, any complaints are likely to arise within a short time and after that you can assume there are no major problems. This can be seen in *Leaf v International Galleries* (1950).

Leaf v International Galleries (1950)

In 1944, the claimant had purchased a picture of Salisbury Cathedral from the defendant. He was told that it was by Constable but found out it was not by the famous artist when he tried to sell it five years later. Even though he had no means of finding out the truth until he came to sell the painting, rescission was not allowed because of the delay in bringing his claim.

A third party has gained rights over the property

Where someone else has gained an interest in the goods, then rescission will not be granted as this would be unfair on the innocent third party. The third party must be an innocent purchaser of the goods for value (for value means that the innocent purchaser must supply consideration), without notice, and he must have acquired title before the victim has communicated the intention to rescind to the rogue, or to someone standing in the place of the rogue, as in *Car and Universal Finance v Caldwell* (1965) (the defendant told police and the AA of the fraud before the car was sold on to the innocent purchaser). This was shown in *Lewis v Averay* (1972).

Lewis v Averay (1972)

Lewis sold his car and let the buyer take the car away in exchange for a cheque. The cheque was worthless. He had accepted it as he was persuaded by the fraudster that he was the well-known actor Richard Greene who had played Robin Hood in the television series. In fact, the rogue posed as Richard Greene but signed the cheque 'R A Green'. The fraudster then sold it on to the defendant, an innocent third party.

The original seller's only effective remedy was to claim rescission and to ask for the car to be returned to him by the innocent third party. The claim for rescission failed as, between the two innocent parties, it would be more unfair to deprive the third party of the car purchased in good faith.

The remedy of damages

There is no right to damages for an innocent misrepresentation. In *Salt v Stratstone Specialist Ltd (t/a Stratstone Cadillac Newcastle)* (2015), Longmore LJ made it clear that the 'normal remedy for misrepresentation is rescission'.

However, the court has discretion to award damages instead of rescission under s 2(2) of the Misrepresentation Act 1967. In *Government of Zanzibar v British Aerospace (Lancaster House) Ltd* (2000), it was stated that damages under s 2(2) were awarded in place of rescission – this meant that a party who had lost the right to rescind the contract, for example because of delay, could also not claim damages under this section.

22.4.2 Negligent misrepresentation

The remedies for negligent misrepresentation are rescission and/or damages. The remedy of rescission has been discussed above. The remedy of damages, if the *Hedley Byrne* principle is applied, are calculated according to the law of tort. It also means that the principle of contributory negligence under the Law Reform (Contributory Negligence) Act 1943 will apply, so damages may be reduced accordingly.

> See *AQA A-Level Law for AS/A Level*, Chapter 26 for more information on damages in tort.

If the claim is under the Misrepresentation Act 1967, damages are again calculated according to a tort measure, because a claim under the Act is made where fraud cannot be proved. In *Royscot Trust Ltd v Rogerson* (1991) the Court of Appeal decided that the measure of damages under s 2(1) is the same as in fraud.

Royscot Trust Ltd v Rogerson (1991)

A car dealer negligently misrepresented to a finance company the amount of a deposit paid for a car by a purchaser. The finance company lost money when the purchaser defaulted on the hire-purchase agreement. The court decided that the damages for negligent misrepresentation under the Act are the same as for fraud.

22.4.3 Fraudulent misrepresentation

The remedies are rescission and damages in the tort of deceit. Both of these have been discussed above. An example of damages in the tort of deceit can be seen in the case of *Smith New Court v Scrimgeour Vickers* (1996), where the court awarded the victim damages based on the difference between the amount paid for shares and the final sale price – more than the usual award of damages in a contract.

Damages based on fraudulent misrepresentation aim to put the victim in the position he or she was in before the tort (the misrepresentation) occurred. However, the court seems willing to take the view that contractual damages may be appropriate in certain circumstances. In *East v Maurer* (1991), the Court of Appeal stated that it was possible in principle to recover damages for loss of profit following a fraudulent misrepresentation.

Tort-based damages do not entirely exclude a possible element of loss of profit, which could be based on the profit that the representee might have made had he not made the contract with the representor but had made a different deal with someone else. This is still not a contractual measure of damages, which would be for the loss of profits expected had the deal gone through and been as represented. The difference between damages in contract and tort are discussed further at section 22.4.5.

East v Maurer (1991)

The claimant had bought a hairdressing salon from the defendant, who continued to trade from another he owned, despite telling the purchaser that he did not intend to continue to work at his other salon. As a result, the purchaser lost business to the defendant. The victim suffered a loss of profit as a result which was only recoverable under breach of contract, not fraudulent misrepresentation.

The court decided the victim would have purchased a different business if the truth had been known. The tort calculation of damages awarded him the profit he would have earned from that business.

22.4.4 Damages and misrepresentation

We have already seen that the normal remedy for misrepresentation is rescission. If the defendant's misrepresentation was relied upon by the claimant and had some influence upon the claimant's entering into the agreement, then the claimant should be entitled to rescind the transaction and be put back into the position he or she was in before the contract was made. However, damages can be awarded in some circumstances:

- Misrepresentation Act 1967, s 2(1) – gives a right to damages for negligent misrepresentation.
- Misrepresentation Act 1967, s 2(2) – gives a court the discretion to make an award of damages in lieu of rescission for a negligent or innocent misrepresentation. In the case of negligent

misrepresentation, this could be in addition to damages under s 2(1) but would have to take account of such damages.
- Damages in the tort of deceit where there is fraudulent misrepresentation.

The circumstances in which a court might regard rescission as inequitable and so make the award of damages instead are provided by s 2(2) of the Misrepresentation Act 1967:

> **if of opinion that it would be equitable to do so, having regard to the nature of the misrepresentation and the loss that would be caused by it if the contract were upheld, as well as to the loss that rescission would cause to the other party.**

This can be seen in the case of *Sindall v Cambridgeshire County Council* (1993).

Sindall v Cambridgeshire County Council (1993)

The claimant paid £5 million to Cambridgeshire County Council for building land, not knowing that it contained a buried sewer pipe which would obstruct its building plans. By the time the claimant found out, the property market had collapsed and the land was worth a much smaller amount, so the claimant wanted to rescind and get back the full purchase price, plus interest. It was held that there was no misrepresentation but, if there had been, it would have been innocent. Then rescission would be denied because the only loss to the claimant was the £18,000 which would have been required to re-locate the pipe. This could easily have been recompensed in damages, whereas rescission would cost the council a huge amount in restoring the purchase price plus interest, and this was inequitable.

The measure of damages under s 2(2) must be recompense for loss related specifically to the misrepresentation. In *Sindall v Cambridgeshire County Council* that would have been the £18,000 necessary to preserve the value of the land as it was agreed in the contract. There would have been no compensation for the loss in market value of the land, which had nothing to do with the misrepresentation.

22.4.5 The difference between damages in contract and in tort

In contract the aim of a damages award is to put the innocent party in the position he or she would have been in had the contract been performed. In tort the claimant is not complaining of failure to implement a promise. Damages in tort aim to restore the claimant to his or her pre-incident position. In tort it is not a question of loss of bargain.

If, for example, D is selling his classic car. He tells C that it was once owned by John Lennon. D genuinely believes this but has no reasonable grounds for doing so. In fact, it is untrue. If true, the car is worth £80,000. If false, it is worth £50,000.

C buys the car from D for £60,000. Assume that the representation becomes a term of the contract. If he had got what he bargained for, the car would be worth £80,000 but it is actually worth only £50,000.

In contract the damages for breach of the term are £30,000 (expected value minus actual value).

If the statement remained a mere representation, the tort measure for negligent (s 2(1)) misrepresentation would be £10,000. He has an asset worth £50,000 but he paid £60,000 for it. To restore him to his position prior to entering the contract, he needs £10,000 (value of purchase minus actual value).

In simple practical terms, if the representee would have made a good bargain had everything been as it was stated to be, he or she should try to sue in contract. If he or she would have made a bad bargain, he or she should try to sue for fraudulent or negligent misrepresentation.

Figure 22.3 Summary chart of types of misrepresentation

Type	Level of truth	Remedy	Example
Innocent misrepresentation	The maker of the statement always believes it to be true	Rescission or damages under Misrepresentation Act 1967, s 2(2)	*Leaf v International Galleries* (1950)
Negligent misrepresentation	The maker of the statement believed the statement to be true, but had no reasonable grounds for believing it to be true	Rescission and damages Misrepresentation Act 1967, s 2(1) and (2)	*Esso Petroleum v Mardon* (1976)
Fraudulent misrepresentation	The maker of the statement knew the statement to be false	Rescission and damages in the tort of deceit	*Cherrilow Ltd v Butler-Creagh* (2011)

Figure 22.4 Key facts chart for remedies for misrepresentation

	Brief legal rule	Case example
Rescission definition	The equitable remedy of rescission means the parties are returned to the positions they were in before the contract was made	
Rescission is not allowed (1) – cannot restore the pre-contract situation	Rescission is not allowed if the parties cannot be restored to their pre-contractual position	*Clarke v Dickson* (1858)
Rescission is not allowed (2) – affirmation	Affirmation is where the innocent party decides to carry on with the contract despite being aware of the misrepresentation	*Long v Lloyd* (1958)
Rescission is not allowed (3) – delay	A delay in bringing the claim for misrepresentation to court will mean rescission is not available as a remedy Delay defeats equity	*Leaf v International Galleries* (1950)
Rescission is not allowed (4) – a third party has gained rights over the property	Where someone else has gained an interest in the goods then rescission will not be granted as this would be unfair on the innocent third party	*Lewis v Averay* (1972)

Figure 22.5 Key cases chart for remedies for misrepresentation

Case	Judgment
Clarke v Dickson (1858)	Rescission was not available as the victim could not return to the original position
Long v Lloyd (1958)	By persevering with the lorry after the first breakdown, he had indicated his willingness to continue with the contract and so affirmed the contract
Leaf v International Galleries (1950)	Even though he had no means of finding out the truth until he came to sell the painting, rescission was not allowed because of the delay in bringing his claim
Lewis v Averay (1972)	The claim for rescission failed as in the circumstances it would be unfair to deprive the third party of the car purchased in good faith
Hedley Byrne and Co. Ltd v Heller and Partners Ltd (1964)	There could be a duty of care in negligence even though there was no contractual relationship
Goodwill v British Pregnancy Advisory Service (1996)	There was no special relationship of proximity between the BPAS and Miss Goodwill Therefore there was no duty of care owed
Esso Petroleum Company Ltd v Mardon (1976)	Here there was proximity, and a duty of care in negligence, between the parties as they were involved in negotiations for a contract between them
Howard Marine v Ogden and Sons (1978)	They had not discharged the burden of proof by demonstrating they had reasonable grounds for believing it to be true; they had the registration document of the barge which stated the correct capacity, so it could not be innocent misrepresentation
Royscot Trust Ltd v Rogerson (1991)	The measure of damages for negligent misrepresentation under the Misrepresentation Act 1967 is the same as for fraud
Derry v Peek (1889)	The directors of the company were only careless as to whether what they said was true, so it was not fraudulent misrepresentation
Smith New Court v Scrimgeour Vickers (1996)	In fraudulent misrepresentation, the remedies are rescission and damages in the tort of deceit
East v Maurer (1991)	It is possible to recover damages for loss of profit following a fraudulent misrepresentation

Activity

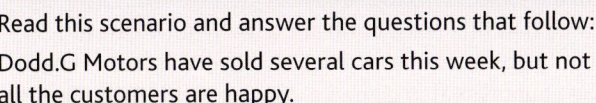

Read this scenario and answer the questions that follow:

Dodd.G Motors have sold several cars this week, but not all the customers are happy.

Alphonso knew nothing about cars so just asked for an Italian car. He was sold a car made for an Italian company in Poland.

Beryl wanted a car with low mileage. She was sold a car with the odometer showing 17,000 miles. Dodd.G Motors knew that it had done 70,000 miles.

Cal asked for a particular make and model of car with the more powerful engine option. The car he was sold had the less powerful engine. Dodd.G Motors could have checked this from the car's identity but did not bother to do so.

Desi bought a car that was described as 'one owner'. The car's document showed one registered keeper, but did not show that it had been specially imported to the UK from Japan where it had had two previous owners. Dodd.G Motors had no reason to believe the car was an import.

1 Decide what type of misrepresentation is present (if any) in each scenario.

2 Explain what remedies might be available in each possible claim against Dodd.G Motors.

22.5 Economic duress – definition

Any contract made where one party is forced into it should not be valid. This could be as result of **undue influence**, **duress** or **economic duress**.

■ Undue influence occurs where one party entered the contract as a result of pressure which deprived that party of independent judgement. This is presumed where the relationship is one of trust and one party will benefit at the expense of another. This includes relationships such as doctor and patient, solicitor and client and religious advisor and disciple, where there is a presumption of undue influence. An example is *Allcard v Skinner* (1882), where a novice nun gave nearly all her money to the mother superior. In that case it was said:

> " The court interferes, not on the ground that any wrongful act has in fact been committed by the donee, but on the ground of public policy, and to prevent the relations which existed between the parties and the influence arising therefrom being abused. "

■ A contract signed under duress might involve threats, such as blackmail, or even violence to persuade one party to sign the contract. The threats of violence to the person would amount to crimes or torts if those threats were carried out. For example, in *Barton v Armstrong* (1976) death threats were made. Threats to property were not always treated as duress but the situation today is that the combination of the ideas of undue influence and duress have led to the development of economic duress.

■ Economic duress – the threat to damage a business or a person financially – is a common form of duress, and the court will consider each case involving economic duress according to its individual circumstances. The threats must be 'improperly coercive', though not necessarily unlawful. The difficulty is to decide when the line is crossed between, say, tough business bargaining, exploiting weaknesses to advantage, and the use of improper pressure.

Key terms

Undue influence – there is a relationship between the parties which has been exploited by one party to gain an unfair advantage.

Duress – when someone enters into a contract as a result of threats of violence to the person which would amount to crimes or torts if those threats were carried out.

Economic duress – when someone enters into a contract as a result of financial threats.

In effect it is saying, make a contract with me on these terms or else there will be no contract and you will be ruined. This can easily be seen where there is a shortage of an item and the supplier of that item can effectively name his price. The court has to distinguish between legitimate commercial pressure and economic duress.

Lord Scarman, in *Universe Tankships Inc. of Monrovia v International Transport Workers Federation (The Universe Sentinel)* (1983), saw duress as recognition of 'the victim's intentional submission arising from the realisation that there is no practical choice open to him'.

In the old and much criticised case of *Skeate v Beale* (1840), the court had decided that a threat towards property as opposed to a person did not constitute duress. However, in the case of *The Siboen and The Sibotre* (1976), the court said that serious threats to property should be considered as duress. In that particular case it was stated that where there exists coercion of the will so as to vitiate consent, it should be possible to set the contract aside. However, commercial pressure was not enough.

This idea was developed in *Atlas Express v Kafco* (1989).

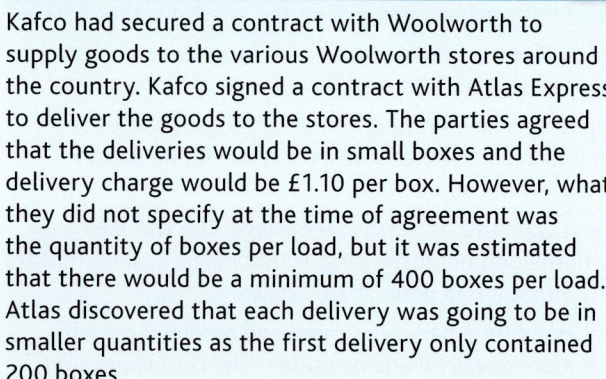

Atlas Express v Kafco (1989)

Kafco had secured a contract with Woolworth to supply goods to the various Woolworth stores around the country. Kafco signed a contract with Atlas Express to deliver the goods to the stores. The parties agreed that the deliveries would be in small boxes and the delivery charge would be £1.10 per box. However, what they did not specify at the time of agreement was the quantity of boxes per load, but it was estimated that there would be a minimum of 400 boxes per load. Atlas discovered that each delivery was going to be in smaller quantities as the first delivery only contained 200 boxes.

Atlas demanded more money per load or it would not deliver the consignments. Kafco had no other option but to agree to pay extra money to Atlas as it was a small company which had just secured a big order from a major company and it was essential that it delivered on time. It was also difficult to find another haulage company quickly. If Kafco failed to deliver the goods in time, that would not only have jeopardised its future dealings with Woolworth, Kafco could also be sued for breach of contract. So Kafco agreed to pay the extra money.

However, when the time came to pay the extra money, Kafco refused and argued that agreement to pay additional money was made under economic duress. The court decided in favour of Kafco. The agreement was made under economic duress as there was illegitimate pressure on Kafco who had no choice but to agree.

Every case where economic duress is argued is considered on its particular circumstances. The key requirements for economic duress are that there must be pressure:

- the practical effect of which is that there is compulsion on, or a lack of practical choice for, the victim
- which is illegitimate, and
- which is a significant cause inducing the claimant to enter into the contract.

This can be seen in *Universe Tankships Inc. of Monrovia v International Transport Workers Federation (The Universe Sentinel) (1983)*.

Universe Tankships Inc. of Monrovia v International Transport Workers Federation (The Universe Sentinel) (1983)

Universe Tankships, and in particular its vessel The Universe Sentinel, was being threatened by the International Transport Workers Federation (ITWF) as it was a vessel sailing under what ITWF regarded as 'a flag of convenience'. The threat was that unless the owners of the vessel comply with ITWF's demands as to the rates of pay and other terms of employment of the crew and also to paying money into a worker's welfare fund, they would not tug the ship, so it could not leave the port. The ship owners agreed so the ship could leave port. The court decided that the money had been extracted as a result of economic duress and must be repaid.

The question is, what makes the pressure illegitimate? The court in *Pao on v Lau yiu Long (1979)* identified the following actors to help decide whether economic duress was present:

- Did the person claiming to be coerced protest about the pressure?

- Did that person have any other available course of action that was reasonable?
- Was he or she independently advised before taking the action?
- After entering into the contract, did he or she take steps to make the contract void?

In *CTN Cash and Carry v Gallagher (1994)*, it was decided that duress was not available when the action threatened was lawful.

CTN Cash and Carry v Gallagher (1994)

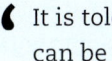

Gallagher sent a consignment of cigarettes to the wrong address and the cigarettes were stolen. Gallagher believed that the cigarettes were at CTN's risk and sent them an invoice for the cigarettes. Gallagher then threatened to withdraw the claimant's credit facility unless the invoice was paid. CTN needed the credit facilities and so paid the invoice. Was this economic duress?

Gallagher genuinely believed the money to be owed to them, so that they were not trying (as they understood it) to exploit a weakness to gain an unfair advantage but were simply trying to get back what they were entitled to.

The court accepted that 'illegitimate' is not synonymous with 'unlawful':

> It is tolerably clear that, at least where they can be confident of a general consensus in favour of their evaluation, the courts are willing to apply a standard of impropriety rather than technical unlawfulness.

In *Progress Bulk Carriers Ltd v Tube City (2012)*, it was decided that pressure could be illegitimate even when lawful.

Progress Bulk Carriers Ltd v Tube City (2012)

Ship owners contracted to hire their ship to charterers to transport a cargo. The charterers had a buyer for the cargo. The ship owners broke the contract by failing to provide the ship but agreed with the charterers to provide a substitute ship and to compensate the charterers for any losses. The delays led to a reduction in the price of the cargo, for which the charterers sought a reduction in the cost of the hire of the ship. By this time, the charterers were under great pressure to deliver the cargo and the ship owners now refused to supply the ship at a discount unless the charterers agreed that no compensation should be paid by the ship owners for the earlier breach of contract. This 'take it or leave it offer' was reluctantly accepted by the charterers, who subsequently sought to sue for losses, arguing that their agreement not to do so was forced on them by economic duress.

The court upheld their claim, arguing that the whole coercive conduct of the ship owners had to be viewed in the light of their initial breach of contract, and their willingness to take advantage of the consequences of that breach. This was 'illegitimate' pressure, even if not unlawful in itself. Cooke J said:

> It is ... clear from the authorities that 'illegitimate pressure' can be constituted by conduct which is not in itself unlawful, although it will be an unusual case where that is so, particularly in the commercial context. It is also clear that a past unlawful act, as well as a threat of a future unlawful act can, in appropriate circumstances, amount to 'illegitimate pressure'.

With economic duress there is no consideration, as the passing of what would otherwise be consideration is not done voluntarily as a part of a freely negotiated contract.

Duress is not concerned with the absence of consent but rather the wrongful nature of threats inducing consent, and thus has a different and separate role to consideration. Duress in most cases relates to contracts that have already been formed but are being varied so as to ensure performance.

Tip

In circumstances where there is a character who is facing financial difficulties, consider whether economic duress might be present.

22.5.1 Effect of a finding of duress

The effect of a finding of duress is always to make the contract voidable. This is exactly the same as for misrepresentation. In other words, it is a valid contract until avoided by the innocent party – the one who has suffered the economic duress.

22.6 Remedies for economic duress

A claim based on economic duress does not result in an award of damages. The courts can make an order for the restitution of property or money extracted under such duress, and also the avoidance of any contract that has been induced by it. Restitution is an equitable remedy that restores a person to the position he or she would have been in if not for the improper action of another. Being an equitable remedy, it is discretionary, as we have seen for rescission.

Figure 22.6 Key facts chart for economic duress

	Brief legal rule	Case example
Economic duress definition	The threat to damage a business or person financially	
Economic duress does not normally cover a threat towards property	Economic duress does not normally cover a threat towards property except in severe circumstances	*Atlas Express v Kafco* (1989)
Economic duress involves (1) – compulsion or a lack of practical choice for the victim	A practical effect must be that there is compulsion on, or a lack of practical choice for, the victim	*Universe Tankships Inc. of Monrovia v International Transport Workers Federation (The Universe Sentinel)* (1983)
Economic duress involves (2) – illegitimate pressure	Commercial pressure is not enough to amount to economic duress There are a number of factors to consider	*Pao on v Lau yiu Long* (1979)
Economic duress involves (3) – actions that are not lawful	Illegitimate is not synonymous with unlawful	*CTN Cash and Carry v Gallagher* (1994)
Economic duress involves (4) – pressure could be illegitimate even when lawful	'Illegitimate pressure' can be constituted by conduct which is not in itself unlawful, although it will be an unusual case where that is so	*Progress Bulk Carriers Ltd v Tube City* (2012)

Figure 22.7 Key cases chart for economic duress

Case	Judgment
Atlas Express v Kafco (1989)	Economic duress was established as the agreement was induced by illegitimate pressure of great magnitude
Universe Tankships Inc. of Monrovia v International Transport Workers Federation (The Universe Sentinel) (1983)	Several demands were made in relation to pay and conditions as well as that the ship owners pay a large sum of money to the Seafarers International Welfare Fund – this amounted to compulsion
Pao on v Lau yiu Long (1979)	The court identified four factors to be considered if there was to be economic duress
CTN Cash and Carry v Gallagher (1994)	The threat to withdraw the credit facility was a lawful threat as Gallagher genuinely believed they were entitled to the money
Progress Bulk Carriers Ltd v Tube City (2012)	The charterers had no other way to ship the goods, and faced 'catastrophic' losses if they delayed any longer The agreement to waive all claims against them arising from the breach was obtained by economic duress

Summary

- Vitiating factors include misrepresentation and economic duress.

- Misrepresentation occurs where a person is induced to enter a contract as a result of statements made that are false.

- There are three types of misrepresentation, each with its own remedies: innocent, negligent and fraudulent.

- Economic duress arises where there is the threat to damage a business or a person financially. The court will consider each case involving economic duress according to its individual circumstances.

23 Discharge of a contract

After reading this chapter, you should be able to:

- Understand the concept of discharge of contract
- Explain discharge by performance
- Explain breach of contract: actual and anticipatory breach, and relevant remedies
- Explain discharge by frustration and relevant remedies

23.1 What is discharge of contract?

The usual method of discharge of a contract is through performance. Both parties have done what they agreed in the contract. But, if the contract has not been performed as agreed, it may be discharged by breach. However, not every breach of contract discharges the contract. The question here is to decide the effect of an individual breach of contract.

A contract may be discharged by frustration where unforeseen events outside the control of the parties make performance impossible.

23.2 Discharge by performance

The strict rule of discharge by performance is that performance must be complete and exact.

Activity

Jen arranged a minicab home from a club late one night for £20. She had given the driver her precise address. The driver was in a hurry to pick up his next, very lucrative, fare so told Jen to get out at the end of her street, about 100 metres from her house, as it was a one-way street and would require him to take a long and time-consuming detour.

- Do you think she should pay the driver £20, a little less than £20 or nothing?
- If you think she should pay nothing, how close do you think the driver should get to her house to be paid?
- Write down the arguments for Jen and the minicab driver.

An early case showing the rule is *Cutter v Powell* (1795).

Cutter v Powell (1795)
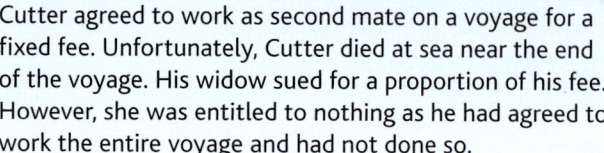

Cutter agreed to work as second mate on a voyage for a fixed fee. Unfortunately, Cutter died at sea near the end of the voyage. His widow sued for a proportion of his fee. However, she was entitled to nothing as he had agreed to work the entire voyage and had not done so.

Another example is *Re Moore and Co. Ltd and Landauer and Co.'s Arbitration* (1921), where even though the total number of the tins was correct, the number of tins in each carton was incorrect and so the goods did not correspond with the description in the contract.

See Chapter 20, section 20.5.2 for full case details of *Re Moore and Co. Ltd and Landauer and Co.'s Arbitration* (1921).

The harshness of the rule has been tempered in several ways:

- divisible contracts
- substantial performance
- prevention of full performance
- acceptance of part performance.

23.2.1 Divisible contracts

Where a contract can be seen as being separate parts, non-completion of one part is not a breach of the whole contract. So, if Mr Cutter's contract in *Cutter v Powell* had been described as, for example, £1 per day, then the contract for the voyage would have been divisible. This can be seen in *Ritchie v Atkinson* (1808).

Ritchie v Atkinson (1808)

A ship owner agreed to carry a cargo at an agreed rate per ton. He carried only a part of the cargo. The ship owner was entitled to be paid for the part of the cargo he had carried at the agreed price per ton, but was liable in damages for breach of contract for not carrying the whole cargo.

23.2.2 Substantial performance

If a party has done substantially what was required under the contract, then the doctrine of substantial performance may apply. Where it does apply, there must be payment of the amount appropriate to what has been done.

This does not apply where the contract is considered to be an entire contract where all of the obligations in the contract are seen as a single transaction that cannot be broken down, as in *Cutter v Powell*.

Substantial performance often occurs in large contracts where little things are not performed exactly, as in *Dakin and Co. v Lee* (1916).

Dakin and Co. v Lee (1916)

Builders agreed to repair the defendant's premises for £1500. They performed the contract completely but there were three relatively poorly performed aspects. These cost £80 to rectify. The court decided that the contract had been substantially, if not precisely, performed. The fact that the work was done badly did not mean it had not been performed at all. The builder was entitled to be paid the price subject to a deduction for the defective work.

The difficulty is in establishing what amounts to substantial performance. No specific percentages for completion are specified as to when work has been substantially completed. It is decided on the circumstances of each case. Two contrasting examples are *Hoenig v Isaacs* (1952) and *Bolton v Mahadeva* (1972).

Hoenig v Isaacs (1952)

A decorator contracted to decorate and furnish a room for £750. Some of the furniture was defective but could be repaired for £55. The court decided that the contract was substantially completed on a financial basis. The decorator was entitled to be paid for what he had done on a *quantum meruit* basis.

Bolton v Mahadeva (1972)

A builder agreed to install a central heating system for £560. However, the installation was defective, as the system gave off fumes and did not work properly. Repairs cost £170. The court decided that the builder was entitled to nothing, as there had not been substantial performance of the contract.

Key term

Quantum meruit – as much as it is worth.

See Chapter 24, section 24.2.6 for more information on *quantum meruit*.

An example of the court's use of discretion to reach a just and fair decision through *quantum meruit* can be seen in *Young v Thames Properties Ltd* (1999).

Young v Thames Properties Ltd (1999)

A contract was made for resurfacing a car park, but the contractor did not resurface to the exact specifications with respect to the depth of some of the materials. The court decided that the defects made little difference to the quality of the car park, so the contractor was entitled to the contract price less the savings to the contractor of not completing the contract with the correct depth of materials.

23.2.3 Prevention of full performance

If one party prevents the other from carrying out his contract, then the innocent party can claim to be paid on a *quantum meruit* basis. This can be seen in *Planche v Colburn* (1831).

Planche v Colburn (1831)

A publisher hired an author to write one of a series of books. When the publisher decided to abandon the whole series, the author was prevented from completing the work through no fault of his own. He was entitled to recover a fee for his wasted work.

23.2.4 Acceptance of part-performance

If one party has agreed the other party need not complete the entire contract then the contract must be paid for on a *quantum meruit* basis. However, the consent must be in the form of a specific acknowledgement that the defaulting party is entitled to be paid for what he or she has completed so far and the agreement was made without undue pressure. If the innocent party has no option but to take the benefit of the work done, this is not considered consent to part-performance. This was shown in *Sumpter v Hedges* (1898).

Sumpter v Hedges (1898)

A builder agreed to build two houses. He completed just over half of the work and then ran out of money. The customer completed the outstanding work. The builder argued that in completing the work himself, the defendant accepted part-performance.

The court said the defendant had no choice but to accept part-performance as he was left with half a completed house on his land. Therefore, the builder was not entitled to be paid for the work he had done so far. The customer had no alternative but to complete the work himself and had not, therefore, consented to the builder's part performance. There was insufficient work done for substantial performance. However, as some of the materials left behind by the builder were used in completing the work, the builder was awarded a sum for the use of those materials.

23.2.5 The effect of a term as to time for performance of a contract

In many contracts it is useful to have a term as to time inserted. This is particularly important when an item is needed at a particular time (for example, a wedding dress). There are often terms in contracts about the time for performance of the contract. The question here is, how exactly must terms as to time be performed? If it is exact, can the injured party repudiate the contract for breach of this term?

The court regards time as a condition if:

- the parties have expressly stated in the contract that time is of the essence of the contract (time of performance of the contract is a critical part of performance)
- in the circumstances time for completion of the contract is critical, or
- one party has failed to perform on time and the other has insisted on a new date for completion of the contract (making time of the essence of the contract).

If none of the above apply, then the time for performance is treated as a warranty rather than a condition. This can be seen in cases such as *Charles Rickards Ltd v Oppenheim* (1950) and *Union Eagle Ltd v Golden Achievement Ltd* (1997).

Charles Rickards Ltd v Oppenheim (1950)

A buyer of a Rolls-Royce car chassis agreed for a body to be built upon it by a fixed date. The body was not completed by that date. The buyer kept pushing for delivery, and eventually gave notice that unless delivery of the car with a completed body was ready within four weeks he would cancel the contract. The car was not delivered within the period of four weeks. When the car was completed, he rejected it. He was entitled to cancel the contract as time had been made of the essence and that term had not been complied with.

A mechanic working on a car

Union Eagle Ltd v Golden Achievement Ltd (1997)

In a contract for the sale of a flat, the time for completion of the contract had been specified as 5.00 p.m. and time was expressly stated to be 'of the essence'. The purchaser delivered the purchase price at 5.10 p.m. and the seller repudiated the contract. The court decided that the seller was entitled to repudiate the contract as the time for completion had been made a condition of the contract.

Most contracts for the sale of land including houses have terms in them with respect to time for performance of the contract. It is essential that once time being of the essence has been waived, it is then reinstated as a term by giving notice if such a term is to be relied on. This is apparent from the case of *Hakimzay Ltd v Swailes* (2015), a case involving the sale of a residential property.

Time and the Consumer Rights Act 2015

Section 52 of the Consumer Rights Act 2015 deals with the time for performance of a contract to which the Act applies. If the contract does not expressly fix time for the service to be performed, and does not say how it is to be fixed, then the contract is to be treated as including a term that the trader must perform the service within a reasonable time. If the trader is in breach of what the contract requires under s 52, the consumer has the right to a price reduction under s 54. The consumer will still have rights to end the contract because of this breach.

The right to a price reduction is explained under s 56 and is to reduce the price to the consumer by an appropriate amount for the trader's failure to perform the contract. This may result in the trader giving a refund, up to the full contract price.

Figure 23.1 Key facts chart for discharge by performance

	Brief legal rule	Case example
Discharge by performance – general rule	Performance must be complete and exact	*Cutter v Powell* (1795)
Some contracts can be seen as divisible contracts	If a contract can be seen as being separate parts, then non-completion of one part is not a breach of the whole contract	*Ritchie v Atkinson* (1808)
The doctrine of substantial performance	If a party has done substantially what was required under the contract, then the doctrine of substantial performance can apply	*Dakin and Co. v Lee* (1916)
Full performance prevented by actions of the other party	If one party prevents the other from carrying out his or her contract, the innocent party can claim to be paid on a *quantum meruit* basis	*Planche v Colburn* (1831)
One party accepts part-performance	If one party has agreed the other party need not complete the entire contract, the strict rule will not apply	*Sumpter v Hedges* (1898)
The effect of a term as to time for performance of a contract	A term as to time is treated as a condition if it falls within one of three categories If not it is treated as a warranty	*Union Eagle Ltd v Golden Achievement Ltd* (1997)
Time can be made of the essence of a contract	This also means the right to treat it as a condition can be waived	*Charles Rickards Ltd v Oppenheim* (1950)

Figure 23.2 Key cases chart for discharge by performance

Case	Judgment
Cutter v Powell (1795)	As the contract was for the whole voyage, he had not performed his contract
Ritchie v Atkinson (1808)	The ship owner was entitled to be paid for the part of the cargo he had carried as the contract was divisible
Dakin and Co. v Lee (1916)	Substantial performance applied as there were relatively minor defects in the work
Hoenig v Isaacs (1952)	*Quantum meruit* was used to establish payment to be made
Bolton v Mahadeva (1972)	The defects were too great to amount to substantial performance
Young v Thames Properties Ltd (1999)	The court used its discretion to reach a just and fair decision
Planche v Colburn (1831)	An author was prevented from carrying out his contract so was paid on a *quantum meruit* basis
Sumpter v Hedges (1898)	The builder was not entitled to be paid for the work he had done so far as the customer had no alternative but to complete the work himself He had not consented to the builder's part performance
Union Eagle Ltd v Golden Achievement Ltd (1997)	The time for completion of the contract had been specified as 5.00 p.m. and time was expressly stated to be 'of the essence' The purchaser delivered the purchase price at 5.10 p.m. and the seller was entitled to repudiate the contract
Charles Rickards Ltd v Oppenheim (1950)	He was entitled to cancel the contract as time had been made of the essence and that term had not been complied with

23.3 Discharge by breach

23.3.1 Actual breach

When a party fails to perform his or her obligations under a contract, that party may be sued for breach of contract. Either or both parties to the contract may be in breach of contract. The victim will always be entitled to claim for damages, but terminating (ending) the contract depends on the type of term that has been breached. Breach of any term of a contract gives the right to claim damages, but only a breach of condition gives the right to repudiate the contract and/or sue for damages. The breach of a condition includes breach of an innominate term where the term is treated as a condition.

Breach can be a total failure to perform, for example non-delivery or non-payment, or it can be failure to perform in accordance with the terms of the contract that could be seen as part-performance.

The three sets of circumstances giving rise to a breach of contract are:

- renunciation by a party of his or her liabilities under it, for example not paying a bill on the due date
- impossibility created by his or her own act, for example closing a hairdresser's business for holidays with appointments during that time
- total or partial failure of performance, for example delivering defective goods.

Repudiatory breach can occur in three ways:

- a breach of condition
- a refusal to perform the contract, such as delivering goods or carrying out contracted work
- a sufficiently serious breach of an innominate term, that is, a breach that would be considered a breach of condition

Key term

Repudiatory breach of contract – this occurs when a party commits a breach of contract that is sufficiently serious that it entitles the innocent party to treat the contract as terminated.

If a repudiatory breach is established, the other party who is not in breach may terminate the contract and claim damages or continue the contract and claim damages.

Sometimes contracts contain express termination provisions as in *Stocznia Gdynia SA v Gearbulk Holdings*

(2009). Where that is the case, the contract can be terminated in the event of any of the circumstances set out in the contract. Typically, this might be non-payment of a stage payment or suspension of work on a project. These rights are in addition to any right to terminate set out by the common law.

23.3.2 Anticipatory breach

An **anticipatory breach** occurs when a party to a contract gives notice in advance to the other party that he or she will not be performing or completing the contract. The innocent party in this situation has a choice – to sue immediately for breach of a condition or to wait for the time agreed for performance of the contract and to sue if performance does not take place then. This means he or she can treat the contract as repudiated immediately and/or claim damages. An example is *Hochster v de la Tour* (1853).

Hochster v de la Tour (1853)

Hochester agreed to work as a courier on a tour due to start in June. However the company told him in May that it no longer required his services. In that situation he was entitled to sue immediately and did not have to wait until the actual breach of contract, which would have occurred in June.

This is a good right to have, as by waiting to see if performance will take place, a company could fall into financial difficulties or there might be other events that result in discharge by frustration.

If one of the parties to a contract, either expressly or by conduct, leads the other party to the reasonable conclusion that he or she does not mean to carry out the contract, this amounts to a repudiation. The other party can treat the contract as at an end.

In *Geden Operations Ltd v Drybulk Handy Holdings Inc. (Bulk Uruguay)* (2014), the principle was summarised as conduct:

> ...which is sufficient to entitle the other contracting party to treat himself as discharged from further performance. It may consist of ... renunciation, [i.e.] words or conduct which evince an intention by the contracting party no longer to be bound by his contractual obligations [or] self induced impossibility, [i.e.] conduct by the contracting party which puts it out of his power to perform his contractual obligations.

In both cases, the inevitability of non-performance entitled the innocent party to treat the contract as at an end prior to the time for performance. However, unlikelihood or uncertainty in future performance do not suffice.

Key terms

Anticipatory breach – when a party to a contract gives notice in advance to the other party that he or she will not be performing or completing the contract.

Actual breach – where the breach occurs at the time or during the course of performance.

23.3.3 Remedies for breach – summary

- If the victim claims an anticipatory breach then the victim may claim damages immediately. These damages are to put the victim in the same position he or she would have been in had the contract been completed. However, the victim must take reasonable steps to mitigate his or her losses.
- The victim may choose not to accept the anticipatory breach but to see if the defendant commits an **actual breach** at the time performance is due. Here, the damages are assessed at the time when performance should occur, and the loss might increase due to a change in market factors. Alternatively, an event may occur which discharges the contract, such as frustration of contract for which there are different remedies.
- The victim may also repudiate the contract under anticipatory breach. The result is that the victim is no longer bound to perform any obligations under the contract.
- For a breach of condition, the right of the victim is to claim for damages and/or repudiation. Damages are again based on putting the victim in the position he or she would have been in had the contract been completed.
- For a breach of warranty, the claim is limited to damages. In Chapter 24 there is much more detail about the award of damages and mitigation of loss.

23.4 Discharge by frustration

Historically the law held that a party was bound to perform his or her obligations under the contract, whatever happened. In *Paradine v Jane* (1647), the defendant was still liable to pay rent on land even though he had been forced off the land by an invading army during the English Civil War!

The injustice of this strict rule led, in the nineteenth century, to the development of a new doctrine. If a party to a contract was prevented from keeping the

Figure 23.3 Key facts chart for discharge by breach

	Brief legal rule	Case example
Discharge by breach – general rule	When a party fails to perform his or her obligations under a contract, that party may be sued for breach of contract	*Poussard v Spiers and Pond* (1876) (see Chapter 20, section 20.2.1)
Types of breach	Breach can be actual breach or anticipatory breach	*Hochster v de la Tour* (1853)
When can it be taken as anticipatory breech?	This can be by renunciation or self-induced impossibility. Unlikelihood or uncertainty in future performance do not suffice	*Geden Operations Ltd v Drybulk Handy Holdings Inc. (Bulk Uruguay)* (2014)
Effect of breach	This depends on the type of term broken	

Figure 23.4 Key cases chart for discharge by breach

Case	Judgment
Hochster v de la Tour (1853)	An anticipatory breach occurs when a party to a contract gives notice in advance to the other party that he or she will not be performing the contract
Geden Operations Ltd v Drybulk Handy Holdings Inc. (Bulk Uruguay) (2014)	Sets out when a breach can be treated as an anticipatory breach.

promise because of an unforeseeable, intervening event, he or she would not be liable for a breach of contract. This was shown in *Taylor v Caldwell* (1863).

Taylor v Caldwell (1863)

The owner contracted to rent out his music hall. Through no one's fault, and before the rental could take place, the music hall burned down. The hirer had spent money advertising the events for which he would not be paid until after the events. As it was now impossible to complete the contract, it was frustrated. This ended the contract and there was no recompense for the wasted expenses.

Two more modern views about frustration of contract can be found in the cases of *Davis Contractors Ltd v Fareham Urban District Council* (1956) and *National Carriers Ltd v Panalpina (Northern) Ltd* (1980).

In the Davis Contractors case, Lord Radcliffe said:

> **❝** Frustration occurs whenever the law recognises that without default of either party a contractual obligation has become incapable of being performed because the circumstances in which performance is called for would render it a thing radically different from that which was undertaken by the contract. **❞**

In the *Panalpina* case, Lord Simon said:

> **❝** Frustration of a contract takes place when there supervenes an event (without default of either party and for which the contract makes no sufficient provision) which so significantly changes the nature (not merely the expense or onerousness) of the outstanding contractual rights and/ or obligations from what the parties could reasonably have contemplated at the time of its execution that it would be unjust to hold them to the literal sense of its stipulations in the new circumstances; in such case the law declares both parties to be discharged from further performance. **❞**

For this reason many contracts contain a **force majeure** clause.

Key term

Force majeure clause – a clause often found in commercial contracts. It excludes liability for the parties for delay in performance or the non-performance if there are extraordinary events.

If the contract does not contain a *force majeure* clause, it may still be possible to rely on frustration to avoid being in breach of contract. However, what may constitute a frustrating event depends on the circumstances of each case.

Frustration requires performance as envisaged in the contract to become impossible as a result of outside events beyond the control and contemplation of the parties.

There is supervening, unanticipated impossibility which is not the fault of either party and is attributable to:

- destruction of the subject matter (including, in a sense, unavailability of a party in a contract for personal services such as through death or serious illness of the performer)
- subsequent illegality, for example by fulfilling a contract for goods that are subsequently banned from being imported
- destruction/frustration of the common venture – this is the situation where there is no physical destruction but the essential commercial purpose of the contract cannot be achieved.

23.4.1 Impossibility of performance

We have already seen this in the destruction of the music hall in *Taylor v Caldwell*. Frustration also applies where the subject matter becomes unavailable through no fault of the contracting parties. An example is *Jackson v Union Marine Insurance Co. Ltd* (1874).

Jackson v Union Marine Insurance Co. Ltd (1874)

A ship was chartered to sail from Liverpool to Newport and from there load a cargo for San Francisco. It ran aground and could not be loaded for a long time. This was seen as 'the perils of the sea'. The court agreed there was an implied term that the ship should be available for loading in a reasonable time, so the long delay frustrated the contract.

In a contract for services, the frustrating event may be the unavailability of the party who is to perform the service because of illness, as in *Robinson v Davidson* (1871), or failure to perform on medical advice as in *Condor v The Baron Knights* (1966).

Robinson v Davidson (1871)

A pianist made a contract to perform. Some hours before the performance was due she became ill and her husband informed the claimant that she would be unable to attend. The court decided that the contract was conditional on the woman being well enough to perform and her illness was a frustrating event.

Condor v The Baron Knights (1966)

A contract entered into by a band required all members of the band to be available to perform for seven evenings a week if necessary. The drummer became ill and was advised to work no more than four nights per week. On occasion, he ignored this advice, but the court still held that the contract was frustrated since it was necessary to have a stand-in musician in case he fell ill.

23.4.2 The contract becoming illegal to perform

A contract may be frustrated as the result of a change in the law that makes the contract illegal to perform, for example as a result of war. Examples include *Denny, Mott and Dickson Ltd v James B Fraser and Co. Ltd* (1944) and *Re Shipton Anderson and Co. and Harrison Bros and Co.* (1915).

Denny, Mott and Dickson Ltd v James B Fraser and Co. Ltd (1944)

The court said that a contract to import certain goods would be frustrated if importing goods of that kind became illegal after the contract was made.

Re Shipton Anderson and Co. and Harrison Bros and Co. (1915)

A cargo of grain was sold, but before it could be delivered, war broke out. The Government requisitioned the cargo so the contract was frustrated.

There is a radical change of circumstances as the essential commercial purpose of the contract cannot be achieved.

If the main purpose of the contract is based on a particular event and the event will not take place, the contract may be frustrated. The contrasting cases of *Krell v Henry* (1903) and *Herne Bay Steamboat Co. v Hutton* (1903) illustrate this.

Krell v Henry (1903)

A man hired a hotel room in order to view Edward VII's coronation procession. The Prince became ill and the coronation and procession were postponed. The court

said that the event was the main purpose of the contract; as it would not occur, the contract was frustrated even though the room could still have been used.

Herne Bay Steamboat Co. v Hutton (1903)

Hutton hired a boat in order to see the fleet when the King reviewed it as part of his coronation celebrations. Hutton claimed he did not have to pay as the King was ill and did not attend. However, the court said the contract was not frustrated as one main reason for the contract still remained, to view the fleet. All that was missing was the King's presence. This was not enough to frustrate the contract.

It can be seen from the above cases that in *Krell* the commercial purpose of the contract was to watch the procession. As the procession did not take place because the king was ill, the commercial purpose was destroyed because of an outside event beyond the control of the parties – frustration of contract.

In *Hutton* the commercial purpose was not destroyed as he could still go and see the fleet of ships that assembled. The only difference is that the king would not be there – no frustration.

23.4.3 When frustration cannot apply

These events are sometimes categorised as:

- self-induced frustration
- the contract becoming less profitable
- the event being a foreseeable risk or the event was mentioned in the contract.

Self-induced frustration

Frustration will not apply when the frustrating event is within the control of one party. This can be seen in *Maritime National Fish Ltd v Ocean Trawlers Ltd* (1935).

Maritime National Fish Ltd v Ocean Trawlers Ltd (1935)

A fishing company owned two trawlers and had a contract to hire a third. The company needed a licence for each vessel but was only allocated two licences, which it allocated to its own boats. The company then claimed frustration of the hire contract as it could not use the hire boat. The court held that frustration did not apply and the contract was still valid. The 'frustrating' event was within the company's control as it could have allocated a licence to the hired boat rather than another of its boats which it had chosen to do.

This can be contrasted with *Gamerco SA v ICM Fair Warning (Agency) Ltd and Missouri Storm Inc.* (1995). Here the lack of a licence was a frustrating event as the issue of the licence was not under the control of either party.

Gamerco SA v ICM Fair Warning (Agency) Ltd and Missouri Storm Inc. (1995)

A Spanish concert promoter and the defendant rock group, Guns N' Roses (their corporate persona is Missouri Storm Inc.) agreed to put on a concert at Atletico Madrid's stadium. Shortly before it was due to take place, the stadium was deemed unfit and its licence withdrawn by the Spanish authorities. No other stadium was available.

The contract had been frustrated, the promoter could not erect the stage and the band could not perform.

Guns N' Roses concert, Los Angeles, 2016

Extension activity

Find the full law report for this case online. It is interesting to read, in terms of the way in which a large rock tour is organised and the amount of money involved.

It is interesting to see how a simple change to words in a contract could have resulted in frustration of contract rather than breach of contract. In *J Lauritzen AS v Wijsmuller BV, (The Super Servant Two)* (1990), just identifying the particular ship would probably have resulted in a frustrated contract. It could be argued this decision is very harsh.

J Lauritzen AS v Wijsmuller BV (The Super Servant Two) (1990)

The defendants agreed to transport an oil rig using one of two ships known as the Super Servant One or the Super Servant Two. The defendants decided to use the second ship

as the first ship was being used for other contracts. However, the Super Servant Two was sunk in Zaire while transporting another rig and it could not then be used to transport the rig in the contract. The defendants argued that the contract has been frustrated as they were incapable of transporting the drilling rig and the claimants argued that the impossibility of performing the contract had been self-induced and, therefore, they should not be discharged of the need to perform the contract. The court stated that there was no frustration of contract as the other ship could have been used, albeit at the expense of breach of the other contract or hiring a substitute vessel for the other contract.

This then leads to the question of the law of frustration and the concept of justice, which is considered below and in Chapter 3.

The contract has become less profitable

A contract becoming less profitable or more difficult to complete is not a reason for frustration of that contract. One example of this is *Davis Contractors Ltd v Fareham Urban District Council* (1956).

Davis Contractors Ltd v Fareham Urban District Council (1956)

Builders contracted to build houses for the urban district council for £94,000 but then discovered it would cost £115,000 to complete the contract due to labour shortages. The builders claimed frustration of the contract but were unsuccessful as the contract was not radically different to what the parties had originally intended, just less profitable.

An even more extreme example can be seen in the case of *Tsakiroglou and Co. Ltd v Noblee Thorl GmbH* (1962).

Tsakiroglou and Co. Ltd v Noblee Thorl GmbH (1962)

The defendants agreed to ship peanuts from Sudan during November or December 1956 to Hamburg. Both parties anticipated that the ship would sail through the Suez Canal but the actual route was not specified in the contract. However, the Suez crisis of 1956 meant that on 2 November the Suez Canal was closed to shipping. The defendant could still have transported the peanuts within the contractually agreed time but this would mean going via the Cape of Good Hope, which would have taken four times as long and increased the cost of transport considerably. The defendants argued that the contract had been frustrated, but, as in the *Davis* case, the court did not agree.

It should be noted that if the contract in the *Noblee Thorl* case had a term in it expressly or impliedly that the transport was to be 'via Suez', the contract might have been frustrated as this had become impossible for the stated shipping period. This is another example of where a simple force majeure term in the contract would have led to a different result.

The event being a foreseeable risk or the event was mentioned in the contract

In *Amalgamated Investment and Property Co. Ltd v John Walker and Sons Ltd* (1977), there was a foreseeable risk.

Amalgamated Investment and Property Co. Ltd v John Walker and Sons Ltd (1977)

This involved a contract to sell a building to the investment company who wanted it for redevelopment. Unbeknown to either party and after the contract was made, the Department of the Environment made the building a listed building, meaning that it could not be used for development. This resulted in a huge drop of the value of the building.

The court rejected a claim of frustration, as listing was a risk associated with all old buildings, of which the developers should have been aware. The pre-contract enquiries showed they were aware of the possibility of the building becoming listed so the contract was not radically different from that contemplated by the parties.

In general, the courts are reluctant to find that there has been frustration of contract. This can be seen in the recent case of *Armchair Answercall v People in Mind* (2016).

Armchair Answercall v People in Mind (2016)

The contract for services was commercially undermined when third-party franchisees eventually refused to agree to vary the way the business was carried out. People in Mind's role was to support Armchair Answercall in moving the business to a new management model for existing franchisees and potential new customers.

The Court of Appeal was clear that for an event to be frustrating, it had to be a 'supervening outside event which the parties could not reasonably be thought to have foreseen as a real possibility'. This was not the case here as the franchisees' departure was promoted by the acts of Armchair Answercall. Clarke LJ concluded

by saying that whether or not a given event is a frustrating one is, once the facts have been determined, a question of law.

> **"** If it was, the fact that the parties did not immediately treat it as such does not alter the position. What the parties did or did not do after the event may, however, be a pointer to whether the event was in truth a frustrating one. **"**

As Armchair Answercall did not treat the contract as frustrated for some five months this was consistent with the court's conclusion that there was no frustrating event. There was no definite event that could be said to have frustrated the contract.

Frustration and justice

We have already seen that in *National Carriers Ltd v Panalpina (Northern) Ltd* (1980) Lord Simon said that it would be unjust to hold the parties to the literal sense of the contract terms in the new circumstances. In *The Super Servant Two*, Bingham LJ stated:

> **"** The object of the doctrine was to give effect to the demands of justice, to achieve a just and reasonable result, to do what is reasonable and fair, as an expedient to escape from injustice where such would result from enforcement of a contract in its literal terms after a significant change in circumstances. **"**

He went on to set out five conditions for frustration:

1 The mitigation of the law's insistence on literal performance of absolute promises so as to avoid injustice.

2 Because frustration operated 'to kill the contract', it was not to be lightly invoked.

3 Frustration brought an end to the contract forthwith.

4 The essence of frustration was that it should not be due to the act or election of the party seeking to rely on it and must instead be due to some outside event or extraneous change of situation.

5 A frustrating event had to take place without blame or fault on the side of the party seeking to rely on it.

The first point stresses justice over a principle of English contract law. The last point stresses the concept of fault in English law. The whole principle of frustration is to sort out a dispute when neither party is at fault but one or both parties have lost out financially. The way in which this is resolved is dealt with by the Law Reform (Frustrated Contracts) Act 1943, dealt with below.

23.4.4 Remedies for frustration

At common law, the frustrating event automatically terminates the contract at the time of the event. Obligations already existing must be completed but future obligations are terminated. This explains why the customer in *Krell v Henry* did not have to pay for the room as the payment was an obligation that only became effective when the room was actually used. This can be contrasted with the similar case of *Chandler v Webster* (1904) where the room had to be paid for in advance. The court decided the contract was frustrated so he still had to pay for the room. His obligation to pay (in advance, on making the booking) arose before the frustrating event (the postponement of the coronation).

The outbreak of the Second World War led to many more cases of frustration. This fact and in particular the *Fibrosa* case (*Fibrosa Spolka Ackyjna v Fairbairn Lawson Combe Barbour Ltd* (1943)) led to the passing of the Law Reform (Frustrated Contracts) Act 1943.

The Act does not affect the law on the situations when frustration may occur; it only applies to situations where frustration is found to exist. What it does is to set out the way in which frustrated contracts are settled.

The key sections of the Act are ss 1(2)–1(4).

Section 1(2) provides that:

- Money paid before the frustrating event occurs is recoverable – this would include paying in advance for goods and then having the order cancelled because those goods have become goods prohibited to be imported under new legislation.
- Money payable before the frustrating event ceases to be payable, whether or not there has been a total failure of consideration. In other words there is no longer an obligation to pay the price agreed for goods or services under a frustrated contract.

- If the party to whom such sums are paid or are payable as above incurred expenses before discharge of the contract resulting from the frustrating event, the court may award him or her such expenses. This sum is limited to a maximum of the sum of money paid or payable before the frustrating event.

In *Gamerco SA v ICM Fair Warning (Agency) Ltd and Missouri Storm Inc.* (1995), mentioned above, the High Court held that the contract was frustrated due to the stadium being unsafe and its use for the contract being banned. The judge ordered the repayment of the whole sum paid in advance of $412,500 and as both parties had incurred some expenditure in advance of the proposed performance, justice would be done by making no deduction from the repayment under the expenses proviso despite the incomplete list of expenses presented to the court.

Section 1(3) provides that:

- If one party has obtained a valuable benefit from the contract before the frustrating event, the court may order him or her to pay a sum in respect of it.
- That sum is what the court considers just, having regard to all the circumstances of the case.

The overarching purpose of judicial discretion on this is to compensate the claimant for not having the sums owed from the date the loss is suffered and to enable the claimant to be compensated fairly in the circumstances of the case. This can be seen in the case of *BP Exploration v Hunt (No. 2)* (1979).

BP Exploration v Hunt (No. 2) (1979)

Hunt had a concession to explore for oil in Libya. BP financed him in return for a half share of the concession. Its expenses would be three-eighths of the oil found until it had recovered 125 per cent of its outlay. Oil came on stream in 1967 but in 1971 the Libyan Government seized BP's interest. BP had not received all its initial expenditure from Hunt's share, and claimed a just sum. Robert Goff J said a just sum under s 1(3) was the sum that would lead to the prevention of the unjust enrichment of the defendant at the claimant's expense; in other words, a just sum at the discretion of the judge on the evidence of the case.

He also addressed the question of interest on money due. He said:

> The fundamental principle is that interest is not awarded as a punishment, but simply because the plaintiff has been deprived of the use of the money which was due to him … the power to award interest is discretionary, and there is certainly no rule that interest will invariably run from the date of loss. It is no part of my task to attempt to define the circumstances in which the court will depart from the fundamental principle; indeed, since the discretion to award interest is unfettered, it would be improper to do so. ”

In this case, the claimant was awarded $35 million in total.

Section 1(4) provides that in estimating the amount of any expenses incurred by any party to the contract, the court may include such sum as appears to be reasonable in respect of:

- overhead expenses
- any work or services performed personally by a party to the contract.

This explains the nature of expenses mentioned in s 1(2) and is subject to the limit stated in that section of a maximum of the sum of money paid or payable before the frustrating event.

The rules may be summarised as follows:

- Money already paid (such as a deposit) is recoverable and money already due under the contract (as in *Chandler*) is not payable.
- The court can use its discretion to order compensation to be paid for work done and expenses incurred under the contract before the frustrating event (provided there was an obligation to pay money before the frustrating event). The quantification of the amount due is based on the principle of *quantum meruit*.
- The court may order compensation to be paid for any valuable benefit one party may acquire under the frustrated contract.

Figure 23.5 Key facts chart for discharge by frustration

	Brief legal rule	Case example
Discharge by frustration – general rule	Where a party to a contract was prevented from keeping the promise because of an unforeseeable, intervening event, he or she would not be liable for a breach of contract	*Taylor v Caldwell* (1863)
For there to be frustration the contract must be impossible to perform	The court must decide whether performance is impossible in fact	*Jackson v Union Marine Insurance Co. Ltd* (1874)
Subsequent illegality can amount to frustration of contract	A contract becoming illegal to perform after it is made frustrates the contract	*Denny, Mott and Dickson Ltd v James B Fraser and Co. Ltd* (1944)
A radical change of the main purpose of the contract can amount to frustration of contract	The main purpose of the contract must be affected by the change, not just some aspect of it	*Krell v Henry* (1903) *Herne Bay Steamboat Co. v Hutton* (1903)
Self-induced frustration is breach not frustration	Frustration will not apply when the frustrating event is within the control of one party	*Maritime National Fish Ltd v Ocean Trawlers Ltd* (1935)
A contract becoming less profitable is not frustration	Merely because a contract becomes less profitable or more difficult to complete is not a reason for frustration of that contract	*Davis Contractors Ltd v Fareham UDC* (1956)
Remedies for frustration of contract	These are dealt with in the Law Reform (Frustrated Contracts) Act 1943	

Figure 23.6 Key cases chart for discharge by frustration

Case	Judgment
Taylor v Caldwell (1863)	As the destruction of the music hall was not the fault of either party, so the contract was frustrated
Jackson v Union Marine Insurance Co. Ltd (1874)	The long delay in loading caused by it running aground amounted to frustration of the contract
Robinson v Davidson (1871)	Illness of a person who is to perform personally can amount to frustration
Condor v The Baron Knights (1966)	Acting on medical advice can be sufficient for frustration of contract
Denny, Mott and Dickson Ltd v James B Fraser and Co. Ltd (1944)	The law was changed so that importing goods of that kind became illegal after the contract was made This frustrated the contract
Re Shipton Anderson and Co. and Harrison Bros and Co. (1915)	The Government requisitioned the cargo so the contract was frustrated
Krell v Henry (1903)	The event, which was the main purpose of the contract, would not occur therefore the contract was frustrated
Herne Bay Steamboat Co. v Hutton (1903)	The contract was not frustrated as one main reason for the contract still remained
Maritime National Fish Ltd v Ocean Trawlers Ltd (1935)	The choice of which boat to allocate a licence to amounted to self-induced frustration
Gamerco SA v ICM Fair Warning (Agency) Ltd and Missouri Storm Inc. (1995)	The licence was withdrawn by a third party so the contract was frustrated
Armchair Answercall v People in Mind (2016)	In general, the courts are reluctant to find there has been frustration of contract

Tip

Consider whether the event preventing the performance of the contract comes from outside the contracting parties. If it does not, breach is a more likely reason for discharge of contract.

Summary

- A contract can be discharged by performance (the usual method), frustration or breach (failure to perform in whole or in part).
- Performance must be complete and exact but there are exceptions such as where part-performance is accepted.
- If the contract is not discharged by frustration, there will be a breach of contract.
- Breach and frustration have different remedies.
- Breach can be of a condition, a warranty or an innominate term.
- Breach can be actual or anticipatory.

24 Remedies

After reading this chapter, you should be able to:
- Understand the way in which compensatory damages are assessed in contract law: categories of recoverable loss, causation, remoteness of damage, mitigation of loss
- Understand equitable remedies of specific performance and rescission
- Understand termination of contract for breach

24.1 What is a remedy?

Remedies in contract law are divided into:
- legal remedies
- equitable remedies
- remedies under a specific statute.

Legal remedies are available against a person in breach of contract as of right. These can be damages, which is financial compensation, or remedies against the goods.

Equitable remedies are discretionary. This means you do not have a right to an equitable remedy, but the court may award one if it thinks the legal remedies are not the most appropriate remedy in the circumstances.

Some Acts of Parliament provide for specific remedies in certain situations. The Acts we have considered in previous chapters are the Law Reform (Frustrated Contracts) Act 1943 and the Consumer Rights Act 2015.

Legal remedies are damages or rights with respect to the goods. So if the goods do not match those required by the contract, the goods can be rejected. There is also the right to repudiate the contract, in other words to treat the contract as at an end.

24.2 Compensatory damages

A claim for damages is always available, as of right, to the claimant when a contractual term has been broken. This means that if the claimant has not suffered any loss, the court must still make an award of damages. See nominal damages below.

The purpose of damages is to put the victim in the position he or she would have been in if the contract

had been properly completed and performed by the defendant. The court is therefore looking at what should have happened and the consequences of non- or part-performance.

The general rule is that damages are meant to place the claimant in the same position as if the contract had been performed. Damages are normally awarded for expectation loss (loss of a bargain) or reliance loss (wasted expenditure).

24.2.1 Types of damages

The problem for the courts is to establish how much the loss will be. As damages are compensatory, they will not include losses that are too remote to be awarded. Compensatory damages are the main type of damages, but other types need to be briefly explained first.

Nominal damages

If no loss is actually suffered but there is breach, the court may award 'nominal damages'. In *Staniforth v Lyall* (1830), the award of nominal damages was made as the claimant had made no loss. In fact, the main purpose of bringing the case was to have proof that the contract was at an end.

Staniforth v Lyall (1830)

Lyall was under a duty to load his cargo onto the claimant's boat by a certain date. He failed and the boat owner, S, sued for breach. S hired his boat out to another party immediately following the breach for a greater profit than he would have made from L. He succeeded in having the contract declared terminated but having suffered no loss, was awarded a nominal sum only.

Therefore, there was no risk of being in breach of contract or of being unable to rehire the boat to someone else without being in breach of contract, as the contract had been terminated by the breach.

In some cases, substantial damages have been awarded where, normally, nominal damages might have been considered more appropriate. One example is *Experience Hendrix LLC v PPX Enterprises Inc.* (2003).

Experience Hendrix LLC v PPX Enterprises Inc. (2003)

After the death of Jimi Hendrix, the defendant had been granting licences to exploit master recordings containing works featuring Hendrix, in breach of a 1973 agreement settling earlier litigation. There was no evidence to show or quantify any financial losses suffered as a result of the breaches. Was there an entitlement to more than nominal damages in respect of the breaches? The court stated that the defendant should make a reasonable payment for its uses of master recordings in breach of the settlement agreement, i.e more than just nominal damages.

This is sometimes called a 'Wrotham Park' award following the case of *Wrotham Park Estate Co. Ltd v Parkside Homes Ltd* (1974).

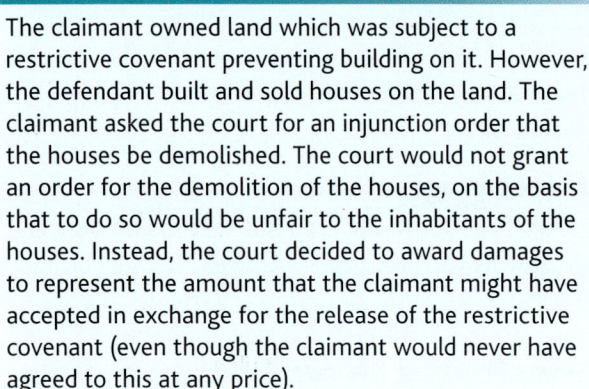

Wrotham Park Estate Co. Ltd v Parkside Homes Ltd (1974)

The claimant owned land which was subject to a restrictive covenant preventing building on it. However, the defendant built and sold houses on the land. The claimant asked the court for an injunction order that the houses be demolished. The court would not grant an order for the demolition of the houses, on the basis that to do so would be unfair to the inhabitants of the houses. Instead, the court decided to award damages to represent the amount that the claimant might have accepted in exchange for the release of the restrictive covenant (even though the claimant would never have agreed to this at any price).

Instead of working out how much the innocent party has lost, or how much the wrongdoer has gained, Wrotham Park damages try to quantify the sum which might reasonably have been negotiated between the parties for giving permission to the wrongdoer to act as he or she did. The difficulty with Wrotham Park damages is that it is not clear when they should be awarded. In *Morris-Garner v OneStep (Support) Ltd* (2016), it was stated that Wrotham Park damages will be awarded where the claimant would have very real problems in establishing financial loss, it is a 'just' response to a breach of contract and such damages should not be restricted to exceptional circumstances.

Extension activity

Research the *Morris-Garner* case. Write down the decision and consider how this case might be used to illustrate the concept of law and justice studied in Chapter 3.

Speculative damages

The courts have been careful to avoid granting damages of a speculative nature when considering the idea of loss of a chance of a benefit that has been denied to the claimant as a result of a breach of contract. In *Addis v The Gramophone Company* (1909), the court refused a claim for damages in contract for injury to reputation and the mental distress caused by the humiliating manner of Mr Addis's dismissal from his job, as this was a matter for the law of tort. He was awarded damages only for the loss of salary and commission owed.

However, in *Chaplin v Hicks* (1911) the claimant succeeded.

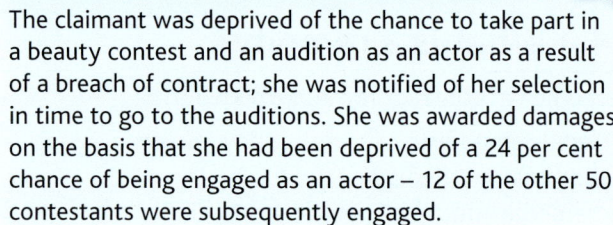

Chaplin v Hicks (1911)

The claimant was deprived of the chance to take part in a beauty contest and an audition as an actor as a result of a breach of contract; she was notified of her selection in time to go to the auditions. She was awarded damages on the basis that she had been deprived of a 24 per cent chance of being engaged as an actor – 12 of the other 50 contestants were subsequently engaged.

There are cases allowing damages of a highly speculative nature for mental distress, while also recognising the problems with respect to privity of contract, such as *Jackson v Horizon Holidays Ltd* (1975) (see Chapter 19, section 19.2.2) and *Jarvis v Swan Tours Ltd* (1973).

More recently, damages for loss of amenity have been allowed where the sole purpose of the contract was for the provision of a pleasurable amenity. In *Ruxley Electronics and Construction Ltd v Forsyth* (1996), damages were awarded for loss of amenity.

Ruxley Electronics and Construction Ltd v Forsyth (1996)

The contract for a swimming pool stated the depth but the builder completed the pool with a depth about 10 per cent less. There was nothing wrong with the pool apart from the depth – it was still worth its cost, it did not affect the value of the property as a whole and it could still be used as originally intended. The cost to correct the pool was £21,650, which was equivalent to the original cost of building the pool.

The court stated that in building contracts there are two bases for quantification of damages – the cost of reinstatement or the difference in value. The cost of reinstatement was totally unreasonable in this case. As there was no real difference in value of the pool, technically, Mr Forsyth was entitled to nothing. However, as he had not received that which he had contracted for, the court awarded him £2500 for loss of amenity.

24.2.2 Causation and remoteness of damage

Compensatory damages are relevant once it has been established which losses are to be compensated. Losses may have been foreseeable at the time of making the contract, but they will only be recoverable if those losses were caused by the breach of contract. Therefore, the claimant must prove that the breach *caused* the loss, not just provided the opportunity for loss. This is the 'but for' test – but for the breach of contract, would the claimant have suffered the loss claimed? If the loss would have happened in any event, then the breach could not be said to have caused the loss.

Remoteness of damage does not establish how much compensation will be payable (damages), but merely which losses can be the subject of compensation (damage).

Tip

To remember the difference between damage and damages, think of damages as being money – damage$. The measure of damages is the term used to describe the quantum (amount) of damages awarded.

The test of remoteness was set out in *Hadley v Baxendale* (1854).

Hadley v Baxendale (1854)

A mill owner made a contract with a carrier to deliver a crankshaft for his mill. The mill was unable to operate as the existing crankshaft was broken. The carrier did not know this. The carrier was late with delivery. The mill owner sued unsuccessfully because the carrier was unaware of the importance of prompt delivery.

Baron Alderson stated:

> Where the parties have made a contract which one of them has broken, the damages which the other party ought to receive in respect of such breach of contract should be such as may fairly and reasonably be considered arising either naturally, i.e. according to the usual course of things, from such breach of contract itself, or such as may be supposed reasonably to have been in the contemplation of both parties at the time they made the contract as the probable result of the breach.

The test is in two parts:

- The first part is measured objectively according to what loss is a natural consequence of the breach – in this case, late delivery.
- The second is subjective, based on specific knowledge of potential losses in the minds of both parties when the contract is formed – did the carrier know that the mill could not operate without the crankshaft?

The test has been developed in subsequent decisions, as in *Victoria Laundry Ltd v Newman Industries Ltd* (1949).

Victoria Laundry Ltd v Newman Industries Ltd (1949)

There was a contract to deliver a boiler to the laundry company but it was not delivered until five months after the contract date. The laundry successfully sued for loss of its usual profits from the date of the breach. This was a natural consequence loss.

The laundry also sued in respect of additional lost profits from a special contract that it had been unable to take up without the boiler. This claim failed as the special contract was unknown to the defendant at the time the contract was made.

The test is:

- Recoverable loss should be measured against a test of reasonable foreseeability.
- Foreseeability of loss is itself dependent on knowledge at the time the contract was made.
- Knowledge is of two types: common knowledge and actual knowledge of the defendant, as in *Hadley v Baxendale* (1854).

Knowledge can be implied on the basis of what a reasonable man may have contemplated in the circumstances. This is shown in *Czarnikow Ltd v Koufos (The Heron II)* (1969).

Czarnikow Ltd v Koufos (The Heron II) (1969)

A contract for the carriage of a cargo of sugar arrived late. The buyers of the cargo had intended to sell the cargo of sugar promptly upon arrival. They claimed for the loss of profit resulting from the fall in the market price of the sugar during the period of delay.

The ship owners did not know what the buyers intended to do with the sugar. But they did know that there was a market in sugar and, if they had thought about it, must have realised that it was 'not unlikely' that the sugar would be sold in the market at its market price on arrival. Since the defendant must have known that market prices fluctuate, he must have contemplated the loss (or equally a profit) as a possible result of the breach.

This principle was considered in *H Parsons (Livestock) Ltd v Uttley Ingham* (1978).

H Parsons (Livestock) Ltd v Uttley Ingham (1978)

The defendants had installed a pig nut hopper. The ventilation hatch was sealed during transit. The installers then forgot to open it. Lack of ventilation caused the nuts that were added by the customer to go mouldy. Many pigs died from eating the mouldy nuts.

The court decided that the death of the pigs would have been within the contemplation of the parties when they made their contract; therefore damages were not too remote.

Thus it is crucial to determine what was in the contemplation of the parties at the time that the contract was made. The case of *Transfield Shipping Inc. v Mercador Shipping Inc. (The Achilleas)* (2008) suggested that the test also concerns whether the damage is of a type that the defendant ought reasonably to have accepted responsibility for.

This has been reviewed again in *Wellesley Partners LLP v Withers LLP* (2015), where the law as it stands was summarised:

> A contract breaker is liable for damage resulting from his breach, if at the time of making the contract, a reasonable person in his shoes would have had damage of that kind in mind as not unlikely to result from a breach.

This case also clarified the position where a claim is made in both contract and negligence, by stating that the contract interpretation of the law as set out here should prevail.

Once the tests of causation and remoteness have established that there is liability for the loss claimed, the court then has to determine how much the claimant can recover.

24.2.3 Summary of the role of the defendant's knowledge

The knowledge that is taken into account to discover what is in the contemplation of the parties is:

- the knowledge of what happens in the ordinary course of things – the parties to the contract are assumed to know this even if they did not
- actual knowledge of special circumstances outside the ordinary course of things but that the defendant knew or was told
- the defendant will be liable if a reasonable person in the defendant's shoes at the time of making the contract would have viewed damage of that kind as not unlikely to result from a breach.

Figure 24.1 Key facts chart for remoteness of damage

	Brief legal rule	Case example
Remoteness of damage	The test is, first, measured objectively according to what loss is a natural consequence of the breach and, second, measured subjectively based on the specific knowledge of potential losses in the minds of both parties when the contract is formed	*Hadley v Baxendale* (1854)

Figure 24.2 Key cases chart for damage

Case	Judgment
Hadley v Baxendale (1854)	Sets out the two-part test for remoteness of damage
Victoria Laundry Ltd v Newman Industries Ltd (1949)	Modifies the test set out in *Hadley v Baxendale* (1854)
Czarnikow Ltd v Koufos (The Heron II) (1969)	The court decided that under the subjective part of the test in *Hadley v Baxendale* it was only necessary to show that the losses were in the reasonable contemplation of the parties as a possible result of the breach
H Parsons (Livestock) Ltd v Uttley Ingham (1978)	The court must determine what was in the contemplation of the parties at the time that the contract was made
Wellesley Partners LLP v Withers LLP (2015)	Summarises the current position on damage

24.2.4 Categories of recoverable loss

There are many ways to assess awards of damages in contract claims.

Loss of a bargain

The idea here is to place the claimant in the same financial position as if the contract had been properly performed. This can be seen in a number of ways:

1 The difference in value between the goods or services required in the contract and those actually provided. An example of this is *Bence Graphics International Ltd v Fasson UK Ltd* (1996).

> ### Bence Graphics International Ltd v Fasson UK Ltd (1996)
>
> The defendant supplied vinyl film on which the claimant printed identifying markers (decals) to put on bulk containers. There was an implied term that the decals would survive in a readable form for five years, but they lasted only two years. The court awarded damages amounting to the actual loss incurred by having to replace the decals.

2 Where there is a market, damages will be the difference between the contract price and the price in the market. If the claimant's profit remains, there is no loss. This can be seen in the case of *Charter v Sullivan* (1957). However, if there is no available market then the claimant can recover the full loss, as in *W L Thompson Ltd v Robinson Gunmakers Ltd* (1955).

> ### Charter v Sullivan (1957)
>
> The defendant contracted to buy a Hillman Minx car then refused to take delivery. Because demand for this particular car easily outstripped supply, the seller could easily sell the car and make his profit. Therefore, only nominal damages were awarded.

> ### W L Thompson Ltd v Robinson Gunmakers Ltd (1955)
>
> The defendant agreed to buy a Standard Vanguard but later refused to accept and pay for it. Supply of Standard Vanguard cars exceeded the demand. Had the garage found another customer and sold to him or her as well as the defendant, then there would have been two sales and two profits. Therefore damages were awarded for the loss of profit on one sale.

3 Loss of profit not just for goods, but also in other contracts – as in *Victoria Laundry Ltd v Newman Industries Ltd* (1949), where the claimant recovered the profit that he would have been able to make but for the breach of contract.

4 Loss of a chance – generally a speculative loss is not recoverable in contract, and most cases are based in negligence rather than contract. There was an exception in *Chaplin v Hicks* (1911), where an actress had a contractual right to attend an audition and she was wrongly prevented from attending. She therefore lost the chance of being selected for the part. The court stated that the mere fact that damages were difficult to calculate should not prevent them being awarded.

Reliance loss

This is the expense incurred by a claimant who relied on a contract being performed. A claimant may also recover expenses he or she has had to spend in advance of a contract that has been breached. An example of this can be seen in *Anglia Television Ltd v Reed* (1972).

> ### Anglia Television Ltd v Reed (1972)
>
> Anglia TV spent a lot of money preparing for a film including fees paid to the director, designer and stage manager. Robert Reed, an American actor, agreed to be the main actor but then pulled out. A suitable replacement could not be found so the film was not made. As Anglia TV could not predict what its profit on the film would have been, the court awarded damages based on reliance loss. Robert Reed must have known that such expenditure was likely and was liable for the expenses incurred by Anglia TV, both before and after the contract was made, up to breach.

It is also possible sometimes to recover damages for the loss of an amenity, as in *Farley v Skinner* (2001).

> ### Farley v Skinner (2001)
>
> The claimant asked the defendant surveyor whether the house he was to buy was subject to aircraft noise. The surveyor incorrectly reassured him that it was not. The court said that an innocent party was entitled to be placed in the position that he or she would have been in had the party in breach exercised due care.
>
> Damages were recoverable for distress and inconvenience where the matter was important to the claimant, that had been made clear to the defendant, and the required action had been incorporated into the contract. The court viewed as appropriate an award of £10,000 for the discomfort of suffering aircraft noise.

The distinction between expectation loss and reliance loss

Expectation loss

This is the normal measure of damages for breach of contract. It refers to the innocent party's loss of bargain. This includes the profits that it would have expected to receive had the contract been performed taking into account the costs it would have incurred to earn that profit. The aim of expectation loss damages is to put the innocent party in the same position as if the contract had been performed.

Reliance loss

This is also known as wasted expenditure. It refers to the expenses incurred by the claimant in reliance of the contract being performed. The aim of damages for reliance loss is to put the claimant in the position he or she would have been in had the contract never been made; here the claimant has incurred expense in preparation for the contract that is expected to be performed, but it has not been performed.

Expectation loss and reliance loss are mutually exclusive to prevent double recovery of damages.

Restitution

This is simply a repayment of any money or other benefits passed to the defendant in advance of the contract that is breached.

Figure 24.3 Key facts chart for damages

	Brief legal rule	Case example
Damages – purpose	The purpose of damages is to put the victim in the position he or she would have been in if the contract had been properly completed and performed by the defendant	
Nominal damages	If no loss is actually suffered but the breach has been established then the court may award 'nominal damages'	*Staniforth v Lyall* (1830)
***Wrotham Park* damages**	Awarded where the claimant would have very real problems in establishing financial loss and it is a 'just' response to a breach of contract	*Wrotham Park Estate Co. Ltd v Parkside Homes Ltd* (1974)
Damages for loss of a bargain	The idea here is to place the claimant in the same financial position as if the contract had been properly performed In other words, the claimant is put in the same financial position as if the main purpose of the contract had been achieved by proper performance	*Bence Graphics International Ltd v Fasson UK Ltd* (1996)
Damages where there is a market	Where there is a market, damages will be the difference between the contract price and the price obtained or required to be paid in the market	*Charter v Sullivan* (1957)
Damages for future contracts	There can be a claim for the profit that he or she would have been able to complete but for the breach of contract	*Victoria Laundry Ltd v Newman Industries Ltd* (1949)
Damages for loss of a chance	In rare circumstances the courts have allowed claimants to recover a loss that is entirely speculative; such claims are normally based on negligence	*Chaplin v Hicks* (1911)
Reliance loss	This refers to the expenses incurred by a claimant who relied on a contract being performed, but it was not performed	*Anglia Television Ltd v Reed* (1972)
Restitution	A repayment of any money or other benefits passed to the defendant in advance of the contract that is breached	
Speculative damages	Contract law has developed cases allowing damages of a highly speculative nature for mental distress while also recognising the problems with respect to privity of contract	*Ruxley Electronics and Construction Ltd v Forsyth* (1996)

Figure 24.4 Key cases chart for damages

Case	Judgment
Staniforth v Lyall (1830)	Upon breach, the claimant hired the boat to someone else for a greater profit than he would have made under the original contract As he had suffered no loss, he was awarded a nominal sum as damages
Wrotham Park Estate Co. Ltd v Parkside Homes Ltd (1974)	The claimant had suffered no loss but damages were awarded on the basis of the hypothetical sum the claimant could have charged to release the covenants
Experience Hendrix LLC v PPX Enterprises Inc. (2003)	The court decided that the publisher should pay a reasonable sum to Hendrix's estate, even though the estate had suffered no actual loss
Bence Graphics International Ltd v Fasson UK Ltd (1996)	Damages are assessed according to the difference in cost of shorter lifespan
Charter v Sullivan (1957)	Where demand exceeds supply, the claimant can still make his or her profit so there is no loss to be compensated
W L Thompson Ltd v Robinson Gunmakers Ltd (1955)	Supply exceeded demand; had the claimant found another customer and sold to him or her as well as the defendant, then there would have been two sales and two profits So loss of profit is the measure of damages
Victoria Laundry Ltd v Newman Industries Ltd (1949)	The claimant may recover for the profit that he or she would have been able to make from contracts but for the breach of contract
Chaplin v Hicks (1911)	The mere fact that damages were difficult to calculate should not prevent them being awarded
Anglia Television Ltd v Reed (1972)	The main actor pulled out and a suitable replacement could not be made so a film was not made The question of damages was decided that, as Anglia TV could not predict what its profit on the film would have been, the court awarded damages based on reliance loss
Farley v Skinner (2001)	It is possible to recover damages for the loss of an amenity under reliance loss
Ruxley Electronics and Construction Ltd v Forsyth (1996)	As he had not received the exact swimming pool that he had contracted for, the court awarded him £2500 for loss of amenity

24.2.5 The duty to mitigate the loss

The injured party must take reasonable steps to minimise the effects of the breach. This is known as **mitigation of loss**. How this works can be seen in *British Westinghouse Electric v Underground Electric Railways* (1912).

Key term

Mitigation of loss – the injured party must take reasonable steps to minimise the effects of the breach.

British Westinghouse Electric v Underground Electric Railways (1912)

The goods delivered were defective. The railway company purchased replacements, which turned out to be more efficient than the original ones. They obtained benefits over and above what they would have got from the original contract. The court said that additional benefits obtained as a result of taking reasonable steps to mitigate loss were to be accounted for when calculating damages. The court will balance loss against gain when calculating the amount of damages.

However, a claimant is not bound to go to extraordinary lengths to mitigate the loss, only to do what is reasonable in the circumstances. In an anticipatory breach, he or she is not bound to sue immediately he or she knows of the possibility of the breach, but may continue until the breach is an actual breach. This can be seen in *White and Carter (Councils) Ltd v McGregor* (1962).

White and Carter (Councils) Ltd v McGregor (1962)

The claimant made a contract to display advertisements of McGregor's garage company for three years on litter bins. The day the contract started, McGregor said they no longer wished to be on bins. The claimants refused cancellation and displayed the ads, and brought an action for the contract price. When the defendant wrongfully ended the contract, the claimants continued to fit the advertisements to the bins. The argument that the claimants might have mitigated the loss by not continuing to fit the bins failed as the contract was essentially a claim for a debt – payment of the price – so mitigation of loss did not apply.

The case of *Thai Airways v K I Holdings* (2015) shows the principle of mitigation in computation of damages.

Thai Airways v K I Holdings (2015)

The defendant company had contracted to supply the claimant with seats for its aircraft, but the seats were delivered either late or not at all. The airline leased substitute planes to mitigate its loss. The leased substitute aircraft were more fuel-efficient and this had to be taken into account. This resulted in damages being reduced by the amount of fuel saved so that the overall effect was that there was no loss and no profit to the claimant.

24.2.6 Liquidated damages

Liquidated damages are where the amount of damages has been fixed by a term in the contract. However, the courts will only accept this sum as the award of damages if the sum identified in the contract represents an accurate and proper assessment of loss. If it is not, it is seen as a penalty and will be unenforceable. The courts developed rules for determining the difference between genuine liquidated damages and a penalty in *Dunlop Pneumatic Tyre Co. v New Garage and Motor Co.* (1914):

- An extravagant sum will always be a penalty.

- Payment of a large sum for failure to settle a small debt is probably a penalty.
- A single sum operating in respect of a variety of different breaches is likely to be a penalty.
- The wording used by the parties is not necessarily conclusive.
- It is no bar to recovering a liquidated sum that actual assessment of the loss was impossible before the contract.

Key term

Liquidated damages – where the amount of damages has been fixed by a term in the contract.

However the Supreme Court has in effect rewritten the rule on penalties. The new rule is found in the conjoined appeals of *Cavendish Square Holding BV v Talal El Makdessi* and *ParkingEye Ltd v Beavis* (2015).

Cavendish Square Holding BV v Talal El Makdessi (2015)

This involved the sale of a Middle Eastern media business. The contract stated that if the seller did not comply with the terms of the contract preventing him from competing with the buyer, then he would lose his right to future payments that would otherwise have been due to him and he would have to sell his remaining shares to the buyer at a greatly reduced price.

The court held that the provisions contained in the agreements were there to protect the legitimate interests of the buyer.

ParkingEye Ltd v Beavis (2015)

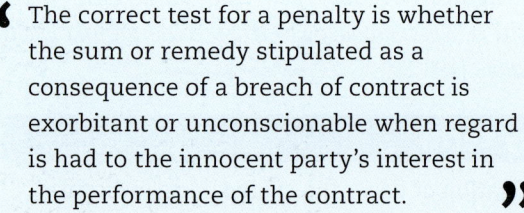

An £85 parking fine was given for overstaying the two-hour parking limit at a privately owned car park. Mr Beavis tried to argue that the fine was a penalty and therefore unenforceable.

Lord Hodge stated:

> 66 The correct test for a penalty is whether the sum or remedy stipulated as a consequence of a breach of contract is exorbitant or unconscionable when regard is had to the innocent party's interest in the performance of the contract. 99

Under the new test, the party seeking to rely on a term in a contract which predetermines the amount of damages to be paid must be able to show that the clause is to protect a legitimate interest and that the amount to be paid is not exorbitant or unconscionable. The following principles will also apply:

- The amount no longer has to be a genuine pre-estimate of loss.
- This rule applies to commercial and consumer cases.
- The party seeking to rely on the term does not have to have suffered loss.
- The purpose of the term can be to act as a deterrent against a specific breach of contract.
- The recompense under the term does not have to be financial.
- The term can only apply to a breach of a primary obligation, not a secondary one, such as not paying a contractual penalty.
- The traditional tests in the *Dunlop* case are useful for cases concerning standard damages clauses but are of little use in more complex cases. The tests are not fixed rules of general application to all situations and were never intended to be this.
- In more complex cases, a broader approach, which focuses on the nature and extent of the innocent party's interest in the performance of the relevant obligation, is more suitable.
- A term with respect to damages may be justified by some consideration apart from the desire to recover compensation for a breach. This is the commercial justification approach.
- The old penalty rule is an interference with freedom of contract. In a negotiated contract between properly advised parties of comparable bargaining power, the strong initial presumption must be that the parties themselves are the best judges of what is legitimate in a provision dealing with the consequences of breach.

This significantly widens the position in relation to the enforceability of 'penalty' clauses. In determining whether such a clause is enforceable, the court will be obliged to consider the wider commercial context of the agreement. If it can be shown that there is a legitimate reason why breach of contract damages would not be sufficient in the case in question, then even if the amount stated in the term seems to have no correlation to the actual loss suffered, it may be enforceable.

Quantum meruit

We have seen the operation of *quantum meruit* in relation to part-performance in Chapter 23.

There are three common circumstances in which such an award is made:

- In a contract for services where no price is stated, as in *Upton Rural District Council v Powell* (1942): a retained fireman provided services with no fixed agreement as to wages – the court awarded a reasonable amount.
- Where the circumstances of the case show that a fresh agreement can be implied in place of the original one, as in *Steven v Bromley* (1919): Steven had agreed to carry steel at a specified rate. When the steel was delivered it contained extra goods. Steven was able to claim extra for the additional items.
- Where a party has elected to consider the contract discharged by the other's breach, or where a party has been prevented from performing by the other party; in either case they might claim for work they have already done as in *De Barnady v Harding* (1853): a principal wrongly revoked his agent's authority to act on his behalf. The agent was then entitled to claim for the work he had already done and for expenses incurred.

Figure 24.5 Key facts chart for mitigation of loss and terms attempting to quantify damages

	Brief legal rule	Case example
The duty to mitigate the loss	The party injured by a breach of contract must take reasonable steps to minimise the effects of the breach	*Westinghouse Electric v Underground Electric Railways* (1912)
Liquidated damages	Liquidated damages are where the amount of damages has been fixed by a term in the contract	*Dunlop Pneumatic Tyre Co. v New Garage and Motor Co.* (1914)
Quantum meruit	Recovery of an unqualified sum for services already rendered	*Upton Rural District Council v Powell* (1942)

Figure 24.6 Key cases chart for mitigation of loss and terms attempting to quantify damages

Case	Judgment
Westinghouse Electric v Underground Electric Railways (1912)	It was necessary to balance loss against gain when the amount of the damages was being calculated
Thai Airways v K I Holdings (2015)	The lease of substitute aircraft which were more fuel efficient had to be taken into account
Dunlop Pneumatic Tyre Co. v New Garage and Motor Co. (1914)	The case sets out the traditional rules as to when the term is a liquidated damages clause or a penalty
Cavendish Square Holding BV v Talal El Makdessi and *ParkingEye Ltd v Beavis* (2015)	Sets out new tests for being able to rely on a penalty clause
Upton Rural District Council v Powell (1942)	Where a contract for services is silent on the issue of remuneration, *quantum meruit* applies
Steven v Bromley (1919)	Where the circumstances of the case show that a fresh agreement can be implied in place of the original one, *quantum meruit* applies
De Barnady v Harding (1853)	Where a party has elected to consider the contract discharged by the other's breach or where a party has been prevented from performing by the other party, *quantum meruit* applies

24.3 Equitable remedies

'Equity mitigates the rigours of strict law', stated Lord Denning in *Crabb v Arun District Council* (1976) and enables 'complete justice' to be achieved. Equitable remedies are awarded where damages is an inadequate remedy and justice would not be served merely by damages. Equitable remedies are not a right as they are at the discretion of the court. Unlike damages, equitable remedies are not constrained by remoteness of damage or causation, so enabling equity to go beyond the common law in providing a remedy that is appropriate and just.

One equitable remedy is an injunction, which aims to prevent a breach of contract. While injunctions are not part of the AQA specification, it should be noted that one type of injunction, a **mandatory injunction**, is very similar to an order for specific performance as it is a court order requiring a party to the contract to do something.

Key term

Mandatory injunction – a court order requiring a party to do something.

24.3.1 Specific performance

This equitable remedy is the opposite of an injunction. When the court orders specific performance, it is ordering one party to perform his or her contractual obligation, rather like a mandatory injunction. There are clear examples of where the judge exercises his or her discretion, such as *Airport Industrial GP Ltd v Heathrow Airport Ltd* (2015). Here the judge was concerned that exercising his discretion to make an order for specific performance would inevitably force a company into liquidation, so he did not make an order for specific performance of the construction of a car park.

In general, equitable remedies such as specific performance will not be available in the following circumstances:

- Where damages would be an adequate remedy, for example where substitute goods are available.
- Contracts involving personal service and contracts of employment, as seen in the case of *Page One Records Ltd v Britton* (1967).

Page One Records Ltd v Britton (1967)

The Troggs agreed that Page One Records would be their manager and sole agent for five years. The Troggs agreed not to appoint anyone else as a manager during the contract. The relationship broke down.

Page One wanted an injunction to prevent The Troggs from appointing a new manager. The injunction was refused and Page One could only claim damages. This was because the contract involved obligations of trust and confidence. An injunction would amount to forcing the band to remain idle, or to continue to employ a manager and agent in whom it had lost confidence. Forcing them to work together could not be supervised by the court.

- Where the court cannot supervise the enforcement of the contract – this would clearly be the case with a contract of personal service such as in Page One Records, but would not be the case where a unique item such as a work of art was the subject matter of the contract. The court could easily enforce delivery of a painting.
- Impossibility – where a defendant cannot perform his or her obligations under the contract, or could only do so illegally, the court will not grant specific performance, for example the export of a famous painting without the required export licence.
- Where the claimant cannot, or it is uncertain that he or she can, perform his or her side of the contract.
- Laches – If a claimant is aware of a breach of contract by the defendant, then the application to the court for an order of specific performance must be made without excessive delay as the passage of

time without complaint suggests contentedness with the contract made. An example of laches can be seen in the case of *Leaf v International Galleries* (1950) (see Chapter 22, section 22.4.1).

- The conduct of the claimant – one of the maxims of equity is 'He who seeks equity must do equity' and the court will not grant a claimant specific performance if he or she has in some way behaved dishonestly or unconscionably.

Activity

Review the scenarios in previous chapters. Where there has been a breach of contract, state the appropriate remedies. Consider, in each case, whether the Consumer Rights Act 2015 would apply, and how remedies under that Act would differ from the remedies where the Act does not apply.

24.3.2 Rescission

This has been dealt with in Chapter 22, section 22.4.1.

Figure 24.7 Key facts chart for equitable remedies

	Brief legal rule	Case example
Specific performance	This is a court order compelling someone to do something – typically hand over property that has been agreed under a contract	*Airport Industrial GP Ltd v Heathrow Airport Ltd* (2015)
Rescission	The equitable remedy of rescission means the parties are returned to the positions they were in before the contract was made	*Clarke v Dickson* (1858) (see Chapter 22, section 22.4.1)

Figure 24.8 Key cases chart for equitable remedies

Case	Judgment
Page One Records Ltd v Britton (1967)	An injunction will not be awarded for a party to complete a personal service as the court is unable to supervise such an order
Airport Industrial GP Ltd v Heathrow Airport Ltd (2015)	Specific performance was not ordered as it would inevitably force a company into liquidation which would be unjust in the circumstances

See Chapter 20, section 20.5.3 for information about remedies under the Consumer Rights Act 2015.

24.4 Termination of contract for breach

This can be a repudiatory breach by the guilty party to the contract.

At common law (therefore not including statutory rights), breach can result in the terminating of the contract, if the affected party so chooses, where:

- there is a breach of a condition or breach of an innominate term construed as a condition
- one party refuses to perform his or her obligations under a contract at all or the substantial part of its obligations, including anticipatory breach
- one party makes it impossible to perform the contract.

24.4.1 Rights against the goods

Rights against the goods include the right to reject the goods for breach of contract. We have already seen this, along with consumer remedies under the Consumer Rights Act 2015. Many contracts include a reservation of title clause in them whereby the title (ownership) of goods remains with the seller until the buyer has paid for them. The Sale of Goods Act 1979 also provides three specific rights for an unpaid seller of goods:

- A lien, which is a right to retain possession of the goods of the debtor until paid. This is an unpaid seller's lien. There are also other liens such as a repairer's lien.

- In case of the insolvency of the buyer, a right of stopping the goods in transit and regaining possession of the goods from a carrier.
- A right of resale as limited by the Act.

Key term

Lien – the right to retain possession of the goods of the debtor until paid.

We have seen that consumers have rights and remedies with respect to the goods. These are:

- the short-term right to reject under s 20
- the right to repair or replacement under s 23
- the right to a price reduction or the final right to reject under s 24.

Summary

- Remedies for breach of contract can be either legal or equitable remedies.

- Damages are the most common form of remedy and are compensation for losses suffered.

- In specific circumstances, more than the actual loss suffered will be awarded.

- Contracts sometimes try to establish what damages will be payable if there is a breach. These are valid terms if considered liquidated damages, but not if they are considered a penalty.
- Equitable remedies are discretionary.
- Specific performance requires delivery of goods but is not available for contracts of service.

Human rights

25 Rules and theory in human rights law

After reading this chapter, you should be able to:

■ Understand the rules and principles of law relating to certain rights recognised by the ECHR, and in the United Kingdom
■ Understand:
 – the theories of rights
 – rights contrasted with liberties
 – the scope of 'fundamental human' rights

25.1 Rules in human rights law

Any discussion of human rights in the UK has to be considered within the constitutional position. Unlike many countries, the UK constitution is not written or contained in a single document or series of documents. Rights in the UK have been protected by:

■ legislation made by Parliament such as HRA 1998
■ judicial decisions (also known as common law)
■ documents such as Magna Carta and the Bill of Rights
■ conventions such as collective cabinet responsibility
■ authoritative writings.

The UK constitution is based on the doctrine of the **separation of powers** and the **rule of law**.

Key terms

Separation of powers – a theory proposed by Montesquieu that the powers in a state should be shared between three bodies: the executive (or government), the legislature (or law makers such as Parliament) and the judiciary (judges in court). This sharing would prevent one body becoming too powerful over the others.

Rule of law – the principle that law should govern a nation, as opposed to it being governed by arbitrary decisions of individuals or government officials. All people and institutions in the state should be subject to, and accountable to, law that is fairly applied and enforced and that no person or institution is above the law.

A common misconception which has applied for a number of years, and still applies, is that the ECHR and its institutions were forced upon an unwilling UK as part of a wider European project. But the reality is that the UK was one of the architects of the human rights agenda that followed the Second World War.

The ECHR has its roots in the philosophical tradition of universal rights which stretches back to the Enlightenment of the eighteenth century and the French Revolution. But the actual spur for creating a model set of rights in the twentieth century was the Allies' determination to bring peace to Europe.

The first international step towards codifying these rights came when the General Assembly of the United Nations adopted the Universal Declaration of Human Rights in 1948. In Europe, largely driven by the UK, work was taking place to create a form of rights customised to the continent, and in 1950 the members of the Council of Europe signed the ECHR, which came into force in 1953. The UK was one of the first members of the Council of Europe to ratify the Convention when it passed through Parliament in 1951. The ECHR allowed an individual with a grievance against a state to challenge his or her treatment in the ECtHR in Strasbourg at international level.

> See Chapter 33 for more detailed information on the ECtHR.

However, it was not until 1966 that the UK granted the right for an individual to take a case to Strasbourg. This meant that UK citizens could only challenge the laws of the state at a European level, which was a costly and lengthy process, and limited compensation was available if a breach of human rights was proved. Breach of ECHR rights could not be argued directly before a UK court.

HRA 1998 was passed by Parliament to deal with this situation and allowed UK citizens to claim remedies for breach of human rights in UK courts. The ECHR was incorporated into UK law and Convention rights became directly enforceable against a public body by an individual who could show that his or her rights had been breached. In addition, HRA 1998 allowed a UK court to declare that a piece of UK legislation was incompatible with a Convention right (though there is no power for a court to overrule the legislation). UK courts can also interpret legislation so that it is compatible with Convention rights.

The ECHR contains 14 Articles, setting out different individual rights which are mainly civil and political in nature. Some ECHR rights are **absolute rights** where a state cannot justify interfering with them. They include the prohibition of torture, inhuman or degrading treatment (Article 3) and the prohibition of slavery and forced labour (Article 4). Other rights are **limited** or **qualified**.

In the AQA specification we are concerned with the following specific rights:

- Article 2 – the right to life. This is an absolute right which cannot be derogated from in peacetime. However, there are exceptions which allow a state to justify killing under certain specified circumstances and allow the right to be derogated from in wartime.
- Article 5 – the right to liberty and security of person. This is a limited right.
- Article 8 – the right to respect for family, private life, home and correspondence.
- Article 10 – the right to freedom of expression.
- Article 11 – the right to freedom of assembly and association.

Articles 8, 10 and 11 are all qualified rights, so that if the state can justify a limitation of these rights that is in accordance with law and meets a legitimate aim, there will be no breach of the EHCR.

Key terms

Absolute rights – this is where a duty is placed upon a state that must be performed in all circumstances, such as the right to life under Article 2 and the right not to be tortured under Article 3.

Limited rights – this is where a right is set out, such as the right to liberty in Article 5, but it sets out circumstances when the right is limited such as imprisonment after conviction.

Qualified rights – this is where, because of public interest, or to protect the rights of others, it is proper to restrict the freedom. In Article 10 there is a general right of freedom of expression, but this can be legitimately restricted, for example by placing reporting restrictions on the media during the course of a criminal trial in order to ensure a fair trial.

25.2 Theories of human rights

If you were to ask the question, 'What are human rights?', you would get many different answers and few people would know all their rights.

A **right** is a freedom of some kind. It is something to which you are entitled by virtue of being human.

Human rights are based on the principle of respect for the individual. Their fundamental assumption is that each person is a moral and rational being who deserves to be treated with dignity. They are called human rights because they are universal. Whereas nations, or groups of people, enjoy specific rights that apply only to them, human rights are the rights to which everyone is entitled – no matter who they are or where they live – simply because they are alive.

Key terms

Rights – things to which everyone is entitled or allowed: they are guaranteed freedoms. They could include the right to life, to liberty and the security of person, to privacy, to freedom of expression, and to freedom of assembly and association as recognised by the ECHR and in the UK.

Human rights – rights and freedoms that everyone in a country and the world are entitled to because they are human.

When asked to name their rights, many people will perhaps list freedom of speech, thought and belief, and perhaps one or two others. These are important rights, but the full scope of human rights is broader. They mean choice and opportunity: the freedom to obtain a job, adopt a career, select a partner of one's choice and raise children. They include the right to travel widely and the right to work without harassment, abuse and threat of arbitrary dismissal. They could even include the right to leisure.

However, these 'universal' rights are not unlimited. The state may restrict some of these rights and may also set out a framework where different individuals' rights conflict. We will see this, for example, in the conflict between freedom of expression and the right to a private life. The extent to which these are limited by the state varies in different countries and at different times. It is sometimes argued that these limitations are set by democratic means, reflecting the views of society and morality and are varied to achieve justice between different parties.

Shortly before his death, and while he was seriously ill, there were suggestions of improper conduct relating to, among others, Lord Britton, a former senior politician. A television van was parked across the road from his country residence, blocking the driveway to another large house in the village. The tenants of that house soon got the van to move so they would not be able to film Lord Britton leaving his house. (In fact he was not living there at the time.)

A photographer placed himself in the churchyard opposite Lord Britton's house and remained there for much of the day with a long lens trained on the front door of the house. The photographer was very annoyed when he was photographed waiting for Lord Britton by a resident of the village.

1 What are the different human rights involved in this situation?

2 Would it matter if Lord Britton had already died?

3 Consider the recent Google 'right to be forgotten' cases. What, if any, is the distinction between the successful and the unsuccessful applicants? Are the rights, freedoms and human rights different?

25.2.1 The development of human rights

Human rights' thinking is almost entirely a creation of the second half of the twentieth century and post-Second World War. However, there were certain thoughts about human rights in ancient times, starting with the ancient civilisation of Babylon.

From Babylon, the idea of human rights spread quickly to India, Greece and eventually Rome. There, the idea of 'natural law' came about due to the fact that people tended to follow certain unwritten laws in the course of life, and Roman law was based on rational ideas derived from the nature of things.

In time documents were made asserting individual rights. These included the *Magna Carta* (1215), the Petition of Right (1628), the US Constitution (1787), the French Declaration of the Rights of Man and of the Citizen (1789) and the US Bill of Rights (1791). They are the written forerunners to many of today's human rights documents. Eventually, in the wake of the Second World War, the Universal Declaration of Human Rights was written, with its 30 rights to which all people are entitled.

See Chapter 26 for more information on the Universal Declaration of Human Rights.

25.2.2 Basic principles

- Human rights belong to every individual regardless of sex, race, nationality, socio-economic group, political opinion, sexual orientation or any other status.
- Ideally, human rights are universal and should apply to everyone simply on the basis of being human. However, as with the following point, not every state will accept their application to everyone or that they cannot be interfered with.
- Human rights are inalienable. They cannot be taken away simply because the state does not like the person seeking to exercise his or her rights. They can only be limited in certain tightly defined circumstances and some rights, such as the prohibition on torture and slavery, can never be limited.
- Human rights are indivisible. The state cannot pick and choose which rights it accepts. Many rights depend on each other to be meaningful – so, for example, the right to free speech must go together with the right to assemble peacefully.
- Human rights are owed by the state to the people. This means that public bodies must respect an individual's human rights and the government must ensure that there are laws in place so that people respect each other's rights. For example, the right to life requires not only that the actions of those working on behalf of the state do not lead to a person's death, but that laws are also in place to protect an individual from the actions of others that might want to cause a person harm.

In addition to these basic rights owed to every individual, the UK Government has, in recent years, tried to address what it refers to as social rights granted to specific groups to improve the quality of their lives. Some of these social rights are:

- equal pay for equal work
- the right not to be unfairly dismissed from work
- the right not to be discriminated against on the grounds of sex, race, or disability
- rights given to consumers when buying goods or services.

Note that there is no one obvious characteristic of being human out of which 'human rights' arise. The Charter of Fundamental Rights and Freedoms referred to below has 'dignity' as its first title but this could be said to raise as many problems as it solves – why is this separated out if 'dignity' is the underlying quality protected by human rights?

Human rights thinking arises out of a view of what we want human beings to be, not out of what they are. It is closely tied to the notion of democracy so a state which professes to be democratic is more likely to promote and protect human rights than an undemocratic state. However, in a democratic state the nature and scope of what is a human right may be contested and subject to agreement, negotiation or challenge.

The boundary between fundamental rights and freedoms on the one hand and social, economic and cultural rights on the other is likely to shift over time, as evidenced by the original content and subsequent interpretation of the EHCR and then the Charter of Fundamental Rights and Freedoms.

25.3 Rights contrasted with liberties

Legal writers and academics have, at various times, attempted to analyse what is meant by a 'right'.

In *Jurisprudence*, Salmond considered a legal right as being separate, from, but connected to, an interest, which was defined as being 'things connected to a man's advantage'. For example, a right to defend one's person or property is separate from, but connected to, protecting one's interests in life and property. However, not all interests are protected by legal rights. It may be in one's interest to take and save money for a comfortable retirement, but the law of theft prevents one from taking another's money or property.

Another thought is that a legal right can only exist where the holder of the right can enforce it by bringing a legal action. However, there may be a complication here, as certain legal actions are time-bound for example, in tort and contract there are limitation periods which prevent an action being brought after a certain number of years.

Another view is that where there is a right there is a corresponding duty on another. For example, if X owes Y £1000, then Y has a legal right to be paid by X and X is under a corresponding duty to pay Y. The right and duty are the opposite of each other. Taking this approach would mean that every right had a corresponding duty and every duty had a corresponding right.

A contrary view to this rights and duties approach was made by Austin, who said that in criminal law everyone has a legal duty not to commit crime, but it is not easy to identify what the corresponding right is.

These views show that no one meaning can be given to the term 'right', though it could be said to revolve around a basic right to be free from unequal treatment.

In its legal definition, a 'liberty' could be defined as 'freedom from government or private interference or constraints' and 'the ability to exercise the rights detailed in a constitution or available or under natural law'. 'Liberties', especially before the Human Rights Act 1998, concerned what was thought to be what an individual could do unless there were specific prohibitions or compulsions. So, for example, demonstrations were allowed unless specifically prohibited by the police under legislation such as the Public Order act 1986. Also freedom of expression was not specifically supported; an individual could say or do what they thought unless the authorities considered it should not be allowed. Since the introduction of the Human Rights Act the approach has changed. An individual has, for example, freedom of expression protected under Article 10 and freedom of assembly and association protected under Article 11. The authorities have to now take these freedoms (liberties) into account when considering what action, if any, to take.

As has been said, one view of a 'right' is that it imposes a corresponding duty to do, or not to do, something, whereas a 'liberty' or freedom merely implies the absence of a prohibition or compulsion.

This distinction between rights and liberties or freedoms is useful, because it helps to clarify the distinction between the approach of English law pre and post HRA 1998.

Before HRA 1998, the extent of 'freedom of expression or speech', for example, could be decided only by examining all the prohibitions or compulsions contained in existing legislation and common law. The approach was to start with a potential unrestrained freedom (for example of expression or speech) and then subtract from it all the constraints or compulsions. What was left was the extent of freedom of expression or speech. Liberty or freedom was 'residual', literally the 'residue' of what was not prohibited or compelled by legislation or common law.

This meant that, for example, prohibitions could be introduced on any form of expression without being subjected to any kind of control that recognised a more general interest in freedom of expression. So, for instance, the legality of police activity in suppressing marches or demonstrations was judged almost entirely by reference to criminal law rules relating to violence, threatening behaviour, disturbing public order or preserving the peace. Sometimes civil law rules of trespass to land or to the person applied as well. Occasionally, judges made reference to some overriding principle of freedom of speech, but rarely in any way that made a difference.

Post HRA 1998, when 'freedom of expression' became a 'right to freedom of expression', this changed. Turning a coach full of protesters back some miles from their intended protest location, or when demonstrators were 'kettled' or arrested for breach of the peace, was no longer simply a matter of applying relevant rules of criminal law to the activities of protesters and the conduct of the police. It also involved an investigation into whether that police conduct engaged Article 10 and/or 11 ECHR. If it did, and the conduct amounted to an interference with those rights, then, in the absence of a justification under Article 10(2) or 11(2), there would be a violation.

After 1966, but before HRA 1998, this would have meant bringing an action in the ECtHR only. After HRA 1998, action could be taken in the English courts, whether by way of a defence to a criminal charge or by way of an action against the police as a public authority to recover damages for breach of ECHR rights

Further, the authorities now have to take ECHR rights into account when considering what action, if any, to take when faced with a protest or demonstration.

The UK does not have a written constitution to set out the rights or **civil liberties** of its citizens. It does, however, have a long history of recognising certain freedoms, and many written constitutions around the world are based on the rights which have for centuries been upheld by UK courts. One example is *habeas corpus*, which has been in effect since at least the fourteenth century. Under this rule, anyone who has been arrested or deprived of his or her liberty may request that he or she is presented before a judge so that the legality of the detention can be judicially decided. Since 9/11, it has been argued that the spirit of this ancient law has been severely undermined in the UK by the introduction of various pieces of anti-terrorism legislation. The government argues that this approach is necessary to ensure the safety of the country and its citizens. Opponents argue that the legislation has gone beyond an acceptable line of what a citizen can and cannot do within a representative democracy. Despite this, successive governments have increased the scope of anti-terrorism legislation.

Key terms

Civil liberties – freedoms guaranteed by a state to people to protect them from an over-powerful government. They are found in democratic states such as the UK but not in undemocratic states such as North Korea.

Habeas corpus – a writ issued by the court which required the immediate production of a detained person so the court could hear arguments for and against the continuation of the detention.

One way to consider the difference between 'civil rights' and 'civil liberties' is to look at:

- what right is affected, and
- whose right is affected.

For example, as an employee, a worker does not have the legal right to be promoted, as obtaining promotion is not a guaranteed 'civil liberty'. However, an employee, whether male, female or disabled, has a right not to be discriminated against in the workplace. By choosing not to promote an employee solely because of the employee's gender or disability, the employer has committed a civil rights violation and has engaged in unlawful employment discrimination based on gender or disability.

25.4 The scope of fundamental human rights

In addition to generally recognised human rights, the concept of fundamental rights to which individuals are entitled has developed.

24.4.1 EU rights

For individuals in member countries of the **European Union** (EU), certain fundamental rights are contained in a Charter which was signed at the same time as the Treaty of Lisbon in 2009. As a result, it became part of EU law and is given effect in the UK while the UK remains a member of the EU. It is separate from the **European Convention on Human Rights**, although there is some overlap.

The Charter of Fundamental Rights and Freedoms brings together all the personal, civil, political and individual rights that are common to EU member states. As part of EU law, it also forms part of the domestic law of each member state. In the UK it may be argued by individuals before UK courts alleging a breach of fundamental rights, as an alternative to, or in addition to claims under HRA 1998 and/or the common law.

Key terms

European Union – a political and economic union of 28 member states of which the UK has been a member since 1973. As a result of the 2016 referendum vote, the UK is committed to leave the EU in 2019.

European Convention on Human Rights – an international treaty signed in 1950 to protect human rights and fundamental freedoms in the 47 states that have adopted it. It is separate from the EU and its terms are overseen by the ECtHR. The UK will not be departing from this treaty when it leaves the EU.

Figure 25.3 Key facts chart on the differences between the EU and the Council of Europe

Institution	European Union	Council of Europe
Establishment	Treaty of Rome 1957 as amended Includes the Charter of Fundamental Rights and Freedoms signed in 2009	European Convention of Human Rights 1953
Membership	28 countries (until UK exits under Brexit)	47 countries who have signed the Convention
UK membership	From 1974 as a result of the European Communities Act 1973 UK due to leave when Brexit takes effect	Ratified by Parliament in 1951 Effective since 1953
Purpose	To break down barriers between member countries in areas such as movement of goods, services and individuals	An individual can take action against a member state to enforce a protected human right
Effect on individuals in UK	Since 1974, an individual or business can take action in UK courts to enforce rights under EU law	Since 1966, an individual could take action in the ECtHR to enforce their rights After HRA 1998, an individual can take action in UK courts to enforce his or her rights If this is not allowed, an individual can appeal to ECtHR
Ultimate arbiter	European Court of Justice	European Court of Human Rights
Rights protected	Under EU law, the right to free movement of goods services and individual movement Under the Charter, 'human' rights of dignity, freedoms, equality, solidarity, citizen's rights and justice can be relied upon in UK courts Charter rights are in addition to and run alongside rights granted by the ECHR	Rights including: ■ life (Art 2) ■ liberty and security of the person (Art 5) ■ privacy (Art 8) ■ freedom of expression (Art 10) ■ freedom of assembly and association (Art 11)

25.4.2 The common law

The Supreme Court has, in a number of judgments, sought to promote the primacy of the common law in the protection of fundamental rights. In a number of recent judgments, the Supreme Court has emphasised the power and primacy of common law rights by underscoring that '[c]onventions, institutions, bills of rights and the like … recognis[e] rather than creat[e]' protections that are inherent in and fundamental to democratic society. The judgments emphasise the common law as the first port of call in claims for breaches of fundamental rights, emphasising that its development was not halted by the incorporation of the ECHR into domestic law. As Lord Toulson stated in *Kennedy v Charity Commission* (2014), 'it was not the purpose of the Human Rights Act 1998 that the common law should become an ossuary'.

There is no definitive list of common law rights, but cases decided by the courts give an idea of rights recognised by the common law. They include rights protected under the ECHR and the Charter and are listed in Figure 25.4.

Figure 25.4 Key cases of rights recognised by common law

Rights recognised by common law	Case
The right to life	R (Amin) v Secretary of State (2004)
The prohibition on torture	A v Secretary of State for the Home Department (No. 2) (2005)
The right to humanity	R v Secretary of State for Social Security, ex parte JCWI (1997)
The right to liberty	A v Secretary of State (2005)
The right to property	HM Treasury v Ahmed (2010)
The right to citizenship	Pham v Secretary of State (2015)
The right of access to justice	R (Medical Justice) v Secretary of State (2011)
The right to confidential communication with a lawyer	R (Daly) v Secretary of State for the Home Department (2001)

As the cases in Figure 25.4 show, many of the successful challenges in recent years to the interference with fundamental rights have been based in part on the common law.

The question of the interrelationship between rights protected by common law and protections guaranteed under HRA 1998/ECHR has been considered by the Supreme Court in claims based on rights arising under HRA 1998/ECHR. They were rights to freedom of speech, to a fair trial and to open justice – all of which are core rights under common law. The Supreme Court made clear its view that the natural starting point in disputes before domestic courts should be the common law – not HRA 1998/ECHR. Thereafter, as a second step, HRA 1998/ECHR may be used as a 'check' or 'fall-back' to find whether further development of the common law is required to keep pace with the protections afforded by it.

The common law does not allow the broad approach to statutory interpretation permitted under HRA 1998. Nor does it allow courts to make declarations of incompatibility between a rights-breaching statute and the common law, nor disapply inconsistent statutory provisions, as required by the Charter. Rights under common law may be overridden or rebutted by a clear, contrary parliamentary intention, set out in a subsequent statute. While lawyers should not overlook the common law, breaches of HRA 1998/ECHR and the Charter should always be pleaded, for the clear, substantive and procedural protections that they give.

Summary

- Human rights belong to everyone; they are universal rights and freedoms to which all people throughout the world are entitled.
- Human rights cannot be removed by the state but can be limited.
- They are owed by the state to their people; they cannot be earned by individuals.
- Civil liberties are rights and freedoms granted by the legislature or the courts.
- Civil liberties prevent governments from abusing their powers and restrict state interference in people's lives.
- Civil liberties are found in democratic states but not in undemocratic states.
- The Charter of Fundamental Rights and Freedoms signed in 2009 is part of EU law and can be relied upon by individuals in national courts.
- Charter rights are in addition to and run alongside rights granted by the ECHR.
- Charter rights cover dignity, freedoms, equality, solidarity, citizens' rights and justice.
- The UK opt-out of the Charter provided that its new rights are not given to UK citizens unless UK law has been introduced to cover Charter rights.
- The Supreme Court's view is that the starting point in disputes before domestic courts should be the common law – not HRA 1998/ECHR. Only as a second step should HRA 1998/ECHR be used as a 'check' or 'fall-back', to find whether further development of the common law is required to keep pace with the protections afforded by it.
- Rights at common law cannot take precedence over statutory provisions.

26 Human rights in international law

After reading this chapter, you should be able to understand:

■ The Second World War and its aftermath in relation to human rights
■ The reasons behind the establishment of the United Nations and the Universal Declaration of Human Rights 1948
■ The reasons behind the establishment of the Council of Europe and the European Convention on Human Rights 1953
■ The relationship between human rights and the European Union

26.1 The Second World War and its aftermath in relation to human rights

Before and during the Second World War, the rights of many individuals had been taken away by totalitarian regimes. National, ethnic and religious groups and individuals had been exterminated, imprisoned, detained, or forcibly resettled or conscripted, and human rights were ignored or abused. Fighting raged from 1939 to 1945, and as the end drew near, cities throughout Europe and Asia lay in ruins. Millions of people were dead; millions more were homeless or starving, and the idea of human rights strongly emerged. The discovery of mass extermination by Nazi Germany of Jews, gypsies, homosexuals and persons with disabilities horrified the world. Trials were held in Nuremberg and Tokyo after the war, and officials from the defeated countries were punished for committing war crimes, 'crimes against peace', and 'crimes against humanity'.

Governments then committed themselves to establishing the United Nations, with the primary goal of bolstering international peace and preventing future conflict. People wanted to ensure that never again would anyone be unjustly denied life, freedom, food, shelter and nationality. The essence of these emerging human rights principles was captured in President Roosevelt's 1941 State of the Union Address when he spoke of a world founded on four essential freedoms:

■ freedom of speech
■ freedom of religion
■ freedom from want, and
■ freedom from fear.

There was an international call for standards of human rights to protect citizens from abuse by government, standards against which governments could be held accountable for the treatment of their citizens. These concerns played a critical role in the San Francisco meeting that drafted the United Nations Charter in 1945.

26.2 The United Nations and the Universal Declaration of Human Rights 1948

In April 1945, delegates from 50 countries met in San Francisco. The goal of the United Nations Conference on International Organization was to fashion an international body to promote peace and prevent future wars. The ideals of the organisation were stated in the preamble to its proposed charter: 'We the peoples of the United Nations are determined to save succeeding generations from the scourge of war, which twice in our lifetime has brought untold sorrow to mankind.'

The Charter of the new United Nations (UN) organisation came into effect on 24 October 1945. The UN came into being as an intergovernmental body with the purpose of saving future generations from the devastation of international conflict.

The Charter of the UN established six principal bodies, including the General Assembly, the Security Council, the International Court of Justice, and in relation to human rights, an Economic and Social Council (ECOSOC). It empowered ECOSOC to establish 'commissions in economic and social fields and for the promotion of human rights'. One of these was the United Nations Human Rights Commission, which, under the chairmanship of Eleanor Roosevelt, drafted the Universal Declaration of Human Rights.

26.2.1 The Universal Declaration of Human Rights 1948

Eleanor Roosevelt in 1949

The Declaration was referred to by Eleanor Roosevelt as the international *Magna Carta* for all mankind and was adopted by the UN on 10 December 1948.

In its preamble and in Article 1, the Declaration sets out the rights of all human beings:

> **Disregard and contempt for human rights have resulted in barbarous acts which have outraged the conscience of mankind, and the advent of a world in which human beings shall enjoy freedom of speech and belief and freedom from fear and want has been proclaimed as the highest aspiration of the common people ... All human beings are born free and equal in dignity and rights.**

The member states of the United Nations pledged to work together to promote the 30 Articles of human rights that, for the first time in history, had been codified into a single document.

It was drafted by representatives of all regions of the world, covering all legal traditions. It is the most universal human rights document in existence, setting out the 30 fundamental rights that form the basis for a democratic society.

The General Assembly called upon all member countries to publicise the text of the Declaration and 'to cause it to be disseminated, displayed, read and expounded principally in schools and other educational institutions, without distinction based on the political status of countries or territories'.

The Declaration is a living document that has been accepted as a contract internationally between governments and their citizens. According to the *Guinness Book of World Records*, it is the most translated document in the world. It provided a long list of rights, most of which are familiar 'political' rights but also 'social' rights, such as the right to work.

The Declaration was not a treaty in the formal sense as it did not create legally binding obligations. It was not ratified by individual nations but approved by the General Assembly, and the UN charter did not give the General Assembly the power to make international law. The rights were described in vague, aspirational terms, which could be interpreted in multiple ways, and national governments – even the liberal democracies – were wary of setting binding legal obligations. The US did not commit itself to eliminating racial segregation, and Britain and France did not commit themselves to liberating the populations in their colonies. Several authoritarian states – including the Soviet Union, Yugoslavia and Saudi Arabia – refused to vote in favour of the Universal Declaration and instead abstained.

In addition, there was disagreement between the US and the Soviet Union. The US argued that human rights consisted of political rights such as the rights to vote, to speak freely, not to be arbitrarily detained and to practise a religion of one's choice, all of which were set out in the US constitution. The Soviet Union argued that human rights consisted of social or economic rights – the rights to work, to health care and to education. Members of the UN tended to support political rights (especially liberal democracies) or economic rights (socialist countries) and negotiations to convert the Universal Declaration into a binding treaty were split. It would take another 18 years for the UN to adopt a political rights treaty and an economic rights treaty. The International Covenant on Civil and Political Rights and the International Covenant on Economic, Social and Cultural Rights finally took effect in 1976.

Look online

Research the 30 Articles of the Universal Declaration of Human Rights at this web address: www.humanrights.com/what-are-human-rights/universal-declaration-of-human-rights/preamble.html. Which of the Articles is of most importance to you?

26.3 The Council of Europe and the European Convention on Human Rights 1953

Formed in 1949, the Council of Europe is completely separate from the EU and much larger, with 47 members compared to the EU's 28. It is an intergovernmental organisation. The UK became a Council member from the start, 24 years before it joined the EU. The UK's membership of the Council of Europe will be unaffected when it leaves the EU.

The aim of the Council of Europe was to protect human rights and the rule of law, and to promote democracy within its members. The member states' first task was to draw up a treaty to secure basic rights for anyone within their borders, including their own citizens and people of other nationalities.

Originally proposed by Winston Churchill and drafted mainly by British lawyers, the European Convention on Human Rights was based on the United Nations' Universal Declaration of Human Rights. It was signed in Rome in 1950 and came into force in 1953.

The Convention consists of numbered 'Articles' protecting basic human rights. The UK eventually made these rights part of its domestic law through HRA 1998. The Convention guarantees specific rights and freedoms and prohibits unfair and harmful practices. It secures:

- the right to life (Article 2)
- freedom from torture (Article 3)
- freedom from slavery (Article 4)
- the right to liberty (Article 5)
- the right to a fair trial (Article 6)
- the right not to be punished for something that was not against the law at the time (Article 7)
- the right to respect for family and private life (Article 8)
- freedom of thought, conscience and religion (Article 9)
- freedom of expression (Article 10)
- freedom of assembly (Article 11)
- the right to marry and start a family (Article 12)
- the right not to be discriminated against in respect of these rights (Article 14)
- the right to protection of property (Protocol 1, Article 1)
- the right to education (Protocol 1, Article 2)
- the right to participate in free elections (Protocol 1, Article 3)
- the abolition of the death penalty (Protocol 13).

The Convention is enforced by the ECtHR in Strasbourg. Any person claiming to be the victim of a violation of one of the above Articles in a member state may take a case to the ECtHR. The claimant must first have exhausted all possible recourse in the courts of their home country and have filed an application for relief with the ECtHR. In 1966, six years after the ECtHR was created, the UK granted what is known as 'individual petition' – the right for individuals who claim their human rights have been breached to take their cases directly to Strasbourg. Since October 2000, when HRA 1998 came into force, UK citizens have been able to enforce their human rights in UK courts without having to go to Strasbourg. However, if they cannot get satisfaction in a UK court, they still have the right to take a case to the ECtHR.

26.4 Human Rights and the European Union

As was mentioned in the previous chapter, the concept of human rights has been developed by the EU. These rights are contained in a Charter which is an instrument of the EU and was signed at the same time as the Treaty of Lisbon in 2009. As it is part of EU law, and while the UK remains a member of the EU, it is given effect in the UK. It is separate from the ECHR, although there is some overlap.

26.4.1 The Charter of Fundamental Rights and Freedoms

This document brings together all the personal, civil, political and individual rights common to EU member states. It forms part of EU law and is subject to rulings of the European Court of Justice (ECJ). As part of EU law, it also forms part of domestic law and may be argued by individuals before UK courts alleging a breach of fundamental rights, as an alternative to, or in addition to, claims under HRA 1998 and/or the common law.

Although decisions of the ECtHR are not directly binding on the ECJ, ECHR law represents a baseline protection of the rights below which EU law cannot fall. While EU law can enhance and extend the protections provided under ECHR law, the protections afforded under the Charter can never be lower than those afforded under the ECHR.

The Charter contains some 54 articles divided into seven titles.

- The first title (Dignity) guarantees the right to life and prohibits torture, slavery, the death penalty, eugenic practices and human cloning.
- The second title (Freedoms) covers liberty, personal integrity, privacy, protection of personal data, marriage, thought, religion, expression, assembly, education, work, property and asylum.
- The third title (Equality) covers equality before the law, prohibition of all discrimination including on the basis of disability, age and sexual orientation, cultural, religious and linguistic diversity, the rights of children and the elderly.
- The fourth title (Solidarity) covers social and workers' rights including the right to fair working conditions, protection against unjustified dismissal, and access to health care, social and housing assistance.
- The fifth title (Citizen's Rights) covers the rights of the EU citizens, such as the right to vote in elections to the European Parliament and to move freely within the EU. It also includes several administrative rights such as the right to good administration, to access documents and to petition the European Parliament.
- The sixth title (Justice) covers justice issues such as the right to an effective remedy, a fair trial, the presumption of innocence, the principle of legality, non-retrospectivity and double jeopardy.
- The seventh title (General Provisions) concerns the interpretation and application of the Charter.

Evidence collected by the British Government indicates that the Charter has had a limited impact on domestic law. This may be due to a lack of awareness about it and confusion about its status in domestic law.

Summary

- The United Nations was established after the Second World War to promote peace and prevent future conflict.
- The Universal Declaration of Human Rights was signed in 1948 and codified internationally individual human rights in 30 Articles.
- The Declaration was not a formal treaty and did not bind individual countries; it was ratified by the General Assembly of the United Nations.
- The ECHR was based on the Universal Declaration and was made between the member states of the Council of Europe.
- The Convention sets out 'articles' which protect individual human rights.
- An individual who claims that one of his or her human rights has been breached may take a state to the ECtHR for a remedy provided he or she has exhausted all domestic remedies.
- The Charter of Fundamental Rights and Freedoms is a document of the EU and can be relied upon by an individual in domestic courts of EU member states in addition to rights under the ECHR.
- The Charter sets a baseline protection of the rights below which EU law cannot fall.

27 Human Rights in the UK before and after the Human Rights Act 1998

After reading this chapter, you should be able to understand:

- The status of the European Convention on Human Rights in the UK before the Human Rights Act 1998
- The impact of decisions of the European Court of Human Rights on the UK before the Human Rights Act
- The effect of the Human Rights Act 1998 on incorporating and interpreting the provisions of the European Convention on Human Rights into UK laws
- The impact on constitutional arrangements and on UK law

27.1 The status of the European Convention on Human Rights in the UK before the Human Rights Act 1998

Before the enactment of HRA 1998, what we now describe as the law on human rights was generally considered to be the law on civil liberties. Liberties were residual, implying that the scope of liberties could be decided only by first establishing the extent of what compulsions, constraints or restrictions were imposed by statute, common law, and any relevant administrative and other procedures. Whatever remained represented the scope of liberties. As the discussion of interests in relation to Article 8 in Chapter 30 will show, this is not the full story, for rights were sometimes in issue. Even so, it is evident in areas such as freedom of expression, discussed in relation to Article 11 in Chapter 32.

The UK was one of the first countries to ratify the ECHR when it was first created in 1953. However, UK citizens were unable to take a case to the ECtHR until 1966, and the ECHR was not formally incorporated into law in the UK until the passing of the HRA in 1998. Since 1966, everyone in the UK has been protected by the Convention; laws in the UK had to comply with the ECHR and claims of a violation of rights could be taken to the ECtHR. This did not mean that the ECHR was totally without impact. The fact that the UK had ratified the ECHR meant that, under international law, the UK incurred obligations. This had three effects:

- Government ministers and, more gener ally, Parliament were required to consider the compatibility of proposed new legislation with the ECHR. The UK is a **dualist system** when incorporating international law into the UK legal system. This means that Parliament must pass legislation in order to make provisions in a treaty between the UK and another country or organisation part of UK law and so directly enforceable in a UK court.
- Courts were required, when interpreting unclear or ambiguous statutory or common law, to attempt to adopt an interpretation consistent with the UK's obligations under the ECHR.
- In any case (brought usually by an individual) after 1966, where the UK was found by the ECtHR to be in breach of the ECHR, the UK was obliged to change the law so as to eliminate the incompatibility. Invariably, the UK fulfilled this obligation.

Additionally, from time to time, courts claimed to acknowledge the importance of certain liberties, without ever going so far as to elevate their status to that of rights.

For example, such an approach was very clear in the decision in *Derbyshire County Council v Times Newspapers Ltd* (1993), where freedom of speech was the underlying value which supported the establishing of the specific rule that a local authority could not sue for libel.

Key term

Dualist system – if a treaty is signed with another country, its provisions must be passed by the domestic parliament before it becomes law.

27.1.1 Effect of decisions of ECtHR after 1966

As stated above, where the UK was found by the ECtHR to be in breach of an obligation under the ECHR, the UK invariably changed the law to eliminate the incompatibility. This can be seen in each of the following cases.

Sunday Times v UK (1979)

The Government applied for an injunction to stop publication of an article which the newspaper planned to publish. The article concerned the cause of birth defects in children whose mothers had used the drug thalidomide during pregnancy. The government applied for the order because it argued that the article might influence negotiations between the drug company and the victims of the thalidomide disaster which, it said, would be a contempt of court.

The ECtHR held that such an injunction violated Article 10 ECHR (freedom of expression). In the court's view, the thalidomide disaster was of public concern and the public and families of victims had a right to know about it. In the court's opinion, there was no greater 'pressing social need' to prevent the newspaper's publication of the article.

As a result of this decision, Parliament passed the Contempt of Court Act 1981 which created a new set of laws covering contempt of court. It gave more weight to freedom of expression of newspapers and media in general. It provided that publication can only be prevented where justice would be 'seriously impeded or prejudiced'. This means the media are prohibited from publishing information that will prejudice ongoing legal cases and, in particular, jury trials.

> See Chapter 31 on Article 10 for more details on the Contempt of Court Act 1981 and *Sunday Times v UK* (1979).

Malone v UK (1984)

The claimant was charged with offences relating to the dishonest handling of stolen goods. He was ultimately acquitted. During his trial, it emerged that a telephone conversation to which he had been a party had been intercepted by the police on the authority of a warrant issued by the Home Secretary. He also believed that his correspondence had been intercepted, his telephone 'tapped' and 'metered' by a device recording all the numbers dialled. The UK Government accepted that, as a

suspected receiver of stolen goods, he was one of a class of persons whose postal and telephone communications were liable to be intercepted.

The ECtHR decided that there had been a violation of the claimant's right to respect for his private life and correspondence, as guaranteed by Article 8 because it was 'not in accordance with the law' but was instead governed by unregulated police discretion. The ECtHR did not say that telephone tapping was illegal, but that unregulated telephone tapping was contrary to Article 8.

The Government reacted to the decision by introducing the Interception of Communications Act 1985 to control telephone tapping by the police.

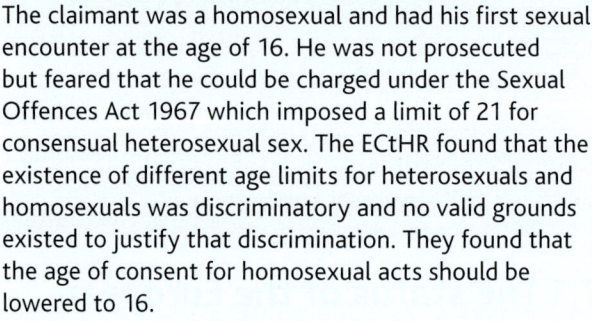

> See Chapter 30 on Article 8 for more details on the right to uninterrupted and uncensored communications with others.

Sutherland v UK (1997)

The claimant was a homosexual and had his first sexual encounter at the age of 16. He was not prosecuted but feared that he could be charged under the Sexual Offences Act 1967 which imposed a limit of 21 for consensual heterosexual sex. The ECtHR found that the existence of different age limits for heterosexuals and homosexuals was discriminatory and no valid grounds existed to justify that discrimination. They found that the age of consent for homosexual acts should be lowered to 16.

This decision led to the equalising of the age of consent for sexual activity between heterosexuals and homosexuals at 16 by the Sexual Offences (Amendment Act) 2000.

Nevertheless, even before the Human Rights Act, the ECHR affected UK law in certain ways.

27.1.2 The ECHR and the courts

The ECHR was not originally part of UK law. The Convention was not enacted by the UK Parliament in the same way as the Treaty of Rome 1957 was incorporated into UK law by the European Communities Act 1972. This meant that, before 2000, a person who alleged a breach of his or her human rights could take a case to the ECtHR but could not argue any of his or her rights given by the ECHR before a UK court. UK courts could use the Convention to help interpret ambiguous wording or clauses in legislation but could not decide a case based purely on a Convention right.

Although before HRA 1998 there was no right for an individual to bring an action for breach of ECHR rights in a domestic UK court, this did not mean that there was no protection of individual rights. Common law, through the *Magna Carta*, protected the right to a fair trial and other fundamental rights and freedoms. These rights were reinforced by the Bill of Rights 1689 and the right of *habeus corpus*. Judicial review gave individuals the right to challenge decisions of government departments and other public bodies. Statutes created express rights for individuals. An example is the Police and Criminal Evidence Act 1984 (seen in Chapter 29 in relation to Article 5), which gives specific rights and procedures to be followed for those arrested and detained by the police.

With regard to statutory interpretation, the courts, adopting the rule of construction that Parliament does not intend to legislate contrary to international law, stated that the requirements of the ECHR ought to be considered by them. However, this applied only where statute law was unsettled or ambiguous or was directly seeking to implement Convention requirements.

As regards the relationship between common law and Convention rights, it is accepted that clear and settled common law which is compatible with the Convention should not be overturned by reference to the Convention, and nor should the Convention be used to decide what the common law is, or to resolve any uncertainty in the common law.

27.1.3 The ECHR and the European Community (Union)

The ECHR is an accepted principle of European Community law (now EU law), so it had to be considered in all cases where Community law (now EU law) was being interpreted or applied. As the EU has developed, a closer relationship has developed between the ECHR and the EU with a greater respect for fundamental rights. This approach can be seen by the adoption of the Charter of Fundamental Rights and Freedoms into EU law in 2009 (see Chapter 26, section 26.4.1).

27.2 Impact of the decisions of the ECtHR prior to HRA 1998

Before HRA 1998, the UK's record in protecting ECHR rights was, to an extent, found lacking. UK citizens made a large number of applications to the ECtHR and many adverse decisions were made against the UK, as is shown in Figure 27.1. But the rate of violation is not completely out of line with other countries of a similar population size, such as France, Italy and Germany. It should also be taken into account that these countries have constitutional courts, which can often mean that the individual does not need to apply to the ECtHR.

Figure 27.1 Impact of European Court of Human Rights by state, 1960–97

State	References to ECtHR 1960–97	Adverse judgments of ECtHR 1960–97
Belgium	40	24
France	99	42
Germany	33	14
Italy	251	98
Spain	19	8
UK	95	47

The following is a selection of cases involving the UK that have been brought before the ECtHR.

Wingrove v UK (1995)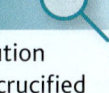

The claimant challenged the refusal of a distribution certificate for a videotape which portrayed the crucified Christ in acts of a sexual nature with a nun. The certificate was refused as it violated blasphemy laws. The claimant alleged a breach of Article 10 – freedom of expression.

The ECtHR found no violation of Article 10. It ruled that blasphemy laws can be necessary in a democratic society and compatible with the Convention if there is a balance of proportionality between the manner in which an anti-religious sentiment is expressed and the state's penalties. They considered that a state must be allowed a degree of flexibility in assessing whether the facts of a particular case fall within the accepted definition of the offence. It is not blasphemous to speak or publish opinions hostile to the Christian religion if the publication is 'decent and temperate'.

Laskey, Jaggard and Brown v UK (1997)

This is a well-known case to law students. A group of men were found in possession of video films depicting sado-masochistic and homosexual activities including maltreatment of genitalia and beatings. These activities were consensual and conducted in private, specially equipped 'chambers'. The men were convicted of a series of offences relating to those activities. Appeals against convictions were rejected by a majority in the House of Lords. The men's complaint was that their acts should be allowed under Article 8 which guaranteed their right to conduct their private life in an undisturbed manner and their convictions were 'an unforeseeable application of the criminal law'.

The ECtHR ruled that the presence of 'a significant degree of injury or wounding' distinguished the case from other cases dealing with 'consensual homosexual behaviour in private between adults' so that the prosecution and conviction of the men were appropriate to safeguard public health within the meaning of Article 8(2).

In a further case of *ADT v UK* (2000), the ECtHR ruled that the prosecution and conviction of a man for engaging in non-violent consensual homosexual acts in private with up to four other men was a violation of Article 8. The Court ruled that the applicant was a victim of an interference with his right to respect for his private life. The interference was not justified as being 'necessary in a democratic society' in the protection of morals and rights and freedoms of others.

> See Chapter 30 on Article 8 for more details on the right to respect for family and private life.

Halford v UK (1997)

The claimant was an Assistant Chief Constable. Her telephone calls were intercepted by senior police officers to obtain information regarding a sex discrimination claim she was pursuing in the employment tribunal. The interception of the telephone calls of an employee in a private exchange was a breach of the right of a private life under Article 8.

> See Chapter 30, section 30.4.2 for more details on *Halford v UK*.

Figure 27.2 Key cases for human rights law prior to HRA 1998

Case	Claim	Outcome at ECtHR
Wingrove v UK (1995)	The claimant challenged the refusal of a distribution certificate for a videotape which portrayed the crucified Christ in acts of a sexual nature with a nun Alleged a breach of Article 10	No violation of Article 10
A v Hoare (2008)	The claimant sought to claim damages for abuse after the expiry of the time limit	House of Lords allowed the claim
Laskey, Jaggard and Brown v UK (1997)	Claimed their Article 8 rights had been infringed by their conviction for taking part in sado-masochistic activities	No violation of Article 8
Halford v UK (1997)	Claimed infringement of Article 8 rights over phone tapping relating to discriminatory claim	Violation of Article 8 for phone tapping at work, but not at home
Malone v UK (1984)	Claimed infringement of Article 8 over police tapping his phone	Violation of Article 8. This led to a change in UK law

27.3 The effect of HRA 1998 on incorporating and interpreting the provisions of the ECHR into UK laws

The Human Rights Act was passed in 1998 and came into effect in October 2000.

By s 3, HRA 1998 imposes an interpretative duty on the courts. Acts of Parliament are to be interpreted for compatibility with Convention rights, so far as it is possible to do so. Legislation is to be interpreted so that the rights, duties, powers and liberties that are set out can only be exercised in ways that are compatible with, and do not lead to breaches of, the ECHR.

But this section applies only 'so far as it is possible to do so'. Section 3(2)(b) makes it clear that legislation that cannot be read or given effect in a way that is compatible remains valid and courts are required to enforce it. Unlike the position in countries such as the USA, courts in the UK are not given the power to strike down or invalidate incompatible legislation. So the Westminster Parliament retains its sovereignty and is free to pass legislation that allows or requires violation of ECHR rights.

'So far as it is possible to do so'

Three general techniques are open to the courts when interpreting a statute to ensure it is Convention compliant:

- 'Reading down' – to introduce limiting words or meanings. For example, where an Act appears to give a minister wide discretionary powers, the scope of the powers might be 'read down' by inserting a provision restricting the powers so they can be exercised in a Convention-compliant manner.
- 'Reading in' – to introduce words or meanings into an Act to create safeguards to ensure the Act is Convention compliant.
- 'Reading out' – where courts remove or will not enforce provisions which would otherwise make the statute incompatible with Convention rights.

Section 3 only applies when under the literal, golden or mischief rules it is not possible to read the legislation as being Convention compatible. Using the literal rule, the intention of Parliament is known through the words in the statute. However, under s 3 the words are no longer decisive and so the intention of Parliament at the time of drafting the Act is no longer followed. So, even if the words are clear when using the literal rule, they can still be departed from, added to or ignored if it is necessary to do so to become Convention compliant.

27.3.1 Primary legislation

Legislation that was in force before HRA 1998 came into force in 2000 is subject to this interpretative duty. To avoid 'a great repeal Act' that amends all incompatible legislation, the courts are given the power to resolve incompatible legislation on a case-by-case basis. Legislation that was brought into force after October 2000 is either capable of being read in an EHCR-compatible way or it is put into effect as legislation which is incompatible but still valid.

27.3.2 Secondary legislation

Secondary legislation (statutory instruments, orders in council or by-laws) that cannot be interpreted in a way that is compatible with the ECHR is invalid and is not to be applied by the courts. The view would be that Parliament cannot have intended to authorise secondary legislation that violates fundamental rights. If Parliament does so intend, then it should say so expressly.

27.3.3 Declarations of incompatibility

If a senior court (the Court of Appeal or Supreme Court) finds that it is not possible to read and give effect to a piece of primary legislation in a way that is compatible with the ECHR, then by s 4 HRA 1998 it has the discretion to make a declaration of incompatibility. Such a declaration does not affect the validity of the legislation or the parties in the case. Before the declaration is made, the Government must be given the opportunity to address the court.

If such a declaration is made, the Government has the choice of:

- doing nothing
- changing the offending law or the practice
- making a remedial order – this can include amending an Act or a piece of secondary legislation, and under s 10 HRA 1998 a piece of legislation can be repealed by ministerial order (a 'Henry VIII clause').

Such a declaration should only be made as a last resort, and s 3 requires the courts to do all they can to achieve compatibility. They should not rewrite legislation or do anything that undermines the relationship between the legislature and the courts.

The following case is an example of when it was argued that legislation was incompatible.

Bellinger v Bellinger (2003)

A woman had been born a man but had gone through gender reassignment so that physically and emotionally she was a woman. She went through a marriage ceremony with a man. She sought a declaration that she was validly married to her husband. The problem was that at law she was a man as her birth certificate could not be changed. The House of Lords decided that s 11(c) of the Matrimonial Causes Act 1973 was incompatible with Articles 8 and 12 ECHR in so far as it made no provision for the recognition of gender reassignment. The Gender Recognition Act 2004 was passed to remedy the defect.

27.3.4 Private law

The main point of the ECHR is to provide rights against the state. This is likely to apply to institutions such as the police, the prison service and the civil service, but could also include the courts and the tribunal service. HRA 1998 does not allow a case to be brought against an individual, a private company or commercial organisation.

However, the duty under s 3 for the courts to interpret legislation in a way so far as possible that is compatible with the ECHR applies to all statutes, including those that cover private law.

The ECHR places duties on the state to secure rights for all its citizens and effective remedies, and this may involve the state taking positive steps. These steps may include changing the law or procedure that applies to private parties. An example may be in employment law, balancing an employee's freedom of expression against employer interests when a dismissal has taken place for something said or written at work. Courts or tribunals will be expected to give effect to positive obligations in the way they develop the law.

27.3.5 Sections 6 and 7 HRA 1998

Section 6 of HRA 1998 places a duty on public authorities not to act incompatibly with certain rights and freedoms drawn from the ECHR. Under s 6(3), a public authority includes a court or tribunal, and any person whose functions are of a public nature. Neither House of Parliament is included as a public authority, nor is a person exercising functions in connection with proceedings in Parliament.

Otherwise, the Act does not define what a 'public authority' is.

A person claiming under the Act can bring a claim under s 7 before a court or tribunal if he or she is a victim of an unlawful act. This means that they consider that they have been affected by a breach of an ECHR right or freedom. The claim must be brought within a year of the unlawful act.

27.4 Impact of constitutional arrangements on the law of the UK including the entrenched nature of HRA 1998 in the devolutionary settlements of Scotland and Northern Ireland

27.4.1 The entrenched nature of HRA 1998

Entrenchment is a procedure which would make an Act of Parliament difficult to repeal or amend in the future. One way of doing this is to include a provision that would require, for example, a 75 per cent majority of votes in the House of Commons before repeal or amendment could take place.

As is well known, under the principle of parliamentary sovereignty, Parliament is the supreme law-making body in the UK, and no single Parliament can bind its successors. This means that, in theory, a future Parliament could repeal or amend HRA 1998. There is no provision in HRA 1998 to stop or limit the powers of a successor Parliament from repealing or amending it.

If a future Parliament did repeal or amend HRA 1998, this would mean withdrawing from respect for the ECHR. In practice this is extremely unlikely because, in a political sense, it would suggest that the UK does not respect human rights.

In its White Paper, 'Rights Brought Home: The Human Rights Bill 1997', the then Government set out its view about entrenchment as follows:

> **2.16 On one view, human rights legislation is so important that it should be given added protection from subsequent amendment or repeal. The Constitution of the United States of America, for example, guarantees rights which can be**

amended or repealed only by securing qualified majorities in both the House of Representatives and the Senate, and among the States themselves. But an arrangement of this kind could not be reconciled with our own constitutional traditions, which allow any Act of Parliament to be amended or repealed by a subsequent Act of Parliament. We do not believe that it is necessary or would be desirable to attempt to devise such a special arrangement for this Bill. **"**

By three separate Acts, Parliament granted devolution, or law-making powers, to Scotland, Wales and Northern Ireland. None of these Acts contained entrenched provisions so again, in theory, these laws could be repealed by a future Westminster Parliament. However, politically, this would be extremely embarrassing and unlikely.

27.4.2 Scotland

Scotland was granted devolved powers by the Scotland Act 1998 and a Scottish Parliament was established. In constitutional terms, the Scotland Act makes provisions for the protection of human rights within Scotland. Specifically, s 57(2) states that:

" ...a member of the Scottish Executive, or government, has no power to make any subordinate, or delegated, legislation or to do any other act, so far as the legislation or act is incompatible with any of the ECHR rights. **"**

Furthermore, schedule 4(1) of the Act states that 'an Act of the Scottish Parliament cannot modify the Human Rights Act 1998'. Any Act which did so would be automatically rendered invalid. A decision on whether a resolution of a minister of the Scottish Parliament or an Act is invalidated by being non-compliant, is ultimately for the UK Supreme Court, in considering any 'devolution issues' brought before it.

It should be noted that Acts of the Scottish Parliament are considered by s 21 HRA 1998 to be subordinate legislation and courts are under the duty imposed by s 3 to read and give effect to them in a way that is compatible with Convention rights.

Scottish Parliament building at Holyrood

27.4.3 Northern Ireland

Northern Ireland was granted devolved powers by the Northern Ireland Act 1998 which established an Assembly with law-making powers. The Act provides, in a similar way to the other devolved countries, in s 7, that the HRA 1998 cannot be modified by an Act of the Assembly or by any subordinate legislation.

In the same way as applies in Scotland, Acts of the Northern Ireland Assembly are considered by s 21 HRA 1998 to be subordinate legislation and courts are under the duty imposed by s 3 to read and give effect to them in a way that is compatible with Convention rights.

27.5 Reform of human rights

Many would argue that the incorporation of the ECHR into UK domestic law is a great moral achievement. However, since 9/11, successive governments have passed a series of laws to deal with the threat of terrorism, which encroach on individual human rights. These laws usually enforce more draconian measures than ordinary criminal laws, as the Government argues that it is necessary to do so to protect its citizens, which is considered as one of the primary functions of a state. This argument is supported by Article 2 ECHR, which imposes a positive obligation on a state to protect people from harm where the state knows, or ought to know, of an immediate risk of harm and can take reasonable steps to protect them.

The case for having new anti-terrorism laws is that, in order to comply with its positive duty, the state needs greater powers. It is argued that existing criminal laws do not cover the terrorist threat, which is often targeted at civilians, and, as a result, there is a greater need than standard criminal law to be able to take preventative measures. In order to take these early measures, there is a need to gather evidence, which has to be done in secret and using sophisticated measures.

The counter-argument is that human rights and the rule of law are the bedrock of democracy, and without respect for these concepts, terrorism can achieve its goal of undermining the state.

It was suggested in the Conservative Party manifesto for the 2015 election that the Human Rights Act could be replaced by a Bill of Rights which could be amended by Parliament. It was argued that human rights could still be protected in ways that did not jeopardise national security or bind Parliament. In addition, it was suggested that a British Bill of Rights could grant additional rights to those available under the Convention, such as the right to trial by jury. However, there was not, and has not been, a political majority for withdrawing from the ECHR and the suggestion for a Bill of Rights appears to have been shelved.

There have been concerns for many years that the approach of the ECtHR has been anti the UK, with decisions such as prisoners being allowed to vote being unpopular with some UK politicians. This could be reinforced by figures showing that, at its peak in 2001–2 the court found against the UK in 30 cases. However, since then the number of decisions against the UK has declined considerably to only four cases in 2014 and a further four in 2015. This reduction could be explained by factors such as the impact of the Human Rights Act or that the UK is committing fewer human rights violations. If this trend continues, the call for a British Bill of Rights seems unnecessary.

Figure 27.3 Key case on the reform of human rights

Case	Facts	Legal principle
Bellinger v Bellinger (2003)	A woman had been born a man but had gone through gender reassignment so that physically and emotionally she was a woman She went through a marriage ceremony with a man. She sought a declaration that she was validly married to her husband	The House of Lords decided that s 11(c) of the Matrimonial Causes Act 1973 was incompatible with Articles 8 and 12 ECHR in so far as it made no provision for the recognition of gender reassignment The Gender Recognition Act 2004 was passed to remedy the defect

Summary

- The UK was one of the first countries to ratify the ECHR.
- UK citizens were unable to take a case to the ECtHR until 1966.
- Since 1966, everyone in the UK has been protected by the ECHR. Laws had to comply with the ECHR and claims of violation of rights could be taken to the ECtHR.
- The UK is a dualist system requiring the Westminster Parliament to pass legislation to make treaty provisions part of UK law and directly enforceable. This did not happen until HRA 1998.
- Before 2000, individuals could rely on common law or statutory rights before UK courts to protect themselves against breaches of human rights.
- If these rights were not upheld by UK courts, an individual could bring an action before the ECtHR.
- If the ECtHR found against the UK, the Government was obliged to take action, which could include introducing legislation.
- Section 3 HRA 1998 requires, so far as it is possible to do so, for primary and secondary legislation to be read and given effect to in a way that is compatible with the ECHR.
- Primary legislation that was in force pre-HRA 1998 is subject to this interpretative duty.
- Post-HRA legislation is either capable of being read in an EHCR-compatible way or it is put into effect as legislation that is incompatible but still valid.
- Secondary legislation that cannot be interpreted in a way that is compatible with ECHR is invalid and is not to be applied by the courts.
- If a senior court finds that it is not possible to read and give effect to a piece of primary legislation in a way that is compatible with the ECHR, it can make a declaration of incompatibility.
- After a declaration of incompatibility, the Government can choose to do nothing, change the law or make a remedial order.
- The main point of the ECHR is to provide rights against the state – it does not directly affect private law.
- HRA 1998 contains no provision to stop or limit the powers of a successor Parliament from repealing or amending it. Any future repeal or amendment is likely to mean withdrawing from respect for the ECHR, which in turn would mean that the UK does not respect human rights.
- When devolved powers were granted to Scotland and Northern Ireland, no entrenched provisions were included. In theory, these laws could be repealed by a future Westminster Parliament but it would be politically embarrassing and unlikely.
- Incorporating the ECHR into UK domestic law is considered a great moral achievement of the UK Government.
- Since 9/11, governments have passed laws dealing with the threat of terrorism which encroach on individual human rights. Governments argue they are necessary to protect individual citizens.

28 Article 2 ECHR: right to life and justified exceptions

28.1 The requirements of Article 2

Article 2 states:

1. Everyone's right to life shall be protected by law. No one shall be deprived of his life intentionally save in the execution of a sentence of a court following his conviction of a crime for which this penalty is provided by law.
2. Deprivation of life shall not be regarded as inflicted in contravention of this Article when it results from the use of force which is no more than absolutely necessary:
    (a) in defence of any person from unlawful violence;
    (b) in order to effect a lawful arrest or to prevent the escape of a person lawfully detained;
    (c) in action lawfully taken for the purpose of quelling a riot or insurrection.

This is one of the most fundamental rights and is based on the inherent dignity of human beings which has been central to the thinking of many legal philosophers. Some, like Thomas Aquinas, argue that this comes from man being made in God's image. Others, such as Thomas Locke, moved away from the idea that this is based on God, arguing that it is based on the idea that man has intrinsic 'goods'. As the state can only rule with the consent of the people, the people have certain rights that the state has a duty not to abuse. The right to life is central to this, and a human being should not be treated without recognition of that dignity. People should not be used by the state as a means to an end, through torture or death.

The right to life is, under Article 2.1, treated as **non-derogable**.

Key term

Non-derogable – this means absolute: it is so important that it cannot be limited or suspended under any circumstance.

Non-derogable rights only apply in peacetime, and in the justified exceptions in Article 2.2 set out above. Note that Protocol 13 provides for complete abolition of the death penalty.

Both the ECtHR and the Supreme Court have found that the ECHR applies not only to acts and omissions attributable to a state on its own territory, but outside it as well. This is shown in cases relating to UK forces in Iraq as in *Al-Skeini v UK* (2011) and *Al-Saadoon v Secretary of State for Defence* (2016). It therefore seems that any operation undertaken by the British Army in the future will lead to legal challenges being brought against almost every aspect of its actions before, during and after any use of military force.

There are a number of issues that may be considered with respect to this Article:
- the beginning of life and the unborn child
- the end of life
- the state's duty to protect life
- the state's duty to make an adequate investigation into loss of life.

28.1.1 The primary obligations on the state as interpreted by the ECtHR

Article 2 contains two elements – an obligation to protect the right to life and a prohibition of deprivation of life set out in the exceptions.

The beginning of life and the unborn child

In Article 2, life means human life, not life of animals. It does not extend to the existence of legal persons such as a limited company. The ECHR does not otherwise clarify what life is, or when it begins or ends. The ECtHR is unwilling to be precise in a definition. This can be seen in the case of *Vo v France* (2005).

Vo v France (2005)

The applicant was a Vietnamese woman living in France. She went to her local hospital for a scheduled ante-natal examination. On the same day another woman, also called Vo, was due to have a coil removed at the same hospital. The hospital mixed up the two Mrs Vos. The doctor, thinking he was removing a coil, pierced her amniotic sac, thus making a therapeutic abortion necessary.

The doctor was charged with unintentional homicide, but was acquitted of these charges as the court did not consider the foetus a human being entitled to the protection of the criminal law.

Mrs Vo complained of the authorities' refusal to classify the unintentional killing of her unborn child as involuntary homicide under Article 2. She argued that France had an obligation, under the right to life, to pass legislation making such acts a criminal offence.

The ECtHR considered that the issue of when the right to life begins was a question to be decided at national level. This was because the issue had not been decided within the majority of the states which had ratified the Convention, and also because there was no European consensus on the scientific and legal definition of the beginning of life.

This has remained the Court's basic position as it has repeated on a number of occasions that the issue of when the right to life begins comes within the **margin of appreciation**, which the Court generally considers that states should enjoy. There is, therefore, considerable freedom to states to regulate matters of life and death. States must give appropriate weight to the various interests at stake and carefully balance those interests.

Key term

Margin of appreciation – the discretion a state has in making rules to comply with the ECHR.

Abortion and the right to life

Applicants in cases relating to abortion have invoked not just Article 2, but also Article 8 and, with respect to information on abortion, Article 10, concerning freedom of expression. Articles 8 and 10 are dealt with in Chapters 30 and 31. With respect to Article 2, the case of *X v UK* (1980) specifically stated that abortion was not noted anywhere in the article, and also that most states that were signatories to the ECHR had some form of abortion law.

The unborn child is not regarded as a person directly protected by Article 2. However, the mother's rights and interests are protected, although this does not mean that there may, in some circumstances, be protection for the unborn child. There is a positive obligation on states to make regulations requiring hospitals to adopt appropriate measures for the protection of patients' lives and an effective system for investigating the cause of death of patients.

In most of Europe, abortion is allowed without restriction up to between ten and 14 weeks' gestation, with a few exceptions such as the Republic of Ireland and Northern Ireland. Abortion is legal in England, Wales and Scotland up to 24 weeks under the Abortion Act 1967. However, if there is a substantial risk to the woman's life or foetal abnormalities are found, there is no time limit. In 2007, the Government's Science and Technology Committee carried out a review of scientific developments since the passing of the 1967 Act. It made several recommendations, including that the latest evidence on foetal viability supported maintaining the 24-week time limit. Given the recent case of twins born at 23 weeks and successfully reared (see 'Look online' below), it may be that this law will be reviewed under Article 2.

Look online

Follow this weblink for the story of twins born at 23 weeks: www.dailyrecord.co.uk/news/scottish-news/they-always-little-miracles-parents-9717722.

Discuss in groups the issues that arise from advancements in medical technology and their potential impact on Article 2.

However, abortion is limited under the law in Northern Ireland although it is permissible to travel to the UK to visit an abortion clinic. The Republic of Ireland has a strict ban on abortion. This is permissible under the ECHR. However, the question of whether information can be provided with respect to abortion was discussed in the case of *Open Door and Dublin Well Woman v Ireland* (1992). Article 2 was not held to be relevant but the claim succeeded under Article 10.

Activity

Research the outcome of the Irish referendum on abortion and any subsequent Irish legislation on the matter.

Figure 28.1 Abortions per 1,000 live births, up to 2013. Note the position in Ireland may change as a result of the 2018 referendum.

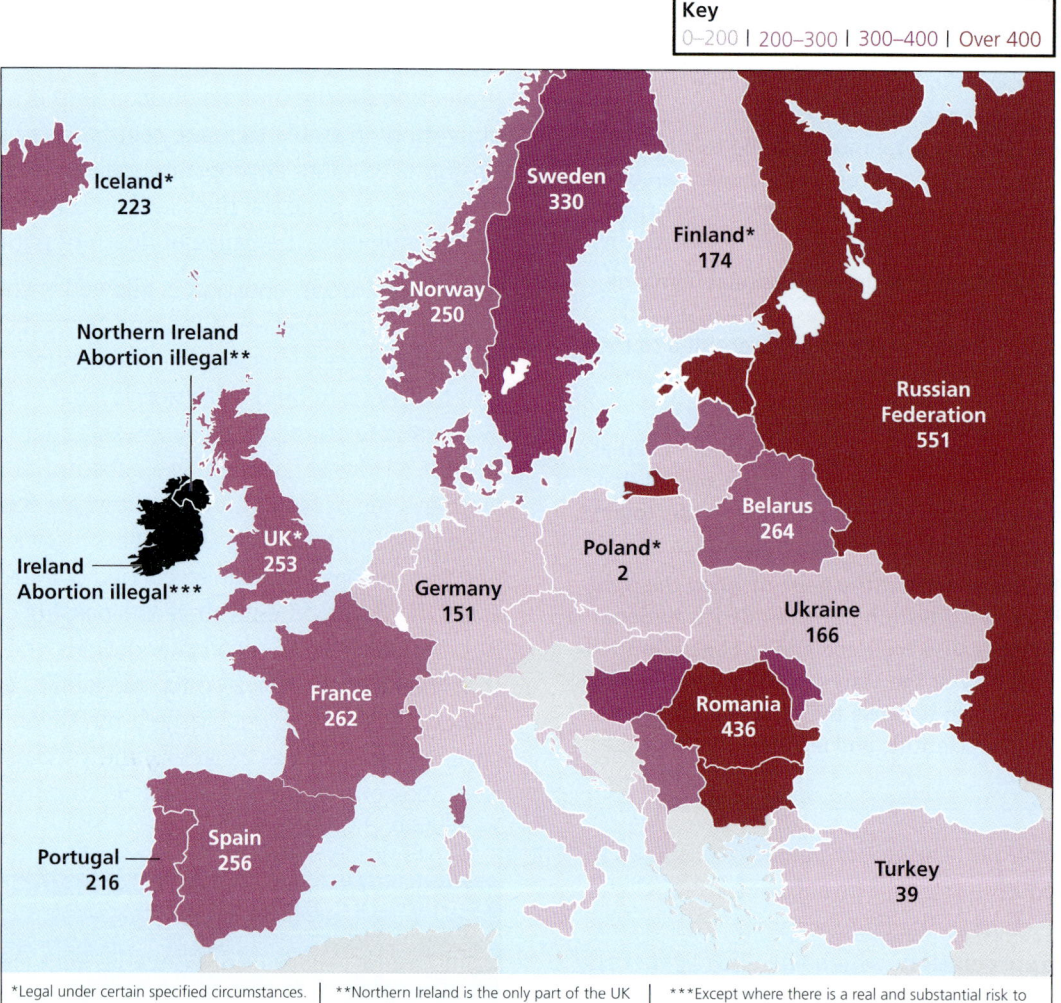

Key
0–200 | 200–300 | 300–400 | Over 400

Iceland*
223

Northern Ireland
Abortion illegal**

Ireland
Abortion illegal***

Norway
250

Sweden
330

Finland*
174

Russian
Federation
551

UK*
253

Germany
151

Poland*
2

Belarus
264

Ukraine
166

France
262

Romania
436

Spain
256

Turkey
39

Portugal
216

*Legal under certain specified circumstances.

**Northern Ireland is the only part of the UK where the 1967 Abortion Act does not apply. It is lawful to terminate a pregnancy where there is a threat to the life of the mother.

***Except where there is a real and substantial risk to the life of the mother. This includes a risk arising from a threat of suicide.

Open Door and Dublin Well Woman v Ireland (1992)

The applicants were two non-profit organisations. Neither advocated or encouraged abortion. They did, however, give information about options to pregnant women. The Supreme Court of Ireland granted an injunction against them against providing information to pregnant women as to the location or identity of, or method of communication with, abortion clinics in Great Britain.

The ECtHR decided that the Supreme Court of Ireland's injunction restraining counselling agencies from providing pregnant women with information concerning abortion facilities abroad violated Article 10 of the Convention. Article 2 did not apply as the case was not concerning the right to an abortion – it was merely about information, which is why Article 10 applied and not Article 2.

The injunction interfered with the right of the applicants by preventing them from providing information about pregnancy-related options and with the ability of women to receive information, so was an infringement of Article 10.

The end of life

Article 2 of the Convention states that everyone's right to life must be protected by law. Apart from the death penalty, it sets out only limited circumstances in which a person can be deprived of this right. In the UK, the death penalty has been abolished. However there are concerns with respect to the death penalty in other states to which UK nationals might be extradited. However, as Article 2 specifically allows the death penalty, the issues in this respect have largely been considered under Article 3.

There are three areas that are not mentioned specifically in the Article: suicide, assisted suicide and euthanasia.

Suicide, assisted suicide and euthanasia

These usually fall within the margin of appreciation that a state has, but the Grand Chamber has considered the issues involved in *Lambert v France* (2015).

Lambert v France (2015)

Vincent Lambert was in a vegetative state for seven years after a motorcycle accident left him tetraplegic. His family had been split over whether he should be kept alive or not. The Court ruled that the French authorities could stop the artificial hydration and nutrition of Mr Lambert.

The court stated that it was primarily for the domestic authorities to verify whether the decision to withdraw treatment was compatible with the domestic legislation and the Convention, and to establish the patient's wishes in accordance with national law. The court's role consisted in ascertaining whether the state had fulfilled its positive obligations under Article 2.

Figure 28.2 Key cases on Article 2(1) regarding the rights of the unborn child and the right to die

Case	Facts	ECtHR decisions
Vo v France (2005)	Mrs Vo complained of the authorities' refusal to classify the unintentional killing of her unborn child as involuntary homicide under Article 2	The issue of when the right to life begins was a question to be decided at national level
Open Door and Dublin Well Woman v Ireland (1992)	The Supreme Court of Ireland granted an injunction against them on providing information on abortion clinics	Article 10 was violated Article 2 did not apply as the case was not concerning the right to an abortion
Lambert v France (2015)	The court ruled that the French authorities could stop the artificial hydration and nutrition of Mr Lambert even with differing views among family members	The court's role consisted in ascertaining whether the state had fulfilled its positive obligations under Article 2

28.1.2 The state's duty to protect life

This is a positive duty under Article 2. There are a number of areas that we can consider:

■ duties of the state in relation to life-threatening environmental risks
■ protection of individuals from violence by others
■ prevention of suicide by prisoners
■ protection against medical malpractice
■ extradition, expulsion and deportation.

While some of these areas overlap with other Articles, it is worth considering some of these in terms of evaluating the UK's response to Article 2.

Duties of the state in relation to life-threatening environmental risks

The court has made it clear that this right does not impose a positive obligation to provide information about this, as is discussed later under Article 10 and the case of *Guerra v Italy* (1998) (see Chapter 31).

However, the overlap between Articles 2 and 8 was brought into the case of *Öneryıldız v Turkey* (2004).

Öneryıldız v Turkey (2004)

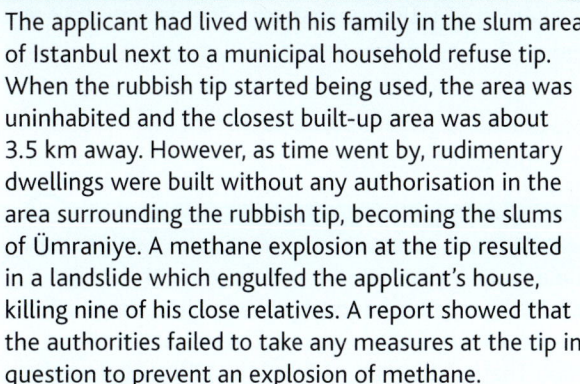

The applicant had lived with his family in the slum area of Istanbul next to a municipal household refuse tip. When the rubbish tip started being used, the area was uninhabited and the closest built-up area was about 3.5 km away. However, as time went by, rudimentary dwellings were built without any authorisation in the area surrounding the rubbish tip, becoming the slums of Ümraniye. A methane explosion at the tip resulted in a landslide which engulfed the applicant's house, killing nine of his close relatives. A report showed that the authorities failed to take any measures at the tip in question to prevent an explosion of methane.

The ECtHR stated that the Turkish authorities had known or ought to have known that there was a real risk to persons living near the rubbish tip. This meant there was an obligation under Article 2 of the Convention to take steps to protect people living near the rubbish tip. As they failed to do so, they breached Article 2.

A Gypsy camp, Istanbul, 2008

While the state enjoys a wide margin of appreciation in this area, merely adopting regulations in conformity with the European standards is not enough to meet the requirements of the Convention. Violation of Article 2 can occur in a number of ways, by a failure to:

- apply the regulations strictly
- provide affected populations with adequate information on the risks
- hold those responsible to account, for example by criminal prosecutions.

Protection of individuals from violence by others

This usually falls within the margin of appreciation. Such cases hinge crucially on matters of law, evidence and procedure. The most relevant decision of the ECtHR involves the UK as defendant. In *Osman v Ferguson* (1993), the police officers knew that there was a real risk of an attack on a schoolboy. The case was taken to ECtHR where it was decided in 1998 as *Osman v UK*. The view of the court was that complete immunity for the police for operational decisions was too wide. It was capable of infringing the human right of protection of life.

Osman v UK (1998)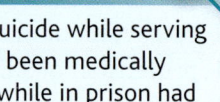

A male teacher developed an obsession with a male pupil. He changed his name by deed poll to the pupil's surname. He was then required to teach at another school. There were many acts of vandalism against the boy's family property. The police investigated these, and interviewed the teacher, who denied responsibility.

The police considered the teacher to be the culprit but had insufficient evidence with which to prosecute him. To the knowledge of the police, the teacher carried out other irrational, criminal acts. The teacher announced, 'In a few months, I'll be doing life'. To his employers he said that he proposed to do 'a sort of Hungerford' (a series of random shootings in Hungerford in 1987, when Michael Ryan shot and killed 16 people, before committing suicide). On three occasions within a week, the teacher was seen, to the knowledge of the police, outside the pupil's family home and, later that week, he killed the pupil's father and seriously wounded the pupil. The claimants asserted that the killer had been known to be a threat, but that insufficient protection had been given by the police.

The ECtHR stated that the UK's then complete immunity for the police for operational decisions was too wide. It was capable of infringing the human right of protection of life. An absolute rule denying access to courts was disproportionate to the needs of the police. Article 2 could impose a duty on a public authority to take all reasonable steps to protect a person from a real and immediate risk to his or her life.

Prevention of suicide by prisoners

The question arises as to whether, and if so when, the state has a duty to prevent individuals from committing suicide. This may be when the individual is in the custody of the state, either as a prisoner or as a patient with a mental illness. Again, the most relevant decision of the ECtHR involves the UK as defendants.

This can be seen in the case of *Keenan v UK* (2001).

Keenan v UK (2001)

The applicant's son had committed suicide while serving a prison sentence for assault. He had been medically monitored by the prison doctor, but while in prison had managed to hang himself.

The ECtHR stated that the prison authorities had done all that could reasonably be expected of them once he had started to display signs of suicidal tendencies. They had placed him in hospital care and subjected him to close scrutiny.

Therefore there had not been a breach of the positive obligation in failing to take steps to prevent the suicide of a mentally ill prisoner.

Protection against medical malpractice

There is an argument that deaths resulting from medical malpractice and negligence should involve the responsibility of the state. They claim that the state has a responsibility for some issues (including allegations of falsification of medical records and of conspiracies between members of the medical professions to cover up their mistakes), and that in serious cases the state has a duty to punish those responsible.

Unfortunately, some of the cases also involve people who were in prison at the time, which can complicate the issue.

In *Erikson v Italy* (1999), the ECtHR stated that Article 2 included:

> **❝** ...the obligation to establish an effective judicial system for establishing the cause of a death which occurs in hospital and any liability on the part of the medical practitioners concerned. **❞**

In *Powell v UK* (2000), it was stated that medical negligence does not result in a breach of Article 2 so long as the state complies with its general duty to protect the lives of patients.

However, in the judgment in *Lopes de Sousa Fernandes v Portugal* (2017), the Grand Chamber appears to limit such claims in the health-care sphere to cases of the denial of life-saving treatment caused by systemic/structural issues rather than individual error. The court has now made clear that 'mere error or medical negligence' is not sufficient.

This is relevant to inquests as the court upheld the finding that there had been a violation of the procedural limb of Article 2 owing to the delay in implementing the state structures to investigate the death.

Extradition, expulsion and deportation

There is, under the Convention, no right not to be extradited, expelled or deported from a country of which one is not a national. However, Article 2 can be applied to situations in which an applicant may suffer in the state to which he or she is to be deported. Most such cases are brought under Articles 3, 5, 6 and 13.

28.1.3 The state's duty to make an adequate investigation into loss of life

The procedural obligation under Article 2, to conduct an effective investigation, applies to any unnatural death which occurs in state detention. The ECtHR has established a number of criteria for an effective investigation which will satisfy Article 2 in the case of *Jordan v UK* (2001).

Where the circumstances of a death are exclusively within the power of the authorities, the burden of proof falls on the authorities. The right could be infringed by a failure to investigate the death properly. In *Jordan v UK* it was stated that:

Figure 28.3 Key cases on Article 2(1) regarding the state's duty to protect life and to make an adequate investigation into loss of life

Case	Facts	Law
Öneryıldız v Turkey (2004)	A methane explosion at a rubbish tip near slum dwellings resulted in a landslide which engulfed the applicant's house, killing nine close relatives	Article 2 was breached There was an obligation to take steps to protect people living near the rubbish tip
Osman v UK (1998)	A male teacher developed an obsession with a male pupil The claimants asserted that the killer had been known to be a threat, but that insufficient protection had been given by the police	Article 2 could impose a duty on a public authority to take all reasonable steps to protect a person from a real and immediate risk to his or her life
Keenan v UK (2001)	The applicant's son had committed suicide while serving a prison sentence for assault He had been medically monitored by the prison doctor	The positive obligations under Article 2 must be interpreted in a way which does not impose an impossible or disproportionate burden on the authorities

> " There must be a sufficient element of public scrutiny of the investigation or its results to secure accountability in practice as well as in theory. The degree of public scrutiny required may well vary from case to case. In all cases, however, the next-of-kin of the victim must be involved in the procedure to the extent necessary to safeguard his or her legitimate interests. "

28.1.4 Justifications stated within the Article for interferences with the rights imposed by primary obligations and by which the state may seek to avoid a finding of a violation

There are a number of issues that need to be considered with respect to Article 2.2:

- the use of force – what is necessary
- in defence of any person from unlawful violence
- in order to effect a lawful arrest or to prevent the escape of a person lawfully detained
- in action lawfully taken for the purpose of quelling a riot or insurrection.

The use of force – what is necessary

As we have seen, the state is expressly forbidden from taking life. However, there will be no breach of Article 2 if death results from the use of force that is no more than absolutely necessary. The question concerns ascertaining whether excess force has been used. Consideration should be given to all dangers and risks and whether a situation was planned and controlled.

The state must also ensure that police and security services that are faced with situations where the use of lethal force is possible must be appropriately trained, instructed and given strict guidance. This was first considered in detail in *McCann v UK* (1995).

McCann v UK (1995)

The case concerned the fatal shooting of three IRA terrorist suspects by the SAS in Gibraltar. The three suspects had travelled to Spain with the intention of detonating a car bomb in Gibraltar and had parked a car next to their intended target. However, at the time they were killed, they were all unarmed and the car did not contain a bomb. A bomb and a timing device were found in the terrorists' hideout in Malaga across the

Spanish border. The court looked in detail at the specified circumstances in which the use of force by these soldiers would be permissible and the nature of warnings that must be given by them.

The court found that the three suspects had been deliberately killed in contravention of Article 2.

The ECtHR Grand Chamber indicated that lethal force used by state agents in self-defence or in the defence of others must be based on 'an honest belief which is perceived, for good reasons, to be valid at the time but which subsequently turns out to be mistaken'. In other words, a test that is in part subjective and in part objective requires an honest and reasonable belief.

In *Matzarakis v Greece* (2004), this was explained further in relation to action by the police, where the consequences were not fatal.

Matzarakis v Greece (2004)

In September 1995 the police tried to stop the applicant, who had driven through a red traffic light in the centre of Athens, near the US Embassy. Instead of stopping, the applicant sped up. He was pursued by several police officers in cars and on motorcycles. During the pursuit, the applicant's car collided with several other vehicles. Two drivers were injured. After the applicant had broken through five police roadblocks, the police officers started firing at his car. The applicant alleged that the police were firing at the car's cab, whereas the Government maintained that they were aiming at the tyres. Eventually the applicant stopped at a petrol station but did not get out. The police officers continued firing. The applicant claimed that he was shot on the sole of his foot while being dragged out of his car. The applicant was immediately driven to hospital, where he remained for nine days. He was injured in the right arm, the right foot, the left buttock and the right side of the chest. One bullet was removed from his foot and another one is still inside his buttock. The applicant's mental health, which had broken down in the past, has deteriorated considerably since the incident.

The use of lethal force by police officers may be justified in certain circumstances but this does not amount to carte blanche. Unregulated and arbitrary action by state officials is incompatible with effective respect for human rights. This means that, as well as being authorised under national law, policing operations must be sufficiently regulated by it, within the framework of a system of adequate and effective safeguards against arbitrariness and abuse of force and even against avoidable accident.

The majority found a violation of Article 2 of the Convention in terms of the action and the investigation that subsequently took place.

The proportionality principle does not appear in the text of Article 2 but is in fact present. This follows from the above cases. Quite often it is not the decision to use force that is the violation, but the way in which it is used and the subsequent investigation of the incident. An example of this can be seen in *Finogenov v Russia* (2011).

Finogenov v Russia (2011)

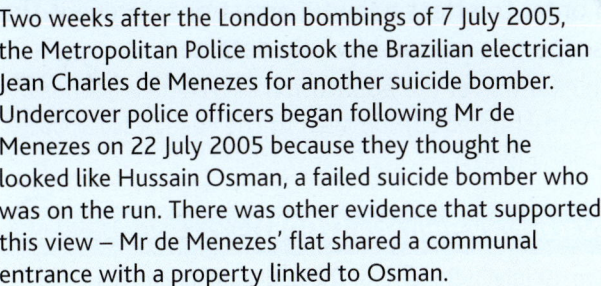

In October 2002, a group of Chechen separatists took more than 900 people hostage in a theatre. To deal with the situation, the Russian security forces pumped an unknown narcotic gas into the auditorium and proceeded to storm the building, killing most of the terrorists and releasing the majority of the hostages.

The applicants from both groups alleged that their relatives had suffered and died as a result of the actions of the Russian security forces. The group of applicants who were hostages themselves alleged that their lives had been put at risk or damaged by it. It was alleged that the use of force by the security forces was disproportionate, the assistance provided to the survivors was inadequate and that the subsequent criminal investigation was ineffective.

The ECtHR examined the complaints under Article 2 and found two violations: one in respect of the inadequate planning and conduct of the rescue operation and another regarding the authorities' failure to conduct an 'effective' criminal investigation into the rescue operation.

No violation of Article 2 was found in relation to the decision made by the authorities to resolve the hostage crisis by ending negotiations, storming the building and releasing the narcotic gas. The ECtHR stated:

> There existed a real, serious and immediate risk of mass human losses and that the authorities had every reason to believe that a forced intervention was the lesser evil in the circumstances and the use of gas was not in these circumstances a disproportionate measure.

This now has to be considered in the context of the three exceptions in Article 2.2 below regarding when officers can use arms.

In defence of any person from unlawful violence

The idea of this is to allow there to be no violation of Article 2 where there is a killing which is strictly proportionate to the aim of defence of others from unlawful violence. As we have seen, this also involves procedural aspects, as in the cases of *McCann v UK* (1995) and *Finogenov v Russia* (2011).

We can examine this in the case of *Armani Da Silva v UK* (2016).

Armani Da Silva v UK (2016)

Two weeks after the London bombings of 7 July 2005, the Metropolitan Police mistook the Brazilian electrician Jean Charles de Menezes for another suicide bomber. Undercover police officers began following Mr de Menezes on 22 July 2005 because they thought he looked like Hussain Osman, a failed suicide bomber who was on the run. There was other evidence that supported this view – Mr de Menezes' flat shared a communal entrance with a property linked to Osman.

The undercover police followed him into an underground station where he was pinned down and shot seven times in the head and once in the shoulder by two officers trained in stopping suicide bombers. The CPS ruled out prosecuting officers in 2006, but they did charge the Metropolitan Police with breaching health and safety laws, leading to a £175,000 fine. The family also received an ex gratia payment. The de Menezes' family brought the case to the ECtHR as none of the individual officers were prosecuted.

The Crown Prosecution Service had considered whether to bring prosecutions against any individual officers for murder, involuntary manslaughter (gross negligence manslaughter), misconduct in public office, forgery or attempting to pervert the course of justice. They decided there was 'insufficient evidence to provide a realistic prospect of conviction against any individual police officer'; that is, it was more likely than not that a jury would not convict.

The court found no violation of Article 2.

The effect of this decision is to bring the test set out in *McCann* much more in line with the test in English law for self-defence and is much more subjective. The court stated:

> The principal question to be addressed is whether the person had an honest and genuine belief that the use of force was necessary. In addressing this question, the court will have to consider whether the belief was subjectively reasonable, having full regard to the circumstances that pertained at the relevant time. If the belief was not subjectively reasonable (that is, it was not based on subjective good reasons), it is likely that the court would have difficulty accepting that it was honestly and genuinely held.

See Chapter 12 for more information on the defence of self-defence.

In order to effect a lawful arrest or to prevent the escape of a person lawfully detained

An example of the application of Article 2 in these circumstances can be seen in the case of *Nachova v Bulgaria* (2005).

Nachova v Bulgaria (2005)

On 19 July 1996, two of the applicant's relatives, Mr Angelov and Mr Petkov, both of Roma origin, who had absconded (not for the first time) from a military construction crew, were shot and killed during an attempted arrest by a Major, and senior officer in charge, of the military police. After the shooting the Major allegedly pointed a gun at a local resident and shouted 'You damn gypsies'. The Major claimed he had aimed at their feet in order to not cause a fatal injury. An autopsy showed Mr Petkov died of a chest wound, and was shot from the front, while Mr Angelov was shot from behind.

Article 2 was obviously engaged here and there were other issues raised including discrimination. The legitimate aim of effecting a lawful arrest can only justify putting human life at risk in circumstances of absolute necessity. The court stated that in principle there can be no such necessity where it is known that the person to be arrested poses no threat to life or limb and is not suspected of having committed a violent offence, even if a failure to use lethal force may result in the opportunity to arrest the fugitive being lost.

In action lawfully taken for the purpose of quelling a riot or insurrection

There were a number of cases with respect to this from Northern Ireland that took place before the *McCann* case. These were not perceived as being satisfactory as there was never a full investigation into the facts, sometimes one version being wholly accepted against another. These decisions and the views of the applicants must be taken in the context of the time – unrest and sectarian killings and bombings and a strong military presence from 'England' on the streets of Northern Ireland.

Farrell v UK (1980)

This case concerned the shooting dead of three robbers by British soldiers who claimed they thought the three were terrorists. The case was settled without a full determination.

Stewart v UK (1984)

A 13-year-old boy was killed after being hit on the head by a plastic bullet fired by a soldier in Belfast during what the military claimed to be serious rioting. The European Commission for Human Rights accepted the facts as determined by the High Court in Northern Ireland and found that the force used was 'absolutely necessary'. The conflicting evidence was as follows:

The applicant provided evidence to the effect that her son did not take part in any aggressive action against the patrol of which Corporal Smith was part at any time before he was struck, and that there was no riotous behaviour in progress at the time of the incident. One witness stated that there was a group of six or seven children, aged seven to nine, nearby who were throwing stones at the soldiers (a regular occurrence, often seen in the media at the time).

A different version of events was given in evidence by army witnesses. They stated that Corporal Smith was a member of an eight-man patrol in the Turf Lodge area of Belfast. They were confronted on either side by a crowd numbered about 150 who showered them with stones and bottles. Lieutenant O'Brien, who was in charge of the patrol, ordered one baton round to be fired, but this had no effect. The stoning was severe and all members of the patrol were hit. Lieutenant O'Brien ordered Corporal Smith to fire a baton round at a leader among the rioters who had been throwing things. He did so, aiming at the youth's legs but he was struck by two missiles on the leg and shoulder which made him jerk as he fired. As a result the baton round hit Brian Stewart who was standing beside the youth.

The European Court of Human Rights accepted the facts as determined by the High Court in Northern Ireland and found that the force used was 'absolutely necessary'.

Kelly v UK (2001)

A 17-year-old 'joy rider' was shot dead by soldiers after his stolen car drove through an army checkpoint (checkpoints were often set up by the army, particularly near police and military establishments to attempt to prevent terrorist attacks). Once again, the Commission uncritically accepted the version of events as found by the High Court in Northern Ireland and declared the case inadmissible, finding the soldiers had acted within Article 2(2)(b) – lawful arrest or preventing escape.

The case of case of *Güleç v Turkey* (1998) shows a different outcome.

Güleç v Turkey (1998)

On 4 March 1991, there were a number of incidents such as spontaneous unauthorised demonstrations, shop closures and attacks on public buildings in the town of İdil in Şırnak Province in Turkey. Two people were killed, one of whom was Ahmet Güleç, aged 15, the applicant's son, and 12 others were wounded.

The owners of 13 rifles, confiscated after the incidents, spent cartridges from which had been collected by the security forces, were prosecuted but acquitted because they had proved that they had not taken part in the events concerned.

According to the Government, Ahmet Güleç was hit by a bullet fired by armed demonstrators at the security forces. According to the applicant, his son was killed by the security forces, who fired on the unarmed demonstrators to make them disperse.

Here there was a violation of Article 2 as even though the demonstration was far from peaceful, security forces called for reinforcements and armoured vehicles were deployed. The allegation that shots were fired at the crowd was corroborated by the fact that nearly all the wounded demonstrators had been hit in the legs, which was perfectly consistent with ricochet wounds from bullets with a downward trajectory, which could have been fired from the turret of an armoured vehicle.

The use of force might have been justified but a balance must be struck between aim and means. A very powerful weapon had been used rather than batons, riot shields, water cannon, rubber bullets or tear gas, for example. This was very odd as the province of Şırnak was in a region where a state of emergency had been declared, and therefore disorder could have been expected.

The force used to disperse demonstrators, which had caused the death of Ahmet Güleç, was not absolutely necessary within the meaning of Article 2.

The court also stated that neither the prevalence of violent armed clashes nor the high incidence of fatalities could displace the obligation under Article 2 to ensure that an effective, independent investigation was conducted into deaths arising out of clashes involving the security forces or, as in the present case, a demonstration, however illegal it might have been – authorities had not complied with this obligation in the present case.

Thus there are two possible violations to Article 2:

■ where the action was absolutely necessary, and
■ where the investigation following the incident has complied with the requirements of Article 2.

Figure 28.4 Key cases for the justified exceptions set out in Article 2(2)

Case	Facts	Law
McCann v UK (1995)	McCann and two others were shot dead in Gibraltar, by the SAS, as they were IRA terrorist suspects	Article 2 was violated Lethal force used by state agents in self-defence or defence of others must be based on a test that is in part subjective and in part objective
Matzarakis v Greece (2004)	The police shot and seriously injured the applicant, who had driven through a red traffic light in Athens, near the US Embassy	Article 2 was violated Unregulated and arbitrary action by state officials is incompatible with effective respect for human rights
Finogenov v Russia (2011)	A group of Chechen separatists held 900 people hostage The Russian security forces pumped an unknown narcotic gas into the auditorium and stormed the building	The use of gas was not a disproportionate measure in these circumstances
Armani Da Silva v UK (2016)	Undercover police officers shot and killed Mr de Menezes, mistaking him for a failed suicide bomber on the run No individual officers were prosecuted	The court found no violation of Article 2 This decision brings the test set out in McCann much more in line with the test in English law for self-defence and is much more subjective
Nachova v Bulgaria (2005)	Two of the applicant's relatives, both of Roma origin, who had absconded from a military construction crew, were shot and killed during an attempted arrest by the military police	Article 2 was engaged The court stated that it cannot be necessary to put human life at risk where it is known that the person to be arrested poses no threat to life or limb
Güleç v Turkey (1998)	The applicant's son was killed in spontaneous unauthorised demonstrations and attacks on public buildings	Article 2 was violated as excessive force was used

28.2 English law and its compatibility with ECHR obligations

So far in this chapter we have considered Article 2 and the way in which it is interpreted by the ECtHR. Aspects of the relevant English law will now be considered so that the match between English law and the obligations under the ECHR can be compared to ensure compliance (or otherwise). You should also be aware of the English law with respect to homicide, dealt with in Chapters 5–7 in this book.

28.2.1 Analysis of relevant English law to determine compatibility with ECHR obligations and the consequences where English law appears to interfere with the ECHR

The beginning of life and the unborn child

We have seen that there is considerable freedom for a state to regulate matters of life and death. English law views that a foetus becomes a person when the baby is born and takes at least one breath outside the womb. In *CP (a child) v First-tier Tribunal and Criminal Injuries Compensation Authority* (2014), the Court of Appeal decided that a foetus could not be 'another person' before birth. This leaves English law muddled as a person cannot claim to be a victim of a crime of violence with respect to injuries caused when he or she is a foetus in the womb for the purposes of criminal injuries compensation, yet can claim for injuries resulting from negligence while a foetus. This seems to be in part consistent with the decision in *Vo v France* (2005).

Abortion and the right to life

Abortion is legal in England, Wales and Scotland up to 24 weeks under the Abortion Act 1967. However, if there is a substantial risk to the woman's life or foetal abnormalities, there is no time limit. This is compatible with Article 2 and the margin of appreciation.

The end of life and the right to die

Suicide

The Suicide Act 1961 decriminalised suicide so that it is not an offence to take one's own life. However, the Suicide Act 1961 makes it a criminal offence for a person to 'Aid, abet, counsel or procure the suicide of another or an attempt of another to commit suicide'.

This has implications for euthanasia in all its aspects. So, while suicide is no longer a criminal offence, all other aspects of assisted dying may be an offence.

Look online

Consider the denial of the 'right to die' in assisted dying CPS policy at https://www.cps.gov.uk/legal-guidance/suicide-policy-prosecutors-respect-cases-encouraging-or-assisting-suicide.

Euthanasia and other aspects of end of life areas in English law

Apart from the death penalty, Article 2.2 sets out the limited circumstances in which a person can be absolved from killing. As we shall see, English law is compatible with Article 2 in this area. End of life areas include:

- euthanasia
- assisted dying
- mercy killing
- withdrawal of treatment
- switching off life-support machines.

The *Pretty* case in 2001 was perhaps the first major case taken through the courts.

R (Pretty) v DPP (2001)

Diane Pretty had motor neurone disease (MND). She wanted to control the time and manner of her death. Because of her condition, she could not commit suicide without the help of her husband. She asked the court to guarantee that her husband would not be prosecuted if he helped her die. The English courts said that the right to life did not include a right to die. They also said that the right to private life (under Article 8) did not include a right to decide when and how to die.

Following that decision, the case went to the ECtHR. She argued that the right to life included a right to choose whether to carry on living. The ECtHR stated that the right to life was not determined by quality of life, so could not be interpreted as also giving a right to die. Unlike the House of Lords, the Court did say that her right to choose how to end her life came within her right to respect for private life. However, the ban on assisted suicide in the UK could be justified to protect vulnerable people. The court did stress that where a state has law that makes assisted suicide legal, that will not be a breach of Article 2.

Sadly, Diane Pretty died the way she always feared, not under her control. Around the same time as Diane Pretty died, the case of *Ms B v An NHS Hospital Trust* (2002) was heard in the UK.

Ms B v An NHS Hospital Trust (2002)

Ms B suffered a haemorrhage and was admitted to hospital. She was informed by doctors that there was a possibility of a further bleed, or she could have surgical intervention, which would result in severe disability. On the basis of this advice she executed a Living Will. The terms of the Living Will stated that should the time come when Ms B was unable to give instructions, she wished for treatment to be withdrawn if she was suffering from, among other things, a life-threatening condition. Unfortunately, she soon become tetraplegic and continued to express her wish not to be kept artificially alive by the use of a ventilator. The court decided that the right to determine what shall be done with one's own body is a fundamental right in our society and the ventilator could be turned off. This is now covered if a person executes a lasting power of attorney.

The case of Debbie Purdy in 2009 took the matter further.

R (Purdy) v DPP and the Society for the Protection of Unborn Children (2009)

Debbie Purdy suffered from primary progressive multiple sclerosis. She accepted that there would come a time when her continuing existence would become increasingly unbearable, at which point she would wish to end her own life. Because of the offence under s 2 of the Suicide Act 1961 of aiding and abetting suicide, if she decided to carry out this wish she would have to travel to a country, such as Switzerland, where assisted suicide is lawful. However, if Ms Purdy's husband were to assist her to make the necessary arrangements – which was likely, given her condition – he would then be at risk of prosecution and conviction under the Act. Ms Purdy and her husband wished to know whether he was likely to be prosecuted in the event that he assisted her in making arrangements to travel abroad for the purpose of assisted suicide.

The House of Lords stated Article 8 was engaged here, but the same issues were in question with relation to the application under Article 2. The law was not clear enough about when people would be prosecuted for encouraging or assisting suicide. They ordered the Director of Public Prosecutions to produce guidance on what makes a prosecution more or less likely. In February 2010 the prosecuting policy on cases of 'Encouraging or Assisting Suicide' was issued. It covers actions that happen in England and Wales, even if the suicide happens abroad.

However, this does not mean that there will be no prosecutions for aiding and abetting suicide.

In the news

Man charged with murder over the death of his father

Bipin Desai has been charged with murder, with assisted suicide in the alternative, in relation to the death of his father, Dhirajlal Desai.

A CPS spokesperson said:

> After an assessment of the evidence provided to us by the police it has been decided that Bipin Desai should face one charge of murder, with assisted suicide in the alternative, in relation to the death of his father, Dhirajlil Desai, on 26 August 2015. He will also face two charges of theft. … This decision was taken in accordance with the Code for Crown Prosecutors and the DPP's guidelines on cases of encouraging or assisting suicide.

Source: Adapted from an article on the Crown Prosecution Service website, 9 November 2016

End of life care and the use of life-support machines

Tip

It would be helpful to remind yourself of the case of *R v Malcherek and Steel* (1981) that you will have studied in criminal law before you study this section. Case details can be found in *AQA A-level Law for Year 1 and AS, Chapter 19*.

Medical and technical advances have enabled doctors to continue to support life with artificial assistance. This then raises the question of when artificial support can be stopped and thus cause the actual death of the person supported. This matter rose to prominence with the case of *Airedale NHS Trust v Bland* (1993).

Airedale NHS Trust v Bland (1993)

As a result of injuries sustained in the Hillsborough football stadium disaster in 1989, Anthony Bland had been in the condition known as persistent vegetative state (PVS) for over three years. The court had to decide whether artificial support could be withdrawn, as otherwise stopping support could amount to unlawful killing. Clearly Tony Bland could not make a decision.

The House of Lords gave permission for doctors at the Airedale General Hospital in West Yorkshire to remove a nasogastric feeding tube from Tony Bland, thus allowing him to die. This led to guidelines being drawn up for doctors in similar circumstances.

This ethical and moral dilemma causes difficulties because of the possibility that some people may wish life to be ended for personal or financial reasons. In *R v Malcherek and Steel* (1981), the court had decided that the doctors' actions in switching off a life-support machine did not constitute a *novus actus interveniens* that broke the chain of causation. Here the support machines were artificially keeping the victims of two serious assaults alive, so that when turned off, a conviction for murder could be allowed. The test of death was said to be where the brain stem has died, which was not the case in the Tony Bland situation.

The law is relatively clear in making decisions with respect to life-support machines, but it may have to cope with new developments, such as the possibility of communicating with people who have 'locked in' syndrome.

Look online

Research online the latest medical developments in treating people with 'locked in' syndrome, and how this might affect their legal position and rights: www.theguardian.com/science/2017/jan/31/groundbreaking-system-allows-locked-in-syndrome-patients-to-communicate-als.

The state's duty to protect life

Duties of the state in relation to life-threatening environmental risks

Much environmental legislation in England and Wales originates from EU law, which is directly applicable or implemented through national legislation. The potential issues for compatibility with Article 2 come from questions of enforcement of the legislation. The Environment Agency is the principal regulator, but it may be argued that lack of resources could result in a violation of Article 2. It will be interesting to see whether this will be considered with respect to the Grenfell Tower disaster and the consequent action needed to prevent a repeat, and also the way in which the disaster is investigated.

Protection of individuals from violence by others

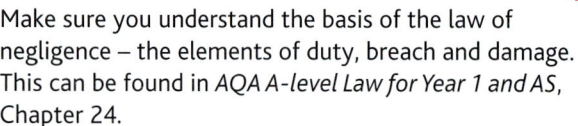

Tip

Make sure you understand the basis of the law of negligence – the elements of duty, breach and damage. This can be found in *AQA A-level Law for Year 1 and AS*, Chapter 24.

There have been a number of cases in which relatives of people killed or nearly killed by other private persons, claimed that the state ought to have protected the victims, but failed to do so.

If you have studied the law of negligence you will probably be familiar with the case of *Hill v Chief Constable of West Yorkshire* (1988), regarding the

Figure 28.5 Key cases regarding the rights of the unborn child and the right to die under English law

Case	Facts	ECtHR decisions
R (Pretty) v DPP (2001)	Diane Pretty asked the court to guarantee that her husband would not be prosecuted if he helped her die	Right to life was not determined by quality of life so could not be interpreted as also giving a right to die
		Where a state has law that makes assisted suicide legal, that will not be a breach of Article 2
Ms B v An NHS Hospital Trust (2002)	Ms B suffered a haemorrhage and executed a Living Will	The right to determine what shall be done with one's own body is a fundamental right and the ventilator could be turned off
R (Purdy) v DPP and the Society for the Protection of Unborn Children (2009)	Would Ms Purdy's husband be prosecuted if he assisted her in making arrangements to travel abroad for the purpose of assisted suicide?	The House of Lords ordered the DPP to produce guidance on what makes a prosecution more or less likely
		The guidance was published in February 2010
Airedale NHS Trust v Bland (1993)	Could artificial support be withdrawn from Anthony Bland, in a PVS state since the Hillsborough Football Stadium disaster?	The House of Lords gave permission for withdrawing support
		Guidelines were subsequently drawn up

murders committed by Peter Sutcliffe and the police actions in protecting the public or not. The question of Article 2 did not arise in that case, but it would have been engaged.

The recent Supreme Court decision in *Robinson v Chief Constable of West Yorkshire Police* (2018) has expressly ruled that the case of *Hill* did not confer on the police a blanket immunity from being sued in negligence. This case involved an injury to a bystander caused by police who were carrying out an arrest. The court decided that as there was a positive act and not an omission, there was a reasonably foreseeable risk of injury to the claimant when the arrest was attempted. This was enough to impose a duty of care on the police.

> **See AQA A-level Law for Year 1 and AS for more details on this area of law.**

The relationship between liability under the law of negligence and the engagement of Article 2 remains difficult. Cases such as *Mitchell v Glasgow City Council* (2009) show that this difficulty is not just related to police action.

Mitchell v Glasgow City Council (2009)

The widow and daughter of an elderly man who was attacked and killed by his next-door neighbour following a long-running dispute claimed for damages from the local authority for the loss, injury and damage they had suffered. Both the deceased and his attacker, Mr Drummond, were tenants of Glasgow City Council. At a meeting with the council, Mr Drummond was advised that the council was considering evicting him because of his behaviour towards Mr Mitchell (and others). After leaving the meeting Mr Drummond attacked and killed Mr Mitchell.

The family claimed that the council was guilty of negligence as it had failed to fulfil its duty of care by warning Mr Mitchell that the meeting was taking place, thereby allowing him to take steps to avoid an attack by Mr Drummond. It also claimed that the council acted in a way that was in breach of the deceased's right to life under Article 2.

The ECtHR decided that the council had not been negligent and did not act in a way that was in breach of the deceased's right under Article 2.

However, there have been many other cases since then. Recently the case of *Michael v Chief Constable of South Wales* (2015) re-examined the problem.

Michael v Chief Constable of South Wales (2015)

The Supreme Court decided this case involving a damages claim against the police for alleged systemic and individual police failings. These failings led to a critical delay in the 999 system and the failure to stop the murder of a Cardiff mother of two by her ex-partner. One aspect was whether the combined faults of separate public bodies can combine to establish a breach of Article 2.

The majority of the Supreme Court rejected the argument that the common law should be developed in harmony with the obligations under HRA 1998. If liability was to arise in cases of pure omission by the police to perform their duty for the prevention of violence, then it was for Parliament to legislate. The *Hill* principle still applied in the law of negligence, but the issues of potential liability for damages under HRA 1998 and Article 2 could proceed to trial as ECHR claims have different objectives from civil actions such as negligence.

It therefore appears that while English law is not in harmony with ECHR, there is no obligation for it to be so, providing that there is accountability by the state for any breaches of the Article.

Extension activity

Look at other recent cases of a similar nature such as:
- *Sarjantson v Humberside Police* (2013)
- *Tyrrell v HM Senior Coroner County Durham and Darlington* (2016)
- *Rabone v Pennine Care NHS Trust* (2013)
- *Hertfordshire Police v Van Colle* (2008)
- *Smith v Chief Constable of Sussex Police* (2008)
- *Rathband v Chief Constable of Northumbria* (2016).

How do these cases reflect the relationship between English law and ECHR?

Prevention of suicide by prisoners

In *Keenan v UK* (2001), there had not been a breach of the positive obligation in failing to take steps to prevent the suicide of a mentally ill prisoner.

This was considered again in the English courts in *Amin v Secretary of State for the Home Department* (2003).

Amin v Secretary of State for the Home Department (2003)

Amin was a young Asian prisoner. He was placed in a cell overnight with a prisoner known to be racist, extremely violent and mentally unstable. Amin was killed. The family sought an inquiry into the death.

The procedural obligation under Article 2 is comprehensively protected under UK law. A public enquiry should be held. Lord Bingham said that an investigation was required:

> ...to ensure so far as possible that the full facts are brought to light; that culpable and discreditable conduct is exposed and brought to public notice; that suspicion of deliberate wrongdoing (if unjustified) is allayed; that dangerous practices and procedures are rectified; and that those who have lost their loved ones may at least have the satisfaction of knowing that lessons learned from his death may save the lives of others.

In other words, all avenues of investigation must be carried out in these circumstances. The question remains as to the nature of the investigation that must be carried out by the state when there is an attempt to commit suicide that nearly succeeds and which leaves the victim with serious injuries. This was considered in *JL v Secretary of State for Justice* (2008).

JL v Secretary of State for Justice (2008)

JL was born in Jamaica and came to the UK in 2002 and shortly afterwards was arrested and charged with possessing cocaine with intent to supply. He was remanded in custody to Feltham Young Offenders Institution, where he was found hanging from the bars of the window of his cell, having used a sheet to make a noose around his neck. He had stopped breathing but was resuscitated. Deprivation of oxygen had resulted in serious brain damage. Was there a human rights duty to hold an investigation into the circumstances leading up to this?

The court decided that there was a similar duty to hold an enhanced investigation as exists after a suicide.

There have been a number of cases with respect to the conduct of inquests following an apparent suicide while in custody. These cases query whether the workings of the inquest have been sufficient to comply with Article 2. The courts generally find that Article 2 has not been breached as the possible errors in procedure have not materially affected the obligations under Article 2. An example of this can be seen in *P v HM Coroner for the District of Avon* (2009).

P v HM Coroner for the District of Avon (2009)

On 5 January 2007, Caroline Jane Powell was found dead in her cell at HMP Eastwood Park. She was hanging from a sheet attached to the wardrobe. An inquest was held and all agreed that she had brought about her own death but there was an issue as to whether she had intended to kill herself or whether what she had done was intended as a cry for help which had unintended consequences. If the former, then the appropriate verdict would have been one of suicide. However, the jury concluded that suicide was not established and that the appropriate verdict was one of accident.

The complaint was that in the inquest, to which Article 2 applied, the Deputy Coroner misdirected the jury because she did not properly explain to them that, if they returned a verdict of suicide or accident, they could also append a narrative about the circumstances of the accident. The verdict did not address the extensive evidence, which was critical of the prison authorities in the way that they had managed and cared for Caroline during her short time in Eastwood Park.

However, given the purpose of an inquest and the fact that there was a Prisons Ombudsman's Report, there had been no breach of Article 2. Maurice Kay LJ, said:

> It is also important to keep in mind that the procedural obligation of Article 2 is imposed not simply on the Deputy Coroner but on the state. To see whether the obligation has been discharged it is necessary to consider the entirety of investigative apparatus deployed by the state. This includes the Ombudsman's Report which, it seems to me, substantially filled the lacuna left by the limited nature of the jury's verdict and thereby rendered the totality of the investigative process Article 2 compliant.

Protection against medical malpractice

We have seen in *Erikson v Italy* (1999) that there is an obligation to establish an effective judicial system for establishing the cause of a death which occurs in hospital and any liability on the part of the medical practitioners concerned. There have been a number of cases where this has been examined by the English courts and there has generally been seen to be compatibility with Article 2.

In *Savage v South Essex NHS Trust* (2008), the question was whether an NHS trust owed an operational obligation to detained mental patients (similar to a prison authority's obligation to prisoners, discussed above) at real and immediate risk of suicide. The House of Lords stated that Article 2 requires the NHS trust to do all that can reasonably be expected to prevent the patient from committing suicide. If NHS trusts fail to do this, not only will they and the health authorities be liable in negligence, but there will also be a violation of the operational obligation under Article 2 to protect the patient's life.

More importantly, it was stated that there should be no distinction between the obligations to prisoners, voluntary patients and detained patients; this would be as unedifying as it is unnecessary. This was confirmed in the case of *Rabone v Pennine Care NHS Trust* (2012).

Rabone v Pennine Care NHS Trust (2012)

In April 2005, Melanie Rabone, who had a history of depression and self-harm, was voluntarily admitted onto the psychiatric ward. Although her admission was voluntary, the hospital noted that if she attempted or demanded to leave, she should be assessed for detention under the Mental Health Act 1983 and could be prevented from leaving the hospital. Melanie was released for home leave on 19 April 2005, despite the concerns of her parents. The next day she hanged herself from a tree in a park near to her house.

The Supreme Court stated that the decision to allow Melanie two days' home leave was one that no reasonable psychiatric practitioner would have made, and recourse to the margin of appreciation was misplaced. The trust had failed to do all that could reasonably have been expected to prevent the real and immediate risk of suicide. It had an operational duty under Article 2 to protect persons from a real and immediate risk of suicide where they were under the control of the state.

It is clear that the scope of Article 2 is widening and can be seen in the approach to claims resulting from death and the procedure that follows a death. A recent case to illustrate the breadth of application of Article 2 can be seen in *Tainton v Preston and West Lancashire Coroner* (2016) (see below).

Extradition, expulsion and deportation

This is the basis of a number of claims, particularly those who do not meet the criteria with UK immigration with respect to refugee status. The 2017 Government report 'Deportation with Assurances' suggests that the main concerns lie with Articles 3, 5 and 6 rather than Article 2.

The state's duty to make an adequate investigation into loss of life

Where a death occurs without engagement of Article 2, the coroner (or jury) will look at who died, when and where, and how he or she came by his or her death. If Article 2 is engaged, the investigation will need to include the wider circumstances of the death. This includes not only how but also in what circumstances the person came by his or her death. This is shown in the case of *Tainton v Preston and West Lancashire Coroner* (2016).

Tainton v Preston and West Lancashire Coroner (2016)

A prisoner died of oesophageal cancer after healthcare staff missed a number of opportunities to identify his condition, thereby delaying diagnosis to a point when no effective treatment options were viable. The healthcare provider admitted failings in relation to the deceased's care. However, medical evidence was not conclusive that earlier identification would have extended his life, particularly as the deceased's ability to tolerate chemotherapy was unknown.

The procedural obligation under Article 2 applied to this inquest. The fact that the coroner did not ask the jury to make findings as to whether the failings in medical care could be said to have caused or hastened the death meant that Article 2 had been breached.

HH Judge Peter Thornton QC produced 'Guidance to Coroners' on 18 June 2016 in connection with this case and suggested a checklist of questions that a coroner sitting with a jury in an Article 2 case such as this should consider. This shows that the UK takes swift and positive steps to remedy any procedural difficulties that are highlighted.

It can also be seen in the context that reporting a death is not always adequate in mental health cases. All deaths in state detention should be examined by a coroner. However, inconsistencies between official data on deaths reported to coroners in England and Wales and notifications sent to health regulators by NHS trusts suggest coroners may not have conducted inquests into every death. Between 2011 and 2014, a total of 373 deaths of people detained under the Mental Health Act were reported to coroners in England and Wales, according to data held by the Ministry of Justice. In contrast, data compiled over the same period by the Care Quality Commission and the Health Inspectorate for Wales, and supplied to the Government's

Figure 28.6 Key cases for Article 2(1) on the state's duty to protect life and to make an adequate investigation into loss of life

Case	Facts	Law
Hill v Chief Constable of West Yorkshire (1988)	The claimant's daughter was the killer's last victim before he was caught The mother claimed that the police owed a duty of care to her daughter	The relationship between the victim and the police was not sufficiently close (proximate) for the police to be under a duty of care
Mitchell v Glasgow City Council (2009)	The widow and daughter of an elderly man who was attacked and killed by his neighbour claimed for damages from the local authority for the loss, injury and damage	The council had not been negligent and did not breach the deceased's rights under Article 2
Michael v Chief Constable of South Wales (2015)	Alleged systemic and individual police failings led to a critical delay in the 999 system and the failure to stop the murder of a mother by her ex-partner	Article 2 was engaged as ECHR claims have different objectives from civil actions such as negligence
Amin v Secretary of State for the Home Department (2003)	Amin was a young Asian prisoner killed by a prisoner known to be racist, extremely violent and mentally unstable	The procedural obligation under Article 2 is comprehensively protected under UK law A public inquiry should be held
JL v Secretary of State for Justice (2008)	JL was remanded in custody and hung himself He was resuscitated but suffered serious brain damage	There was a similar duty to hold an enhanced investigation as exists after a suicide
P v HM Coroner for the District of Avon (2009)	A suicide verdict did not address the extensive evidence which criticised prison authorities	Article 2 was not breached as a Prison's Ombudsman's Report was published
Rabone v Pennine Care NHS Trust (2012)	Rabone was released for home leave from a psychiatric ward despite the concerns of her parents The next day she committed suicide	The trust had failed to do all that could reasonably have been expected to prevent the real and immediate risk of suicide Article 2 was violated
Tainton v Preston and West Lancashire Coroner (2016)	A prisoner died after health care staff missed a number of opportunities to identify his condition	Article 2 had been breached

Independent Advisory Panel on Deaths in Custody, show a total of 1,115 deaths – 742 more than was reported to coroners. (Source: Shaun Lintern, 'Trusts fail to report hundreds of mental health patient deaths to coroner', *Health Service Journal*, 9 August 2016.)

The justified exceptions set out in Article 2(2)

Look online

The investigation of deaths attributable to police officers and other agents of the state is dealt with by the Independent Office for Police Conduct (IOPC), Coroners' Inquests. See, for example: https://policeconduct.gov.uk/, https://www.gov.uk/government/publications/guide-to-coroner-services-and-coroner-investigations-a-short-guide and https://www.cps.gov.uk/legal-guidance/coroners.

We have already seen that the ECtHR found that the three suspects in the *McCann* case had been deliberately killed in contravention of Article 2 and that this was not necessary force. What is necessary force as seen by English law is considered below.

In defence of any person from unlawful violence

In *Armani Da Silva v UK* (2016) the court set out a test that was much in line with the English law on self-defence.

See Chapter 12 for more information on the defence of self-defence.

In order to effect a lawful arrest or to prevent the escape of a person lawfully detained

All police officers have a duty to act professionally and only use force that is proportionate, reasonable and justifiable in the circumstances; otherwise it is unlawful.

Section 3 of the Criminal Law Act 1967 states:

> " A person may use such force as is reasonable in the circumstances in the prevention of crime, or in effecting or assisting in the lawful arrest of offenders or suspected offenders or of persons unlawfully at large. "

Section 117 of the Police and Criminal Evidence Act 1984 also states that force may be used when permitted in any other legislation. The Act also requires codes of practice to be established. Typically, these set out what is considered reasonable force.

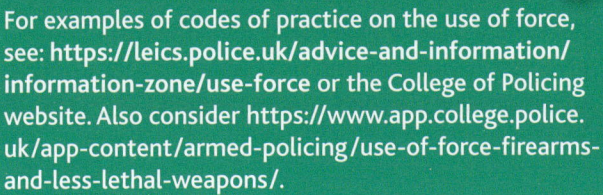

Look online

For examples of codes of practice on the use of force, see: https://leics.police.uk/advice-and-information/information-zone/use-force or the College of Policing website. Also consider https://www.app.college.police.uk/app-content/armed-policing/use-of-force-firearms-and-less-lethal-weapons/.

These regulations and Acts seem to confirm that English law is intended to comply fully with Article 2 and the decisions thereunder.

Look online

Read the following news article for an example of the consequences of failing to comply: www.dailymail.co.uk/news/article-4746786/Police-removed-duty-beating-suspects.html.

In action lawfully taken for the purpose of quelling a riot or insurrection

As we have seen, there are two possible violations to Article 2:

- the question of whether the action was absolutely necessary, and
- whether the investigation following the incident has complied with the requirements of Article 2.

While it is clear that the question of absolute necessity is a question that is open to debate, the subsequent investigation is important in ensuring that Article 2 has not been violated. The civil consequences of a riot in terms of compensation are now covered by the Riot Compensation Act 2016 which sets out 'the framework for a modern, fair and affordable compensation scheme that supports communities that are recovering from riots, without placing unreasonable burdens on the taxpayer'.

Look online

The case of *Commissioner of Police of the Metropolis v DSD and another* (2018), while relating specifically to Article 3, has relevance to Article 2. Here, the workings of the Parole Board were called into question. The press summary of this case can be seen at: https://www.supremecourt.uk/cases/docs/uksc-2015-0166-press-summary.pdf.

Summary

- Both the ECtHR and the Supreme Court have found that the ECHR applies not only to acts and omissions attributable to a state on its own territory, but outside it as well.

- In Article 2, life means human life, not life of animals. It does not extend to the existence of legal persons such as a limited company. The ECHR does not otherwise clarify what life is, or when it begins or ends.

- The unborn child is not regarded as a person directly protected by Article 2.

- Article 2 of the Convention states that everyone's right to life must be protected by law. Apart from the death penalty, it sets out only limited circumstances in which a person can be deprived of this right.

- Suicide is not a criminal offence in the UK, but all other aspects of assisted dying may be an offence, even if the actual death is to take place in a state where assisted suicide is legal.

- The law in the UK is relatively clear in making decisions with respect to life-support machines, but there remain ethical and moral dilemmas in other medical conditions.

- The relationship between liability under the law of negligence and the engagement of Article 2 remains difficult.

- For a positive obligation to arise, it must be established that the authorities knew or ought to have known at the time of the existence of a real and immediate risk to the life of an identified individual.

- The scope of Article 2 is widening in the approach taken to claims resulting from death and the procedure that follows a death.

- The use of lethal force by police officers may be justified in certain circumstances but this does not amount to *carte blanche*. The test is that the use of force is no more than absolutely necessary. This requires that consideration be given to all dangers and risks and whether a situation was planned and controlled.

29 Article 5 ECHR: the right to liberty and security of person

After reading this chapter, you should be able to:
- Understand the scope of Article 5 – the right to liberty and security of person
- Understand English law and its compatibility with ECHR obligations

29.1 The requirements of Article 5 ECHR

The focus of the discussion in this chapter is on Article 5.1 (a)–(c). The relevant sections of Article 5 state:

1. Everyone has the right to liberty and security of person. No one shall be deprived of his liberty save in the following cases and in accordance with a procedure prescribed by law:
   (a) the lawful detention of a person after conviction by a competent court;
   (b) the lawful arrest or detention of a person for non-compliance with the lawful order of a court or in order to secure the fulfilment of any obligation prescribed by law;
   (c) the lawful arrest or detention of a person effected for the purpose of bringing him before the competent legal authority on reasonable suspicion of having committed an offence or when it is reasonably considered necessary to prevent his committing an offence or fleeing after having done so.
2. Everyone who is arrested shall be informed promptly, in a language which he understands, of the reasons for his arrest and of any charge against him.
3. Everyone arrested or detained in accordance with the provisions of paragraph 1(c) of this Article shall be brought promptly before a judge or other officer authorised by law to exercise judicial power

and shall be entitled to trial within a reasonable time or to release pending trial. Release may be conditioned by guarantees to appear for trial.
4. Everyone who is deprived of his liberty by arrest or detention shall be entitled to take proceedings by which the lawfulness of his detention shall be decided speedily by a court and his release ordered if the detention is not lawful.
5. Everyone who has been the victim of arrest or detention in contravention of the provisions of this article shall have an enforceable right to compensation.

29.1.1 The meaning of 'deprivation of liberty'

A distinction has to be made between what amounts to a 'deprivation of liberty' and a general restriction of movement of an individual.

As stated in *HM v Switzerland* (2002):

> In order to determine whether there has been a deprivation of liberty, the starting-point must be the specific situation of the individual concerned and account must be taken of a whole range of factors such as the type, duration, effects and manner of implementation of the measure in question. The distinction between a deprivation of and restriction upon liberty is merely one of degree or intensity, and not one of nature or substance.

In this case, an elderly woman was placed in an open ward in residential accommodation and was able to contact friends. She was found not to have been deprived of her liberty.

Generally, confinement will be due to an arrest by a public authority on suspicion of having committed an offence, imprisonment following court conviction, or due to a hospital order. It does not always depend on being locked up. As Lord Hope said in *Austin v Commissioner of Police of the Metropolis* (2009) (also shown as *Austin v UK* (2015)):

> A person can be deprived of his liberty even if his departure is not prevented by a locked door or other physical barrier and even though he may be allowed extensive social and other contact with the outside world.

It is clear that holding someone in prison or a secure hospital is a common example of detention. However, there are other situations where the courts have had to consider whether interference with a person's liberty amounts to a deprivation of liberty and the following cases illustrate the approach of the ECtHR as to what can amount to a deprivation of liberty. This can depend on the circumstances of each case.

HL v UK (2004)

HL was informally detained for mental health reasons under the common law doctrine of necessity and not subject to the standard compulsory detention procedures. He did not have the capacity to refuse or consent to detention and was subject to continuous supervision and control. The ECtHR ruled (in contrast to *HM v Switzerland* (2002) above) that this detention was arbitrary as there were no clear rules in place to provide HL with any safeguards.

Amuur v France (1996)

The applicants, who were four Somali nationals, arrived in France by airplane after fleeing Somalia due to fear for their lives there. They were held in the airport's transit zone under strict police surveillance and without access to legal or social assistance.

They applied for asylum but the Minister of the Interior refused them the right to enter and therefore they were returned. They complained that holding asylum-seekers in the international zone of an airport was in violation of Article 5.1.

The court took note that holding third country nationals in international zones involved restrictions upon liberty. It accepted that such confinement was acceptable if it was accompanied by the appropriate safeguards for the person concerned, in order to enable a state to prevent unlawful immigration while respecting its international obligations provided that such restriction was not prolonged excessively. In this case, the court decided that holding the applicants in the transit zone of the airport was a deprivation of liberty.

Austin v UK (2015)

The police stood in lines across the exits from Oxford Circus in London during an anti-globalisation demonstration. People were allowed to leave the cordon or 'kettle' only with permission but many were held for over seven hours. The detention was challenged by one of the detained demonstrators and by some passers-by who were not involved in the demonstration. It was

argued that this restriction on movement in the 'kettle' amounted to a deprivation of liberty contrary to Article 5.

The ECtHR referred to a number of general principles established in its case law:

1 The ECHR was a 'living instrument', which had to be interpreted in the light of present day conditions. Even by 2001, advances in communications technology had made it possible to mobilise protesters rapidly and covertly on a previously unknown scale. Article 5 did not have to be construed in such a way as to make it impracticable for the police to fulfil their duties of maintaining order and protecting the public.

2 The ECHR had to be interpreted harmoniously, as a whole. It had to be taken into account that various Articles placed a duty on the police to protect individuals from violence and physical injury.

3 The context in which the measure in question had taken place was relevant. Members of the public were often required to endure temporary restrictions on freedom of movement in certain contexts, such as when travelling on public transport, or on a motorway, or when attending a football match or an event.

The court did not consider that such commonly occurring restrictions could properly be described as 'deprivations of liberty' so long as:

- they were rendered unavoidable as a result of circumstances beyond the control of the authorities
- they were necessary to avert a real risk of serious injury or damage, and
- they were kept to the minimum required for that purpose.

The court further emphasised that, within the Convention system, it was for the domestic courts to establish the facts and the court would generally follow the findings of facts reached by the domestic courts. In this case, there had been a three-week trial which considered substantial evidence and appeals to the House of Lords.

The police had anticipated a real risk of serious injury, even death, and damage to property if the crowds were not effectively controlled and they had decided to impose an absolute cordon as the only way to prevent violence and the risk of injured people and damaged property.

There had been space within the cordon for people to walk about and there had been no crushing. But, there was no shelter, food, water or toilet facility. The police had tried to start releasing people but their attempts were repeatedly suspended because of the violent and uncooperative behaviour of a significant minority both within and outside the cordon.

The court found that the cordon was imposed to isolate and contain a large crowd in dangerous and volatile conditions and in the circumstances an absolute cordon had been the least intrusive and most effective means available to the police to protect the public, both within and outside the cordon, from violence. As a result, the ECtHR decided that the people within the cordon had not been deprived of their liberty.

Despite this finding, the court emphasised the fundamental importance of freedom of expression and assembly in all democratic societies and underlined that national authorities should not use measures of crowd control to stifle or discourage protest, but rather only when necessary to prevent serious injury or damage.

Police kettling students during an education cuts demonstration

Shimovolos v Russia (2011)

S was Russian and his name had been registered in a surveillance database containing information about people perceived by the authorities as 'potential extremists'. When he got on a train to travel to an EU–Russia summit and protest march, his identity documents were checked several times, and when he got off the train, he was threatened with force if he did not go to the police station. He was kept there for 45 minutes and questioned about the purpose of his trip and his acquaintances. The police report indicated that he had been stopped and questioned, acting on information in order to prevent him from committing administrative or criminal offences.

The ECtHR ruled that, as he had been taken to the police station under threat of force and had not been free to leave without permission, he had been deprived of his liberty, even for a short time. Article 5.1(c) did not allow detention, as a general policy of prevention of people who were perceived by the authorities to be dangerous or likely to offend. He had been arrested arbitrarily, in violation of Article 5.1.

Kasparov v Russia (No. 2) 2016

Garry Kasparov, the former world chess champion, and a second claimant were detained at a Moscow airport before they could board a flight to Samara to attend a rally at an EU–Russia summit. The second claimant's ticket and passport were confiscated and he was taken to a police office and questioned for five hours about whether his ticket was forged. He was prevented from leaving the office for 48 hours and an armed officer guarded the door. The prescribed detention period for administrative offences is three hours.

The authorities claimed they had been investigating Kasparov and the second claimant for committing the crime of forgery. However, there was no evidence that any forgery had taken place, or any reasonable suspicion that such offence had been committed. The ECtHR decided that there had been unlawful deprivation of liberty which was not justified for any lawful purpose.

Ostendorf v Germany (2013)

The claimant was a known problem football supporter. He was on his way to a high-profile match and had been in a group which had been given directions by the police over where they could go in order to avoid violent confrontations between rival supporters. In an apparent bid to evade the policing operation, the claimant hid in a pub toilet. He was found, arrested and detained for about four hours until after the match had ended

He claimed a breach of his rights under Article 5.1(b) and 5.1(c).

The ECtHR found that where Article 5.1(b) is relied upon to justify a pre-emptive arrest, the legal obligation said to apply to an individual must be 'very closely circumscribed'. The place and time of the imminent commission of the offence and its potential victim(s) must be sufficiently specified. A general obligation to keep the peace is not sufficient to justify arrest under Article 5.1(b) but may be relevant to Article 5.1(c).

In order to ensure under Article 5.1(b) that individuals are not subjected to arbitrary detention, it is necessary, *before* concluding that a person has failed to satisfy his or her obligation at issue, that the person concerned:

1 was made aware of the specific act that he or she was to refrain from committing, and

2 that the person showed him- or herself not to be willing to refrain from so doing.

On the facts, the claimant had been ordered to stay with the group of supporters he had arrived with and had been warned, in a clear manner, of the consequences of his failure to comply with that order, as the police had announced that any person leaving the group would be arrested. The court found that the claimant's arrest was lawful under Article 5.1(b), but *not* under Article 5.1(c).

29.1.2 The additional positive duty

Article 5.1 states that 'Everyone has the right to liberty and security of person'. This must be considered as laying down a positive obligation on the state to protect its citizens. Any conclusion to the effect that this was not the case would not only be inconsistent with the Court's case law, notably under Articles 2, 3 and 8 ECHR. It would, moreover, leave a sizeable gap in the protection from arbitrary detention which would be inconsistent with the importance of personal liberty in a democratic society.

This positive obligation requires a state to explain where an individual is when taken into detention or custody, to prevent the individual's disappearance and to conduct an investigation where a person is held in state custody but has not been seen since. State agents could spirit dissenters away in the night but claim never to have done so. The dissenter's bodies may never be found. Under the ECHR, the state should still carry out proper investigations.

This obligation would also extend to taking action where the deprivation of liberty is attributable to private individuals rather than to agents of the state, such as in human trafficking. In *Rantsev v Cyprus and Russia* (2010), the applicant, who was a Russian national, brought a complaint against the Republics of Cyprus and Russia in relation to the death of his 20-year-old daughter. The ECtHR found a violation of Article 4 ECHR – the prohibition of slavery and forced labour. It also clarified the positive obligations upon states to investigate allegations of trafficking and to implement measures to prevent and protect people from human trafficking. This obligation would presumably extend to other instances of false imprisonment such as kidnapping, forced labour, domestic abuse, etc. Obviously, such cases will involve other ECHR Articles as well, such as Articles 3 and 8. The obligation may require investigation of instances of unexplained disappearances which are not state-related but which the state is not then simply allowed to ignore.

29.1.3 In accordance with procedure prescribed by law

Article 5 then provides that 'No one shall be deprived of his liberty save ... in accordance with a procedure prescribed by law'.

Conformity with domestic law

This law will be the domestic law that is in issue. Whether an action is in conformity with the relevant domestic law is a question for the state but the ECHR will scrutinise the measure to be certain that this is the case. The ECtHR will then look at the quality of the domestic law to consider whether it is arbitrary.

Is the measure arbitrary?

The measure must have some basis in domestic law so, for example, detention on remand before trial must be a practice based on a law passed by the state.

A measure will be arbitrary if there is no link between the detention and the reason given for it. In England, **indeterminate prison sentences** are compatible with Article 5 as long as there is a link between the sentence passed by the court and the reason for the continued detention. This form of sentence was challenged in *Stafford v UK* (2002).

Key term

Indeterminate prison sentence – an indeterminate prison sentence can be imposed if a court thinks an offender is a danger to the public and is one where:

- no date is set when the prisoner will be released
- the prisoner has to spend a minimum amount of time in prison (called a 'tariff' period) before he or she is considered for release
- the Parole Board decides if the prisoner can be released – often on licence.

Stafford v UK (2002)

Having been released on licence from a life sentence for murder, the claimant was re-sentenced for a cheque fraud. He was not released at the end of the sentence he served for the fraud offence. He claimed that there was no evidence that he would continue to be a danger to the public, and the system provided no way for him to test his continued detention. The House of Lords decided that the Home Secretary had the right not to follow a Parole Board's recommendation to release a prisoner after the service of the tariff part of his or her sentence, where the Home Secretary was satisfied that the offender would commit further offences, even if those offences might be expected to be non-violent.

The ECtHR decided that there was a breach of Article 5 as there was no sufficient connection between his original conviction for murder and any risk that he might commit further non-violent offences after release.

It observed that it is wrong to regard a sentence of life imprisonment as a sentence that the prisoner be imprisoned for life. It was never expected that prisoners serving mandatory life sentences would stay in prison for life, save in exceptional cases. The mandatory life sentence does not impose imprisonment for life as a punishment. It is the tariff period, which reflects the individual circumstances of the offence and the offender, that represents the element of punishment.

Is there legal certainty?

Any measure should be based on legal rules and should not be vague, unclear or unpredictable. An offender should be able to reasonably foresee what action may be taken by the state and when any detention may happen.

29.1.4 Justified deprivation of liberty

Any deprivation of liberty must be justified by reference only to Article 5.1(a)–(c). These provisions are strictly construed and are exclusive.

Crime

Article 5.1(a) allows for an individual to be detained following a conviction. As has been seen above with the case of *Stafford v UK* (2002), continued detention after conviction cannot be arbitrary and must be linked to the conviction. The conviction must be by a competent court, which means it must be independent and impartial.

Article 5.1(c) allows for the lawful arrest or detention of a person suspected of having committed an offence. There must be some facts or information which satisfies the requirement of the police having reasonable suspicion and a person can be arrested for questioning in order to obtain evidence. In *Fox, Campbell and Hartley v UK* (1990), the applicants were arrested under a law that required a police constable to 'genuinely and honestly' suspect a person of being a terrorist. The question before the court was whether this amounted to reasonable suspicion that would satisfy an objective observer. In the case there was not enough evidence that the honest belief of the police constable was strong enough to be reasonable. By contrast, in *Murray v UK* (1994) there was no violation of this provision where a suspected terrorist was detained on 'honest suspicion based on reasonable grounds'.

Non-compliance with a court order

Article 5.1(b) allows for the lawful arrest or detention in cases such as arrest under a warrant for non-payment of a fine, contempt of court and breach of a bail condition. This covers measures where a court order has already been made and may include civil orders such as matrimonial orders or psychiatric confinement. It allows the police to detain to administer criminal law, for example to require a motorist to take a drink- or drug-driving test at the roadside. The measures must be necessary and the obligation must be 'specific and concrete' so that the detention is not based on vague grounds.

29.1.5 Articles 5.2–5.3: additional requirements to justify deprivation of liberty in cases of lawful arrest or detention

Article 5.2: promptly given reasons

Everyone who is arrested, or detained, shall be informed promptly, in a language which he or she understands, of the reasons for the arrest or detention and of any charge against him or her. In England, the provisions of this Article are mostly covered in the Police and Criminal Evidence Act (PACE) 1984, which allows a person to know why he or she has been arrested. The reason does not have to be given in full at the very moment of arrest but should be given promptly. In general, an explanation by the custody officer at the police station will be sufficient.

> For details of PACE 1984, see section 29.2 below.

In *Fox, Campbell and Hartley v UK* (1990), referred to above, the ECtHR decided that a delay of seven hours was acceptable. In most cases a delay of a few hours will be accepted as this will allow the police to make further enquiries and prepare for an interview. The ECtHR seems to be flexible on the level of detail that has to be given to the person detained as long as reasons for the arrest or detention are clear from the start.

Article 5.3: brought promptly before judicial officer and trial within reasonable time

This provision contains three separate parts:

1 The individual should be brought promptly before a judge or other officer authorised by law to exercise judicial power. The judicial officer should not be part of the investigation and should be able to make a binding decision which cannot be overturned by the Government.

2 The right to release on bail, except when custody is justified. The right to bail is not absolute, but if objected to, the objection must be justified by the judge. This provision is covered in England by the Bail Act 1976, by which there is a presumption in favour of bail and the court must give reasons for its refusal.

3 The right to be tried within a reasonable time. The purpose of this provision is to ensure that no one spends too long in detention before trial. Time starts when the accused is first remanded into custody and ends when the court gives judgment. What is a reasonable time depends on the circumstances of each case including the seriousness of the charge. It will also be necessary to consider whether continued detention while awaiting trial is required or whether bail can be granted.

> For more detail on bail, see section 29.2.4 below.

29.1.6 Article 5.5: right to compensation

This provides that everyone who has been the victim of unlawful arrest or detention shall have a right to compensation. This right arises for breach of Articles 5.1 and 5.4 and is mandatory – if there has been a breach, compensation must be awarded. The amount of compensation will be assessed by the court finding the detention unlawful. It is unlikely that compensation will be awarded for feelings of disappointment or frustration, though actual financial loss caused by the unlawful detention can be recovered.

Tip

Not every scenario that you have to consider will involve a breach of Article 5. Discuss the issues both for and against a possible breach before coming to a conclusion.

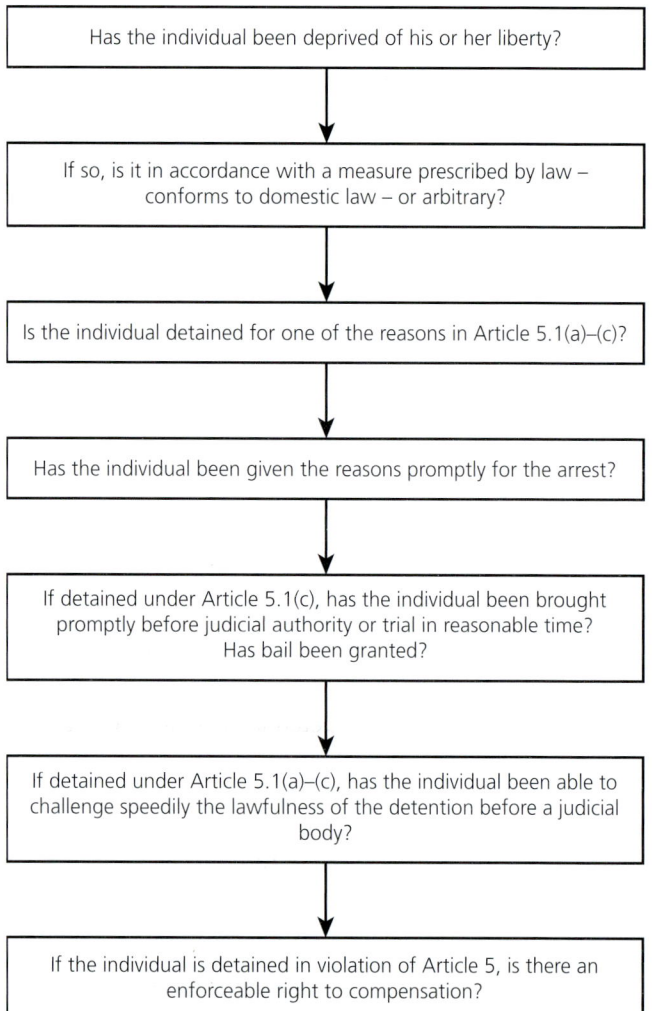

Figure 29.1 Steps to bringing a case to the ECtHR under Article 5

Figure 29.2 Key cases for Article 5 ECHR

Case	Facts	Law
HL v UK (2004)	HL was informally detained for mental health reasons under the common law doctrine of necessity and not subject to the standard compulsory detention procedures	This detention was arbitrary as it was non-statutory and there were no clear rules in place to provide HL with any safeguards

Case	Facts	Law
Amuur v France (1996)	Four Somalis applied for asylum in France but were held in the airport's transit zone under strict police surveillance and without access to legal or social assistance Their asylum was refused and they were returned	Holding the applicants in the transit zone of the airport was a deprivation of their liberty
Austin v UK (2015)	Police 'kettled' demonstrators and passers-by for over seven hours	Article 5 should not make it impracticable for the police to carry out their duties of maintaining order and protecting the public There was a duty on the police to protect individuals from violence and physical injury The context is relevant and the public may be required to suffer temporary restrictions on freedom of movement in certain contexts and these do not amount to 'deprivations of liberty' so long as they were unavoidable, necessary and were kept to the minimum There was no breach of Article 5 as the measures were taken in good faith, proportionate, and enforced for no longer than necessary
Shimovolos v Russia (2011)	S had his ID checked several times on a train journey, was forced to go to a police station and was questioned about the purpose of his trip and his acquaintances	S had been arbitrarily arrested in breach of Article 5.1
Kasparov v Russia (No. 2) (2016)	Garry Kasparov and another were detained and their tickets and passports were confiscated Detention and questioning at a police office followed Kasparov was prevented from leaving the office for 48 hours and an armed officer guarded the door There was no evidence of forgery as the authorities claimed	There had been unlawful deprivation of liberty which was not justified for any lawful purpose
Ostendorf v Germany (2013)	A football supporter was on his way to a match and had been given directions by the police where to go to avoid fights with rival supporters He was found hiding in a toilet, arrested and detained until after the match had ended He claimed a breach of Articles 5.1(b) and 5.1(c)	The claimant had been ordered to stay with the group of supporters and clearly warned of the consequences of his failure to comply with that order His arrest and detention were lawful under Article 5.1(b), but *not* under Article 5.1(c)
Stafford v UK (2002)	S was released on licence from a life sentence for murder, but re-sentenced for fraud and not released after the end of the fraud sentence	This was a breach of Article 5 as there was no sufficient connection between his original conviction and any risk that he might commit further non-violent offences after release

29.2 English law and its compatibility with ECHR obligations

29.2.1 In respect of Article 5(1)(a): lawful detention after conviction by a competent court

This principally involves examining the imposition of sentences of life imprisonment following conviction and there are several forms it can take.

The mandatory life sentence

This has to be imposed when the offender has been convicted of murder – the judge has no option. The Criminal Justice Act 2003 sets out guidelines for how long murderers should spend in prison before being considered for parole. Judges do not have to follow the guidelines, but must give reasons in court if they depart from them – whether recommending a lesser or higher minimum term.

> **Extension activity**
>
> Research the guidelines set by the Criminal Justice Act 2003 for mandatory life prisoners. List the types of murder that could result in the imposition of a whole life sentence.

- Release on licence following the serving of a tariff period – when imposing the life sentence, the judge will fix a minimum term (the tariff period) that the murderer must serve before being considered for release on licence. Release on licence is not automatic but the Parole Board will consider if the offender is fit for release.
- Conditions will be imposed, such as where the offender lives and works and reporting to the authorities. If any conditions are breached, the offender can be recalled to prison to serve a further term.
- Sentencing of minors – life imprisonment is only applicable to offenders aged 21 or over. Those aged between 18 and 20 are sentenced to custody for life. Those aged under 18 are sentenced to detention during Her Majesty's pleasure for murder. Offenders aged under 21 may not be sentenced to a whole life order and so must become eligible for release on licence.

> **Extension activity**
>
> There are currently about 70 prisoners serving 'whole life' sentences for murder. Research the case of one such prisoner and the reason given for the imposition of a whole life term.

Political interference

Before the Criminal Justice Act 2003, the Home Secretary, a government minister, was responsible for setting the tariff period. Increasingly, this was considered to be an Executive action and setting the tariff could be seen as being a political action. In some cases the Home Secretary increased the tariff period after the offender had served a number of years of the tariff. For example, when Myra Hindley was sentenced the judge indicated she should serve a minimum of 25 years. When the majority of this period had been served the Home Secretary at the time increased the tariff period to 30 years and subsequently to a whole life term. In *Thompson and Venables v UK* (1999), the murderers of James Bulger challenged the power of the Home Secretary to fix their tariff period and the ECtHR confirmed that this should be a judicial decision in relation to offenders aged under 18. A similar decision was made in *Anderson v UK* (2002) for adult murderers. The UK took note of these decisions and, since the 2003 Act, judges have set the tariff period, which can only be varied by appeal judges. Even though politicians can no longer decide the length of the tariff period, the Attorney-General, another government minister, still has the power to petition the Court of Appeal if he or she considers that the set tariff is unduly lenient. In the case of *Stafford v UK* (2002), above at section 29.1.3, the ECtHR also decided that decisions of the Parole Board to release an offender on licence could not be overturned by the Home Secretary.

> **Extension activity**
>
> Research the guidelines set out by the Criminal Justice Act 2003 for judges sentencing murderers and find the minimum terms for the following:
> - a murder involving a firearm or explosive
> - a murder involving a knife
> - a multiple murder, and
> - a basic murder.
>
> Do you consider these terms as being fair?

The discretionary life sentence

This type of sentence has always been imposed by judges and as such does not fall foul of Article 5.1(a). For offences such as manslaughter (either voluntary or involuntary) or certain other offences such as s 18 OAPA 1861, the maximum sentence set by law is life imprisonment. The judge is able to set the length of imprisonment, up to the maximum, depending on relevant aggravating and mitigating factors. This is purely a judicial decision, though again the Attorney-General has the power to petition the Court of Appeal if he or she considers that the sentence is unduly lenient, and it will be for the court to either agree the sentencing judge's decision or to vary the sentence.

Maximum sentences

Less serious offences will have a maximum sentence set by the Act that creates the offence. For example, theft has a maximum sentence of seven years set by the Theft Act 1968. The Criminal Damage Act 1971 sets different maximum sentences depending on the value of the property destroyed or damaged, whether the offence is a basic or aggravated offence, if it is arson or if it is racially or religiously aggravated. For an offender convicted of an offence under this Act, the sentence will again be a judicial decision, either by magistrates or a judge. This will not offend Article 5.1(a).

29.2.2 In respect of Article 5.1(b): non-compliance with a court order or to secure an obligation required by law

Article 5.1(b) allows for the lawful arrest or detention in cases such as arrest under a warrant for non-payment of a fine, contempt of court and breach of a bail condition. This covers measures where a court order has already been made and may include civil orders such as matrimonial orders or psychiatric confinement. It allows the police to detain to administer criminal law, for example to require a motorist to take a drink- or drug-driving test at the roadside. The measures must be necessary and the obligation must be 'specific and concrete' so that the detention is not based on vague grounds.

29.2.3 Articles 5.1(c) and 5.2

PACE 1984 was introduced to provide specific rules for the police when dealing with stopping, arresting, detaining and questioning suspects. The statutory provisions are supplemented by Codes of Practice. Failure to follow the rules and Codes will not result in action against the police officers concerned but will mean that evidence obtained in breach will be inadmissible at trial.

The relevant provisions of Article 5 to this section are:

1. No one shall be deprived of his liberty save in the following cases and in accordance with a procedure prescribed by law:

…

(c) the lawful arrest or detention of a person effected for the purpose of bringing him before the competent legal authority on reasonable suspicion of having committed an offence or when it is reasonably considered necessary to prevent his committing an offence or fleeing after having done so;

and

2. Everyone who is arrested shall be informed promptly, in a language which he understands, of the reasons for his arrest and of any charge against him.

The meaning of 'arrest'

This is not defined by PACE 1984 but there are considered to be three main parts to an arrest:

- there is a submission by the arrested person to the police or some physical restraint to enforce the arrest
- the arresting officer must clearly show, as soon as practicable, that he or she is arresting the person, and
- the arresting officer must make the grounds for arrest clear as soon as practicable.

Stop and search

The police have powers to stop and search members of the public in a public place. This does not amount to an arrest, provided the person co-operates, although it may be a precursor to an arrest. A stop and search power could be said to be a deprivation of liberty of an individual during the process.

Under ss 1 and 2 PACE 1984, a police officer may search any person or vehicle and detain the person or vehicle for the purposes of the search. The search can only be carried out to look for certain items such as stolen items and prohibited items such as offensive weapons or articles adapted for, or used for, criminal offences. The officer can only stop and search a person if he or she has reasonable grounds for suspecting he or she will find one of these items. This is an objective test and not just the officer's personal opinion. The reasonable grounds must exist before the person is stopped – an officer cannot stop in order to find grounds for a search. The reasonable grounds must generally be based on some form of intelligence and should never be based on personal beliefs or on a suspect's behaviour. If the reasonable grounds for suspicion cease to exist, the officer cannot search the person, and if there are no other grounds to detain, the person is free to leave. Provided the stop and search is based on reasonable grounds, it is unlikely that it will breach Article 5.

Arrest with a warrant

The police can apply to a magistrate for a warrant to authorise an arrest. Reasons have to be given for the need to arrest a person, and the magistrate should satisfy him- or herself that the reasons are sufficient. The warrant may also authorise the police to enter and search premises and seize any property they suspect being there.

Arrest without a warrant

Section 24 PACE 1984 allows a police officer to arrest a person without a warrant where he or she is committing an offence or is about to commit an offence or where the officer has reasonable grounds to suspect the person is going to or has already committed an offence. If the offence has been committed, the officer can arrest anyone who he or she has reasonable grounds for suspecting is guilty of the offence.

A lawful arrest requires:

- a police officer knowing or having reasonable grounds for suspecting a person to be guilty of an offence, and
- a police officer having reasonable grounds for believing that the arrest is necessary.

The reasonable grounds are objective and the arrest must be based on one or more of the following:

- it gives the police time to check the name or address of the person arrested
- it prevents the person from causing or suffering injury or damage to property
- it allows the effective investigation of an offence
- it prevents the person from disappearing.

Reasonable grounds for suspecting a person to be guilty of an offence.

In *Castorina v Chief Constable of Surrey* (1988), the Court of Appeal lay down the following test to satisfy this condition:

- Did the officer suspect the person was guilty? (A subjective test)
- Did the officer have reasonable proof for that suspicion? (Objectively)
- If yes to both the above, was the arrest reasonable? Did it take into account all relevant factors and ignore non-relevant matters? Was it made for a proper purpose? Would a reasonable officer have come to the same decision?

In *Hayes v Chief Constable of Merseyside Police* (2011), the Court of Appeal set out the test to be applied when deciding whether the necessity criterion is satisfied, it being a two-stage test. First, that the officer actually believes that arrest is necessary for one of the above reasons. Second, that objectively, that belief was reasonable. The court rejected the argument that there was also a requirement, in order to make a lawful arrest, that the arresting officer should have actively considered all possible courses of action alternatives to arrest, to have taken all relevant considerations into account and have excluded all irrelevant ones.

Reasonable grounds for believing that the arrest is necessary

Code of Practice G states that an officer has discretion as to what action to take and which reason to apply but at least one of the above reasonable grounds for arrest must apply. The officer must justify the reason or reasons why the person should be taken to the police station and for a custody officer to decide whether the person should be placed in detention.

Tip

Having the power to arrest does not automatically allow a police officer to arrest without further consideration of the reasonable grounds for arrest. The responsibility for the arrest lies with the arresting officer, not his or her superiors. It is the arresting officer's beliefs and considerations that are relevant.

Informing the arrested person

Section 28 PACE 1984 provides that the arrested person must be informed that he or she is under arrest and of the grounds for the arrest as soon as practicable. It is not necessary to use the words 'you are under arrest', as long as the person understands he or she is under arrest. The amount of detail the person must be told will depend on each case. In *Murphy v Oxford* (1985), the person was told he was being arrested on suspicion of a burglary but as there was no mention made of a date, or that it was a burglary of a hotel, the arrest was unlawful. In *Moses Adler v Crown Prosecution Service* (2013), an off-duty, plain-clothed police officer had not used the words 'I am arresting you' when arresting a person. However, there was sufficient evidence that a lawful arrest had been made as the officer had explained that he was a police officer and was detaining the person because he had seen him smash a car window.

Once at the police station, the arrested person will be in the care of the custody officer, who will not have been involved in the original arrest. This officer will ensure that the arrested person understands the reason for his or her arrest and can arrange for an interpreter or suitable adult to be contacted to ensure the arrested person is aware of his or her situation and his or her rights while in custody.

Arrest to prevent a breach of the peace

This is a common reason to arrest would-be offenders. It can be regarded as a more flexible power of arrest than arrests under PACE 1984 because it is based on common-law powers. The police are entitled to arrest a person where there is a breach of the peace under this offence. Where there is an anticipated breach of the peace the power of arrest should only be used where there is a sufficiently serious and imminent threat.

An arresting officer has to identify what a breach of the peace is and that it has taken place or that a breach of the peace is imminent. It is commonly used to arrest what are suspected to be would-be offenders.

A breach of the peace was defined in *R v Howell* (1981) as being a positive act that harms a person or his or her property, which is likely to cause harm or which puts someone in fear of such harm being done. This does not have to be unlawful but must give rise to a fear of violence.

This power of arrest was challenged in the 'kettling' case of *Austin v Commissioner of the Police of the Metropolis* (2009), the facts of which were described in section 29.1.1. above under the case name *Austin v UK*. Before taking their case to the ECHR, the claimants had taken action in English courts for false imprisonment and breach of Article 5.

The House of Lords decided that where Article 5 is engaged – for crowd control reasons – account must be taken of the rights of the individual and the interests of the community. Any steps taken (by the police) must be taken in good faith and proportionate to the situation which made the measures necessary. In this case it was decided that the measures taken by the police were necessary to allow the protestors and other people caught up in the 'kettle' to eventually disperse safely and that the 'kettling' involved no breach of Article 5.

Note the case of *Mengesha v Metropolitan Police Commissioner* (2013), referred to in Chapter 2, section 2.4.2, provides that videoing a member of the public engages Article 8 ECHR when the video was taken as the price of being required to leave a containment area or 'kettle'. The retention of the video was not 'in accordance with the law' and the retention was therefore a breach of Article 8.

The right of the police to arrest for breach of the peace has also been considered by the Supreme Court in the recent case of *R (on the application of Hicks) v Commissioner of Police for the Metropolis* (2017).

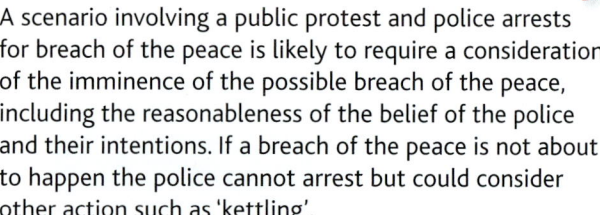

R (on the application of Hicks) v Commissioner of Police for the Metropolis (2017)

The case concerned the arrest and detention of four people on the day of the wedding of the Duke and Duchess of Cambridge. They were arrested in separate incidents at various places in central London on the grounds that their arrest was reasonably believed to be necessary to prevent an imminent breach of the peace. They were all released without charge once the wedding was over and the police considered the risk of a breach of the peace had been passed. Their period of custody ranged from two-and-a-half hours to five-and-a-half hours.

It was alleged that the detention violated their Article 5 rights. The police argued that the detention was lawful under Article 5.1(c), the offence being a breach of the peace.

The court considered that Article 5.1(c) is capable of applying to a case of detention for preventive purposes followed by early release such as in this case. They considered it would be irrational if the law was that in order to be lawfully able to detain a person so as to prevent a breach of the peace, the police must intend to continue the detention, after the risk has passed, until the person could be brought before a court for an order to being bound over to keep the peace in the future. This would lengthen the period of detention and place an unnecessary burden on police resources.

Early release from detention for preventive purpose does not breach Article 5 if the lawfulness of the detention can subsequently be challenged and decided by a court.

In a free society, there is a balance between the right to protest and meet in groups and the need to maintain public order and security. The court observed that the fundamental principle underlying Article 5 is the need to protect the individual from arbitrary detention, and an essential part of that protection is timely judicial control. However, Article 5 (and the common law relating to arrest for breach of the peace) must not be interpreted in such a way to make it impracticable for the police to perform their duty to maintain public order and protect the lives and property of others. The ability of the police to perform their duty would be severely hampered if they could not lawfully arrest and detain a person for a relatively short time – too short for it to be practical to take the person before a court.

Tip

A scenario involving a public protest and police arrests for breach of the peace is likely to require a consideration of the imminence of the possible breach of the peace, including the reasonableness of the belief of the police and their intentions. If a breach of the peace is not about to happen the police cannot arrest but could consider other action such as 'kettling'.

29.2.4 In respect of Article 5.3: PACE 1984 and bail

The relevant provision of Article 5 to this section is:

> 3. Everyone arrested or detained in accordance with the provisions of paragraph 1(c) of this Article shall be brought promptly before a judge or other officer authorised by law to exercise judicial power and shall be entitled to trial within a reasonable time or to release pending trial. Release may be conditioned by guarantees to appear for trial.

This contains three separate parts:

1. The right to be brought promptly before a judge or other officer authorised by law to exercise judicial power. The judicial officer should not be part of the investigation and should be able to make a binding decision which cannot be overturned by the Government.

2. The right to release on bail, except when custody is justified. The right to bail is not absolute, but if objected to, the objection must be justified by the judge. This provision is covered in England by the Bail Act 1976 by which there is a presumption in favour of bail and the court must give reasons for its refusal.

3. The right to be tried within a reasonable time. The purpose of this provision is to ensure that no one spends too long in detention before trial. Time starts when the accused is first remanded into custody and ends when the court gives judgment. What is a reasonable time depends on the circumstances of each case including the seriousness of the charge. The ECtHR has been reluctant to set specific time limits on what amounts to a reasonable time so as long as national law provisions are complied with there will be no breach of Article 5.

Detention and custody time limits

Once a person is arrested he or she is generally taken to a police station. The purpose of detention is to allow the police to question the suspect and obtain enough evidence in order to decide whether a charge can be brought. A suspect is entitled to legal advice while he or she is being held in detention.

PACE 1984 limits the amount of time a person charged with a criminal offence can be kept in custody at a police station. The time limit is overseen by the custody officer and must be strictly observed. A suspect can be held for up to 24 hours before being charged. If the suspect is not charged within this time limit he or she has to be released.

In the case of a serious crime such as murder, the time limit can be extended before a charge of up to 36 hours if the approval of a senior officer is obtained, or up to 96 hours if the approval of a magistrate is obtained. Again, if the suspect is not charged within these time limits the suspect has to be released. This maximum time limit cannot be extended except in the case of terrorism offences where a suspect can be held without charge for up to 14 days.

Bail decision by the police

The suspect can be released on police **bail** if there is not enough evidence for a charge. He or she may be required to return to the police station at a later date for further questioning.

Once a suspect is charged with an offence, the custody officer has to decide if bail can be granted or if the suspect should be held in custody until a first court appearance. The officer can impose conditions on bail if it is thought that another offence may be committed, the accused may fail to turn up at court, may intimidate witnesses or obstruct the course of justice. These conditions are likely to restrict the accused's freedom in some way, as the conditions may relate to the accused's residence or movements such as a curfew. If the accused fails to turn up at court or breaks one of the conditions, an offence is committed and the accused can be arrested for that offence.

If the accused is held in police custody, he or she must be brought before a Magistrates' Court on the next sitting day.

Key term

Bail – where an accused is allowed to leave police custody until attendance at trial or required pre-trial hearings. Conditions may be imposed on the grant of bail. Failure to attend a court hearing or observe conditions will be an offence. The grant of bail is covered by the Bail Act 1976.

Bail decision by a court

Any person accused of committing a crime is presumed innocent until proven guilty, so a person charged with a crime should not be denied freedom unless there is a good reason.

When an accused is held in custody, he or she is entitled under the Bail Act 1976 to have his or her custody reviewed. This can be done either at the first appearance at a Magistrates' Court or at subsequent appearances. An appeal lies from refusal to grant bail by a magistrate to a Crown Court judge. The Act sets a presumption that bail should be granted unless there is sufficient reason not to grant it. However, where the accused has previous convictions for certain homicide or sexual offences, the burden of proof is on the accused to rebut a presumption against bail.

The main reasons for refusing bail are that the accused is charged with an imprisonable offence and there are *substantial grounds* for believing that the defendant would either:

- abscond
- commit further offences while on bail, or
- interfere with witnesses.

Extension activity

1 Research the reasons why a court can refuse to grant bail.
2 Research the conditions that a court can impose when granting bail.

Failing to attend court on time, as required, is an offence and bail is likely to be revoked until the end of the trial. The sentence for breaching bail is usually custody and consecutive to any other custodial sentence that may be imposed following conviction.

On the face of it, the law of bail and pre-trial detention is compliant with the ECHR and compares well with other ECHR members. The following features are in its favour:

- the initial presumption of the granting of bail
- the speedy production of accused persons before a court following charge
- the limited use of financial conditions on the granting of bail, and
- the limited use of custody where an accused is charged with a non-imprisonable offence.

However, there are problems including the following:

- A large number of people are placed in pre-trial detention at any one time – it is suggested around 12,000, which amounts to about 14 per cent of the total prison population. This percentage compares favourably to the rest of the world but still represents a large number of people.
- A large number of accused remanded in custody are acquitted at trial or their case is dropped, or ultimately receive a non-custodial sentence.
- Courts deciding bail often do so under pressure, without full knowledge of the case or the accused's background and defence lawyers are given limited initial information by the police to represent their clients effectively. Failure to automatically supply information contravenes the EU Directive on the Right to Information (June 2014) which states that an accused must be provided with documents that are essential to challenging effectively the lawfulness of detention. Neither the Bail Act nor the Criminal Procedure Rules have been amended to give effect to the Directive.
- The Bail Act 1976 has been amended by subsequent legislation and, as a complex regulatory framework, is difficult to apply by magistrates (who make the bulk of decisions) and judges.
- Few magistrates or judges are aware of the Law Commission guidance, published in 2001, on applying bail law in compliance with the ECHR or received training on the application of the ECHR to pre-trial detention decision making since HRA 1998 came into force.
- On occasions, limited reasons are given by courts for the decision to remand in custody to enable the accused to understand the explanations, especially if unrepresented.
- There are procedural issues once bail has been granted, including inconsistent and inadequate provision of bail information schemes, a lack of sufficient bail hostel places and a lack of routine monitoring of bail conditions.

Figure 29.3 Key cases on unlawful detention

Case	Facts	Law
R (on the application of Hicks) v Commissioner of Police for the Metropolis (2017)	Four people were arrested and detained on the day of the wedding of the Duke and Duchess of Cambridge They were arrested in separate incidents on the grounds that their arrest was reasonably believed to be necessary to prevent an imminent breach of the peace They were all released without charge once the wedding was over Their period of custody ranged from two-and-a-half hours to five-and-a-half hours It was alleged that the detention violated their Article 5 rights The police argued that the detention was lawful under Article 5.1(c) – the offence being a breach of the peace	The court considered that Article 5.1(c) can apply to detention for preventive purposes followed by early release They considered it would be irrational if the law was that in order to be lawfully able to detain a person so as to prevent a breach of the peace, the police must intend to continue the detention, after the risk has passed, until the person could be brought before a court for an order to being bound over to keep the peace in the future This would lengthen the period of detention and place an unnecessary burden on police resources Early release from detention for preventive purposes does not breach Article 5 if the lawfulness of the detention can subsequently be challenged and decided by a court

Summary

- Article 5 ECHR protects a person's liberty and security.
- A person's liberty has been deprived when the person has not consented to being held, it is more than a temporary restriction on movement and there is a reason for it.
- 'Kettling' does not offend Article 5.
- There is a positive obligation on a state to protect its citizens; this includes explaining where an individual is when taken into detention or custody, preventing the individual's disappearance and carrying out an investigation where a person Is held in state custody but has not been seen since.
- No one shall be deprived of his or her liberty except in accordance with a procedure set out in domestic law which is not arbitrary and there is legal certainty.
- There is a right to compensation if Article 5 rights have been broken.
- Mandatory life sentences do not breach Article 5 when imposed by a court and the tariff or minimum term to be served is set by judges.

- Stop and search is a statutory power and does not offend Article 5 as it involves a temporary deprivation of liberty.
- Formal arrest and detention before charge must follow prescribed procedures – in the UK this is laid down by PACE 1984. Provided the procedures have been followed, there is no breach of Article 5.
- An arrest can be made following the issue of a warrant, on suspicion of committing an offence and after conviction is authorised.
- The person detained must be promptly informed of the reasons for his or her detention.
- Any person detained must be brought before a judicial officer promptly, bail must be considered and the person must be tried within a reasonable time.
- The presumption of the grant of bail, unless there are grounds for not granting it, are complaint with Article 5.

30 Article 8 ECHR: the right to respect for family and private life

30.1 Article 8 ECHR

❝ 1. Everyone has the right to respect for his private and family life, his home and his correspondence.
2. There shall be no interference by a public authority with the exercise of this right except such as is in accordance with the law and is necessary in a democratic society in the interests of national security, public safety or the economic well-being of the country, for the prevention of disorder or crime, for the protection of health or morals, or for the protection of the rights and freedoms of others. ❞

The primary purpose of Article 8 is to protect against arbitrary interferences with private and family life, home and correspondence. Member states also have positive obligations to ensure that Article 8 rights are respected between private parties despite the fact that the object of Article 8 is to protect the individual against arbitrary interference by public authorities. Additionally, there may be positive obligations to secure respect for private life between individuals.

30.2 General aspects of qualified rights

Article 8 is a qualified right and as such the right to a private and family life and respect for the home and

correspondence may be limited. So, while the right to privacy is engaged in a wide number of situations, the right may be lawfully limited. Any limitation must have regard to the fair balance that has to be struck between the competing interests of the individual and of the community as a whole.

Under Article 8(2), any limitation must be:

■ in accordance with law
■ necessary and proportionate, and
■ for one or more of the following legitimate aims:
  – the interests of national security
  – the interests of public safety or the economic well-being of the country
  – the prevention of disorder or crime
  – the protection of health or morals, or
  – the protection of the rights and freedoms of others.

When someone can show that there is an interference with his or her rights, it is then up to the state to show that the interference is justified. This can only be done if it is in accordance with the law. It also has to be necessary in a democratic society and has to be proportional.

If it is proportional, the court must ensure that:

■ the objective of the legislation is sufficiently important to justify some interference with a person's basic rights
■ the measure is rationally connected with the objective in question
■ it is not arbitrary, unfair or based on other irrational considerations
■ the limitation must impair the right as little as possible
■ the interference must not be so severe in effect that it outweighs the objective for which it would otherwise be permitted.

Thus, 'in accordance with the law' means there must be a specific legal rule to which the citizen must have access that authorises the interference and that the law must be formulated with sufficient precision to enable the citizen to foresee the circumstances in which the law would or might be applied. This also applies to Articles 10 and 11 set out in Chapters 31 and 32 of this book.

'Necessary in a democratic society' means it must be shown that:

■ an interference corresponds to a pressing social need
■ it is proportionate to the legitimate aim pursued.

'Proportionality' means that the exercise of the rights and their protection by the courts have to be done in a way that is proportional to the needs of society, or a 'pressing social need' for interference.

The margin of appreciation is the state's leeway in adopting the measures it considers most appropriate to pursue that aim. In the area of public morals, for example, state authorities have been considered to be in a better position than the Court itself to determine restrictions on the sale of pornography (*Handyside v UK* (1976)) or the legal recognition of transsexuals (*Rees v UK* (1986)).

30.3 Background to Article 8: who is 'everyone'?

The ECtHR's view of the importance of these rights can be seen in the case of *Klass v Germany* (1978), which raised a question about mail opening and telephone tapping. The Court said that the powers of secret surveillance of citizens are tolerable under the ECHR only in so far as strictly necessary for safeguarding the democratic institutions.

This also raises the question as to who is an individual – does it include a business? In certain circumstances it appears to include business life.

If businesses are entitled in certain circumstances to assert a right to privacy, then we need to establish when they should be able to do so. A lawyer's office was private in *Niemietz v Germany* (1992) (see section 30.4.2 below). Does the business itself have that right? This is important as many celebrities have corporate persona. In *Gamerco v ICM Fair Warning (Agency) Ltd and Missouri Storm Inc* (1995), the defendant rock group, Guns N' Roses, had made a contract through their corporate persona, Missouri Storm Inc. (see Chapter 23, section 23.4.3).

We know that limited companies are in law individuals ever since the famous case of *Salomon v Salomon and Co. Ltd* (1897), where the limited company was stated to be a completely separate legal person to Mr Salomon who owned virtually all the shares in the company and thus controlled it. It can therefore be argued that companies and other business organisations with separate legal persona have human rights under the Convention.

This seems to be the case, as the ECtHR has ruled in *Vinci Construction and GTM Génie Civil et Services v France* (2015) that wholly generalised document seizures during dawn raids conducted by the French Department for Competition, Consumer Affairs and Fraud Prevention violated the fundamental rights of both Vinci Construction and GTM Génie. The inspections and seizures violated Article 8 because the indiscriminate nature of the seizures was disproportionate and interfered with rights to respect for home, private life and correspondence under Article 8.

30.4 The scope of Article 8

Article 8 has four protected interests. **Everyone** has the right to respect for:

- private life
- family life
- home
- correspondence.

These concepts will be considered in turn together with the relevant law, although the separate interests overlap as part of the general idea behind the Article.

Key term

'**Everyone**' – so far as Article 8 is concerned, this includes businesses.

30.4.1 'Respect'

The word '**respect**' means that primarily the state must not interfere as stated in Article 8(1), with the qualifications in Article 8(2). It also means that the state must take positive steps to protect these rights. This was considered by the ECtHR in *Sheffield and Horsham v UK* (1999).

Key term

'**Respect**' – with regard to Article 8, this requires the state not to interfere and has positive aspects.

Sheffield and Horsham v UK (1999)

The two applicants had undergone gender reassignment surgery from male to female. The state would not recognise their new status as women or take steps to allow this to be officially recognised. There had been no breach of Article 8(1) as a nation could refuse to re-register birth details of people who had undergone gender reassignment surgery. Similarly, the state could refuse to permit post-operative transsexuals to marry. However the ECtHR criticised the UK's apparent failure to take any steps to keep this area of the law under review. The Court recognised increased social acceptance of transsexualism and the problems that post-operative transsexual people encounter.

English law has now been changed by the Gender Recognition Act 2004, which allows transsexual individuals to apply for legal recognition for their new gender. The Marriage (Same Sex Couples) Act 2013 is also now in place, so fulfilling positive obligations.

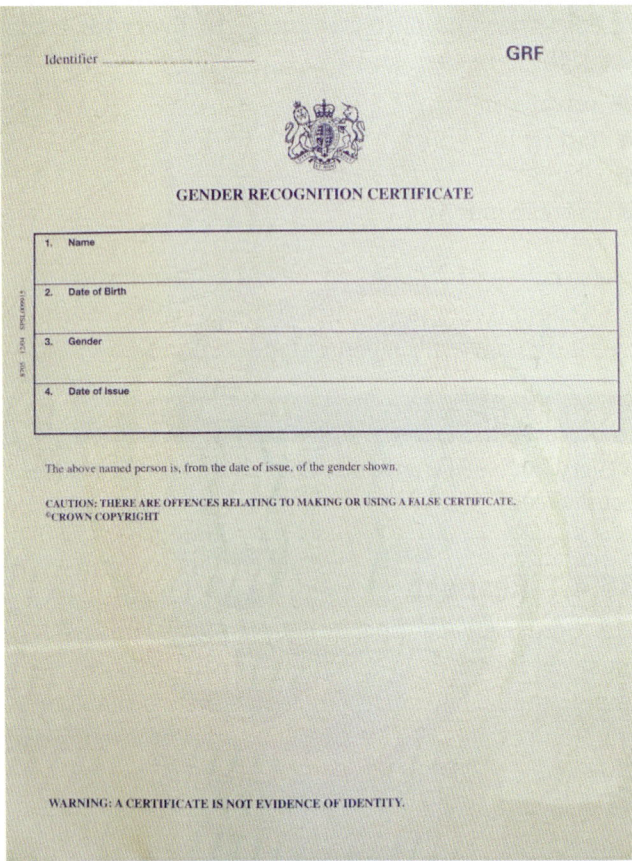

30.4.2 'Private life'

The meaning of **'private life'** is very wide and is not the same as privacy. There is some overlap with Article 10, freedom of expression. Aspects of the right to private life include:

- the physical and psychological integrity of a person
- sex life and gender
- personal data
- reputation
- names
- photos.

Key term

'Private life' – with regard to Article 8, this includes matters such as physical and psychological integrity, sex life and gender, personal data, reputation, names and photos.

Niemietz v Germany (1992)

The police searched a lawyer's offices to try to identify a suspect. The search was part of home and the lawyer's private life.

The court attempted to define private life and said:

> It would be too restrictive to limit the notion of an 'inner circle' in which the individual may live his own personal life as he chooses and to exclude therefrom entirely the outside world not encompassed within that circle. Respect for private life must also comprise to a certain degree the right to establish and develop relationships with other human beings.

This included being at work.

Surveillance is included, as shown in *Halford v UK* (1997).

Halford v UK (1997)

The claimant was Assistant Chief Constable of a police force. Following a refusal to further promote her in the force, she claimed that she had been discriminated against on grounds of her sex, and that there had been an interception of her home and office telephone calls to obtain information against her in the discrimination proceedings. She claimed a breach of Article 8 – the right to private life.

The ECHR held that conversations made on the telephones in her office fell within the scope of 'private life' and 'correspondence' in Article 8 and that there had been violations of her right to privacy for these conversations. However, there was no interference with Ms Halford's rights to respect for her private life and correspondence in relation to her home telephone.

Personal information and data is also included. This means things such as DNA details and medical records. In *MS v Sweden* (1999), it was stated that 'respecting the confidentiality of health data is a vital principle in the legal systems of all contracting parties to the Convention'.

Figure 30.1 Key cases for Article 8 – the right to a private life

Case	Facts	Law
Niemietz v Germany (1992)	Police searched a lawyer's offices to try to identify a suspect	The search was part of the lawyer's home and private life
Halford v UK (1997)	Telephone calls were intercepted by senior police officers to obtain information	Interception of the telephone calls of an employee in a private exchange was a breach of the right of a private life

Private life and the extent of intrusion by the media can be observed through the ECtHR's decisions in a series of cases involving perceived intrusions into one family's life, the *Von Hannover* cases.

Background to the cases

Caroline, Princess of Hanover, the eldest daughter of Prince Rainier III of Monaco, had for some time attempted to prevent pictures being published of her in the German press. Some of her complaints related to photographs of her with her husband and children as well as some, apparently, of her homes. The question of privacy and photos taken by the paparazzi were the issues behind each of the cases. In each case she was trying to supress publication of the photos by means of an injunction. The cases also involve the ECtHR balancing Articles 8 and 10 (see Chapter 31).

Von Hannover v Germany (No. 1) 2004

In this case, the German court granted an injunction restraining the publication of photographs in which Princess Caroline appeared with her children. The basis for this was that the need for protection of the children was greater than that of adults. It was taken into account that she was a contemporary 'public figure' and therefore must put up with the publication of photographs of herself in a public place, even if only showing her daily life rather than any official duties. The court also recognised the freedom of the press and the public's legitimate interest in knowing how such a person generally behaved in public.

The ECtHR stated that the general public did not have a legitimate interest in knowing her whereabouts or how she behaved generally in her private life, even if she appeared in places that were not private. Everyone, including celebrities, had a legitimate expectation that his or her private life would be protected. There had been a violation of Article 8.

Von Hannover v Germany (No. 2) 2012

In this case, some German magazines published a series of photographs showing Princess Caroline and her husband on skiing holidays. One accompanied an article about the ill health of her father. Other photographs in the magazines were stated by the German court to be an invasion of privacy but the one accompanying the article about the ill health of her father was said to be connected to a matter of public interest.

The Grand Chamber noted the German courts' change of approach since the first von Hannover judgment and having regard to the margin of appreciation enjoyed by national courts when balancing competing interests, the court found no violation of Article 8.

Von Hannover v Germany (No. 3) 2013

A German magazine published an article about celebrities renting out their holiday homes. It described in detail the von Hannover family villa on an island off the Kenyan coast. The article included several photographs of the villa, as well as one photograph showing Princess Caroline and her husband on holiday in an unidentifiable location. The photograph had been taken without their knowledge, but they were in the company of others and it disclosed no information about the location or how they were spending their holidays.

The ECtHR stated that the German courts had given due consideration to the criteria and had complied with its positive obligations under Article 8.

30.4.3 'Family life'

Article 8 gives the right to enjoy family relationships without interference from the state. This includes the right to live with a family and, where this is not possible, the right to regular contact with a family. 'Family life' can include the relationship between an unmarried couple, an adopted child and the adoptive parent, and a foster parent and fostered child.

Key term

'Family life' – with regard to Article 8, the right to enjoy family relationships without interference from the state.

There are many aspects of family life that can be affected by the state. For example:

- care proceedings and the possibility of a child being removed from the family home
- access to a child
- forced breakup of a relationship as a result of immigration rules.

The protection of Article 8 always extends to marriages that can be shown to be lawful and genuine. So, for example, a sham marriage to avoid immigration rules or to acquire nationality may not be protected. A child born to parents who are married will therefore also always fall within Article 8. Unmarried couples who live together with their children fall within the Article, as the stable nature of the relationship makes it effectively the same as marriage.

The scope of the margin of appreciation differs according to the context of the case. It is particularly wide in child protection cases. It takes this into account when examining such cases under the Convention by allowing states a measure of discretion. An example of this can be seen in *Gaskin v UK* (1989).

Gaskin v UK (1989)

Graham Gaskin was placed in care when he was a baby. He complained of ill treatment while he was in the care of a local authority and living with foster parents. He wanted access to his case records held by the local authority but his request was denied. He applied to the ECtHR.

The refusal to allow him access to his records involved a breach of his rights under Article 8. This was because there was no independent mechanism to decide whether or not access should be permitted if the consent of

third-party contributors, such as care workers who made the decisions at the time, could not be obtained. There must be specific justification for preventing individuals from having access to information which forms part of their private and family life. The court stated that relationships between children and foster parents or carers fall within the definition of 'family' within the meaning of Article 8.

In *Johannsen v Norway* (1996), the court had to consider a permanent placement of a child with a view to adoption in opposition to the natural parents' wishes. The question was, under Article 8, how the rights of the child and the parents should be balanced.

Johannsen v Norway (1996)

The natural parents of a child opposed the decision of the state with respect to adoption. The mother had been subject to domestic violence and suffered a chaotic lifestyle. There had been several interventions by Norwegian social services.

The court stated that particular weight should be attached to the best interests of the child, which may override those of the parent.

In *Yousef v Netherlands* (2003), the court reiterated that in judicial decisions where the rights under Article 8 of parents and those of a child are at stake, the child's rights must be the paramount consideration. This is entirely consistent with the principles in English family law.

Extension activity

Look in detail at the case of *Yousef v Netherlands* (2003) for further examples of how Article 8 operates.

These cases can be seen as the way in which different states' legal frameworks operate in a positive way to prevent harm to an individual who is part of a family.

Figure 30.2 Key cases for Article 8 – respect for family life

Case	Facts	Law
Gaskin v UK (1989)	The applicant had been in care as a baby and then fostered He wanted access to his case records held by the local authority to support claims of abuse, but his request was denied	Refusal to allow him access to his records involved a breach of his rights under Article 8
Johannsen v Norway (1996)	The natural parents of a child opposed the decision of the state with respect to adoption	Particular weight should be attached to the best interests of the child, which may override those of the parent

30.4.4 'Home'

Respect for your **'home'** means that public authorities should not stop you from entering or living in your home without good reason, nor should they enter without your permission. This applies whether or not you own your home.

Attempts have been made to extend Article 8's remit to social and economic claims for welfare, such as access to medical treatment and specific drugs. The courts have resisted such claims by repeatedly holding that Article 8 cannot be invoked in relation to the provision of medical and other resources.

> ### Key term
>
>
> **'Home'** – with regard to Article 8, this is a right to enjoy your existing home peacefully, rather than a right to a house.

30.4.5 'Correspondence'

Respect for **'correspondence'** under Article 8 covers all forms of communication including phone calls, letters, text messages, emails and other communication methods.

In *Klass v Germany* (1978), the powers of secret surveillance of citizens were tolerable under the ECHR only in so far as strictly necessary for safeguarding the democratic institutions.

This means that, in some circumstances, a public authority may be able to interfere with your right to a private and family life in order to protect public safety or the freedoms of others. This has interesting but untested possibilities, including the operation of the Investigatory Powers Act 2016. This Act legalises a whole range of tools for snooping and hacking by the security services unmatched by any other country in Western Europe and the USA.

> ### Key term
>
>
> **'Correspondence'** – with regard to Article 8, this means the right to uninterrupted and uncensored communications with others.

We have seen that the right of privacy extends to an office. With respect to private communications made while at work, the case of *Bărbulescu v Romania* (2017) indicates the current position.

> ### Bărbulescu v Romania (2017)
>
>
> At his employer's request, Mr Bărbulescu set up a Yahoo Messenger account to deal with client enquiries. However, he also used the account to send personal messages, which was not allowed under the company rules. The company investigated his communications including his personal messages and dismissed him for unauthorised use of the internet.
>
> The ECtHR said that his Article 8 rights had been engaged, but that the interference had been proportionate within the state's margin of appreciation. In the absence of a warning to the contrary, an employee can expect privacy of telephone calls, emails and internet usage. Here personal internet use was strictly forbidden. Although the employer had examined the messages, it had only done so after Mr Bărbulescu told them that the messages were all professional communications. The employer had not looked at any other data or documents on his computer.
>
> The Grand Chamber ruled by 11 to 6 that the original judgment given by the Romanian Court had failed to protect Mr Bărbulescu's rights under Article 8. The judges established that employers were able to monitor workers' emails, provided the employee is informed of this. The employee must also be made aware of any potential consequences for using his or her email for personal reasons, making reference to the employer's specific policy against such use.

30.4.6 Justifications stated within the Article for interferences with the rights imposed by primary obligations and by which the state may seek to avoid a finding of a violation

Under Article 8(2), any limitation must be:

- in accordance with law
- necessary and proportionate, and
- for one or more of the following legitimate aims:
    - the interests of national security
    - the interests of public safety or the economic well-being of the country
    - the prevention of disorder or crime
    - the protection of health or morals, or
    - the protection of the rights and freedoms of others.

We have already considered the ideas of the limitations above, and the legitimate aims are set out to demonstrate the categories to be considered.

30.5 English law and its compatibility with ECHR obligations

In this section, we analyse relevant English law to determine compatibility with ECHR obligations and the consequences where English law appears to interfere with the ECHR. There is a particular difficulty for English courts as they attempt to provide law on privacy by using the law of breach of confidence and its development into the tort of misuse of private information. This area is worthy of greatest investigation as it is more complex than the other areas, which fit more neatly with the ECHR law.

30.5.1 'Private life'

In English law, there has never been a right to privacy. While there was the possibility for a claim in the tort of breach of confidence, this was restricted to confidential information and confidential relationships. Lord Hoffmann, in *Wainwright v Home Office* (2003), said that English law contains no specific tort of invasion of privacy and does not need to create one. However, Article 8 is not available in private disputes. It can only be raised in cases involving a public authority, which includes a judge deciding a case in court. As a result, once a claim is brought before a court, the judge must take into account the ECHR, as a decision that is incompatible with the ECHR cannot be made.

There are many parts of English law which relate to privacy. These include:

- the tort of misuse of private information
- the tort of defamation
- the Protection from Harassment Act 1997
- the Data Protection Act 1998
- the Regulation of Investigatory Powers Act 2000
- the Investigatory Powers Act 2016 (not fully in force).

Tort of misuse of private information

The case of *Vidal-Hall v Google* (2014) confirmed that misuse of private information is a tort.

The intrusion into private life has always been a feature of the tabloid press. The principle of freedom of expression under Article 10 is considered in Chapter 31, but the two articles do overlap. The difficulty is in establishing what is in the public interest and what is a mere invasion of privacy. The courts have had to balance individual rights to privacy and to freedom of expression.

The cases of *Wainwright v Home Office* (2003) (appealed to ECtHR in and decided in 2007) and *Campbell v MGN Ltd* (2004) show a contrast in the development of the law in England.

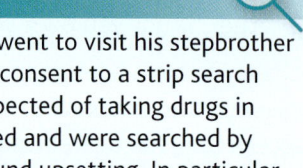

Wainwright v UK (2007)

The claimant and his mother went to visit his stepbrother in prison. They were asked to consent to a strip search because the prisoner was suspected of taking drugs in jail. They reluctantly consented and were searched by prison officers, which they found upsetting. In particular, Wainwright was handled in a way that was later conceded amounted to a battery.

The claimant had physical and learning difficulties, and was diagnosed by a psychiatrist as suffering from PTSD following the strip search experience.

At trial, the judge awarded damages, holding that the searches were wrongful because of the battery and that the claimant's right to privacy had been invaded. The Court of Appeal disagreed with the finding that the prison officers had committed any wrongful act of trespass against the person. They set aside the judgments with the exception of the damages for battery, which was valued at £3,750. Further, the House of Lords did not support a claim under Article 8 – the right to privacy and family life, or Article 3 – inhuman and degrading treatment, and the appeal was unanimously dismissed.

The claimant appealed to the ECtHR which decided:

1. The treatment to which the claimant had been subjected was negligent and fell short of the level of severity required to constitute a breach of Article 3.
2. However, Article 8 also protects physical and moral integrity. As the searches had not been proportionate to the aim of preventing crime and disorder in the manner in which they had been carried out, there was a violation of Article 8.
3. The absence of an effective domestic remedy, in particular the absence of a general tort of invasion of privacy, resulted in a breach of Article 13.
4. The applicants were awarded €3,000 each in damages for the distress caused to them.

Campbell v MGN Ltd (2004)

Naomi Campbell was photographed coming out of a Narcotics Anonymous meeting in London. The newspaper published these photographs with the faces of others attending the meeting pixelated to protect their identities. The headline alongside the photograph read 'Naomi: I'm a drug addict'.

Because she was a model who had proclaimed publicly that she did not take drugs, this might be a legitimate matter to discuss under Article 10, freedom of expression. The question was whether this was a breach of her right to a private life and whether Article 8 takes precedence over Article 10.

The court stated that Articles 8 and 10 are now part of a claim for breach of confidence. There is no question of priority of Article 10 over Article 8 or a presumption in favour of one rather than the other. The publication of photographs of her outside a rehabilitation clinic was a disproportionate interference with her right to privacy, even though the fact that she was receiving treatment was in the public domain.

Naomi Campbell started proceedings in 2001, after the coming into force of HRA 1998. Her appeal to the House of Lords succeeded in 2004. She succeeded even though the newspaper publisher was not a public authority.

Although Article 8 is, under s 6 HRA 1998, only applicable against public authorities, the court saw no logical grounds for saying that a person should have less protection against a private individual than they would have against the state for the publication of personal information for which there is no justification.

The question of priority has been raised on a number of occasions, most recently in *PJS v News Group Newspapers Ltd* (2016). Here it was stated that case law establishes that neither Article 8 nor Article 10 has preference over the other. When the court is considering an injunction with respect to the right of an individual to a private life, it focuses on the comparative rights being claimed in the individual case.

PJS v News Group Newspapers Ltd (2016)

The claimant applied to the court for an injunction to prevent publication of the fact that, in 2011, he had a three-way sexual encounter. The Supreme Court decided that neither Article 8 nor Article 10 has preference over the other. Furthermore, criticism of a person's conduct cannot be a pretext for invasion of privacy by disclosure of alleged sexual infidelity, which is of no real public interest in a legal sense. This rules out one defence to a claim for defamation.

Thus it seems that there is, as yet, no full privacy law in the UK, but Article 8 together with law on breach of confidence and defamation give adequate, if confused, protection.

There is a similar issue in the English courts' approach to access to information, particularly where a child is involved. The ECtHR and English law have always been keen to consider the interests of a child as paramount. This has some consequences when it is appreciated that a person is still a child until the age of 18, but that the under-18s gain certain rights and obligations at different ages as they grow up.

This can be seen with cases involving an attempt to protect the confidentiality of health information concerning a young person. This was the issue in *Axon v Secretary of State for Health* (2006). The case discussed the relationship of **'Gillick competence'**, Article 8 and the right to keep medical records private.

Woolf, J stated:

> Whether or not a child is capable of giving the necessary consent will depend on the child's maturity and understanding and the nature of the consent required. The child must be capable of making a reasonable assessment of the advantages and disadvantages of the treatment proposed, so the consent, if given, can be properly and fairly described as true consent.

Key term

'Gillick competence' – a term used to help assess whether a child has the maturity to make his or her own decisions and to understand the implications of those decisions. The term is taken from the case of *Gillick v West Norfolk AHA* (1984).

Axon v Secretary of State for Health (2006)

Sue Axon sought a declaration that a doctor was under no obligation to keep confidential advice and treatment proposed to a young person, under the age of sixteen, in respect of contraception, sexually transmitted infections and abortion. She wanted a declaration from the court that a doctor must inform the parents unless that might prejudice the child's physical or mental health. At the time, medical professionals were bound by advice contained within professional guides. The claimant sought a declaration that this guidance was unlawful.

The court rejected the claimant's argument; provided the child is Gillick competent, the parental right to determine medical treatment is ended.

The right to a private life also includes sexual identity. We have seen this in terms of transsexuals. Same-sex marriage need not, yet, be treated in the same way as heterosexual marriage although it is in the UK. As the ECtHR is a dynamic institution, its decisions reflect the situation at the time of a decision. The growing view of marriage being made available to all regardless of their sexual orientation is not yet sufficiently firm that the Court will find that a state has an obligation to provide identical rights. However, where a state provides a civil partnership possibility, it should not do so in a discriminatory manner. This can be seen from the case of *Vallianatos v Greece* (2013).

The UK does not allow a civil partnership to be registered between persons of the opposite sex. This was confirmed by the Court of Appeal in *Steinfeld v Secretary of State for Education* (2017).

Look online

Check whether *Steinfeld v Secretary of State for Education* (2017) has been appealed to the Supreme Court and investigate the application of Article 8 in particular in this case.

Extension activity

There are many other cases that have helped develop English law in this area. Some of the more important cases that you can research online are:

- *Douglas v Hello! Ltd* (2001)–(2005) – a series of cases of which No. 1 and No. 8 are the most interesting
- *HRH Prince of Wales v Associated Newspaper Ltd* (2006)
- *McKennitt v Ash* (2006)
- *A v B plc (Flitcroft v MGN Ltd)* (2002)
- *Mosley v NGN Ltd* (2008)
- *Ferdinand v MGN Ltd* (2011)
- *Weller v Associated Newspapers Ltd* (2014).

Figure 30.3 Key cases for Article 8 – tort of misuse of private information

Case	Facts	Law
Wainwright v Home Office (2003)	There was a strip-search by prison officers of Mrs Wainwright and her son during a visit to Armley Prison, Leeds	Article 8 does include touching of the body as part of the right to private life
Campbell v MGN Ltd (2004)	Naomi Campbell was photographed coming out of a Narcotics Anonymous meeting in London	Articles 8 and 10 are now part of a claim for breach of confidence There is no question of priority of Article 10 over Article 8 or a presumption in favour of one rather than the other
PJS v News Group Newspapers Ltd (2016)	PJS applied to the court for an injunction to prevent publication of the fact that, in 2011, he had a three-way sexual encounter	Neither Article 8 nor Article 10 has preference over the other Criticism of a person's conduct cannot be a pretext for invasion of privacy by disclosure of alleged sexual infidelity, which is of no real public interest in a legal sense
Axon v Secretary of State for Health (2006)	Mrs Axon queried whether a doctor was under an obligation to keep confidential advice and treatment proposed to a young person, under the age of 16, in respect of contraception, sexually transmitted infections and abortion	Provided the child is *Gillick* competent, the parental right to determine medical treatment is ended or else there is a potential violation of Article 8

The tort of defamation

In the UK, the law of defamation sets out a position that is largely compatible with the ECHR. Defamation comes in two forms, libel and slander. Libel is defamation in permanent form including broadcasting, slander in transient form – spoken, conduct or gestures. In defamation the words are taken to have their normal or natural meaning.

A claimant needs to show that the statement complained of:

- is defamatory, meaning that an ordinary person would think worse of the claimant as a result of the statement
- identifies or refers to him or her, and
- is published to a third party.

The Defamation Act 2013 requires claimants to show that the publication of the statement caused them, or is likely to cause them, serious harm. In the case of businesses, 'serious harm' means caused them, or is likely to cause them, serious financial loss.

A claim for slander also requires proof of special damage. This means financial loss. There are two exceptions to this requirement:

- a statement that the claimant has committed a criminal offence punishable by imprisonment, such as 'X is a thief', or
- where the words are calculated to disparage the claimant in any office, profession, calling, trade or business carried on by him or her at the time of publication such as 'X is a doctor who is always amputating the wrong limb'.

Defences to a claim for defamation

There are a number of defences in English law with respect to defamation:

- Truth – this is a statutory defence under s 2 of the Defamation Act 2013. It is a complete defence if the defendant can show that the imputation conveyed is substantially true.
- Honest opinion – this is a statutory defence under s 3 of the Defamation Act 2013. It provides a defence if the statement complained of was one of opinion which could have been held by an honest person on the basis of any fact which existed at the time the statement was published. If a claimant can show that the defendant did not hold the opinion, the defence will fail.

- Publication on a matter of public interest – this is set out in s 4 of the Defamation Act 2013. Here the defendant has to show that the statement complained of was, or formed part of, a statement on a matter of public interest, and a reasonable belief that publishing the statement complained of was in the public interest.
- What is in the public interest is potentially very wide. It is not just that it is considered newsworthy. Whether the defendant has a reasonable belief includes attempts made to verify the truth of what is being published, the nature of the sources of information and the extent to which the claimant was given an opportunity to respond or comment. You will often see an article in a newspaper that 'X declined to comment'.
- Internet defences – there are also a number of defences available to internet intermediaries, including innocent dissemination and a website operator's defence, as well as defences under the E-Commerce Regulations of 2002.
- Privilege – this comes in two forms, absolute and qualified. Absolute privilege applies if there are clear public policy reasons for ensuring that there is a limit on the freedom of speech. Such situations include statements made in the course of judicial proceedings, parliamentary proceedings or papers, and contemporaneous reports of judicial proceedings.

Qualified privilege covers the publication of any fair and accurate report or statement on a matter of public interest. This defence can be defeated if there is evidence that the publication was made with malice. Examples of statutory qualified privilege include fair and accurate reports of proceedings in public or Parliament or the courts, or courts or international organisations anywhere in the world, or at a UK public company general meeting or reporting. This has been extended to cover peer-reviewed statements published in scientific or academic journals.

UK legislation

Parliament has created a number of Acts to help protect a person's private life. The Acts provide a range of civil and criminal sanctions, but in most cases an injunction preventing publication or access to information is the most sought-after remedy, as we have seen from ECtHR and UK cases.

Protection from Harassment Act 1997

The Protection from Harassment Act 1997 was originally introduced to deal with the problem of stalking. The Act in fact covers a range of conduct, including harassment motivated by race or religion, some types of anti-social behaviour and some forms of protest.

The Act gives both criminal and civil remedies. There are two criminal offences:

- pursuing a course of conduct amounting to harassment
- a more serious offence where the conduct puts the victim in fear of violence.

Harassing a person includes alarming the person or causing the person distress.

A 'course of conduct', which can include speech, must normally involve conduct on at least two occasions, although there are exceptions to this.

In addition to the criminal offences, a civil court can impose civil injunctions in harassment cases as well as awarding damages to the victim for the harassment. Breach of such an injunction is a criminal offence.

Malicious Communications Act 1998

The Malicious Communications Act 1998 states that it is an offence to send another person a letter, electronic communication or article of any description which conveys:

- a message which is indecent or grossly offensive
- a threat
- information which is false and known or believed to be false by the sender.

Guilt requires the intention to cause distress or anxiety to the recipient or any other person. This is increasingly relevant with respect to cyber bullying.

The Data Protection Act 1998

The Data Protection Act 1998 controls how personal information is used by organisations, businesses or the government. Everyone responsible for using data has to follow the strict rules – the 'data protection principles'. We can see this in relation to medical records in the *Axon* case (see above), but the law has developed in other ways to give some protection from what might be considered an invasion of privacy and thus a person's right to a private life.

An example of this can be seen in the case of *Murray v Big Pictures (UK) Ltd* (2008).

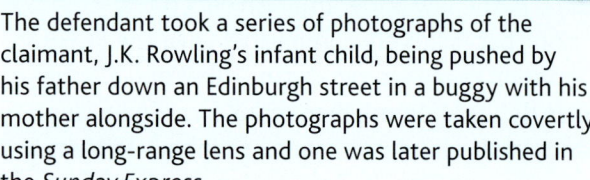

Murray v Big Pictures (UK) Ltd (2008)

The defendant took a series of photographs of the claimant, J.K. Rowling's infant child, being pushed by his father down an Edinburgh street in a buggy with his mother alongside. The photographs were taken covertly using a long-range lens and one was later published in the *Sunday Express*.

The court stated that claims for misuse of private information and under the Data Protection Act 1998 were permissible:

> " It seems to us that, subject to the facts of the particular case, the law should indeed protect children from intrusive media attention, at any rate to the extent of holding that a child has a reasonable expectation that he or she will not be targeted in order to obtain photographs in a public place for publication which the person who took or procured the taking of the photographs knew would be objected to on behalf of the child. "

The Investigatory Powers Act 2016

As we have seen, most UK employers allow or at least tolerate some personal internet and telephone use at work, so the situation is unlikely to be replicated in the UK. To what extent is it the same for members of the same family or for someone using facilities in a hotel or holiday cottage, or for teachers and pupils at a school?

Look online

Read the article entitled 'Three quarters of secondary schools "spying on pupils" devices' at: www.miltonkeynes.co.uk/news/three-quarters-of-secondary-schools-spying-on-pupils-devices-1-7682795.

Make a list of the arguments for and against this form of surveillance being in breach of Article 8 ECHR. Prepare for and hold a debate on whether a school or college is justified legally or morally in 'spying on pupils' devices' and restricting access through school internet servers.

The much-criticised Data Retention and Investigatory Powers Act 2014 gave the Home Office powers to issue a data retention notice to telecommunications operators to retain the personal data of subscribers and registered users without overview by a judge. While this piece of legislation has now come to an end as the result of a sunset clause, its replacement has many similar characteristics. The Act required communications companies (telephone companies) to retain data for 12 months following the giving of a notice by the Secretary of State, irrespective of whether the data subject was suspected of committing any crime. This is done in order to combat crime.

Its replacement, the Investigatory Powers Act 2016, has similar provisions. The aims of the Act are to:

- combine the powers already available to law enforcement and the security and intelligence agencies to obtain communications and data about communications
- introduce a 'double-lock' for interception warrants, so that, following Secretary of State authorisation, they cannot come into force until they have been approved by a judge
- create an Investigatory Powers Commissioner to oversee how these powers are used
- ensure the powers are fit for the digital age.

However, this may not be seen as being compatible with EU law and the ECHR, as shown in the ruling from the Court of Justice of the European Union in the joined cases of *Tele2 Sverige and Watson* (2016).

Tele2 Sverige and Watson (2016)

The court stated:

> " That data taken as a whole is liable to allow very precise conclusions to be drawn concerning the private lives of the persons whose data has been retained, such as everyday habits, permanent or temporary places of residence, daily or other movements, the activities carried out, the social relationships of those persons and the social environments frequented by them ... In particular that data provides the means ... of establishing a profile of the individuals concerned, information that is no less sensitive, having regard to the right to privacy, than the actual content of communications. "

Where national legislation provides for data retention, any retention must be strictly necessary for the purposes of investigating serious crime and linked to the investigation of serious crime.

This strongly suggests that the Investigatory Powers Act 2016 is likely not to be compatible under Article 8 as its powers are too wide-reaching and indiscriminate. The challenge now rests in the English courts' hands to decide on this or for the new Act to be amended.

30.5.2 'Family life'

The Human Rights Act 1998, along with Article 8, has influenced the development of the law in the UK. Some examples have been seen above. More recent examples often relate to immigration, in cases such as *Agyarko and Ikuga v Secretary of State for the Home Department* (2015).

In *Wood v Commissioner of Police for the Metropolis* (2009), the question again arose about the taking of photographs and their retention.

Wood v Commissioner of Police for the Metropolis (2009)

The taking and retention of photographs by the police of a person connected with a group opposed to the arms trade as he left the annual general meeting of a company that organised a trade fair for the arms industry, was an interference with that person's right to respect for his private life under Article 8 and the police failed to justify that interference as being proportionate.

The police action was a sufficient intrusion by the state into the individual's own space and integrity as to amount to a violation of Article 8.

In terms of sexuality and gender, the courts in England have been quite clear in their engagement of Article 8. In *AB v Secretary of State for Justice* (2009), it was decided that the continued detention of a pre-operative transgender woman in a male prison breached her right to privacy under Article 8.

AB v Secretary of State for Justice (2009)

The claimant asked for judicial review of a decision to keep her in a male prison and to not transfer her to a female prison. She suffered gender dysphoria and had been granted a certificate under the Gender Recognition Act 2004 (UK). The certificate provides that for all purposes the claimant is a female. The claimant wanted to have gender reassignment surgery to complete her female transition. However, the Gender Identity Clinic would not approve her for surgery until she had lived as a woman for a period of time within a female prison. Her claim was that the failure to transfer her to a female prison prevented her from attempting to meet the conditions for surgery.

The court said that the failure to transfer her violated her Article 8 rights. Justification for the infringement of her rights must be clear and weighty in order to be proportionate and there was no justification in this case.

Other UK regulations have also been questioned. Under s 82 of the Sexual Offences Act 2003, all persons sentenced to 30 months' imprisonment or more for a sexual offence become subject to a lifelong duty to keep the police notified of where they are living and of travel abroad. There is no right to a review of the necessity for the notification requirements. Is this a violation of Article 8? This was considered in *F and Thompson v Secretary of State for the Home Department* (2010).

F and Thompson v Secretary of State for the Home Department (2010)

The two convicted sex offenders were subject to the notification requirements. They claimed that the absence of a right of review of the requirements was disproportionate to the pursuit of the legitimate aim of preventing crime and violated Article 8.

The Supreme Court stated that the notification requirements may not be disproportionate, but there must be a way for the offender to seek a review of his or her status. Therefore the current law was incompatible with Article 8.

Guidance was issued on this matter by the Home Office in November 2016.

The result of this and other decisions is that UK law is amended so as to comply with Article 8.

Extension activity

Look at the issue of warnings and cautions that were raised in cases such as *R (T) v Chief Constable of Greater Manchester* (2013) and the Law Commission review on Criminal Record Disclosure (Law Com No. 371) (2017).

Do you consider that English law breaches Article 8 now, and will recommendations made by the Law Commission be sufficient? What are the interests being balanced here?

Figure 30.4 Key cases for Article 8 – family and private life in the UK

Case	Facts	Law
Wood v Commissioner of Police for the Metropolis (2009)	The police took and retained photographs of a person connected with a group opposed to the arms trade as he left the annual general meeting of a company that organised a trade fair for the arms industry	The photography had to be considered in context, and here it was an interference under Article 8
AB v Secretary of State for Justice (2009)	The claimant, a pre-operative transgender woman who was in a male prison, asked for judicial review of a decision not to transfer her to a female prison	The court said that the decision not to transfer her to a female prison was in violation of her Article 8 rights
F and Thompson v Secretary of State for the Home Department (2010)	Two convicted sex offenders claimed that the absence of a right of review of the notification requirements was disproportionate and breached their right to privacy under Article 8	The notification requirements may not be disproportionate, but there must be a way for the offender to seek a review of his or her status The current law is incompatible with Article 8
R (T) v Chief Constable of Greater Manchester (2013)	In T, the police issued warnings in 2002 to an 11-year-old boy for theft, which were disclosed in 2008 and again in 2010 when he applied for positions that might have involved contact with children	The court agreed that the 1997 Act is incompatible with Article 8

30.5.3 'Home'

As we have seen, respect for your **'home'** means that public authorities should not stop you from entering or living in your home without good reason, nor should they enter without your permission. This applies whether or not you own your home.

> #### Key term
>
>
> **'Home'** – with regard to Article 8, this is a right to enjoy your existing home peacefully, rather than a right to a house.

Article 8 operates only with respect to an individual's claim against a public body. Bizarrely, this would appear to include publicly owned housing rented to a tenant, but not where private landlords were concerned. This is seen in the case of *McDonald v McDonald* (2016).

> #### *McDonald v McDonald* (2016)
>
>
> Fiona McDonald suffered with mental health issues. Her parents decided to purchase a property for her to live in, with the assistance of a mortgage on the property. The parents ran into financial difficulties and therefore the mortgage company wished to evict her and then sell the property. The Supreme Court decided that HRA 1998 and Article 8 do not require a court to consider whether it is proportionate to evict a residential occupier in a possession claim brought by a private residential landlord.

30.5.4 The overlap of Articles 8 and 10

There are often occasions where these two Articles overlap. These are explored more in the next chapter.

> ## Summary
>
> - Article 8 has four protected interests: private life, family life, home and correspondence.
> - Article 8 is a qualified right.
> - Under Article 8(2), any limitation must be in accordance with law, necessary and proportionate, and for one or more of the five legitimate aims.
> - Private life and privacy are not the same.
>
> - Article 8 is not available in private disputes. It can only be raised in cases involving a public authority.
> - Family life means that you have the right to enjoy family relationships without interference from the state.
> - Respect for home is a right to enjoy your existing home peacefully, rather than a right to a house.
> - Respect for correspondence is a right to uninterrupted and uncensored communications with others.

31 Article 10 ECHR: right to freedom of expression

After reading this chapter, you should be able to:

- Understand the scope of Article 10(1), the right to receive and communicate information and ideas
- Understand the restrictions permitted by Article 10(2)

31.1 Article 10

> 1. Everyone has the right to freedom of expression. This right shall include freedom to hold opinions and to receive and impart information and ideas without interference by public authority and regardless of frontiers. This Article shall not prevent States from requiring the licensing of broadcasting, television or cinema enterprises.
>
> 2. The exercise of these freedoms, since it carries with it duties and responsibilities, may be subject to such formalities, conditions, restrictions or penalties as are prescribed by law and are necessary in a democratic society, in the interests of national security, territorial integrity or public safety, for the prevention of disorder or crime, for the protection of health or morals, for the protection of the reputation or rights of others, for preventing the disclosure of information received in confidence, or for maintaining the authority and impartiality of the judiciary.

Article 10(1) contains the meaning of expression and Article 10(2) sets out how the state can justify an interference with Article 10(1).

In his *Essays, Moral and Political* (1741), the eighteenth century Scottish philosopher David Hume wrote:

> Nothing is more apt to surprise a foreigner, than the extreme liberty, which we enjoy in this country, of communicating whatever we please to the public, and of openly censuring every measure, entered into by the king or his ministers. "

The concept of free speech has been with us for many years, and attempts to restrict it have been met with an outcry throughout history. Speakers' Corner is an area of Hyde Park, London, which is set aside for public speaking. The Parks Regulation Act 1872 passed that anyone can turn up here unannounced to speak on any subject, as long as the police consider their speeches lawful. The spot is near to where the Tyburn gallows were situated, and the creation of Speakers' Corner stems from 1866, when the Government suppressed a meeting of the Reform League demanding the extension of the right to vote.

A gathering at Speakers' Corner in Hyde Park

Before HRA 1998, freedom of expression was permitted as long as the law did not prevent it.

31.2 The key provisions of Article 10

Article 10(1) gives everyone the right to **freedom of expression**, which includes the freedom to hold opinions and to receive and communicate information and ideas without state interference. This is much more than free speech. Freedom of expression includes the right to communicate and to express oneself in any medium, including through words, pictures, images and actions. Actions include public protest and demonstrations; this therefore overlaps with Article 11, the right to freedom of assembly and association.

Key term

Freedom of expression – the freedom to hold opinions and to receive and communicate information and ideas without state interference.

The right to receive information does not, however, place a duty on the state to provide information. In *Guerra v Italy* (1998), a case about toxic emissions, it was stated that freedom to receive information prohibits a government from restricting a person from receiving information that others wish or may be willing to give. There is no positive obligation to collect and disseminate information.

There are three components of the right to freedom of expression:

- freedom to hold opinions
- freedom to communicate information and ideas
- freedom to receive information and ideas.

31.2.1 Freedom to hold opinions

Freedom to hold opinions is a prior condition to the other freedoms guaranteed by Article 10. The possible restrictions set out in Article 10(2) do not apply. Any restrictions to this right will be inconsistent with the nature of a democratic society.

This means that states must not try to indoctrinate their citizens and should not be allowed to distinguish between individuals holding one opinion and another. The idea is to prevent prejudice against an individual because of his or her views by public authorities such as the police or a school. This can be seen in the operation of the equality duty under the Equality Act 2010 where there is a potential conflict with Article 10. For example, a university must prevent unlawful discrimination and promote equality of opportunity, fostering good relationships between different groups, including those with 'protected characteristics' as designated in the Act.

Look online

Read the article at www.theguardian.com/education/2015/feb/02/free-speech-universities-spiked-ban-sombreros.

1 Consider the arguments for and against the bans being outside the apparent scope of freedom of expression under Article 10.

2 Debate this within a small group and consider the justifications for some bans.

3 Revisit this when you have finished this chapter and review your findings.

This indoctrination could include the promotion of information by the state unless it promotes a balanced view.

An individual's freedom to hold opinions includes the negative freedom of not being forced to communicate his or her opinions.

31.2.2 Freedom to communicate information and ideas

The right to freedom of expression includes the right to 'offend, shock and disturb'. In *Handyside v UK* (1976), the ECtHR stated:

> ❝ The Court's supervisory functions oblige it to pay the utmost attention to the principles characterising a 'democratic society'. Freedom of expression constitutes one of the essential foundations of such a society, one of the basic conditions for its progress and for the development of every man. ❞

Freedom of speech was not applicable only to inoffensive material, but also extends to protect activity that others may find shocking, disturbing, or offensive.

Handyside v UK (1976)

Mr Handyside had published a 'Little Red Schoolbook'. He was convicted under the Obscene Publications Acts 1959 and 1964 on the basis that the book was obscene, as it tended to deprave and corrupt its target audience, children. The book claimed that it was intended to teach school children about sex, including recommending the use of pornography.

The court found there was no breach of Article 10 and the UK law fell within the margin of appreciation of the member state (this means the discretion allowed to a state). This is in line with the idea of human rights and their interpretation being dynamic and not bound by precedent.

The type of expression protected includes:

- political expression (including comment on matters of general public interest)
- artistic expression
- commercial expression, particularly when it also raises matters of legitimate public debate and concern.

Political expression is given particular precedence and protection. This was the case with respect to Speakers' Corner too. This is described as high-value expression, which means that there is less margin of appreciation.

Freedom of the press

The freedom to communicate ideas requires freedom of the press. To ensure that free expression and debate are possible, there must be protection for elements of a free press, including protection of journalistic sources. The public and the media should be able to comment on political matters without hindrance. This includes a journalist being able to protect his sources.

Look online

Much more detail can be seen in *A Journalist's Guide to the Human Rights Act*, published by Liberty and available online at: www.liberty-human-rights.org.uk/sites/default/files/journalist-s-guide-to-the-human-rights-act-january-2011.pdf.

There have been many cases with respect to this aspect of Article 10, such as *Goodwin v UK* (1996).

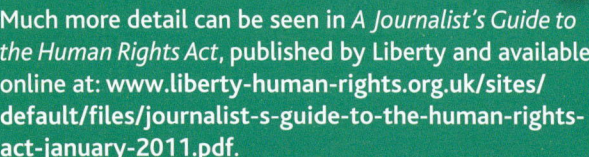

Goodwin v UK (1996)

Mr Goodwin was a trainee journalist with *The Engineer* magazine. He got information by phone from a source who wished to remain anonymous about company financial information from a confidential corporate plan. The company obtained various court orders, including one under s 10 of the Contempt of Court Act 1981, which required him to divulge the identity of his source. The applicant appealed unsuccessfully to the English courts, but still failed to disclose his source and was fined £5,000 for contempt of court.

The ECtHR stated that as publication of the confidential information was already prohibited by injunction, the order for disclosure of the source was not necessary, and so was a breach of Article 10.

This decision was repeated in *Financial Times Ltd v UK* (2009), when the ECtHR held unanimously that an order requiring various media organisations to disclose original leaked documents that might have led to the revelation of a journalistic source was an unjustified interference with Article 10.

One of the main problems with freedom of the press is the balance between Articles 10 and 8. As we have seen with the limitations under Article 8(2), the balance is difficult.

Tip

Review the material on Article 8, as questions may well require a discussion of both Articles. Note that Articles 8, 10 and 11 are closely connected.

The case of *Axel Springer AG v Germany* (2012) set out criteria to be used in balancing the two articles. These criteria are:

- whether the information contributes to a debate of general interest
- the notoriety of the person concerned and the subject matter of the report
- the prior conduct of the person concerned
- the method of obtaining the information and its veracity
- the content, form and consequences of the publication
- the severity of the sanction imposed.

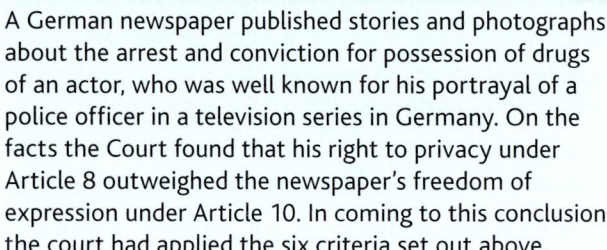

Axel Springer AG v Germany (2012)

A German newspaper published stories and photographs about the arrest and conviction for possession of drugs of an actor, who was well known for his portrayal of a police officer in a television series in Germany. On the facts the Court found that his right to privacy under Article 8 outweighed the newspaper's freedom of expression under Article 10. In coming to this conclusion, the court had applied the six criteria set out above.

Activity

Find some recent sensational newspaper headlines about an individual. Consider the criteria for the balance between Articles 8 and 10 for that individual and the newspaper.

Political expression

Meaningful free elections are not possible in the absence of this freedom. A wide range of views were expressed during the 2016 referendum campaign on Britain's withdrawal from the EU, and a Remain-supporting MP, Jo Cox, was murdered by a man who disagreed with her views. In December 2016, after the conviction of Mrs Cox's murderer, a man was arrested over a Twitter post calling for people to 'Jo Cox' an MP.

The difficulty is when political expression contravenes the criminal law relating to protests, or, indeed, as to what is considered political. The limits of acceptable criticism are wider with respect to a politician as such than as regards a private individual. A politician inevitably lays him- or herself open to close scrutiny of his or her every word and deed by both journalists and the public at large, and therefore must display a greater degree of tolerance.

However, the reporting needs to be at the standard of responsible journalism and reportage.

Civil or public interest expression

This is where the expression raises matters of legitimate public debate and concern. This might be with respect to the building of a motorway or rail line, hunting, fracking or activities by commercial enterprises. An example of this is the case of *Steel and Morris v UK* (2005), where the Court found that there had been a violation of Article 10.

Steel and Morris v UK (2005)

McDonald's brought a libel action against Helen Steel and David Morris. The defendants had published a leaflet against the claimants making various allegations against them. Legal aid was not available for libel cases and the defendants had to represent themselves, despite each being on a low wage. McDonald's employed experienced senior barristers. The trial lasted 313 days and the defendants lost their case.

The ECtHR decided that the complexity of the case and the different levels of legal support were so great to make the case unfair under Article 6. It also decided that the level of damages awarded against the defendants was so great that it breached Article 10.

Helen Steel and David Morris in London, 2005

Artistic expression

This is vital for fostering individual fulfilment and the development of ideas. There is much variety between states as to what is acceptable – in other words, a wide margin of appreciation to reflect different cultures and values in different states.

For example, in *Otto-Preminger-Institut v Austria* (1994) there was a conflict between freedom of expression and religion.

Otto-Preminger-Institut v Austria (1994)

The institute tried to show a film that offended the Catholic religion and the religious feelings of the people of Tyrol, a region of Austria that consists of a large majority of Catholics in whose lives religion plays a very important role. The authorities had banned the showing of the film in an art cinema and confiscated the film. The institute claimed a violation of its freedom of speech under Article 10 but the ECtHR found no violation.

Hate speech or incitement to hatred

The ECtHR distinguishes between 'hate speech' and 'incitement to hatred'. The difference between the two is not clear. Hate speech therefore falls outside the scope of Article 10, but if the material is found to be incitement to racial hatred, the ECtHR will allow it to be argued under Article 10(1) and the state may therefore justify restriction under Article 10(2). This has been seen in the case of *Garaudy v France* (2003). This case is very important, because it calls into question the extent to which a person can rely on freedom of expression under Article 10 to challenge established 'truth'.

Garuady v France (2003)

Garuady's book, *The Founding Myths of Modern Israel*, challenged certain historical orthodoxies about the Holocaust and the existence of Hitler's 'final solution'. Criminal proceedings were brought against him and he was found guilty of disputing the existence of crimes against humanity, public defamation of a group of people (the Jewish community) and incitement to discrimination and racial hatred.

He argued that under Article 10, his right to freedom of expression had been unjustifiably infringed. He also argued that his book was a political work written with a view to combating Zionism and criticising Israeli policy, and had no racist or anti-Semitic content. He argued he should have unlimited freedom of expression.

The court found that there could be an interference with his right to freedom of expression. However unpalatable his views, his publication contained ideas and as such should be protected under Article 10. Therefore there was no breach of Article 10.

Figure 31.1 Key cases for Article 10 – freedom to communicate information and ideas

Case	Facts	Law
Handyside v UK (1976)	Handyside was convicted under the Obscene Publications Acts 1959 and 1964	There was no breach of Article 10 and the UK law fell within the margin of appreciation of the member state
Goodwin v UK (1996)	Goodwin failed to disclose the source of company financial information and was fined	The order for disclosure of the source was not necessary and so was a breach of Article 10
Axel Springer AG v Germany (2012)	A newspaper published stories about the arrest and conviction for possession of drugs of a well-known TV actor, together with photographs of him	The actor's right to privacy under Article 8 outweighed the newspaper's freedom of expression under Article 10 The court had applied six criteria
Steel and Morris v UK (2005)	Steel and Morris (and others) libelled and were ordered to pay damages to McDonald's in 1997 after handing out leaflets attacking the company's working practices and policies	Given the lack of procedural fairness and the disproportionate award of damages, the court found that there was been a violation of Article 10
Otto-Preminger-Institut v Austria (1994)	The institute tried to show a film that offended the Catholic religion but the authorities banned it and confiscated the film	The institute claimed a violation of its freedom of speech under Article 10 of the Convention but failed in its attempt
Garuady v France (2003)	Garuady was found guilty of disputing the existence of a number of crimes in relation to a book he had written	However unpalatable his views, his publication contained ideas and as such should be protected under Article 10. But restriction was justifiable under Article 10(2) (so there had been no breach of Article 10)

31.2.3 Freedom to receive information and ideas

The freedom to receive information includes the right to gather information and to seek information through all possible lawful sources, including international television broadcasts and the internet. This freedom enables the media to communicate such information and ideas to the public, who have a right to be adequately informed, in particular on matters of public interest. This relates to freedom of information.

This right does not create a general positive obligation to provide the information. This can be seen in *Guerra v Italy* (1998).

Guerra v Italy (1998)

The applicants complained that the Italian state had failed to provide information about potentially hazardous industry near where they lived.

ECtHR stated that Article 10 of the Convention 'basically prohibits a government from restricting a person from receiving information that others wish or may be willing to impart to him'. The ECtHR stated that the freedom cannot be construed as imposing on a state positive obligations to collect and disseminate information on its own accord.

In the UK, the Freedom of Information Act 2000 gives everyone the right to access recorded information held by public sector organisations. Any request for information under the Act will be handled under different regulations depending on the kind of information requested, and an organisation could refuse a request if the information is sensitive or the costs are too high.

The other side of freedom of information is the Investigatory Powers Act 2016.

See Chapter 30, section 30.5.1 for more details of the Investigatory Powers Act 2016.

Whether this Act will have an effect on the interpretation of Articles 8 and 10 (as well as other Articles of the ECHR) remains to be seen.

Without interference by public authority

The whole question of freedom of information and when a response can be refused under the ECHR has been reviewed in *Magyar Helsinki Bizottság v Hungary* (2016). The ECtHR tied access to information to freedom of expression.

The scope of access to information is narrowly defined: it applies to state-held information and ensures access in the public interest and for recipients who seek access to information in order to contribute to the public debate in a watchdog capacity. The audience's potential 'wish for sensationalism or even voyeurism' is not sufficient reason to provide access to information under Article 10. Where access to the information is 'instrumental' for the individual's exercise of his or her right to freedom of expression, the information must be disclosed.

Whether it is instrumental requires consideration of four indicative criteria:

- The purpose of the information request – which must be to receive and communicate information and ideas to others, and necessary for the exercise of freedom of expression.
- The nature of the information sought – it needs to meet a public interest test in order to prompt a need for disclosure under Article 10.
- The role of the applicant – journalists, social watchdogs, non-governmental organisations (NGOs), researchers and academics are in a privileged position, so long as they seek the information with a view to informing the public in the capacity of a public watchdog.
- Ready and available information.

If the right is engaged (as the court held it was for the NGO in *Magyar*), it is necessary to consider whether the interference is justified under Article 10(2).

'Not prevent States from requiring the licensing of broadcasting, television or cinema enterprises'

This allows the state to license such media companies as, when the ECHR was drafted, there were only a limited number of broadcasting frequencies available and most European states had control of these frequencies.

Later ECtHR decisions, such as *Groppera Radio AG v Switzerland* (1990), recognised that the technical progress that had been made meant that the justification of these restrictions could no longer be supported on this basis. Public monopolies within the audio-visual media were seen by the court as contrary to Article 10.

31.2.4 Justifications stated within the Article for interferences with the rights imposed by primary obligations and by which the state may seek to avoid a finding of a violation

The limitations are set out in Article 10(2). These limitations are only permissible if they fulfil three criteria:

- The interference (formality, restriction, condition, or penalty) is prescribed by law. This means that it is part of the relevant state's law. In the UK this includes statutory and common law rules. For instance in *Sunday Times v UK* (1979), the court found that the British common law rules on contempt of court were sufficiently precise as to fall under the requirement 'provided by law'.
- The interference is aimed at protecting one or more of the following legitimate aims:
  - the interests of national security
  - territorial integrity or public safety
  - the prevention of disorder or crime
  - the protection of health or morals
  - the protection of the reputation or rights of others
  - preventing the disclosure of information received in confidence
  - maintaining the authority and impartiality of the judiciary.

  This list is exhaustive; no other ground may be relied on.
- The interference is necessary in a democratic society. Here the national courts must apply the principle of proportionality, answering the question: 'Was the aim proportional with the means used to reach that legitimate aim?' In *Observer and Guardian v UK* (1995), the ECtHR stated that 'necessary', within the meaning of Article 10(2), means the existence of a pressing social need.

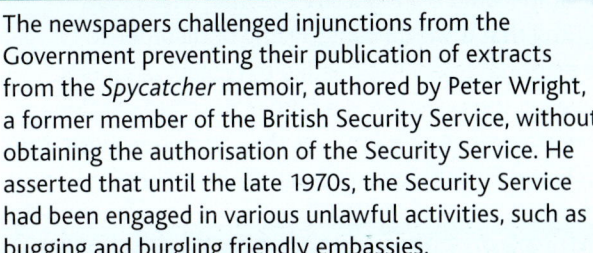

Observer and Guardian v UK (1995)

The newspapers challenged injunctions from the Government preventing their publication of extracts from the *Spycatcher* memoir, authored by Peter Wright, a former member of the British Security Service, without obtaining the authorisation of the Security Service. He asserted that until the late 1970s, the Security Service had been engaged in various unlawful activities, such as bugging and burgling friendly embassies.

In July 1986, the courts granted an interim injunction to prohibit publication, but by the time of the hearing for a permanent injunction, the book was published abroad, including in the USA, and many copies had been imported into the UK.

The ECtHR stated that the temporary injunctions were justified prior to the publication in the United States. At that point, the information lost its confidential character and so the interference was no longer permissible.

Where the ECtHR finds that all three requirements are fulfilled, the interference will be considered legitimate. The burden of proof is on the state. The ECtHR examines the three conditions in the order set out. As soon as the state fails to prove one of the three requirements the interference is unjustified and freedom of expression violated.

Tip

When considering the application of Article 10(2), follow the order set out here to examine the three conditions.

We therefore need to consider how these limitations operate and the reasons for permitted interference by the state, listed under the second bullet point above.

31.2.5 In the interests of national security

The court rarely challenges the legitimate national security aim argued by the state. *Hadjianastassiou v Greece* (1992) is an example of this, where a report the applicant had written for a private company gave some hints of the military capabilities of the Greek Air Force where he was an aeronautical engineer.

31.2.6 With respect to territorial integrity or public safety

Territorial integrity means the borders of the state. Public safety would include legislation to prevent bomb hoaxes.

31.2.7 For the prevention of disorder or crime

The state could try to justify the interference by arguing that it would cause crime or disorder so the criminal offence is needed to protect against it. However, the question is whether the state's actions are proportionate. An example of this (and other limitations) can be seen in the case of *Surek v Turkey* (1999).

Surek v Turkey (1999)

The applicant was the major shareholder in a company that owned a weekly review. Two readers' articles

were published in the weekly review in which the state authorities were severely criticised for their part in the massacres in Kurdistan in south-eastern Turkey. The letters used labels such as 'fascist Turkish army' and 'murder gang' alongside references to 'massacres', 'brutalities' and 'slaughter'. In the court's view they amounted to an appeal to revenge.

The applicant was convicted of the offence of disseminating propaganda against the indivisibility of the state and provoking enmity and hatred among the people. Surek argued that this was an interference by a public authority under Article 10. However, the ECtHR stated that the applicant's conviction was both relevant and sufficient and that therefore the interference was proportionate to its legitimate aim so there was no violation of Article 10.

31.2.8 For the protection of health or morals

There are areas of expression that no society or state is likely to allow. This might be incitement to murder, or the sale of pornography to or involving children.

However, one difficulty is that different states have different views of morals and obscenity. In *Müller v Switzerland* (1988), this was one of the main arguments.

Müller v Switzerland (1988)

This involved a claim that Article 10 had been infringed by the applicant's conviction of an offence of publishing obscene items, consisting of paintings which were said 'mostly to offend the sense of sexual propriety of persons of ordinary sensitivity'. The court stressed the need to consider the principle of necessity for limitation in this context, and stated: 'The adjective "necessary" implies the existence of a "pressing social need".'

The ECtHR recognised that standards of sexual morality do change, but it did not find the view of the Swiss courts to be unreasonable. Therefore, fining the exhibition organisers was not a violation of the right to freedom of expression.

The debate about abortion combines the issues of both health and morality. Article 10's application will reflect the prevailing views at the time of any complaint brought before the court as each case is based on the standards of the day rather than strict precedent. In *Open Door and Dublin Well Woman v Ireland* (1992), the views prevailing then were in issue.

See Chapter 28, section 28.1.1 for full case details.

Figure 31.2 Key cases for Article 10 – freedom to receive information and ideas (1)

Case	Facts	Law
Guerra v Italy (1998)	The applicants lived about 1 km from a chemical factory and demanded a right to receive information	The court held there is no positive obligation to collect and disseminate information
Observer and Guardian v UK (1995)	The newspapers challenged injunctions preventing their publication of extracts from *Spycatcher*	The ECtHR stated that the temporary injunctions were justified prior to the publication of the book but not thereafter
Surek v Turkey (1999)	The applicant was convicted of the offence of disseminating propaganda against the indivisibility of the state and provoking enmity and hatred among the people	S argued that this was an interference by a public authority with his right to freedom of expression No breach of Article 10 was found
Müller v Switzerland (1988)	M was convicted of an offence of publishing obscene items, consisting of paintings	Fining the exhibition organisers was not a violation of the right to freedom of expression
Open Door and Dublin Well Woman v Ireland (1992)	The applicants were prohibited from providing any information to pregnant women about abortion clinics in Great Britain	This prohibition was a breach of Article 10

31.2.9 For the protection of the reputation or rights of others

The case of *Bédat v Switzerland* (2016) is interesting as the Grand Chamber had to balance the conflicting rights of the right to fair trial and presumption of innocence under Article 6 and the right to privacy in Article 8 on the one hand, and freedom of expression under Article 10 on the other hand.

Bédat v Switzerland (2016)

In 2003, the applicant published an article in *L'Illustré* dealing with criminal proceedings against a motorist who had crashed his car into passers-by on the Lausanne Bridge, resulting in three deaths and injuries to eight people. The article questioned the motorist's state of mind and included a personal description as well as photographs of letters sent by him to the investigating judge. Criminal proceedings were brought against the journalist by the public prosecutor for having published secret documents, in breach of the Swiss Criminal Code.

The Grand Chamber found no violation of Article 10 and found that the fine imposed on Mr Bédat was necessary in a democratic society. In doing so, the Grand Chamber took into account six criteria relating to the case. The Grand Chamber expanded its approach of balancing the competing interests of privacy protection of Articles 8 and 10 to the situation of conflict between the right to fair trial under Article 6 and freedom of expression.

Restrictions on human rights law – defamation

In the UK, the law of defamation sets out a position that is largely compatible with the ECHR. Defamation comes in two forms, libel and slander. Libel is defamation in permanent form, including broadcasting slander in transient form – spoken, conduct or gestures. In defamation the words are taken to have their normal or natural meaning. This has been dealt with under Article 8.

31.2.10 For preventing the disclosure of information received in confidence

In *Bédat v Switzerland* (2016), the court suggested that the journalist had not obtained the information by unlawful means. However, as a professional journalist he must have been aware of the confidential nature of the information.

In *Guja v Moldova* (2008), it was decided that the public interest in having the information about undue pressure and wrongdoing within public office was so important in a democratic society that it outweighed the interest in maintaining public confidence in that office.

The ECtHR used this case to stress that open discussion of topics of public concern, such as the separation of state powers and the independence of investigating authorities, was essential to democracy and it was of great importance for civil servants and members of the public not to be discouraged from voicing their opinions on such matters.

In *Heinisch v Germany* (2011), the ECtHR considered the need to strike a fair balance between the need to protect the employer's reputation and rights on the one hand and the need to protect the right to freedom of expression of the whistleblower on the other. Here the failure of the domestic courts to order the whistleblower's reinstatement (she had been dismissed following her whistleblowing) had violated her rights under Article 10.

31.2.11 For maintaining the authority and impartiality of the judiciary

There are usually restrictions on the press disclosing details in advance of a trial so that the case can proceed fairly, without those involved being swayed by views in the media. There are usually restrictions on recordings and photography in court, punishable as a criminal offence. This is usually less of a problem in the UK than in some other states, but the idea can be seen in the case of *Sunday Times v UK* (1979). The Government justified injunctions against publication of a newspaper article on the basis of this limitation.

Sunday Times v UK (1979)

The use of the prescribed drug thalidomide resulted in side effects where many children were born with severe malformations. In the UK the drug was produced and sold by Distillers Company Ltd, which withdrew it from the market in 1961. Parents sued the company and negotiations continued for many years. Settlements had to be approved by the courts. This was covered by the press in great detail.

In 1971, the parties started negotiations to set up a charity fund for the children with malformations. In September 1972, the *Sunday Times* published an article entitled 'Our thalidomide children: a cause for national shame', criticising the company for the financial payments the company were to pay. The *Sunday Times* also announced that it would run a detailed analysis of the circumstances of the tragedy in future editions of the paper.

The Attorney-General asked the court to grant an injunction against the newspaper as the publication of the announced article would obstruct justice. The *Sunday Times* claimed a violation of Article 10. Since thalidomide cases were still pending before the courts, the Attorney-General claimed that there was no violation of Article 10.

The ECtHR stated that the thalidomide disaster was a matter of public concern. The families involved in the tragedy as well as the public at large had the right to be informed on all the facts of this matter. The Court concluded that the injunction ordered against the newspaper 'did not correspond to a social need sufficiently pressing to outweigh the public interest in freedom of expression within the meaning of the Convention'.

While the *Sunday Times* case was not critical of the judiciary, recent criticisms of the judiciary with respect to the challenge to the UK's handling of the referendum on leaving the EU and Article 50 has led to lively debate.

Look online

Read newspaper articles such as www.theguardian.com/politics/2016/nov/04/enemies-of-the-people-british-newspapers-react-judges-brexit-ruling. List arguments stating whether or not these pieces violate Article 10.

The ECtHR has considered 'maintaining the authority and impartiality of the judiciary' in the case of *Pinto Coelho v Portugal (No. 2)* (2016).

Pinto Coelho v Portugal (No. 2) (2016)

Ms Pinto Coelho is a journalist and crime reporter for a Portuguese television channel. On 12 November 2005, the news programme on the channel broadcast a report prepared by her about the criminal conviction of an 18-year-old man for aggravated theft of a mobile phone. The programme claimed that the young man was innocent and that the judges had made a mistake. She included in her report shots of the courtroom, extracts of sub-titled sound recordings and the questioning of prosecution and defence witnesses, in which their voices and those of the three judges were digitally altered.

She was fined for broadcasting unauthorised audio recordings of a criminal trial. The ECtHR said that her rights under Article 10 had been breached. The sound recordings were from the official tape recording of the proceedings which was available to the parties, but their use in a broadcast had not been authorised. The court balanced the rights of the media to report on a matter of public interest with the interests of the participants, witnesses and judiciary and the necessity in a democratic society to impose restrictions on the use of recordings.

There may be a further appeal in this case.

Figure 31.3 Key cases for Article 10 – freedom to receive information and ideas (2)

Case	Facts	Law
Bédat v Switzerland (2016)	In 2003, the applicant was fined for publishing an article questioning an accused motorist's state of mind and included a personal description as well as photographs of letters sent by him to the investigating judge	The court found no violation of Article 10 and found that the fine imposed on Mr Bédat was necessary in a democratic society
Sunday Times v UK (1979)	The Attorney-General asked the court to grant an injunction against the *Sunday Times* as the publication of the article on thalidomide victims would obstruct justice. The *Sunday Times* claimed a violation of Article 10	This was a matter of public concern. The injunction was not granted
Pinto Coelho v Portugal (No. 2) (2016)	The applicant was fined for broadcasting unauthorised audio recordings of a criminal trial	The court balanced the rights of the media to report on a matter of public interest with the interests of the participants. It found a breach of Article 10

31.2.12 Article 10 and the internet

Technology has progressed significantly since the ECHR was conceived. *Editorial Board of Parvoye Delo and Shtekel v Ukraine* (2011) deals with the internet aspects of Article 10.

Editorial Board of Parvoye Delo and Shtekel v Ukraine (2011)

Ukrainian legislation exempts journalists from civil responsibility for referencing materials that have already been published by another press outlet. However, the local courts held that the exemption does not apply to material obtained from publications that are not registered with the Ukrainian authorities. However, Ukrainian law does not regulate registration of internet media. *Pravoye Delo*, a Ukrainian newspaper, published an anonymous letter posted on an internet site that accused senior local officials of involvement in various criminal activities.

The ECtHR stated that since Ukrainian domestic law was not clear on the use of information received from the internet, the applicants could not have foreseen that the exemption did not apply. Therefore, the Ukrainian ruling failed to meet the Article 10 requirement that any limitation of freedom of expression should be based on a clear, accessible and reasonably foreseeable law.

In *Yildirim v Turkey* (2013), the ECtHR unanimously held that the blanket blocking of access to sites.google.com breached the right to freedom of expression. In *Delfi AS v Estonia* (2015), the Grand Chamber commented:

> While the Court acknowledges that important benefits can be derived from the Internet in the exercise of freedom of expression, it is also mindful that liability for defamatory or other types of unlawful speech must, in principle, be retained and constitute an effective remedy for violations of personality rights.

Activity

Research the following cases (and similar ones you can find). Consider the arguments for and against the merits of the decisions with respect to Article 10 and any other Articles you have studied.

- *Delfi AS v Estonia* (2015)
- *Ashby Donald v France* (2013)

Figure 31.4 Key cases for Article 10 and the internet

Case	Facts	Law
Editorial Board of Parvoye Delo and Shtekel v Ukraine (2011)	*Pravoye Delo*, a Ukrainian newspaper, published an anonymous letter posted on an internet site that accused senior local officials of involvement in various criminal activities	The Ukrainian ruling failed to meet the Article 10 requirement that any limitation of freedom of expression should be based on a clear, accessible and reasonably foreseeable law
Yildirim v Turkey (2013)	The state had ordered blanket blocking of access to sites.google.com	This breached the right to freedom of expression

31.3 English law and its compatibility with ECHR obligations

As we have seen, the framework of human rights law in the UK is designed to encourage compliance with the Convention. The Freedom of Information Act 2000 attempts to promote freedom of expression by providing public access to information held by public authorities. This is done in two ways:

- public authorities are obliged to publish certain information about their activities
- members of the public are entitled to request information from public authorities.

Public authorities include government departments, local authorities, the NHS, state schools and police forces.

Recorded information includes printed documents, computer files, letters, emails, photographs, and sound or video recordings.

The Act does not give people access to their own personal data such as their health records or credit reference file. If a member of the public wants to see information that a public authority holds about him or her, he or she must make a subject access request under the Data Protection Act 1998.

In the UK, there are a number of restrictions on freedom of expression. These relate to:

- protecting reputation and physical/mental integrity
- protecting the secrecy of non-public information
- protecting an interest in the proper administration of justice
- protecting society from depravity, corruption and offence
- protecting from offence directed at religious beliefs and race
- preserving public order and the peace.

31.3.1 Protecting reputation and physical/mental integrity

Defamation and protection from harassment have been dealt with under Article 8.

31.3.2 Protecting the secrecy of non-public information

The law of confidentiality and misuse of personal information has been considered with respect to

Article 8 under the Data Protection Act 1998 and the Investigatory Powers Act 2016. As we have seen, the Investigatory Powers Act 2016, which is not yet fully in force, may well be incompatible with Article 8 and also Article 10.

The Official Secrets Acts 1911–1989 provide the main legal protection against espionage and the unauthorised disclosure of information. Section 1 of the Official Secrets Act 1911 (as amended by the 1920 and 1939 Official Secrets Acts) sets out offences related to spying, sabotage and related crimes. The Official Secrets Act 1989 creates an offence for the unlawful disclosure of information in six specific categories by employees and former employees of the security and intelligence services, and for current and former Crown Servants and government contractors.

'Official information' means any information, document or article which a Crown servant or government contractor has or has had in his or her possession by virtue of his or her position. This is obviously a situation which falls within Article 10 and will be subject to consideration of the margin of appreciation principle. There is, however, no public interest defence available to offences under the Official Secrets Act 1989. This was decided in the case of *R v Shayler* (2002).

R v Shayler (2002)

The defendant had been a member of the security services. He had signed the Official Secrets Act as required by the security services. However he disclosed a number of documents to journalists from the *Mail on Sunday*. A large number of documents were later returned by the newspaper. Most of them appeared to relate to security and intelligence matters and were classified at levels ranging from 'Classified' up to and including 'Top Secret'.

His defence that the disclosures had been made by him in the public or national interest failed.

It is argued that this is not a violation of Article 10.

The Leveson Inquiry and the Crime and Courts Act 2013

The Leveson inquiry was a judicial public inquiry into the culture, practices and ethics of the British press following the News International phone hacking scandal, chaired by Lord Justice Leveson. The Inquiry published the Leveson Report in November 2012, which reviewed the general culture and ethics of the British media and made recommendations for a new, independent, body to replace the existing Press Complaints Commission, which would have to be recognised by the state through new laws. These laws were set out in the Crime and Courts Act 2013, although many of the relevant sections of the Act have not yet been brought into force.

Whistleblowing

In the UK, the Public Interest Disclosure Act 1998 protects workers who disclose information about malpractice at their workplace provided certain conditions are met. The conditions concern the nature of the information disclosed and the person to whom it is disclosed. If these conditions are met, the Act protects the worker who made the disclosure.

However, the English courts tried to limit this right to employees and the public as opposed to members of the firm. It was not until the case reached the Supreme Court in *Clyde and Co LLP v van Winklehof* (2014) that a member of a limited liability partnership firm of solicitors was able to come within the definition of a worker and so be protected.

Figure 31.5 Key cases for Article 10 and protecting the secrecy of non-public information

Case	Facts	Law
R v Shayler (2002)	S had been a member of the security services and disclosed documents to journalists that related to security and intelligence matters	S argued that the disclosures were in the public or national interest. This defence failed

Look online

The following newspaper article expands on this area of law: www.theguardian.com/law/2011/sep/19/official-secrets-act-human-rights-act.

31.3.3 Protecting an interest in the proper administration of justice

The law of contempt of court was established at common law as 'an act or omission calculated to interfere with the administration of justice.' The common law is still the starting point for determining what constitutes a contempt, and case law has established the powers of courts to deal with contempt. There are many Acts of Parliament relating to contempt of court. The main one is the Contempt of Court Act 1981 relating to publications creating a 'substantial risk of serious prejudice' unless a discussion in good faith of public affairs or other matters of general public interest where 'the risk of impediment or prejudice to particular legal proceedings is merely incidental to the discussion'.

Section 9 prohibits the use of tape recorders and similar devices in court or bringing sound recording equipment into court without leave of the court and deems publication of a sound recording as a contempt. Section 10 provides limited protection against contempt for a person refusing to disclose the source of information contained in a publication for which he or she is responsible.

Elsewhere, the law prohibits disclosure of what happens in the jury room as misconduct by jurors. These are prosecuted under the Juries Act 1974. The restrictions may be compatible with Article 10.

Look online

Consider the following article and discuss whether Article 10 might be engaged in these situations: www.belfasttelegraph.co.uk/news/northern-ireland/online-comments-by-rugby-rape-trial-juror-investigated-36759210.html.

31.3.4 Protecting society from depravity, corruption and offense

There is no problem with law where the expression reflects views with which everyone agrees. The real test is to permit expression of views with which most people do not agree or which the state wishes to discourage or suppress.

Obscene publications are governed by the Obscene Publications Act 1959 and the Obscene Publications Act 1964. The 1959 Act sets out the legal test for obscenity. Section 1(1) of the Obscene Publications Act 1959 describes an 'obscene' item as one that has the effect of tending to deprave and corrupt persons likely to read, see or hear it. This statutory definition is largely based on the common law test of obscenity, as laid down in the case of *R v Hicklin* (1868), namely:

> *...whether the tendency of the matter charged as obscenity is to deprave and corrupt those whose minds are open to such immoral influences, and into whose hands a publication of this sort may fall.*

Famous cases in the UK include those involving the books *Lady Chatterley's Lover* and *Last Exit to Brooklyn*. The courts have defined 'deprave' as meaning to make morally bad, to debase, to pervert or to corrupt morally, and 'corrupt' as meaning to render morally unsound or rotten, to destroy moral purity or chastity, to pervert or ruin a good quality, and to debase or defile.

Section 4 of the Obscene Publications Act 1959 provides a defence of 'public good'. This requires proof that publication of the article in question is justified as being for the public good on the grounds that it is in the interests of science, literature, art or learning, or of other objects of general concern. Publication of a film or soundtrack is justified as being for the public good on the grounds that it is in the interests of drama, opera, ballet or any other art, or of literature or learning. In this respect, the opinion of experts as to the literary, artistic, scientific or other merits of an article may be admitted either to establish or to negate the grounds.

It should also be noted that ss 63 to 67 of the Criminal Justice and Immigration Act 2008 create the offence of possession of extreme pornographic images. The offence requires proof that the image:

1 is pornographic, and
2 is extreme, i.e. grossly offensive, disgusting or otherwise of an obscene character, and
3 portrays in an explicit and realistic way any of the extreme acts set out in s 63(7) of the Act.

The painting by Michelangelo 'Leda and the Swan' would also not be caught by the new offence because it would not meet the explicit and realistic test.

There are also a number of defences, such as where the material is a *complete* film that has been passed by the British Board of Film Classification, or where the material is held by a person who has a legitimate work reason for being in possession of the image, for example a child protection officer.

The Theatres Act 1968 applies a similar definition of obscenity to plays and performances. This is also extended to live broadcasts under the Broadcasting Act 1990.

There is also a possible lesser offence of outraging public decency. Public decency requires a level of behaviour which is generally accepted by the public and is not obscene, disgusting or shocking for the observers. A recent example is the case of a man arrested after being spotted urinating on Manchester's city centre war memorial.

Another case that demonstrates this is *R v Gibson* (1991).

R v Gibson (1991)

In December 1987, an artist, Rick Gibson, exhibited a pair of earrings made with freeze-dried human foetuses attached to a mannequin's head at a London art gallery. Gibson and the gallery owner were convicted of the common law offence of outraging public decency.

Thus galleries (and their staff, officers or directors) may be committing a criminal offence if, for example, they sell, show or distribute work that is considered to be obscene or which causes public outrage. It could be argued that this is incompatible with Article 10 because of the decision in *Müller v Switzerland* (1988) and *Handyside v UK* (1976) (above). In *Handyside,* the ECtHR stressed that the freedom of expression protected by Article 10 is:

> *...applicable not only to information and ideas that are favourably received or regarded as inoffensive ... but also to those that offend shock and disturb the State or any sector of the population. Such are the demands of that pluralism, tolerance and broadmindedness without which there is no democratic society.*

Extension activity

In 2015, the Law Commission reported on 'Simplification of Criminal Law: Public Nuisance and Outraging Public Decency' (Law Com No. 358). Find its main recommendations with respect to outraging public decency and consider arguments for and against the proposals.

English law is not necessarily compatible with the ECHR in this area.

31.3.5 Protecting from offence directed at religious beliefs and race

Stirring up hatred against people because of their race, or because of religious beliefs or sexual orientation, in the form of making or publishing a threatening statement is an offence under the Public Order Act 1986 as amended by the Racial and Religious Hatred Act 2006.

A racial group means a group of people who are defined by reference to their race, colour, nationality or ethnic or national origin; this therefore includes, for example, gypsies and travellers, refugees and asylum seekers, as well as religious groups such as Muslims, Hindus and Christians. It also includes people with no religious belief at all.

The Acts make it an offence to use threatening, abusive or insulting words or behaviour with intent to stir up racial hatred in the street or in a public speech. The Acts also made it an offence to display, publish or distribute written material that is threatening, abusive or insulting with intent to stir up racial hatred.

Look online

Look at the recent publication of the 2018 House of Commons and House of Lords Joint Committee on Human Rights entitled 'Free Speech: Guidance for Universities and Students Organising Events' at: https://publications.parliament.uk/pa/jt201719/jtselect/jtrights/589/589-annex.pdf.

31.3.6 Preserving public order and the peace

In the UK, this can be seen through the mechanisms used by the Government to ensure compliance of legislation with the various Articles in ECHR. For example, the memorandum by the Home Office and Ministry of Justice with respect to the Serious Crime Bill (now the Serious Crime Act 2015) and the impact of the ECHR, states that:

- Serious Crime Prevention Orders may interfere with a person's rights under Articles 8, 10 and 11
- any order would be in pursuit of a legitimate aim, and necessary in a democratic society, in that the action that interfered with the right would meet a pressing social need and be proportionate to the legitimate aim relied on.

Tip

Legislation may have to reflect more than one Article of the ECHR. When considering if UK legislation meets the requirements of the ECHR remember to consider all relevant Articles.

The Terrorism Act 2006 makes it an offence to publish, or cause another to publish, a statement intending members of the public to be directly or indirectly encouraged to commit, prepare or instigate acts of terrorism, or being reckless as to whether such a result will occur. This is clearly compatible with Article 10.

The Public Order Act 1986 overlaps with Article 11 and will be considered in Chapter 32.

31.4 Overlap of Articles 8 and 10

There are obviously a number of cases where there is an overlap between these two Articles. There is a potential conflict between the individual's right to a private life and freedom of expression. We have seen a typical example of this in the *Von Hannover* cases (see Chapter 30, section 30.4.2) and other examples considered under Article 8, as well as those set out in this chapter.

31.4.1 Criteria for balancing Articles 8 and 10

In the second *Von Hannover* case, the Court set out five relevant criteria for domestic courts to consider when balancing rights under Articles 8 and 10:

- whether the information contributes to a debate of general interest
- the notoriety of the person concerned
- the prior conduct of the person concerned
- the way the material is published
- the circumstance in which photos were taken.

Whether the information contributes to a debate of general interest

The primary criterion is the contribution by the photographs or articles to a debate of general interest. What constitutes a matter of general interest will depend on the circumstances of the case. Where an article was merely a pretext for publishing a photograph of a prominent person, the individual's rights would prevail over the media's Article 10 rights.

The notoriety of the person concerned

Public figures cannot claim the same protection for their private life as ordinary individuals. Public figures must expect their lives to be of public interest so the media's rights under Article 10 are more likely to prevail.

The prior conduct of the person concerned

The mere fact that a public figure has cooperated with the press on previous occasions does not mean he or she must do so on all future occasions. However, previous attempts to enforce privacy will not normally be sufficient for Article 8 to prevail over Article 10.

The way the material is published

The way in which the photograph or article is published, the manner in which the person concerned is represented therein and the extent of dissemination can be important factors. This includes the context of the photograph and the publication.

The circumstance in which the photos were taken

Whether the person photographed gave his or her consent to the taking of the photographs and subsequent publication clearly allows Article 10 to prevail. Where photographs were taken without the person's knowledge or where he or she was tricked are relevant considerations that may allow Article 8 to prevail. The nature or seriousness of the intrusion and the consequences for the person concerned must also be considered.

Summary

- Article 10 covers freedom of expression in all its forms.
- Whether a restriction on the right contained within Article 10 can be justified depends on whether it comes within the terms of Article 10(2). The *Sunday Times* case explained that the test is as follows:
  - Is the restriction prescribed by law?
  - Does it have a legitimate aim?
  - Is it necessary in a democratic society?
  - Is it within the margin of appreciation?
- The list of the possible grounds for restricting the freedom of expression is exhaustive – this means that no other ground may be relied on.
- There are three components of the right to freedom of expression:
  - freedom to hold opinions
  - freedom to communicate information and ideas
  - freedom to receive information and ideas.
- The case of *Axel Springer AG v Germany* (2012) set out criteria to be used in balancing Articles 10 and 8.
- There is a wide margin of appreciation as to what is acceptable with respect to artistic expression to reflect different cultures and values in different states.
- Incitement to racial hatred can be dealt with under Article 10.

32 Article 11 ECHR: right to freedom of assembly and association

32.1 Article 11

> 1. Everyone has the right to freedom of peaceful assembly and to freedom of association with others, including the right to form and to join trade unions for the protection of his interests.
>
> 2. No restrictions shall be placed on the exercise of these rights other than such as are prescribed by law and are necessary in a democratic society in the interests of national security or public safety, for the prevention of disorder or crime, for the protection of health or morals or for the protection of the rights and freedoms of others. This Article shall not prevent the imposition of lawful restrictions on the exercise of these rights by members of the armed forces, or the police, or of the administration of the State.

32.2 The rights under Article 11

There are three rights under Article 11(1):
- freedom of peaceful assembly
- freedom of association with others
- the right to form and to join trade unions for the protection of an individual's interests.

These are qualified rights. The limitations are set out in Article 11(2):
- prescribed by law
- necessary in a democratic society

- for a legitimate aim:
  - in the interests of national security or public safety
  - for the prevention of disorder or crime
  - for the protection of health or morals
  - for the protection of the rights and freedoms of others.

The right must fulfil the criterion of proportionality. This involves looking at the following questions:
- Is the limitation effective?
- Is it the least intrusive measure possible?
- Does it deprive the very essence of the right?
- Is it balanced between the competing interests as a whole?

As with other Articles, the margin of appreciation will vary from case to case. However the Council of Europe has expressed concerns about developments in some states during 2015 such as:
- in Turkey, with the adoption in March 2015 of the Security Bill, which extends the powers of the police to use firearms
- in Spain, with the adoption in March 2015 of the law on citizen's security, which allows heavy fines against organisers of spontaneous protests
- in the Russian Federation, with an amendment to the law on public gatherings, which permits the detention of any person participating in an unauthorised public assembly.

Article 11, as interpreted by the courts, has two closely related rights:
- the right not to be prevented or restricted by the state from meeting and associating with others to pursue particular aims, except to the extent allowed by Article 11(2) – a negative obligation
- the duty on the state to take positive measures, even in the sphere of relations between individuals, to ensure that the rights provided are secured – a positive obligation.

Freedom of assembly is not a mere duty on the part of the state not to interfere. Where individuals or businesses act in a way that undermines Article 11 rights, the state may be required to intervene to secure the protection of those rights.

In the view of the ECtHR, Article 11 is closely associated with Article 10, in that freedom of assembly and association supports freedom of expression, an integral component of the proper functioning of a democratic society.

Keep in mind that Article 11 has both a positive and a negative obligation.

32.2.1 The primary obligations on the state as interpreted by the ECtHR

There are three rights under Article 11(1):

- freedom of peaceful assembly
- freedom of association with others
- the right to form and to join trade unions for the protection of an individual's interests

The freedom of peaceful assembly

This applies to static meetings, marches, public processions and demonstrations. The right must be exercised peacefully, without violence or the threat of violence, and in accordance with the law. Freedom of **peaceful assembly** under Article 11 is broadly interpreted to include the organisation of, and participation in, marches or processions, static assemblies or sit-ins and both public and private events, whether formal or informal. Article 11 will cover any gathering for a common economic or political purpose, but it is unlikely to be applicable to gatherings that are purely social or sporting in character. This seems to indicate that a football match or an unauthorised music festival will not be covered.

Key term

Peaceful assembly – in human rights, under Article 11 a person is allowed to meet in public, march, process and demonstrate without state interference.

A totally peaceful assembly can still be disbanded without a violation of Article 11, as can be seen from the case of *Cisse v France* (2002).

Cisse v France (2002)

The applicant was a member of a group of people without residence permits who in 1996 decided to take collective action to draw attention to the difficulties they were having in obtaining a review of their immigration status in France. A group of some 200 illegal immigrants occupied a church as a protest about their plight, ten of whom began a hunger strike. The Paris Commissioner of Police signed an order for the total evacuation of the church on the grounds that the occupation of the premises was unrelated to religious worship, and there were serious sanitary, health, peace, security and public order risks.

The assembly was peaceful and did not cause any disturbance of public order or prevent churchgoers from attending services. However, after two months of continued occupation of the church, the hunger-strikers' health had deteriorated and sanitary conditions become wholly inadequate. There was no breach of Article 11.

Assemblies may be peaceful even though they may lead to counter demonstrations. The case of *Plattform 'Ärzte für das Leben' v Austria* (1988) shows that a peaceful demonstration may annoy or give offence to persons opposed to the ideas or claims that it is seeking to promote.

Plattform 'Ärzte für das Leben' v Austria (1988)

Plattform 'Ärzte für das Leben' was an association of doctors who were campaigning against abortion, which organised a religious service and a march to the surgery of a doctor who carried out abortions. The ECtHR stated that a demonstration may annoy or give offence to persons opposed to the ideas or claims that it is seeking to promote. The participants must, however, be able to hold the demonstration without fear of physical violence by their opponents. Fear might deter associations or other groups supporting common ideas or interests from openly expressing their opinions on highly controversial issues affecting the community. While there is a right to counter-demonstrate, sometimes the state must interfere to protect its citizens and maintain order.

Tip

As with Article 10, a situation involving Article 11 sometimes requires positive measures to be taken to comply with the ECHR.

However, where the assembly is designed to cause disorder, this would not be within Article 11. *G v Federal Republic of Germany* (1989) concerned an illegal demonstration in front of US military barracks in support of nuclear disarmament. Here, demonstrators blocked the road for 12 minutes every hour, but the sit-in still fell within the accepted definition of a 'peaceful assembly'.

There is an increasing recognition that some tolerance of demonstrations that may shock, annoy or distress others is an integral part of ensuring that these rights are properly protected. This was the view taken in *Faber v Hungary* (2012), where restrictions on the display of a flag during a demonstration were a breach of Article 10.

Tip

Note the clear link between Articles 10 and 11 in *Faber v Hungary* (2012).

Where the assembly takes place on private land, the owner of that land is able to prohibit the assembly, providing this does not prevent lawful protest taking place in a suitable alternative place or by an alternative method. This can be seen in *Appleby v UK* (2003).

Appleby v UK (2003)

The claimants wanted to demonstrate against a development in their town. The shopping mall, which dominated the town centre, had been built by public funds but sold to a private company. The company refused to allow the claimants to demonstrate in the mall or to distribute protesting leaflets. The claimants complained of interference with their rights to free speech and expression.

Shopping centres, though primarily for private commercial interests, increasingly serve as gathering places and events centres. Despite the importance of freedom of expression, Article 11 does not grant any freedom as to where an individual may exercise that right. Therefore, no violation had occurred.

All demonstrations affect others who are not part of them. The authorities must bear that in mind and make a decision that results in any restriction being proportionate. No permissions would ever be granted if any effect of the demonstration on others would always be enough to deny permission.

The freedom of association with others

Freedom of association is the right to come together with others to form an association. This includes the right to form and join trade unions, and to join with others to pursue or advance common causes and interests. Equally, it is the right not to belong to an association. This was stated in *Young, James and Webster v UK* (1981), where the ECtHR stated:

> Article 11 guarantees not only freedom of association, including the right to form and to join trade unions, in the positive sense, but also, by implication, a 'negative right' not to be compelled to join an association or a union.

Key term

Freedom of association – the right to come together with others to form an association.

G20 protest march, London, 2009

Figure 32.1 Key cases for Article 11 – peaceable assembly

Case	Facts	Law
Cisse v France (2002)	The applicant was a member of a group of people without residence permits who in 1996 decided to take collective action to draw attention to the difficulties they were having in obtaining a review of their immigration status in France	In the circumstances there was no violation of Article 11 The restrictions on the exercise of the applicant's right to assembly may have become necessary
Plattform 'Ärzte für das Leben' v Austria (1988)	Plattform 'Ärzte für das Leben' held two demonstrations which were disrupted by counter-demonstrators despite the presence of a large contingent of police	A demonstration may annoy or give offence to persons opposed to the ideas or claims that it is seeking to promote, but sometimes the state must interfere
Appleby v UK (2003)	The claimants wanted to demonstrate against a development in their home town of Washington	Where the assembly takes place on private land, the owner of that land is able to prohibit the assembly, providing this does not prevent lawful protest taking place in a suitable alternative place or by an alternative method

The meaning of association is not defined, as is the case in many states. It is not just spending time in other people's company, as seen in *McFeeley v UK* (1981).

McFeeley v UK (1981)

The claimants had been convicted of offences relating to anti-terrorist legislation in Northern Ireland and were serving prisoners in the Maze prison. There was a change of regime in 1976, resulting in them not being permitted association with the rest of the prison community. This was decided on the basis of Article 3; Article 11 did not apply to association in this sense.

Similarly, association does not include professional regulatory bodies set up by the state to regulate professions, as in *Le Compte, Van Leuven and De Meyere v Belgium* (1981), a case involving doctors and their regulatory body.

Political parties have been found to be an association, as in *Redfearn v UK* (2012).

Redfearn v UK (2012)

The appellant was a bus driver driving children and adults with physical and mental disabilities. He worked in and around Bradford and most of his passengers were of Asian origin. He was summarily dismissed, after nearly seven months' employment, following his election to the local council representing the British National Party. Concerns were voiced by unions that their members could be at risk of harm or abuse. However, there were no allegations against him and he had been nominated as a 'first class employee' by his line manager, who was of Asian origin.

In the ECtHR, he successfully argued that for an employee to lose his or her job for exercising his or her right to freedom of association 'struck at the "very substance" of that right', and that the Government had a positive obligation under Article 11 to enact legislation that would protect that right even though he could not claim for unfair dismissal.

The right to form and to join trades unions for the protection of an individual's interests

Trades unions are specifically recognised as associations, as is the right to form and join one. The state can restrict the right if the restriction can be justified. This might be the restriction on secondary picketing and the right of a trades union to expel members.

32.2.2 Justifications stated within the Article for interferences with the rights imposed by primary obligations and by which the state may seek to avoid a finding of a violation

As this Article contains a qualified right, any interference depends on the conditions set out below.

'Prescribed by law'

This means there must be a clear, precise and predictable legal basis for the interference with Article 11.

'Necessary in a democratic society'

'Necessary in a democratic society' implies two conditions:

- there has to be a pressing social need for the interference, and in particular
- the interference should be proportionate to the legitimate aims pursued.

National authorities need to decide whether or not there is a pressing social need in a particular case. There is a margin of appreciation, although the assessment of the national authorities is subject to supervision by the ECtHR. Furthermore, the court's task is not to substitute its own view for

Figure 32.2 Key cases for Article 11 – freedom of association with others

Case	Facts	Law
McFeeley v UK (1981)	The claimants had been convicted of offences relating to anti-terrorist legislation, and after a change of regime imposed in 1976, they were not permitted association with the rest of the prison community	The meaning of association is not defined, as is the case in many states It is not just spending time in other people's company
Redfearn v UK (2012)	The appellant was a bus driver and elected local councillor representing the British National Party He was summarily dismissed after his election	While association does not include professional regulatory bodies set up by the state to regulate professions, it does include political parties, so there was a violation of Article 11

that of the national authorities, but to review under Article 11 the decisions it delivered in the exercise of its discretion. This means that the court must look at the interference complained of in the light of the case as a whole and determine whether it was 'proportionate to the legitimate aim pursued' and whether the reasons adduced by the national authorities to justify the interference are 'relevant and sufficient'.

In *Ezelin v France* (1991), the ECtHR said:

> The freedom to take part in a peaceful assembly – in this instance a demonstration that had not been prohibited – is of such importance that it cannot be restricted in any way, even for an avocat [a French lawyer roughly equivalent to a barrister], so long as the person concerned does not himself commit any reprehensible act on such an occasion.

In *Ziliberberg v Moldova* (2004), the court observed at the outset of its findings that:

> The right to freedom of assembly is a fundamental right in a democratic society and, like the right to freedom of expression, is one of the foundations of such a society.

32.2.3 'For a legitimate aim'

The legitimate aim must fall under one of the following categories:

- in the interests of national security or public safety
- for the prevention of disorder or crime
- for the protection of health or morals
- for the protection of the rights and freedoms of others.

In the interests of national security or public safety

The *Laporte* case, considered below, may well be argued on the basis of public safety as well as the prevention of disorder or crime. This will include counter-terrorism measures and counter-extremism measures, and will inevitably overlap with freedom of expression. The ECtHR seems quite willing to accept that the state has a wide margin of appreciation on this.

For the prevention of disorder or crime

The majority of references to the ECtHR are dismissed as the court takes the view that each state recognises the need to protect public safety. We have seen one example of the state being heavy handed in the *Laporte* case. However, states have a relatively wide margin of appreciation in this area, as we have seen in *Cisse v France* (2002).

For the protection of health or morals

One case with respect to Article 11 and health and morals is *Larmela v Finland* (1997). Here the Cannabis Association of Finland aimed 'to influence intoxicant policy and legislation with a view to making the personal use of cannabis legal for Finnish citizens'. The Finnish Minister of Justice refused to register the association. The state was permitted to deny this association registration with the aim of protecting the health and morals of the country.

This would also apply to banning a march in favour of drug-taking if the authorities thought this would have a detrimental effect on the health or morals of the country.

For the protection of the rights and freedoms of others

The protection of others' rights and freedoms ensures that the law must balance those interests using the principles of proportionality. As we have seen, proportionality means that the interference must be no more than is absolutely necessary to achieve one of the aims in the ECHR. The impact of the restriction on the individual must not be excessive in relation to the legitimate interests pursued. In other words, the state must not use a sledgehammer to crack a nut. The more severe the interference with an individual's rights, the more is required to justify it.

32.3 English law and its compatibility with ECHR obligations

Here we need to concentrate on:

- control of processions
- breach of the peace and important associated police powers.

The remaining material in this chapter is designed to give a broad picture of the relevant English law. The focus of study for the AQA specification should be on the knowledge and understanding of English law on the restrictions on assembly and association on grounds of public order, and the protection of the rights of others:

- notice, control and prohibition of public 'processions' under ss 11–13 of the Public Order Act 1986
- control of public 'assemblies' under s 14 of the Public Order Act 1986
- prohibition of trespassory assemblies under s 14A–C of the Public Order Act 1986
- prohibition of aggravated trespass under ss 68–69 of the Criminal Justice and Public Order Act
- breach of the peace – note the connection with material in Article 5, Chapter 29.

32.3.1 Analysis of relevant English law to determine compatibility with ECHR obligations and the consequences when English law appears to interfere

For the protection of the rights and freedoms of others

When deciding in the case of *Countryside Alliance v Attorney General* (2007), Baroness Hale said:

> **❝** Article 10 protects freedom of expression, the freedom to hold opinions and to receive and impart information and ideas. But it does not expressly protect the right to meet or associate with other people in order to do this. This, it might be said, is separately provided for in article 11. It protects the freedom to meet and band together with others in order to share information and ideas and to give voice to them collectively. While democracy values each individual, it also knows that individuals cannot get much done unless they band together. These articles, then, are designed to protect the freedom to share and express opinions, and to try to persuade others to one's point of view, which are essential political freedoms in any democracy. On this view, the right of the hunt and its followers to gather together publicly to demonstrate in favour of their sport and against the ban, perhaps even by riding over the countryside to demonstrate what they do, is protected by article 11. But the right to chase and kill the fox or the stag or the mink or the hare is not. **❞**

Proportionality

The question of proportionality arose in the case of *R (Laporte) v Chief Constable of Gloucestershire* (2006).

R (Laporte) v Chief Constable of Gloucestershire (2006)

Officers from seven police forces, acting under the direction of the Gloucestershire constabulary, stopped three coaches from London carrying 120 anti-Iraq war protesters in March 2003. The protesters had been planning to join thousands of people in a demonstration against the war at RAF Fairford in Gloucestershire, from which part of the US-led attack on Iraq had been launched two days before. At least some of the protesters, including Laporte, had purely peaceful intentions, but some items that suggested a more violent intent were apparently discovered by the police on the coaches.

The coaches were returned to London under police escort, without any opportunity for any of the passengers to get off the coaches. It was decided that the Chief Constable's actions were unlawful because they were not prescribed by law and were disproportionate.

Principle of proportionality and police powers

The core principles and legislation guidance set out by the College of Policing requires there to be a link between the purpose for the restriction and the measures employed to achieve proper treatment of minorities and avoid any abuse of a dominant position. The following need to be considered in making a decision as to proportionality:

- Is the purpose sufficiently important to justify the restriction (i.e. are there relevant and sufficient reasons to justify the restriction)?
- Will the measures proposed achieve that purpose?
- Are the measures to be taken the least restrictive to achieve the intended purpose?
- Are the restrictions to ECHR rights necessary to meet the legitimate aims set out in the ECHR rights concerned?

Figure 32.3 Key case for assembly in a public place

Case	Facts	Law
DPP v Jones (Margaret) (1999)	21 people protested peacefully on the verge of the A344, next to the perimeter fence at Stonehenge The officer in charge concluded that they constituted a 'trespassory assembly'	A peaceful assembly on the highway, which did not unreasonably interfere with or obstruct the highway, was not a trespassory assembly

If the answer to all four questions is yes, then the conditions or restrictions imposed on a public procession or public assembly under s 12 or 14 of the Public Order Act 1986 will be proportionate.

Assembly in a public place

In the UK, the position can be seen in the case of *DPP v Jones (Margaret)* (1999).

DPP v Jones (Margaret) (1999)

There was a peaceful protest on the main road next to the perimeter fence at Stonehenge. Some carried banners saying things such as 'Stonehenge Campaign 10 years of Criminal Injustice'. The officer in charge concluded that they constituted a 'trespassory assembly' and told them so. When asked to move off, some people were determined to remain and were convicted. On appeal, the appeal was allowed. A peaceful assembly on the highway, which did not unreasonably interfere with or obstruct the highway, was not a trespassory assembly. The existence of a public right of way entitled the public to have the right of public assembly so long as such assembly does not unreasonably obstruct the highway.

However, there are restrictions on processions or marches and demonstrations and the police have to keep order based on the idea of preventing a breach of the peace.

Breach of the peace, trespass to land, control of processions and associated police powers

Breach of the peace

Breach of the peace is used to prevent unlawful violence against people or property. 'Peace' in this context refers to the Queen's peace. 'Peace' also occurs in the definition of the crime of murder. Peace is the opposite of war. The definition of breach of the peace can be found in *R v Howell* (1981):

> **❝** There is a breach of the peace whenever harm is actually done or is likely to be done to a person or in his presence to his property or a person is in fear of being so harmed through an assault, an affray, a riot, unlawful assembly or other disturbance. **❞**

Key term

Breach of the peace – this is defined in *R v Howell* (1981).

The wide powers available to stop or prevent a breach mean that any use of the powers is closely examined by the courts to ensure that there has been no undue interference with respect for human rights. Examples of this can be seen with respect to kettling tactics by the police in *McClure and Moos v Commissioner of Police of the Metropolis* (2012) and *Austin v Commissioner of Police of the Metropolis* (2009).

> See Chapter 29, section 29.1.1 for a case study of *Austin v Commissioner of Police of the Metropolis* (2009).

Look online

Read the material at http://criminology.leeds.ac.uk/2013/09/05/kettling-protests-and-the-limits-of-the-european-convention-on-human-rights/.

How does this help to explain the relationship between Articles 5, 10 and 11?

Trespass to land

Trespass to land is a tort and so the remedies would be damages or an injunction to stop the trespass. It is not a criminal offence unless some special statutory provision makes it so. Any damage done by a trespasser while trespassing may amount to the offence of criminal damage.

Trespass to land consists of any unjustifiable intrusion by a person upon land in the possession of another. It is actionable in the courts, whether or not the claimant has suffered any damage. This rule may seem harsh but in modern practice an action will not normally be brought for trespass without damage unless the claimant wishes to deter persistent trespassing or there are disputes over boundaries or rights of way.

Key term

Trespass to land – any unjustifiable intrusion by a person upon land in the possession of another.

Technically, the slightest crossing of the claimant's boundary is sufficient to result in a trespass. In the case of *Ellis v Loftus Iron Co.* (1874), the court stated:

> **❝** If the defendant place[s] a part of his foot on the claimant's land unlawfully, it is in law as much a trespass as if he had walked half a mile on it. **❞**

This principle was used to evict travellers parked on land belong to others, typically the owners of woodland, as in the case of *Drury v Secretary of State for Environment, Food and Rural Affairs* (2004) and those involved in sit-ins such as that at Essex University in *University of Essex v Djemal* (1980). These cases had mixed results for the landowners and so the criminal law was strengthened, as will be seen later in this chapter.

Examples of civil trespass include removing any part of the land in the possession of another, or any part of a building or other erection attached to the soil. It can also be a trespass to place something on, or in, land in the possession of another – such as dumping rubbish.

There are a number of legal justifications to trespass, including:

- licence to enter by law
- justification by right of way or easement (the use of someone else's property or land for a stated reason, such as permitting the underground services of one property (such as drains) to pass beneath the land of a neighbouring property)
- justification by licence or necessity
- various powers of entry granted to officers of the law, such as the police.

Statutory restrictions

Removing trespassers from land

Section 61 of the Criminal Justice and Public Order Act (CJPOA) 1994 applies to trespassers who are on the land of another with the common purpose of remaining there. This section enables a police officer to direct trespassers on the land to leave the land where the occupier has already taken steps to ask them to do so, and either:

- they have damaged the land
- they have used threatening, abusive or insulting behaviour to the occupier, the occupier's family, employees or agents, or
- between them they have six or more vehicles on the land.

Failure to obey a direction to leave or returning to the land as a trespasser within three months is an offence. This deals with the problems occurring in *Drury v Secretary of State for Environment, Food and Rural Affairs* (2004) and *University of Essex v Djemal* (1980).

Section 62 provides a power for the police to seize vehicles of persons failing to comply with a direction under s 61.

Raves

A rave is defined as a gathering on land in the open air of 20 or more persons at which amplified music is played during the night, and as such, by reason of its loudness and duration and the time at which it is played, is likely to cause serious distress to the inhabitants of the locality.

Section 63 CJPOA 1994 provides the police with powers to direct persons (other than exempt persons such as the occupier of the land and his or her family or assistants) gathering on land for a rave to leave. Failure to comply with a direction or returning to the site within seven days are offences.

Aggravated trespass

Section 68(1) CJPOA 1994, as amended, states that a person commits the offence of aggravated trespass if he or she trespasses on land and, in relation to any lawful activity which persons are engaging in or are about to engage in on that or adjoining land, does anything there which is intended by him or her to have the effect of:

- intimidating those persons or any of them so as to deter them or any of them from engaging in that activity
- obstructing that activity
- disrupting that activity.

Following the case of *DPP v Chivers* (2010), the word 'land' includes a building.

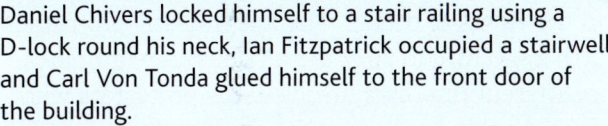

DPP v Chivers (2010)

Daniel Chivers locked himself to a stair railing using a D-lock round his neck, Ian Fitzpatrick occupied a stairwell and Carl Von Tonda glued himself to the front door of the building.

The court decided that land includes a building so all three had been correctly charged with aggravated trespass.

The s 68 offence is capable of being committed by hunt saboteurs, motorway protesters or any protesters who are trespassing on land, but it is not formally limited to protest groups. It was used with respect to the UK Uncut protest in Fortnum & Mason.

In the news

Why the Fortnum & Mason protesters' case matters

If 300 football fans chant together and then one assaults a rival supporter, are they all responsible? If you're on a protest and someone commits a crime and you don't leave immediately, can you be held to account for the person's actions? That was the question put before Westminster Magistrates' Court as we, the first ten defendants in the trials of those arrested for staging a sit-in at Fortnum & Mason on 26 March 2011, faced our verdict. We were found guilty of aggravated trespass; nine of us were given a conditional discharge and order to pay costs of £1,000 each, while the tenth was also fined ...

The prosecution was required to prove an act beyond ordinary trespass – which on its own is not a crime. In this case, it argued that the protesters demonstrated intent to intimidate. Michael Snow, the district judge, accepted in his sentencing that none of us had been personally intimidating towards staff and shoppers, but said that under the terms of 'joint enterprise' we were responsible for the actions of other protesters.

... There is some evidence that a small number of acts inside the store may have been intimidating. There is no evidence that any of us on trial was responsible for these. ... But the prosecution maintained that we were guilty because we didn't leave when the intimidating acts allegedly took place. We will find out if the high court agrees when we take the case to appeal.

Source: Blog by Adam Ramsay in the New Statesman *online, 17 November 2011*

In *Edward Bauer v DPP* (2013), the appellants appealed a decision of a District Judge convicting them of aggravated trespass following occupation of the Fortnum & Mason's store by demonstrators in protest against tax avoidance. The court upheld the conviction as the demonstration was an additional act distinct from the trespass and it could be inferred that by demonstrating they intended to intimidate.

This additional conduct can be anything. There is no requirement that the additional conduct should itself be a crime, so activities such as playing a musical instrument or taking a photograph would suffice. What limits the scope of 'anything' is the intention that must accompany it: the intention to obstruct, disrupt or deter by intimidating.

Ramblers for instance, may trespass, and may disrupt a lawful activity such as rounding up sheep by doing so, but unless they have the intention to obstruct, disrupt or deter, they do not commit the offence of aggravated trespass.

Trespassory assemblies

Section 70 CJPOA 1994 amends the Public Order Act 1986 by inserting two new sections, ss 14A and 14B, in respect of trespassory assemblies.

A chief officer of police who reasonably believes:

- that an assembly will be held on land (being land to which the public has no or only a limited right of access)
- that the assembly is likely to take place without the permission of the occupier, and
- that it may result in serious disruption to the life of the community or damage a site of historical archaeological or scientific importance,

may apply for an order prohibiting the holding of all trespassory assemblies for a period of not more than four days. To organise a prohibited assembly, to take part in one and to incite others to take part in one are all offences.

It is also an offence to fail to comply with a direction not to proceed to a trespassory assembly.

The Public Order Act 1986

The Public Order Act 1986 sets out various offences which can occur where there are demonstrations or protests. The Act replaces and largely replicates existing common law offences. Other offences include obstructing the highway under the Highways Act 1980 and aggravated trespass under the Criminal Justice and Public Order Act 1994.

This means that when Article 11 is considered, the state may have to show that the offence was committed and that the offence is a proportionate response to a legitimate aim. These offences include:

Riot

Riot comes under s 1 of the Public Order Act 1986 and is used for the most serious cases, usually linked to planned or spontaneous serious outbreaks of sustained violence.

Violent disorder

Violent disorder comes under s 2 of the Public Order Act 1986 and is used in relation to instances of serious disorder falling short of riot.

Affray

Affray comes under s 3 of the Public Order Act 1986 and is used where the behaviour of the accused puts in fear members of the public. There must be some conduct, beyond the use of words, which is threatening and directed towards a person or persons.

Causing fear or provocation of violence; causing intentional harassment, alarm or distress (s 4); causing harassment, alarm or distress (s 5)

These offences come under s 4 and s 5 of the Public Order Act 1986. They include behaviour such as making threats to innocent bystanders or individuals carrying out public service duties or the throwing of missiles by a person taking part in a demonstration or other public gathering where no injury is caused. Section 5 is used in cases which amount to less serious incidents of anti-social behaviour, such as persistently shouting abuse or obscenities at passers-by.

> **Look online**
>
> Read through this document to see how the police are trained to respond to protests: http://library.college.police.uk/docs/APPref/police-response-to-protest.pdf.

Control of processions etc.

Restrictions on the right to demonstrate are always controversial and the courts have to rule on the balance between protecting the workers at a site, the right to protest and the need to protect public order and the rights of others. The antifracking protests in North Yorkshire in 2017 are an obvious example of the different interests involved: the protestors who believe fracking is bad for the environment; people who wish to travel past the protest site; those living in the locality whose lives are disrupted; those who have to pay for the police presence; the disruption and cost to the fracking business; those supplying materials to the fracking site, and so on. Depending on your point of view, there is always an argument that the state, through the police, did or did not do enough.

The state is obliged to deal with these conflicting interests using the principle of proportionality. Proportionality is the balance between the individual right and others in the community. The criteria used for this include the effectiveness of the measures taken, the balance achieved, whether the actions of the state operate in the least intrusive manner possible and whether the effect is to deprive the individual of the right under Article 11.

A 'public procession' constitutes any number of people (the law does not specify a minimum) moving along a route.

A 'public assembly' is two or more people gathered together in a public place. This includes highways, parks, shopping precincts, shops and offices, restaurants, pubs or any other place to which the public have access or partial access.

With respect to processions and marches, the main UK legislation is found in ss 11–14 of the Public Order Act 1986, trespassory assemblies in s 14A–C (dealt with above), as well as the offence of wilful obstruction of the highway (s 137 of the Highways Act 1980), as was argued unsuccessfully in *DPP v Jones (Margaret)* (1999) (above). The legislation works as follows:

- Section 11 of the Public Order Act 1986 sets out requirements to give advance notice of public processions.
- Section 12 of the Public Order Act 1986 permits the police to impose conditions on public processions.
- Section 13 of the Public Order Act 1986 gives power to prohibit processions.

- Section 14 of the Public Order Act 1986 gives power to impose conditions on public assemblies.
- Section 137 of the Highways Act 1980 creates the offence of wilful obstruction of the highway and gives power to order removal of the obstruction.

Section 11 of the Public Order Act 1986 sets out requirements to give advance notice of public processions

Written notice must be given to hold a public procession intended to demonstrate support for or opposition to the views or actions of any person or body of persons, to publicise a cause or campaign, or to mark or commemorate an event. This does not apply to a procession that is one commonly or customarily held (perhaps a Good Friday Christian walk of witness) or a funeral procession organised by a funeral director acting in the normal course of his or her business.

The notice must specify the date when it is intended to hold the procession, the time when it is intended to start it, its proposed route, and the name and address of the person (or of one of the persons) proposing to organise it. The notice has to be taken to a police station.

Sections 12 and 14 of the Public Order Act 1986 permit the police to impose conditions on public processions and assemblies

Under these sections, conditions can be set which restrict the place, the duration and the numbers of people allowed. Conditions can be imposed in advance, or by the senior police officer who is at the scene. The conditions can be imposed 'as they appear necessary to prevent serious disorder, disruption of the life of the community, or intimidation'.

Section 13 of the Public Order Act 1986 gives power to prohibit processions

This section allows a chief officer of police to apply to the local council for an order prohibiting the holding of a public procession for a period of up to three months where the chief officer of police reasonably believes that in the particular circumstances the powers to impose conditions on a public procession will not be sufficient to prevent serious public disorder. The council must obtain the consent of the Secretary of State before making a banning order.

The blanket application of a ban of all public processions in a particular district raises issues regarding proportionality, as there is no ability to consider the particular circumstances of each individual procession when such a ban is imposed.

Section 137 of the Highways Act 1980 creates the offence of wilful obstruction of the highway and gives power to order removal of the obstruction

Section 137 states:

> If a person, without lawful authority or excuse, in any way willfully obstructs the free passage along a highway he is guilty of an offence and liable to a fine not exceeding level 3 on the standard scale.

This offence is useful in assisting the police in removing demonstrators but leads to few prosecutions. A freedom of information request shows the following for the Metropolitan Police District:

Figure 32.4 Data extracted from the National Strategy for Police Information Systems (NSPIS)

	2013/14		2014/15		2015/16	
	Number of arrests	Number of charges	Number of arrests	Number of charges	Number of arrests	Number of charges
Wilful obstruction of a highway	23	11	30	17	44	30
Wilfully obstruct a highway with a non-motor vehicle	26	7	6	2	3	1
Total	49	18	36	19	47	31

These are further broken down at:

www.whatdotheyknow.com/request/365602/response/893973/attach/html/3/HUMPRHRIES%20Copy%20of%206954%20Arrests%20for%20Highway%20Obstructions%20report.xlsx.html.

Notice Under Section 12 of the Public Order Act 1986
– Conditions for Processions

I am Chief Constable Simon Richard Cole of the Leicestershire Constabulary and Chief Officer of Police for Leicester, Leicestershire and Rutland.

Having regard to the time or place at which, and the circumstances in which public processions are intended to be held by the English Defence League (EDL) and Leicester Unite Against Fascism (LUAF), and including non-affiliated groups intending to demonstrate against EDL on Saturday 4 February 2012, I reasonably believe that they may result in serious public disorder, serious damage to property and serious disruption to the life of the community.

I have made this decision having considered the history of previous events involving the EDL and Unite Against Fascism (and non-affiliated groups), a number of which have led to serious public disorder and serious damage to property, and on the more general basis that any event involving simultaneous marches involving several hundreds of people in a busy City Centre environment is likely to cause serious disruption to the life of the community.

I direct that the following conditions will be imposed as necessary to prevent such disorder, damage and disruption:-

In the case of persons in and attending the City of Leicester in support of the EDL

The initial assembly point for the EDL procession will be the car park of St Margaret's Pastures recreation area, accessed from St Margaret's Way, postcode LE1 3EA. Coach parking will be available at this site.

Individuals intending to support the EDL at this event are required to arrive at this location between 11.00 am and 12.00 midday. A failure to arrive by this time may result in being excluded from the event.

A further period of time between 12.00 midday and approximately 12.30 pm will be allowed for organisers and stewards to brief and prepare EDL supporters for the procession through Leicester, which will follow the following prescribed route under the direction and to specific timings directed by the Senior Police Officer present at the time:

Route:
- From St Margaret's Pastures,
- Left onto St Margaret's Way,
- Left onto Burleys Way,
- Right onto Abbey Street,
- Right onto Belgrave Gate and continuing onto Haymarket,
- Right onto Church Gate and continuing onto St Margaret's Way,
- Right into St Margaret's Pastures.

There is no provision for a static assembly during the course of this route.

A person who takes part in a public procession and knowingly fails to comply with a condition imposed under Section 12 of the Public Order Act 1986 is guilty of an offence for which they may be arrested.

S. R. Cole   0830hrs, 30 January 2012
Chief Constable

A typical notice as to conditions with respect to a procession

Notice Under Section 14 of the Public Order Act 1986
– Conditions for Assemblies

I am Chief Constable Simon Richard Cole of the Leicestershire Constabulary and Chief Officer of Police for Leicester, Leicestershire and Rutland.

Having regard to the time or place at which, and the circumstances in which public assemblies are intended to be held by the English Defence League (EDL) and Leicester Unite Against Fascism (LUAF), and including non-affiliated groups intending to demonstrate against EDL on Saturday 4 February 2012, I reasonably believe that they may result in serious public disorder, serious damage to property and serious disruption to the life of the community.

I have made this decision having considered the history of previous events involving the EDL and Unite Against Fascism (and non-affiliated groups), a number of which have led to serious public disorder and serious damage to property, and on the more general basis that any event involving simultaneous marches involving several hundreds of people in a busy City Centre environment is likely to cause serious disruption to the life of the community.

I direct that the following conditions will be imposed as necessary to prevent such disorder, damage and disruption:-

In the case of persons in and attending the City of Leicester in support of the EDL

The initial assembly point for the EDL will be the car park of St Margaret's Pastures recreation area, accessed from St Margaret's Way, postcode LE1 3EA. Coach parking will be available at this site.

This assembly will follow on from a procession as directed under Section 12 of the Public Order Act 1986 referred to overleaf.

Individuals intending to support the EDL at this assembly are required to arrive at this location between 11.00 am and 12.00 midday. A failure to arrive by this time may result in being excluded from the event.

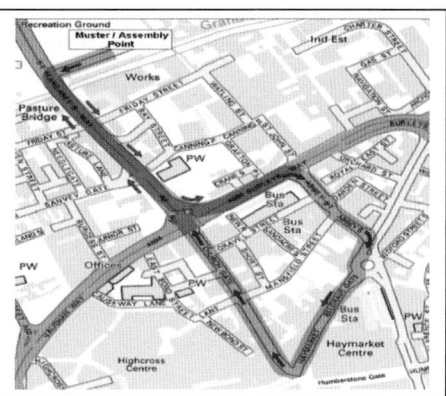

They may either remain at the location until the return of the procession, or take part in the procession, returning to the assembly point at its conclusion.

Following the conclusion of the procession there will be an opportunity for a static assembly.

Persons attending the assembly will then disperse as directed by the Senior Police Officer present at the scene, before or by 4pm.

A person who takes part in a public assembly and knowingly fails to comply with a condition imposed under Section 14 of the Public Order Act 1986 is guilty of an offence for which they may be arrested.

S. R. Cole   0830hrs, 30 January 2012
Chief Constable

A typical notice as to conditions with respect to an assembly

Look online

Read the article at: www.nicholashancox.co.uk/highway_obstruction.htm.

Do you think this gives a fair reflection of the law today and how it relates to Article 11 ECHR?

Activity

As you have now studied this section on English law, construct a chart that lists all the offences available to the authorities with respect to assemblies. Alongside each offence, give a brief note that helps you identify the key aspects of that offence.

Figure 32.5 Key cases for Article 11 in English law

Case	Facts	Law
DPP v Chivers (2010)	The activity complained of took place inside a house	Section 68 could be used as the court decided that land includes a building
R (Laporte) v Chief Constable of Gloucestershire (2006)	Police officers stopped three coaches from London carrying 120 anti-Iraq war protesters in March 2003 and returned the coaches to London Some protesters had purely peaceful intentions, but police discovered some items which suggested a more violent intent	The Chief Constable's actions were unlawful because they were not prescribed by law and were disproportionate

Summary

- Article 11 has three protected interests:
  - freedom of peaceful assembly
  - freedom of association with others
  - the right to form and to join trades unions for the protection of an individual's interests.
- Article 11 is a qualified right.
- Under Article 11(2), any limitation must be in accordance with the law, necessary and proportionate and for one or more of the four legitimate aims.
- As with other Articles, the margin of appreciation will vary from case to case.
- There are restrictions under common law and statute.
- The common law restrictions are based on breach of the peace and trespass to land.
- Restrictions under statute are many and varied, so the authorities have a variety of possible offences available to help control assemblies of people.

33 Enforcement

For the doctrine of Parliamentary Supremacy see AQA *A-level Law for Year 1 and AS*, Chapter 3, section 3.5.

After reading this chapter, you should be able to:
- Understand claims under HRA 1998 in English courts
- Understand claims before the ECtHR
- Understand the process of judicial review

33.1 Claims under HRA 1998 in English courts

By s 6(1), it is unlawful for a public authority to act in a way which is incompatible with a Convention right.

By s 7(1), a person who claims that a public authority has acted (or proposes to act) in a way which is made unlawful by section 6(1) may:

(a) bring proceedings against the authority under this Act in the appropriate court or tribunal, or

(b) rely on the Convention right or rights concerned in any legal proceedings, but only if he is (or would be) a victim of the unlawful act.

By s 8 (1), in relation to any act (or proposed act) of a public authority which the court finds is (or would be) unlawful, it may grant such relief or remedy, or make such order, within its powers as it considers just and appropriate.

33.1.1 Requirements of s 6 HRA 1998

It is unlawful for a public authority to act in a way which is incompatible with a Convention right.

HRA 1998 does not define what a 'public authority' is (except for Parliament and the courts) so it is a matter for interpretation in each case whether the ECHR rules apply to the claim. The general approach of HRA 1998 is that if a claimant could take an action before the ECtHR, then it should be possible to take a claim before a domestic court.

Parliament

Parliament is specifically stated in HRA 1998 as not being a public authority. This is because of the doctrine of Parliamentary Supremacy and s 3 HRA 1998, which recognises that Parliament can make law even if it is incompatible with the ECHR.

The courts

HRA 1998 provides that courts and tribunals are public authorities all the way up to the Supreme Court. The role of the courts is to apply ECHR rights in cases involving statutes or actions of public authorities. When doing so they assess the proportionality of the action of a public authority. Proportionality assesses the relative importance of an individual's rights under the ECHR against other individuals of the general public interest.

In *R v Secretary of the State for the Home Department, ex parte Daly* (2001), the test for proportionality was said to require a court to ask whether:

1 the legislative objective is sufficiently important to justify limiting a fundamental right

2 the measures designed to meet the objective are rationally connected to it, and

3 the means used which impair the right or freedom are no more than necessary to achieve the objective.

Who is a public authority?

The following are all considered to be public authorities for the purposes of HRA 1998:
- government departments
- local authorities
- the armed forces
- the civil service and bodies that have had their service contracted out by the Government, such as the Prison Service, and HM Revenue and Customs.

Other bodies are included within the scope of a public authority if they have the general characteristics of:
- special powers that are likely to have been given by Parliament
- democratic accountability, and
- public funding.

Such bodies are likely to have a constitution set or required by statute and an obligation to act in the public interest. Both state schools and NHS trusts will come within this definition. By s 6(3), public authorities also include bodies whose functions are of a public nature, so this will include:

- the BBC
- universities
- charities
- docks and airport operators, as they have a responsibility for safety of members of the public
- airlines, as they have responsibilities for checking on the status of immigrants, and
- professional regulatory bodies such as the Solicitor's Regulatory Authority and the Bar Council.

It should be noted that only public acts carried out by these bodies will be covered by HRA 1998 so that decisions relating to the employment of their workers, property ownership and the management of the organisation are all considered to be private acts and not subject to HRA 1998.

In recent years, many services have been contracted out by public authorities to private companies – for example, local authorities contracting out the provision of care services for the elderly. Issues may arise in relation to ECHR rights – for example, under Article 8 if a decision is taken to close a residential care home. It has been decided that in this type of situation an individual cannot take action to enforce his or her ECHR rights as the rights between the local authority and the care service provider are private as they are contained in a contract between the two.

A public authority is given a defence to an action under HRA 1998 by s 6(2) if statute requires it to act in a way which is incompatible with ECHR rights.

33.1.2 Actions against public authorities

Section 7(1) HRA 1998 provides that a person who claims that a public authority has acted (or proposes to act) in a way which is made unlawful by s 6(1) may:

(a) bring proceedings against the authority under this Act in the appropriate court or tribunal, or

(b) rely on the Convention right or rights concerned in any legal proceedings, but only if he is (or would be) a victim of the unlawful act.

Appropriate court or tribunal

In most claims this will be bringing a claim before any English court. There are some exceptions:

- in some cases the action should be dealt with by way of appeal – for example, where an accused has been remanded in custody before trial and

there is an alleged breach of Article 5 rights, the proper course of action would be to appeal against the remand decision

- some specialist tribunals have been established and the appropriate action should be taken in that tribunal – an example is the Investigatory Powers Tribunal which is the only body that can hear matters about the intelligence services
- if a claim should be made by judicial review rather than under HRA 1998 (for judicial review claims see below).

Time limits

A claim against a public authority must be brought within one year. Compare this with the time limit for a judicial review claim at section 33.4.3 below.

Who can bring an action?

To bring an action under HRA 1998, the claimant must be a victim – this is an individual who is directly affected by the act or omission that is in issue. This could also include an individual who is in a class of persons who may be potentially affected. Organisations such as trade unions and pressure groups can bring an action in respect of a wrong done to them as an organisation. For example, a trade union can bring a case when the issue is a matter of trade union law. A claim cannot be brought by, for example, a pressure group, on behalf of the public or a section of the public.

33.1.3 Remedies

By s 8 (1), in relation to any act (or proposed act) of a public authority which the court finds is (or would be) unlawful, it may grant such relief or remedy, or make such order, within its powers as it considers just and appropriate.

This section allows a court to grant whatever remedy it considers just and appropriate to the claimant, provided it is allowed to grant that remedy. The court cannot create a new remedy for the claimant.

A court cannot grant a remedy it is not entitled to make so, for example, a criminal court cannot grant an award of damages as damages can only be granted by civil courts. The remedy will often be in a judicial review action – see section 33.2.4 below for a list of remedies available in judicial review.

Damages in HRA actions are discretionary and the principles to be applied by the English courts mirror those before the ECHR – see section 33.2 below. The priority in an action under HRA 1998 is protection of human rights and the balancing of public and private interests rather than the award of compensation. The point of taking action under HRA 1998 is to allow victims to obtain from English courts what they would otherwise obtain from the ECtHR.

Damages can be awarded by civil courts in just satisfaction of a claim, bearing in mind that the ECtHR will often hold that finding in favour of the applicant without further remedy.

33.2 Claims before the ECtHR

The ECtHR is an international court established by the ECHR. It hears applications alleging that a state, which has subscribed to the Convention, has broken a provision of the Convention.

An application to the court can be lodged by an individual after all domestic remedies have been tried and exhausted. The Court can issue both judgments and advisory opinions. It is based in Strasbourg, France.

33.2.1 Making a claim

The majority of claims before the court are brought by individuals who allege that their Convention rights have been violated and the courts in their own country have been unable to provide an effective remedy. The purpose of bringing a claim is to obtain a ruling that a Convention right has been violated and the state will have to change the law or its practice in the future. In some cases, the state will be ordered to pay compensation.

A person wishing to make a claim must lodge a written application which must set out:

- the facts
- the Article in the Convention that he or she alleges has been violated
- that the claim is admissible
- the remedy sought.

The applicant must also show that he or she has exhausted all domestic remedies; therefore he or she must pursue the alleged violation in his or her national courts to the highest level. In the UK this means taking a claim to the Supreme Court. It must also be shown that the loss or suffering is more than trivial. The importance of the claim to the applicant and what is objectively at stake will be considered.

A claim must be admissible and relate to an issue which the court can deal with and show a possible violation of the Convention. The decision on admissibility is taken either by a single judge, or a committee of judges, and there is no appeal against

European Court of Human Rights building, Strasbourg

refusal. More than 90 per cent of initial applications are declared inadmissible.

The claim must be brought within six months from the date when the applicant became aware that his or her domestic remedy had been exhausted. The claim will not be accepted if it relates to an issue that has already been decided by the court. About 60 per cent of applications that are accepted are found to be repetitive cases, where there is already well-established case law on a similar issue.

The court can take interim measures such as, for example, ordering the prevention of deportation until a full hearing takes place.

Once a claim has been accepted, the court is under a duty to examine the case, which will often involve relying on representations from both parties. The burden of proof will not always rely on the applicant.

33.2.2 Precedent

The ECtHR treats the ECHR as a 'living instrument' and not something as fixed at the time it was written in 1950. The aim is to apply the Convention as society and values of members states change. This means that the court tends to follow the principles and decisions made in previous cases but does not consider itself strictly bound by precedent. It is willing to depart from previous decisions in order to provide effective protection of human rights in a modern society.

33.2.3 The margin of appreciation

States have direct democratic legitimation and it is for national authorities to assess how and whether to interfere with a Convention right or freedom. The role of the ECtHR is supervisory and subsidiary to member states as they are better placed to look after local needs. The ECtHR has recognised the need to take into account the different conditions and standards that apply in different member countries, so states have certain freedom of choice of the measures they take to comply with certain ECHR Articles. National authority decisions are subject to review by the ECtHR to ensure conformity with the ECHR. The decisions of the ECtHR are variable depending on matters such as:

- how much of a balance has to be struck between competing interests – this applies particularly to Article 8
- the importance of the matter to the individual

- the nature of the activities restricted, and
- the nature of the interference by the state.

There is little or no margin of appreciation where:

- absolute or unqualified rights are in issue
- where there is a clear consensus among member states – an example being on the rights of transsexuals, as in *Goodwin v UK* (2002)
- where an important principle needs to be upheld – an example being any attempt to restrict political speech in breach of Article 10.

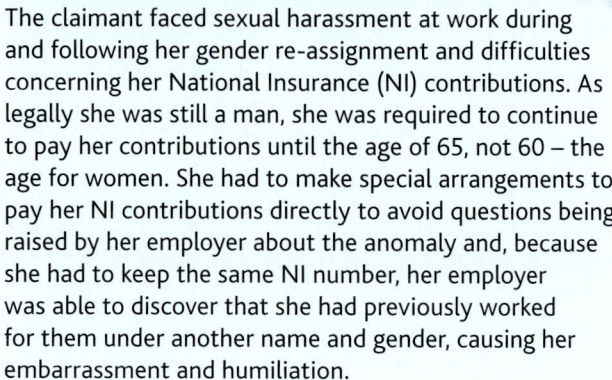

Goodwin v UK (2002)

The claimant faced sexual harassment at work during and following her gender re-assignment and difficulties concerning her National Insurance (NI) contributions. As legally she was still a man, she was required to continue to pay her contributions until the age of 65, not 60 – the age for women. She had to make special arrangements to pay her NI contributions directly to avoid questions being raised by her employer about the anomaly and, because she had to keep the same NI number, her employer was able to discover that she had previously worked for them under another name and gender, causing her embarrassment and humiliation.

Relying on Article 8 and other Articles in the ECHR, she complained about the lack of legal recognition of the post-operative sex and legal status of transsexuals in the UK, especially about the treatment in relation to employment, social security and pensions and the inability to marry either as a man or a woman.

The ECtHR ruled that UK law violates the rights of transsexual people and that the UK lagged behind most of the rest of Europe in its treatment of transsexuals, in ways that discriminate by forcing this intensely private information into the public domain without a clear necessity.

There is a wider margin where:

- the issue is of a moral nature – for example, issues of sado-masochism as in *Laskey, Jaggard and Brown v UK* (1997)
- matters of social policy such as housing, health care or the environment, and
- matters over which a state has exclusive knowledge, such as when dealing with national security issues.

See Chapter 27, section 27.2 for full case details of *Laskey, Jaggard and Brown v UK* (1997).

The margin of appreciation can be considered controversial, as it appears to undermine the universal nature of human rights across member states and it could allow oppressive actions to continue unchallenged.

On the other hand, it can be said to recognise the different standards in member countries which ensure the continuing support of the Convention. It also supports the principle of democracy by ensuring that decisions are taken locally by democratically elected bodies rather than by unelected judges.

33.2.4 Remedies

As has been stated above in relation to English courts, damages can be awarded in just satisfaction of a claim, bearing in mind that the ECtHR will often hold that finding in favour of the applicant without any further remedy may be sufficient. The following general principles have been adopted by the ECtHR:

- if damages are awarded, the general principle is to restore the claimant back to the position he or she would have been in if his or her rights had not been violated
- the court is unlikely to award punitive damages but money loss, such as loss of income could be awarded and, in certain cases, such as Article 5 claims for false imprisonment, certain non-pecuniary losses such as anxiety, distress and psychological trauma could be compensated
- costs can be awarded to a claimant, but only for the action before the ECtHR and not for any part of the action before the English courts.

33.3 The relationship between the ECtHR and other bodies and rules

33.3.1 The European Court of Justice

The Court of Justice of the European Union (ECJ) is not related to the ECtHR. However, since all EU member states are members of the Council of Europe and have signed the Convention on Human Rights, there are concerns about consistency in case law between the two courts. The ECJ refers to the case law of the ECtHR and treats the Convention on Human Rights as though it was part of the EU's legal system, since it forms part of the legal principles of the EU member states. Even though its member states are party to the Convention, the EU itself is not a party, as it does not have competence under the treaties. However, EU institutions are bound under Article 6 of the EU Treaty of Nice to respect human rights under the Convention.

33.3.2 English courts

Section 2(1) HRA 1998 says:

A court or tribunal determining a question which has arisen in connection with a Convention right must take into account any—

(a) judgment, decision, declaration or advisory opinion of the European Court of Human Rights

The effect of this section is to require English courts to take into account any previous decisions of the ECtHR. This affects judicial precedent as it allows for the overruling of any previous English precedent that was in conflict with the ECHR.

This provision was commented on by Lord Slynn in R (Holding and Barnes plc) v Secretary of State for the Environment, Transport and the Regions (2001):

> **Your Lordships have been referred to many decisions of the ECtHR on Article 6 of the Convention. Although the Human Rights Act 1998 does not provide that a national court is bound by these decisions, it is obliged to take account of them so far as they are relevant. In the absence of some special circumstances it seems clear to be that the court should follow any clear and constant jurisprudence of the ECtHR. If it does not do so there is at least a possibility that the case will go to that court which is likely in the ordinary case, to follow its own jurisprudence.**

Most of the signatory states to the ECHR, including now the UK, have incorporated the Convention into their own national legal systems, either through constitutional provision, statute or judicial decisions.

33.3.3 The UK Parliament

An adverse judgment by the Court may, in the UK, require the amendment of an Act of Parliament. In Chapter 31 there is the example of the result of the case of Sunday Times v UK (1979) bringing about the introduction of the Contempt of Court Act 1981.

See Chapter 31, section 31.3.7 for full case details of Sunday Times v UK (1979).

Another example of a case resulting in legislative change is *ADT v UK* (2001).

ADT v UK (2001)

The applicant alleged that his conviction for gross indecency violated his Article 8 rights. He was a practicing homosexual. Police officers conducted a search under warrant of his home, seizing various items including photographs and videotapes. He was charged with gross indecency between men contrary to s 13 of the Sexual Offences Act 1956. The evidence consisted of videotapes showing him with four other consenting men in the privacy of his house. Following conviction he was conditionally discharged.

The court found that as there was no likelihood of the tapes being made public, in view of the applicant's desire for anonymity and that he concealed his sexual orientation, his right to respect for his private life had been interfered with.

The court observed that the Sexual Offences Act 1956 failed to secure the private life of homosexual men. As a result Parliament introduced the Sexual Offences (Amendment) Act 2000 which, in turn, was replaced by the Sexual Offences Act 2003.

There is an assumption that Parliament intends to legislate in a manner compatible with the UK's international obligations, including the ECHR.

33.3.4 UK delegated legislation

The UK courts developed the rule, before HRA 1998, that delegated legislation is void if it is incompatible with fundamental rights, including the ECHR.

R v Secretary of State for Social Services, ex parte Joint Council for the Welfare of Immigrants (1996)

Regulations were introduced that required immigrants to apply for benefits instantly on arriving in the UK. This caused a dilemma for immigrants between applying for asylum but having no money while the process was going on, or giving up their claim and facing deportation but being fed while the process was going on. The Court of Appeal decided that the regulations were void as a policy required express, unambiguous legislation.

33.3.5 UK administrative policies

The state must ensure that its policies and the activities of its agents are compatible with the Convention. This will include the activities of the police, prison officers and civil servants.

A large number of cases involving the UK concern prisoners' rights and the policies of the Prison Service. This has affected issues such as prisoners' correspondence with their lawyers, the right to effective health care and to have the length of a sentence decided by the judiciary rather than the Home Secretary. It has not yet brought about a change in prisoners' rights to vote.

Another example of the effect of the ECHR on English law is the removal of the general ban on homosexual men and lesbian women in the military, due to the decision in *Smith and Grady v UK* (2000).

Smith and Grady v UK (2000)

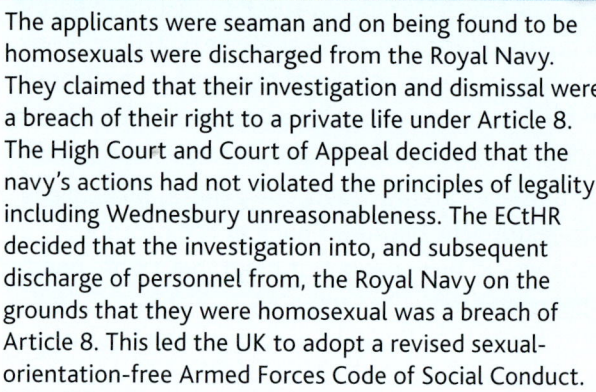

The applicants were seaman and on being found to be homosexuals were discharged from the Royal Navy. They claimed that their investigation and dismissal were a breach of their right to a private life under Article 8. The High Court and Court of Appeal decided that the navy's actions had not violated the principles of legality including Wednesbury unreasonableness. The ECtHR decided that the investigation into, and subsequent discharge of personnel from, the Royal Navy on the grounds that they were homosexual was a breach of Article 8. This led the UK to adopt a revised sexual-orientation-free Armed Forces Code of Social Conduct.

33.4 The process of judicial review

Judicial review is a form of court proceeding, usually in the Administrative Court, in which the judge reviews the lawfulness of a decision or action, or a failure to act, by a public body exercising a public function. It is only available where there is no other effective means of challenge. The Administrative Court is part of the Queen's Bench Division of the High Court.

Judicial review is concerned with whether the law has been correctly applied, and whether the correct procedures have been followed. The court's role is supervisory only, and any remedies are discretionary.

In order to succeed, the claimant will need to show:

- a public body is under a legal duty to act or make a decision in a certain way and is unlawfully refusing or failing to do so, or
- a decision or action has been taken by a public body that is beyond the powers it is given by law.

33.4.1 Whose decisions can be challenged by judicial review?

Decisions made by public bodies in a public law capacity may be challenged by judicial review. Examples of the bodies whose decisions can be challenged are:

- government ministries and departments
- local authorities
- health authorities
- chief constables
- prison governors
- some tribunals (but not if an appeal is available to a higher tribunal or court).

If a public body is not exercising a public function, for example where it is an employer, or there is a claim of negligence against it, its actions are governed by private laws and its decisions will not be subject to judicial review.

Increasingly, public functions are contracted out to a private company, for example a private company running a prison. In this case, the private company is carrying out a public function and so its actions in the running of the prison are governed by public law and are subject to judicial review.

33.4.2 Who can bring a judicial review action?

The person bringing the action has to have an interest in the decision being challenged. This is called 'standing'. That means the claimant has to have sufficient connection to the subject matter of the claim.

33.4.3 Time limits

A judicial review action must be brought within three months of the decision or action that is being challenged.

33.4.4 The grounds for judicial review

Illegality

Public bodies can only generally do what the law allows them to do and their powers are usually contained in legislation. Public bodies must correctly apply the law that set their powers. If they do not follow the law correctly, their decision, action or failure to act will be unlawful. This is known as being **ultra vires** and the decision will be void and of no effect. An action or decision may be unlawful if the decision maker had no power to make it or exceeded the powers given to him or her, or if it misapplies the law, or if the correct procedure was not followed.

> **Key term**
>
> *Ultra vires* – this is when a decision has been made beyond the power of the decision maker or when the wrong procedure has been followed. If the court finds a decision to be *ultra vires* the decision will be void and of no effect.

> See AQA A-level Law for Year 1 and AS, Chapter 4, section 4.2.3 for judicial review as a control of delegated legislation which is *ultra vires*.

Fairness

A public body should never act so unfairly that it amounts to an abuse of power. If there are set procedures that it must follow in order to reach a decision, then it must follow them. The claimant must be given a fair hearing which includes knowing the case against him or her and having the opportunity to present his or her case.

A public body must be impartial and not biased. The public body must consult the people it has a duty to consult before a decision is made, or who have a legitimate expectation that they will be consulted, perhaps because they have been consulted in the past or because they have an obvious interest in a matter.

Irrationality and proportionality

The court may quash a decision when it is considered to be so demonstrably unreasonable as to be 'irrational' or 'perverse'. In practice this is very difficult to show, and it is usually argued alongside other grounds. The test, per Lord Greene in *Associated Provincial Picture Houses Ltd v Wednesbury Corporation* (1948) is:

> If a decision on a competent matter is so unreasonable that no reasonable authority could ever had come to it, then the courts can interfere ... but to prove a case of that kind would require something overwhelming.

R (Rogers) v Swindon NHS Trust (2006)

A woman with early stage breast cancer was prescribed Herceptin by her GP. The NHS Trust refused to supply the drug as it said it was non-approved and because – it said – her case was not exceptional. The trust was not able to put forward in court any clear reasons for allowing some patients to have the drug treatment and not others, and it was ruled as irrational and unreasonable.

33.4.5 The orders that the court can make

When a case is being brought for judicial review, a remedy will also be asked for. The remedies the Administrative Court can give are:

1   A quashing order – this is an order which overturns or undoes a decision already made.
2   A prohibiting order – this stops a public body from taking an unlawful decision or action it has not yet taken.
3   An injunction – this is a temporary order requiring a public body to do something or not to do something until a final decision has been made.
4   A mandatory order – this makes a public body do something the law says it has to do.
5   A declaration – the court can state what the law is or what the parties have a right to do.

These remedies are discretionary. Even if the court finds that a public body has acted wrongly it does not have to grant a remedy. It might decide not to do so if it thinks the claimant's own conduct has been wrong or unreasonable, for instance where the claimant has delayed unreasonably, has not acted in good faith, or where a remedy would impede a public body's ability to deliver fair administration.

There is a right of appeal from the Administrative Court to the Court of Appeal. The party that wants to appeal must first ask permission from the Administrative Court, and if that is refused, he or she can ask permission from the Court of Appeal directly. A further appeal may lie to the Supreme Court if the case is one of public importance.

Figure 33.1 Key cases on enforcing the ECHR

Case	Facts	Law
ADT v UK (2001)	The applicant was convicted for gross indecency based on videos showing him engaged in sexual activity with consenting men in his own home	The Sexual Offences Act 1956 breached his Article 8 rights As a result Parliament had to amend the law
R v Secretary of State for Social Services, ex parte Joint Council for the Welfare of Immigrants (1996)	Regulations were introduced requiring immigrants to apply for benefits instantly on arriving in the UK	The Court of Appeal decided that the regulations were void
R (Rogers) v Swindon NHS Trust (2006)	An NHS trust refused to supply the drug Herceptin to a patient as it said it was non-approved and her case was not exceptional	The trust's decision was irrational and unreasonable It was overturned

Summary

- HRA 1998 creates the legal framework for the rights and freedoms in the ECHR to be given further effect in English law.

- It does this by imposing a duty on the courts to interpret legislation, so far as is possible to do so, to be compatible with the ECHR and by placing legally enforceable duties on public authorities to act compatibly with ECHR rights.

- Public authorities perform public functions. HRA 1998 does not impose duties on private individuals or companies.

- The courts are public authorities but Parliament is not and Parliament can enact legislation that contravenes the ECHR.

- Under HRA 1998 an individual can bring a claim against a public authority claiming his or her ECHR rights have been violated if he or she has 'standing' – he or she is a 'victim' and could have brought a claim before the ECtHR.

- Remedies available under HRA 1998 are English law remedies fashioned to mirror the remedies available at the ECtHR.

- An individual can only bring a claim to the ECtHR if he or she has exhausted all domestic remedies.

- The claim will be considered for admissibility before it is investigated and considered by the ECtHR.

- The ECtHR is not bound by its previous precedent as it treats the ECHR as a 'living instrument', allowing the ECHR to evolve to match changes in society.

- The role of the ECtHR is supervisory and subsidiary to member states and recognises the need to take into account the different conditions and standards that apply in different member countries, so states have a certain freedom of choice of measures they can take to comply with certain ECHR Articles – this is the 'margin of appreciation'.

- All UK courts are bound to give effect to decisions of the ECtHR.

- A judgment against the UK may require the amendment of an existing Act of Parliament.

- Delegated legislation that is contrary to the ECHR may be declared void by UK courts.

- Administrative policies that are contrary to the Convention may have to be changed.

- A claim for judicial review can be brought in the Administrative Court by a person with sufficient interest in a decision of a public body and within three months of the decision.

- The grounds for judicial review are illegality, fairness, irrationality and proportionality.

- The court can make any one of a number of discretionary orders if it finds the public body has acted *ultra vires*.

Glossary

Absolute rights – this is where a duty is placed upon a state that must be performed in all circumstances, such as the right to life under Article 2 and the right not to be tortured under Article 3.

Acceptance – a final and unconditional agreement to all the terms of the offer.

Actual breach – in contract law where the breach occurs at the time of, or during the course of, performance.

Agent – a person who is authorised to act for another (the principal) in the making of a contract with third parties. The resulting contract is made between the principal and the third party, and not with the agent.

Anticipatory breach – when a party to a contract gives notice in advance to the other party that he or she will not be performing or completing the contract.

Attempt – in criminal law, an attempt occurs where a person with the relevant *mens rea* does an act which is more than merely preparatory to the commission of an offence.

Automatism – a defence to a criminal offence. It is an act done by the muscles without any control by the mind, such as a spasm, a reflex action or a convulsion; or an act done by a person who is not conscious of what he or she is doing such as an act done while suffering from concussion or while sleep-walking.

Bail – where an accused is allowed to leave police custody until attendance at trial or required pre-trial hearings. Conditions may be imposed on the grant of bail. Failure to attend a court hearing or observe conditions will be an offence. The grant of bail is covered by the Bail Act 1976.

Basic intent offences – offences where recklessness is part of the *mens rea*. This includes manslaughter, ss 20 and 47 OAPA 1861 and some property offences such as criminal damage.

Bilateral contract – this requires both offeror and offeree to do something. Both parties have obligations.

Breach of the peace – a criminal offence committed when it is alleged that harm has been done, or is likely to be done, to a person or to property or when a person fears harm by an assault, affray, riot, unlawful assembly or some other disturbance.

Civil liberties – freedoms that are guaranteed by a state to people to protect them from an over-powerful government. They are found in democratic states such as the UK but are not found in undemocratic states such as North Korea.

Condition – a term in a contract that is central to the contract, breach of which may allow the contract to be repudiated.

Consumer – described in the Consumer Rights Act 2015 as 'an individual acting for purposes that are wholly or mainly outside that individual's trade, business, craft or profession'. Note that a company cannot be a 'consumer', as it is not an 'individual'.

Contra proferentem – where there is doubt about the meaning of a term in a contract, the words will be construed against the person who put them in the contract.

Corrective justice – this is sometimes known as restorative justice and is when the law restores the imbalance that has occurred between two individuals or an individual and the state.

'Correspondence' – with regard to Article 8 ECHR, this means the right to uninterrupted and uncensored communications with others.

Counter offer – a response to an offer which makes a firm proposal that materially alters the terms of the offer.

Diminished responsibility – a partial defence to a charge of murder which reduces the offence to one of voluntary manslaughter.

Direct intent – where the defendant deliberately intends the result – for murder, the death of the victim.

Disclaimer – a statement informing the claimant that the company does not accept responsibility for the advice being given.

Dualist system – if a treaty is signed with another country, its provisions must be passed by the domestic parliament before it becomes law.

Duress (1) – a full defence in criminal law based on the fact that the defendant has been effectively forced to commit the crime.

Duress (2) – when someone enters into a contract as a result of threats of violence to the person which would amount to crimes or torts if those threats were carried out.

Economic duress – when someone enters into a contract as a result of financial threats.

Estoppel – being prevented from making assertions that contradict what has previously been said to be a fact.

European Convention on Human Rights – an international treaty signed in 1950 to protect human rights and fundamental freedoms in the 47 states that have adopted it. It is separate from the EU and its terms are overseen by the ECtHR. The UK will not be departing from this treaty when it leaves the EU.

European Union – a political and economic union of 28 member states of which the UK has been a member since 1973. As a result of the 2016 referendum vote, the UK is committed to leave the EU in 2019.

'Everyone' – so far as Article 8 ECHR is concerned, this includes businesses.

Exclusion clause – a term in a contract that prevents one party being liable for a breach of contract.

Executed consideration – an act in return for a promise.

Executory consideration – a promise for a promise.

'Family life' – with regard to Article 8 ECHR, the right to enjoy family relationships without interference from the state.

Force majeure clause – a clause often found in commercial contracts. It excludes liability for the parties for delay in performance or the non-performance if there are extraordinary events.

Freedom of association – in Human Rights under Article 11 ECHR, it is the right for a person not to be prevented or restricted by the state from meeting and joining with others to follow a particular aim.

Freedom of expression – in Human Rights under Article 11 ECHR, the freedom for a person to hold opinions and to receive and communicate information and ideas without state interference.

Gillick competence – a term used to help assess whether a child has the maturity to make his or her own decisions and to understand the implications of those decisions. The term is taken from the case of *Gillick v West Norfolk and Wisbech Area Health Authority* (1984).

Gross negligence manslaughter – a form of involuntary manslaughter committed where D is grossly negligent in breach of a duty of care towards V and this results in V's death.

Habeas corpus – a writ issued by the court which required the immediate production of a detained person so the court could hear arguments for and against the continuation of the detention.

'Home' – with regard to Article 8 ECHR, this is a right to enjoy your existing home peacefully, rather than a right to a house.

Human rights – rights and freedoms that everyone in a country and the world are entitled to because they are human.

Indeterminate prison sentence – an indeterminate prison sentence can be imposed if a court thinks an offender is a danger to the public and is one where: no date is set when the prisoner will be released; the prisoner has to spend a minimum amount of time in prison (called a 'tariff' period) before he or she is considered for release; the Parole Board decides if the prisoner can be released – often on licence.

Innominate term – a term in a contract that is not defined as a condition or a warranty. Whether it is regarded as a condition or a warranty depends on the severity of the consequences of any breach of the term. Instead of insisting at the outset of the contract, the parties wait until the effect of the breach makes it a condition or warranty.

Insane automatism – where the cause of the automatism is a disease of the mind within the *M'Naghten* Rules and comes within the defence of insanity.

Insanity – a full defence to a criminal offence requiring *mens rea*. The defendant must be labouring under such a defect of reason, from disease of the mind, as not to know the nature and quality of the act he or she was doing, or if he or she did know it, that he or she did not know he or she was doing what was wrong.

Intention to create legal relations – the parties to a contract expressly or impliedly agree that the contract is legally binding and therefore enforceable in court.

Invitation to treat – an indication that one person is willing to negotiate a contract with another, but that he or she is not yet willing to make a legal offer.

Involuntary manslaughter – an unlawful killing where the killer does not have the *mens rea* of murder. It can be committed either by an unlawful act or by being grossly negligent.

Legal positivists – the theory of law that is based on the idea that laws are valid where they are made by the recognised legislative power in the state and do not have to satisfy any higher authority.

Letter of comfort – a written assurance usually provided by a parent company in respect of its subsidiary's financial obligations to a bank. It is usually where the parent company wishes to give some assurance to the lender in respect of the subsidiary's ability to repay the loan but has no obligation to pay on its behalf.

Lien – the right to retain possession of the goods of the debtor until paid.

Limitation clause – a term in a contract that sets an upper limit on liability for breach of contract.

Limited rights – this is where a right is set out, such as the right to liberty in Article 5, but it sets out circumstances when the right is limited such as imprisonment after conviction.

Liquidated damages – where the amount of damages has been fixed by a term in the contract.

Loss of control – a partial defence to a charge of murder which reduces the offence to voluntary manslaughter under s 54(1) of the Coroners and Justice Act 2009.

Mandatory injunction – a court order requiring a party to do something.

Margin of appreciation – the discretion a state has in making rules to comply with the ECHR.

Misrepresentation – a false statement of material fact made by a party to the contract that induces the other party to enter the contract.

Mitigation of loss – in contract law the injured party must take reasonable steps to minimise the effects of a breach of contract.

Murder – 'the unlawful killing of a reasonable person in being and under the King's (or Queen's) Peace with malice aforethought, express or implied'.

Natural law – a moral theory of jurisprudence, which maintains that law should be based on morality and ethics.

Non-derogable – this means absolute: it is so important that it cannot be limited or suspended under any circumstance.

Non-insane automatism – a complete defence where the cause of the automatism is external.

Novus actus interveniens – an intervening act which breaks the chain of causation.

Oblique or indirect intent – where the defendant's aim or purpose was not to bring about the consequence (the death). It will be sufficient for a charge of murder if the defendant foresees death or serious injury as a result of their actions.

Offer – proposal (or offer) showing a willingness to contract on firm and definite terms.

Offeree – in contract law the person to whom an offer is made.

Offeror – in contract law the person who makes an offer to another.

Peaceful assembly – in human rights, under Article 11 a person is allowed to meet in public, march, process and demonstrate without state interference.

Pluralism – a form of society in which the members of minority groups maintain their independent cultural traditions.

Primary victim – a victim of an accident who suffers physical or mental injuries, or both.

'Private life' – with regard to Article 8 ECHR, this includes matters such as the physical and psychological integrity; sex life and gender; personal data; reputation, names and photos.

Private nuisance – a tort claim where someone's use or enjoyment of their property is affected by the unreasonable behaviour of a neighbour.

Privity of contract – only those who are parties to a contract are bound by it and can benefit from it.

Procedural justice – this is concerned with making and implementing decisions according to fair processes.

Promisee – in contract law a person to whom a promise is made.

Promisor – in contract law a person who makes a promise to another.

Promissory estoppel – an equitable doctrine which can prevent a person going back on a promise which is not supported by consideration.

Psychiatric injury – also known as nervous shock. A severe, long-term mental injury which is more than shock or grief.

Qualified rights – this is where, because of public interest, or to protect the rights of others, it is proper to restrict the freedom. In Article 10 there is a general right of freedom of expression, but this can be legitimately restricted, for example by placing reporting restrictions on the media during the course of a criminal trial in order to ensure a fair trial.

Quantum meruit – as much as it is worth.

Repudiation – the ending of a contract due to a refusal by one of the parties to perform the duty or obligation owed to the other party.

Rescission – this is an equitable remedy that is made at the discretion of the judge. The purpose of rescission is to place the parties back in their pre-contractual position.

'Respect' – with regard to Article 8 ECHR, this requires the state not to interfere and has positive aspects.

Rights – things to which everyone is entitled or allowed: they are guaranteed freedoms. They could include the right to life, to liberty and the security of person, to privacy, to freedom of expression, and to freedom of assembly and association as recognised by the ECHR and in the UK.

Robbery – theft with the use or threat of force.

Rule – this has been defined by Twining and Miers in *How to Do Things with Rules* (2014) as 'a general norm mandating or guiding conduct'.

Rule of law – the principle that law should govern a nation, as opposed to it being governed by arbitrary decisions of individuals or government officials. All people and institutions in the state should be subject to, and accountable to, law that is fairly applied and enforced and that no person or institution is above the law.

Rylands v Fletcher – where a person's property is damaged or destroyed by the escape of non-naturally stored material onto adjoining property.

Secondary victim – a person who suffers mental injury after witnessing an accident or its immediate aftermath.

Separation of powers – a theory proposed by Montesquieu that the powers in a state should be shared between three bodies: the executive (or government), the legislature (or law makers such as Parliament) and the judiciary (judges in court). This sharing would prevent one body becoming too powerful over the others.

Social control – the ways in which our behaviour, thoughts and appearance are regulated by the norms, rules, laws and social structures of society.

Specific intent offences – criminal offences for which the *mens rea* required is only intent. These offences include murder and s 18 OAPA 1861. For both these offences the *mens rea* is intent only.

Substantive justice – the content of the law itself must be just.

Theft – A person is guilty of theft if he or she dishonestly appropriates property belonging to another with the intention of permanently depriving the other of it.

Trader – described in the Consumer Rights Act 2015 as 'a person acting for purposes relating to that person's trade, business, craft or profession, whether acting personally or through another person acting in the trader's name or on the trader's behalf'. Note that a trader can be a sole trader or a company or business partnership or any other form of business organisation.

Trespass to land – any unjustifiable intrusion by a person upon land in the possession of another.

Ultra vires – this is when a decision has been made beyond the power of the decision maker or when the wrong procedure has been followed. If the court finds a decision to be *ultra vires* the decision will be void and of no effect.

Undue influence – a principle of contract law where there is a relationship between the parties which has been exploited by one party to gain an unfair advantage.

Unilateral contract – an agreement to pay in exchange for performance, if the potential performer chooses to act. There is no obligation to perform the act.

Unlawful act manslaughter – where the defendant causes a death through doing an unlawful act that is objectively dangerous with the necessary *mens rea* for the unlawful act.

Vicarious liability – where a third person has legal responsibility for the unlawful actions of another. It is commonly seen in employment where the employer is responsible for the actions of an employee who acted in the course of his or her employment.

Vitiating factor – something that makes a contract void or voidable.

Void – a void contract is one that is declared to be a nullity, in other words, it never had legal effect. A void contract is said to be void ab initio (from the beginning).

Voidable – a voidable contract can be made void in certain circumstances. If the right to make it void is not exercised then the contract remains valid.

Voluntary manslaughter – the verdict where the defendant has a partial defence to murder where the killing was carried out when the defendant was suffering from diminished responsibility or loss of control.

Warranty – a minor term in a contract, breach of which does not end the contract but allows a claim for damages only.

Index